The Third Reich's Intelligence S

CW00967826

The Career of Walter Schellenberg

This is the first-ever analytical study of Nazi Germany's political foreign intelligence service, Office VI of the Reichssicherheitshauptamt and its head, Walter Schellenberg. Katrin Paehler tells the story of Schellenberg's career in policing and intelligence, charts the development and activities of the service he eventually headed, and discusses his attempts to place it at the center of Nazi foreign intelligence and foreign policy. The book locates the service in its proper pedigree of the SS as well as in relation to its two main rivals – the Abwehr and the Auswärtige Amt. It also considers the role Nazi ideology played in the conceptualization and execution of foreign intelligence, revealing how this ideological prism fractured and distorted Office VI's view of the world. The book is based on contemporary and postwar documents – many recently declassified – from archives in the United States, Germany, and Russia.

KATRIN PAEHLER is Associate Professor at Illinois State University. She was a member of the "Independent Historians' Commission on the German Foreign Office and Nazism and its Aftermath." She is co-editor of *A Nazi Past: Recasting German Identity in Postwar Europe* (2015).

The Third Reich's Intelligence Services

The Career of Walter Schellenberg

Katrin Paehler

Illinois State University

CAMBRIDGE
UNIVERSITY PRESS

CAMBRIDGE
UNIVERSITY PRESS

University Printing House, Cambridge CB2 8BS, United Kingdom

One Liberty Plaza, 20th Floor, New York, NY 10006, USA

477 Williamstown Road, Port Melbourne, VIC 3207, Australia

314-321, 3rd Floor, Plot 3, Splendor Forum, Jasola District Centre, New Delhi - 110025, India

79 Anson Road, #06-04/06, Singapore 079906

Cambridge University Press is part of the University of Cambridge.

It furthers the University's mission by disseminating knowledge in the pursuit of education, learning and research at the highest international levels of excellence.

www.cambridge.org
Information on this title: www.cambridge.org/9781316610145
DOI: 10.1017/9781316661826

First published 2017
First paperback edition 2019

A catalogue record for this publication is available from the British Library

Library of Congress Cataloging in Publication data
Names: Paehler, Katrin, author.
Title: The Third Reich's intelligence services : the career of Walter Schellenberg / Katrin Paehler, Illinois State University.
Other titles: Career of Walter Schellenberg
Description: New York : Cambridge University Press, [2017] | Includes bibliographical references and index.
Identifiers: LCCN 2016048263 | ISBN 9781107157194 (alk. paper)
Subjects: LCSH: Schellenberg, Walter, 1910–1952. | World War, 1939–1945 – Secret service – Germany. | Nationalsozialistische Deutsche Arbeiter-Partei. Schutzstaffel. Reichssicherheitshauptamt. | Nationalsozialistische Deutsche Arbeiter-Partei. Schutzstaffel. Sicherheitsdienst. | Nazis – Biography. | Intelligence officers – Germany – Biography. | Nationalsozialistische Deutsche Arbeiter-Partei. Schutzstaffel – Biography.
Classification: LCC DD247.S338 P34   2017 | DDC 940.54/8743092 [B] – dc23
LC record available at https://lccn.loc.gov/2016048263

ISBN   978-1-107-15719-4   Hardback
ISBN   978-1-316-61014-5   Paperback

Für Vater und Mutter

Contents

Figures

Acknowledgments

When, years ago, I met David Kahn, author of *Hitler's Spies*, I told him that I was writing about Office VI of the Reich Security Main Office. Without missing a beat he blurted out, grinning, "I am so sorry." I have thought about this comment frequently and it always made me chuckle. This has been a long process, and it is with great pleasure and enormous gratitude that I write these sentences acknowledging the many who have supported me over the years.

I thank Richard Breitman for his unfailing support, impeccable advice, and incredible patience. He was the best *Doktorvater* I could have wished for, and he has been an inspiration, a wonderful colleague, and a great supporter ever since. The same is true for Peter Black whose great kindness has been humbling and deeply appreciated. Gerhard Weinberg took an early in interest in my work and over the years, I have enjoyed tremendously his and his wife's friendship and hospitality. Along the way, he has helped me in more ways than I can count, and I owe him a debt of gratitude (and my introduction to Wyoming!)

My colleague John Freed read the manuscript several times. A distinguished historian of Medieval History, he professed an "amateur interest in Nazi Germany." His interest might be so, but his knowledge is shockingly in-depth. I will always be thankful for his support, his counsel, and for teaching me how "to not split every infinitive." I would also like to thank the two anonymous reviewers who pushed me: first to the proverbial brink and then to strengthen my argument and to streamline as much as possible the stories I tell. I also owe much to Lew Bateman at Cambridge University Press, who reacted with compassion when tragedy struck.

Friends and colleagues near and far and too numerous to list have been fountains of advice, information, and spirited discussions – and served as wailing walls more frequently than I care to recall. I want to thank Florian Altenhöner, Shlomo Aronson, Tracy Brown, Kyle Ciani and Doug Cutter, Tania and Robert Coderre, the late Elisabeth Dulleck, Hilary Earl, Max Friedman, the late Valerie French, Thomas Gebauer,

Hanna Gersmann, Christopher Griffin, Hans Joachim Langhans, James Lide, David Kahn, Greg Kocourek, Kerstin von Lingen, Wendy Lower, Jörg Marciniak, Christoph Mauch, Geoff Megargee, David Messenger, Liesl Nieswand, Sarah and Eric Myers, Patrice Olsen, Adrian O'Sullivan, Melanie Oelgeschläger, Julia Pähler, Erika Quinn, Vanda Rajcan, Touré Reed, Anne and Phil Rush, David Schuchat, Susanna Schrafstetter, Carsten Schreiber, Natalia A. Smirnova and her husband Anatol, Alan Steinweis, Vanette Schwartz, Stephen Tyas, Katharina Vester, Christine Varga-Harris and Glen Harris, Alexandra Wenck, and Jürgen Wittner. I am certain that I am missing a good number of friends and colleagues who should be on this list, but this mistake, like the many others one will surely find in this book, are my responsibility.

Over the years, various institutions have supported my research and have given me wonderful opportunities. I am keenly aware that I would not have been able to research and to write this book without their financial and moral backing. I thank the Department of History, the Department of Jewish Studies, and the College of Arts and Science at American University; the United States Holocaust Memorial Museum and the German Historical Institute in Washington, DC; and the Holocaust Educational Foundation in Skokie, Il. I am also grateful for the support Illinois State University has extended to me over the years; both the Department of History and the College of Arts and Sciences have been generous.

I wish to thank the publishers for permission to use and rework materials that appeared in the following articles and chapters: "Creating an Alternative Foreign Office: A Reassessment of Office VI of the Reich Main Security Office," in *Journal of Intelligence History* 8 (Winter 2008/2009): 27–42 [www.tandfonline.com]; "Foreign Intelligence in a New Paradigm: Amt VI of the Reich Main Security Office (RSHA)," in David Bankier, ed., *Secret Intelligence and the Holocaust. Collected Essays from the Colloquium at the City University of New York Graduate Center* (New York and Jerusalem: Enigma Books and Yad Vashem, 2006), 273–299; "Im Spiegel seiner Selbst. Der SD-Ausland in Italien," in Michael Wildt, ed., *Nachrichtendienst, Politische Elite und Mordeinheit. Der Sicherheitsdienst des Reichsführers SS* (Hamburg: Hamburger Edition, 2003), 241–266; and "Auditioning for Postwar: Walter Schellenberg, the Allies, and Attempts to Fashion a Usable Past," in David Messenger and Katrin Paehler, eds., *A Nazi Past: Recasting German Identity in Postwar Europe*, (Lexington: The University of Kentucky Press, 2015), 29–56.

Finally, I thank those who told me to go and chase my dreams, in particular my parents Reinhold and Hildegard Pähler. They were always proudest of their ability to let go of their children, and so am I. I know, though, that it was not easy on them when I moved halfway across the world, but they took this much like they took on life in general: with great humor and grace. I guess my father never quite understood what his eldest child was doing when she was researching this or why it took so long. My mother, for her part, was just flabbergasted how much time one could spend on revisions. I would sometimes try to explain it to her and she would listen carefully, nod her head in seemingly complete understanding, only to say, "That makes sense. Now get it done already." When I close my eyes, I can see them: father's half-smile and a spark in his eyes, saying "finally" with exasperated pride. And mother rolling her eyes (she had a great eye roll!), muttering, "I told you so." So here it is, and it is for my parents.

Katrin Paehler
Normal, IL and Berlin, Germany
2016

Archives

Bundesarchiv, Berlin-Lichterfelde, Germany (BAL)
Bundesarchiv, Zwischenarchiv Dahlwitz-Hoppegarten, Germany (BA-DH)
Hessisches Staatsarchiv, Marburg, Germany (HStA)
Institut für Zeitgeschichte, Munich, Germany (IfZ)
Politisches Archiv des Auswärtigen Amtes, Berlin (PAAA)
Rossiiskii Gosudarstvennyi Voennyi Archiv, Moscow (RGVA)
National Archives and Record Administration, College Park, MD (NA)
United States Holocaust Memorial Museum, Washington, DC (USHMM)

Introduction

> Schellenberg's name was known to have received a certain prominence in the World Press, not only because of the important position in the G.I.S. [German Intelligence Service], that he held during the greater part of the war, but also on account of the leading part he had played in certain peace negotiations.
>
> Final Report on the Case of Walter Schellenberg[1]

Intelligence combines information and understanding. In spring 1952, an unexpected piece of information rippled through the international postwar intelligence community: Walter Schellenberg, the head of Nazi Germany's political foreign intelligence service, *Amt* VI of Heinrich Himmler's *Reichssicherheitshauptamt* (RSHA) – Office VI of the Reich Security Main Office – and advisor to and confidant of Himmler had died in Italy. A flurry of intelligence activity took place, meant to confirm a death that despite the man's longstanding ailments came as a surprise. An understanding and appreciation of the facts settled in soon. There would be no further need by the various intelligence services to concern themselves with the former spymaster.[2]

Walter Schellenberg's career had been illustrious. Born in 1910, he was fresh out of law school when Adolf Hitler was appointed chancellor on January 30, 1933. Quickly aligning himself with the new government, Schellenberg joined the NSDAP and SS, *Schutzstaffel* – Protective Squads – and was shortly thereafter recruited into the SD,

---

[1] Final Report on the Case of Walter Schellenberg, NA, RG 319, IRR, XE 001725, Walter Schellenberg, Folders 7 and 8. Until recently, this report was among the lesser-known documents about Walter Schellenberg and could only be found in RG 319. The declassification effort at the National Archives in Washington, DC, has uncovered the same document in both the CIA and FBI files. Reinhard Doerries has published the report, including its twenty-three appendices, introduced by a biographical sketch, as *Hitler's Last Chief of Foreign Intelligence: Allied Interrogations of Walter Schellenberg* (London: Frank Cass, 2003).

[2] Chief of Station, Frankfurt to Chief WE, Specific—Dr. Walter Schellenberg, May 6, 1952, NA, RG 263, Entry ZZ-18, Box 112, File: Schellenberg, Walter, vol. 2, 2 of 2.

Sicherheitsdienst – Security and Intelligence Service – of the SS. Over the course of the next decade, Schellenberg, taking all opportunities given to him and creating additional ones along the way, made a stellar career that brought him close to the head of the SD, Reinhard Heydrich and Himmler. In the summer of 1941, Walter Schellenberg was appointed to lead Office VI, the political foreign intelligence service, of Heinrich Himmler's main instrument of power and terror, the RSHA. Having headed the Gestapo's counterintelligence department in the two years prior to this, Schellenberg was no stranger to intelligence matters. He had written on it, tried to define it in its new, Nazified context, and played a prominent role in broadly defined counterespionage matters, notably in the abduction of two British intelligence officers across the Dutch border in November 1939. Until the end of the war, Schellenberg strove to create in Office VI what he deemed a unified, objective, and infallible foreign intelligence service for all of Germany. Along the way, Schellenberg's upstart agency swallowed Germany's seemingly well-entrenched military intelligence service, the *Abwehr* – literally: the Defense – in February 1944 and battled the *Auswärtige Amt* – Foreign Office – under Minister Joachim von Ribbentrop. Prominently involved in Himmler's last-ditch efforts to negotiate ith the Western Allies in the spring of 1945, Schellenberg managed to extract himself from the fate that befell many of his SS and SD peers. The end of the war found him in Sweden and he subsequently managed to parlay his short-term stint as Himmler's peace emissary, his perception of himself as a reasonable politician, and his knowledge about the inner workings of Nazi Germany into the role of a friendly witness for the Western Allies. Put on trial during the so-called subsequent Nuremberg proceedings, Schellenberg found himself on the docket with members of the Foreign Office. The erstwhile spymaster had morphed into a diplomat. At Nuremberg, he received a lenient sentence of six years but was released on a medical pardon in 1950. Schellenberg spent the last months of his life near Lake Como in Italy, furtively writing and editing his memoirs, which were published after his death, and regaling visitors with his wartime exploits. A myth of Schellenberg's making gained currency.

Walter Schellenberg has remained an enigma and so has the organization he headed. Who was this man? What did he and his organization stand for? What did Office VI do? How did Office VI collect intelligence and how did it use it? How Nazified, how ideological was Office VI? Where was Office VI's locus in Nazi Germany's intelligence universe? Should Office VI be considered an intelligence service in the first place? Schellenberg's own answers to these broad questions – given in interrogations and in his memoir – are as straightforward as they are predictable:

he was not a Nazi but a German patriot doing his selfless best in trying times; Office VI was an ordinary intelligence service intent on collecting up-to-date and relevant information needed for Germany's leadership to make informed decisions; and Nazi ideology and its adherents played a perfunctory and marginal role in the intelligence service, unless Hitler, Himmler, or Heydrich ordered the opposite.

This book is the first analytical study of Nazi Germany's political foreign intelligence service and the man who led it. It addresses two broad historiographical needs at once. As a biographical treatment – not a full biography – it follows Schellenberg's career, paying due attention to his many activities, largely at Heydrich's behest, as an administrator of the *Sicherheitsdienst*, who tried to define policing and intelligence in the context of the National Socialist state, and as the head of the Gestapo's counterintelligence department before his 1941. It then discusses Schellenberg's role and activities at the helm of Office VI. It is also an institutional history of Office VI and its forerunner, the *SD-Ausland* – literally: SD-Abroad – even though it does not account for all its activities. Taking this institutional-biographical approach, the book tells the story of Schellenberg and the service he eventually headed. It locates the service in its proper pedigree of the SS; investigates the office's activities; discusses Office VI and its activities in relation to its two main rivals – the Abwehr and the Auswärtige Amt; considers the role Nazi ideology played in the activities of the office's leading personnel and in their conceptualization and execution of foreign intelligence; and shows that Schellenberg attempted to make Office VI into an Alternative Foreign Office, based solidly in Himmler's universe.

In the early 1930s, when Heinrich Himmler's recently founded SD was consolidating, "foreign intelligence" was already a crowded field in Germany. Civilian and military entities collected foreign intelligence, focusing on information at the core of their respective mandates. The most important civilian, ministerial organization collecting information was the diplomatic service.[3] It was – and is – at the core of a diplomat's brief to gather political intelligence but diplomats' positions and roles are clearly circumscribed: per longstanding international customs, they are not to engage in espionage or run agents. Rather, they collect political information from open sources such as the media or by using general

---

[3] Other ministries kept information-gathering entities as well, see: Michael Geyer, "National Socialist Germany: The Politics of Information," in Ernest R. May, ed., *Knowing One's Enemy: Intelligence Assessment Before the Two World Wars* (Princeton: Princeton University Press, 1984), 322–325; David Kahn, *Hitler's Spies: German Military Intelligence in World War II* (New York: Macmillan, 1978; reprint, Cambridge, MA: DaCapo Press, 2000), 55.

4 The Third Reich's Intelligence Services

contacts established in their host countries.[4] Their primary customer is their minister and other foreign policy decision makers in their home countries. International diplomatic customs also provide an above-board venue for the collection of military information: the military attaché. His job is to keep tabs on the military developments in the host country and to liaise with its military personnel. He is a snoop rather than a spy and in a perfect, theoretical world the exchange of military attachés should safeguard countries from surprises. A military attaché's customers are the foreign minister and decision makers in the military. The Auswärtige Amt of the early 1930s adhered to established international norms; it was, argues Michael Geyer, "static" and had largely withdrawn "from military matters."[5]

Straight military intelligence – for operational and tactical purposes – was collected and evaluated by the services' separate intelligence entities.[6] In this context, the army's intelligence service is the most relevant one. Its evaluation section, the *Nachrichtenabteilung*, Intelligence Branch, originated with the Prussian Great General Staff during the wars of 1866 and 1870/71 but was always drawn down at the end of the military campaigns. Intelligence held a low priority in the Prussian – and later the German – military and was also not considered a place in which ambitious military men could make great careers. Indeed, for the longest time intelligence gathering was not regarded as a separate activity and designated intelligence officers did not exist at the lower levels. This changed during the Great War and in June 1917, the evaluation section, the Intelligence Branch of the General Staff was renamed *Abteilung Fremde Heere*, Foreign Armies Branch. After the war and in violation of the Versailles Treaty, the General Staff remained in a disguised existence as the *Truppenamt*, Troops Department, and so did Foreign Armies, reemerging in the open with the remilitarization of Germany in 1935. Foreign Armies focused on operational and tactical matters – this is what interested its leadership most – but was not averse to bringing into its analyses nonmilitary issues and thus an "aura of completeness." Part of the *Oberkommando des Heeres*, High Command of the Army, Foreign Armies was divided into *Fremde Heere West*, Foreign Armies West, and *Fremde Heere Ost*, Foreign Armies East, in 1939. With this, the former "nerve center of the army's foreign intelligence mutated into a system of theater-intelligence forces,"

[4] "Political Intelligence," in Bruce W. Watson, Susan M. Watson, and Gerald W. Hopple, eds., *United States Intelligence: An Encyclopedia* (New York: Garland Publishing, 1990), 447–449.
[5] Geyer, "Politics of Information," 312; Kahn, *Spies*, 55.
[6] "Military Intelligence," in *United States Intelligence: An Encyclopedia*, 353–354.

yet it is worth keeping in mind that the so-called nerve center largely
restricted itself to operational military foreign intelligence.[7]

What came to be known in the 1920s as the Abwehr also originated
with the General Staff of the Prussian Army during the German War of
1866 when General Helmuth von Moltke created the *Nachrichtenbüro*,
the Intelligence Bureau, to gather covertly foreign intelligence with a
focus on, but not restricted to, military matters and strategic military
intelligence. It took some time before this entity found a permanent
institutional locus in the General Staff but it was eventually designated
O.Q. III b, Oberquartiermeister III B and by the turn of the century, its
funds and staffing levels were rising. By 1901, III b employed some 120
officers, running agents from War Intelligence Posts abroad. Yet there
existed a great schism between the acquisition of foreign intelligence and
espionage, handled by III b, and its evaluation, which took place in the
Intelligence Branch of the General Staff.[8] Before the Great War, then,
the acquisition of foreign intelligence had become largely the military's
responsibility; foreign intelligence was understood primarily as intelligence related to military matters; there was no centralized evaluation
of all intelligence; there was little communication between military and
civilian entities; and the military as a whole continued to underappreciate
intelligence as a field. And there was little interest or patience for "politics, psychology, economics, social problems, and other intangibles,"
as these were unlikely to influence the military's immediate – tactical –
decision-making process.[9] If anyone dealt with these intangibles, it was
the Auswärtige Amt. Certainly not the best set-up, it was workable still
and in a society as dominated by the military as Wilhelmine Germany,
it is not surprising that the military – and not civilian entities – dominated the collection and evaluation of foreign intelligence or that foreign
intelligence was conceived as military intelligence.

After the Great War, during which III b, then headed by Walther
Nicolai, saw both success and lackluster performances, the entity came
to the Troops Department as well.[10] Renamed *Abwehr Gruppe*, Abwehr

---

[7] Kahn, *Spies*, 30–31, 35, 50; Geyer, "Politics of Information," 319, 330–335.
[8] Kahn, *Spies*, 32. Different in Gert Buchheit, *Der Deutsche Geheimdienst: Die Geschichte der militärischen Abwehr* (München: List Verlag, 1966), 19–20. See also Tom Polgar, "The Intelligence Services of West Germany," *International Journal of Intelligence and Counterintelligence*, 1, no. 4 (1986), 82–83.
[9] Heinz Höhne, *Der Krieg im Dunkeln: Macht und Einfluß der deutschen und russischen Geheimdienste* (Gütersloh: Bertelsmann, 1985; reprint Berlin: Ullstein, 1988), 48.
[10] On the Great War, see: Kahn, *Spies*, 34–41; Polgar, "The Intelligence Services," 83–84; Buchheit, *Geheimdienst*, 20–31; also Walter Nicolai, *Geheime Mächte: Interna-tionale Spionage und ihre Bekämpfung im Weltkrieg und Heute* (Leipzig: K.F. Köhler, 1923).

Group – to put adequate emphasis on its supposedly defensive nature, and as Kahn stresses to "camouflage [its] espionage functions" – it was a small entity with big tasks: the collection of intelligence, espionage, and counterintelligence and counterespionage. The late 1920s saw an attempt to centralize foreign intelligence. In 1928, defense minister Wilhelm Groener pulled the Abwehr out of the Troops Department and the naval intelligence out of the Naval Command. Combining it with the Cipher Service, it became the *Abwehr-Abteilung*, the Abwehr Branch. It was eventually integrated into the *Ministeramt*, Ministry Office and declared its sole intelligence-gathering unit. The Abwehr was to focus on strategic and military-political information for the minister, its main customer, and his office "as the military-political nerve center of the state." The plan did not work out, as there was a lack of cooperation and no consensus on national strategies, the precondition, as Geyer emphasizes, for any centralization of German intelligence efforts to work out.[11] In 1932, the Abwehr was placed under naval Captain Konrad Patzig and another navy man, Wilhelm Canaris, replaced Patzig in January 1935. Patzig's appointment can be read as indicative of the Abwehr's limited relevance in the eyes of career army personnel, yet naval officers had a leg-up on their army colleagues: they tended to have more foreign experience. This was certainly true in the case of Wilhelm Canaris.[12] Put differently, directing the Abwehr was not the most coveted assignment but there was also the growing realization that some foreign experience was a useful precondition for it. Geyer argues that at the time of Canaris' appointment in 1935, the Abwehr was on a downward slope. Some of the changes of the late 1920s had been undone: communication intelligence had been returned to the respective services and some of the more ambitious cipher personnel had joined Hermann Göring's *Forschungsamt*, Research Office. Canaris then focused his office's work on something in which nobody else wanted to engage: espionage, counterespionage, and sabotage.[13] And he did well. In 1938, after the dismissal of the War Minister Werner von Blomberg

[11] Kahn, *Spies*, 224; Geyer, "Politics of Information," 316–317; Thomas Menzel, "Organisationsgeschichte des Amtes Ausland/Abwehr im Spiegel der Aktenüberlieferung im Bundesarchiv-Militärarchiv Freiburg i. Br.," *Militärgeschichtliche Zeitschrift* 67/1 (2008), 105–115.
[12] Normal Polmar and Thomas B. Allen, *Spy Book: The Encyclopedia of Espionage* (New York, NY: Random House, 1997), 4. On Canaris, see: André Brissaud, *Canaris: The Biography of Admiral Canaris, Chief of German Military Intelligence in the Second World War*, trans. Ian Colvin (New York, NY: Grosset & Dunlap, 1974); Ian Goodhope Colvin, *Master Spy: The Incredible Story of Admiral Wilhelm Canaris, Who, While Hitler's Chief of Intelligence, Was a Secret Ally of the British* (New York: McGraw-Hill, 1951); Heinz Höhne, *Canaris*, trans. by J. Maxwell Brownjohn (New York, NY: Doubleday, 1979), and Kahn, *Spies*, 226–230.
[13] Geyer, "Politics of Information," 317–318.

and the abolishment of the ministry, the *Oberkommando der Wehrmacht* (OKW), High Command of the Armed Forces, was created; it inherited the Abwehr from the ministry and created, in essence, a new entity, as of October 1939 called *Amt Auslandsnachrichten und Abwehr*, Office for Foreign Information and Counterintelligence. Its Foreign Information section collected and disseminated foreign political material, sometimes likened to "news update[s] in a good newspaper," but its key activities happened in the three branches of the Abwehr. Abwehr I focused on military espionage; Abwehr II on sabotage and covert operations; and Abwehr III on counterespionage. The Office provided both the OKW and OKH – and anyone else who showed interest – with situation reports that also included some rudimentary evaluation.[14] The dislocations of the early 1930s notwithstanding, domestically and abroad the Abwehr was understood as Germany's foreign intelligence service and it was considered successful.

The German case was unusual, then, in that the entity that had the greatest potential and the strongest claim to become a centralized organization for the collection and evaluation of military and political foreign intelligence, the Abwehr, was part of the military. Yet the military held intelligence in low estimation and was primarily interested in operational and tactical and not in strategic intelligence, which went beyond its immediate interests. In Great Britain, in contrast, the services' intelligence units addressed the respective intelligence needs of the services while MI 6, a centralized, clandestine collection agency, answered primarily to the Foreign Office, where most evaluation took place. MI 6 also enjoyed reasonable relations to MI 5, which dealt with counterintelligence in Britain and the colonies, except India, where counterintelligence fell under the responsibility of the Government of India. No integrated service existed, on the other hand, in the United States in the 1930s. Indeed, there – as well as in France – the division between military and political information was more clearly defined and seemingly more workable.[15] Put differently,

[14] Kahn, *Spies*, 47; Geyer, "Politics of Information," 336–337. Menzel, "Organisationsgeschichte," 118–121.
[15] Philip H.J. Davies, *Intelligence and Government in Britain and the United States: A Comparative Perspective. Vol I: Evolution of the US Intelligence Community* (St. Barbara: Praeger, 2012), 167–172; Keith Jeffery, *MI 6: The History of Secret Intelligence Service, 1909–1949* (London: Bloomsbury, 2010), IX–XII; 725–747; Robert J. Young, "French Military Intelligence and Nazi Germany, 1938–1939," in Ernest R. May, ed., *Knowing One's Enemy: Intelligence Assessment Before the Two World Wars* (Princeton: Princeton University Press, 1984), 272–279; Cameron Watt, "British Intelligence and the Coming of the Second World War in Europe," in Ernest R. May, ed., *Knowing One's Enemy: Intelligence Assessment Before the Two World Wars* (Princeton: Princeton University Press, 1984), 242–244; Wesley Wark, *The Ultimate Enemy: British Intelligence and Nazi Germany, 1933–1939* (Ithaca: Cornell University Press, 1985), 20–22.

while not free of conflict, Western intelligence universes, notably the admired British one, had developed reasonable and workable structures. The German intelligence universe, on the other hand, remained in flux, especially after 1933 and its soft spots – fragmentation, decentralization, lack of evaluation, and the unresolved tension between military and political information, tactical and strategic intelligence, domestic and foreign issues – obvious. It was a potential opening for ambitious men and organizations that believed themselves to be the state's elite and to have – qua ideology – the correct answers to questions and problems that had vexed many before them.

There is no shortage of publications about Nazi foreign intelligence efforts, ranging from the sensational to the scholarly with the former outnumbering the latter. Most studies focus on the military intelligence service, the Abwehr.[16] All of them, although for different reasons, declare German foreign intelligence efforts a failure. David Kahn's seminal study *Hitler's Spies*, which focuses on the Abwehr but mentions Office VI, proposes convincing and nuanced explanations for this failure. Unjustifiably arrogant, Germany lost touch with reality; waging an aggressive war, Germany ignored the need for good intelligence until the tide of the war turned against it; many high ranking officers were hostile to the very concept of foreign intelligence; the authority structure of Nazi Germany and the inefficiency of the party state led by a charismatic *Führer* impaired the collection of foreign intelligence; and anti-Semitism deprived the German intelligence community of many scholars who could have benefitted it. Most importantly, Hitler's and Himmler's ideological irrationalism impeded foreign intelligence, "Hitler's charisma devastated German intelligence."[17] In short: already in dire straits due to German hubris, arrogance, and hostility toward the concept of foreign intelligence, Nazi Germany's ideology, structure, and Hitler's personality administered the death blow to German foreign intelligence efforts. Rebecca Ratcliff, on the other hand, focuses more on German traditions than on Nazism. She argues that the German failure to realize that Enigma, the German code-system, had been broken is to be found in German military, intelligence, and cultural traditions. Ratcliff highlights the German penchant for decentralization and specialization; the lack of cooperation; the permanent rivalries for funds and personnel;

---

[16] Kahn, *Spies*; Lauran Paine, *The Abwehr: German Military Intelligence in World War II* (London: Robert Hale, 1984); Richard Breitman et al., eds., *U.S. Intelligence and the Nazis* (Washington, DC: National Archives Trust Fund for the Nazi War Crimes and Imperial Japanese Records Interagency Working Group, 2004).

[17] Kahn, *Spies*, 524–536.

the wish to hire the "right people," as defined by race, class, and military loyalty; and the low priority of intelligence work in the thinking of the military leadership with its concomitant focus on the instant gratification of tactical intelligence. The latter was of particular importance for the practitioners of intelligence; not considered real military men, their need for tangible, quick successes was tantamount – as was their desire to give their work a particular intellectual sheen. Ratcliff posits that many of these traits suited Hitler and the Nazi leadership but came courtesy of German traditions. Nazi rule exacerbated the existing systemic and cultural issues – and associated blind spots – of the German military.[18] How did these issues play out in Office VI, a foreign intelligence outfit that originated with the SS, Nazi Germany's ideological elite? The answer – oftentimes a resounding "it depends" – adds additional nuance to the question and talks broadly to matters of foreign intelligence in the German context.

Most serious studies of German intelligence efforts are written outside of Germany. In the same way that intelligence held low priority among military planners, the study of intelligence has held low priority among historians in Germany – a situation that is slowly changing. There is scant information on intelligence in the official, multivolume, (West-) German study of World War II, *Das Deutsche Reich und der Zweite Weltkrieg*.[19] And the few German-language books on German intelligence efforts are dated and were frequently penned by authors who had been involved in the activities they describe.[20] While both the Abwehr as well as army intelligence efforts find mention in any number of studies on World War II, broad scholarly studies on foreign intelligence efforts, thematic or synthetic, as they are common in the United States or Great Britain, do not exist in the German case.[21] As a consequence, it is, for example, surprisingly difficult to piece together something as basic as the structure and institutional affiliations of the component parts of Germany's

---

[18] Rebecca A. Ratcliff, *Delusions of Intelligence: Enigma, Ultra, and the End of Secure Ciphers* (Cambridge: Cambridge University Press, 2006).

[19] Militärgeschichtliches Forschungsinstitut, ed., *Das Deutsche Reich und der Zweite Weltkrieg*.

[20] For example: Buchheit, *Geheimdienst.*

[21] For example: Davies, *Vol. I: Evolution of the US Intelligence Community*; Philip H.J. Davies, *Intelligence and the Government in Britain and the United States. Vol. II: Evolution of the UK Intelligence Community* (Santa Barbara: Praeger, 2012); Barry M. Katz, *Foreign Intelligence Research and Analysis in the Office of Strategic Service 1942–1945* (Cambridge, MA: Harvard University Press, 1989); Jeffery, *MI 6: The History of Secret Intelligence Service, 1909–1949*; Wark, *The Ultimate Enemy.* For a recent organizational history of German intelligence: Menzel, "Organisationsgeschichte," 105–136.

intelligence universe – military and civilian – before and after 1933, their relationships with each other, and their respective customers.[22] Much work still needs to be done.

These general problems come into even starker relief in the few works on Office VI and its forerunner, the SD-Ausland. Memoirs and thinly disguised memoirs, problematic primary sources at best but rarely treated as such, make up much of the field.[23] Sensationalist journalistic accounts, relying heavily on the aforementioned memoirs and other problematic accounts, round out these offerings.[24] These works hold that Hitler, Himmler, and Heydrich thwarted good intelligence work for ideological reasons. Different from what Kahn argues when it comes to Hitler's role, here these statements are meant to exculpate. That said, like many other politicians, Hitler, Himmler, and Heydrich were, indeed, allergic to intelligence they did not like and which did not conform to perceptions; an extensive literature on the role of perceptions among intelligence customers and its contribution to intelligence failures speaks to this.[25] Yet the leadership's dislike of some of Office VI's findings does not make it good intelligence. However, the focus on the leadership's distaste for certain information, carefully selected parts of Kahn's book, and exculpatory explanations peddled by former Office VI men came to define the understanding of Office VI. Differentiations between the Abwehr, the military foreign intelligence service, and Office VI, the political foreign intelligence service, disappeared or conclusions initially germane – if not necessarily accurate – to studies of the Abwehr were furthermore transferred to Office VI. In addition, scholars and journalists alike did not seem to know what to make of Office VI and its head Schellenberg. There is a palpable uneasiness with an entity that does not conform to what one

---

[22] Still most useful but focusing on 1933 to 1941: Geyer, "Politics of Information," 310–346.

[23] Walter Schellenberg, *The Labyrinth: Memoirs of Walter Schellenberg, Hitler's Chief of Counterintelligence*, intr. Allan Bullock, trans. Louis Hagen (New York: Harper & Brothers, 1956; reprint, Cambridge, MA: Da Capo Press, 2000); Wilhelm Höttl, *Die Geheime Front: Organisation, Personen und Aktionen des deutschen Geheimdienstes* (Linz and Vienna: Nibelungen, 1950); Wilhelm Höttl, *Unternehmen Bernhard: Ein historischer Tatsachenbericht über die größte Geldfälschaktion aller Zeiten* (Wels: Westermühl, 1955); Wilhelm Höttl, *Im Einsatz für das Reich: Im Auslandsgeheimdienst des Dritten Reiches* (Koblenz: Verlag S. Bublies, 1997). Abwehr personnel also wrote exculpatory memoirs.

[24] For example: Andre Brissaud, *The Nazi Secret Service*, trans. Milton Waldman (New York: Norton & Company, 1974); Edmond L. Blandford, *SS Intelligence: The Nazi Secret Service* (Shrewsbury, UK: Airlife Publishing Ltd., 2000).

[25] Richard K. Betts, "Analysis, War, and Decision: Why Intelligence Failures are Inevitable," *World Politics. A Quarterly Journal of International Relations* 31 (1978/1979), 61–89; Michael I. Handel, *War, Strategy, and Intelligence* (London: Frank Cass, 1989), Chapter 4.

would expect of an intelligence service. There are, for example, few missions one can describe, let alone successful ones. Yet the question of intelligence failure is the least of the researcher's problems. There are no clear customers beyond, if at all, Himmler. The office's structure seems in perpetual upheaval and Schellenberg – by his own accounts – focused his attention on peculiar and far-fetched foreign political endeavors. Yet Office VI has always been treated as an intelligence service, maybe a slightly strange one. This book makes the case that this explanatory model falls short and proposes the additional reading of Office VI as a nascent Alternative Foreign Office.

Leaving aside these interpretative questions for the moment, the strong reliance on a few key texts, interrogations, and interviews has proven harmful to scholarly and journalistic endeavors alike – even if it cannot be avoided. Schellenberg's memoirs, for example, can become a liability to historians, but at least his writings can be considered "set," as the author has been dead for decades. Oral histories, interviews, and evolving interpretations by former officials, such as Wilhelm Hoettl, the highest-ranking member of Office VI to live a long life, constitute a greater problem.[26] A prolific postwar information peddler and a member of Austrian and South German neo-Nazi circles, Hoettl, who held a postwar doctorate in history, fashioned himself as the historian of Office VI. Aside from his own publications, he spent his long postwar life talking to historians and journalists, disseminating much dubious information along the way. Many journalistic and scholarly accounts are poorer for their reliance on interviews of Hoettl and others, their descriptive nature, and their lack of analytical rigor.[27] Yet, it is impossible to write about Office VI without using Schellenberg's apologetic memoirs or without paying attention to Hoettl's musings. Schellenberg, for one, impresses less with his ability to tell a tall tale made from whole cloth than by his talent to mix fact with fiction, lie with truth, half lie with full truth, and full lie with half-truth with fiction. Within one sentence, one story, one can find it all. And sometimes Schellenberg is as truthful as a man can be, even though he rarely appears to be without an endgame. Schellenberg was as much a liar as he was a master dissembler, and it is the latter that makes dealing with his statements so difficult. I found that keeping in mind what he possibly wanted to achieve with a certain account provides for a decent window into its likely truthfulness. Like any historical source – maybe even more so – statements by Schellenberg and the

[26] Hoettl, who died in 1999, was of immense interest to US intelligence services after the war. See his voluminous CIA records. NA, RG 263, Entries ZZ-16 and ZZ-18.
[27] For example: Thorsten J. Querg "Spionage und Terror: das Amt VI des RSHA, 1939–1945" (Ph. D. diss., Freie Universität Berlin, 1997).

like have to be evaluated and contextualized carefully, and, if possible, confirmed and reconfirmed independently. Yet still, dealing with Schellenberg's statements is akin to a master class in sources analysis and there is ample room for misinterpretation, as the historian never sees the entire picture but frequently follows a trail someone else has laid for particular reasons. All one can do is to try one's best and keep in mind the sources' possible shortcomings.

Writing intelligence history is a tricky business. In a perfect world one would write a book like this exclusively from contemporaneous records, but this is impossible. In many cases no written record was ever created; existing documents were destroyed or dispersed at the end of the war; or the evidence is fragmentary. I have tried my best to piece together stories from disparate sources held at archives in the United States, Germany, and Russia. There exists no distinct, separate record group for Office VI, let alone its component parts. A great many documents dealing with Office VI can be found among the records of the RSHA and those of Himmler but combining them into a reliable institutional history remains difficult. The matter is made even more difficult by the fact that copies of this record group – organized differently and not always containing the same materials – can be found in different archives in the United States and Germany.[28] The disjointed nature of these sometimes overlapping and sometimes complementary collections makes the work in these records both cumbersome and exciting while records from other German authorities – for example the Auswärtige Amt, held at the *Politische Archiv des Auswärtigen Amts*, Political Archives of the Foreign Office, in Berlin – help to complement and to illuminate further the fractured historical record of Office VI.

A short but intensive research trip to Moscow – during the boiling hot summer of 2006 – yielded additional finds of the contemporaneous sort. *Fond*, record group, 500 of the *Rossiiskii Gosudarstvennyi Voennyi Archiv*, RGVA, Russian State War Archive, in Moscow holds documents from the various RSHA offices and its predecessors. Before their transfer to

---

[28] At the National Archives and Records Administration in Washington, DC, the documents of the *Reichsführer* SS Heinrich Himmler are in RG 242, T-175. The same collection of documents, plus additional documents acquired by the German Federal Archives after the return of the so-called Captured German documents, can be found as Record Group 58 [BAL, R 58] in the Bundesarchiv. The Americans catalogued the documents the way they received them at war's end; the West German archivists attempted to recreate the documents' original structure. The United States Holocaust Memorial Museum holds a copy of the Bundesarchiv's version of this record group [USHMM 14.016 M]; however, this collection does not include documents the Bundesarchiv gained after Germany's reunification from GDR holdings or copies of documents acquired in Poland later.

the RGVA, these materials were held in Moscow's famed KGB archive, known by its shorthand *osobyi* ("special"). Over the years bits and pieces of this record group found their way abroad and former East German archives held some materials dealing with foreign intelligence matters. It appears that the German Democratic Republic acquired these materials in the 1960s, presumably as ammunition in the German-German propaganda wars. These materials are now part of the German *Bundesarchiv*, Federal Archive, in Berlin. And in the early 1990s, the United States Holocaust Memorial Museum, USHMM, in Washington, DC, obtained microfiche copies of documents from fond 500 that deal with the Holocaust.[29] Parts of fond 500 can thus be accessed in the West – and I have seen some documents there – but the majority of documents dealing with foreign intelligence can be used only in Moscow, where I found most of the fond 500 documents I have used in this book. This substantial collection of SD-Ausland/Office VI materials deals with the intelligence service's structure and day-to-day operations in Central, Eastern, and Southeastern Europe and is untouched by archivists' ordering hands. The documents were filmed, to the best of my knowledge with the financial support of the USHMM, but its order is as it must have been at the end of the war when the files were shipped to Moscow. Working with those files has improved tremendously my understanding of the organization, its personnel, and its operations. There is, however, much more to be had in those records, especially when it comes to piecing together operations in various countries. I hope that soon another enterprising historian will delve into these sources.

This book is also among the first to make extensive use of the declassification effort at the National Archives in Washington DC, for I began my investigation of Schellenberg and his office at a fortuitous point in time.[30] There was always material available on Schellenberg and

---

[29] Bundesarchiv-Zwischenarchiv Dahlwitz-Hoppegarten (BA-DH); RSHA Film A to G. When I used these films in Berlin in 2001, they were not yet catalogued and had no official signature or designation. The designation above is my own design, reflecting the information available then. At the United States Holocaust Memorial Museum (USHMM), the collection is labeled "11.001 M, *Osobyi* Archive Moscow." The Bundesarchiv, Berlin Lichterfelde owns a German translation of the Russian finding aid; Western historians also created finding aids to *fond* 500. George C. Browder, "Captured German and Other Nations' Documents in the Osoby (Special) Archive, Moscow," *CEH* 24 (1991), 424–445; George C. Browder, "Update on Captured German Documents in the Former Osoby Archive, Moscow," *CEH* 26 (1993), 335–342.

[30] Other scholars have used these newly declassified materials as well. Stephen Tyas, "Allied Intelligence Agencies and the Holocaust: Information Acquired from German Priosners of War," *Holocaust and Genocide Studies* 22 (Spring 2008), 1–24; Kerstin von Lingen, "Conspiracy of Silence: How the 'Old Boys' Network of American Intelligence Shielded SS General Karl Wolff from Prosecution," *Holocaust and Genocide Studies* 22

on Nazi Germany's foreign intelligence efforts at the National Archives – Captured German Documents as well as documents originating with the Office of Strategic Services, OSS, the Army Staff, or created and pulled together during and for postwar trials, many of them interrogations – but President Clinton's Nazi War Crimes Disclosure Act of 1998 opened the historian's equivalent of Pandora's Box. It declassified documents dealing with Nazi Germany and the CIA, the US Army, and the FBI's postwar recruitment efforts among Nazi officials that had been held back during earlier declassification efforts and eventually – in fits and starts and with delays owed to different administrations' definitions of national security – released almost nine million pages.[31] Among these were unknown interrogations of Schellenberg and other members of Office VI, decodes of Office VI communications, Allied analyses of German intelligence efforts and their practitioners, and a myriad of other documents relevant to my area of interest. These documents complement, expand, and sometimes call into question the existing historical record.

These recently declassified documents are not without problems either. There is, of course, the issue of interrogations and memoirs, which I already touched upon. It is only greater now that there are more of them. But as no declassification effort in the United States will make up for contemporaneous German documents lost, destroyed, or never created, the historian has to rely on interrogations and testimonies in which people – caught red-handed – are trying to put their best foot forward. After the war most of the men involved in German foreign intelligence efforts talked like waterfalls. That does not mean that their statements are reliable. Office VI was an agency permanently in flux; what some of them believed to be true and permanent – from policies to job assignments – was oftentimes but a snapshot. Office VI was also a secretive organization; policies, let alone intentions were not communicated widely. Consequently, some postwar testimonies, even those given with the best intentions, amount to little more than glorified office gossip. Thirdly, Office VI was defined by intense rivalries between individuals and fiefdoms; these rivalries color interrogations vividly. Fourthly, everyone had activities to hide and activities to highlight; for many, their interrogations were akin to step dancing on a tightrope. It is also worth recalling

(Spring 2008), 74–109; Hilary Earl, *The Nuremberg SS-Einsatzgruppen Trial: Atrocity, Law, and History* (New York: Cambridge University Press, 2009); Kerstin von Lingen, *SS and Secret Service. "Verschwörung des Schweigens": Die Akte Karl Wolff* (Paderborn: Ferdinand Schöningh, 2010).
[31] Breitman et al., eds., *U.S. Intelligence*, 4; *Nazi War Crimes & Japanese Imperial Government Records Interagency Working Group. Final Report to the United States Congress*. April 2007. http://www.archives.gov/iwg/reports/final-report-2007.html, accessed May 25, 2015.

that interrogation reports, even stenographic versions, rarely allow for the true voice of the interrogated to be heard – and that is without even considering issues of translation. Lastly, the quality of an interrogation is contingent on an interrogator's level of knowledge at a certain point in time and space. In short: interrogations are the things of which historians' nightmares are made. I have attempted to navigate their pitfalls in a way similar to which I have treated Schellenberg's memoir. I assume the worst and always keep in mind the potential endgame of the interrogated.

Also prominent among these recently declassified documents are Allied analyses of events, organizations, and people. Some of these reports, especially those based on interrogations – well intended and in all likelihood put to together with the greatest possible care – perpetuate the mistakes, misunderstandings, misinformation, and sometimes plain old lies discussed above. Other intelligence briefs, pulled together from anything available then appear brilliantly perceptive, but the historian is well advised to keep in mind the dangers of falling for a short-circuited argument: analysts back then and researchers right now are looking at much of the same materials. Seen in that light, then, allied perceptiveness loses some of its luster. Only additional documents not available at the time of the initial analysis – or not taken into account then – have the potential to break this cycle. It is worth keeping this dynamic in mind. Yet despite all of this, these documents presented me with an unsurpassed opportunity and they will do the same for others. Put differently, I have collected documents here and abroad; I have had the opportunity to work with documents few, if any, other historians have seen; and all my sources – prewar, wartime, and postwar – are fraught with problems. It is a truism of the worst kind that all historical sources have to be evaluated carefully. Yet, it is a particularly true truism when it comes to the topic and the sources at hand here, for they present a perfect archival storm. That said, all history remains estimation; the hope and the goal is to make it as precise, coherent, and waterproof as possible. History is a debate, but in it, we understand the past a bit better.

Even the most comprehensive research remains just that. No single historian can see all documents pertaining to the issue of interest. And the (archival) law of diminishing returns remains a potent reminder that it might not be worth it. Yet there still remains the inkling that some files remain just outside the reach of even the most committed researcher. Richard Breitman notes that "[t]here are strong indications that additional information resides in unreleased British files," drawing attention to a peeved FBI agent who observed that a certain Mr. Johnson, a special interrogator of the War Office in London, had a leg-up on him: "Johnson is a man who has made a study of Schellenberg for the last five years and has had a penetration Agent in close contact with the man for some time. In fact he knows Schellenberg almost as well as he knows himself." The possibilities as to who his penetration agent might have been, if s/he indeed existed, are as endless as they are intriguing, as is speculation about the materials that might remain classified in British archives – dealing with Office VI or with Walter Schellenberg. Similarly, Adrian O'Sullivan makes a strong case that Roman Gamotha of Office VI was turned by the Soviets while on assignment in Persia; here, too, there is no knowing what files might be hidden in Moscow collections and what they might reveal.[32] Yet there is plenty of material available.

No book-length biography exists on Walter Schellenberg – in much the same way that there is no true institutional history of Office VI and its forerunner. Aside from shorter biographical treatments, Reinhard Doerries' most recent book, which also provides a good overview of some of office's activities and is based on an amazing array of documents, comes closest to it.[33] This lacuna is even more surprising if one considers Schellenberg's exculpatory memoir, which is still in wide circulation and a perennial favorite of World War II buffs. Yet it might well be that this, and Schellenberg's talent as a master dissembler, is exactly the reason why. Schellenberg is hard to pin down. On the other hand, there is no private Schellenberg to be found in the sources. The man and private individual remain an enigma and the few glimpses one does get, for example in his divorce proceeding, are unpleasant. The upshot is that the historian is unlikely to get too close to the object of her research or to develop empathy – a concern of many who write biographies of Nazi officials. It is worth noting, though, that slightly different versions of Schellenberg's memoirs are in circulation and there is an indication that his widow held on to "several suit cases [sic] additional material."[34] Whatever those suitcases might have held and wherever they might be today, a scholarly edition of Schellenberg's memoir – as well as an analysis of the changes imposed on it over the years – would

[32] Richard Breitman, "Nazi Espionage: The Abwehr and the SD Foreign Intelligence," in Richard Breitman et al., eds., *U.S. Intelligence and the Nazis* (Washington, DC: National Trust Fund for the Nazi War Crimes and Japanese Imperial Government Records Interagency Working Group, 2004), 114; Adrian O'Sullivan, *Nazi Secret Warfare in Persia (Iran): The Failure of the German Intelligence Services, 1939–1945* (Basingstoke: Palgrave Macmillan, 2014), 136–141, 204–205, 248.

[33] Reinhard R. Doerries, *Hitler's Intelligence Chief Walter Schellenberg: The Man Who Kept Germany's Secrets* (New York: Enigma Books, 2009); Doerries, *Hitler's Last Chief of Foreign Intelligence*; George C. Browder "Walter Schellenberg: Eine Geheimdienst-Phantasie," in Ronald Smelser and Enrico Syring, eds., *Die SS: Elite unter dem Totenkopf. 30 Lebensläufe* (Paderborn: Schöningh, 2000), 418–430.

[34] Berlin to Director, July 2, 1957, NA, RG 263, Entry ZZ-18, Box 112, File: Schellenberg, vol. 2, 2 of 2.

be beneficial to any debate about Nazi Germany and about postwar apologetic tendencies and their influences on (West) German society and beyond.[35]

For many years the biographical approach to writing history, especially biographies of so-called lesser Nazis – a flexible term, indeed – was unfashionable among historians. Structures trumped individuals.[36] This trend turned in the aftermath of Ulrich Herbert's masterful study on Werner Best and recent years have seen several fine biographies of Nazi officials – and an excellent collective biography of the "unbound generation" at the helm of the RSHA – that have paid due attention to structural issues and considered questions of individual ideological steadfastness and convictions.[37] This book does tackle these same issues in discussing Schellenberg's life, career, and politics, but does not claim biographical comprehensiveness. And attentive readers will notice that Reinhard Doerries and I disagree quite frequently on the evaluation and interpretation of Schellenberg's activities, for he is more willing to follow Schellenberg's lead than I am. Reasonable people can disagree and I remain indebted to Doerries, who pushed me to reconsider – if rarely to revise – my assessments.

This book, then, based on a broad document base, combines a biographical treatment of Walter Schellenberg with the institutional history

---

[35] Schellenberg, *Labyrinth*. For an overview on its genesis, see Allan Bullock's introduction. The memoirs have seen numerous editions; Browder, "Schellenberg," 418–430. The original manuscript is held at the Institut für Zeitgeschichte (IfZ) in Munich: IfZ, ED 90/1–5. I use the reprint of the original English-language edition for its readily available translations. The newer edition of the original German version is slightly more detailed but not more truthful. Many historians dealing with the waning months of the Third Reich, for which Schellenberg's memoirs provide one of the few detailed accounts, have relied too heavily on him. Peter Padfield, *Himmler: Reichsführer SS* (New York: Holt, 1991) and Yehuda Bauer, *Jews for Sale? Nazi-Jewish Negotiations* (New Haven: Yale University Press, 1995).

[36] Catherine Epstein, *Model Nazi: Arthur Greiser and the Occupation of Western Poland* (Oxford: Oxford University Press, 2010), 342–344.

[37] Ulrich Herbert, *Best: Biographische Studien über Radikalismus, Weltanschauung und Vernunft 1903–1989*, 2nd ed. (Bonn: Dietz, 1996). See also, for example: Lutz Hachmeister, *Der Gegnerforscher: Die Karriere des SS-Führers Franz Alfred Six* (München: Beck, 1998); Claudia Steur, *Theodor Dannecker: Ein Funktionär der "Endlösung"* (Essen: Klartext Verlag, 1997); Andreas Seeger, *"Gestapo-Müller": Die Karriere eines Schreibtischtäters* (Berlin: Metropol Verlag, 1996); Epstein, *Model Nazi;* Robert Gerwarth, *Hitler's Hangman: The Life of Reinhard Heydrich* (New Haven: Yale University Press, 2011); Peter Longerich, *Heinrich Himmler*, trans. by Jeremy Noakes and Lesley Sharpe (Oxford: Oxford University Press, 2012). An exception to this trend was Peter Black, *Ernst Kaltenbrunner: Ideological Soldier of the Third Reich* (Princeton: Princeton University Press, 1984). See also: Michael Wildt, *Generation des Unbedingten: Das Führungkorps des Reichssicherheitshauptamtes* (Hamburg: Hamburger Edition, 2002) [published in English as *An Uncompromising Generation: The Nazi Leadership of the Reich Security Main Office* (Madison: University of Wisconsin, 2010).]

of the SD-Ausland/Office VI. It consists of nine chapters and revolves around three thematic complexes: Walter Schellenberg's biography and career; Nazi conceptualizations of foreign intelligence; and the development and activities of what came to be known as Office VI of the Reich Security Main Office. Despite the three thematic complexes, this book is visualized best as a braid of two strands – one biographical and the other institutional. These two themes weave in and out and, especially in the first half of the book, seem to exist alongside each other. This changes in the second half of the book when they join together. After the war, US intelligence analysts stated that Schellenberg's personality defined the foreign intelligence service he led, and there is a great deal of truth to that assessment.[38] This was, after all, a state organized by the *Führerprinzip*, leadership principle. Thus, both the organization and its leader need to be investigated, as only then does either one come into view.

Chapter 1 deals with Schellenberg's political socialization, the slow but steady rise of the SD, and Schellenberg's early career within it. It depicts an organization and a man defining and then filling a need, more frequently than not by using ideological precepts. Chapters 2 and 3 are devoted to Schellenberg's rapid rise and surreptitious, yet palpable importance and influence in the Reich Security Main Office and with its leaders. These chapters also consider Schellenberg's role as the head of the Gestapo's counterintelligence department and his attempts to remake it – and intelligence in general – according to Nazi ideology. Chapter 3 draws particular attention to and analyzes several of Schellenberg's ideologized initiatives, which broke new, Nazified ground, and his intimate involvement in many of Nazi Germany's core racist and genocidal policies. Chapter 4 takes a step back from Schellenberg and investigates the activities of Office VI and its forerunner under Heinz Jost and then considers Schellenberg's attempts to remake the office into an ideologized intelligence service upon his appointment to its leadership. Chapter 5 investigates the conflict between the military intelligence efforts and Office VI, focusing, as an example, on Office VI's attempts at mass espionage in the Soviet Union that, in the minds of its instigators, highlighted the office's ideological firmness. The chapter concludes with the absorption of the better part of the Abwehr into Schellenberg's service. Chapter 6 constitutes a case study of Office VI intelligence efforts in Italy and conflict and competition with other German entities there, showcasing an ideologically and racially homogenous intelligence agency

---

[38] The German Intelligence Service and the War, December 1, 1945, NA, RG 319, Entry 134 A, Box 5, XE 003641, German Intelligence Service, 3 of 3.

that deprived itself of any reach beyond Italian Fascists with pro-Nazi leanings. It also delineates various other activities, such as lootings and deportations, in which Office VI engaged under the guise of foreign intelligence. Chapter 7 focuses on the strained relationship between Himmler, Schellenberg, and Office VI on the one hand and Joachim von Ribbentrop and the Auswärtige Amt on the other. It highlights Office VI's attempts to dispose of Ribbentrop – some of them camouflaged as foreign intelligence, some outright bureaucratic attacks on the man and his ministry – and to create what I have termed an "alternative foreign office" at Himmler's disposal. Taken together, Chapters 5–7 argue that even conflicts that appeared functional and driven by bureaucratic or organizational considerations were fought with ideological means and with a keen eye toward ideological considerations. The penultimate chapter (Chapter 8) discusses the last-minute peace feelers of this nascent alternative foreign office, which used concentration camp inmates as pawns in an attempt to either break up the anti-Hitler alliance outright or to reach a separate agreement with the Western Allies, which would have broken up the alliance by default. The chapter contends that these efforts were not the aberration but rather consistent with basic tenets of Nazi ideology – most notably the existence of "Jewish World Conspiracy" – and with the foreign political role that Schellenberg and Himmler envisioned for Office VI. The last chapter (Chapter 9) focuses on Schellenberg in Allied captivity and discusses his and his captors' use of his knowledge in the postwar period; it details Schellenberg's fate and considers questions of postwar justice and myth making. I draw together the study's findings in the Concluding Thoughts.

My study proposes several revisions to the understanding of Office VI and its forerunner. For one, it shows that Nazi Germany's political foreign intelligence service can be understood only through its pedigree. Office VI was not simply yet another, if somewhat peculiar, German intelligence service but needs to be placed in its concrete institutional and ideological context, and this context was the SS and the SD. The service habitually used ideology to conceptualize foreign intelligence; ideology was the defining feature and lodestar of Office VI. It determined the mandate of Office VI and expanded its role vis-à-vis other entities and thereby advanced the functional radicalization of Nazi Germany and its bureaucracy. Ideology was fundamental in winning bureaucratic conflicts and in breeding, preserving, and extending power; it determined personal advancement and institutional success. Always present, the importance of ideology was, however, not static. Within certain parameters, ideology was adjustable to the pragmatic needs of the day, especially when it came to conflicts with other party and state authorities. And Schellenberg was a master at finding the appropriate mixture between ideology and pragmatism.

Ideology – racism, anti-Semitism, and anti-Bolshevism – was Office VI's key ingredient but it was not brought to bear on the service from without, as many claimed after the war. Instead, the policies and activities of the service were shaped by ideological leanings coming from inside the office. Ideology was the prism through which the personnel of the service conceived, executed, and evaluated their work, and this ideological prism seriously – and on every level – fractured and distorted their view of the world and its realities. It was not Hitler's (or Himmler's or Heydrich's) ideologically slanted judgments, imposed from above, that damaged foreign intelligence. Rather, ideological convictions coming from within the service, its homogenous nature, and the groupthink these conditions created made for poor intelligence.

Conflicts between the component part of a country's intelligence universe, intensive intramural fights for dominance, preconceptions guiding the collection and evaluation of intelligence, and spectacular intelligence failures are, however, by no means a specialty of Office VI or Nazi Germany. What, if anything, makes this different then? Much of the answer can be found in Nazi ideology and its wish for totality. Information was a "passkey to power," for it could provide access to Hitler; was a lever in the "struggle for power;" expanded power bases; and gave access to additional resources.[39] But intramural fights went beyond anything that seems reasonable, yet it is worth recalling that the stakes were high. The losing party – oftentimes irreconcilably tainted as ideologically lacking – would find it difficult to recover its standing and influence. Other parts of the answer can be found in the state's structure, for the point of intelligence was not to have ample information to guide a decision. Rather, it was to have the right information. Intelligence meant to divine what customers, Himmler and most notably Hitler, were about to decide: to "work toward the Führer" (Ian Kershaw) and to create a situation or to collect the information that would make this decision appear correct. It was intelligence as activism. Intelligence collection and its evaluation, if the latter happened, was also, and on every level, conducted by men who shared their leaders' ideological make-up. This congruence of ideological convictions also existed when reports did not hit the mark with the customers, for sometimes they divined wrongly or erred on the side of ideological pragmatism when their customers were not inclined to do so. It is also worth noting that these men were amateurs who shared similar generational and social experiences and lacked the familiarity with the

---

[39] Geyer, "Politics of Information," 329, 339.

countries in which they were supposed to collect information; they were, indeed, a group of homogenous provincials. However, they were certain that National Socialist ideology transcended these shortcomings and allowed them to understand the world correctly, for "[w]hat outsiders saw as ideology, Nazis experienced as truth."[40] Put differently: the state's structure, its ideology, and its servants transformed a common problem of intelligence services into an inherently unsolvable mess.

I also show that, although conceived and branded as a foreign intelligence service and studied as such, Office VI was – simultaneously – both less and more. Schellenberg was readying Office VI to function as an alternative Foreign Office at Himmler's disposal, as evidenced, for example, in Office VI's conflict with Ribbentrop's Auswärtige Amt and its forays into negotiations with the Western Allies.[41] It remains patently unclear what exactly Schellenberg envisioned for the future, but he clearly held that he and Himmler would do better than Ribbentrop. Here, too, an ideological view of the world, leavened by a dose of pragmatism, determined Schellenberg's and the office's activities. Focusing on what Schellenberg and Office VI did – as opposed to what they were supposed to do according to their names and titles – interesting new vistas open up: Office VI was anything but an intelligence service and its forays into foreign policy were not aberrations but at the core of what Schellenberg's envisioned his office to be – the center of foreign intelligence and foreign policy efforts. Put differently, I set forth a more sophisticated and nuanced interpretation of Nazi Germany's political foreign intelligence service and its main proponents that removes it from the "oddity" column and takes seriously an entity that, despite its spectacular intelligence failures, wielded tremendous influence and strove to conduct foreign policy. The ramifications of this approach – for the understanding of the Nazi state, intelligence matters, and the course of World War II – are far-reaching and apparent. In recent years, the investigation of foreign intelligence efforts and its role in the political decision making process has garnered more attention among historians.[42] Here I show that for Germany's Office VI, ideology, the fight for additional resources and power, wrested from entities deemed ideologically unsound, and the vision of itself as an ideologically sound but still pragmatic foreign policy center, not only mattered but was

---

[40] Claudia Koonz, *The Nazi Conscience* (Cambridge, MA: The Belknap Press of Harvard University Press, 2003), 2.

[41] Richard Breitman, among others, alludes to Schellenberg's foreign policy efforts; Breitman, "Nazi Espionage, "106.

[42] David Bankier, ed., *Secret Intelligence and the Holocaust: Collected Essays from the Colloquium at the City University of New York, Graduate Center* (New York and Jerusalem: Enigma Books and Yad Vashem, 2006); Breitman et al., eds., *U. S. Intelligence.*

fundamental. And it spelled failure on each and every level with ideology taking the pride of place.

The investigation of Office VI also enhances the understanding of the SD, the Reich Security Main Office, and Nazi Germany's functional elites. Studies of the SD oftentimes focus on its formative years and do not address Office VI and its forerunner in any detail.[43] This study begins to plug this hole, which is of particular import as a number of recent studies have focused on particular branches of the SD or on SD investigations of certain *Lebensgebiete*, areas of life.[44] Office VI constitutes a missing piece in this historiography and this study allows for a more comprehensive understanding of the SD and the RSHA, achievements like Michael Wildt's magisterial study of the "unbound generation," which led these entities, notwithstanding. Lastly, the book adds to the study of those men who are at the core of a key debate about Nazi Germany's nature: what made it function the way it did? Investigating Walter Schellenberg and Office VI is one step in answering this question.

[43] Shlomo Aronson, *Reinhard Heydrich und die Frühgeschichte von Gestapo und SD* (Stuttgart: Deutsche Verlagsanstalt, 1971); George C. Browder, "Sipo and SD, 1931–1940: Formation of an Instrument of Power" (Ph.D. diss., University of Wisconsin, 1968); George C. Browder, "Die Anfänge des SD: Dokumente aus der Organisationsgeschichte des Sicherheitsdienstes des Reichsführers SS," *VfZ* 27 (1979), 299–32; George C. Browder, *Foundations of the Nazi Police State: The Formation of Sipo and SD* (Lexington: University Press of Kentucky, 1990); George C. Browder, *Hitler's Enforcers: The Gestapo and the SS Security Service in the Nazi Revolution* (New York: Oxford University Press, 1996); George C. Browder, "Die frühe Entwicklung des SD. Zur Entstehung multipler institutioneller Identitäten," in Michael Wildt, ed., *Nachrichtendienst, Politische Elite und Mordeinheit: Der Sicherheitsdienst des Reichsführers SS* (Hamburg: Hamburger Edition, 2003), 38–56. See also: Michael Wildt, "Einleitung," in Michael Wildt, ed., *Nachrichtendienst, Politische Elite und Mordeinheit. Der Sicherheitsdienst des Reichsführers SS* (Hamburg: Hamburger Edition, 2003), 7–37. For an East German treatment of the SD, based on sources maintained by the East German Stasi (State Security Service), see: Ramme, *Sicherheitsdienst*. For a discussion of the leadership corps of Sipo and SD, see: Jens Banach, *Heydrichs Elite: Das Führerkorps der Sicherheitspolizei und des SD, 1936–1945* (Paderborn: Schöningh, 1998). On the SS with a good discussion of Office VI, see: Höhne, *Orden*.

[44] Wolfgang Dierker, *Himmlers Glaubenskrieger: Der Sicherheitsdienst des SD und seine Religionspolitik 1933–1941* (Paderborn: Schöningh, 2002) and Michael Wildt, *Die Judenpolitik des SD 1935–1938: Eine Dokumentation* (München: Oldenbourg Verlag, 1995); Carsten Schreiber, *Elite im Verborgenen: Ideologie und regionale Herrschaftspraxis der Sicherheitsdienstes der SS und seines Netzwerkes am Beispiel Sachsens* (München: Oldenbourg Wissenschaftsverlag, 2008); Michael Wildt, ed., *Nachrichtendienst, Politische Elite und Mordeinheit: Der Sicherheitsdienst des Reichsführers SS* (Hamburg: Hamburger Edition, 2003).

1   Gaining a Foothold

Friends and foes alike agreed upon his intellectual abilities and his work ethic, attributes that helped his career. Alternately described as charming and personable or as evasive and cunning, Walter Friedrich Schellenberg was barely over thirty when, after an almost meteoric ascent through the ranks of the SD, he was appointed to head the foreign intelligence section of Heinrich Himmler's Reich Security Main Office in the summer of 1941. He thus became one of the six (sometimes seven) RSHA department heads and moved in the highest circles of Nazi Germany's elites. Who was this man? Where did Schellenberg come from?

In his postwar memoir, a self-promotional and exculpatory spymaster's tale as well as in testimonies given in allied captivity, Schellenberg told a simple story that must have resonated with many of his German contemporaries. It also captured the imagination of his allied interrogators. The youngest of seven children, Schellenberg was born in Saarbrücken in 1910. His father was a piano manufacturer whose business fell on hard times in the aftermath of the Great War and the French occupation of the Saar territory. The family eventually relocated to Luxembourg; Schellenberg stated that his interest in foreign policy began then. Schellenberg's mother was a homemaker, and – postwar – he credited her with his "Christian upbringing." His father's "liberal philosophy and outlook," he claimed to have felt later in his youth.[1] After graduating from the *Realgymnasium*, high school, Schellenberg began his studies in the summer term of 1929. He allegedly matriculated in medicine but switched to law for economic considerations, passing his first judicial state exam at the University of Bonn in early 1933. He joined the NSDAP and the SS the same spring.[2]

Schellenberg proffered various postwar explanations for his decision to join the party and the SS: when he attempted to secure a state grant for

---

[1] Walter Schellenberg, *The Labyrinth: Memoirs of Walter Schellenberg, Hitler's Chief of Counterintelligence*, intr. Allan Bullock, trans. Louis Hagen (New York: Harper & Brothers, 1956; reprint, Cambridge, MA: Da Capo Press, 2000), 2.

[2] Schellenberg, *Labyrinth*, 1–2.

his mandatory traineeship in law, the judge who reviewed Schellenberg's application "suggested that my chances of securing a grant would increase *appreciably* [emphasis added] if I were a member of the Nazi Party and one of its formations, the SA or the SS." Schellenberg did not hesitate taking this advice.[3] While his immediate reason to join the Nazis was, then, mercenary, in his memoir Schellenberg justified his decision to join the NSDAP in generalized political terms:

It was obvious that a more vigorous program was needed which would overcome the social injustices of the Weimar Republic and bring about some equal status for Germany among the nations, as well as a revision of the Versailles Treaty. It seemed to me only just that Germany should strive for those rights which every sovereign nation, and especially France, had fought to secure for itself. [. . .] I was certain, as was the majority of these people [rushing to join the Nazi party], that Hitler was a political realist and that having gained power he would now drop the more extreme and unreasonable aspects of his program – such as the measures against the Jews. These might have been useful to gain adherents in the past, but they certainly could not serve as principles on which to run a modern state.[4]

Schellenberg also joined the SS, Nazi Germany's ideological elite. His postwar explanation is a peculiar combination of social ambition and protestations of naïveté:

All young men who joined the Party had to join one of its formations as well. The SS was already considered an 'élite' organization. The black uniform of the Fuehrer's special guard was dashing and elegant, and quite a few of my fellow-students had joined. In the SS one found the 'better type of people' and membership in it brought considerable prestige and social advantages, while the beer-hall rowdies of the SA were beyond the pale.[5]

Schellenberg's initial experience with the SS was typical, tiresome, and much less glamorous than he had anticipated. However, within short order he secured a task he deemed more "suitable" than monotonous

---

[3] Schellenberg, *Labyrinth*, 3. There is some confusion as to when Schellenberg joined the party and SS. According to his handwritten *Lebenslauf*, he joined the SS in March 1933 and the party in April. His SS *Stammkarte*, on the other hand, notes that he joined the SS on April 1, 1933 and the party on May 1, 1933. See Schellenberg's SS file, NA, RG 242, BDC, A 3343, SSO, Reel 074B. A 1944 promotion request states that Schellenberg joined both party the and SS on April 1, 1933, see IfZ, FA 74, 11–12. His party membership card records May 1, 1933 as Schellenberg's entry into the party; see NA, RG 242, BDC, A 3343, MFKL, Reel 0047. Another document suggests that Schellenberg's initial party membership did not go through, as his initial application for membership lacked his signature; NSDAP Gauleitung, Köln-Aachen, Ortsgruppe Bonn-Süd to Walter Schellenberg, December 12, 1933, NARA, RG 469, Entry 11, Folder Schellenberg 40F8. This might explain the difference. The secondary literature relies on his *Stammkarte*.
[4] Schellenberg, *Labyrinth*, 3.   [5] Schellenberg, *Labyrinth*, 3.

military drills, for he was tasked to deliver indoctrination talks at the university. Most of his talks and lectures allegedly dealt with historical matters, such as the development of Germanic law or consisted of attacks on the Catholic Church. These speeches facilitated Schellenberg's initial contact with the SD, the *Sicherheitsdienst*, security and intelligence service of the SS.

Two professors, both honorary, unsalaried members of the SD, asked Schellenberg to join Himmler's intelligence service. They also introduced him to the entity's function: gathering "information that could help the government to form policy or to evaluate the results of policy decisions already taken." Indicating that Schellenberg might be able to parlay his interest in foreign policy into a career with the SD's foreign section, they suggested that he should continue his legal career and become an honorary member of the SD. This piqued Schellenberg's interest, but he was also pleased that as an SD member he would be relieved of all regular SS duties.[6]

Subsequently, Schellenberg continued his legal training. He initially worked at the Police Headquarters in Frankfurt/Main where, according to his memoir, he was always assigned to the most interesting cases against *Gauleiter*, party district leaders. He twice went to Berlin to report to the Interior Minister and eventually met with Heinrich Müller, the head of the political police, who told him that Reinhard Heydrich, the head of the SD, had taken an interest in him. The next day Schellenberg had an appointment at the *Sicherheitshauptamt*, SD Main Office, where he was assigned to the administrative department, working under the supervision of SS Oberführer Herbert Mehlhorn. While Schellenberg stated that Mehlhorn "built up for Heydrich the machinery with which he could secretly survey every sphere of German life," Schellenberg does

---

[6] Schellenberg, *Labyrinth*, 4–5. Schellenberg was then still a member of the Catholic Church. He stated that his first lecture with "an outspoken anti-Catholic bias" captured the interest of Reinhard Heydrich. His later colleagues were keenly aware that Schellenberg's career commenced with teaching *Weltanschauung*; see SS Sturmbannfuehrer Dr. Wilhem Hoettl, A Character Sketch of Schellenberg: Chief of Germany's Espionage Service, July 12, 1945, NA, RG 226, Entry 199A, Box 55, Folder 1602 [hereafter: Hoettl/Character Schellenberg]. Schellenberg names one of the professors: Prof. Ne(h)lis, a philologist; Final Report on the Case of Walter Schellenberg, NA, RG 319, IRR, XE 001725, Walter Schellenberg, Folder 7 and 8 [hereafter: Final Report]. Nelis joined the NSDAP in 1933 and was active in the NS-*Dozentenbund*. He was an instructor at the Teachers' Seminary in Bonn in 1934/35; appointed professor in Berlin in 1935. Hochschullehrerkartei, BAL R 4901/13272. I owe this information to Hans-Joachim Langhans, Berlin. In his memoir, Schellenberg notes that he performed SS guard duties for the last time when the Nazi leadership met at Hotel Dreesen in Bad Godesberg to decide the fate of Ernst Röhm and his SA, providing a vivid description of seeing a discussion among Hitler, Göring, Goebbels, and others through a window while in the midst of a thunderstorm.

not give any indication of his own tasks.[7] Thus goes the bare outline of Schellenberg's rendition of his political socialization and early career.

For a man of Schellenberg's importance and standing within the Nazi hierarchy, little solid information is available. Evidence is fragmentary at best and the differences between Schellenberg's own renditions of his early life appear minute and have received little attention. Consequently, Schellenberg's own, accessible account defines the literature, albeit with additions and qualifications.[8] It is, however, worthwhile exploring Schellenberg's personal and political background in detail. How did the youngest son of a Catholic, lower middle-class piano manufacturer rise so rapidly in the ranks of the SD? What was Schellenberg's political and ideological make-up?

Fragmentary evidence brought together in order to locate Walter Schellenberg in his ideological and political milieu shows an ambitious, almost mercenary young man with a taste for elite organizations and an unquenchable thirst for societal ascent. It reveals a man who moved comfortably on the right fringes of a decidedly National Conservative milieu and then cast his lot with those who were most likely to determine Germany's future: the Nazi Party and its most elite organizations. The fragmentary evidence also allows for deliberations about Schellenberg's "battle with the truth," to use Gitta Sereny's apt term, that permeates all his statements and makes into such a challenge the study of his person, activities, and the organization he led. The following pages also touch upon Schellenberg's attempts to fashion a respectable, Catholic, and National Conservative postwar identity through his finely calibrated narrative strategies. This chapter then provides insight into Schellenberg's early career, his motivations, and his pathology. Schellenberg was a careful and accomplished obfuscator, keenly aware of audiences and accomplished at dispensing the one statement that successfully straddled the line between half-, quarter-, and non-truths – and always to his benefit.

---

[7] Schellenberg, *Labyrinth*, 7–9.
[8] David Kahn, *Hitler's Spies: German Military Intelligence in World War II* (New York: Macmillan, 1978; reprint, Cambridge, MA: Da Capo Press, 2000), 255; Thorsten J. Querg "Spionage und Terror: das Amt VI des RSHA, 1939–1945" (Ph. D. diss., Freie Universität Berlin, 1997), 224–225; Michael Wildt, *Generation des Unbedingten: Das Führungskorps des Reichssicherheitshauptamtes* (Hamburg: Hamburger Edition, 2002), 262–263; George C. Browder, *Hitler's Enforcers: The Gestapo and the SS Security Service in the Nazi Revolution* (New York: Oxford University Press, 1996), 224–226; Reinhard R. Doerries, *Hitler's Last Chief of Foreign Intelligence: Allied Interrogations of Walter Schellenberg* (London: Frank Cass, 2003), 3–55; George Browder "Walter Schellenberg. Eine Geheimdienst-Phantasie," in Ronald Smelser and Enrico Syring, eds., *Die SS: Elite unter dem Totenkopf. 30 Lebensläufe* (Paderborn: Schöningh, 2000), 418–430.

There are no blatant lies in Schellenberg's postwar renditions of his life. Additional materials do, however, provide a fuller, more nuanced picture or call into question some of his assertions and their implications. There is, for example, no independent confirmation that Walter Schellenberg lived in Luxembourg as a teenager; his early introduction life abroad and his alleged cosmopolitanism seem a figment of his imagination. Conversely, Schellenberg's childhood and youth in the Saar territory, which under the Treaty of Versailles came under a League of Nations mandate that was lifted after the plebiscite in 1935, does not seem to have influenced or politicized him at all, as had been the case with many of his later SD peers.[9] Schellenberg's political inactivity is noteworthy as he presented himself as older and more aware than his years in his writings, highlighting experiences and memories that aligned him with the members of the "war youth generation." Born in 1910, however, Schellenberg can barely be considered part of this generation.[10] Schellenberg stressed that he was just old enough to remember the terrors of war, and the "hard winter of that year, the hunger, the cold, and the misery." Similarly, Schellenberg tied the family's alleged relocation to Luxembourg, his decision to forgo the study of medicine, and his financial situation as a student to postwar economic deprivations, noting these as the most

---

[9] Wildt, *Generation*, 60–63; Catherine Epstein, *Model Nazi: Arthur Greiser and the Occupation of Western Poland* (Oxford: Oxford University Press, 2010).

[10] The concept of "generations" as a tool to understand mentalities has seen a renaissance; Ulrich Herbert's seminal study, *Best: Biographische Studien über Radikalismus, Weltanschauung und Vernunft 1903–1989*, 2nd ed. (Bonn: Dietz, 1996). Herbert's classification is based in on E. Günther Gründel, *Die Sendung der Jungen Generation: Versuch einer umfassenden revolutionären Sinndeutung der Krise* (München: C.H. Beck'sche Verlagsbuchhandlung, 1932). It is worth noting that Gründel's book was a proto-fascist rallying call for the "generations" he discussed but it also describes their self-perception. Gründel defines three generations in their relation to the Great War: the "young front generation," born between 1890 and 1900; the "war youth generation," born between 1900 and 1910; and the "postwar generation," born after 1910. The "young front generation" was defined by its front experience, which translated into their later radicalism. The numerically largest "war youth generation" lacked the frontline experience, but was old enough to remember the euphoria of 1914, early successes, and a Volk-centered nationalism. They also remembered the end of the war and its aftermath. This generation compensated for their lack of frontline experience by espousing a passion for objectivity, coldness, rationality, and economic thinking. These tendencies were exacerbated among youths growing up in the borderlands that came under temporary foreign occupation, which they regarded as "their war." Lastly, the "postwar generation" had no active recollection of the war but was defined by the war and its aftermath still. Gründel saw this generation as industrious, determined, and capable of expertly running the world. Gründel, *Sendung*, 57–58; Herbert, *Best*, 43–45. Gründel's definitions are less precise than Herbert's and he has reservations about including boys born between 1906 and 1910 into the "war youth generation," but notes that they experienced postwar deprivation. Gründel, *Sendung*, 42–44.

important experiences of his early life.[11] In his construction of a postwar identity Schellenberg clearly aligned himself with the generation of men influential in Nazi Germany. He saw himself as one of them.

Schellenberg's politically apathetic tone in his memoir is therefore unexpected. He stated that before 1933 he "had not paid much attention to the political questions of the day, but [...] was not unaware of the severity of the social crisis."[12] Similarly, his justification as to why he joined the Nazi Party in 1933 lacks ideological fervor. Focusing on the dire economic and social situation of the late Weimar Republic and the perceived injustices of the Versailles Treaty, Schellenberg portrayed himself as someone with a common political outlook. Even more so, Schellenberg emphasized that he was one of the many supporters of the Nazi Party who believed that the party's radical days were over after Hitler's appointment as chancellor. Stock explanations, which played well with his postwar audiences, give few insights into Schellenberg's motivations. A closer look at Schellenberg's university studies, however, allows for a valuable window into his political socialization and overall leanings.

Schellenberg neither matriculated in Bonn nor did he switch from medicine to law. He spent the first two and a half years of his law studies at the Philipps-Universität in Marburg; there he also joined the elitist *Corps Guestphalia*.[13] As a university and a town, Marburg had a peculiar reputation during the Weimar Republic, and it is possible to draw a few conclusions about Schellenberg from his choice to commence his studies there. The Philipps-Universität was a renowned school. Founded as the first Protestant university in Germany in the mid-sixteenth century, it had undergone a major expansion in the years before the Great War that transformed it into one of Germany's best-equipped universities. Even the economic decline after the Great War did not tarnish its reputation. It counted several of Germany's best-known scholars among its faculty.[14] Marburg was a prestigious and proudly Protestant environment.

Marburg was also known for its vibrant social scene, regarded by many (male) students as the perfect "summer university," at which to enjoy

---

[11] Schellenberg, *Labyrinth*, 2. Both Schellenberg's Lebenslauf and files at the University of Marburg show that Schellenberg matriculated in law. *Lebenslauf*, n.d., NA, RG 242, BDC, A 3343, SSO, Reel 074B; Hessisches Staatsarchiv (HStA) Marburg, Bestand 305 a, Acc 1963/13, No.90, No. 95, No. 100, No 105; Bestand 305 a, Acc. 1971/26, No. 350.

[12] Schellenberg, *Labyrinth*, 3.

[13] *Lebenslauf*, n.d., NA, RG 242, BDC, A 3343, SSO, Reel 074B; Final Report.

[14] Anne Chr. Nagel, ed., *Die Philipps-Universität im Nationalsozialismus: Dokumente zu ihrer Geschichte* (Stuttgart: Franz Steiner Verlag, 2000), 1; Rudy Koshar, *Social Life, Local Politics and Nazism: Marburg 1880–1935* (Chapel Hill: University of North Carolina Press, 1986).

the social life of the various students' associations, fraternities, and corps. These student associations and their shared characteristics defined university and city. Most student associations were dueling, conservative, and elitist; their networks of *Alte Herren*, senior members, provided ambitious young men with good networking opportunities.[15] The corps, inaccurately tracing their origins to medieval university life, were the most conservative organizations among the various fraternities and student associations. In their modern form, most of these corps originated in the early nineteenth century; Guestphalia, founded in 1806, was among the oldest. The corps considered themselves an "elite within the [student] elite" and as the "intellectual leadership of the nation." Corps students were recruited from circles that made up Germany's higher civil service: the aristocracy and highest rungs of the bourgeoisie.[16] Even though over time recruitment standards had been lowered to include students of lesser social standing, the corps remained the most prestigious student associations. The fraternities and corps, increasingly attracted by radical and *völkisch* politics, defined the political disposition of the city in the Weimar Republic and made it into an antirepublican and anti-Semitic environment. This reputation was owed partly to the student associations and their history during the Weimar Republic, in particular the so-called Murders at Mechterstädt.[17] In March 1920, Marburg fraternity and corps students were called into action by the government to stifle Communist and Independent Socialist activities in neighboring Thuringia. The unrest had broken out in reaction to the preceding right-wing Kapp *Putsch*, attempted coup, in Berlin. The corps' political loyalties were, however, largely with the defeated antirepublican *putschists* in

---

[15] For different evaluations of the corps and fraternities, see: R.G.S. Weber, *The German Student Corps in the Third Reich* (New York: St. Martin's Press, 1986); Helma Brunck, *Die Deutsche Burschenschaft in der Weimarer Republik und im Nationalsozialismus* (München: Universitas Verlag, 1999); Hans Peter Bleuel and Ernst Klimmert, *Deutsche Studenten auf dem Weg ins Dritte Reich: Ideologie-Programme-Aktionen, 1918–1935* (Gütersloh: Siegfried Mohn Verlag, 1967); Alexandra Kurth, *Männer – Bünde – Rituale: Studentenverbindungen seit 1800* (New York and Frankfurt: Campus Verlag, 2004), esp. 110. Senior members traditionally functioned, "bei der Ämterpatronage als bekannteste Verteilerzentrale."

[16] Kurth, *Männer*, 171; Die Altherrenschaft, ed., *Die Guestphalia zu Marburg*, 2 vols. (Melsungen: Bernecker, 1937 and 1938); Bleuel and Klimmert, *Studenten*, 84.

[17] Nagel, *Philipps-Universität*, 1. On the "Mechterstädt" and its repercussions Peter Krüger and Anne Chr. Nagel, eds., *Mechterstädt – 25.3.1920. Skandal und Krise in der Frühphase der Weimarer Republik* (Münster: Lit Verlag, 1997); Koshar, *Marburg*, 1880–1935, 152; Hellmut Seier "Radikalisierung und Reform der Universität Marburg, 1918–1933," in Walter Heinemeyer, Thomas Klein, Hellmut Seier, eds., *Academia Marburgensis: Beiträge zur Geschichte der Philipps-Universität Marburg*, vol. 1 (Marburg: N.G. Elwert Verlag, 1977), 303–352; James Weingärtner, "Massacre at Mechterstädt," *The Historian* 73 (1975), 598–618.

Berlin. Deployed near Mechterstädt, the students from Marburg, led by a Guestphalia member and including several other Guestphalia students among their ranks, killed fifteen men in their captivity. In subsequent years, the Murders at Mechterstädt defined preconceptions about the Marburg and its university on both sides of the political divide. Supporters of the Weimar Republic saw Marburg as a hotbed of the reaction, while the Marburg fraternity and corps students and their supporters argued that the government had called into action the students but later abandoned them – in the court of law and in the court of public opinion. In the aftermath of the "Mechterstädt," many students grew ever more suspicious of and antagonistic toward the Weimar Republic; through customs, habits, and political persuasions the student associations became the "counter-image of the Weimar democracy."[18] The political leanings of many of the fraternities and corps and their overall suspicion of and antagonism toward the Weimar Republic frequently translated into pro-Nazi or Nazi activities. A small chapter of the *Nationalsozialistischer Deutscher Studentenbund*, National Socialist German Students' Association, not yet a significant organization, was founded in Marburg in 1926.[19] University students also constituted Weimar Germany's anti-Semitic avant-garde. During the 1920s, most fraternities and corps officially adopted anti-Semitic admission practices; unofficially, Jews had not been welcome in these student associations for many years prior. Guestphalia had been among the first corps to introduce anti-Semitic admission policies; it had done so in 1920. Any member had to be of "Aryan" descent.[20] With the preponderance of the student associations in Marburg, the university came to be known as an inhospitable place among Jewish students. They tended to avoid Marburg.[21]

The antirepublican and anti-Semitic disposition of the city was, however, not solely of the students' making or restricted to them. The Marburg citizenry, too, leaned right. In the elections of September 1930, the NSDAP reached 18.3 percent nationally. In Marburg, the NSDAP received 28.8 percent of the vote, making it the strongest party there. This stunning result was not a fluke. During the 1932 election for Reich President, Paul Hindenburg defeated Hitler on the national level.

[18] Kurth, *Männer*, 168.
[19] Nagel, *Philipps-Universität*, 58. Also Geoffrey Giles, *Students and National Socialism in Germany* (Princeton: Princeton University Press, 1985); Anselm Faust, *Der Nationalsozialistische Deutsche Studentenbund: Studenten und Nationalsozialismus in der Weimarer Republik*, 2 vols. (Düsseldorf: Schwann, 1973).
[20] Bleuel and Klimmert, *Studenten*, 148; Kurth, *Männer*, 122–128; Siegfried Weichlein "Studenten und Politik in Marburg. Die politische Kultur einer Universitätsstadt 1918–1920," in Krüger and Nagel, eds., *Mechterstädt.*, 32.
[21] Nagel, *Philipps-Universität*, 59.

In Marburg, Hitler received the majority of votes. And in the national elections for parliament later that year, the NSDAP received almost 50 percent of the votes in Marburg, 16 percent more than the German average. This was nothing short of a sensational result.[22] When it came to the envisioned National Socialist revolution, Marburg was ahead of the national curve.

It is tempting to overstate the importance of politics for Walter Schellenberg's decision to commence his university studies in Marburg, in particular due to the lack of other materials illuminating his political socialization. However, Schellenberg's decision for Marburg gives indication of his political leanings and future ambitions. He chose an elite institution and religious concerns did not temper Schellenberg's ambitions, opted for an intensely Protestant environment: 86.8 percent of Marburg's students were Protestant, 11.2 percent Catholic, and 0.9 percent Jewish. But attending Marburg University and embracing its Protestant mainstream culture could afford Schellenberg professional advantages well beyond the restrictions of his social and religious milieu; indeed, Schellenberg's father apparently supported the son's decision.[23] Conversely, Schellenberg's postwar intimation that he spent his entire university career in Bonn suggests an attempt to recast himself in a more Catholic and less radical mold.

Schellenberg took his studies in law seriously. There is no evidence that he had to switch his field of study, but his postwar suggestion that he had to forgo medical studies for economic reasons probably resonated with his readers. It also cast in a different light his later career: as a road taken by circumstances, not by choice. While Schellenberg, like many others, paid his student fees in installments, his finances appear stable; he maintained matriculation for five terms, thus spending the majority of his university career in Marburg.[24] Schellenberg took the opportunities that the university's stellar faculty presented, by, for example, attending lecture courses in economics. In the early 1930s, Marburg was home to two famous proponents of historical national economics: Walter Troeltsch and Wilhelm Röpke, both staunch supporters of the Weimar Republic. He also took "Socialism and its Greatest Representatives" with Erwin Wiskemann, Troeltsch's and Röpke's rising nemesis who,

[22] Hellmut Seier, "Marburg in der Weimarer Republik 1918–1933," in Erhart Dettmering and Rudolf Grenz, eds., *Marburger Geschichte: Rückblick auf die Stadtgeschichte in Einzelbeiträgen* (Marburg: Magistrat, 1980), 561; 563–564. Nagel, *Philipps-Universität*, 2.
[23] Nagel, *Philipps-Universität*, 59–60; Schellenberg, *Labyrinth*, 2.
[24] Hessisches Staatsarchiv (HStA) Marburg, Bestand 305 a, Acc 1963/13, No.90, No. 95, No. 100, No 105; Bestand 305 a, Acc. 1971/26, No. 350.

within a year of the Nazi seizure of power, was appointed full professor in Berlin.[25] Schellenberg took full advantage of his university's academic range.

In his free time, Schellenberg was active with his corps, Guestphalia. The Marburg chapter of Guestphalia was one of the oldest and most prestigious student associations in town. It recruited from Germany's social elite and was meant to provide young men a boost when they began their careers. Schellenberg pledged with the corps his first semester and remained active for the next years.[26] Active members were committed to keep out the riff-raff that, according to an official history, had been flooding Guestphalia, but despite his lower middle-class background, Schellenberg passed the hurdle. A history of Guestphalia indicates its culture during the Weimar Republic. It presented Guest-phalia as nationalist, *völkisch*, and conservative organization, which adopted a "military-manly tone," such as when discussing the corps' "stubborn (trotzig), manly confirmation of our German specificity." The book also established a close connection between the corps' activities during the Weimar Republic and National Socialism and noted that Guestphalia stood "always... with both feet on the ground of the [Nazi] movement."[27] In other words, Guestphalia conceived of itself as having been part of the Nazi movement well before January 1933. These pronouncements were not simply a function of the late 1930s when the book was published: since 1920, the year of the Murders at Mechterstädt, Guestphalia had been an "Aryan" corps. Schellenberg's social life as a student was proto-Nazi, elitist, and "Jew-free."

It is impossible to ascertain the precise extent to which Schellenberg shared the antirepublican and anti-Semitic sentiments prevalent among his corps brothers and dominant in the city, but Schellenberg's choices as a young student offer a window into his political leanings and ambitions. He opted for a town and a university with a known right-wing, antirepub-lican, anti-Semitic reputation. He chose a corps on the right fringes of this right-wing environment, presumably expecting that the connections made with other students, and with senior members above his social standing, would help him. In his memoir, Schellenberg portrayed himself

---

[25] Erwin Wiskemann (1896–1941) most famous book is *Mitteleuropa: Eine Deutsche Aufgabe* (1933). It proposes the creation of a German-led economic space in central Europe for which the "absurd borders created by the Versailles Treaty" had to be abolished. When Troeltsch died in February 1933 and Röpke's eulogy made clear that his opposition to National Socialism remained intact, Wiskemann was appointed to Troeltsch position. He later became a full professor in Berlin. Röpke emigrated to Turkey, then to Switzerland.

[26] Altherrenschaft, ed., *Guestphalia*, vol. 2, 322, 327–328.

[27] Altherrenschaft, ed., *Guestphalia*, vol. 1, 326, 333.

as apolitical and apathetic, but evidence suggests overall agreement with proto-Nazi organizations. Not an apparent activist, Schellenberg participated fully. Even in the earliest stages of his professional life, then, three traits can be discerned in Schellenberg's personality. Politically, Schellenberg was comfortable in an anti-republican and anti-Semitic environment. Socially, Schellenberg had a taste for elitist organizations that claimed leadership roles. Guestphalia had this self-image and the SS appealed to him for the same reasons. Professionally, Schellenberg was focused and ambitious, joining organizations he deemed most beneficial for his career and ascent in society. Seen in this context, Schellenberg's matter of fact explanation as to why he joined the SS, Nazi Germany's most ideological organization, appears far less naïve but indicative of his mercenary motives. Schellenberg wanted to move beyond the sphere defined by his class and religious background, and he actively pursued these goals. Joining the SS was a step along the way, a vehicle to further his professional and social ambitions, and not necessarily an expression of deeply held political convictions. Yet Schellenberg was clearly comfortable in a conservative, völkish, anti-Semitic, and proto-Nazi environment.

After five semesters in Marburg, Schellenberg transferred to the university at Bonn. He took his first judicial state exam in March 1933, joined the Nazi Party and the SS, and began his association with the SD. In his memoirs, Schellenberg presented his first SS assignment as that of an ideological speaker but in at least one other document, he suggested that he prepared ideological training plans. In the end, the upshot remains the same: Schellenberg's task was the transmission of Nazi ideology, and he focused on Germanic law, attacks on the Catholic Church, and similar issues.[28] If he ever had to fake his ideological leanings, he had little problem doing so and was convincing. His almost immediate promotion and the invitation to join the SD were based on his strengths as an ideological indoctrinator or, at least, his persuasive performance thereof.[29]

The *Sicherheitsdienst*, abbreviated SD, was the security, intelligence, and surveillance service of Heinrich Himmler's SS; when Schellenberg joined it, it was still a young organization. As early as 1927 Himmler had ordered all SS men to regard reporting on enemy infiltration as well as on the problems in the Party as their daily duty; its founding myth as

---

[28] Schellenberg, *Labyrinth*, 2, 4; Brigadeführer Schellenberg, Amtschef VI, Autobiography compiled during his stay in Stockholm, June 1945, NA, RG 226, Entry 125A, Box 2, Folder 21. [Hereafter: Autobiography/Stockholm]

[29] Similar, Browder, "Schellenberg," 420.

a service directed against external enemies notwithstanding.[30] Himmler formalized the organization in spring 1931. Taking his lead from the military, Himmler created intelligence positions, labeled Ic, in all SS units to collect information gathered in their units and to report them up the chain. That summer Himmler also created an intelligence position on his staff to formalize and to organize better his nascent intelligence service. Himmler interviewed Reinhard Heydrich for this position and had him write down his ideas for a party intelligence service. Heydrich complied, showing off his military jargon. Himmler hired the man – who also looked the Aryan part – on the spot.[31] When Heydrich took over, the service probably consisted of forty-nine Ic officers, forty-one serving with the regiments and eight on the divisional and regional level in Germany, Austria, and the Free City of Danzig. Their majority was amateurs but theoretically, 15,000 SS men should have been reporting regularly to their Ic officers. Himmler's service was only one among many. Ernst Röhm's SA, the *Sturmabteilung*, Storm Troopers, and the Propaganda Headquarters of the NSDAP also maintained intelligence services. Theoretically, the organizations were to collaborate, but in reality rivalries were fierce.[32]

In the short term, the SD contended with the realities of the Weimar Republic. Fearing a Nazi coup and capitalizing on the population's unease after the so-called Boxheimer Documents, which detailed how a Nazi government would deal with a Communist coup, became public, the government of Heinrich Brüning banned the SA and SS.[33] Heydrich's Ic unit was lucky, as it could take cover under Himmler's immunity as a member of parliament and thus avoid disbandment. When the ban against SA and SS was lifted in June 1932, the Ic unit reemerged under a new name, *Sicherheitsdienst*, a new structure, and closely aligned to Heydrich. Throughout 1932, Heydrich traveled across Germany recruiting local leaders to build SD networks; he also moved the office from shabby Schwabing to an imposing building near Nymphenburg Palace.[34] This move was a fitting symbol of Heydrich's aspirations and his and Himmler's vision for the SD. Yet in the months before and after Hitler's appointment as chancellor, the SD was a small, haphazardly organized,

---

[30] Browder, *Enforcers*, 105; Richard Breitman and Shlomo Aronson, "Eine unbekannte Himmler-Rede vom Januar 1943," *Vierteljahrshefte für Zeitgeschichte* 38 (1990), 537–548.
[31] Himmler interviewed Heydrich either in June or July 1931. Browder, *Enforcers*, 105; Kahn, *Spies*, 56; Shlomo Aronson, *Reinhard Heydrich und die Frühgeschichte von Gestapo und SD* (Stuttgart: Deutsche Verlagsanstalt, 1971), 37–38, 208. On Himmler mistaking "signals officer" for "intelligence officer" before interviewing Heydrich, see Breitman and Aronson, "Himmler-Rede 1943."
[32] Browder, *Enforcers*, 108.   [33] Herbert, *Best*, 112–119.
[34] Browder, *Enforcers*, 109–111.

financially strapped entity without a clear task. It had no regular operating budget and was dependent on the charity of other Nazi organizations, which were not doing well themselves. The headquarters' staff consisted of six underpaid members clipping newspapers and filing these. The entire SD consisted of thirty to forty members; even the most generous estimates – including unofficial members loosely associated – do not exceed one hundred men. The SD also lacked a clear mandate. Himmler and Heydrich retreated to a "grand but elusive" definition of the SD and appealed to romanticized cloak-and-dagger visions of intelligence work. This was also meant to disguise the unsavory fact that the SD spied primarily on party organizations and their members – especially after police attempts to infiltrate the Nazi Party and movement ended with Hitler's appointment as chancellor.[35] However, the lack of a clear mandate also presented an opportunity: it allowed the leaders to change or to broaden the SD's purview as they saw fit.

Under the new circumstances, the precise position of the SD in the new state and among state and party entities needed clarification. How would the SD fit in with other party organizations? How would it relate to state organizations, most notably the police that was undergoing its own adjustment to the new government? In November 1933, the SD became an independent SS office, the *Sicherheitsamt*, Security Office, with Heydrich at the helm. The Security Office consisted of five departments – six if one is to include the registry Department Z – and two independent desks. Departments I and II dealt with organization, personnel matters, and administrative issues. The two Independent Desks monitored and evaluated the press, served as an information service, and provided technical and organizational support. The office's core were Departments III, IV, and V. The former was charged with domestic surveillance and focused on six areas: right-wing opposition; Marxism; religion, science, and education; constitution and law; and the strengthening of public ideological awareness – the latter a possible indication that the SD intended to monitor and also to shape German society. Department V dealt exclusively with Freemasonry, focusing on an ideologically loaded, but numerically insignificant movement.[36] Identified as a Jewish-led threat to the new state, the Freemasons provided the SD with a wide-open entry into anything one saw fit. Lastly, Department IV, the earliest incarnation of the political foreign intelligence service, dealt with "Counterespionage and Foreign Inquiry."[37] It comprised six sections and

---

[35] Browder, *Enforcers*, 109, 112–113.   [36] Browder, *Enforcers*, 118–119.
[37] "Appendix B 3: Organization of the Security Office, 1933–1934," Browder, *Enforcers*, 252–253.

was riddled with peculiarities indicative of the lack of a well-defined mandate. With some grandeur but without additional explanations, the first section was labeled Foreign Intelligence. The second section focused on Jews – defined in accordance with Nazi ideology as a foreign problem – as well as pacifists, anti-Nazi propaganda, and emigrants. The third section dealt with the Soviet intelligence service, espionage in general, and immigrants, and the fourth was devoted to military and economic counterespionage. The fifth section concerned itself with armaments. Lastly, section six dealt with the economy and corruption.[38] In short, Department IV was a hodgepodge of poorly differentiated areas of inquiry with ample opportunity for overlap and friction. This problem was not restricted to competing sections within Department IV or even within the SD, but extended to state and military institutions. The Counterespionage and Foreign Inquiry section of the SD collided with several departments of the *Geheime Staatspolizeiamt*, the Secret State Police Office.[39] Similarly, Department IV of the SD was on a collision course with the Abwehr. Except for ideologically defined subjects such as Jews, pacifists, anti-Nazi propaganda, emigrants, and immigrants, the Abwehr investigated the same issues in which the SD was interested. The Security Office thus revealed the political foreign intelligence service in its embryonic form and foreshadowed future conflicts with other institutions.

After the establishment of the Security Office, ten months into the new, Nazi-dominated government, the SD's finances and overall standing began to improve. Well into 1933, the SD financed itself through extortion, blackmail, and "fundraising" in the German industry. In July 1933, shortly after the dissolution of all German political parties, their organizations, and the trade unions, the SD began receiving regular funding from the Party Treasury, even though the SD's professed needs remained a hard match for the party's coffers.[40] The financial commitment of the party was a good indication that the SD was there to stay, despite persistent rumors that the SD was to be abolished. Reasons ranged from its surveillance of party rank and file to the wish to streamline policing after Himmler's takeover of the German Political Police in May 1934.[41] By late spring 1934, though, the SD and its leaders were solidly entrenched in the emergent policing and surveillance system; disposing them would

[38] Browder, *Enforcers*, 119.
[39] Johannes Tuchel and Reinhold Schattenfroh, *Zentrale des Terrors. Prinz-Albrecht-Strasse 8: Hauptquartier der Gestapo* (Berlin: Siedler, 1987), 66–82; "Appendix B.1: The Geheime Staatspolizeiamt Organization Plan for September 1, 1933," Browder, *Enforcers*, 249–250.
[40] Browder, *Enforcers*, 128–129.
[41] Heinz Höhne, *Der Orden unter dem Totenkopf: Die Geschichte des SS* (Munich: Bertelsmann, 1967; reprint, Augsburg: Weltbild Verlag, 1998), 194; Browder, *Enforcers*, 124.

not be an easy task.[42] Indeed, the SD was about to be designated the sole intelligence service of the party.

In June and July 1934 – around the time of and related to the Röhm Purge – the role of the SD was redefined; it simultaneously contracted and expanded. On June 9, 1934, Hitler's deputy Rudolf Hess decreed the SD the sole intelligence service of the Nazi Party. All other intelligence services still in existence, for example in the Propaganda Ministry, and regardless of whether they dealt with foreign or domestic matters, were to be abolished or transferred into the SD. At the same time, Hess' decree stressed that the SD was not authorized to spy on any party formations or their members; its activities were to be directed exclusively against the enemies of the party. It is likely, though, that the designation of the SD as the party's sole intelligence service was tied to the need to keep informed about Ernst Röhm and his SA, whose activities were increasingly seen as a threat to Hitler and the stability Nazi Germany had achieved.[43] The SD, although still prone to investigate party formations and individual party members and thus despised, had achieved a status congruent with its ambitions.

Himmler's order of July 4, 1934, on the other hand, issued immediately after the purge, restricted the SD's purview and barred it from executive powers. This was surely intended to calm the frayed nerves of the state bureaucracy – most notably among the police and the lower ranks various ministries – after the bloodshed that had engulfed SA personalities as well as prominent national conservatives, such as former chancellor Kurt von Schleicher and his wife or Edgar Julius Jung, the author of vice-chancellor Franz von Papen's "Marburg Speech." Himmler's decree addressed the issue of the executive and detailed the relationship between SD and Gestapo and the organizations' respective tasks. The decree is thus a forerunner of the so-called Functional Order of 1937, which set out to achieve the same.[44] Himmler's decree reinforced that the right to arrest remained the sole prerogative of the police. Since January 1933, the SD has on occasion usurped executive powers, arresting people and brutally interrogating them, for example in Berlin's Columbia House. This was to come to an end. The Gestapo, for its part, recognized the SD as the only "political and counterintelligence service" and committed itself to

---

[42] Auskunftserteilung in Landesverrats- und Spionagesachen und Zusammenarbeit mit den Organisationsbeauftragten der Wehrmacht, May 16, 1934, USHMM, 14.016 M, 242.

[43] Hess Decree of June 9, 1934, NA, RG 242, T-580/93, Ordner 457; Aronson, *Frühgeschichte*, 196.

[44] Gemeinsame Anordnung für den Sicherheitsdienst des Reichsführer-SS und die Geheime Staatspolizei, July 1, 1937, USHMM, 14.016 M, 239; Aronson, *Frühgeschichte*, 196.

the suppression of any other intelligence services. The SD was defined as the Gestapo's "essential supplement," the moniker circumscribing the extent of the SD's role in police work. While the Gestapo was charged with combating the enemies of the National Socialist State and defending it against these enemies, the SD was to identify (*ermitteln*) the enemies of the National Socialist idea and bring them to the Gestapo's attention for further policing measures.[45] In short and reflective of the two organizations' background and pedigree, the police was in charge of the Nazi state while the SD was responsible for the Nazi idea.

The precision was, however, only surface deep. Overlap and conflict, likely intended, remained. The restriction of the SD to ideological surveillance must have appeared to many of its members as a step back. Yet it was also a step forward: the SD took on ideological surveillance forcefully, thus proving its worth vis-à-vis the Gestapo, which still counted many people from before the seizure of power among its personnel. The SD, an organization lacking institutional traditions and eager to find its place, was likely to engage in more militant and radical solutions.[46] Furthermore, the SD had acquired the power of definition: as the Gestapo's "essential supplement," it had the right to suggest whom and what to investigate. The SD defined what constituted an ideological transgression and was in a position to further encroach on the Gestapo and its tasks and move the policing as a whole. The "essential supplement" could possibly wag the dog, as the saying goes, and thus bolster its reputation and role as the ideological flag-bearer of the new state.

The SD, while still a small organization, made quick progress in its relationship to the Gestapo, as a 1935 memorandum indicated.[47] It described the SD as an "auxiliary organ" (*Hilfsorgan*) and asserted the primacy of the police, but considered the SD part of the state security system and ultimately equal to the police (*stehen rangmäßig nebeneinander*). Police and SD were to collaborate as closely as possible in the interest of state security, but particular importance was ascribed to the SD's wider reach into society. Despite its status as an auxiliary organ and its lack of executive powers, the SD was allowed to conduct its own investigations. And as long as these investigations were "within the law," the police was to

---

[45] Aronson, *Frühgeschichte*, 196; Michael Wildt, *Die Judenpolitik des SD 1935–1938: Eine Dokumentation* (Munich: Oldenbourg Verlag 1995), 18; Browder, *Enforcers*, 115; 123–124.

[46] Browder, *Enforcers*, 124; Aronson, *Frühgeschichte*, 196–197.

[47] Organisation der Geheimen Staatspolizei, n.d., USHMM, 14.016 M, 243; Aronson, *Frühgeschichte*, 197. The number and classification of SD members is in doubt. Compare Browder, *Enforcers*, 127; George Browder "The Numerical Strength of the Sicherheitsdienst RFSS," *Historical Social Research* (1983), 32, especially Table 1; and Wildt, *Generation*, 243.

follow the SD's lead. The SD was only required to inform the police of its investigations in a timely manner and to terminate them upon request. The police, in turn, was to inform the SD about any executive steps it had taken based on SD investigations. And in the regulations regarding Freemasons and Catholics a division of labor emerged: the police had to transfer all information regarding these groups to the SD. As it was, the police had little legal way of addressing these ideologically defined issues, as neither being a Freemason or a Catholic was illegal. However, the SD could put them under surveillance. Invented by Himmler and Heydrich, initially underfunded and made up by staff members long on ideological allegiance and short on intelligence experience, the SD had come a long way in a short period of time. And there was the aspiration to make the SD into the state's foremost intelligence service, domestically and abroad. Schellenberg had clearly joined an organization that stood at the forefront of national-socialist thinking about surveillance and policing, and he had done so when it was a small entity if with much potential. Schellenberg and the SD were, indeed, rather alike: unformed but full of possibilities.

Schellenberg spent the two, perhaps close to three years after passing his initial exam as a *Referendar*, a judicial trainee, receiving on-the-job training in different branches of the legal system. Considered part of the legal education, a trainee only becomes *Volljurist*, a full member of the profession, upon passing a second state exam at the end of the meagerly reimbursed traineeship; a set-up that privileged students from wealthy backgrounds. Schellenberg's need for a state grant was therefore unsurprising. He took his second exam in December 1936, receiving the grade *befriedigend*, satisfactory, which translated into a distinction.[48] Schellenberg did not simply rely on social and political connections; he also made the grade.

The stations of Schellenberg's traineeship included an array of judicial and police institutions. He worked at the *Amtsgericht*, District Court, in Sinzig/Rhine; the *Land- und Amtsgericht*, State and District Court, in Bonn; the *Staatsanwaltschaft*, Prosecutor's Office, in Bonn; *Staatspolizeistelle*, State Police Office, in Frankfurt; the *Geheime Staatspolizeiamt*, Secret State Police Office, in Berlin; and the *Oberlandesgericht*, Superior State Court, in Düsseldorf. While at the State Police Office in Frankfurt, Schellenberg's SD contact in Bonn put him in touch with Dr. Wilhelm Albert, who was then the head of the *SD-Oberabschnitt* West, Superior District West, in Frankfurt. Wilhelm Albert has the distinction to be the first of Schellenberg's superiors who chose to foster his career.

[48] Zeugnis, December 17, 1936, BAL, R 58 Anhang I/ 48; Final Report.

Albert organized comparatively successful and substantial espionage efforts against France and Schellenberg claimed that he spent a month at the Sorbonne in Paris on an intelligence mission. There is no independent confirmation of this but if it is true, it would have been Schellenberg's first endeavor into his later area of expertise.[49] Little else is known about Schellenberg's actual work, but Albert seems to have assisted Schellenberg in attaining his initial, short-term appointment to the newly established *Sicherheitshauptamt*, SD Main Office, in Berlin in early 1935.

The SD Main Office owed its existence and shape to Werner Best's efforts in the preceding year. When he took over Department I, Administration, of the then Security Office in March 1934, he did much to streamline it. Best also began to recruit new members for the SD, focusing his attention on recent university graduates who had been active in radical university groups, but had only recently joined the party and the SS. Supposedly, this allowed for a certain distance from the NSDAP and a "cool rationality," a trait both Best and Heydrich prized in their ideal SD member. But Best's prominence as well as some of his recruitment decisions – especially regarding recent law graduates – also foreshadowed future conflicts with Heydrich. For the time being, however, all was well: Heydrich was stretched thin with his Gestapo obligations and Best was the perfect man as Heydrich's second in command. When Best left this position and began his new appointment with the Gestapo in January 1935, the SD had been consolidated into an entity capable of fulfilling its potential. Consisting of three offices – Office I dealing with administrative issues; Office II focusing on domestic surveillance; and Office III charged with foreign intelligence matters – it was elevated to main office status.[50] Himmler and Heydrich clearly saw an important role for the SD in the future. Schellenberg, for his part, was a perfect fit for both the organization and Best's recruitment profile. From here on out, Schellenberg and the development of the SD become almost inextricably linked.

Schellenberg's first, brief stint with the SD was in its Administrative Department. Interior Minister Wilhelm Frick attempted to centralize under the control of his ministry the police; not surprisingly, Himmler and Heydrich, who had different plans for the police, put up a determined fight against this.[51] Schellenberg was likely involved in thwarting Frick's attempts, but, curiously, Schellenberg claimed that under a special

[49] Schellenberg, *Labyrinth*, 8; Lebenslauf, n.d., NA, RG 242, BDC, A 3343, SSO, Reel 074B; Aronson, *Frühgeschichte*, 163.
[50] Browder, *Enforcers*, 125; Herbert, *Best*, 141–145.
[51] On the *Reichsreform*: Günter Neliba, *Wilhelm Frick. Der Legalist des Unrechtsstaates: Eine politische Biographie* (Paderborn: Schöningh, 1992), 141–159, 247–258.

agreement he received some of his pay from the Ministry of the Interior as a "probationary assessor" while also collecting an SD salary.[52] But perhaps this was simply another of his postwar attempts to put some distance between himself and the SD. In early 1936, Schellenberg briefly worked at the Superior State Court in Düsseldorf. However, he was also involved with a law firm owned by a friend of his father that Schellenberg was to take over, or so he claimed. Another source suggests that a senior member of Guestphalia owned the firm and if that were the case, Schellenberg had made good use of his Marburg connections. However, after passing his second state exam, Schellenberg decided to forgo private practice. He and his senior friend believed that there would be no professional future in a private legal practice, as it was deemed too liberal a profession.[53] Again, Schellenberg's writings allude to a road not taken. The road taken returned Schellenberg to the SD's Administrative Department. He now began a career that would lead him to the pinnacles of Nazi power.

Minute as they are, the subtle differences between Schellenberg's various accounts of his early career tell an important story. In his postwar accounts, Schellenberg's initial position with the SD Main Office gains the air of a regular station of his legal traineeship and Schellenberg also chose to emphasize that his position was partially financed by the Interior Ministry, a state institution. He likely assumed that this made his activities more reputable, as the Interior Ministry was commonly seen a less-Nazified institution – even if under Wilhelm Frick this amounted to a dubious claim – not to mention that Schellenberg's position in the SD set him in opposition to Frick and his plans. Yet Schellenberg's careful calibration of information for postwar audiences shows his overall intent. This observation is made even more interesting because Schellenberg's exact function in the Administrative Department remains patently opaque. Indeed, Schellenberg's official SS resume indicates that he was not working in the SD Main Office, but for the Secret State Police Office.[54] But even if it remains unclear what he was doing where, he was doing it well. Schellenberg was laying the foundations for his future.

---

[52] Final Report. The stations of his traineeship indicate that he was officially assigned to the Geheime Staatspolizeiamt; this might explain why he was paid by Interior Ministry. In addition, he relied on the income of his live-in girlfriend.

[53] Final Report; Autobiography/Stockholm. Theodor Paeffgen suggests that the law practice was owned by a senior member of Guestphalia; Affidavit, Dr. Theodor Paeffgen, March 12, 1948, NA, RG 238, M 897, Reel 114. Beginning October 1, 1936, "Walter Schellenberg, Gerichtsreferendar," received a monthly stipend of 160 RM from a certain Schellenberg, Luxembourg. NA, RG 319, IRR, Box 195. The money possibly came from Schellenberg's father; Doerries, Last Chief, 3 note 6.

[54] Lebenslauf, n.d., NA, RG 242, BDC, A 3343, SSO, Reel 074B.

Schellenberg's career between 1933 and 1936 makes it tempting to construct a teleological development. Shlomo Aronson, for example, notes that Schellenberg's career began to blossom after he served as an informant in academic circles in Bonn. Following Schellenberg's rendition, Aronson concludes that Schellenberg's reports must have garnered interest in the SD Main Office in Berlin, leading to Schellenberg's various assignments with the "internal administration in Frankfurt" and as an operative on a foreign intelligence mission of the SD to France. As the penultimate step Schellenberg worked for some time in the Secret State Police Office, from where he was transferred to the SD Main Office.[55] However, taking into account that Schellenberg was also fulfilling the requirements of his traineeship and the different renditions of Schellenberg's early career, Aronson might be overstating the teleological thrust of Schellenberg's early path. Schellenberg, for his part, was keenly aware that he was given many opportunities at a young age; he met "officials at all levels" who were "most friendly and courteous," and "every door was opened [. . .] as though some unseen power was working silently." Incidentally, Schellenberg came to believe that Reinhard Heydrich was the moving force behind his ascent.[56] This is an intriguing reflection of Schellenberg's sense of self. His assumption that the head of the SD actively supported the career of a twenty-five- or twenty-six-year-old judicial trainee shows an enormous level of self-assuredness. Schellenberg's records do not support this assumption and George Browder relegates the idea to the realm of Schellenberg's fantasy. Many of Schellenberg's immediate colleagues, friends, and foes alike, seemed to have shared the notion that Schellenberg was under Heydrich's special protection, though.[57] Whether Heydrich's patronage was real or not is then actually beyond the point. Such rumors – sheer buzz, as it was – likely contributed substantially to Schellenberg's status. Ultimately, it was not relevant whether Heydrich was indeed looking out for Schellenberg, but that everybody believed so and acted accordingly made all the difference. Schellenberg was also the right man at the right time; he was well educated and adaptable and it is not surprising at all that Himmler and Heydrich "recognized the talented young man." Schellenberg, for his part, recognized the opportunities and became a dedicated functionary for Heydrich.[58] People far less educated and talented were making stunning careers; for a man of Schellenberg's education, talent, adaptability, and industriousness, the sky was the limit.

[55] Aronson, *Frühgeschichte*, 210. Aronson relies exclusively on Schellenberg's memoir.
[56] Schellenberg, *Labyrinth*, 8–9.
[57] Browder, "Schellenberg," 420; Hoettl/Character Schellenberg.
[58] Doerries, *Last Chief*, 5.

Once Schellenberg joined the SD Main Office permanently, he was promoted speedily. In March 1937, Schellenberg was made SS-Untersturmführer. The SD Main Office was clearly pleased with Schellenberg's job performance and the evaluation for promotion supports that Schellenberg had a knack for being in the right place at the right time. His promotion was necessitated as he fulfilled tasks above his initial rank, interacting regularly with the heads of the central departments. His promotion became all but mandatory to maintain proper structures. His evaluation was glowing: racially, he was "pure Nordic" with an "open, unobjectionable, ingenuous" character, and "firm, tenacious" willpower. He was deemed a precise thinker full of general knowledge and able to discern quickly the core of any problem. Ideologically, Schellenberg was deemed "altogether firm" [*durchaus gefestigt*] and his "soldierly bearing inside and outside the office" was noted favorably.[59] Schellenberg, for his part, did what he could and needed to do to advance: he left the Catholic Church and became *gottgläubig* [believer in God, not a member of any church].[60] This was the logical endpoint of a route that had led him first to the Protestant university of Marburg and then to his role as an anti-Catholic SS indoctrinator. A mere six months later Schellenberg received yet another promotion, as he had replaced Dr. Mehlhorn at the head of *Hauptabteilung*, Main Department, I/II.[61] Schellenberg had also played a prominent role in the preparation for Mussolini's Berlin visit in the fall of 1937 and was credited with most of the security work for a visit that was fundamental in the creation of the Axis Rome-Berlin.[62] Once again, then, Schellenberg's promotion was based on a dual reasoning. He needed to be promoted for his rank to be in sync with those of the people with whom he dealt regularly and his work performance had been outstanding. The suggestion for Schellenberg's preferential promotion came immediately on the heels of

[59] Personalbericht/Beurteilung, March 27, 1937, NA, RG 242, BDC, A 3343, SSO, Reel 074B. Hoettl stressed that "the SD was still at its formative stage and consequently Amt I was of pivotal importance. [. . .] he soon began to exert considerable influence;" Hoettl/Character Schellenberg.
[60] Kirchenaustritt per April 30, 1937, BAL, R 58, Anhang I/48. The evaluation, dated March 27, 1937, lists Schellenberg as *gottgläubig* already.
[61] On Mehlhorn, who left his position "more or less voluntarily:" Aronson, *Frühgeschichte*, 58; 161; Höhne, *Orden*, 198; Jens Banach, *Heydrichs Elite: Das Führerkorps der Sicherheitspolizei und des SD, 1936–1945* (Paderborn: Schöningh, 1998), 285. In 1941, he was in charge of all "Jewish questions" in the Warthegau, Epstein, *Model Nazi*, 143–144.
[62] Personalbericht/Beurteilung, March 27, 1937, NA, RG 242, BDC, A 3343, SSO, Reel 074B. For a description of the visit, see Dennis Mack Smith, *Mussolini* (New York: Knopf, 1982), 215–216.

Mussolini's visit.[63] Again, Schellenberg took an opportunity and made the best of it.

It had been only five years since Hitler was appointed chancellor, and less than five years since Schellenberg, fresh out of law school, joined the Nazi Party and the SS and became involved with the SD. In these years, Schellenberg rose meteorically from a low-level ideological speaker in Bonn to a department head in the SD Main Office in Berlin. In January 1938 Walter Schellenberg turned 28, and he had parlayed his abilities into a position with the SD Main Office's upper management. There were two more rungs above the position Schellenberg held after replacing Mehlhorn. One consisted of the heads of the three offices; above them was only Heydrich. Building on his university training in law, his sheer industriousness, and the ability to recognize an opportunity and willingness to chase it, Schellenberg had attained a position of considerable influence and tremendous potential. And it was with one of Germany's most Nazified institutions.

What, then, was Schellenberg's relationship to Nazi ideology? After war's end, Schellenberg always insisted on his nonideological, non-Nazified worldview, yet it is hard to fathom that one could become as high ranking a member of Nazi Germany's elite as quickly as Schellenberg without the proper ideological convictions. Others have noted before the conspicuousness of a man who prided himself on his ideological aloofness commencing his career with the SD as an ideological speaker. Even if Schellenberg might not have always been fully convinced himself, he certainly was convincing. Attempting to bridge the gap between Schellenberg's self-image and his role in the SD, Browder observes:

Schellenberg absorbed and conformed as necessary to the prevalent values of the environment in which he sought to succeed. Like any successful status seeker, he had acquired this skill as a second nature. Although his polish required him to reserve a certain haughty detachment, especially from crude and offensive extremists, he conformed tacitly with the dominant values. Although luckier than Ohlendorf in avoiding the evil demands of ideology, he was not nearly as free from its contamination as his self-image demanded, or as he insisted in his memoirs. [...] What Schellenberg had embraced was an intellectual's 'critical' brand of National Socialism, making him susceptible to the SD's dedicated-intellectual image.[64]

---

[63] Beförderungsurkunde, January 22, 1938. BAL, R 58 Anhang I/48. Kahn claims that in preparation of Mussolini's 1937 visit, Schellenberg spent four weeks in Italy and "took the opportunity to gather some intelligence on Italian foreign policy." Kahn, *Spies*, 256. Schellenberg did not mention a trip in 1937 but frequently referred to a four-week stay in Rome in 1938.

[64] Browder, *Enforcers*, 225.

This description of Schellenberg's brand of ideology rings true. Schellenberg was absolutely willing to conform to the ideological norms of his environment, because this was the environment in which he was trying to succeed professionally. Yet, to see Schellenberg's careerism and sheer ambition as the main reason for his willingness to conform ideologically does not completely convince. An explanation Browder offers elsewhere is more compelling. It posits that the existence of "a broader cultural conjunction of assumptions, values, and beliefs characterized the antiliberal, anti-Marxist, nationalist, xenophobic, social-Darwinist, culturally reactionary mentality" allowed the Nazis to reach beyond the few radical adherents of their ideology and "suck in vast numbers of allies."[65] Or, put differently, the dividing line between National Socialism and National Conservatism was fluid and easy to cross, as men like Schellenberg show. The fluidity and the amorphous nature of National Socialism has been a matter of scholarly interest for years and Browder's observations touch on an interesting inverse effect of this fluidity. In the same way that the nature of the beast allowed the Nazis to woo and incorporate many into the movement, it allowed for people in positions of responsibility and importance in Nazi Germany to (re-)construct themselves – after 1945 – as National Conservatives, as largely non-Nazified, as generally aloof from Nazi ideology, or as having embraced selected aspects of National Socialism only. These ideological conjunctions also served as a tool of ideological compartmentalization. They allowed people – and not only the Schellenbergs – to focus on those elements of Nazi ideology with which they felt comfortable while largely, and for quite some time, ignoring the less palatable.[66]

Walter Schellenberg certainly did well. His ascent in the SD Main Office was swift, and what was as a promising career in 1937 gained even more momentum in 1938. In a year when two new territories, Austria and the Sudetenland, were to be incorporated into the German Reich and major decisions about the structure of Germany's police were on the horizon, there was an undeniable demand for ideologically conversant lawyers with ample ambition.

[65] Browder, *Enforcers*, 7.
[66] Broadly: Peter Fritzsche, *Life and Death in the Third Reich* (Cambridge: Harvard University Press, 2009).

2   Rising Star

Schellenberg is one of my best and work-wise one of my most reliable
supports.

Reinhard Heydrich, 1939

In the last years of the 1930s, and under the tutelage of Reinhard Heydrich, Walter Schellenberg ascended rapidly through the ranks of the
SD. Beginning in 1938 and making use of Schellenberg's legal training, his keen understanding of key administrative issues, his ability as
a negotiator, and his zealous drive to succeed, Heydrich began to rely
on Schellenberg for the solution of complicated legal and administrative
issues and, due to the former's conflict with Werner Best, Schellenberg
moved into position as Heydrich's legal expert of choice.[1] By late 1939,
Schellenberg had parlayed his abilities and ambitions into the position of
a department head in the Gestapo and had acquired the reputation of a
rising star. He was on good terms with Heydrich – and his wife Lina –
and increasingly also with Heinrich Himmler. How did this development
come about and what does it say about Walter Schellenberg, the SD, and
Nazi Germany's intelligence and security complex?

In 1938 and 1939, long-simmering institutional conflicts between the
Security Police and the SD came to the fore, as the respective leaderships
became embroiled in an argument of far-reaching ramifications. The
initial issue at stake was the planned amalgamation of the Security Police,
a state organization, and the SD, a quintessential party organization,
into one entity. In this process, which led to the establishment of the
Reichssicherheitshauptamt, Reich Security Main Office, in the fall of 1939,
both the Security Police and, even more so, the SD, its role, and mandate
were defined. Much of this was Schellenberg's doing. This discussion
then led to a debate about career paths in both Security Police and SD.

---

[1] George C. Browder "Walter Schellenberg: Eine Geheimdienst-Phantasie," in Ronald
Smelser and Enrico Syring, eds., *Die SS: Elite unter dem Totenkopf. 30 Lebensläufe* (Paderborn: Schöningh, 2000), 422.

Outwardly a curious development, the latter debate went to the core of the issue: who was to lead in the new state based on which qualifications? Ultimately, the question was about how far the Nazi revolution would go and how radical and ideologically defined the new state – and its coming Empire – would be. Would it displace German bureaucratic and civil service traditions and create a new caste of leaders? The debate pitched two people against each other: Heydrich, representing the SD, who did not hold a university degree, and Werner Best, who had a doctorate in law and represented the Security Police. Heydrich and Best had worked together amicably for years and their collaboration had been fundamental in bringing the German police under Himmler's oversight. Both men were committed National Socialists but disagreed on who was to lead the state: Best was convinced that ideologically committed jurists, political lawyers as he called them, were suited best for leadership positions. Heydrich desired political soldiers, men whose primary qualification was their ideological commitment, to gain preeminence in the state. Both men wanted to create a new leadership caste in their own image.

Enter Walter Schellenberg, who then occupied a position in the SD's administrative department. Outwardly, Schellenberg fit Best's profile perfectly: he was a trained lawyer, a dedicated bureaucrat, and apparently committed to National Socialism. And while working on Heydrich's plans for the amalgamation of the Security Police and the SD, Schellenberg initially appeared sympathetic to Best's opinions about leadership qualifications, even if he did not agree with his stand on the SD's future role. However, Schellenberg soon realized that it would serve his career better if he were to express Heydrich's views. In the escalating and eventually rather public conflict with Best, Schellenberg skillfully filled the role of Heydrich's legal expert of choice. This episode is not simply yet another example of Schellenberg's chameleon-like character. In these arcane yet fundamental debates, Schellenberg positioned himself as the preeminent expert on the role and the mandate of the SD. Schellenberg also began to display a skill that he then honed in the coming years: his ability to move from ideologically based to bureaucratically based arguments – and back – as he and his superiors saw fit. These disputes and an understanding of Schellenberg's role in them ultimately provide a missing link in the understanding of his personality, strategy, and his visions for the future of Germany's security and intelligence complex and the SD's role in it.

On March 12, 1938, German troops marched into a largely welcoming Austria, bringing the country, as the slogan went, "home into the

Reich."[2] On the day of the *Anschluß*, annexation, Heydrich dispatched Walter Schellenberg and Adolf Eichmann, the SD's emerging specialist on Jewish matters, to Vienna. The men carried with them a list of political and racial enemies slated for arrest, which was Eichmann's task, while Schellenberg seized documents relating to Austrian military and political intelligence.[3] In effect, then, Schellenberg was part of the Austrian *Einsatzkommando*, as these intelligence and policing units came to be known, and – like Eichmann – a member of the SD. He should thus not have been involved in executive matters but principles jealously guarded in Germany were not stringently applied in Austria that, for some time, became a laboratory for all kinds of Nazi policies – and not only vis-à-vis its Jews. Schellenberg's postwar description of his month-long stay in Austria is a study in contradiction. On the one hand, he self-importantly stressed the role he played when Heinrich Müller, head of the Gestapo and as such responsible for executive matters, was out of the country, leaving the impression that he deputized for "Gestapo-Müller," as the latter was commonly called. On the other hand, Schellenberg attempted to construct his activities in Austria as simple legal and administrative tasks.[4] He was representing the SD in its most political and ideological form yet details remain hazy.

---

[2] Gerhard L. Weinberg, *The Foreign Policy of Hitler's Germany: Starting World War II, 1937–1939* (Chicago: University of Chicago Press, 1980), 261–312; Detlev Wagner and Gerhard Tomkowitz, *Anschluss: The Week Hitler Seized Vienna*, trans., Geoffry Strachan (New York: St. Martin's Press, 1971); Evan Burr Burkey, *Hitler's Austria: Popular Sentiment in the Nazi Era, 1938–1945* (Chapel Hill: University of North Carolina Press, 2000).

[3] Peter Black, *Ernst Kaltenbrunner: Ideological Soldier of the Third Reich* (Princeton: Princeton University Press, 1984), 109. Black stresses that Heydrich dispatched Schellenberg and Eichmann to curb Ernst Kaltenbrunner's influence early and thoroughly. Schellenberg wrote that he flew to Vienna with Himmler; he did not mention Eichmann; Walter Schellenberg, *The Labyrinth: Memoirs of Walter Schellenberg, Hitler's Chief of Counterintelligence*, trans. Louis Hagen (New York: Harper & Brothers, 1956; reprint, Cambridge, MA: Da Capo Press, 2000), 30. Hachmeister indicates that Eichmann arrived in Vienna on March 16, 1938. Lutz Hachmeister, *Der Gegnerforscher. Die Karriere des SS-Führers Franz Alfred Six* (München: Verlag C.H.Beck, 1998), 194. Himmler's appointment book indicates that he was in Vienna from March 12 to 24, 1938; Terminkalendar, January 1938–March 1939, NA, RG 242, T 581, Reel 37 A, but does not indicate who accompanied him.

[4] Final Report on the Case of Walter Schellenberg, NA, RG 319, IRR, XE 001725, Walter Schellenberg, Folders 7 and 8 [hereafter: Final Report]; Schellenberg, *Labyrinth*, 29–32. Schellenberg allegedly fulfilled similar administrative tasks in subsequent German campaigns; he "worked on questions of international law, legal questions concerning Sudetenland, Danzig, Austria and at the same time I was occupied with mobilizing an entire Reich Administration."Autobiography, compiled during his stay in Stockholm, June 1945, NA, RG 226, Entry 125 A, Box 2, Folder 21 [hereafter: Autobiography/Stockholm].

Schellenberg returned to Berlin on April 15, 1938 and was almost immediately dispatched to Rome.[5] Here he assisted Müller with the security preparations for Hitler's visit to the Italian capital, scheduled for the next month. Concerned about Italian security preparations and trying to circumvent the Italian opposition to using German Security Police for that purpose, German authorities decided to bring some 70 SD Main Office members posing as civilians to Italy.[6] Schellenberg interviewed and briefed the secret contingent of SD men for their tasks; his was a role was important yet subordinate. But, much like his work in Austria, it also established him as more than an able administrator but a practitioner on the ground.

Schellenberg's next assignment coincided with his official position in the SD's administrative department, as he became involved in the contentious discussion about the future face of the Security Police and the SD; the closely related issue of the *Laufbahnrichtlinien*, career path regulations, in these two organizations; and the deliberations about the future amalgamation of these two entities into the Reich Security Main Office. This debate pitched two people against each other: Reinhard Heydrich and Werner Best. The deliberations about these issues as well as their fallout, namely the eventual ouster of Werner Best and a partial victory for Heydrich, are known – as is Schellenberg's authorship of the memoranda coming from Heydrich's camp.[7] Yet Schellenberg's role warrants a careful and detailed discussion, for he did more than fight Heydrich's battles for the preeminence of the radically ideological. Schellenberg also attempted to define the role and mandate of the SD and the qualifications of its personnel and to provide needed theoretical underpinnings. Schellenberg's memoranda thus offer a window into attempts to define an "SD-philosophy" in general and the SD as an organization in particular; Schellenberg emerged as a vocal proponent of an independent and eventually meaningful SD as an intelligence service, defending and defining the SD in the process. The debates are key to understanding Schellenberg's thoughts, priorities, career strategies, and later positions. Over the course of the debate, Schellenberg morphed into a forceful opponent of all of Best's plans and established himself as an alternative to Best.

---

[5] Final Report. The document states that Schellenberg and Müller were in Rome in preparation for a Duce visit. However, it was Hitler who visited Mussolini that year. Dennis Mack Smith, *Mussolini* (New York: Knopf, 1982), 215–216; 220.

[6] Final Report.

[7] Jens Banach, *Heydrichs Elite. Das Führerkorps der Sicherheitspolizei und des SD, 1936–1945* (Paderborn: Schöningh, 1998), 287–297; Ulrich Herbert, *Best: Biographische Studien über Radikalismus, Weltanschauung und Vernunft 1903–1989*, 2nd ed. (Bonn: Dietz, 1996), 230–233; Michael Wildt, *Generation des Unbedingten. Das Führungkorps des Reichssicherheitshauptamtes* (Hamburg: Hamburger Edition, 2002), 264–276.

Much of Schellenberg's later authority – and some of his positions – was owed to Best's eventual resignation from his positions in the Security Police–SD complex. Schellenberg's spirited work for Heydrich, marked by substantial initiative, also cemented his relationship with Heydrich, for he established himself and came to be regarded as Heydrich's man, his favored protégé. This made Schellenberg virtually untouchable.

Himmler and Heydrich – and Best – intended to integrate the Security Police, abbreviated Sipo, a state organization staffed by civil servants, into the SS, a party organization, and, subsequently, amalgamate the Security Police and SD into a new agency. The envisioned end result was to be a completely Nazified policing and intelligence system. The creation of the Inspector of Security Police and SD positions in fall 1936 and of the Higher SS- and Police Leaders as Himmler's regional representatives a year later, the so-called Functional Order of 1937, and several decrees regulating the induction of Security Police members in the SS or the SD were steps taken toward this end: a "unified State Security Corps of a new mould," as Werner Best phrased it. In this new State Security Corps, the Sipo and the SD were to be the "elite's elite, the racial and ideological core of SS and the future State Security Corps alike."[8] However, problems abounded. Two issues were key: one was the question of leadership – was it going to be Sipo or SS/SD personnel? The other was the eventual structure of the super-agency, initially labeled "Reich Security Service" or "State Security Corps," and the respective responsibilities of its integral, but frequently rival parts.

The difficulty of integrating the Security Police and the SD into a single supra-agency is revealed in an undated and unsigned document that shows all the indications of Schellenberg's handiwork.[9] The document delineates the main differences between Security Police and SD and argues that the two entities are "genetically" different – meaning they have different backgrounds – and have different tasks. In effect, the document argues for the independence and specificity of the SD and – slyly, palpably, and supported by a smattering of Nazi history and pseudo-scientific language – for the preeminence of the SD. The author argues that the police emerged from the judicial-administrative necessities of the state and constitutes, much like the state itself, a judicial-administrative apparatus. In such an apparatus people of different ideologies could co-exist. However, after 1933 it became apparent that this was not suitable to guarantee the protection of the new National Socialist state. The

---

[8] Wildt, *Generation*, 251–259.
[9] Die Eigenständigkeit des Sicherheitsdienstes, no author, no date, USHMM, 14.016 M, 826. It is likely that Schellenberg authored the document.

creation of a state security system based on and fueled by the political will of the (Nazi) movement therefore became a necessity. The SD is identified as the carrier of this will. The author suggests that the difference between the police and the SD might appear negligible during peacetime and that the SD might be considered irrelevant. Ultimately, though, the SD, ideologically firm and reflecting the will of the movement, would be the decisive protector of the (Nazi) state. The document then discusses the respective tasks of the police and the SD as well as their fundamental differences. Faintly echoing of the so-called Functional Order of 1937, which demarcated the areas of responsibility between Gestapo and SD, it notes that the police is to focus on infractions against the state and its laws, using judicial categories to determine offenses, while the SD concentrates on attacks against the racially defined volk, which are not part of the judicial code but even more dangerous to volk and state. As judicial instruments to combat these offenses do not exist – one is tempted to add "yet" – they have to be addressed differently. Put differently: it is the SD's task to deal with offenses that cannot be addressed judicially, but put volk and state in the gravest danger. Defining the normative and the prerogative state, to use Ernst Fraenkel's terminology, the document gives clear preeminence to the latter.[10] Only the SD can protect the new state but its position does yet not reflect its relevance.

The problems anticipated with the planned induction of Security Police members into the SS/SD were not based on the organizations' different mandates alone but also related to professional qualifications. The qualifications of SS/SD men oftentimes differed from those in the Security Police. Who was to lead the future State Security Corps – SS/SD men or jurists who had been with the Security Police first and with the SS/SD second? This question informed much of the debate. Werner Best argued that only jurists were suitable for leadership positions; he favored "political-ideological jurists" and hired accordingly. Diametrically opposed was the view espoused by Hitler, Himmler, and Heydrich and shared by many younger members of both organizations, but the SD in particular. They held that "political-ideological leaders," trained in future National Socialist leadership schools, would be better equipped to fill leadership positions in the administration of the new Germany. Ultimately, the issue boiled down to the question of whether the future State Security Corps was to be led by bureaucrats with appropriate legal and police training or whether it would be defined in a new way, namely by

---

[10] Ernst Fraenkel, *The Dual State: A Contribution to the Theory of Dictatorship*, trans. by E.A. Shils, in collaboration with Edith Lowenstein and Klaus Knorr (New York: Oxford University Press, 1941; reprint, New York: Octagon Books, 1969.)

the ideological needs of the Volk. In the latter case, legal training would be irrelevant, and the SD would take a leadership role.[11]

Schellenberg's initial, June 1938 contribution to the debate, written at Heydrich's behest, criticized Best's suggestions regarding the personnel structure of the future State Security Corps that favored Sipo personnel; compared and contrasted Sipo and SD through a series of examples; and developed suggestions for the future.[12] Heydrich must have deemed Schellenberg an excellent choice for the assignment. Schellenberg headed Department I 11 of the SD and was known for his good grasp of complicated legal and administrative issues. An SD member and a trained jurist, Schellenberg was also in an excellent position to contribute to the debate and to be taken seriously by his counterpart. Schellenberg's memorandum also came at an important time: an earlier decree by Himmler, which allowed for Security Police members to be inducted into the SS/SD after three years of post-1933 service, was seen as an indication that Best's vision was gaining currency. It was feared that the Security Police, with its better-educated personnel, would soon dominate the SD.[13] Concerns voiced by the SD, Schellenberg wrote disapprovingly, were ignored.[14] If the SD wanted to retain a modicum of control, it needed to engage actively in the developments taking place now.

Schellenberg's memorandum was ambitious, as he focused on the fundamental differences between Sipo and SD and thereby called into question the overall wisdom of Best's suggestions, which gave primacy to the Sipo.[15] He construed his argument along the differences between Sipo and SD, as defined by the Functional Order: the Sipo was in charge of executive policing of single cases while the SD was a political intelligence service. Their different structures and approaches reflected their difference in mandate, his argument went: the Main Office Security Police was a ministerial unit and involved in administrative and legal issues pertaining to the executive. The SD, on the other hand, was "the moveable instrument, the tactile and sensual organ on the body of the folk, in all enemy circles, in all living spheres, [that] must have a different

[11] Wildt, *Generation*, 259–262.

[12] Stabskanzlei, I 11, Sche/Ld, Vermerk, July 5, 1938, USHMM, 14.016 M, 827. Note the earlier version with its handwritten comments: Stabskanzlei, I 11, Sche/Ld, Vermerk, July 1, 1938, USHMM, 14.016 M, 827. Wildt, *Generation*, 262–264.

[13] Regarding Himmler's February 18, 1938 decree, see Banach, *Führerkorps*, 287.

[14] Stabskanzlei, I 11, Sche/Ld, Vermerk, July 5, 1938, USHMM, 14.016 M, 827.

[15] Schellenberg mentioned four problems: (1) the coordination (*Angleichung*) of SS ranks in the SD with those in the Security Police; (2) a comparative listing of the activities of SD members and members of the Security Police; (3) the adjustment of pay scales upon reaching the next level; and (4) financial issues arising from retirement and untimely deaths. All the issues related to the status of civil servants.

structure than the State Police, based necessarily on its own viewing method of all things relevant for intelligence." The SD, Schellenberg posited, attempted to gain an "organically seen picture of any given enemy sphere or living sphere" through the "systematic compilation of individual information." This approach necessitated the peculiar structure of the SD. Seemingly redundant and overwrought to the uninitiated, as Schellenberg admitted, this structure allowed for cross-pollination between the different offices and guaranteed the SD's ability to "impose order on the immense amount of available information about all enemy and living spheres in order for the intelligence service to fulfill its ultimate mission in the first place, namely to be a constant source of information for the leadership of the state [...]." Put differently, there was a method to the madness and to illustrate his point, Schellenberg chose an ideologized example. He raised the specter of a Jew involved in stock market fraud and currency smuggling who, through the cooperation of various SD departments, was discovered to be a leading member of Freemasonry abroad. "[A]ny intrusion into this organic structure [of the SD]," Schellenberg warned, would destroy and "lead to a complete failure of the entire intelligence service." In essence, Schellenberg argued that the SD structure grew "organically" out of its tasks as an intelligence service and could not be changed without impeding its work and success. The Security Police's structure, on the other hand, was based on different premises. Coordinating the two agencies based on a primacy of the Security Police was thus a foolish and shortsighted step.

Schellenberg also rejected suggestions to restructure the SD, based on the ranks and the capabilities of the individual members, to allow for its easy coordination with the Security Police. "Rather the opposite would be advisable," Schellenberg wrote and recommended creating a characteristic (*arteigene*) pay scale within the SD. Then, Schellenberg opined, everything else would fall into place, and an easy exchange between Security Police and the SD would be possible. However, Schellenberg also posited that higher-ranking SD men should be able to switch over to the Security Police only, "as long as they possess the needed judicial or other preconditions." In other words, Schellenberg, much like Best, believed legal training to be a precondition for most leadership positions in the Security Police but left other options open. Summarizing his suggestions, Schellenberg stressed that under his plan the SD would remain "characteristic," thereby giving the organization the opportunity to "become, maybe, some day the envisioned, great intelligence service, comparable to the [British] 'Intelligence Service'."[16]

[16] Stabskanzlei, I 11, Sche/Ld, Vermerk, July 5, 1938, USHMM, 14.016 M, 827.

Schellenberg clearly addressed two main issues facing the SD and its members at this time. For one, there were mundane, yet far-reaching financial issues that would affect SD members if and when the two organizations were to be combined. Many of the leading members of the Security Police had better credentials than their SD counterparts and combined with SS ranks, this would allow them to surpass their SD colleagues when it came to promotions. As civil servants, they were also eligible for many financial perks. SD members wanted access to those benefits. But Schellenberg's memo was not simply about finances or even the fear that less ideologically sound, but academically qualified Sipo members would flood and overtake the SD. Rather, Schellenberg defended what he deemed special about the SD and its approaches.[17] The SD was not to become a branch of the Sipo, but should remain true to its defining characteristics as an ideologically bound surveillance and intelligence service. Otherwise, Schellenberg left no doubt, it would never reach greatness. His intention was, at least at this point, not the creation of the new State Security Corps along the lines of the SD, as Michael Wildt suggests.[18] His goals were both commonplace and fundamental: to gain ground lost in the debate thus far; to put the SD on an equal footing for the anticipated showdown with the Sipo; and to define clearly the SD's role, mandate, and specificity.

Schellenberg's defense of SD and its characteristics must have pleased Heydrich, for he subsequently asked Schellenberg to consider the future role of the SD.[19] Schellenberg had also been involved with various restructuring efforts of Office III in the SD Main Office and was clearly committed to the SD's future.[20] He now was to focus on several interconnected issues: the SD's role as an intelligence organization, its funding, its future career paths, and its relationship with the Security Police in the envisioned State Security Corps while retaining its independence from the Sipo as a separate cadre. This was a monumental assignment and Lutz Hachmeister thus dubbed Schellenberg "Heydrich's RSHA-planner."[21] Heydrich had, indeed, asked Schellenberg to draft the future

[17] Wildt, *Generation*, 266.   [18] Wildt, *Generation*, 265.

[19] Schellenberg to Heydrich, February 27, 1939, USHMM, 14.016 M, 826; Wildt, *Generation*, 266. Banach claims that Heydrich gave this order to Schellenberg in February 1938, but seems mistaken; Banach, *Führerkorps*, 287–288. Banach references Höhne, who, incidentally, assumes that Schellenberg received said order in the fall of 1938; Heinz Höhne, *Der Orden unter dem Totenkopf. Die Geschichte der SS* (Munich: Bertelsmann, 1967; reprint, Augsburg: Weltbild Verlag, 1998), 253.

[20] See, for example: Befehl für den SD, Nr. 36/38, Neugliederung Sachgebiete III, Leiter Zentralabteilung I 1 a.A. Schellenberg, June 18, 1938; Anlage "Organisationsplan des Sachgebietes III im SD (June 1, 1938)," RGVA, Fond 500, Opis 1, film 907, roll 3.

[21] Hachmeister, *Gegnerforscher*, 208.

Reich Security Main Office, arguably Heinrich Himmler's most important instrument of terror and power.

Schellenberg soon presented a detailed memorandum.[22] It first surveyed the status quo: the SD's shortcomings and problems as an intelligence outfit with a poorly defined mandate and in competition with
the Security Police; the incomparability of SD and Sipo career paths
and the financial insecurity for SD members; and the challenges arising
from the planned creation of a State Security Corps. Schellenberg suggested an ambitious restructuring program. And with it, the SD, a small,
ill-defined, and not firmly entrenched entity – and Walter Schellenberg
personally – staked a claim in any further reorganization or integration
of SD and Sipo. Schellenberg's basic tenet was that the militarized and
ideologically firm SS should incorporate the police.[23] Initial steps in
this direction had already been taken. Soon all members of the police
would also be SS members and promotion within the police would be
matched by promotion within the SS. The establishment of clear SD
career paths would then allow for the SD to synchronize its promotions
as well. Yet all plans remained contingent on adequate state funding
for the SD and Schellenberg stressed that by taking the Party Treasury
out of the financial equation, the SD would become independent from
"internal party-political constellations." Put simply, the SD wanted to
achieve two mutually exclusive objectives. While nominally and struc-
turally remaining a party and SS institution and independent of state
structures, its formalized civil service qualifications, and its career paths,
the SD wanted the state, which had deeper pockets than the party, to foot
the bill. The incorporation of the police into the SS would have meant
that within the State Security Corp the SD would be dominant. Yet in
terms of concrete, ordinary policing work, the SD remained the police's
junior partner without executive powers.

To argue for the SD's future preeminence, Schellenberg posited the
existence of two separate SDs. As part of the SS, it was the carrier of a
"political finish line," but there was also the "purely practical work of the
total political intelligence service." This dual role of the SD was at its
core and brought about its own dynamics; it presented, explained Schellenberg, a complicated and challenging issue that needed to be balanced
out carefully. The understanding of the SD's dual role, Schellenberg
stressed, formed the basis for his suggestions. Schellenberg primarily

---

[22] Reorganisation des Sicherheitsdienstes des Reichsführers SS im Hinblick auf eine organ-
isatorische und personelle Angleichung mit der Sicherheitspolizei, Stabskanzlei I 11,
Sche/Ld, Berlin, February 24, 1939, USHMM, 14.016 M, 826 [hereafter: Reorganisa-
tion/Sicherheitsdienst].
[23] Reorganisation/Sicherheitsdienst.

defined the SD in its difference to the military intelligence service. He argued against redistricting the SD along army lines, as this would go against the "basic principles" of SD intelligence work and might constitute a prelude to a "cold reform of the Reich" by the military. Even though the specter of the military taking over must have played well with his audience, Schellenberg largely couched his argument in technical terms: the military intelligence service and the SD fulfilled different tasks. For the former, security concerns and changing strategic situations defined geographical organization and priorities, which were subject to change. The SD, on the other hand, was defined by "economic, ethnological and other factors," and while these factors were nebulous, they helped to make the point that the SD was a separate entity and had different tasks not to be confused with military intelligence collection. Schellenberg consequently proposed a new regional set-up that favored the long-term plans for SS, Police, Security Police, and SD and emphasized the main goal: the simultaneous development of a State Security Corps (by amalgamating SS and Police) and a Reich Security Service (by amalgamating SD and Security Police).[24]

For the SD, the regional restructuring posed a risk, in particular when it came to the leadership positions in the *Unterabschnitte*, Lower Districts. Schellenberg opposed the idea that the same person should head the regional SD and the Sipo section but was quick to emphasize that this had nothing to do with the assumption that the Sipo officer – likely a trained in law – would be appointed to a leadership position almost by default. "Short courses" and exams, Schellenberg curtly pointed out, would be enough to allow the uninitiated SD-leader to gain the needed qualifications. Instead, Schellenberg pointed out that the Functional Order of 1937 precluded joint appointments and did not regulate "the needed gear-like interlocking of different work functions (intelligence service – executive evaluation)."[25] The Functional Order provided neither for a clear division between the intelligence service and the executive nor gave it primacy to either one branch and Schellenberg noted that the planned amalgamation would not solve this issue either. It was therefore mandatory that the leaders of the State Police Office and the SD Lower District Leaders remain responsible for their distinct branches. Otherwise,

---

[24] Reorganisation/Sicherheitsdienst. In the short term, Schellenberg pointed to the amount of work involved in the proposed restructuring process; in the long term, he highlighted the sheer size of the different areas of responsibility, which should preclude any leader from attempting to fill more than one position. The term "Reich Security Service," used throughout the early discussions, was later abandoned, as an entity with that name already existed. I use it here until Heydrich rejected the term in April 1939.
[25] Reorganisation/Sicherheitsdienst.

Schellenberg prognosticated, the intelligence service would be broken up into many different entities, each of them under the control of the executive branch. If that were the case, the envisioned totality of the intelligence service would be lost.[26] And this was Schellenberg's main concern.

In the latter part of his memorandum, Schellenberg focused on the organizational structure of the planned Reich Security Service. Schellenberg suggested establishing six offices. Office I was to deal with administrative and legal matters; Office II was to become the SD-dominated research office; Office III the domestic intelligence service; and Office IV the foreign intelligence service. Counter-intelligence and "political executive," that is the Secret State Police, would form Office V, and Office VI would be the new home of the criminal police. The SD as an intelligence service would remain unchanged in its structure but improve its operations. As Office III, the domestic intelligence service was to be built into a "powerful (*schlagkräftig*) intelligence service in all living spheres (*Lebensgebieten*)."[27] Schellenberg barely mentioned the planned foreign intelligence service, noting that he was not content with his current ideas but promised future suggestions. Instead, he focused on issues that needed to be addressed immediately: the creation of the new districts; the transfer of the Superior Districts' responsibilities to the Lower Districts; the organization of the new middle instances; financial matters; coordinated career paths; training for new recruits; and the merger between the administrative section of the SD and the administrative section of the Security Police, Werner Best's domain. As a deadline for these preliminary measures, Schellenberg proposed June 1, 1939; he anticipated the creation of the new entity to be finished by October 1, 1939. Schellenberg suggested how to meet these tight deadlines: Heydrich was to call a meeting soon and deliver a speech that Schellenberg had drafted for him. Time was of the essence: insecurity about the future of the service was creeping into the ranks of the SD and people were leaving the organization. Schellenberg regarded the insecurities, the gossip, and the men leaving the SD as a "vote of distrust" against the leadership that needed to be dealt with immediately.[28] Schellenberg laid out a tight and ambitious blueprint for a service befitting Heydrich and Himmler's plans that combined Schellenberg's judicial training, his understanding of administrative details, and his knack for couching these elements in the

---

[26] Reorganisation/Sicherheitsdienstes.
[27] Reorganisation/Sicherheitsdienst. Schellenberg suggested broadening the intelligence-gathering basis by using more people, for example, Robert Ley's German Workers' Front (DAF). This was directed against the "research-oriented" approaches favored by Six; Hachmeister, *Gegnerforscher*, 208.
[28] Reorganisation/Sicherheitsdienst.

appropriate language. It was a workable blueprint that went beyond the theoretical and included concrete steps to achieve the goals in a timely manner. And while the later Reich Security Main Office took a slightly different shape and not every suggestion was realized, Schellenberg was one of its main creators. He had also established himself as its resident expert, in particular for its intelligence sections, and made himself all but indispensable, even when in the short term the discussion took a different but not unexpected turn.

On February 28, 1939, Heydrich reviewed Schellenberg's memorandum, called him in for further discussions, and also met with Werner Best.[29] The next day, Best pushed the discussion into a different direction. He presented Heydrich, and by extension Schellenberg, with his deliberations about career paths in what he labeled the German Security Police.[30] Heydrich and Schellenberg were prepared. Based on an earlier draft, Schellenberg had also prepared a memorandum on career paths, dated February 28.[31] Apparently, Heydrich and Schellenberg were expecting a showdown with Best. February had been busy.

The career paths issue now came to a boil. On the basic level, the debate was about the role and the position of jurists in the Security Police and the SD. On the meta-level, the institutional relationship between Security Police and SD was the crux of the matter. Best conceptualized the SD as one branch of his German Security Police and not as something apart from it and worthy of special consideration.[32] Accordingly, Best proposed unified training and career paths for all leading members of the German Security Police, based on the study of law. This, he argued, was the best and only way to ensure that everyone would be able to fill any position within the administration. Upon passing the first judicial state exam, every candidate would attend the leadership school of the Security Police and pass a test equivalent to the old *Kriminlapolizeiprüfung*, the Criminal Police Exam. Most candidates would take their second judicial

[29] Wildt, *Generation*, 268.
[30] Grundzüge der Ausbildung und der Laufbahn der Führer (leitenden Beamten) der Deutschen Sicherheitspolizei, March 1, 1939, USHMM, 14.016 M, 827 [hereafter: Grundzüge/Ausbildung].
[31] Stabskanzlei I 11, Die Laufbahnrichtlinien im Sicherheitsdienst, February 28, 1939, USHMM, 14.016 M, 826; Stabskanzlei I/11, Pl./Sa., Vermerk, Betr: Laufbahnrichtlinien im Sicherheitsdienst/RFSS, Berlin, February 24, 1939, USHMM, 14.016 M, 827 [hereafter: Laufbahnrichtlinien, February 24, 1939]. It is not clear whether Heydrich read this memorandum before his meeting with Best; Best's cover letter to Schellenberg does not answer this question. It calls into question Wildt's statement that Best expected blanket approval from Heydrich. Best's cover letter suggests that Best saw his (draft) memorandum as a starting point and emphasized his interest in Schellenberg's comments before further discussions.
[32] Grundzüge/Ausbildung.

state exam in due time, with a few candidates entering specialized two-year programs in "history, economics, theology, chemistry or languages" that would be useful for the work of the German Security Police. Having passed their first judicial state exam with their cohort, even these men, posited Best, would be able to move into higher positions by eventually fulfilling the additional requirements germane to the study of law. By limiting the numbers of those embarking on specialized studies, Best believed it is possible to offer the select few guaranteed employment. Mainly, though, Best suggested relying on temporarily hired experts paid according to their fields' prevalent rates. In other words, Best suggested creating a different, effectively lower stratum of employees, lacking in payment and prestige, for the specialized tasks that Schellenberg regarded as the core of the SD's mission. Best, for his part, envisioned recruitment and training programs that would allow its graduates to fill any position in the state, making possible the complete infiltration of the state by ideologically firm jurists. The study of law was the plan's centerpiece, for as much as Best was a man of the new times and actively dismantling the normative state, he still believed in the benefits of creating elites by sending them through the proper, state-sanctioned training and making all full members of the German Security Police, including its SD personnel, into civil servants.[33] His parting shot at the SD illustrates vividly Best's disdain for a leadership lacking judicial training: his reforms, he opined, would end the "the highhandedness and short-sightedness of self-reliant praetorians (to which professional party institutions tend)."[34] Best was set to rein in the unruly praetorians.

Schellenberg, though, did not regard the SD as part of the German Security Police but as a separate entity defined by its unique mission – intelligence. As early as the summer of 1938, Schellenberg had argued that the SD had to remain "characteristic" if it ever wanted to amount to anything.[35] Using the pseudo-biological terminology prevalent in Nazi ideology, Schellenberg's memorandum on career paths sounded a similar tune, foregrounding the future role of the SD.[36] Schellenberg laid out the three areas the SD was to cover – domestic intelligence, foreign intelligence, and research – and its three main approaches: intelligence gathering, intelligence evaluation, and research. In a seeming bid for symmetry, Schellenberg also proposed three leadership levels for the

---

[33] On Best's understanding of SD, Security Police, and the role of the law in this conflict: Wildt, *Generation*, 268–276; Herbert, *Best*, 228–233.
[34] Grundzüge/Ausbildung.
[35] Stabskanzlei, I 11, Sche/Ld, Vermerk, July 5, 1938, USHMM, 14.016 M, 827.
[36] Stabskanzlei I 11, Vermerk, Betr.: Die Laufbahnen im Sicherheitsdienst, February 28, 1939, USHMM, 14.016 M, 826 [hereafter: Laufbahnen, February 28, 1939]

SD.[37] The ability to fill these positions depended on recruitment, training, and clear career paths. Once more, Schellenberg did more than simply address the issue at hand but also took the opportunity to define his vision for the future SD as a viable intelligence service. He warned that under the current training, which focused on policing expertise, SD work was bound to become a subfield of policing and lose its independence. He argued that the SD needed specialists with expert knowledge in the living spheres they investigated and doubted that police officers could easily acquire this specialized knowledge. Instead, he suggested recruiting experts in institutions of higher learning, forgoing any specialized SD schools, and supporting them with stipends.[38] In short, Schellenberg laid out career paths closely tied to the mandate of the SD and his vision for its future: an independent, total intelligence service with a strong research component, active domestically and internationally.

Schellenberg's suggestions were based on a document that, by drawing on the SD's history, provided an even broader rationale for the service's specialized status and separate career paths. It is not clear to which extent Schellenberg was involved in drafting the document, but tone and diction suggest that his influence was substantial.

This document defined the role of the SD as twofold: defensive, by securing and protecting the National Socialist ideology, and offensive, by moving into the enemy's sphere. "The task of the SD is therefore, as before, to penetrate the enemy's spiritual and material sphere of power, to identify him by gathering intelligence on him, and to strike him dead in evaluating that intelligence."[39] As the enemy reacted, the argument went, battlefields as well as the enemies' tactics, weapons, and allies changed. Therefore, the service needed to be able to adjust its work and its organizational structure, especially as six years into the Third Reich, the ideological and political enemy was not out in the open anymore. Instead, he hid in various living spheres. However, the "rigid SD" had difficulties in adjusting to these changes, as the internal organization of the SD did not correspond with the enemy groups anymore: "[s]imilarly, after the final solution (*nach der endgültigen Lösung*) of the Jewish question after November 1938, the Jews do not exist as an organized enemy anymore."[40] Indeed, the document noted that by now the Jewish Department in the SD focused exclusively on speeding up the emigration process. Yet at the same time, pro-Jewish attitudes would persist, even after all Jews left Germany. This then created an entirely different task for the

---

[37] Laufbahnen, February 28, 1939.   [38] Laufbahnen, February 28, 1939.
[39] Laufbahnrichtlinien, February 24, 1939.
[40] Laufbahnrichtlinien, February 24, 1939.

SD. Germany, the argument went, was now encircled by countries "inoc-
ulated with the spirit of Jewish and Jew-friendly emigration, supported
by the world fraternization tendencies of freemasonry and following the
equalizing tendencies of German Catholicism, fighting against Germany
with all intellectual, technical, and economic means."[41] Consequently,
it was suggested to create an organization and a staff able to respond to
new political situations as they arose. However, only personnel trained for
these specific tasks would be able to do so. The SD should thus take the
lead and the Security Police should simply serve as the arresting power.

On the surface, Best and Schellenberg addressed two different things in
their pieces. The former focused on the Security Police and career paths
while the latter concerned himself with the particularities of the SD and
their implications for the career paths of the SD officers. However, as the
two organizations were to be merged soon, their different visions were
on silent a collision course. Any decision would have far-reaching consequences. At stake was the nature of the new organization, the relevance
of its respective parts, the independence – or lack thereof – of the SD as
an intelligence service, and the new organization's leadership: political-
ideological jurists or political-ideological soldiers trained on the job.

Schellenberg also engaged directly Best's suggestions for the career
paths and despite "some objections," he indicated general agreement
and did his best to reach a compromise. In light of the ensuing conflict,
it is noteworthy that Schellenberg agreed with Best that all candidates
for leadership positions should train in law and take their first judicial
state exam. Beyond that, Schellenberg focused on maintaining the SD's
independence and suggested that the course after the first state exam
should accentuate the military and ideological basics of the SS.[42] As
"SS-capabilities" were required for Sipo and SD officers anyhow, this
appeared to be wholly reasonable. Schellenberg also wanted the training
to take into account the requirements of the intelligence service, but
noted, seemingly graciously, that Best's suggestions had done so to some
extent. In another contentious area he construed a line of reasoning
that allowed Best to save face if he chose to do so. Best had stated
that even men who opted for a "specialized, two-year training" could
attain other positions later on – implying, though, that they needed
to fulfill the judicial preconditions beforehand. Schellenberg opted to
assume that these men would be able to enter the higher administrative
service as long as they successfully finished their specialized degrees.
Indeed, Schellenberg slyly claimed that Best had not included this

[41] Laufbahnrichtlinien, February 24, 1939.
[42] Stabskanzlei I 11, Sche./Fh., Vermerk, March 8, 1939, USHMM, 14.016 M, 827.

provision for tactical reasons, but he expressed concern nonetheless. If not included now, it would be forgotten in the future. This was a willful misunderstanding of Best's succinct statements, but Schellenberg was prepared to find common ground with Best, as long as the needs of the SD, as he defined them, were recognized.

Heydrich was a different matter, though, and Schellenberg was paying attention. Heydrich's handwritten remarks on his copy of Best's draft convey his discontent. Commenting on the suggestion that all candidates should study law, Heydrich jotted in the margins that – depending on a person's capabilities and planned employment – law should be one possibility among several. Best's reasoning for mandatory studies elicited a large question mark from Heydrich. And while Best distinguished between jurists and specialists, Heydrich angrily noted that jurists were specialists. A few days earlier, Heydrich had polemicized that fifty years onwards he did not want the SD to be a "bureaucratic civil servants' shop" – *bürokratischer Beamtenladen* – and now Best's draft raised that specter.[43] Heydrich disdained civil servants and unequivocally rejected any preeminence for jurists. In his mind, both were part of the old system. Schellenberg eventually realized the full extent of Heydrich's anger, as on April 4, 1939, he remarked in a notation to Heydrich that it could not be that only academics had a right to exist in the SD and suggested taking a clear stand against this.[44] Schellenberg's indignation is palpable, but whether it was genuine or a reflection of Heydrich's apparent ire remains unclear. However, taking into account Schellenberg's exchanges with Best thus far, the latter seems likely. After treading carefully for months and taking a neither–nor approach that tried to find a leadership role for SD members without a background in law while agreeing on the usefulness of a law degree, Schellenberg now unequivocally came down on one side of the argument. He threw in his lot with the man whom he assumed to have the more promising future: Heydrich.

Precisely now and presumably both unaware and unconcerned about Schellenberg's evolving stand, Werner Best accelerated the conflict. He published his essay *"Kritik und Apologie des Juristen"* (Critique and Apologia of a Jurist) in the academic journal *Deutsches Recht* and in other venues.[45] Noting that jurists were the most severely criticized professionals, a situation comparable only to the criticisms levied against military officers during the Weimar Republic, Best made it his task to get to the bottom of this "relentless critique." In a stylistic gamble, he used his

[43] Wildt, *Generation*, 270.   [44] Herbert, *Best*, 231 note 274.
[45] Werner Best, *"Kritik und Apologie des 'Juristen',"* *Deutsches Recht des NSRB*, Heft 8/9, 9. Jhg., April 8 and 15, 1939, BAL, NSD 56/1 Jahrgang 1939. Herbert, *Best*, 231 note 275.

own political socialization and career in a law to show that jurists should occupy top positions in the state. Never a shrinking violet, Best suggested that the new generation of leaders should be created in his image. Best noted that "the [racial] folk" was critical of jurists because they did not fulfill its expectations, because the folk wanted jurists to be political, true representatives of the people, instead of neutral deciders. But, Best wrote, the jurists' role in a *völkisch* state was different from their role in a liberal, democratic state defined by the separation of powers. In the *völkisch* state, the jurist imparted order on the folk, served as a steward (*Ordner*), and "masters the techniques of command."[46] Rather than interpreting the existing body of law, the jurist set the law for the Volksgemeinschaft. Law thus became politics, but in order to avoid chaos, jurists – experts in the technique of giving orders and formulating the law – were still needed, even though Best conceded that their training should be improved.[47] Indeed, Best deemed the jurist to be the most political professional of all and jurists the Volksgemeinschafts's natural leaders. Indeed, the folk wanted the jurist as the executor of its will, or so Best argued.

Best's decision to take the controversy into the public sphere was a tremendous provocation. Conflicts within the Nazi hierarchy were normally not aired in public and Heydrich, who had no academic training at all, was incensed. The same was certainly true for many in the leading ranks of the SD; their careers and reputations were suddenly and publicly on the line.[48] The public nature of the debate also opened the SD – an organization far from secure in its funding, mandate, and future and regarded with suspicion by many – to questions and attacks from other party or state authorities. A serious and fiery rebuttal was needed, and Walter Schellenberg was just the right person to pen it. This he did.

In this piece, Schellenberg constructed a historical-ideological argument that made a mockery of Best's seemingly measured but also strikingly self-pitying article. Commencing his critique with doubts that the time for a defense of jurists had arrived, Schellenberg summarized Best's view as focusing on the accusation of formalism as the jurists' main shortcoming. Schellenberg did not see this as the central issue and focused his critique on the jurists' other objectionable characteristics. And there were many: jurists were out of touch with reality, self-important, lacked common sense, and restricted their thinking to the formal and the existing. Schellenberg also deemed jurists arrogant, enamored with so-called objectivity, and unable to think "subjectively-factually" along broader political lines. Modern jurists, argued Schellenberg, thought of

[46] Herbert, *Best*, 231–232.   [47] Wildt, *Generation*, 273.
[48] Herbert, *Best*, 231–232; Wildt, *Generation*, 272 note 185.

themselves as the "rulers in all living spheres," while historically a jurist had not been much more than an assistant and advisor, *Rat*. This was, indeed, opined Schellenberg, the jurists' proper place in the world. Liberalism – with its separation of power into three equally important branches, all of them run by jurists – had destroyed this natural state. Rejecting this erroneous liberal view, Schellenberg then extolled the "modern German idea" that he described as a "remembrance of the primacy of a stronger leadership," which returned jurists to their natural position as advisors. Their role was to assist the leaders in defining facts and "wording orders." They were cogs in the system and not its motor; the law was a tool and not a purpose in itself.[49] Despite his strong rhetoric, Schellenberg did not reject outright the notion that a jurist, if qualified, could be a leader, but the article clearly meant to put jurists into their proper, subordinate place.

Schellenberg's strengths rested in his ability to attack his opponents forcefully without burning all bridges. He displayed this when he stressed that there was no intention to create a separate caste of professional political leaders, but argued instead that neither jurists nor those trained in party leadership schools were leaders by virtue of their training. Both were assistants, as "[n]either the 'state' with its professional leadership staff of jurists nor the 'party' with its professional leadership staff of party officials know how to rule." Schellenberg made his case based on the *Führerprinzip*, the leadership principle, noting that "[i]ndividuals of leadership talent" from all walks of life and regardless of their professional background could and should become leaders. Resonating *Mein Kampf*, Schellenberg stated that no one could learn to lead; rather, one was born for it.[50] Schellenberg thus envisioned the establishment of a new leadership, growing out of the people's community and thus superseding differences between state and party. The conflict between Best's and Schellenberg's views is salient. Best wanted to have it both: the end of traditional jurisprudence in the normative state and a preeminent role for jurists in the *völkisch* state. Schellenberg agreed with the importance of jurists – he was, after all, one of them – but intended to move beyond this group by creating a new leadership, selected on an ideological basis and grounded in the "real life" of the Nazi state.[51]

Schellenberg's attack on Best was strikingly personal. Tersely commenting that the biographical approach of Best's article was a matter

---

[49] Schellenberg to Chef des Sicherheitshauptamts, April 25, 1939, USHMM, 14.016 M, 827.

[50] Schellenberg to Chef des Sicherheitshauptamts, April 25, 1939, USHMM, 14.016 M, 827. For the allusion to *Mein Kampf*, see Wildt, *Generation*, 274 notes 188 and 189.

[51] Wildt, *Generation*, 275.

of taste, he left little doubt about his own. Schellenberg then described jurists as generally arrogant but his implication was particular: Best was arrogant. Most damning was doubtlessly Schellenberg's statement that despite condemning liberalism, Best had not yet fully disavowed it.[52] In short, Schellenberg portrayed Best as the man of the transitional period, not fully free of the old traditions and unable to move beyond them completely. This was a personal and vivid attack against a man who had been crucial to the development of the Nazi police and who was the main theorist of *völkisch* justice. Heydrich must have been pleased.

Schellenberg's rebuttal of Best's article was never published and it remains unclear who read it. But it must have had some impact, as the debate lost some of its fervor. Heydrich and Schellenberg had put Best on notice. By no means any less ideologically committed than Heydrich, Best was still more traditional in his approaches: he saw political jurists as dismantling the remaining normative state from within.[53] In the sixth year of the Third Reich, though, the stock of those clamoring for comparatively careful approaches was falling. Heydrich was ready to dismantle the traditional state, its elites, and its processes quickly and entirely. And Schellenberg forcefully made the case for separate, yet equally well-paid and professionally secure SD career paths and against the preeminence of jurists while positioning himself as the man of the new times, cognizant of the future and its demands. He portrayed himself as Best's inverse image.

Did his argument reflect Schellenberg's ideological beliefs? After the war, Schellenberg went to great lengths to brandish his belief in due process and to construct himself as, at best, wary of Nazi ideology and removed from any ideologized, radical, destructive, and nontraditional activities. Schellenberg's initially positive reaction to Best's proposal indicates that his personal views might have been closer to Best's than to Heydrich's. But it did not take Schellenberg long to realize how the wind was blowing, and he certainly knew how to acquire convictions – or close approximations thereof – quickly and forcefully. And by structuring his arguments around *Mein Kampf*, Schellenberg made his writings and himself unassailable.

The war of words notwithstanding, everybody knew that the issue remained and that a solution had to be found. Best and Schellenberg kept exchanging memos. In late May, it was Best's turn; he sent over a

---

[52] Herbert, *Best*, 232; Schellenberg to Chef des Sicherheitshauptamts, April 25, 1939, USHMM, 14.016 M, 827.

[53] Herbert, *Best*, 229. Note Herbert's words of caution about the overall meaning of Best's standpoints. When it came to the actual policies of these months – the *Einsatzgruppen*, the police in Poland, and the anti-Jewish policies in the Reich – there was no difference between Heydrich and Best.

memo and a draft decree, noting that he had also sent it to Heydrich for approval.[54] In it Best tried to defuse many of the earlier criticisms and was less contemptuous of people educated in fields other than law. But he did not concede his main point: men trained in law should populate the higher administrative service of the planned new super office – and everything else. However, Best's new suggestions allowed for specialized studies as an alternative path after the first judicial exam. All candidates would also be required to take a course at a Reich Security Service leadership school, finishing it with the police inspector exam. Best saw this is a way to keep open career opportunities for those who had embarked on specialized studies. "SS-suitability" and ideological firmness, on the other hand, were to be achieved by inducting all candidates into the SS. Best then detailed what would be achieved: selection and training combining the best of all three career paths; suitability for all tasks the Reich Security Service might be asked to fulfill; equal status and remuneration for members of the Reich Security Service vis-à-vis their counterparts in the state administration; and, consequently, the possibility of having members of the Reich Security Service serve in any administrative branch of the state.[55] Best had largely met Heydrich's and Schelleberg's demands; his insistence on the study of law as the gold standard was little more than a way to save face. Best's plan had many advantages, such as the interchangeability of personnel or, more precisely, the possibility to move SS/SD members into the civil administrative positions. A cold take-over of the civil administration, which still harbored a fair share of insufficiently Nazified experts, would have been within reach. But this was apparently not good enough for Heydrich and Schellenberg, as administrators trained in law would still occupy central positions in the new service and in any effort to take over the civil service. Sipo personnel would remain dominant. Conversely, the SD – defined by the particular needs of an intelligence service, as Schellenberg never tired to emphasize, and with fewer jurists on staff – would still occupy a position of lesser importance. And lastly, while Best contemplated the cold take-over of the civil administration, Schellenberg's writings indicate that he and Heydrich called into question the existing structure as a whole. They envisioned much more radical changes.

Schellenberg laid out these ideas in August 1939, and the coming war of imperial conquest clearly informed the memorandum.[56] Schellenberg

---

[54] Best to Schellenberg, May 25, 1939, USHMM, 14.016 M, 827.
[55] Best to Schellenberg, May 25, 1939, USHMM, 14.016 M, 827.
[56] Stabskanzlei I 11, Sche./Fh., Vermerk: Stellungnahme zum letzten Entwurf der Laufbahnrichtlinien durch SS-Brigadeführer Dr. Best, Berlin, August 28, 1939, USHMM, 14.016 M, 827. Schellenberg referred to Best's "secret reasoning," and thus presumably

made the case for a new, radically redefined administrative structure that would break with tradition, be based on the will of the Führer, and meet the demands of an Empire. And with its reliance on Hitler's writings and comparisons to the British Empire, Schellenberg put Best on the ideological and practical defensive. Schellenberg pointed out that Hitler wished the state to be run by a smallest number of people possible. Thus, there existed a need to create a new administrative apparatus that was responsible, detail-oriented, and flexible enough to govern the Empire. However, Schellenberg did not simply base his argument on Hitler's wish, important as it was. He also compared to devastating effect, as it showed German inefficiency, the British administration of India with the German administration of the Protectorate of Bohemia and Moravia, the since early 1939 German-occupied Czech crown-lands. This was not an academic problem but a concrete one: the future empire needed to be administered and Schellenberg suggested doing so with a thoroughly reformed system centered on the "ideologically sound human, educated in the new way." Incidentally, he saw Best as too grounded in traditions that even Best's suggested reforms would not jettison and argued that the new generation of leaders would, due to their specialization, not be more flexible than the last and almost as uniform. Schellenberg also scathingly suggested Best's plan was likely to create "poor jurists, poor criminal officers, and poor SD-men." There was nothing to recommend Best's plan. In contrast, Schellenberg proposed unified career paths enhanced by specialized courses, based, surely no accidentally, on comments Heydrich had made during a meeting in April.[57] This, Schellenberg argued, would guarantee flexibility and make it possible to move personnel from one position to the next. Early recruitment was key and SS training would form the initial phase of the candidates' education. After earning an SS rank, candidates would decide on a university program, balancing the need of the Reich Security Service with their interest and talents. Subsequently, their SS and university education would proceed hand-in-hand and the men would eventually be deployed based on their exams and educational backgrounds. Decisions about leadership positions, Schellenberg wrote, would be taken much later but a candidate's academic background would be irrelevant for these. His personality and his political and ideological prowess would be the determining factors then.[58]

---

not to Best's May 25, 1939 proposal. The gist of Best's argument is, however, the same. The literature makes no mention of a document containing "secret reasoning."

[57] Vermerk, n.d., signed Schellenberg, USHMM, 14.016 M, 826.

[58] Stabskanzlei I 11, Sche./Fh., Vermerk: Stellungnahme zum letzten Entwurf der Laufbahnrichtlinien durch SS-Brigadeführer Dr. Best, Berlin, August 28, 1939, USHMM, 14.016 M, 827.

Schellenberg's blueprint was ideologically sound, as it embraced the leadership principle and was based on Hitler's writing; appeared egalitarian but was still academically inclined, as it embraced university degrees; and was efficient, as it promised to create a new caste of effective administrators for Germany and its future Empire. When Schellenberg wrote this, the debate was at an impasse and the attack on Poland a few days away.

The discussion about the career paths, which all involved must have initially regarded as a minor issue in the grand scheme of things, had evolved into a major stumbling block. There was no doubt that the career paths needed to be unified or at least synchronized, if only for practical reasons like the cohesion of the planned super-office or the SD's wish to acquire state funding. But ideological questions, tied to different personalities, soon overshadowed the issue. Heydrich's radicalized ideological vision, in which the civil administration could be replaced and new career paths could be established quickly, collided with Best's more traditional ideological approach. Ultimately, the question was in whose image the new leaders would be created: Heydrich's or Best's. The eventual outcome was a draw; none of the problems was solved for good.[59] Yet, it was also a debate about the administration of the Empire and those bound by tradition – however tenuously, as in the case of Best – were not winning it, an ominous development. Schellenberg's role in what was officially a conflict between Heydrich and Best went beyond that of a high-level scribe, who put into writing the boss' ideas. Rather, Schellenberg imprinted them with his own vision for the future of the SD as an intelligence service and its relationship to the Security Police. He fashioned himself as the theorist of the SD as an intelligence service, keeping its "characteristics" and its future on the agenda while defending the qualifications of the SD officers and arguing for their comparability with those of Sipo officers.[60] This was no mean feat, as qualifications often differed enormously. Schellenberg achieved much of his success by the structure of his arguments. These combined the down-to-earth practical with the ideological, creating a mixture that appears to have stumped Best. Best surely encountered much more resistance to his plans than ever expected – and Schellenberg was the key player.

The debates were eventually overtaken by reality. On September 1, 1939 German troops invaded Poland and the ideological-racial war for which they had been planning became an actuality. The SD and

---

[59] Banach, *Führerkorps*, 294.
[60] Also unhappy with Best's plans was the head of the Gestapo, Heinrich Müller. Banach, *Führerkorps*, 294 note 199.

Sipo functionaries involved in the debate now had to contend with bigger issues of immediate concern.[61] The speedy establishment of the Reich Security Main Office, which had spawned the debate about the synchronization of career paths in the first place, became a priority, for this institution was to racially and ideologically police the Reich and the Empire. The basic idea was clear: the RSHA was to amalgamate into a policing and intelligence super-agency the Security Police and the SD. Schellenberg's initial memorandum had addressed these issues and laid out a tight timeline, but his suggestions were soon overshadowed by the related conflict on the career paths. However, this does not mean that all discussion ceased; indeed, Schellenberg remained active on this administrative front as well. On April 4, 1939, Schellenberg drafted a long memorandum summarizing a discussion with Heydrich who wanted to move quickly, also in light of the SD's intent to become part of the state budget by the next fiscal year.[62] Billed as Heydrich's thoughts on the matter, the document has Schellenberg's fingerprints all over it and sheds an interesting light on the relationship between the two men, as Schellenberg used it to self-promote, either gracefully or slyly. He noted, for example, that Heydrich had made only minor changes and had reacted positively to his, Schellenberg's, suggestions. Heydrich and Schellenberg were clearly of one mind when it came to the RSHA.

Key issues for Heydrich were the creation of a personnel office under his immediate control and the relationship between sections of the SD's domestic intelligence service and the police. Heydrich's idea to create in Office I a personnel office answering directly to him was thinly veiled attempt to circumvent the contested career path issue and to recruitment his responsibility. This was to be charged with the "SS-related care of all SD members" and with the recruitment, training, and mentorship of younger members of both the Security Police and the SD. Heydrich's other concern was the role of the SD. Office II would be in charge of "broad scholarly investigation of ideological enemies" and report on enemy ideologies and programs and not on the enemies as such. Its reports would then serve as guidelines for the concrete work of the other offices. In contrast, Office III was to function as the domestic intelligence service, relying on networks of informers. Its mainstay would be the rapid collection and dissemination of short reports. For executive matters it would call upon Office V, the Secret State Police. The division between investigative and executive work remained a problem, as this ideologically and theoretically logical but practically

[61] Banach, *Führerkorps*, 294.
[62] Stabskanzlei I 11, Sche/Ld, Vermerk, April 4, 1939, USHMM, 14.016 M, 826.

unworkable suggestion, which echoed the Functional Order, shows. The memorandum attempted to split the difference by positing the existence of two different domestic intelligence services and rid them of the biggest overlap. Office III was defined as the political intelligence service that guaranteed the uniform scanning – *abtasten* – of all living spheres. The intelligence service section of the police, on the other hand, was billed as the "executive intelligence service," and thus as specialized by definition. It is not clear who came up with this shrewd construction but, reminiscent of Schellenberg's reasoning, this construction nicely veiled the limitations of the SD's domestic intelligence. Nobody seemed convinced that the service succeeded in gathering the information needed to prepare executive measures.[63] This construct allowed to avoid conflict with the Gestapo and to save the SD's face.

Little was said about the SD's foreign section. It was to combine Central Department III 1 "Countries" and Central Department III 3 "Political Intelligence Service Abroad." Central Department III 2, "Defense," that is the counterintelligence section, was to become part of the Gestapo. Most interesting are passing references to deliberations about the political foreign intelligence service in III 3, which were not disseminated widely, and to a report by Best on the work and workings of the British Intelligence Service. However, neither Heydrich nor Schellenberg were – to their irritation – apprised of any details.[64] Heydrich and Schellenberg had even picked the future heads of the offices: Werner Best was to head the administrative office; Heinrich Müller the Gestapo; and Arthur Nebe the criminal police. Of the three SD offices, Franz Alfred Six was to head the SD research office; Erich Ehrlinger the domestic intelligence service; and Heinz Jost the foreign intelligence service.[65]

The ideological make-up of the personnel remained Heydrich's primary concern. On his copy of Schellenberg's memorandum he noted an additional suggestion: the creation of a separate office for recruitment and education, to be headed by Wilhelm Albert. This was an attempt even bolder than the earlier personnel office to gain authority over the career

---

[63] Stabskanzlei I 11, Sche/Ld, Vermerk, Berlin, April 4, 1939, USHMM, 14.016 M, 826. The sentence about the domestic intelligence service's capabilities is dubious. My reading is that the two men had questions about the service's capabilities, as the structure of the sentence counterweighs the double negation. This I see as a grammatical error in a document full of grammatically adventurous constructions.

[64] Stabskanzlei I 11, Sche/Ld, Vermerk, April 4, 1939, USHMM, 14.016 M, 826.

[65] Andreas Seeger, "*Gestapo-Müller.*" *Die Karriere eines Schreibtischtäters* (Berlin: Metropol, 1996); Peter Black "Arthur Nebe: Nationalsozialist im Zwielicht," in Ronald Smelser and Enrico Syring, eds., *Die SS: Elite unter dem Totenkopf. 30 Lebensläufe* (Paderborn: Schöningh, 2000), 365–378; on Six see Hachmeister, *Der Gegnerforscher*; on Erich Ehrlinger see Wildt, *Generation*, 92–96, 99.

paths and over education based on SS principles.[66] A meeting between
Heydrich, Albert, and Schellenberg eleven days later covered much of
the same territory and included the separate office for recruitment and
education into the planned set-up of the RSHA.[67] Heydrich discussed
the newly included office – especially in relationship to the debate about
the career paths – in some detail. Schellenberg, for his part, used Heydrich's comments about the career paths in a later exchange with Werner
Best.[68] Several other issues, most notably budgeting and pay scales for
SD members and their career paths, were still up in the air. Heydrich's
suggestions and ideas bespoke the SD's dire financial situation as much
as the wish to maintain its independence, while also indicating their disdain toward the civil administration. Heydrich pictured receiving a lump
sum from the Reich Finance Ministry, allowing him to pay SD members along SD criteria and without any oversight from the ministry.[69] He
clearly wanted to combine the best of all worlds.

   In early July 1939, Heydrich sent a draft decree for the establishment of the new agency to all office heads of the Security Police and
SD, inviting their comments.[70] Heinrich Müller and Franz Alfred Six's
responses – both of them designated office heads – dealt with their fiefdoms. Most of Müller's suggestions, pertaining to the internal structure
of the Gestapo, found approval with Heydrich.[71] The same was true
for Six's suggestions.[72] Neither man questioned the overall usefulness
of the planned amalgamation of Security Police and SD. A fundamental critique emanated from a different source altogether: Lothar Beutel,
SS member since 1930 and a full-time SD functionary since 1934.[73] It
showed vividly that Schellenberg's defense of a "characteristic SD" was
not simply one ambitious man's quest. Beutel and Schellenberg disagreed
on many details, but both envisioned a total intelligence service. Yet Beutel seized the opportunity to criticize the basis of the planned merger of

[66] Stabskanzlei I 11, Sche/Ld, Vermerk, April 4, 1939, USHMM, 14.016 M, 826.
[67] I follow Wildt here; my copy of the document gives no indication about the meeting's
   date or that Albert attended it. Wildt, *Generation*, 277–278; Vermerk, n.d., signed
   Schellenberg, USHMM, 14.016 M, 826.
[68] Stabskanzlei I 11, Sche./Fh., Vermerk: Stellungnahme zum letzten Entwurf der Laufbahnrichtlinien durch SS-Brigadeführer Dr. Best, Berlin, August 28, 1939, USHMM,
   14.016 M, 827.
[69] Wildt, *Generation*, 277–278; Vermerk, n.d., signed Schellenberg, USHMM, 14.016 M,
   826.
[70] Chef der Sicherheitspolizei und des Sicherheitshauptamtes, Neuorganisation der
   Sicherheitspolizei und des Sicherheitsdienstes, July 5, 1939, USHMM, 14.016 M, 826.
[71] Vermerk, n.d., USHMM, 14.016 M, 826. The author was most likely Müller; Wildt,
   Generation, 335–336.
[72] Wildt, *Generation*, 364–367; Hachmeister, *Gegnerforscher*, 210–213.
[73] On Beutel see Wildt, *Generation*, 931–932.

Security Police and SD in one office on every level. Beutel feared that it would change completely the role of the SD from a "total intelligence service of party and state to a specialized intelligence service and evaluation instrument of the police." Different from its initial mandate of working for all state and party organizations, the SD nowadays mostly assisted the police, Beutel claimed. He traced this problem back to earlier definitions of the SD as an "essential supplement" of the police, and not, as it should have been, as an "essential supplement" of all state and party entities. While Security Police and SD supplemented each other well in their fight against ideological enemies, Beutel drew attention to their overlap and rivalry in other areas. In a bold move, he then suggested putting the investigation of ideological enemies completely under the purview of the police while upholding SD intelligence traditions. The investigation of living spheres, he argued, was to be conducted by a "total, incorruptible intelligence service," completely independent from the police. This, Beutel stressed, was the intelligence service for which SD leaders and volunteers had worked "tirelessly and under many personal sacrifices." A complete integration of the SD into the new office would make this independence, the non-negotiable precondition for an intelligence service supposed to be "practically and ideologically better qualified" than any other intelligence entity, unattainable. Beutel disagreed with the establishment of the RSHA as a central office as much as he disagreed with the integration of the Security Police and SD. He suggested different set-ups on all administrative levels. His ideas about the career paths were as contrary to the established wisdom as were all his other propositions. He rejected, for example, the notion of special schools and argued that SD men should be as academically specialized as possible. He also proposed cherry-picking among the most qualified and ideologically firmest employees in the civil administration, transferring them to the SD for several years and using them as voluntary SD members, informants, after their return to their original positions.[74] His was an SD vision through and through. Beutel's rejection of Heydrich's and Schellenberg's plans exemplifies the variety of visions long-serving SD men had for their organization. However, it also positioned Heydrich and Schellenberg on the practicable middle ground in the reconfiguration of Security Police and SD. While they wanted to achieve the independence of the SD as a total intelligence service as much as Beutel, they also understood the financial and political limitations to their plans. Rather

---

[74] Beutel to Heydrich, Betr.: Neuorganisation der Sicherheitspolizei und des Sicherheitsdienstes, Munich, August 10, 1939, BAL, R 58/7093. Beutel cc-ed Six.

than chasing an unattainable vision, they pushed for the most that was possible under the circumstances. And Schellenberg was the expert for this tightrope walk.

The actual establishment of the Reich Security Main Office and the solution of many of the problems under discussion for about a year, such as the regional restructuring, were anticlimactic. With the beginning of the war, time was essential and far-reaching plans had to be abandoned for short-term solutions. A day before the German invasion of Poland, Heydrich issued a decree streamlining the Gestapo. During the war, the Gestapo was to focus on its most important tasks. An analogous decree was issued for the SD.[75] And on the day German forces invaded Poland, Heydrich and Schellenberg met again to discuss the establishment of the RSHA.[76] Schellenberg then drafted a decree for Heydrich. A little more than three weeks later, Himmler issued the decree finalizing the establishment of the RSHA.[77] Aside from the fact that the offices were arranged differently, Heydrich suffered one defeat. His brainchild, an office for recruitment and education, was not included in Himmler's decree, which established six offices under the umbrella of the RSHA. Werner Best headed Office I, which combined most of the administrative departments of the Security Main Office, the Secret State Police, and the Security Police Main Office. Alfred Six was appointed to run Office II, Scientific Research, combining two Central Departments of the Security Main Office. Office III, run by Otto Ohlendorf (and not Erich Ehrlinger), equaled Central Department II 2 of the former Security Main Office.[78] It was the domestic intelligence service. Heinrich Müller ran Office IV, the Gestapo. The criminal police became Office V; Arthur Nebe was at the helm. Heinz Jost headed the political foreign intelligence section, Office VI, which came out of the foreign intelligence department of the SD. At its core, the RSHA did not change much over the next six years; most changes, and there were many, occurred at the departmental level.

The establishment of the RSHA was, at best, a partial success. The amalgamation of the offices did not touch upon their respective relationships to party and state and no office merged party and state elements

---

[75] Wildt, *Generation*, 280; 291 note 203; Stabskanzlei I 11, Sche./Fh., Vermerk, September 2, 1939, USHMM, 14.016 M, 826.

[76] Stabskanzlei I 11, Sche./Fh., Vermerk, September 2, 1939, USHMM, 14.016 M, 826.

[77] Der Reichsführer SS und Chef der Deutschen Polizei, Himmler, Die Zusammenfassung der zentralen Ämter der Sicherheitspolizei und des SD, September 27, 1939, USHMM, 14.016 M, 240.

[78] On Ohlendorf see Hilary C. Earl, *The Nuremberg SS Einsatzgruppen Trial 1945–1958: Atrocity, Law, and History* (Cambridge: Cambridge University Press, 2008).

into something new. The SD offices remained party entities, financed by the Party's Treasury and career paths, training, and pay scales were not altered either. The RSHA constituted, in Werner Best's words, a "curiosum," not much more than a combined reference sign for offices subsumed under it.[79] Yet even if unification was not achieved, the broad political goals the establishment of the RSHA was to realize became clearer and more easily attainable: the creation of an unambiguously National Socialist policing and surveillance entity that understood its tasks politically, fought the ideologically and racially defined enemy, and was unimpeded by any judicial norms: "the executive of a racist 'people's community'."[80]

Most objectives Schellenberg had championed – some clearly at Heydrich's behest – were not fulfilled. However, 1938 and 1939 had been pivotal for both Schellenberg and the SD. Both came of age. Seizing documents in Austria during the country's annexation and conducting security screenings in Italy when the Axis Rome-Berlin came into being might have been interesting, but Schellenberg's involvement in the discussion about the career paths and the establishment of the Reich Security Main Office was a different business altogether. Here, he gained a foothold among the leading personalities of the RSHA and established a close relationship with Heydrich. He became Heydrich's legal expert of choice – thus far a position expertly filled by Werner Best – when complex and complicated issues needed to be addressed. Schellenberg took on the task with much gusto. He had the same legal training, if not experience, as Best, but was far more accommodating to Heydrich. Schellenberg was also – by age, experience, and nature – less of a rival to Heydrich and became his eager proxy in the conflict with Best. However, the discussion about the career paths initially found Schellenberg on the fence. His initial contributions indicated that he was in agreement with Heydrich about the role and mandate of the SD as the future intelligence service, which he theorized. And like Heydrich, Schellenberg did not want to see the SD disappear in the Security Police's warm embrace. It was likely Schellenberg's clear defense of the SD and its characteristics that persuaded Heydrich to entrust him with further work on this issue. Yet Schellenberg initially did not object to a prominent place for jurists but was amenable to Best's suggestions. Soon enough, though, after having played it until he was confident of the winner, Schellenberg voiced Heydrich's view and did so forcefully. Schellenberg then also emerged as a man unusually adept in finding the most suitable way to further Heydrich's agenda, easily able to counter formal arguments with objections

---

[79] Herbert, *Best*, 233 note 279.   [80] Wildt, *Generation*, 282.

based on ideology or vice versa. Walter Schellenberg was an SD bureaucrat intent on leaving a mark, on furthering his career, and on staking a
claim in the future of the RSHA. He was a man on the rise, who – even
when the destination of his career was still undecided – embraced every
opportunity to further it.

3   Intelligence Man

Major Schaemmel was the picture of a German military man, down to his impressive monocle. And the two British Secret Service agents with whom he met were delighted, because they had finally made contact with a member of the German military resistance. The initial meetings went well. Then, on November 9, 1939, a gun battle disrupted the quiet Dutch border town of Venlo. A Dutch officer died of the wounds sustained during the shoot-out, and the two Englishmen, Sigismund Payne Best and Richard Stevens, having fallen into a trap set by Gestapo and SD, were spirited off to Germany.[1] Schaemmel, alias Schellenberg, arrived in Berlin to a hero's welcome. He had been in the thick of things; Hitler personally pinned the Iron Cross on his chest.[2]

The kidnapping and gun battle at Venlo are the hinge between Schellenberg's past and future careers. Thus far, Schellenberg's career had rested on his administrative and legal expertise with the creation of the Reich Security Main Office as its capstone. It was to be seen whether Schellenberg would do equally well in the Gestapo's counterintelligence department, Department IV E. The incident at Venlo allowed Schellenberg to combine his cerebral image with a new reputation as a successful activist and bona fide intelligence man, and it served him well in his new position, for Schellenberg attempted to remake the department

---

[1] Schaemmel is alternatively spelled Schemmel. On Venlo, see Heinz Höhne, *Der Orden unter dem Totenkopf: Die Geschichte der SS* (Munich: Bertelsmann, 1967; reprint, Augsburg: Weltbild Verlag, 1998), 263–265; David Kahn, *Hitler's Spies: German Military Intelligence in World War II* (New York: Macmillan, 1978; reprint, Cambridge, MA: Da Capo Press, 2000), 257–258; Florian Altenhöner, '*Der Mann, der den Zweiten Weltkrieg begann. Alfred Naujocks: Fälscher, Mörder, Terrorist* (Münster: Prospero-Verlag, 2010), 123–136; Walter Schellenberg, *The Labyrinth: Memoirs of Walter Schellenberg, Hitler's Chief of Counterintelligence*, intr. Allan Bullock, trans. Louis Hagen (New York: Harper & Brothers, 1956; reprint, Cambridge, MA: Da Capo Press, 2000), 63–80; Payne Best, *The Venlo Incident* (London and New York: Hutchinson, 1950).

[2] Meldung, Berlin, November 1939, NA, RG 242, BDC, A 3343, SSO, Reel 074B, Frame 218; Beförderung des SS-Obersturmbannführer Walter Schellenberg, SS Nr. 124 817, zum SS-Brigadeführer, May 12, 1944, NA, RG 242, BDC, A 3343, SSO, Reel 074B, Frame 229–230; Schellenberg, *Labyrinth*, 83–92.

into a more ideologized entity with a broader mandate. He also became involved with some of the core developments related to the implementation and operations of Germany's nascent genocidal campaigns. Indeed, the years at the helm of IV E gave Schellenberg personal stature and presaged his later position as the head of the foreign intelligence. Poorly documented, these were formative years for an intelligence man and a differently conceptualized foreign intelligence service in the making.

Although the creation of the RSHA was imminent and no big administrative tasks were on the horizon, Schellenberg was not lacking prospects. Like for many men of his generation, the war brought excitement and opportunities. Schellenberg spent the first three weeks of World War II as a liaison between Heinrich Himmler and the *Oberkommando der Wehrmacht* (OKW), the High Command of the Armed Forces, traveling on Himmler's special train.[3] It remains impossible to ascertain the full extent of the interactions between the two men or Himmler's motives in appointing Schellenberg; other than maybe trust in Heydrich's man Schellenberg. Schellenberg, for his part, tied his presence on Himmler's train to his new position with the Gestapo's counterintelligence department; "[s]omeone had to be on hand who could deal on the spot with urgent intelligence matters."[4] The realities are less clear. Schellenberg was appointed deputy to the head of the IV E – under its nominal head Werner Best – in late November, well after Venlo and after a short-term stint with the State Police Office in Dortmund.[5] However, Schellenberg relished the time on Himmler's train in war-torn Poland; it presented him with new opportunities to prove his worth. He was enthralled by his proximity to power and claimed to have met regularly with Himmler and spent time on Hitler's train.[6] Schellenberg came to see himself as an insider, and he liked what he saw. Yet it was "Venlo" that added the needed spice to his already impressive resume and made Schellenberg into a foreign intelligence activist not to be ignored.

[3] Terminbuch, March 17, 1939–December 31, 1939, NA, RG 242, T-581, Reel 38 A.
[4] Schellenberg, *Labyrinth*, 51; Interrogation of Walter Schellenberg by Dr. R.W.M. Kempner, November 13, 1947, IfZ, ZS291/V, 00031; SS Sturmbannfuehrer Dr. Wilhelm Hoettl, A Character Sketch of Schellenberg: Chief of Germany's Espionage Service, July 12, 1945, NA, RG 226, Entry 199A, Box 55, Folder 1602 [hereafter: Hoettl/Character Schellenberg].
[5] CdS to Office Heads and Department Heads of RSHA, November 27, 1939, USHMM, 14.016 M, 16. Schellenberg apparently spent October 1939 in Dortmund to survey industrial security and to reorganize countermeasures. Schellenberg, *Labyrinth*, 59; Final Report on the Case of Walter Schellenberg, NA, RG 319, IRR, XE 001725, Walter Schellenberg, Folders 7 and 8 [hereafter: Final Report].
[6] Schellenberg, *Labyrinth*, 51–55; Final Report. Regular meetings with Himmler cannot be corroborated. Terminbuch, March 17, 1939–December 31, 1939, NA, RG 242, T-581, Reel 38 A.

The exact details of the events at Venlo as well as the thought processes of the main players remain shrouded in mystery. No contemporaneous account of Schellenberg exists and all postwar accounts are determined by their audiences. His memoirs read like a colorful spy novel with Schellenberg as a well-prepared hero willing to take serious risks and about to go to London for "negotiations." The ploy went on until Georg Elser's failed attempt on Hitler's life on November 8, 1939 that left over seventy casualties and destroyed the venue where Hitler had spoken earlier that evening. Elser was arrested the same night while trying to cross the border into Switzerland.[7] German officials blamed Elser's attempt to kill Hitler not on a single man, a carpenter without any political connections, but believed Elser to be in the employ of the British Intelligence Service. Consequently, Himmler ordered Schellenberg to arrest the British agents without further ado or any consideration of Dutch neutrality. This Schellenberg did.[8] And he reaped the benefits.

In Allied captivity and given the evidence against him, Schellenberg tried to minimize his role at Venlo.[9] He emphasized the part Helmut Knochen and Office VI, the political foreign intelligence service, had played. An expert on Freemasonry, Knochen had initially been with the domestic section of the SD; by November 1939, he was with Office VI. Later on, Knochen later held various senior positions with the Security Police and the SD in German-occupied France and Belgium and was involved in the deportation of the French Jews.[10] In short, Knochen was a known entity to Schellenberg's interrogators and as he had been prominently involved in the events at Venlo, Knochen was an ideal person on whom to fix the Allies' gaze. Schellenberg was equally adamant that Venlo had been the brainchild of Office VI and that plans were far advanced when he, representing the Gestapo's counterintelligence department, became involved. Schellenberg also claimed to have raised objections against the planned kidnapping with Himmler and Heydrich, but, due to his low rank, remained unheard. Bigger issues were at stake:

[7] Anton Hoch, "Das Attentat auf Hitler im Münchener Bürgerbräukeller 1939," *Vierteljahrshefte für Zeitgeschichte* 17 (1969), 583–413.
[8] Schellenberg, *Labyrinth*, 63–80. Imprisoned in Germany, Payne Best gave his rendition of the events "Translation from The German. Translation of the deposition of Captain Best." NA, RG 65, Entry A 1–136 P, Box 50, Folder 65–47826, EBF 293, 2 of 3. The English original of Best's written statement (*Niederschrift*) is not included among the declassified FBI documents. The materials were "[b]elieved to have been contained in the personal files of Walter Schellenberg" and were secured in a highly confidential manner;" Frederick Ayer to Director, FBI, Re.: R.S.H.A. Espionage – G, June 8, 1945, NA, RG 65, Box 50, Folder 65–47826, Section 12, 4 of 4.
[9] Final Report.
[10] Wildt, *Generation*, 370–371; "Helmut Knochen," in *Enzyklopädie des Holocaust*.

Office VI, newly minted with the creation of the RSHA a few weeks earlier, largely untested, and predominantly staffed by intelligence laymen,
needed a success to "stifle any criticism of the S.D. and even enhance its
prestige."[11] Schellenberg intimated that he came along for the ride.

The abduction at Venlo originated, indeed, with Office VI and involved
a host of SD men beyond Knochen, most importantly Alfred Naujocks.
Office VI had worked on the penetration of British MI 6 operations in
the Netherlands for a while and had managed to do so – in addition to
the establishment of contact with Best and Stevens. It remains unclear
what Office VI wanted to achieve, beyond enhancing its prestige. Florian
Altenhöner suggests that the operation was meant to create a pretext
for a German invasion of Holland and his circumstantial evidence is
strong. Naujocks had been among the men who created the incident at
the Gleiwitz station that gave the pretext for the German invasion of
Poland on September 1, 1939; he was, so to speak, the resident expert;
the decision to abduct the two men was taken a day before the failed
assassination attempt against Hitler; and the abductions largely coincided
with the date for which the invasion of Holland was initially planned. The
argument hinges on when the order for the abduction was given – before
or after the attempt on Hitler. After the war, Schellenberg consistently
noted that it happened after; however, consistency, even under oath, does
not truth make. Ultimately, it remains impossible to get to the bottom
of this, as different recollections, driven by postwar agendas, collide. Be
that as it may, German authorities saw a propaganda value in the events
at Venlo: when German troops invaded the Low Countries six months
later, the "continuing breach of Dutch neutrality for the benefit of Great
Britain" was given as a justification.[12]

Schellenberg was one of the ploy's main beneficiary. He took home the
biggest trophy: the two British Secret Service officers who interrogated by
a special commission, "Secret Intelligence Service" (S.I.S.), established
in the Gestapo department he headed. By December 19, 1939, Best and
Stevens had been subjected to numerous interrogations. Schellenberg
himself interrogated Best and Stevens some four or five times. Interest

[11] Final Report.
[12] Altenhöhner, *Naujocks*, chapter 4.3. Altenhöner also raises the possibilities that the ini-
    tial idea to make contact "with Dutch and British circles" originated with the Abwehr. I
    thank Florian Altenhöner, Berlin, for his generosity in sharing materials and ideas. For a
    different reading, see: Reinhard R. Doerries, *Hitler's Intelligence Chief Walter Schellenberg:
    The Man Who Kept Germany's Secrets* (New York: Enigma Books, 2009), 255. Farago
    argues that Schellenberg dealt the British Intelligence Service a serious blow, as afraid
    to be double-crossed again, it never again trusted members of self-proclaimed German
    resistance groups. Ladislas Farago, *Burn After Reading: The Espionage History of World
    War II* (Annapolis, MD: Naval Institute Press, 2003), 37–49.

was intense: Hitler received daily reports on the interrogations. A full report about Best and Stevens was projected for early January 1940, but the main responsibility as well as the "leadership" – as Schellenberg penciled in – for the "case Best and Stevens" would remain, "as before," with the same people.[13] Schellenberg was not to relinquish his catch.

A preliminary report on the interrogations, summarizing the most relevant findings about the British Intelligence Service and its activities in the Low Countries, was sent from Heydrich's office to Hermann Göring in December.[14] Section one dealt with Stevens, describing his biographical and linguistic background and his training in intelligence matters. It then discussed his actual activities while heading the Passport Control Office (PCO) in The Hague as well as his collaboration with other Western intelligence services. The report stressed that friendly personal relations among leading officers of the services – some of them Jews, as the report pointed out – led to good relations between the British, Dutch, Belgian, and French services. It also emphasized that Stevens gave detailed insight into the British Intelligence Service, its working methods, officers in leadership roles, orders received from London, and agents and informers. At the end of this section the question why Stevens was so forthcoming was raised. The report suggested that Stevens was not aware of the importance of the information he provided, but it also brought up the possibility that Stevens, aware that he had bungled a major operation, knew that his career was over and had therefore decided to part with his knowledge. It is, however, also possible that Stevens assumed that his captors knew more than they did. Overestimating the German intelligence services, he unwittingly handed them a success.

The report's section on Best was constructed along the same lines. Some biographical and educational background was followed by a discussion of his work as an intelligence officer during the Great War and his subsequent life as a businessman in Holland. Best also provided

---

[13] Vermerk, December 19, 1939, NA, RG 65, Entry A 1–136 P, Box 50, Folders 65–47826, EBF 293, 1 of 3. Only some of the interrogations have survived. Thus, the picture available is far from complete, see: NA, RG 65, Entry A 1–136 P, Box 50, Folders 65–47826, EBF 293. The document listing the materials received by the FBI mentions an "over-all report, written in large print, of the information obtained from Best and Stevens." The reference to "large print" indicated that this document was prepared for Hitler. This document is likely to be contained in box 51 of the same collection; when I worked on this section, the box was missing. Doerries notes that at another time, Schellenberg claimed that he did not interrogate the men himself, however, the statement sounds decidedly like Schellenberg. Reinhard Doerries, *Hitler's Last Chief of Foreign Intelligence: Allied Interrogations of Walter Schellenberg* (London: Frank Cass, 2003), 14 note 67.

[14] CdS to Göring, Berlin, December 1939, NA, RG 65, Entry A 1–136 P, Box 50, Folders 65–47826, EBF 293, 1 of 3.

detailed information on "Organization Z," a separate and secret entity of
the British Intelligence Service, and changes brought about by the war.
In addition, he gave his captors historical information on his employer,
deemed of utter importance by them. However, Best did not measure
up to German expectations about a British intelligence officer; his captors saw him as a businessman and coward who lacked loyalty to his
country.[15] The mythical, imaginary British intelligence officer was the
yardstick against which Best was measured. He fell short.

German disappointments about Best's character notwithstanding, the
interrogations were an information bonanza. The German intelligence
and policing systems gained first-hand information about the British
Intelligence Service in general and about British activities in the Low
Countries and in Germany in particular.[16] Agents and informants in
these countries were identified, as were collaborators in Germany; arrests
now became possible. The two men also confirmed long-held suspicions
about collaboration among the Western European intelligence services.
And, last but not least, the two men, who would spend the coming years
in German concentration camps, were to remain a source for future use.[17]
Schellenberg's tenure with the Gestapo's counterintelligence department
was off to a promising start.

Schellenberg soon began to remake his department, IV E, to his liking.
Strictly speaking, Schellenberg served as the deputy to Werner Best, who
also headed the administrative and legal office of the RSHA (Office I),
but as this was a time-consuming position, Schellenberg was left with
a reasonably free rein over IV E. Best's stock was, indeed, falling: the
firm integration of the counterintelligence department into the Gestapo
can be read as a sign of Best's waning influence and personnel politics
augmented Best's problems.[18] His former deputy in the counterintelligence department, Heinz Jost, was promoted to the helm of Office VI,
the political foreign intelligence service. The replacement of Jost, a Best
intimus, with Schellenberg, a Heydrich confidant and protégé, suggests
Best's diminishing importance in the RSHA and indicates Heydrich's

---

[15] CdS to Göring, Berlin, December 1939, NA, RG 65, Entry A 1–136 P, Box 50, Folder
65–47826, EBF 293, 1 of 3.

[16] Reichsminister des Innern, Bericht, gez. Frick and Himmler, Berlin, March 20, 1940,
NARA, RG 238, M 946, Reel 1, WA # 4. A translation can be found in NA, RG
65, Entry A 1–136 P, Box 50, Folder 65–47826, EBF 293, 1 of 3 as "Geheimes
Staatspolizeiamt, Service Report from the Gestapo to the Government," no date.

[17] Schellenberg, *Labyrinth*, 80. Schellenberg's postwar claim that he tried to include the
two men in prisoner of war exchanges with Great Britain but had this idea always
rejected by Himmler cannot be confirmed.

[18] Michael Wildt, *Generation des Unbedingten: Das Führungkorps des Reichssicherheitshauptamtes* (Hamburg: Hamburger Edition, 2002), 285–301, 349.

intention to keep him in check. Best was saddled with a deputy who had earned some of his reputation by questioning each and every one of Best's actions a few months earlier. And as early as summer 1939 rumors abounded that Best intended to leave the Security Police and the RSHA, as his standing had sustained damage during the discussions about the career paths.[19] Where Best was, there would soon be a vacancy. Schellenberg, who had helped to create it, and he also intended to fill it. In June 1940 Schellenberg officially replaced Best at the helm of IV E.[20] He now had a wide field in front of him.

More than any other organization, the Gestapo had "pride of place" within the RSHA and became the epitome of National Socialist terror and oppression. The Gestapo and its leading members were at the center of the National Socialist project; they constituted the "motor of the radicalization."[21] Among the offices integrated in the RSHA, the Gestapo could be considered the main beneficiary, for it transcended the Functional Order and expanded its purview beyond the executive. By early 1940, it engaged in "enemy surveillance and battle," *Gegnererforschung und –bekämpfung*, and effectively took over part of the SD's intelligence mandate. With parts of the mandate came some of the personnel: for example Adolf Eichmann and Albert Hartl.[22] Both men had their

[19] Herbert, *Best*, 233.
[20] Schellenberg, Heydrich to Verteiler C, im Hause, Übernahme der Leitung der Gruppe IV E durch den SS-Sturmbannführer Regierungsrat, Berlin, June 12, 1940, USHMM, 14.016 M, 240. Schellenberg was possibly slated for this position months earlier, see: Geschäftsverteilungsplan des Reichssicherheitshauptamtes (Stand vom 1.2.1940), CdS, Berlin, February 1, 1940, USHMM, 14.016 M, 840.
[21] Gerhard Paul and Klaus-Michael Mallmann, eds., *Die Gestapo im Zweiten Weltkrieg: 'Heimatfront' und besetztes Europa* (Darmstadt: Primus Verlag, 2000); Gerhard Paul and Klaus-Michael Mallmann, eds., *Die Gestapo – Mythos und Realität* (Darmstadt: Primus Verlag, 1996); Andreas Seeger, *"Gestapo-Müller:" Die Karriere eines Schreibtischtäters* (Berlin: Metropol, 1996). Gerhard Paul, "'Kämpfende Verwaltung.' Das Amt IV des Reichssicherheitshauptamtes als Führungsinstanz der Gestapo," in *Die Gestapo im Zweiten Weltkrieg: 'Heimatfront und besetztes Europa*, eds., Gerhard Paul and Klaus-Michael Mallmann (Darmstadt: Primus Verlag, 2000) 42. Wildt comments on the difference between old and new Gestapo members – the former created in Heinrich Müller's and the later in Werner Best's image. The newer members were men trained in law and began their career after 1933; they found themselves at the forefront of the *"Entgrenzung der Feindgruppen,"* the definition of increasing numbers of people as enemies of National Socialism; Wildt, *Generation*, 362–364.
[22] Gerhard Paul, "'Kämpfende Verwaltung," 47–49. Wildt states that Eichmann's transfer to the Gestapo made administrative sense and did not violate the functional, as beginning with his activities in Austria, Eichmann's function became executive. Wildt, *Generation*, 360. By 1941, Hartl headed IV B while Eichmann was in charge of IV B 4. However, Eichmann's direct access to Müller allowed him to bypass his superior. On the early history of Hartl, see Wolfgang Dierker, *Himmlers Glaubenskrieger: Der Sicherheitsdienst des SD und seine Religionspolitik 1933–1941* (Paderborn: Schöningh, 2002); on Eichmann's universe, Yaacov Lozowick, *Hitler's Bureaucrats: The Nazi Security Police and the Banality of Evil*, trans. by Haim Watzman (London: Continuum, 2002).

established areas of expertise – Jews and Political Churches, respectively – and this distinguished them from Schellenberg, who had to transform his interest in intelligence matters into accepted expertise. Schellenberg's area of responsibility, IV E, one of several Gestapo departments, consisted of the entire former counterintelligence office of the Main Office Security Police and the counterintelligence department of Office III of the former SD Main Office; it comprised six sections.[23] Its task was defense against foreign espionage and treason. Schellenberg's new area was small but had its advantages. Combining two well-established departments and building on their expertise, its structure was sensible and its task clear. The department's leadership shared a background in police work and different degrees of expertise in counterintelligence matters.

Schellenberg lacked these credentials, but he plunged into his new field full of zeal, convictions, and ideas. He regarded the department's structure and its approach to counterintelligence as obsolete and ineffective – and many of its ranking members as too old, possibly coded language for their not being sufficiently Nazified. Three section heads were soon replaced, but the department's overall structure remained unchanged. Schellenberg also took steps to rationalize and improve the department's performance: he created a more efficient filing system and had a counterintelligence handbook prepared.[24] He then took on the department's mandate, defined as *Spionageabwehr*, defense against espionage. In the German context of the time and within the framework of the police, *Spionageabwehr*, counterintelligence, was seen as a defensive exercise intent on thwarting active espionage efforts of other countries' intelligence services in the country. *Gegenspionage*, counterespionage, on the other hand, included penetration and manipulation of foreign services and attempts to control them – at home and abroad. The latter still fell under the purview of the *Abwehr*, the military intelligence service, and was envisioned as a potential field for Office VI.[25] Schellenberg attempted to

---

[23] IV E 1 dealt with counterintelligence and military matters (*Abwehr- und Wehrmachtsangelegenheiten*); IV E 2 focused on economic espionage, respectively, the defense against it. Sections IV E 3 through IV E 6 approached counterintelligence geographically, defining *Angriffsländer* (attacking [foreign] countries) and *Anfallgebiete* (affected [German] territories).

[24] Wildt, *Generation*, 349–352, notes 198 and 199; Geschäftsverteilungsplan des Reichssicherheitshauptamtes (Stand vom 1.2.1940), CdS, Berlin, February 1, 1940, USHMM, 14.016 M, 840. Geschäftsverteilungsplan des RSHA vom 13.3. 1941, USHMM, 14.016 M, 1076; Final Report.

[25] Historians find themselves with several problems when dealing with definitions in intelligence in a multilingual environment: different cultures of intelligence at the time; translation issues; changing understandings over time; and no commonly shared definitions. The precise differences between counterespionage and counterintelligence, Gegenspionage and Spionageabwehr, remain hazy. I use counterintelligence for Spionageabwehr

break out of this mold. He argued that "counterintelligence should begin on the other side of the frontier in order to control internal foreign activities," and mixed together elements of counterespionage, counter-intelligence, and espionage.[26] His conception of counterintelligence was offensive, proactive, and meant to engage enemy intelligence services active or soon to be active in Germany and do so outside of Germany. Schellenberg attempted to create a new, integrated approach to coun-terintelligence and intelligence. He held that "active counterespionage," which was still with the Abwehr, belonged together with "defensive coun-terintelligence," his department. Similarly, Schellenberg saw a growing necessity to combine his counterintelligence department and the for-eign intelligence service; in this combination, "active counterespionage" would serve as the bridge between the two elements. In short, Schellen-berg suggested the creation of super-agency with his own department in a key position. It was to take over "active counterespionage" and then combine it with the intelligence service.[27] Schellenberg's ambition far outstripped his current department, which he later described in a curt one-liner: "Was half an intelligence service."[28]

The precise activities of IV E are hard to ascertain or mainly known from postwar interrogations, which focus on the mundane and go to great lengths in creating distance to Gestapo matters. According to the interro-gations, the Gestapo's counterintelligence department mostly engaged in the surveillance of embassies, consular offices, and suspicious individuals and did not share the Gestapo's focus on ideologically or racially defined enemy groups and its executive powers.[29] After the war, Schellenberg also stressed his conviction that counterintelligence should not be part of the executive. While at the helm of the department, though, Schel-lenberg bemoaned the lack of a centralized Reich executive and created

and counterespionage for matters of Gegenspionage. For different conceptualizations, see: John Laffin, *Brassey's Book of Espionage* (London/Washington: Brassey's, 1996), 5, 7; Norman Polmar and Thomas B. Allen, *Spy Book. The Encyclopedia of Espionage* (New York, NY: Random House, 199), 138–139; *United States Intelligence: An Encyclopedia*, eds., Bruce W. Watson, Susan M. Watson, and Gerald W. Hopple (New York: Garland Publishing, 1990), 124–126.

[26] Final Report.
[27] Affidavit, Hans O'gilvie, February 16, 1948, NA, RG 238, M 897, Reel 114, Frame 901; Final Report. Both statements were made after the war and might misrepresent the counterintelligence department.
[28] Interrogation of Walter Schellenberg by Dr. R.W.M. Kempner, November 13, 1947, IfZ, ZS291/V, 00030.
[29] Final Report; Counter-Espionage Cases dealt with by Amt IV (Group IVE) in the period of August 1939–June 1941 and known to Schellenberg, NA, RG 26, Entry 119A, Box 26, File 646. Schellenberg's rendition is more spirited and self-important in his memoirs; Schellenberg, *Labyrinth*, 125–135, 145–157.

"flying commandos" to deal with expected enemy activities.[30] Interest in executive matters clearly existed.

The cases described by Schellenberg after the war also all took place on his side of the border, thus contradicting his theorem that "counter-intelligence should begin on the other side of the frontier." This notion was also supported by affidavits that likened the Gestapo's counterintelligence department to the Federal Bureau of Investigation (FBI). In the same vein, Schellenberg stressed his department's cooperation with the Abwehr. These statements conjured a department tied only nominally to the Gestapo; mainly engaged in defensive matters; and barely interested in executive issues.[31] This approach was successful: Department VI E became a footnote in accounts of the Gestapo, in investigations into intelligence matters, or in discussions of Schellenberg's career, but never a topic in its own right.

VI E was, however, part of the Gestapo. In December 1939, Schellenberg suggested using the war as the justification to create a centralized identification system for all foreigners. Schellenberg's overall proposal looked beyond a step not unusual in wartime, for he planned to maintain the database after the war's successful end.[32] Schellenberg was clearly in tune with the workings and the needs – current and future – of the Gestapo and so was his department. Among its tasks was the vetting process of workers in the war industry, the registration and surveillance of former soldiers of the French Foreign Legion and of carrier pigeon keepers, as well as the issuance of "residency permits for Polish civilian workers."[33] Schellenberg's protestations notwithstanding, this was Gestapo work.

With the broadening of the war after attack on the Low Countries and France in May 1940, Schellenberg's vision of a new form of counter-intelligence gained currency. At the outset of the campaign, Schellenberg was again part of the entourage assembled on Himmler's special

---

[30] Affidavit, Hans O'gilvie, February 16, 1948, NA, RG 238, M 897, Reel 114, Frame 900–901; Hoettl/Character Schellenberg; Vermerk, IV E [likely Schellenberg], February 16, 1940, USHMM, 14.016 M, 572. Schnellbrief, Betr.: Einsatz fliegender Kommados, RSHA IV E 3, im Auftrag Schellenberg, April 20, 1940, USHMM, 14.016 M, 240. Schellenberg also complained about the lack of personnel and remarked on the difficulties of surveillance during dark-out. See also Paul, "Kämpfende Verwaltung," 59.

[31] Final Report; Affidavit, Hans O'gilvie, 16 February 1948, NA, RG 238, M 897, Reel 114, Frame 900–905.

[32] Vermerk, RSHA Amt IV, Schellenberg, 8 December 1939, USHMM, 14.016 M, 572.

[33] Einschränkungen des Dienstbetriebes in den Stapostellen, IV E 1 to Referat IV E 6, 25 June 1940, USHMM, 14.016 M, 241.

train.[34] The ongoing operations and the subsequent establishment of a German occupational regime, defined by National Socialist ideology, dominated their meetings. In the morning of May 23, Schellenberg presented Himmler with material on the "population composition in Holland and Belgium;" in the afternoon, their conversation focused on the "arrest of known hostile Dutch people." They also conferred about "Methodists," apparently an issue of concern as it had been a topic the day before and was revisited again five days later. In addition, they discussed the readiness of a certain SS-Sturmbannführer for deployment in Holland. Later that evening, Himmler and Schellenberg discussed the "law about legal support for ethnic Germans in Baltic prisons."[35] The new notion of counterintelligence opened a wide field. In occupied Poland it was already at work and Schellenberg was involved in it.

In the spring of 1940 Germany embarked on the so-called *AB-Aktion*, Extraordinary Pacifying Action, a "massive program to exterminate the Polish intelligentsia in the General Government."[36] It was a follow-up to Operation Tannenberg, which began immediately after the German invasion and encompassed the murder of a broadly defined Polish *intelligenstia* as well as of members of the Polish clergy and aristocracy. Also murdered were thousands of Polish Jews while tens of thousands of ordinary Poles were driven from their homes to make space for ethnic Germans. In November 1939, German authorities arrested two hundred professors of the Jagiellioan University in Cracow and other institutions of higher education. The Western world reacted with shock, especially to the latter developments. Consequently, the A-B Aktion was scheduled to coincide with the German campaign against the Low Countries and France. With the eyes of the world resting on Western Europe, mass executions in Poland would be less newsworthy. On June 6, Schellenberg reported to Himmler about "executions in the Polish General Government." Four days later, Himmler discussed "leading Poles in Posen [Poznań]" with Hitler, presenting him with lists of people slated for execution.[37] These were likely the same executions about which Schellenberg had briefed

---

[34] Terminbuch, January 1940–December 1940, NA, RG 242, T-581, Reel 38A, Entry 15 May to 5 July 1940. After the war, Schellenberg stated that he attended a "military exercise" as Himmler's messenger and travel companion; Final Report.

[35] Terminbuch, May 1940–December 1940, NA, RG 242, T 581, Reel 39 A, Entry May 23, 1940. The SS-Sturmbannführer's name is not quite legible.

[36] Richard C. Lukas, *The Forgotten Holocaust: The Poles under German Occupation, 1939–1944*, 2nd rev. ed. (New York: Hippocrene Books, 1997), 9; Alexander B. Rossino, *Hitler Strikes Poland: Blitzkrieg, Ideology, and Atrocity* (Lawrence: University Press of Kansas, 2003), 58–87.

[37] Terminbuch, May 1940–December 1940, NA, RG 242, T 581, Reel 39 A, Entry June 6, 1940 and June 10, 1940. I thank Richard Breitman for bringing the relationship between these two meetings to my attention.

Himmler four days earlier. At least 6,000 people were murdered during the A-B Aktion; in addition, several thousand men were rounded up and sent to Auschwitz, then known as a particularly brutal concentration camp largely for Poles. There were few survivors.[38] This was a new approach to counterintelligence that considered the murder of perceived racial and ideological enemies as a viable method of preventing espionage. Racial–ideological cleansing had entered German counterintelligence efforts and, even if the exact details remain unclear, Schellenberg was involved in this metamorphosis.

The German victory in the West, on the other hand, created a fundamentally new situation for the Gestapo and for Schellenberg's department in particular. Schellenberg found himself in a counterintelligence and foreign intelligence quagmire endemic to the thinking about intelligence matters in the RSHA: once a country was occupied – "pacified" – by German troops, it was not considered an *Angriffsland*, attack country, anymore and came under the purview of IV D, Occupied Territories. Ironically, the better the war was going for Germany, the more limited the role of the RSHA's (counter)intelligence entities became. Schellenberg strove to get ahead of potential issues. In a memorandum written in late May 1940, he explored the impact of the *völkisch*, political, and economic reorganization of Western Europe on the institution.[39] It was an attempt to maintain the initiative and to benefit from a puzzling situation. If implemented, Schellenberg's ideas would have joined together the responsibility for geographically and ideologically defined enemies in his department and, along the way, might have even imploded the new Office VI under Jost. As a first step, Schellenberg suggested moving the sections for France and the Low Countries from his counterintelligence department to IV D, Occupied Territories; its personnel would assume leadership in any Gestapo matters in these countries. Schellenberg envisioned a similar move for the section on Great Britain and Switzerland, two "centers of foreign espionage," that he expected to be occupied by German forces soon. Conversely, Schellenberg suggested focusing his department's efforts on four other countries, three of which were allied with Germany: Russia, Japan, Italy, and the United States. Outwardly a plan advantageous for Office IV D, the Schellenberg's department would reap the benefits. IV D had no department head and the little institutional knowledge the Gestapo had about these countries would still reside in Schellenberg's department. Schellenberg also attempted to

[38] Lukas, *Forgotten Holocaust*, 8–9.
[39] Vermerk, IV E, Schellenberg, May 30[?], 1940, USHMM, 14.016M, 572. On IV D, see Wildt, *Generation*, 352–358.

use the changing situation to press for another reorganization benefiting his department. He suggested that a previously discussed integration of VI H, Ideological Enemies Abroad, into his department go forward. IV E would have thus had under its purview the four main powers that Schellenberg expected to be there in the longer run and all ideologically defined enemy groups operating abroad while still holding most of the knowledge needed in IV D – thus surreptitiously folding it into IV E as well. Nothing came out of these suggestions, but Schellenberg had his eyes set on what he deemed the relevant parts of the RSHA's foreign intelligence complex. Running "half an intelligence service" was not to be enough.

Germany's expansionist policies kept the office busy. In preparation for the planned invasion of the British Isles, Schellenberg was asked to oversee the compilation of an *Informationsheft*, a handbook, and *Sonderfahndungsbuch*, a Special Wanted List, for Great Britain.[40] This was a prototypical RSHA project, because it prepared for the racial–ideological cleansing of the soon-to-be vanquished Great Britain. Since the German occupation of Great Britain never came to happen, this document has become the subject of ridicule; some consider it "among the more amusing" Nazi documents.[41] In his memoirs, Schellenberg intimates the same by juxtaposing the efforts that went into its creation with the fact that some 20,000 copies went up in flames during a later – presumably British – air raid on Berlin.[42] Yet, the fact that occupational forces or *Einsatzgruppen* – mobile policing, intelligence, and later murder squads – never used the handbook to detain and murder racial and ideological enemies should neither detract from its existence nor from the efforts of its creation. Department IV E and its peculiar mixture of intelligence gathering, analysis, and ideology is evident in this ideological manifesto on the nature of Great Britain.

The responsibility for the handbook rested with men whose background was with the SD and not with traditional policing and the main responsibility was Schellenberg's. Also prominently involved were Walther Zur Christian and Alfred Six. Zur Christian was part of Office VI, the political foreign intelligence service, and Six headed Office II (later Office VII), *Weltanschauliche Gegnerforschung*, Research

---

[40] Walter Schellenberg, *Invasion 1940: The Nazi Invasion Plan for Britain*, intr. John Erickson (London: St. Ermin's Press, 2000). The *Informationsheft* and the *Sonderfahndungsheft* can also be found in BAL, R 58, 3507a and 3507b. Schellenberg always admitted freely to his leadership in these tasks; Schellenberg, *Labyrinth*, 106.

[41] William L. Shirer, *The Rise and Fall of the Third Reich: A History of Nazi Germany* (New York: Simon and Schuster, 1960), 784.

[42] Schellenberg, *Labyrinth*, 106.

into Ideological Enemies, of the RSHA.[43] Hitler initially vacillated about the decision to invade Great Britain, as hopes for a political solution and the logistics of such an invasion made it difficult. At the end of June, after the success in the West, Hitler settled on a plan by Alfred Jodl, chief of the operations staff, to weaken Great Britain by air and sea attacks, thus readying it for a German landing.[44] The handbook was part of the preparation process for the invasion and many things at once: an overview of Great Britain, an occupational manual, and a manifesto on the nature of the country. At the basic level, it provided information on the country's size, topography, climate, economy, finances, constitutional structure, government, law and administration, military, educational and cultural institutions, media, religious life, and political parties. The Special Wanted List resembled lists compiled for earlier invasions, focusing on people to arrest and objects of interest, with another section presenting the same information broken down geographically, thereby making it more user friendly.[45] This was not the equivalent of "an educational video intruded by ideological basis."[46] Rather, and regardless of its prima facie organization, Nazi ideology, especially its vision of World Jewry and Freemasonry, formed the basis for the understanding of Great Britain, its structure, and its customs. It is, indeed, a snapshot of how parts of Nazi Germany's ideological elite viewed Great Britain and planned to treat it after a successful German invasion.

"England is the country of the Freemasonry," posited the handbook, putting this elusive enemy ideology at the core of the British fabric of life. Yet the influence of British Freemasons was not restricted to Great Britain. Ideologically indebted to English Enlightenment clerics, Freemasons had expanded their influence overseas in the wake of and aided by Great Britain's growing economic, cultural, and political influence. Freemasonry provided the main link between Great Britain and its colonies, making it "an invisibly effective, important political instrument for the internal structure of Great Britain and its Empire, and for

---

[43] Nigel West, "Preface," in *Invasion 1940*, xxx; Lutz Hachmeister, *Der Gegnerforscher: Die Karriere des SS-Führers Franz Alfred Six*. (Munich: Verlag C.H.Beck, 1998), 228–230.
[44] Hitler abandoned plans for an invasion in 1940 on September 17. Peter Fleming, *Invasion 1940: An Account of the German Preparations and British Counter-Measures* (London: Rupert Hart-Davis, 1957); Ronald Wheatly, *Operation Sea Lion: German Plans for the Invasion of England, 1939–1942* (Oxford: Clarendon Press, 1958); Gerhard Weinberg, *A World at Arms: The Global History of World War II* (Cambridge: Cambridge University Press, 1994), 152, 171; John Erickson, "Introduction," in *Invasion 1940: The Nazi Invasion Plan for Britain* (London: St. Ermin's Press, 2000), ix–xii.
[45] Compare to the preparations for the Anschluß and for the occupation of the Sudeten German territories discussed below. See also Rossino, *Hitler Strikes Poland*, 15–16.
[46] Erickson, "Introduction," in *Invasion 1940*, xxx.

British imperialism" with the royal family serving as the Empire's political and Masonic leadership.[47] Freemasonry was to blame for the spread of liberal and democratic ideas in England and elsewhere as well as for the emancipation of the Jews and their eventual acceptance among the British ruling class and among members of church. "[T]he essence of Puritanism [. . .], the handbook argued, is close to ideas from Judaism and the Old Testament," as both Jews and Britons believe to be the chosen people, either of the "earth," in the case of the Jews or "the world," in case of the British.[48] The latter idea formed the foundation of the British Empire and its world rule with "English Freemasonry regard[ing] itself as the organization for the realisation of this idea." Freemasons were present at every level of British imperial society and located at the center of the British imperial project; " . . . it does not require specific political goals, since it significantly controls the domain of English politics. Under the guise of a humanitarian welfare organization, English Freemasonry is a pivotal element of English Imperialism, and therefore to the British Empire." Even more so, Freemasonry was a "dangerous weapon in the hands of Britain's plutocrats against national socialist Germany."[49] Great Britain, the handbook declared, was the Freemasons' country and Nazi Germany was under attack.

The handbook identified the Jews as the second pillar of Great Britain. It attributed the revival of Jewish life in England after the expulsion of 1290 to the rise of Puritanism and Oliver Cromwell's influence. Cromwell "recognized the similarities between the English scheme for world domination and the Jewish version. [. . .] This set the foundation for an Anglo-Jewish alliance."[50] It then described the current state of this alliance and illuminated the perceived exceptional importance of Jews in politics, finance, economy, and the media. Unsurprisingly, Benjamin Disraeli, the former British prime minister, and the role he played in the creation of the British Empire served as Exhibit A but the handbook also emphasized that no British cabinet in recent memory was formed without Jews. The handbook then traced Jewish influence in finance, the economy, and the media and argued, "the anti-German attitude of these instruments of propaganda is mainly due to the large number of Jews working for them." It opined that two Jewish film producers, Ivor Montagu and S. Bernstein, "hold positions akin to film censors" and noted that Great

---

[47] *Invasion 1940*, 87–88.
[48] *Invasion 1940*, 89. The distinction between "earth" and "world" is rather capricious; the general idea seems to be that the Jews considered themselves to be the chosen people in a spiritual sense, while the British believed themselves to be chosen in a political sense.
[49] *Invasion 1940*, 88, 89, 93.   [50] *Invasion 1940*, 94.

Britain served as the headquarters for all types of international Jewish organizations.[51] Orthodox National Socialism's understanding of Great Britain and the colonies becomes apparent here: a worldwide Empire run by a Jewish-Freemason conspiracy and, accordingly, Nazi Germany's natural enemy. However, much of the handbook recounted Wolf Meyer-Christian's *The English–Jewish Alliance*, which gave an "anti-Semitic interpretation of four centuries of English history," and had been highlighted in directives from the Reich Press Office in October and November 1940.[52] Without reference to Meyer-Christian, the handbook transformed ideology and propaganda into intelligence.

Other parts of the handbook provide the basic material one expects but enlivened by snide comments. Britain's constitutional structure, for example, was evaluated as undemocratic; the opposition parties were faulted for having abandoned their task of criticizing the government.[53] This was, however, not a misplaced lesson in civics for the handbook's expected audience. Rather, these statements as well as comments about the British class system, conceptualized as the opposite of Germany's Volksgemeinschaft, reinforced the notion of British hypocrisy and of the Reich's superiority.

The Special Wanted Lists consisted of two registries of individuals: a subject index and a register of locality, thus making it user-friendly for the Einsatzgruppen. A second, "special" Special Wanted List contained information and photos of thirty people of different nationalities who were to be arrested on sight. Everyone on this list was of particular interest to IV E and had presumed or real connections to matters of foreign intelligence. It was a counterintelligence wish or shopping list. Approximately 2,800 individuals were marked for arrest on the regular Special Wanted List; the pertinent office in the RSHA must have worked overtime to cull the information.[54] The targets fell into three groups: emigrants from the continent; British and continental intelligence operatives; and British politicians, officials, and personalities. Section one ranged from ordinary

[51] *Invasion 1940*, 99; 100–103.
[52] Jeffrey Herf, *The Jewish Enemy: Nazi Propaganda During World War II and the Holocaust* (Cambridge: The Belknap Press of Harvard University Press, 2008), 71–75; Gerwin Strobl, *The Germanic Isle: Nazi Perceptions of Britain* (Cambridge: Cambridge University Press, 2000). The same materials makes it into educational materials for SS and Police: Stoffsammlung (A 76) für die weltanschauliche Schulung der Ordnungspolizei, "Juda in England," USHMM, 15.007 M, Reel 11.
[53] *Invasion 1940*, 9, 15–16.
[54] The office designations behind a person's name indicated which department would handle the arrestee; they were likely also the source of the information. Shirer, *Rise and Fall*, 784.

workers, such as a certain Josef Kroll, to clergy members, such as the Polish priest Piotr Bzdyl to well-known artists and writers such as the painter Oskar Kokoschka, the writer Stefan Zweig, and the novelist Heinrich Mann. Also prominent in this group were Central European politicians, such as the former Czechoslovak president Eduard Beneš, mentioned twice and spelled differently, to Jan Masaryk, the former Czechoslovak diplomat in London and son of the Republic's first president, or the Polish General Władysław Sikorski. The group also included former German and Austrian politicians of different backgrounds, such as Gottfried Reinhold Treviranus, a former German minister who had fled the country to avoid being murdered in the Röhm Purge of 1934; Hermann Rauschning, the former President of the Danzig Senate and Nazi turned anti-Nazi; the former German diplomat Wolfgang von Putlitz; or Hitler's old nemesis and founder of the Black Front, Otto Strasser. The second group comprised British and presumed continental intelligence operatives of different standing. They ranged from apparently ordinary agents, like a certain Bell, assumed to be a British agent, to W. Edward Hinchley-Cooke, the head of MI 5, the British military intelligence service. The group also included continental intelligence operatives, such as the head of the Czechoslovak Military Intelligence Service, František Moravec, to unknowns or people whose connection with intelligence work was based on the RSHA's conjecture. The list's last group ran the gauntlet from British politicians, such as the former and the current prime ministers, Neville Chamberlain and Winston Churchill, to the head of the Labour Party, Clement Attlee, to the founder of the Boy Scout Movement, Lord Baden-Powell, to the "minister, trade-unionist" Ernest Bevin, described as an "encirclement politician," to artists such as Vic Oliver – identified as a "Jewish actor" – to bankers like Anthony James Rothschild, to senior historians like R. Williams Watson-Seton, to rising academic stars like the Hungarian-born nuclear physicist Leo Szilard, spelled Szillard here, to writers and opinion makers such as Noel Coward, Aldous Huxley, Vera Brittain, and Virginia Woolf. The list also included quite a few curiosities. Not included was the royal family and many of the descriptions given were vague or inaccurate. Leo Szilard, for example, had left Great Britain for the United States in 1938.[55] Ultimately, this list included almost everyone who had run afoul of Nazi Germany and was deemed to be in Great Britain as well the main representatives – in the RSHA's understanding – of British politics, economics, and society. The list might not have been the best showcase of precise information,

---

[55] "Leo Szilard-A Biographical Chronology," www.dannen.com/chronbio.html, accessed March 11, 2008.

but comprehensive it was and, without any doubt, real.[56] Great Britain was to experience a thorough and crippling arrest wave.

The handbook also included a substantial section on the British Intelligence Service that oscillates between contempt and grudging admiration and allows for insights into the thinking of the German compilers. Much of the information is attributed to the recently kidnapped members of the British Intelligence Service – a matter of contention for many years – but in light of the now available interrogations, it is clear that the balance of the information originated with Best and Stevens. Only a few statements cannot be traced to them.[57] But this section is more than a detailed and admiration-tinged description and a showcase of available information. Using the two Britons as witnesses, the section implicitly suggests remedies to Germany's foreign intelligence malaise. The handbook linked the British service's amorphous structure to that of the Freemasons' Lodges. In both entities, the claim went, the individual is largely "an instrument on which, and with whom, mysterious people play." Some of the service's successes – and its mystique – derived from this unseen, omnipotent puppet-master. Taking a holistic approach, the British Intelligence Service did not distinguish between counterintelligence and espionage; as Steven and Best put it, "they overlap so much, there can be no division." The Service also benefited from its ample sources and connections; "[w]hatever is known to Shell is also known to the SIS." The service saw success due to "international capitalist networking, the vast scale of the British Empire, national character and a centuries-old tradition and practice" of intelligence work. Access to valuable information was easy and cheap; the service used journalists, study commissions, and the like for intelligence gathering purposes; and it was adept at exploiting talkative and admiring foreigners. Noteworthy was also the British use of "private, financially independent individuals" for intelligence-gathering efforts. Paid agents and traitors were used only on a limited basis. "[E]very British expatriate is an agent for his country, and each expatriate German a traitor by negligence," the adage went, and the authors of the handbook certainly agreed with it.[58] The reasons for this difference, the handbook counseled, were grounded in different national characters: the British regard the Intelligence Service highly,

---

[56] Fleming doubts that this was an actual arrest list; Fleming, *Invasion*, 195. Some of the biographical information provided here originates with Fleming.

[57] See Erickson "Introduction" and West, "Preface" in Schellenberg, *Invasion 1940*. West attributes most of the information to Colonel C.H. ("Dick") Ellis, who collaborated with the *Abwehr* from 1923 on and even raises the hypothetical specter of another German Abwehr agent in Great Britain. CdS to Göring, December 1939, NA, RG 65, Entry A 1–136 P, Box 50, Folders 65–47826, EBF 293, 1 of 3.

[58] *Invasion 1940*, 125, 131, 137–140.

while Germans detest it as an occupation for lowlifes. The strength of the British Intelligence Service thus rested on its holistic approach that combined counterintelligence and intelligence, its ample resources and connections, and the conviction that intelligence gathering was an honorable, patriotic undertaking.

The handbook stressed that even though it remained an example, there was no reason to admire the British Intelligence Service too much or to regard it as infallible. As the British national character put a high premium on tradition, its organizations tended to be inflexible, the handbook counseled. One also drew hope from Payne Best's description of the British Intelligence Service as bureaucratic, greedy, and heavy-handed. Similarly, the handbook cited a French newspaper article that emphasized the service's political and diplomatic failures and stressed that its omnipotence was evaporating. However, a quick transformation back to its old glory remained a possibility. Consequently, the British Service remained the one Germany should emulate, for "[n]evertheless, it is certain that the Service has helped significantly to construct and support the Empire. The motto: 'My country, right or wrong' does not have to be a British monopoly and, having been adapted to suit our ideology, it can and should be transferred to Germany."[59] Implicitly and explicitly, the handbook thus advocated changes to Germany's approach to foreign intelligence as well as to the structure of its foreign intelligence complex. Some of these Schellenberg, the handbook's main author, already had in mind; others he tried to implement in the years to come.[60] To assume that these statements were made by chance in a handbook of which 20,000 copies were printed and which every ranking member of the German invasion and occupational forces to be employed in Great Britain was expected to use, would be to underestimate Schellenberg and his ambitions for Germany's foreign intelligence complex. It was a call to create an ideologically bound intelligence service supporting Germany's imperial ambitions.

In the summer of 1940, and despite other tasks, such as the Ribbentrop-planned abduction of the Duke of Windsor from his Portuguese domicile, the compilation of the handbook was among Schellenberg's priorities.[61] Much of the information derived from open sources

---

[59] *Invasion 1940*, 142, 144.
[60] Vernehmung von Walter Schellenberg vom 24.11.1947 durch Mr. Bahr, IfZ, ZS 291/III, 00067–00070.
[61] On the attempt to abduct the Duke of Windsor, see Schellenberg, *Labyrinth*, 107–125; Final Report; Michael Bloch, *Operation Willi: The Plot to Kidnap the Duke of Windsor, July 1940* (London: Weidenfeld and Nicolson, 1984). Schellenberg's Portuguese itinerary can be found in USHMM, 14.016 M, 572.

but the act of compilation made the handbook valuable. There is no way to ascertain whether Schellenberg, or other men working on it, were fully convinced by, for example, Meyer-Christian's anti-Semitic line of reasoning. Yet, Schellenberg's distrust and dislike of the British system – grudging admiration notwithstanding – must have been grounded in his own ideological convictions, so that using literature pushed by the Propaganda Ministry seemed a logical step, which would also please his supervisors and ensure the work's positive reception. The manual as such held great import for different groups: it was to guide military and civilian personnel; the political police intent on understanding and locating their enemy; and the so-called experts raiding museums and archives – it was a "chop-licking" looter's to-do list.[62] It was also a showcase for information gathered by the different offices of the RSHA and their efficiency in fulfilling this task. Lastly, it was a platform for Schellenberg on which to display his personnel and time-management abilities. The task and its realization allowed for Schellenberg's department to shine and to take the lead on a matter where other offices, for example, Jost's political foreign intelligence service, should have done so. Schellenberg's department spearheaded the effort instead, breaking out of its role as "half an intelligence service," functioning in a subordinate position. Along the way, it articulated the precepts of the proper ideological interpretation of Great Britain as seen by the ideological avant-garde. It would have been difficult to devise a more radically ideological interpretation of British society and politics and even harder for a rival agency to win support for a more nuanced view.

During the two years in which Schellenberg worked on transforming his image from an administrator to an intelligence man as well as on a new vision of foreign intelligence, he was subordinate to Heinrich "Gestapo" Müller, the head of the Gestapo. Their relationship illuminates Schellenberg's position in the Gestapo between 1939 and 1941 – he had exceptional insights into the Gestapo's workings – as well as his later professional trajectory which brought him into conflict with Müller; it also throws into sharp relief some of Schellenberg's postwar defense strategies. The crux of the matter is Schellenberg's role in the Gestapo hierarchy: Schellenberg signed documents for Müller when the head of the Gestapo, who did not have a designated deputy, was absent but adamantly denied having been Müller's deputy. He also made it known that he had disliked Müller intensely.[63] Some of Schellenberg's erstwhile

---

[62] Fleming, *Invasion*, 193.
[63] Zum Thema der Anklage in ihrem Opening Statement, Schellenberg, January 14, 1948, IFZ, ED 90/5. Seeger, *Gestapo-Müller*, 77. Seeger notes that Walter Huppenkothen, who

subordinates supported this notion, expounding on personal and professional differences between the two men: the professional policeman, Müller, blindly obedient and expecting the same from his subordinates on the one hand, and the freethinking Schellenberg, disdainful of *Kadavergehorsam*, blind obedience, on the other. In short, Müller was a "typical Nazi," and Schellenberg was not and thus, the argument went, Schellenberg could not have been Müller's deputy. Furthermore, Müller would not have wanted Schellenberg to be privy to his plans, while, conversely, Schellenberg would have rejected any official deputyship due to the differences between the two men. Decrees that Schellenberg signed for Müller were explained away by spatial closeness: the two men's offices were near each other. Schellenberg might have signed for Müller "by chance occasionally" (*zufällig fallweise*), but only in the well-intentioned effort not to disrupt normal business when Müller was away.[64] Put differently, Schellenberg's signatures were favors and not representations of an official position as Müller's deputy; an indication of Schellenberg's involvement in Gestapo matters; or suggestive of a close and amenable relationship with "Gestapo-Müller." Yet, Schellenberg did sign documents for Müller. Not officially designated as Müller's deputy, he still functioned as such and on occasion, Schellenberg's temporary role as Müller's deputy was formalized, as when Müller went on vacation in March 1940.[65] Between 1939 and 1941 Schellenberg was the closest to a deputy Müller had.

The most infamous document Schellenberg signed on Müller's behalf is a May 1941 decree regulating the emigration of Jews.[66] In essence, the decree privileged the emigration of Jews from Germany and the so-called Protectorate, German-occupied Bohemia and Moravia, to areas outside the German sphere of influence over similar emigration attempts by Jews residing in German-occupied France or Belgium, even if the latter were refugees from Germany or the Protectorate. In addition, the decree discussed Jewish emigration from the Reich and the Protectorate

---

headed IV E after Schellenberg's departure, and Friedrich Panzinger, who was friendly with Müller, deputized for the head of the Gestapo.

[64] Affidavit, Hans O'gilvie, February 16, 1948, NA, RG 238, M 897, Reel 114, Frame 902.

[65] Beurlaubung, Berlin, March 1, 1940, USHMM, 14.016, 246.

[66] Auswanderung von Juden aus Belgien, dem besetzten und unbesetzten Frankreich – Auswanderung von Juden aus dem Reichsgebiet in das unbesetzte Frankreich, RSHA IV B 4 b, in Vertretung Schellenberg, May 20, 1941, NA, RG 238, M 946, Reel 1, WA #16 Frame 0133–0136. The document originated with IV B 4, and Lozowick identifies Richard Hartman as the author of the document. Lozowick states that there is no way of knowing why Schellenberg signed the document – "apparently [he was] filling in for Müller" – but he is confident that "it can not be attributed to him [Schellenberg]." Lozowick, *Bureaucrats*, 52, 74.

to unoccupied France, establishing German financial gain as the guiding principle: a destitute Jew able to live off his family in unoccupied France was allowed to leave, but if the Reich could gain financially, permission for emigration was not to be granted. To ensure that Germany would not lose any spoils of persecution, every emigration request was to be reviewed individually. The emigration ban was issued "in view of the certainly coming Final Solution of the Jewish question" ["*im Hinblick auf die zweifelsohne kommende Endlösung der Judenfrage*"].[67] After the war, Schellenberg tried to mitigate the impact of this document, its wording, and his signature underneath it. In a telling note prepared in his defense, Schellenberg mixed together several lines of defense ranging from not having signed the document to a discussion of illegal and Jewish border-crossings as a well-established security problem.[68]

The document brings to the fore questions about the precise extent of Schellenberg's involvement in the planning of the annihilation of European Jewry, for he played a role in the establishment and the deployment of the Einsatzgruppen in the Soviet Union. This puts him in the middle of one of the crucial steps in the "genesis of the final solution." Schellenberg indubitably knew more about this than he let on after the war.[69] His role in the negotiations likely stemmed from his administrative abilities and his association with earlier incarnations of the Einsatzgruppen as well as his relationship with Heydrich. In light of Schellenberg's role in the A-B Aktion in Poland a year prior, his position in the Gestapo's counterintelligence department clearly played a role as well. The Einsatzgruppen were, after all, commonly justified by security and counterintelligence needs, even if by 1941 their mandate changed and they turned into instruments of mass murder. In the summer of 1941, Einsatzgruppen entered the Soviet Union in the wake of the German Army Groups. Their task was to round up Jews and other racial–ideological enemies behind the advancing German front and murder them. They were deadly efficient. When the German advance came to a first halt in December 1941, they had already murdered hundreds of thousands of mostly Soviet Jews of both genders and all ages. The metamorphosis of the Einsatzgruppen from racial–ideological policing and intelligence entities to organizations of mass murder was thus complete.

---

[67] Auswanderung von Juden aus Belgien, dem besetzten und unbesetzten Frankreich – Auswanderung von Juden aus dem Reichsgebiet in das unbesetzte Frankreich, RSHA IV B 4 b, in Vertretung Schellenberg, May 20, 1941, NA, RG 238, M 946, Reel 1, WA #16 Frame 0133–0136.

[68] Vermerk zum Thema der Anklage in ihrem Opening Statement, January 14, 1948, IfZ, ED 90/5, 772–774.

[69] Richard Breitman, *Official Secrets: What the Nazis Planned, What the British and the Americans Knew* (New York: Hill and Wang, 1998), 35 note 33.

Precursors of the Einsatzgruppen, consisting of Security Police and SD members, were first deployed during the annexation of Austria in 1938. Mobile policing and intelligence-gathering squads, they collected information and made arrests based on information compiled in the Security Main Office. They operated outside any traditional judicial norms and were only legitimized by the will of the Führer.[70] Their personnel structure integrated party and state policing agencies and thus backhandedly granted the SD executive powers it did not have inside Germany. Foreign conquest benefited the SD. After a few days, the Einsatzgruppen active in Austria were transformed into a permanent police and SD structure mirroring that in the Reich. In September of the same year, Einsatzgruppen were deployed in the Sudeten German territories. They again arrested ideologically and sometimes racially defined enemies and collected intelligence until the new status of the Sudeten territories as part of the Reich was consolidated.[71] Poland was the next step in the radicalization of the Einsatzgruppen's mandate. On July 5, 1939, Heydrich assembled in his home a small group of men to discuss the deployment of Einsatzgruppen in the campaign against Poland. Schellenberg was among the invitees. Thus far, his involvement with the Einsatzgruppen had ranged from having been part of one in Austria to having dealt with administrative matters half a year later.[72] Also in attendance, in addition to Heydrich and his adjutant, were Werner Best, Heinz Jost, Helmut Knochen, and "Gestapo-Müller." The RSHA did not yet exist, but the meeting brought together those men who were about to be in charge of policing, intelligence, and counterintelligence. Discussion notwithstanding, the mechanics of any Einsatzgruppen operation were well established by this point, even though their relationship to the military remained contentious.[73]

[70] Helmut Krausnick, *Hitlers Einsatzgruppen: Die Truppe des Weltanschauungskrieges, 1938–1942* (Frankfurt: Fischer TB Verlag, 1985), 13. Krausnick suggests that Office II under Six played the main role in compiling arrest lists for Austria. Newly available documents indicate that Office III, the foreign intelligence section, had a substantial role in the preparation of the Anschluß; for details see below.

[71] Document 509-USSR, IMG, vol. XXXIX.

[72] II 12 Dr. Kno/Scho, Aktenvermerk, July 8, 1939, BAL, R 58/7154. Wildt writes that Schellenberg was present at this meeting due to his position in Jost's office but Schellenberg had no association with the foreign intelligence section of the Security Main Office then. He was more likely invited due to the work he had done at Heydrich's behest on the establishment of the RSHA and might have already been slated for IV E. Wildt, *Generation*, 422. Document 509-USSR, IMG, vol. XXXIX.

[73] Rossino, *Hitler Strikes Poland*, chapter 1. Krausnick argues that during the Sudeten German campaign the Einsatzkommandos remained outside of the military's authority, as had been the case in Austria. Krausnick, *Einsatzgruppen*, 21. Documents suggest that the relationship between Einsatzgruppen and military was never precisely defined, but left to solve itself. Richtlinien für den auswärtigen Einsatz der Sicherheitspolizei und des

The invasion of Poland was different from earlier German expansions and marked a turning point for the Einsatzgruppen. Capitalizing on the actual fighting and ideological perceptions of the Polish population, including its substantial number of Jews, it allowed for the role of the Einsatzgruppen to be pushed to a new level. The mere existence of Polish "insurgents," frequent reports about irregular fighters attacking the Germany military, and overblown reports about Polish riots and atrocities inflamed German soldiers imbued with anti-Polish ideology and added to the military's willingness to use extreme force to "avenge Polish atrocities," such as the Bromberger *Blutsonntag*, Bloody Sunday, on September 3, 1939 when ethnic Germans were killed in the Polish town of Bydgoszcz. Himmler and Heydrich now quickly and substantially expanded the role of the Einsatzgruppen; Hitler eventually sanctioned this move. Nominally still under the authority of the military, the Einsatzgruppen received their orders directly from Heydrich and thereafter embarked on a murderous campaign against Poland's ruling elite and its Jews.[74] In Poland the role of the Einsatzgruppen transformed from ruthless racial–ideological policing to racial–ideological murder campaigns. Concurrently, the Einsatzgruppen's relationship with the military shifted and its command structure changed. By the end of the Polish campaign, the Einsatzgruppen operated largely outside the authority of the military.[75] But their activities would reach their apex in the campaign against the "Judeo-Bolshevik" Soviet Union.

On December 18, 1940, Hitler issued "Weisung Nr. 21 (Fall 'Barbarossa')," ordering war against the Soviet Union.[76] The RSHA began to plan its role in the campaign: Einsatzgruppen were to be formed; the details of their deployment had to be discussed; and their relationship to the military had to be negotiated. The last item was of particular importance as Heydrich and Himmler intended to use the Einsatzgruppen

SD", Geheim, n.d. [July 31, 1939], USHMM, 14.016 M, 241; Document 509-USSR, IMG, vol. XXXIX; Richtlinien für die Tätigkeit der Einsatzkommandos der Geheimen Staatspolizei in den Sudetendeutschen Gebieten, USHMM, 14.019 M, 241.

74 Rossino, *Hitler Strikes Poland*; Krausnick, *Einsatzgruppen*, 27–89; Wildt, *Generation*, 419–455; and Michael Wildt, "Radikalisierung und Selbstradikalisierung: Die Geburt des Reichssicherheitshauptamtes aus dem Geist des völkischen Massenmordes," in Gerhard Paul and Klaus Michael Mallmann, eds. *Die Gestapo im Zweiten Weltkrieg: 'Heimatfront' und besetztes Europa* (Darmstadt: Primus Verlag, 2000), 11–41. Wildt argues that the SS leadership had no intention of living up to its agreements with the military, which deprived them of executive powers and regards the events in Poland as a turning point in the radicalization of Security Police and SD personnel.

75 Krausnick, *Einsatzgruppen*, 65–89.

76 Document printed in: Gerd R. Überschär and Wolfram Wette, eds., *Der deutsche Angriff auf die Sowjetunion: 'Unternehmen Barbarossa' 1941* (Frankfurt/Main: Fischer Taschenbuch Verlag, 1991), 244–246.

primarily as killing squads.[77] Complete independence from the military would make this task much easier. Negotiations with the military took place in March and April and an agreement was reached by the end of April 1941. On April 28, 1941, the commander-in-chief of the army, General Walther von Brauchitsch, issued an order detailing the future cooperation between the army and the Einsatzgruppen.[78] Heydrich and Himmler's success was all but complete: the Einsatzgruppen were to be independent from the military and to receive their orders directly from the chief of the Security Police and SD, Heydrich, and remain under the jurisdiction of the SS. The army commander-in-chief had to approve Einsatzgruppen operations possibly affecting military operations, but the order also included the establishment of small *Sonderkommandos*, special commandos, that were to operate directly at the front. Only in terms of marching orders, quarters, and rations were the Einsatzgruppen subordinated to the military. In effect, the military was to house and feed the Einsatzgruppen but would not have any authority over them. Himmler and Heydrich had reached their goals.

Schellenberg claimed that he played an important role in the process leading to Brauchitsch's order, but precise details remain murky. Initially, Heinrich "Gestapo" Müller and the army's Quartermaster General Eduard Wagner conducted the negations but to no avail. Exasperated, Wagner allegedly asked Heydrich for a different negotiator and Heydrich picked his trusted administrator Schellenberg, after admonishing him that he needed to gain the army's full support for all Einsatzgruppen activities. Schellenberg took over the negotiations and soon drafted an

---

[77] Some historians have argued that the decision to exterminate all European Jews dates to the spring of 1941, with the Einsatzgruppen killings of the Soviet Jews representing the first phase of the Final Solution. See, for example, Helmut Krausnick, "Judenverfolgung," in Martin Broszat et al., eds. *Anatomie des SS-Staates*, vol. 2, 5th ed. (Munich: Deutscher Taschenbuch Verlag, 1989), 297–313; Richard Breitman, *The Architect of Genocide: Himmler and the Final Solution* (Hanover, MA: Brandeis University Press, 1991), 145–166; 244–250. Christopher Browning argues for a decision-making process divided in two stages: one concerning the Soviet Jews in July 1941 and the other, encompassing all European Jews, in October 1941; Christopher R. Browning, *The Origins of the Final Solution: The Evolution of Nazi Jewish Policy, September 1939–March 1942* (Lincoln: University of Nebraska Press and Jerusalem: Yad Vashem, 2004). For a different assessment and timing, see Christian Gerlach, "Die Wannsee-Konferenz, das Schicksal der deutschen Juden und Hitler's politische Grundsatzentscheidung, alle europäischen Juden zu ermorden," *Werkstatt Geschichte* 18 (1997), 7–44.

[78] Document printed in: Überschär and Wette, *Überfall*, 249–250. Fundamental for understanding the establishment and deployment of the Einsatzgruppen in the Soviet Union is still Krausnick, *Einsatzgruppen*. See also: Ralf Ogoreck, *Die Einsatzgruppen und die "Genesis der Endlösung"* (Berlin: Metropol, 1996); Andrej Angrick, *Die Einsatzgruppe D: Struktur und Tätigkeiten einer mobilen Einheit der Sicherheitspolizei und des SD in der deutsch besetzten Sowjetunion* (Ph.D. Diss., Berlin, 1999). Wildt has been able to flesh out details on the negotiations: Wildt, *Generation*, 538–546.

agreement that found Wagner's approval. This draft formed the basis for subsequent negotiations between Heydrich and Wagner, leading to Brauchitsch's order. Once more, Schellenberg came through for the head of the RSHA. All of this, Schellenberg claimed, happened towards the end of May 1941.[79]

At Nuremberg, Schellenberg described the terms of the agreement he allegedly negotiated with Wagner in May. Stressing that it was based on a Führer order, Schellenberg noted that the agreement laid out that the Einsatzgruppen were dependent on the military at the front as well as in disciplinary matters. Only in the rear were they allowed to operate independently and to receive their orders from the RSHA. Heydrich and Wagner signed this agreement in Schellenberg's presence, but after he left the room, the two men discussed additional details based on another, secret, Führer order. Schellenberg opined that Heydrich and Wagner "most probably discussed and determined" the planned mass shootings in the "context of the fighting troops of the army" then.[80] In short, Schellenberg played an important role in key negotiations but was not involved with their most unsavory facets.

Schellenberg's testimony does not track. There is no doubt about the prominent role of German military in the murders of Jews and others, but Schellenberg's description downplays the agreement's ultimate purpose: the Einsatzgruppen's independence from the military. Also curious is his skewed timeline. Possibly, then, the agreement brokered by Schellenberg, which fell behind common ground reached between the negotiators by March 26, 1941, existed only "in his [Schellenberg's] testimony," as Michael Wildt suggests. Indeed, he argues that Schellenberg admitted

---

[79] Affidavit Walter Schellenberg, November 26, 1945, Document 3710-PS, IMG, vol. XXXII; Testimony Walter Schellenberg, January 4, Internationaler Militärgerichtshof. Amtlicher Text in Deutscher Sprache (Nürnberg 1947), vol. IV. In his memoirs, Schellenberg gives a more colorful rendition of events; Schellenberg, *Labyrinth*, 196.

[80] Affidavit Walter Schellenberg, November 26, 1945, Document 3710-PS, IMG, vol. XXXII. The German version of Schellenberg's affidavit is ambiguous. The context suggests that Schellenberg meant to say that the army was fully informed about the murderous plans of the Einsatzgruppen, which can also be deduced from his assertion that otherwise the close collaboration between Einsatzgruppen and military during the campaign, described in detail in the Einsatzgruppen reports, cannot be explained. However, Schellenberg used the phrase "*bis auf*," which normally means "excluding". The context suggests that Schellenberg meant to say "*bis (hin) zu*," meaning "including." Schellenberg stressed that he was not aware of any plans for mass murder when he negotiated with Wagner, but on May 16, 1941 he signed an order dealing with the deployment of Einsatzgruppen in Yugoslavia. After the war, he emphasized that this order was identical to earlier orders given to Einsatzgruppen employed in the Sudeten German territories. Interrogation Walter Schellenberg by Dr. R.M.W. Kempner, December 18, 1947, IfZ, ZS 291/V, 00036.

to his – in Wildt's estimation – minor role in the negotiations to lay blame at the feet of the German military.[81] But if Schellenberg's role was that minor, he would have done even better by downplaying it further, as he did with other elements of his career; laying blame at the feet of the military does not appear a good reason for Schellenberg to stick out his neck. Indeed, Schellenberg left the impression that without him there would have been no agreement. A different explanation is more consistent with Schellenberg's character and approaches. The timing could be a simple mistake or an attempt to obfuscate.[82] The latter is supported by a close reading of the testimony. Schellenberg showed a consistent proclivity for selectively drawing the prosecutors' attention to minute facts and spinning them to his benefit. Brauchitsch's April 28, 1941 order stated that Einsatzgruppen operations possibly affecting military operations would need approval by the army commander-in-chief.[83] Self-servingly and attempting to shift a share of the responsibility on to the military, Schellenberg focused his attention, and that of the prosecutors, not on the independence gained for the Einsatzgruppen, but on the areas in which the military retained some nominal authority over them. Schellenberg's emphasis on the military's responsibility for food, gas, and housing served the same purpose, as did his false statement that the Einsatzgruppen personnel remained under the disciplinary authority of the military. Shrewdly calculating that these minor points would neither generate much debate nor additional questioning by the prosecution, they helped Schellenberg to establish an overall picture of Einsatzgruppen by and large subordinated to the military. Schellenberg did not describe a different document here; he described a document differently.

And despite a lack of contemporaneous documentation bearing Schellenberg's signature, there can be little doubt that he was involved in these negotiations. Aside from his incriminating postwar statements, his position as the head of the counterintelligence department in Office IV necessitated it. After all, the Einsatzgruppen were also supposed to gather information connected to foreign intelligence services. His relationship to Heydrich made his involvement likely as well; Schellenberg was his trusted advisor, even regarded as a deputy by many. He was the

---

[81] Wildt, *Generation*, 546; 546 note 180. Wildt posits that the same held true for Ohlendorf and suggests that both men were involved with the negotiations on a lower level. Hilary Earl's extensive research on Ohlendorf produced no archival evidence on the extent of his involvement. For a reading amenable to Schellenberg's statements, Doerries, *Intelligence Chief*, 245–247.

[82] Breitman, *Architect*, 150 note 24.

[83] Document printed in: Überschär and Wette, *Überfall*, 250. For a different interpretation of this document, Wildt, *Generation*, 546 note 180.

man to whom Heydrich turned when complicated issues needed to be solved.

Schellenberg's involvement with the Einsatzgruppen did not reach the extent of many of his peers; he did not become a murderer. Four of the office heads of the Reich Security Main Office commanded Einsatzgruppen or Sonderkommandos; the assignment was not a punishment, as it has sometimes been asserted, but the men were selected based on their abilities.[84] It is possible that Schellenberg was not tapped as Heydrich and Himmler had different plans for him; in spring 1941, his appointment to Office VI's leadership was already on the horizon. It probably also had to do with Schellenberg's then position in the RSHA.[85] The Gestapo's counterintelligence department was arguably an important entity during the upcoming campaign against the Soviet Union; sending its leader into the "field" was counterintuitive at best. Whether officially or de facto, Schellenberg also deputized for Müller. The head of the Gestapo was not called to Einsatzgruppen duty either, as leading Gestapo personnel were less expendable than other Sipo and SD personnel. And Schellenberg clearly had no interest to volunteer, but there is little reason – or evidence – to construe his lack of voluntarism as a rejection of policies.[86] A smart career move for others, it was already below Schellenberg's status; he had distinguished himself from many of his peers and staying close to the center of powers was a much better course of action. And by the time the invasion of the Soviet Union began, Schellenberg was appointed acting head of Office VI. Many could head an Einsatzgruppe, but only Schellenberg would be able to create the formidable political foreign intelligence service Himmler and Heydrich envisioned.

Much about Schellenberg's two years at the helm of the Gestapo's counterintelligence department remains shrouded in mystery, but his experiences in this department and his additional activities at Himmler's and Heydrich's behest indubitably prepared him for his later position as the head of Office VI. Schellenberg gained valuable experience, learned the lay of the land in Germany's intelligence complex, cut his teeth in the interoffice wrangling for responsibilities, and took on a substantive role in the Gestapo. Arguing that counterintelligence should be less of a defensive and more of a proactive endeavor and not be separated completely from intelligence efforts, Schellenberg attempted to remake his department. He was not planning to be the head of "half an intelligence service" for long; rather, Schellenberg encroached on

[84] Wildt, *Generation*, 546–553.
[85] See Otto Ohlendorf's testimony, Doerries, *Last Chief*, 52 note 265.
[86] Doerries, *Intelligence Chief*, 248. Doerries choice of words "without risking his entire family's and his personal extermination [sic]" is dubious.

other departments' areas of responsibility. His efforts did not meet with much success but clearly illustrate his determination. Schellenberg also enjoyed an amenable working relationship with Heinrich Müller and it was only after Schellenberg became the head of the Office VI that professional rivalries defined their interactions. As long as he headed the Gestapo's counterintelligence department, Müller supported Schellenberg's attempts to broaden his purview in intelligence matters, as this would also benefit the Gestapo. Schellenberg apparently also served as Müller's deputy, even though the arrangement was never formalized. This informality served Schellenberg well after the war, as it helped him to mitigate his responsibility for Gestapo policies. Whether the two liked each other or not is beyond the point. For as long as they were both Gestapo, there is no indication that their professional relationship was strained: between 1939 and 1941, what was good for Schellenberg was good for Müller.

Schellenberg's informal role as the number two in the Gestapo hierarchy also raises questions about the role of his department in the Gestapo. IV E was not a straightforward counterintelligence entity primarily occupied with defensive measures in Germany and removed from any Gestapo terror and nor was Schellenberg a run-of-the-mill bureaucrat. The counterintelligence department and Schellenberg had a stake in the A-B Aktion in Poland. Schellenberg briefed Himmler on ideological and racial enemies in the Low Countries and oversaw the preparation of the invasion handbook for Great Britain. If this is counterintelligence, it is certainly a different, Nazified approach to it – "proactive," just as Schellenberg envisioned it. Heading the Gestapo's counterintelligence department was Schellenberg's apprenticeship for a leadership position in the RSHA.

Schellenberg also played a significant role in the negotiations about preceding the deployment of the Einsatzgruppen in the Soviet Union, solving, by his own recounting, an impasse between Wagner and Müller. Due to his position, ambition, and relationship to other major figures in the decision-making process, Schellenberg clearly knew more about genesis of the Final Solution than he let on after the war.[87] But among Schellenberg's many characteristics was his ability to be very close to the fire and cunning enough not to get burnt.

[87] Breitman, *Secrets*, 35 note 33.

4   Office VI and Its Forerunner

> You will recognize from this that even Office VI fulfills its responsibility
> and duty, and that it is surely worth the support by other offices and
> departments, if this is possible in the first place.
>
> Speech prepared for Heinz Jost, *Amtschef* Office VI 12 June 1941

On September 19, 1939 the office heads of the newly established RSHA
convened for a meeting during which Heydrich took aim at the political foreign intelligence service, Office VI. Dr. Albert Filbert stood in
for Heinz Jost, who was still on duty in Poland. In front of his peers
and "[i]n unequivocal form," Heydrich told Filbert that "the foreign
reports were poor and had to be reorganized substantially. In their existing form they were a poor compilation of newspaper and radio news of
foreign senders." Heydrich impatiently requested the "commencement of
the work, and [he] wishes [to receive] only those reports that are acquired
through direct intelligence work."[1] Jost and his foreign intelligence service had been put on notice.

Under Jost's leadership Office VI was engaged in an uphill battle.
During the years that Schellenberg worked on remaking the Gestapo's
counterintelligence department into an intelligence service with a broad-
ened mandate and new methods, Office VI strove to establish itself as a
respected foreign intelligence entity. Jost's office attempted to transcend
its many conceptual problems – many of them related to its pedigree as
part of the SS – and to forge a new identity in an environment defined
by intense internal competition and the beginning of the Second World
War. For Jost, this process ended in failure; in July 1941, Schellenberg
took over the office's leadership. The following pages describe the history
of Office VI and its predecessor and discuss their place and role in Nazi
Germany's foreign intelligence universe. How did Office VI and its forerunner conceptualize, execute, and evaluate political foreign intelligence?

---

[1] Stabskanzlei I 11, Bf./Fh. Betr. Amtschefbesprechung am 19.9.39, USHMM, 14.016
M, 825.

Early SD foreign intelligence efforts were associated with Heinz Jost. Office VI of the RSHA had its origins in Office III of the *Sicherheitshauptamt*, SD Main Office, created in early 1935.[2] The SD Main Office found itself in conflict with the police on the one hand and the *Abwehr*, Germany's military intelligence, service on the other: a party organization rooted in the SS, it intended to take on policing and intelligence functions in the state. The 1930s saw a slew of agreements meant to settle or subdue these conflicts and to find a suitable role for the SD as a domestic and as a foreign intelligence service. The fact that some of the leading police personnel, such as Heydrich and Werner Best, who were then still cooperating, had a stake in the development of the SD as well, did much to make possible these early understandings. The 1935 agreement between Gestapo, SD, and the Abwehr is an excellent example of how these administrative connections and political ambitions gained advantages for the nascent SD.

In January 1935, shortly after Wilhelm Canaris' appointment as the head of the Abwehr, leading members of the three organizations met to discuss the future division of labor between the Abwehr, Gestapo, and, in its wake, the SD. Six men participated in the meeting: Canaris and Rudolf Bamler represented the Abwehr; Heinz Jost, who had been recruited by Best in 1934, was there on behalf of the SD's foreign intelligence office; Best and Dr. Günther Patschowski represented the Gestapo. Also in attendance was Heydrich, presumably focusing on the Gestapo. Yet the three men representing the Gestapo were also SD members: Heydrich headed the SD while Best had left his position as the SD's number two for his position in the Gestapo a mere three weeks before the meeting. Patschowski, head of the Gestapo Office IV, Treason and Espionage, in 1934 and of Department III, Counterintelligence, in early 1935, was also connected to the SD and had been Heydrich's man in initial attempts to extend the SD's influence over the police.[3] In later years the rivalry between the Gestapo and SD could be intense but the situation was different in January 1935, when Gestapo and SD were still intent on jointly wresting areas of responsibility from Canaris' Abwehr.

---

[2] David Kahn, *Hitler's Spies: German Military Intelligence in World War II* (New York: Macmillan, 1978; reprint, Cambridge, MA: DaCapo Press, 2000), 252–254; Michael Wildt, *Generation des Unbedingten: Das Führungkorps des Reichssicherheitshauptamtes* (Hamburg: Hamburger Edition, 2002), 936–937. Kahn ties Jost career to that of his friend and mentor Werner Best. This was also true after the war, yet as before Best held more prominent positions.

[3] Shlomo Aronson, *Reinhard Heydrich und die Frühgeschichte von Gestapo und SD* (Stuttgart: Deutsche Verlagsanstalt: 1971), 156–157; George Browder, *Foundations of the Nazi Police State: The Formation of Sipo and SD* (Lexington: University Press of Kentucky, 1990), 182–183.

And Patschowski's Gestapo department served as the SD's wedge to become involved in foreign intelligence matters.[4]

The January 1935 agreement was the first that defined in ten points the roles of the Gestapo and the Abwehr in counterintelligence matters; the role of the SD was covered outside of these points.[5] The Abwehr was charged with five functions. Military espionage and counterespionage rested exclusively with the Abwehr; it was also responsible for counterintelligence in military and industrial complexes owned by the military. In addition, the Abwehr vetted new members of the military and retained its leadership role in all matters of national defense. However, not all was as clear-cut as it seemed: in industrial security, further regulations were to define cooperation with the Gestapo. And while the Abwehr was responsible for all counterespionage regulations and measures, it was to collaborate with the Gestapo and the SD. In other words, in two of the five Abwehr areas, it was to collaborate with Gestapo and SD and in others intrusions became a possibility. The role of the Gestapo, defined in five points as well, encompassed tasks associated with the political police: the fight against all enemies of the state. The Gestapo was also in charge of the border police and the border intelligence service, the policing of foreign nationals in Germany, and all issues related to passports. It was furthermore responsible for all counterintelligence and counterespionage matters within the Reich and industrial counterintelligence and counterespionage. Lastly, in accordance with pertinent agreements between the Abwehr and Hermann Göring's *Forschungsamt*, Research Office, the Gestapo handled the surveillance of the mail and telecommunications. Ultimately, then, the Gestapo ended up with the bigger part of the pie: it was in charge of or involved with all matters of counterintelligence and counterespionage in the Reich, short of those pertaining exclusively to military matters and installations. Several rules and regulations toward the document's end, rarely discussed in the literature, show the extent to which the Gestapo and, in its wake, the SD were encroaching on Abwehr tasks.[6] The Abwehr was to share formerly restricted information with the

---

[4] George C. Browder, *Hitler's Enforcers: The Gestapo and the SS Security Service in the Nazi Revolution* (New York: Oxford University Press, 1996), 197–198.

[5] Ergebnisse der Besprechung im Reichswehrministerium am 17.1.1935, 15–18 Uhr, Berlin, January 17, 1935, USHMM, 14. 016 M, 242.

[6] Geyer posits that through this agreement Canaris secured the "new" Abwehr as a "specialized executive for unconventional or political warfare." This appears to be a positive reading of the Abwehr's position. Michael Geyer, "National Socialist Germany: The Politics of Information," in Ernest R. May, ed., *Knowing One's Enemy: Intelligence Assessment Before the Two World Wars* (Princeton: Princeton University Press, 1984), 318. For a reading that suggests that Abwehr regained territory lost: Horst Mühleisen, "Das letzte Duell: Die Auseinandersetzungen zwischen Heydrich und Canaris wegen der Revision der 'Zehn Gebote'," *Militärgeschichtliche Mitteilungen* 58/2 (1999), 400.

Gestapo and to assist the Gestapo in fulfilling its newly gained obligations. In effect, the Abwehr was tasked to facilitate the Gestapo's expansion.

The agreement accorded the SD a minor role but it represented a major shift. Its tasks briskly defined as "collaborating in intelligence matters (without any executive powers) in areas of plant security, industrial counterintelligence, and border intelligence," the SD was piggybacking on the expanding role of the Gestapo. It was defined through what it was not to be or to do: the SD was not concerned with military intelligence, as this was the task of Abwehr. It had no executive powers, as these rested with the Gestapo. It was to assist the Gestapo, but the extent of the assistance remained undefined. Yet at the same time, the Abwehr recognized the SD as part of the new German counterintelligence complex.[7] And the agreement's overall vagueness could benefit the SD, as it lent itself to future expansion and renegotiation. From the SD's vantage point this was a step forward: four years after its founding, the SD sat at the table when the future of Germany's (counter-)intelligence structure was negotiated. Later agreements and renegotiations – including the so-called Ten Commandments of December 1936 – reiterated and refined the understanding reached in January 1935.[8] The Ten Commandments of December 1936 set forth that military espionage and counterespionage fell under the purview of the Abwehr, while searches and arrests relating to espionage and treason were to be handled by Gestapo and SD. The distinction between military and non-military matters must have appeared clear enough but realities were muddy. The Gestapo became more and more involved with Abwehr matters, and in the Gestapo's wake came the SD.

Joined in their encroachment on Abwehr responsibilities, the relationship between the Gestapo and the SD was fractious in its own right. At the center of the debate were the issue of executive powers and the overall division of labor. Himmler initially addressed these concerns in July 1934; subsequent orders, such as the Functional Order of July 1, 1937, defined the respective areas of responsibility for the Gestapo and the SD and established procedures for sharing information.[9] The Functional

---

[7] Browder, *Foundations*, 180–181.
[8] Regarding the term Ten Commandments and its application to other Abwehr/Gestapo/SD agreements, see Browder, *Foundations*, 180 note 33; 182–184; Peter Black, *Ernst Kaltenbrunner: Ideological Soldier of the Third Reich* (Princeton: Princeton University Press, 1984), 190. Mühleisen, "Duell," 401 notes a defeat for the police. Grundsätze für die Zusammenarbeit zwischen der Geheimen Staatspolizei und den Abwehrdienststellen der Wehrmacht vom 21.12. 1936 NA, RG 242, T-77/1449, Frame 00484–000487.
[9] Gemeinsame Anordnung für den Sicherheitsdienst des Reichsführer-SS und die Geheime Staatspolizei, July 1, 1937, USHMM, 14.016 M, 239. This was the *Funktionsbefehl*, Functional Order.

Order was basically the Gestapo-SD equivalent of the Ten Commandments. It loftily announced that the relationship between the Gestapo and the SD was defined by unity rather than by subordination or rivalry and divvied up responsibilities between the two organizations. The SD's areas included science, *Volkstum* – racial folkdom – and *völkisch* science, art, education, party, state, constitution, administration, foreign countries, Freemasonry, and associations. The Gestapo, on the other hand, was in charge of Marxism, treason, and emigrants. Both organizations shared responsibility regarding the churches, religious and *weltanschauliche*, ideological, groups, pacifism, Jewry, rightist movements, "other" opposition groups such as the Black Front, *Bündisch* youth movements, and the press. In these areas of joined responsibility, the Gestapo handled concrete cases and their prosecution, while the SD dealt with their broader ideological implications. If the SD deemed executive measures necessary, it was to request the Gestapo's support. The Functional Order thus codified the role of the SD in matters traditionally restricted to the political police. Executive powers remained beyond the SD's reach but it became privy to information gathered as well as to measures taken by the police. Within a few short years, the SD had become entrenched in both Abwehr and Gestapo matters.

The overall progress of the SD was undeniable, but internally it remained an institution in flux. Various efforts to define its mandates and to create appropriate structures are symptomatic of this fluidity; they should be read as a thinking process about role and mandate of the SD even when the SD Main Office's structure remained stable. An order by Heydrich in January 1936 shows that the SD Main Office consisted of the same three offices that already existed in 1935, but it also provides a clearer picture of the SD's mandate and structure.[10] Office I, divided into the Staff Chancellery and the Central Department, dealt with financial, administrative, and personnel issues and included a section for press evaluation and other research tasks. Office II, known as *Inland*, Interior, was focused on domestic issues. It has the task to determine the activities of the opponents of the National Socialist ideology [*Weltanschauung*] in its different forms and to evaluate them in such a form that the impact of the foreign ideologies becomes clearly visible in the present, past, and future in order to give the leadership of the state and the

---

[10] Gliederung SD/SD Hauptamt, January 15, 1936, gez. Heydrich, RGVA, Fond 500, Opis 1, film 907, roll 3. The translations are mine. See also: Michael Wildt, *Die Judenpolitik des SD 1935–1938: Eine Dokumentation* (Munich: Oldenbourg Verlag, 1995), Dokument 4, Befehl des Chefs der Sicherheitspolizei zum organisatorischen Aufbau, 1936, 73–80; Browder, *Enforcers*, Appendix B 5 "Organization of the SD Main Office 1936–1937," 255–258. Browder incorporates various sources into this chart; note the changes in Amt III, Abwehr, marked in parentheses.

movement the basis to take measures for defense and battle [*Abwehr und Bekämpfung*].

Office II was divided into two Main Departments: II 1 *Weltanschauliche Auswertung*, Ideological Evaluation and II 2 *Lebengebietsmäßige Auswertung*, Evaluation by Living Sphere. Main Department II 1 concerned itself with "ideologies," among them Freemasonry, Judaism, Zionism, "religious-political" movements such as Catholicism, especially in its politicized version, and "enemy forms," such as Marxism and the *völkisch* opposition. Main Department II 2, on the other hand, covered cultural life, societal life, and material life. In effect, *Inland* focused on ideological enemies and surveyed domestic life. Office III dealt with foreign matters. Labeled *Abwehr*, defense, like the military's intelligence service, its tasks were described briefly, betraying its vague mandate. "Office III (Abwehr) has the task to support the appointed state organization in the defense against espionage and sabotage." This was a decidedly second-tier role and a far cry from the tasks of its better-developed counterpart, Office II.

Office III's set-up betrayed larger ambitions, though. It, too, was divided into two Central Departments. Main Department III 1 focused on *Fremdländische Lebensgebiete*, Foreign Living Spheres. It was subdivided into a European and a non-European area and below that into regional and country desks. Main Department III 2, under Jost, dealt with *Aussenpolitische Abwehr*, Foreign Defense. Conceived as a counter-intelligence section, III 2 was divided by form and target of espionage, for example "military espionage, navy" or "political espionage, diplomacy," and area of enemy service activity plus the likely predominant foreign service, for example "West, French Intelligence Service," or "South, Switzerland."[11] The new structure pointed to a future in which Office III was meant to do more than support the appointed state organizations in the defense against espionage and sabotage.

Creating grand structures was one thing, but the formulation of a well-defined mandate was a different issue. In that sense, the incessant reorganization showed the entity's search for a mandate and concomitant approaches. A December 1936 order, which begins with the mantra "The SD is an intelligence service," illustrates the SD's quandary: it

[11] In the SD *Abschnitte*, Districts, und SD *Oberabschnitte*, Superior Districts, the offices were organized accordingly but with fewer sub-fields. Based on their geographical location, they were also expected to include a foreign country in their work. Wildt, *Judenpolitik*, 78–79; Alwin Ramme, *Der Sicherheitsdienst der SS: Zu seiner Funktion im faschistischen Machtapparat und im Besatzungsregime des sogenannten Generalgovernements Polen* (Berlin, East Germany: Deutscher Militärverlag, 1970), 57 asserts that Office III worked mainly against the Soviet Union. The structure for Western Europe was much better developed, though.

shows great aspiration, but is also indicative of the SD's lackluster performance thus far. It calls for the collection of information from non-open sources and the reporting on future developments through the creation of networks. The order's ambition is total: the SD is to "record completely" everything there is and to provide "complete situation reports without any gaps [. . .] from each place where facts of political relevance could happen." Meant for Office II, the order applied to Office III as well: III 1 and III 2 were each given 999 code numbers for informers.[12] Yet there is little indication as to what was done or achieved.

By the mid-1930s, then, Office III, headed by Jost, boasted an ambitious structure and an impressive-sounding mandate, but a clear understanding of its set-up and activities, or even Jost's precise role, remains out of reach. Reliable documentation does not exist.[13] One of the office's mainstays in the early 1930s was clearly its security function in the German industry, counterintelligence, and Office III worked closely with the pertinent sections of the Gestapo and Abwehr.[14] The SD's role in counterintelligence is often regarded as an exercise in redundancy, as both Gestapo and Abwehr fulfilled these tasks already. Acidly, George Browder remarks that only ideologues could have believed that the SD, as a valuable ideological supplement, could recruit better – ideologically more committed – people than the Gestapo, or that special attention should be paid to Jews and Gypsies as potential foreign agents.[15] Yet that was exactly the point. The SD was playing up its ideological prowess. The Gestapo still had among its ranks many who had been members of the police during the Weimar Republic and were not deemed fully trustworthy. Abwehr personnel, on the other hand, was often deemed old-school reactionary and eyed with suspicion. And, ultimately, the SD was not trying to convince the Gestapo or Abwehr personnel that its members

---

[12] Befehl für den SD, 76/36, December 15, 1936, RGVA, Fond 500, Opis 1, film 941.

[13] By some accounts, Jost headed Central Department III 1 and III 2, as Heydrich, the office's nominal leader, was busy. Jost also ran the counterintelligence department of the Gestapo, working closely with Best. This dual appointment represented a personal link between the two sometime warring departments. Browder, *Enforcers*, 201–202. Preussische Geheime Staatspolizei, Stellvertretender Chef und Inspekteur, Berlin, January 2, 1936, USHMM 14.016 M, 239. Other documents suggest a less prominent role for Jost, at least intermittently. Personalbefehl des CdS, January 25, 1936. RGVA, Fond 500, Opis 1, film 907, roll 3.

[14] Counter Intelligence War Room, Situation Report No. 10, Amt VI of RSHA, Gruppe VI E, NA, RG 319, IRR, Box 1, XE 002303 [hereafter: Situation Report No. 10]. Browder asserts that the SD focused on industrial counterintelligence in its early years. Ramme, however, suggests that early on Office III was mainly occupied with active intelligence and espionage efforts and reads the emphasis on defensive measures as a smokescreen. Browder, *Enforcers*, 198; Ramme, *Sicherheitsdienst*, 57.

[15] Browder, *Enforcers*, 198.

were better suited for intelligence work but Himmler and Hitler. And they were swayed by ideological commitment.

Office III performed, for example, a number of operations abroad. One such case is the murder of Rudolf Formis, a radio operator for Otto Strasser's Black Front, in the Czecho-Slovak Republic (ČSR) in late 1935. This was a special assignment that could not be undertaken by the Gestapo and, since it involved the murder of a man associated with Hitler's rival Otto Strasser, the operation was too ideological to be entrusted to the Abwehr. Abroad and under special circumstances, the SD retained a "capacity for executive action," and was an instrument for the execution of sensitive covert operations.[16] However, until the late 1930s, such operations remained an exception.

Postwar reports emphasize that Office III moved slowly from its initial counterintelligence focus to intelligence-gathering efforts. The early focus on plant security had allowed Office III "to provide the SD-Hauptamt with a fairly clear picture of German industry and its productive capacity." Subsequently, Jost was asked to "exploit the industrial connections to establish good contacts in business circles and to develop the facilities which the *Oberabschnitte*, Superior Districts, near the German frontier provided for espionage activities outside of the Reich." Office III began to act as a "positive espionage system."[17] But the fact of the matter was that Office III had always attempted to do that but simply not seen a lot of success. The Berlin headquarters played little role in these early efforts; rather, Office III functioned in a decentralized fashion through the SD districts and outposts. The lack of qualified personnel with experience abroad made the situation even more difficult.[18] Unevenness resulted and some districts were more effective than others: between 1933 and 1935, for example, Wilhelm Albert appears to have mounted reasonably successful intelligence efforts against France from his headquarters in Frankfurt. In the years before the 1935 plebiscite, which decided whether the region would return to Germany, his district focused on the Saar region and prepared "well informed assessments from a Nazi ideological perspective." The effort purportedly won praise from the Abwehr. The same has been said for the SD Superior Region South West, which from 1933 to 1935 was led by Werner Best and focused on France, Switzerland, and Alsace-Lorraine while also paying

---

[16] Browder, *Enforcers*, 202–203.

[17] Situation Report No. 10. Note that the SD's foreign department saw it as part of its responsibility to investigate the "productive capacity" of the German industry.

[18] Allgemeine historische Entwicklung des Nachrichtendienstes, n.a., n.d., BA-DH, ZR 920/59 [herafter: Allgemeine Entwicklung]; Situation Report No. 10.

due attention to the Saar.[19] Localized but largely unconfirmed successes notwithstanding, these networks were haphazard.[20]

In Eastern Europe, the SD relied on "large pro-German minority groups" – pro-Nazi ethnic Germans – who "served as a source of information through their constant passage backwards and forwards across the border."[21] Many of these individuals were personal acquaintances of the SD officers in charge in the districts. Living across the border, they were either imbued with the National Socialist spirit or, at least, not opposed to Germany's new order.[22] Unsurprisingly, these informants came with their own issues.

The situation in Austria perfectly illustrates some of the SD's problems. In the mid-1930s Austria should have been the easiest place for the SD's foreign department to penetrate. Austria had an active Nazi movement that included a *Nachrichtendienst* (ND), intelligence service. Nevertheless, after the failed Austrian Nazi coup in 1934, collaboration across the border remained sporadic. Austrian ND members were not officially affiliated with the SD and the central ND in Vienna served as the personal intelligence service of the Austrian SS leader, Ernst Kaltenbrunner.[23] Reporting directly to Himmler, Heydrich, and Jost about the Austrian Nazi underground and providing other information his men gleaned Kaltenbrunner maintained a fair degree of independence from the SD still. And despite the many émigrés staffing the Austrian desks at the Superior Districts, the SD did not penetrate even the Austrian Nazi movement, let alone the Austrian government or military. The situation only began to look up shortly before the annexation of Austria in 1938.[24]

Overall, Office III's fortunes began to improve once Germany embarked on expansionist foreign policies toward the late 1930s. It played a substantial role in the preparation and execution of the Austrian *Anschluß*, annexation, in March 1938 but was involved even more in the takeover of the Sudeten German territories that fall. Little concrete is known about the SD's activities in Anschluß, but an Office III summary of the year's activities provides valuable insights into the office's

[19] Aronson, *Frühgeschichte*, 163; Browder, *Enforcers*, 208, 121. Sixth Detailed Interrogation Report on SS Sturmbannführer Huegel Dr. Klaus, June 21, 1945, NA, RG 226, E 119A, Box 71, Folder 1828.

[20] Kahn, *Spies*, 253; Browder, *Enforcers*, 201. Very few documents from this early period survive, thus making it difficult to gauge seriously the intelligence efforts at this point.

[21] Situation Report No. 10.   [22] Allgemeine Entwicklung.

[23] Black, *Kaltenbrunner*, 69–103; Browder, *Enforcers*, 205.

[24] Browder, *Enforcers*, 205–206. For a positive assessment of SD work in Austria; Black, *Kaltenbrunner*, 83.

role, even if the document is self-congratulatory.[25] Austria was subsumed under "Enemy Intelligence Services/Department South-East" in Office III's structure; the department focused on the services of the "Danube region, the Balkans, and Asia." On June 13, 1936, Himmler had given the department the additional task of creating an intelligence operation reaching into Austria; the department was to undertake the "preparatory work for the annexation of Austria to the Reich." Incidentally, Himmler issued this order almost exactly a month prior to the German–Austrian Treaty of July 1936 through which Germany recognized Austrian independence and renounced future interference in Austrian affairs.[26] The new task indicates just how seriously the treaty was taken in Germany.

The department focused on preparing memoranda on Austria; these eventually played an important role in the *Anschluß* of March 1938. One dealt with planned Austrian measures in case of a German invasion; its sections discussed military and political matters, the economy, and popular mood while additional memoranda delineated the postannexation security structure of Austria. At least two indices were put together in direct preparation for the Anschluß. One planned the deployment of individual Austrians living within the Reich while the other was a "special index," which consisted of a "search index, a subject index, and a special index." It included objects of special interest to German security forces entering Austria and, presumably, an arrest list. This was, in effect, a forerunner of the Special Wanted List Great Britain prepared under Schellenberg's oversight two years later. During the Anschluß, the indices came in handy: the report self-congratulatory remarked the department's preparatory work had facilitated the quick establishment of the Gestapo and *Kriminalpolizei* (Kripo), criminal police, network in Austria.

The report also noted the creation of a well-developed "political intelligence service" that provided valuable information in the run-up to the annexation. Through this service the department received communications between the Austrian Chancellery and embassies abroad, economic reports, and all decrees sent from the General Directorate of Public Security to its agencies. This information allowed the department to prepare memoranda and reports for Hermann Göring, the economic service of the plenipotentiary for Austrian affairs, and interested state and party agencies. Office III did not share its knowledge with the military, though. The report also emphasized that one had gleaned relevant knowledge

---

[25] Browder, *Enforcers*, 205; III 2 to I/1, Vortragsthemen zur SS-Gruppenführer-Tagung am 26. Januar 1939, January 12, 1939, BA-DH, ZR 920/148.

[26] III 2 to I/1, Vortragsthemen zur SS-Gruppenführer-Tagung am 26. Januar 1939, January 12, 1939, BA-DH, ZR 920/148 [hereafter: Vortragsthemen 26. Januar 1939.]

about other intelligence services active in the greater region. It is not clear how Office III acquired this information, though. Postwar interviews suggest that the Austrian ND had a contact person in the confidential mail division of the Austrian Foreign Office, which would account for much of the information listed above. Kaltenbrunner is believed to have carried materials across the border.[27] In short, the annexation of Austria, Nazi Germany's first territorial expansion, was the first time that the SD's foreign department played a significant and systematic role: it served as an annexation think tank and as an intelligence-gathering entity and laid the groundwork for future activities.

Likely in recognition of its efforts in Austria, Office III occupied a more prominent role six months later when, with the assistance of French and British appeasement politicians, Hitler pried the Sudeten German territories from the Czecho-Slovak Republic.[28] But even before the Sudeten Question became a foreign policy flashpoint of Hitler's making, SD Superior Districts attempted to gather information on the country. These activities throw into sharp relief the office's conceptual problems; among them – but as the tip of the iceberg – Office III's preoccupation with issues inside the Sudeten German Nazi Movement. With the help of Wilhelm Krichbaum, an SD operative in the Dresden Gestapo, the SD had gained access to the vetting process of émigrés at the Sudeten German Control Post in Dresden as early as late 1933. Three other SD Superior Districts – South, Middle, and Southeast – also focused some of their attention on the ČSR.[29]

The Sudeten German Movement, consisting of ethnic Germans dissatisfied with their status in the ČSR, split into a traditional-völkish and a radical wing. Konrad Henlein, the leader of the *Sudetendeutsche Partei*, Sudeten German Party (SdP), initially belonged to the former; he only aligned himself with Hitler in late 1937. However, even before the alignment, both Henlein and his party represented a thorn in the side of the government in Prague and a growing threat to its stability. To Henlein's universe also belonged the *Kameradschaftsbund*, Comradeship Circle. In Germany, the SdP and the Kameradschaftsbund found an ally in the Abwehr and Canaris. The *Aufbruch Kreis*, Departure Circle, which took its name from a Sudeten German newspaper, represented the radical side of the Sudeten German Movement. While some of its members also

---

[27] Black, *Kaltenbrunner*, 83.   [28] Vortragsthemen 26. Januar 1939.
[29] The control post had been established under a Hess order to stave off attempts by the Czecho-Slovak intelligence service to infiltrate the Reich; the SD apparently used the control post without the knowledge of Hess. Ronald M. Smelser, *The Sudeten Problem, 1933–1938: Volkstumspolitik and the Formulation of Nazi Foreign Policy* (Middletown, CT: Wesleyan University Press, 1975), 169; Browder, *Enforcers*, 203–204.

held a membership with the SdP, it represented the movement's younger, radical elements and was critical of what it considered Henlein's failures in his dealings with Prague. Former members of the *Deutsche National-sozialistische Arbeiterpartei* (DNSAP), German National Socialist Workers' Party, a Sudeten German offshoot of the NSDAP, were numerous in the Aufbruch Kreis. National Socialist ideology, great-German ideas, anti-Semitism, and racism defined the Aufbruch Kreis.[30] The SD sided with the Aufbruch Kreis and SD reports that "actually attempt[ed] to affect the outcome of the situation about which they were supposedly merely reporting," facilitated Himmler's positive outlook on the most radical wing of Sudeten German movement and his negative view of Henlein. The reports thus shaped attitudes and, ultimately, decisions.[31] The SD's focus on Nazi movements and their personalities abroad highlights its conceptual and actual weaknesses as a foreign intelligence entity. Finding it difficult or all but impossible to collect information about foreign governments, Office III adopted the approaches of the SD's domestic intelligence service. It largely conceptualized its work as that of an ideological watchdog abroad.

Collecting information on the rest of the ČSR was an uphill battle and reports were defined by Nazi ideology. The Superior Districts as well as headquarters in Berlin were, for example, interested in intelligence services operating out of the ČSR and the structure of the police. Reports, though, remained vague.[32] The Superior District Elbe, on the other hand, tried to concern itself with political matters, as can be seen in a report that evaluated various members of the Czechoslovak government. But rather than focusing on the ministers' politics or activities, the report evaluated them through the SD's ideological prism. Accordingly, and in a willful interpretation of his international educational background with some racist innuendo thrown in for good measure, Czechoslovak president Eduard Beneš is described as having "significant Jewish blood," being "tied to Paris," and as the grandmaster of the Freemason Lodge "Grand Orient de France." He is also portrayed – correctly, one hastens to add – as an opponent of state theories based on racial science and as proponent of the League of Nations and the Danube Pact. In short,

[30] Smelser, Sudeten Problem, 166–184; Volker Zimmermann, Die Sudetendeutschen im NS-Staat. *Politik und Stimmung der Bevölkerung im Reichsgau Sudetenland 1938–1945* (Essen: Klartext, 1999), chapter I.2.

[31] Smelser, *Sudeten Problem*, 170; Browder, *Enforcers*, 203.

[32] "Nachrichtendienst der tschechoslowakischen politischen Organisationen," SD-OA Südost, September 10, 1936; "Tschechoslowakische Politische Polizei," SD-OA Süd, June 30, 1936; "Nachrichtendienst der tschechoslowakischen Wehrmacht," SD-OA Süd, June 30, 1936; "Nachrichtendienst der deutschen Emigration in der ČSR," SD-OA Elbe, no date, RGVA, Fond 500, Opis 1, film 870, rolls 1–3.

Beneš signified the polar opposite of National Socialism. The health minister Dr. Czech "is a Jew!" In addition, he is described as a Social Democrat supported by Freemasons.[33] The main office clearly valued this type of information. In the summer of 1937, in the middle of a developing political crisis in Prague, it charged the Superior District to follow the crisis and supply bimonthly reports on it. The main office was particularly interested in changes at the cabinet level, "if possible with a characterization of new cabinet members."[34] Clearly, then, the ideological characterizations of Czechoslovak politicians was what Office III had in mind.

Other reports provided information about domestic and economic policies in the ČSR, but the SD's primarily focused on the alleged plight of the Sudeten Germans and issues within the Sudeten German Nazi movement.[35] The latter reports were highly critical of Konrad Henlein and the SdP. A report of February 1937, for example, described Henlein as a hapless tool of the Czechoslovak politicians and deviant circles within the Sudeten German movement.[36] This was clearly not the case but reflected the views of the Aufbruch Kreis at a time when Henlein still kept some distance from Hitler. Where the Sudeten Germans were concerned, the information collected and reported by the SD was precise in its partisanship while SD reports on general developments in the ČSR showed intelligence efforts in an analogous ideological stranglehold.

The information gathered was a function of the informers used by the Superior Districts; they were a homogenous and parochial group of people.[37] These men – and few women – were not simply pro-German or pro-Nazi. Rather, a good number of them were critical of Henlein and his policies, as they were members of the Aufbruch Kreis, or former members of the DNSAP. The SD regarded them as "exponents of a more correct and, from a National Socialist sensibility, more broadly conceived understanding [of the realities]."[38] These sensibilities were

---

[33] SD-OA Elbe an III 1, March 15, 1937, RGVA, Fond 500, Opis 1, film 891, roll 2. I thank Vanda Rajcan for perusing the pertinent Czech and Slovak literature on Beneš' religious background; he was Catholic.

[34] III 1114 to SD-OA Elbe, June 21, 1937, RGVA, Fond 500, Opis 1, film 891, roll 2.

[35] For a number of these reports, dating to 1936, 1937 and 1938: RGVA, Fond 500, Opis 1, film 891, roll 2 and 3.

[36] SD-OA Ost an SD-HA, Lagebericht aus der ČSR – Stand Ende Januar 1937, February 24, 1937, RGVA, Fond 500, Opis 1, film 891, roll 2.

[37] For lists of informers: RGVA, Fond 500, Opis 1, film 906, roll 1.

[38] SD-UA Chemnitz/Zwickau to SD-OA Elbe, Verbindungen des SD nach der Tschechoslowakei, June 13, 1938, RGVA, Fond 500, Opis 1, film 906, roll 1. Zimmermann and Smelser stress that after the annexation of the Sudeten German territory, a minimum of sixty-five Sudeten German informers were suggested for admission into the SD. Zimmermann, *Sudetendeutschen*, 49–5; 56; Smelser, *Sudeten Problem*, 178. On the

their primary qualification for their work with the SD. Conversely, their political and ideological make-up prevented these informers from having any substantial contacts outside the Sudeten German areas and beyond their political circles. In the same way that Sudeten Germans who had transcended the minority's initial "negativist" stance toward the ČSR were unlikely to work for the SD, those who did were unlikely to be privy to confidential information emanating from the government in Prague. The SD informers' qualification was not their reach but their ideological firmness. Success begat success, though: many of the informers listed in a June 1938 report had volunteered their services after the annexation of Austria. Driven by a "fundamental [*lebensanschaulichem*] need and based on a strengthened feeling of a connection with German folkdom [they] had the desire to inform the entities of state in charge of these matters about all special measures and developments and thus to become active in terms of intelligence collection."[39] The SD Lower District Chemnitz, located on the Czechoslovak–German border, found itself – short-staffed as it was – with more volunteers than it could handle.

The haphazard and peculiar nature of the SD's approaches became particularly obvious in the spring and summer of 1938, when, after the annexation of Austria and while the Sudeten Crisis was beginning to take center stage, Office III was restructured. This was possibly also a belated reaction to the dismissal commander-in-chief Werner von Fritsch and War Minister Werner von Blomberg and the transfer of the ministry's duties, including the Abwehr, to the newly established *Oberkommando der Wehrmacht* (OKW), High Command of the Armed Forces, under Wilhelm Keitel earlier that year. It is likely that these developments added to the impression that it was time to remake Office III. Main Department III 2, Foreign Defense, which in 1937 attempted to use ideological categories, such as Freemasonry, Jews, Political Churches, Communism and Marxism, Liberalism, and Rightist Movements, as its efforts organizing principles – thus becoming the mirror image of Main Department II 1, Domestic Ideological Surveillance – reverted back to a set up reminiscent of January 1936.[40] In addition, Main Department III 3, rarely

DNSAP: Andreas Luh, "Die Deutsche Nationalsozialistische Arbeiterpartei im Sudetenland: Völkische Arbeiterpartei und faschistische Bewegung," *Bohemia* 32 (1991), 23–38; Ronald Smelser, "Hitler and the DNSAP: Between Democracy and Gleichschaltung," *Bohemia* 21 (1979), 137–155.

[39] SD-UA Chemnitz/Zwickau to SD-OA Elbe, Verbindungen des SD nach der Tschechoslowakei," June 13, 1938, RGVA, Fond 500, Opis 1, film 906, roll 1. My translation reflects the diction of the original letter.

[40] Ramme, *Sicherheitsdienst*, Schema 1: Struktur des Sicherheitshauptamts der SS nach dem Stand vom Januar 1937; Browder, *Enforcers*, Appendix B 5 "Organization of the SD Main Office 1936–1937," 255–258.

mentioned in the literature but seemingly important in the development of the office and in the minds of the SD's intelligence practitioners, surfaced. Contemporaneous as well as postwar documents suggest that Main Department III 3 was, indeed, the birthplace of the later political foreign intelligence service.[41]

A number of orders from June and July 1938, many of which originated from Schellenberg's desk at a time when he was also doing Heydrich's bidding in the conflict with Werner Best and attempting to define the role and mandate of the SD, allow for a window into the development of Office III and the role Main Department III 3 was to play in it. Office III was now divided into three Main Departments: III 1 *Fremdländische Lebensgebiete*, Foreign Living Spheres; III 2 *Abwehr*, Defense; and III 3 *Politischer Nachrichtendienst im Ausland*, Political Intelligence Service Abroad. Main Department III 1 "has the task," an order went, "to investigate the entire foreign living sphere," which was defined as "not simply survey[ing] German foreign policy in its relationships." Rather, III 1 was to "penetrate the different countries in their geographical, economic, and other structures and to investigate the problems occurring in these countries and to summarize them [the problems] under the set perspective of an overarching, general-staff-like [*generalstabsmässig*] surveillance, [and] to report about the complete living sphere situation in each country under consideration." To achieve this, the Main Department was divided into East and West and below this into country or regional desks.[42] In effect, III 1 was the equivalent of the domestic SD intelligence service, which was geared toward a total observation of all domestic living spheres. III 1 was to do so abroad. The task of Main Department III 2 was equally ambitious, "to take care of the entire interior living sphere in defensive/counerintelligence terms (including sabotage [against Germany]), which means supporting the appointed offices in the battle against enemy intelligence services." This was largely in sync with earlier definitions of its role, even harking back to language used in prior agreements with the Gestapo and the Abwehr. In addition, III 2 was to "conduct systematic

---

[41] Sicherheitsdienst des RFSS-SD Hauptamt, Neuer Plan mit Wirkung vom 20. April 1938, RGVA, Fond 500, Opis 1, film 907, roll 1. Most authors mention only two Main Department in 1937 and 1938, but some documents in their appendices indicate the existence of three; Browder, *Enforcers*, Appendix B 5 "Organization of the SD Main Office 1936–1937," 255–258; Ramme, *Sicherheitsdienst*, 57; Schema 1: Struktur des Sicherheitshauptamts der SS nach dem Stand vom Januar 1937. Situation Report No. 10. Verfügung, Stabskanzlei I 11, Sche/Ld, April 4, 1939, USHMM 14.016 M, 826.

[42] Befehl für den SD, Nr. 36/38, Neugliederung Sachgebiete III, Leiter Zentralabteilung I 1 a.A. Schellenberg, June 18, 1938; Anlage "Organisationsplan des Sachgebietes III im SD (June 1, 1938)," June 18, 1938, RGVA, Fond 500, Opis 1, film 907, roll 3 [hereafter: Neugliederung Sachgebiete III.] The translations, meant to capture the convoluted nature of the German original, are mine.

checks of all foreigners present in Germany," traditionally a policing task. But even more far-reaching was III 2's last task: "the SD-type [*SD-mäßige*] surveillance of all other domestic defense organizations."[43] Here, the SD leadership showed its cards. Instead of working in support of state organizations, it attempted to nudge III 2 into a position that included oversight of Gestapo and Abwehr.

III 1 and III 2 were expanding their projected roles, but III 3 was the Trojan horse. It had "the task to build and maintain a political foreign intelligence service and to facilitate – through the central collection of information and its distribution to the relevant departments [*Sachabteilungen*] of the entire SD – its factual evaluation and processing [*Sachauswertung und Bearbeitung*]. In addition, III 3 is tasked to function as the relay station [*Vermittlungsstelle*] for orders [*Aufträge*] and tasks to all SD offices [*Dienststellen*] that can only be fulfilled and solved by the political foreign intelligence service [operating] abroad, meaning not domestically."[44] Main Department III 3 had three subdivisions. III 31, "Organization," consisted of four sections: one dealing with the overall organization of the intelligence service, domestically and abroad; one concerned with collaboration with other German intelligence services (state, military, economy); one dealing with non-SD personnel working for the SD; and one focused on training. Main Department III 32, "Distribution and Issuance of Orders," was divided into geographical target regions, and III 33 concerned itself with the technical matters of the political foreign intelligence service. Thus, a catch-all Main Department had been created; it was a potential ram in the SD's attempts to wrestle more and more authority from other state and military organizations involved in intelligence work abroad. In addition, it was to evaluate the materials, thereby making it an entity of central import for policy-making.

III 3 was clearly meant to be the nucleus of an altogether new intelligence service, even if it had to be built up by shifting SD members from other departments, as there was not money for additional hires. In July 1938, the branches of the SD, the leaders of the SD Superior Districts, and the Gestapo were ordered to transfer all their existing and developing informer nets to Main Department III 3. From here on out, the order emphasized, political intelligence activities abroad had to be approved by III 3.[45] With the creation of Main Department III and these orders the SD staked a forceful claim in foreign intelligence, taking a total approach

---

[43] Neugliederung Sachgebiete III.   [44] Neugliederung Sachgebiete III.
[45] Befehl, CdS, Ergänzung, July 8, 1938, RGVA, Fond 500, Opis 1, film 907, roll 3. See also: Befehl für den SD, 37/38, gez. Schellenberg, June 18, 1938, RGVA, Fond 500, Opis 1, film 907, roll 3.

that rested on the SD's pedigree as an ideologically firm party organization. It would do a better job, the implicit argument went, because its men were the better servants of the Nazi state and more clearly in tune with its demands and approaches. These new structures were soon overtaken by the political developments – and eventually by the creation of the RSHA with Office VI as the political foreign intelligence service – but the gauntlet had been thrown.

In the meantime, as Hitler escalated the crisis over the Sudeten Territories, a "Special Department ČSR" – III 225 – was created in Jost's Office III. Yet again, Schellenberg drafted the decree for Heydrich but its creation made a bad situation worse. The special department was to register and to evaluate centrally, based on "ideological, living-sphere-related and countermeasure-related" viewpoints, all incoming information for the purpose of the SD, and to prepare the annexation. The Superior Districts, for their part, were to collect and to sort information and keep it accessible. No other SD departments were to concern themselves with the ČSR, but if there existed connections into the country – or possibilities of such – in these, they were to be reported to Main Department III 3, the newly minted, broadly conceived intelligence service.[46] All of this created havoc within an already less than stellar system. Files were redistributed for the benefit of the Special Department while, once vetted, particularly valuable informers were to be transferred to the Main Department.[47] This created two separate informer networks: one at the regional and one at the central level. To make matters worse, a *Blockstelle*, a temporary intelligence collection point, existed in Hof near the German–Czech border. In charge was Hans Daufeldt who also served as Henlein's SS adjutant, even though Heinlein mistrusted him "utterly."[48] The attempts to ready the SD for a starring role in looming foreign adventures threw a poorly conceived intelligence effort into even greater turmoil.

The Special Department, scrambling to gain traction while the crisis over the Sudeten German territories was already under way, went into overdrive. There were attempts to demarcate clearly the extent of Special Department's authority. In a letter to Göring, drafted by Schellenberg, Heydrich took issue with an ill-conceived "leaflet-action" conducted under the auspices of the Wehrmacht, which did more harm than

---

[46] I 113 to Führer SD-OA und Zentralabteilung, Sonderabteilung Tschecho-Slowakei, August 4, 1938, gez. Schellenberg, RGVA, Fond 500, Opis 1, film 907, roll 3; Vortragsthemen 26. Januar 1939.

[47] RGVA, Fond 500, Opis 1, film 906, roll 1–6.

[48] Florian Altenhöner, *Der Mann, der den Zweiten Weltkrieg began. Alfred Naujocks: Fälscher, Mörder, Terrorist* (Münster: Prospero-Verlag, 2010), 87.

good in the Sudeten German territories and to their inhabitants, as it led to arrests and economic hardship for the population.[49] The army's attempt to bring Sudeten Germans across the border to create special "SA-Formations" for the territories did not find the support of the SD either. While it is safe to assume that the SD was not keen on having "SA-Formations" resurrected, Office III focused its criticism on the exodus of the best men and the consequential weakening of "Germandom" in the territories.[50] The need to build up a new department quickly did nothing to mute existing rivalries but exacerbated them, as new responsibilities became an incentive to focus on a rival's shortcomings and to gather evidence for future use.

Yet the Special Department also realized how poorly positioned it was. In June 1938 it began to search high and low for SD members with Czech-language capabilities. Lists of Czech speakers of various proficiency levels were compiled, but the Special Department also inquired where one could learn Czech and how long it would take to become proficient. The answer – seven semesters of regular or four semesters of intensive study – must have been frustrating, as knowledge was needed immediately. Soon, the Special Department began to feel the heat of unmet expectations: for Heydrich, things were not moving quickly enough.[51]

In the end, the Special Department served as a think-tank preparing the annexation. Based on reports compiled at lower SD levels, III 225 created general memoranda on the ČSR and planned the activities of the Einsatzgruppen. It created lists of targets – objects and people – as well as mobilization plans and indices. Reviewing its efforts after the fact, the Special Department was particularly proud of its indices' user-friendliness, which allowed the Einsatzgruppen to add and remove sections easily. Maps and sometime blueprints, marking the location of important installations and individual offices, augmented the object lists.[52] Exhaustive lists of individuals included "elements hostile to the

---

[49] III 225/3 to Göring, Flugblatt-Aktion der Wehrmacht am 14. und 15.5.38, June 10, 1938, RGVA, Fond 500, Opis 1, film 939, roll 2.

[50] III 22 to III 2, Maßnahmen der dt. Wehrmacht in der ČSR, June 27, 1938, RGVA, Fond 500, Opis 1, film 939, roll 4.

[51] RGVA, Fond 500, Opis 1, film 939, roll 5–6.

[52] Vortragsthemen 26. Januar 1939. One of the memoranda mentioned dealt with the political administration of the country, including the police, and contained a cartographical addendum and was distributed to governmental institutions. A second memorandum suggested the future structural outlines for the security police in ČSR territories. Purportedly divided into two parts, one focused on the history of security institutions in this area, while the second part gave concrete suggestions that took into account "economic structures, transportation issues, tourism, enemies of the state, geographical contexts, and, above all, population policy basics." The memorandum described the new order down to the town level. Augmented by two volumes of images and maps, it was an

[Nazi German] state" – people who were to be arrested, to be expelled from their current positions, or to be put under special surveillance – as well as information on "reliable groups of people."[53] For the former, the informers frequently provided detailed biographical information and political evaluations; they also reported on the whereabouts of Jews, taking note if they had displayed enmity toward Germany.[54] The informers knew what type of knowledge the SD desired and shared the sentiment. Information about "immediate measures," such as "occupation of the state police office in A., the closure of the lodge in B., the closure of the Social Democratic club house in C. [. . .]," road maps and a "schematic depiction of the entire deployment" rounded out the offerings.[55] As the extent and nature of the activities in the ČSR kept changing due to political circumstances, the Special Department adjusted its plans several times and prepared for contingencies, ranging from the annexation of the Sudeten German territories to an occupation of the entire country.[56] And nobody expected the engagement in the ČSR to be easy or unopposed: the SD mobilization plan called for reliance on personnel with military training. They would be operating in a "war zone" after all.[57] Little was left to chance.

The Special Department was also involved with the staging of the Einsatzgruppen deployment and tried to carve out additional responsibilities for the SD. The Special Department created assembly and training points in the Reich, from where the Einsatzgruppen, on the heels of the military, were to converge on the territory to secure "political life" and the economic facilities. The different operational areas foreshadowed, rather efficiently, the envisioned postannexation administrative set-up. The Einsatzgruppen were to become the permanent policing and security organization in their areas, but staffing remained a concern. SD personnel as well as volunteers were to take on prominent positions but one also needed to make sure not to strip the SD offices in the Reich of their most qualified personnel. The Einsatzgruppen ranks were thus to be augmented by Sudeten German fellow travelers. Forewarned of the operation's commencement, these men were also expected to protect important facilities until the arrival of the Einsatzgruppen.[58] In the

internal document. See also: "III 225 Mob.-Vorbereitungen," RGVA, Fond 500, Opis 1, film 939, roll 6; film 939, roll 5–7.

[53] Vortragsthemen 26. Januar 1939.

[54] RGVA, Fond 500, Opis 1, film 876, roll 2.   [55] Vortragsthemen 26. Januar 1939.

[56] RGVA, Fond 500, Opis 1, film 939, roll 6; Vortragsthemen 26. Januar 1939.

[57] "M-Plan ČSR," no date, RGVA, Fond 500, Opis 1, film 939, roll 6.

[58] Vortragsthemen 26. Januar 1939; "M-Plan ČSR," no date, RGVA, Fond 500, Opis 1, film 939, roll 6.

planning process, the issue of executive power, a bone of contention between Gestapo and SD in the Reich, loomed large. Officially, it remained the sole prerogative of the Gestapo, but the SD planners capitalized on the opportunities the situation presented: SD personnel received the right to take executive measures if needed, especially at the beginning of the deployment and in emergency situations. "Comradely collaboration" was the order of the day.[59] Yet it was the SD that benefited most, as it would extend its responsibilities beyond its by now traditional norms.

Over the course of 1938 – with its two annexations – the SD's foreign department came into its own and found, at a time when Himmler's interest in foreign policy was growing, an officially sanctioned function in Germany's expansionist policies. Commenting on the domestic activities of the SD, Browder states that it monitored German society and attempted to shape it. The activities of the Special Department ČSR illustrate that the SD's foreign department fulfilled this dual role as well: it did not simply report on political developments abroad but also attempted to shape Germany's activities there.[60] The activities of the SD's foreign department toward the annexation of the Sudeten Territories also allowed other entities to recognize it as a foreign intelligence entity capable of fulfilling its ambitions. Former SD personnel recalled after the war that Heydrich ordered the establishment of a proper SD foreign intelligence service during the Anschluß and that "from the preparatory work in the Sudeten German territories and in Austria a well-informed political and economic intelligence service developed."[61] In 1938, a year of change and radicalization – from the domestic to the foreign policy developments to the increasingly concerted actions against Jews that culminated in the November Pogrom – both Schellenberg, as Heydrich's legal expert with a strong interest in intelligence matters, and the SD, as a foreign intelligence service, came of age.

The establishment of the Reich Security Main Office in September 1939 destroyed the embryonic political foreign intelligence service, and the new Office VI had to be fashioned from its former incarnation's lesser pieces. Main Department III 2, the best-established department of the office, was transferred to the Gestapo. The new political foreign intelligence service was made up of Main Departments III 1 and III 3, with the latter, headed by Albert Filbert, oftentimes regarded as the birthplace

[59] "Von III 225 getroffene Vorbereitungen für den Einsatz des SD in der ČSR," no date, RGVA, Fond 500, Opis 1, film 939, roll 7.
[60] Browder, *Enforcers*, 118. See also Zimmermann, *Sudetendeutschen*, 59–60; Smelser, *Sudeten Problem*, 180–189.
[61] Allgemeine Entwicklung.

of Office VI as an "offensive and not a defensive service."[62] Jost certainly
had his work cut out for him when he returned to Berlin in the fall of
1939; indeed, David Kahn has pronounced it "heartbreakingly difficult
even in peace: creating an espionage organization to spy in belligerent
countries."[63] Office VI was reorganized into groups along geographical
lines and also included two technical groups. Each group, in turn, was
divided into *Referate*, sections, referred to by Arabic numerals and led
by a *Referent*, specialist, commonly assisted by two *Sachbearbeiter*, clerks.
One dealt with the collection of intelligence and the other with its evaluation. Additional office personnel was assigned to the groups as well
and the groups occasionally also included specialized area desks. The reestablishment of the political foreign intelligence service as Office VI did
not bring about a sharpening or clarification of its mandate; a postwar
report stated blithely, "Jost was given his general instructions without any
clearly defined policy."[64] Trying to find a model for conducting political
foreign intelligence remained difficult. Visions of the British Secret Service notwithstanding, the only actual blueprint available for the foreign
intelligence service was the domestic section of the SD.[65] The transfer
of some members of the former domestic intelligence service – most
notably Helmut Knochen and Herbert Hagen – to Office VI likely fostered this overall reliance on internal models of intelligence collections
and evaluation.

A more concrete definition of the office's mandate can be found in a
speech drafted internally for Heydrich in early 1940. It illuminated Office
VI's mandate on two different, yet interconnected levels: it depicted what
SD members believed their mandate and tasks to be and described what
they actually did. The office's task was basically twofold. On the one
hand, Office VI was to create and maintain a political and economic
intelligence service. On the other hand, it was to serve as a centralized collection agency for all information gathered abroad, systematically

---

[62] Stabskanzlei I 11/ Sche/Ld, Vermerk, April 4, 1939, USHMM, 14.016 M, 826; Die
Zusammenfassung der zentralen Ämter der Sicherheitspolizei und des SD, September
27, 1939, USHMM 14.016 M, 240; Situation Report No. 10. On Filbert: Wildt,
Generation, 195–197.
[63] Kahn, *Spies*, 253.   [64] Situation Report No. 10.
[65] Paul comments on the declining importance of the domestic SD vis-à-vis the Gestapo
after the establishment of the RSHA. However, during the 1930s the domestic intelligence service had been the more successful element of the SD and thus provided the
SD's foreign intelligence section a blueprint. Gerhard Paul, "'Kämpfende Verwaltung':
Das Amt IV des Reichssicherheitshauptamtes als Führungsinstanz der Gestapo,"in Gerhard Paul and Klaus-Michael Mallmann, eds., *Die Gestapo im Zweiten Weltkrieg: 'Heimatfront' und besetztes Europa* (Darmstadt: Wissenschaftliche Buchgesellschaft, Primus Verlag, 2000), 42–48.

analyzing and evaluating it. Consequently, the office would be able to recognize and address "any problem in any country at any time."[66] Its claim was unlimited. Yet what exactly political intelligence was – information on the politics and policies of a given country or reports on moods and attitudes among the population or something entirely different – or how the office was to go about its task was not addressed.

The activity report for 1940 by the section dealing with Switzerland, describing its task as equivalent to Office VI as a whole, clarified this somewhat.[67] The report divided the office's tasks into three areas: political tasks; tasks related to the intelligence service; and "[c]reation of a net of politically and economically influential Swiss citizens in order to influences Swiss politics." On the political side, the section provided general situation reports and kept abreast of important developments in the country, from the economy to the political parties. In addition, it observed the country's economic life as well as cultural or international institutions that could serve as conduits for foreign propaganda. The section was also interested in the country's foreign relations, especially with France and Great Britain. In addition, the section focused on the recruitment of new informers; the observation of activities by the British and the French intelligence services; the investigation of people working for foreign intelligence services; the methods of foreign intelligence services; and any possibilities to extend its own reach beyond Switzerland. It also tried to create a network of politically and economically important Swiss citizens with the goal of influencing Swiss politics.[68] This was a broad mandate, and some of the work Office VI took on was of the type that was customarily performed by embassy and consulate personnel. Other parts fell more in line with traditional intelligence service work. But either way: Office VI believed to be able to do it all and do it better than anyone else.

Office VI also engaged in clandestine activities abroad: the destabilization of foreign countries and the creation and procurement of "useful and usable" information. As the January 1940 speech put it: "Certain orders

[66] Vortrag, Vorlage C., January 23, 1940, BA-DH, ZR 920/57 [hereafter: Vortrag January 1940.] Compare this to a notation by Filbert, taken in June 1941: "Office VI of the RSHA has the task to create and maintain a political and economic intelligence service abroad; it is its goal to record the complete economic and political structure abroad according to its living spheres and to evaluate it like a general staff (generalstabsmässig) [. . .] In addition, the surveillance of the ideological enemy abroad was conferred to Office VI." VI A Fi/Th, Vermerk, June 12, 1941, BA-DH, ZR 920/59.

[67] Nachrichtendienstliche Arbeit des Referates VI F 3 nach der Schweiz [1940], BA-DH, ZR 920/64.

[68] Nachrichtendienstliche Arbeit des Referates VI F 3 nach der Schweiz [1940], BA-DH, ZR 920/64.

given by the Foreign Minister and the *Führer* were executed so unobjectionably that a situation developed in Slovakia at the desired moment that gave the Reich the right to intervene and solve the issue."[69] After the annexation of the Sudeten German territories, the then-Office III had supplied a steady stream of reports from Bohemia, Moravia, and Slovakia on the alleged plight of the German population in the Czech crown-lands as well as on the overall situation there and in Slovakia.[70] These reports advocated the destruction of the so-called *Rest-Tschechei*, the "Czech-leftover" and the creation of a nominally independent Slovak State, ultimately paving the way for it. The collection of intelligence had an activist agenda as a matter of design: "[i]n coming foreign political decisions as well, the SD has the ambition to be the tool that procures information useful and usable for a successful foreign policy...."[71] This was not useful information in a traditional sense, in that it would be useful for the decision-making process. Rather, it was meant to be "useful and usable" for the execution of a political agenda defined by ideology. Office VI was meant to be more than a broadly conceived intelligence gathering agency or an information clearing house: it was to function clandestinely as an active force in the preparation and execution of pre-existing National Socialist foreign policy goals. Office VI clearly conceptualized its tasks differently from older, less predetermined approaches to foreign intelligence gathering.

Consequently, then, the question becomes: how did Office VI expect to achieve these goals? Who worked for the office? What were the approaches taken? How was this particular foreign intelligence service imagined and ultimately constructed? Like most intelligence services, Office VI, as well as its predecessor, collected much information through open sources. However, individuals were the backbone of the intelligence-gathering efforts. Generally speaking, the SD distinguished between *Beobachter*, observers; *Vertrauensleute* and *Vertrauensmänner*, trusted men; *Zubringer*, feeders or stringers; and *Agenten*, agents.[72] Abroad, the position of a *Hauptbeauftragte*, main representative augmented the cast of characters.[73]

---

[69] Vortrag January 1940, BA-DH, ZR 920/57. Note the similar comment regarding Poland.

[70] For example: RGVA, Fond 500, Opis 1, film 1022, roll 2; RGVA, Fond 500, Opis 1, film 1031, roll 1.

[71] Vortrag, January 1940, BA-DH, ZR 920/57.

[72] Befehl für den SD Nr. 76/36, Nachrichtenerfassung, December 15, 1936, USHMM, 11.001 M.01, Reel 1, 1–16.

[73] Situation Report No. 10; Stellvertreter des Führers, Anordnung, Nr. 201/38, Betr. Die Stellung des Sicherheitsdienstes des Reichsführers SS (SD) in der Partei, December 14, 1938, USHMM, 14.016 M, 243; Leiter II to Leiter Abtlg. II 112, gez. Six, September 16, 1938, Unterscheidung zwischen Zubringern, Agenten, Vertrauenspersonen

Observers and trusted men worked closest with the SD; they were SD members but not professional SD men. Expected to wear uniform, they were trained by the SD/SS and fell under its disciplinary authority. They reported under an assigned number. In fact, all SD members who were not professional SD men were considered observers.[74] Simply by default, this construction created an impressive and wide-ranging network, even if it was based on a totalitarian illusion. Trusted men or *V-men* were defined as "individuals with whom durable trusting relationships exist, without the trusted person being a member..." Sworn to secrecy in writing, V-men were unpaid and worked in voluntary support of the "great cause." They answered to the observer they worked for. Trusted men did not have to possess SS suitability (*"SS-mäßige Eignung"*) but a "pure character and unobjectionable National Socialist convictions" remained mandatory.[75] In short, they had to be good ideologues.

The ideological preconditions for feeders and agents were less stringent, but this mainly denoted the lesser trust put in them and their information. The SD's relationship to feeders was fraught with ambiguity. At times, feeders – neither sworn to secrecy nor part of a trusting relationship – were regarded as individuals who provided observers and trusted men with information on a case-by-case basis.[76] At other times, their role was likened to those of V-men, who were expected to be of good National Socialist character. Most importantly, they were "not agents, who work only for money."[77] Conversely, the SD felt somewhat responsible for their V-men. Agents, on the other hand, inhabited the lowest rung on the SD's totem pole; they were defined as "people who gather information for payment," whose mercenary status and presumed lack of loyalty and ideological conviction made them suspicious. Accordingly, the use of agents had to be approved on a case-by-case basis, and they were not

und Beobachtern, BA-DH, ZR 909/3; Allgemeine Entwicklung. The documents focus on the domestic intelligence service but information about the use of personnel abroad can be extrapolated. I use the appropriate terms if distinctions matter; otherwise, I use "operative" or the even broader designation of "informers." For the domestic application, see Carsten Schreiber, "'Eine verschworene Gemeinschaft': Regionale Verfolgungsnetzwerke in Sachsen," in Michael Wildt, ed., *Nachrichtendienst, Politische Elite und Mordeinheit: Der Sicherheitsdienst des Reichsführers SS* (Hamburg: Hamburger Edition, 2003), 67–72.

74 Befehl für den SD Nr. 76/36,. Nachrichtenerfassung, December 15, 1936, USHMM, 11.001 M.01, Reel 1, 1–16.

75 Leiter II to Leiter Abtlg. II 112, gez. Six, September 16, 1939, Unterscheidung zwischen Zubringern, Agenten, Vertrauenspersonen und Beobachtern, BA-DH, ZR 909/3.

76 Leiter II to Leiter Abtlg. II 112, gez. Six, September 16, 1939, Unterscheidung zwischen Zubringern, Agenten, Vertrauenspersonen und Beobachtern, BA-DH, ZR 909/3.

77 Stellvertreter des Führers, Anordnung, Nr. 201/38, Die Stellung des Sicherheitsdienstes des Reichsführers SS (SD) in der Partei, December 14, 1938, USHMM, 14.016 M, 243.

to be engaged for tasks relating to the country's security. Neither the SD offices nor professional SD men were to engage directly with agents.[78] The focus on the ideological qualifications and the ideologically defined character of observers, trusted men, and feeders goes to the core of the SD's notion of a viable political intelligence service. For an organization steeped in the ideological elite of the Nazi Party, ideological firmness was the key to the perception of its role and mandate. Individuals lacking these preconditions were considered unqualified or, at best, viewed with serious suspicion.

Office VI was an extremely homogenous entity, down to its lowest levels. In Switzerland, for example, almost all of the SD's collaborators were Swiss National Socialists. Leadership as well as courier positions were staffed with German citizens.[79] The same personnel situation prevailed in Sweden and in Finland, or, as indicated above, in the ČSR.[80] Intelligence contacts in the Soviet Union consisted primarily of German officials engaged in government-sponsored contacts with the country and a number of presumably anti-Bolshevik – as well as anti-Semitic – Ukrainians.[81] There is no indication that the homogeneity raised any concerns about the political intelligence service's ability to fulfill its tasks, even though an internal description of the service's development noted the lack of personnel that combined experience abroad with political reliability.[82] However, concerns did not go any further.

Several reports covering the office's activities in 1939 and 1940 provide insights into the realities of intelligence gathering and analysis in Jost's Office VI. Meant to summarize activities and to showcase successes, these reports actually reveal the extent of the office's disarray, its attempts to cover up these failings, and future plans presented with much panache. In early 1940, the overall picture was bleak, although the reports tried to put the best spin on the situation. Country Group VI A, charged with the surveillance of the Baltic States, Russia, and the Far East, stressed that the repatriation of many Baltic Germans in the fall of 1939 – after the Baltic States came within the Soviet sphere of influence according to the secret

---

[78] Leiter II to Leiter Abtlg. II 112, gez. Six, September 16, 1939, Unterscheidung zwischen Zubringern, Agenten, Vertrauenspersonen und Beobachtern, BA-DH, ZR 909/3. In this particular document, agents and feeders are lumped into one category.

[79] Rechenschaftsbericht des Referates VI F 1 für das Jahr 1940, BA-DH, ZR 920/64.

[80] Rechenschaftsbericht über die nachrichtendienstliche Arbeit des Referates VI G 3 für das Jahr 1940, n.d., BA-DH, ZR 920/63.

[81] Rechenschaftsbericht des Referates VI C 1 bis zum 30. November 1940, BA-DH, ZR 920/64. Compare to the Allied observation, "Typical agents are recruited from pro-German and Nationalist party leaders, chiefs of police, and Foreign Office Clerks," R.I.S.16/27.9.43, NA, RG 226, Entry 108 B, Box 286, Folder: RIS Reports.

[82] Allgemeine Entwicklung.

amendment of the Molotov–Ribbentrop agreement of August 23, 1939 – had severely damaged the capabilities of the foreign intelligence service in that part of Europe. Virtually all trusted men had been among the ethnic Germans repatriated to Germany. Contacts with pro-German and anti-Bolshevik Latvian, Estonian, and Lithuanian opposition groups allegedly helped to remedy this situation. The Country Group also claimed to receive secret statements by Stalin and Molotov from these groups.[83]

The Soviet Union, regarded as difficult to penetrate by foreign intelligence services, remained virtually closed to Office VI. Most information about the Soviet Union was gathered by way of neighboring states; at this point, Poland – that is, German-occupied Poland – served as a base for "constant forays" into the Soviet Union. "Single representatives," the document claimed, were crossing regularly into the Western Soviet Union, reporting on the situation and moods and attitudes there. Yet, most of the information about the Soviet Union, "a vivid picture of a different world," was gathered differently, as some 80 SD men had augmented the staff of the VoMi, the *Volksdeutsche Mittelstelle*, during the repatriation of ethnic Germans from Wolhynia and Galicia; they gathered information for Office VI. Similarly, the Country Group was trying to integrate their men into commissions, agencies, or companies dealing with the Soviet Union. In addition, a special representative in Helsinki provided information about the "Russian–Finnish War" and the Red Army in general.[84] In effect, Office VI was on a broadly conceived fishing expedition.

The situation that presented itself to Country Group VI B – Danube Region, Balkans, and the so-called Near Eastern State Bloc – was slightly better, or so the report maintained. The group was particularly active in Southeastern Europe, an area in which the British Intelligence Service was active and which was also central to Germany's supply of raw materials. The group claimed to have good contacts, if not always trustworthy ones, in Slovakia and Hungary, two countries allied with Germany but bemoaned the lack thereof in Romania, Yugoslavia, and Turkey. The political foreign intelligence service was supposed to identify "unobjectionably" the members of enemy intelligence services tasks in these countries and to neutralize them. However, at the time of the report, the German intelligence net was restricted to "unobjectionable" surveillance and reporting about developments in the region. As was the case elsewhere, the net of informers consisted of ethnic Germans, or Reich Germans working for local employers; in addition, the group had members

---

[83] Vortrag January 1940.   [84] Vortrag January 1940.

embedded in German companies and maintained special representatives "supposed to be supporting the Foreign Office in its tasks."[85]

The efforts of Country Group VI C, working on the countries of "Roman mentality and language," a large swath of the territory stretching from Italy, Spain, Portugal to South and Central America, had been hurt by the beginning of the war. Contacts with South America had been severed and the Country Group was working on their reestablishment. Allegedly, it was still receiving constant information about South America from members of those countries' diplomatic missions in Germany, allowing for "unobjectionable" insights into the political situation there. Plans for future activities, such as sabotage missions, had been hatched and were ready to be implemented.[86] Foreign intelligence efforts against Italy were allegedly prohibited, but Office VI used Italy as a base for work against other countries. Information from the Western Hemisphere was routed, for example, through Italy. In addition, the Country Group focused on the activities of the British Intelligence Service in Italy. The situation was allegedly favorable in Spain. Taking advantage of the good contacts made during the Spanish Civil War, the Country Group gathered information about the Spain and its relationship with France and Great Britain. In Portugal, similar plans were underway. Spain allegedly also served as a base for activities in France and French Morocco, such as the establishment of an informer network in France, the sabotage of enemy objects, and the "neutralization," murder, of enemy agents. In French Morocco the objective was to make contact with the Arab national movement.[87]

Western Europe – Holland, Belgium, Luxembourg, still neutral at the time of reporting, and Switzerland – fell under Country Group VI D; France, at war with Germany since September 1939, was this group's responsibility as well. Not only since the kidnappings at Venlo was VI D acutely aware that many of the French and British Intelligence Services' activities originated in the Low Countries and Switzerland; conversely, though, these countries were also bases for German intelligence efforts. But in Belgium and Holland only a small percentage of the population was willing to work for Nazi Germany and many ideological fellow travelers with whom the office was in contact were too exposed to be of any value. Consequently, Office VI knew a lot about developments in these pro-Nazi movements and believed it could influence these groups for the benefit of the Reich. For intelligence gathering beyond the narrow confines of these movements, these organizations were quite

[85] Vortrag January 1940.   [86] Vortrag January 1940.   [87] Vortrag January 1940.

useless, though.[88] The same situation applied to Switzerland. In the neutral countries, Office VI focused its attention on enemy intelligence services active there, especially on the British service and Office VI held an advantage: information gathered could be checked against the knowledge gained from the two agents abducted at Venlo. VI D was purportedly also informed about developments in French government circles and about the domestic situation in France in general and claimed good contacts within the Dutch Foreign Ministry and with government circles in Belgium, Luxembourg, and Switzerland. Who provided the office with this information remains a mystery, though.[89]

Country Group VI E dealt with Scandinavia, the British Empire, and the United States. It focused much of its attention on Scandinavia and on the war between the Soviet Union and Finland. What was true in Western and Southern Europe also held true in Northern Europe: capital cities became centers of interest for all foreign intelligence services. VI E had allegedly established "main trusted men" in the three Northern capitals to run nets of informers and to keep in contact with the Country Group. Their work was regarded as successful: contact had been made with the Swedish king himself, or so the report claimed, and with Finnish military headquarters. Therefore, the Country Group deemed itself well informed about the Soviet–Finnish War and successful Finnish propaganda against the Red Army. From Copenhagen, the country group was attempting to establish contact with Russian nationalist groups all across Europe. In addition, a nationwide intelligence network of Danish National Socialists had been created, which one expected to use for Germany's purposes in the future. The Country Group also claimed to be in contact with "pro-German" Danish officers' circles. In Sweden, on the other hand, contact had been made with a new press agency, which was to expand into other countries and serve as a cover for the intelligence service and its clandestine transmitters. Activities in Scandinavia were described as both successful and extremely promising.

VI E was also in charge of Ireland, the United States, and Great Britain; the former was seen as an opportunity while the latter two represented a myriad of problems. Ireland and the Irish people were seen as of great promise for Germany and the Country Group believed to have found a champion of Nazi Germany in the former Irish ambassador to Berlin, Charles Bewley. Living in Italy, he was using his good contacts in diplomatic circles for Germany's benefit.[90] Bewley apparently also

---

[88] Vortrag January 1940.   [89] Vortrag January 1940.
[90] Vortrag January 1940; Mark M. Hull, *Irish Secrets: German Espionage in Ireland, 1939–1945* (Dublin: Irish Academic Press, 2003), 190–191.

assisted the Country Group in selecting suitable members of the Irish Republican Army to mobilize the Irish against the British. The Country Group also believed that with sufficient funds, the Irish population in the United States was destined to become a key element in Germany's intelligence gathering and overall political efforts.[91] The United States and Great Britain, on the other hand, presented the Country Group with problems. The transmission of information from the United States was difficult, in particular, as the British kept a close tap on postal communications. Accordingly, the Country Group wanted to establish wireless communications and had trained some out of the "significant number of American [radio] engineers living in this country" for this purpose. One man had already left for his overseas mission. Until then, information about the United States was mainly acquired through connections inside the US Embassy in Berlin. At the suggestion of the Country Group, a *Rückwanderer*, German-American returnee, had gained employment there. He now provided the country group with "all embassy material" on a daily basis.[92] Great Britain remained largely closed to the country group as well. An Irishman who had been sent to scout out places for radio transmitters had not yet returned and the plan to bring "suitcase transmitters" to suitable V-men had not moved beyond the initial stage yet. For the time being, the country group relied on the debriefing of neutral foreigners.[93] And while there were ambitious plans to use Danish and Swedish Communist and Social Democratic circles to make contact with similarly minded circles in England, the Country Group gave no indication how this feat was to be accomplished, especially in light of Office VI's ideologically handicapped networks.

The same problems that plagued the various Country Groups – the stark dichotomy between a dire reality and grand plans for the future obfuscated by detailed descriptions that made and still make it hard to distinguish between plans and realities – defined Country Group VI F, at that point in charge of the "Investigation of Ideological Enemies Abroad." It was to monitor the activities and methods of enemy ideologies and gather all information needed to defend Nazi Germany against them. Envisioned as a Special Intelligence Service, the group was to focus on the links between the remnants of enemy ideologies still active in Nazi Germany, the middlemen abroad, and the presumed headquarters of these enemy ideologies. Ultimately, the group was to gather constant and reliable information from the imagined headquarters and to create a

---

[91] Vortrag January 1940.
[92] Vortrag January 1940. I reckon that the engineers were *Rückwanderer*, returnees, as well.
[93] Vortrag January 1940.

"defensive apparatus." This apparatus would then be able to attack the enemy on "political, scholarly, and propagandistic grounds." Eventually, the group was expected to be able to destroy the ideological enemy abroad as the ideological enemy had been destroyed domestically. In addition, and using a purely ideological viewpoint, the group was to investigate politically various countries. Due to the nature of the task, the members of this group had to be especially qualified: they had to know the enemy, his tactics and methods, and had to be capable of counteracting him.[94] Among many difficult and broadly defined tasks, VI F had the most difficult and broadest but it proudly broadcast its triumphs. One of the alleged headquarters of the "world Masonic movement" had been penetrated and important material had been acquired; information about the plans of international Jewry was gained through Jewish agents and much was known about conflicts among Jewish organizations, especially regarding Palestine. The group claimed to have scuttled the alleged joint policies of the British Empire and the Jews. Similarly, the group had purportedly gained information about Jesuits. But not all was well: other movements needed to be covered better and the group wanted to make better use of emigrants, especially in light of the role emigrants had played in the ruse that led to the kidnapping of Best and Stevens.[95] The report concluded with some comments about the section "Colonies." Liaising with other government agencies dealing with the colonial question, the group monitored developments in the former German colonies and prepared for the creation of a colonial Security Police. Plans for Togo and Cameroon were already complete.[96]

The detailed listing of real and imagined activities was clearly an attempt to present Office VI in the best possible light but could not mask its shortcomings. By early 1940, prewar informer nets consisting of ethnic Germans were in shambles, as, for example, in the Baltic States, while in other countries, such as Holland and Belgium, Germany's ideological fellow travelers were too exposed to be of any use. The tribal and ideological selection of collaborators was already approaching its limits, unless one wanted to know about developments among ethnic German groups or in pro-Nazi movements abroad. Other countries, such as those in the Americas or the British Empire or the Soviet Union, were all but completely outside the office's reach. On the other hand, existing

---

[94] Vortrag January 1940. Later Ideological Enemies Abroad fell under VI H.
[95] Vortrag January 1940. Taking into account the role the group – and its leader Knochen – had played in the kidnapping of the two British Intelligence officers, it is surprising that the abductions at Venlo were not covered in detail. By early 1940, Schellenberg and the Gestapo had seemingly taken possession of "Venlo."
[96] Vortrag January 1940.

contacts appear to have been trumped up much beyond their actual viability, as, for example, in the Baltic States, the Balkans, or in Spain. The lack of precision when it came to information gained from much-trumpeted sources speaks volumes about their quality. Office VI attempted to mitigate these shortcomings by focusing on future plans, yet these frequently lacked any connection to reality, such as when VI E assumed that it would be able to rely on two million ethnic Irish living in the United States. Clearly meant to portray Office VI in the best possible light, the report did little to inspire confidence.

The 1939 and 1940 annual reports of the individual Country Groups indicate that the realities on the ground were even worse. Most of the activities touted in the talk prepared for Heydrich were barely more than broadly conceived initiatives or visions for the future. In Italy, only a few contact addresses and courier routes existed. The supposedly excellent foreign intelligence situation in Spain consisted of an SD Representative residing in Madrid, where he worked under the cover of a translator for the German postal system. He headed a net of thirteen V-men who provided reports on Spanish "living spheres." The situation in South America was vastly exaggerated; VI C had one V-man in one South American embassy.[97] Country Group VI D, Western Europe, did not fare much better, but, according to its report, it was not to blame. Rather, its work was impeded by the "basic liberalistic, anti-National-Socialist, simply 'westernized' attitude" of the population in its target countries.[98] In other words, the Country Group fared poorly due to a lack of indigenous Nazis; it had to rely on foreigners. However, good contacts in Paris allowed for the group to compile reports on the domestic situation – "living spheres" – in France. The Country Group used its limited intelligence connections for economic pursuits as well.[99] Unsuccessful in the gathering of intelligence and its analysis, it helped to secure raw materials.

The situation did not change for the better over the next few months, as activity reports from late 1940 and early 1941 show. Incidentally, these are even more candid than their forerunners, displaying the shortcoming of Office VI to a surprising extent. The office's progress in its work against the Soviet Union, for example, remained abysmal. There were

---

[97] Bisherige Tätigkeit und Aufgaben der Gruppe VI C, January 22, 1940, BA-DH, ZR 920/57.

[98] Ländergruppe West, January 22, 1940, BA-DH, ZR 920/ 57. Without ever addressing it, the report indicates the shortcomings of foreign intelligence efforts based on racial and ideological coherence.

[99] Ländergruppe West, January 22, 1940, BA-DH, ZR 920/57. It proudly reported that in the last few days alone, Office VI had been able to forward offers for "35,000 tons of ore, 70,000 faucets of pure brass and several hundred thousand pairs of military boots."

no contacts inside the country; Soviet border fortifications resembled "a Chinese Wall;" illegal traffic across the border did not happen; and the SD men engaged in the repatriation of ethnic Germans had done exactly that. Only one informer network, which SD members working for VoMi had established in the Bukovina, remained active. The group also used members of German industry to gather information, but their knowledge remained restricted to the industrial centers for which they received visas. And a V-man in Moscow, who presumably worked in the German Embassy, had been drafted for military service for a few months. But then, it did not make a difference at all, for the creation and maintenance of an intelligence network in the Soviet Union was deemed impossible. Ultimately, the group was best informed about the mood and opinions of Soviet representatives posted in Germany. By its own exasperated admission, intelligence gathering in the Soviet Union was simply impossible.[100]

The situation was almost as bad in the United States where Office VI's attempts to create an intelligence network were still in its early stages and never made it much beyond. Most information was gained through open sources and returnees – German-Americans returning to Germany – provided additional information. The few contacts that existed in the United States, mostly with journalists, petered out with the beginning of the European war. The reasons for this exemplify the amateurish nature of the SD's approaches: information was transmitted via regular mail and no contingency plans existed. However, since the journalists' reports had been poor in the first place – they were mostly copies of stories the journalists had filed with their papers beforehand and arrived irregularly in Germany – none of this was a great loss. But failure to establish intelligence-gathering networks in the United States before the beginning of the war came back to haunt the organization, as it was too late now. The United States, with British help, also began to mount an active defense against German attempts to create a viable foreign intelligence service in the country, focusing its attention on foreign ethnicities living in the United States, for one assumed that these groups could serve as an important entry point for propaganda and foreign intelligence efforts.[101] In the case of Office VI, the fears of US officials proved largely accurate. The US authorities' exhaustive counterintelligence and counterespionage measures effectively countered the approaches of the

---

[100] Rechenschaftsbericht des Referates VI C 1 bis zum 30. November 1940, BA-DH, ZR 920/64. Only in the Far East was the situation worse: Rechenschaftsbericht des Referates VI C 3 bis zum 30. November 1940, BA-DH, ZR 920/64.

[101] Rechenschaftsbericht über die nachrichtendienstliche Arbeit des Referates VI G 2 für das Jahr 1940, BA-DH, ZR 920/57.

SD with their reliance on ethnic Germans, ideological fellow travelers, German companies operating abroad, and financial means already in the country. The sheer distance between the two countries accomplished the rest.

The section in charge of the United States tried to offset this disadvantage by focusing its attention on US representatives outside the country and by entertaining plans for a future network in the country – despite the correct assessment that current problems would become more insurmountable in the future. One plan was to deploy operatives capable of establishing a circuitous wireless connection to Germany and once war broke out between the two countries, sabotage was to commence magically; until then, it remained prohibited.[102] There is no indication how the section was to accomplish this. But there was also little indication that Office VI appreciated mundane details over exciting plans. And as not to present too bleak a picture, the report claimed that the section had managed to deepen its political connections in the United States; allegedly, two unnamed operatives were to unite opponents of President Roosevelt, such as

The Senators Watson, Lodge, Robert Reynolds, additionally Chas. G. Davis, Wintrop [sic] Aldrich, the president of the Board of Directors of the Chase National Bank, John D. Rockefeller jr., Mr. Goodhue, president of the Board of Directors of the Import- and Export Bank, all directors of the First National Bank, Nicolaus [sic] Murray Butler, President of the Columbia University, John Cudahay [sic], former ambassador to Belgium, Joe Kennedy, former ambassador to Great Britain, Thomas Lemont [sic], from the Finance Trust Morgan, Henry Ford, General Robert E. Wood, Cordell Hull, Foreign Minister of the United States, Henry Wallace, the new Vice President of the United States, and William Knudson, the head of the Defense Council.[103]

This list was little more than a slightly misspelled "Who's Who" of official Washington and New York, representing the office's wishful thinking. It included some well-known and sometimes outspoken critics of President Roosevelt, both Democrats and Republicans, such as Joe Kennedy, or the North Carolina Democrat with pro-Fascist leanings, Robert R. Reynolds, or the Republican Senator Henry Cabot Lodge Jr., who, incidentally, served with distinction at the African front during World War II. Conspicuously missing was Charles Lindbergh, who perhaps did not occupy an official enough position, but it included men who were part of Roosevelt's administration, such as Cordell Hull and Henry Wallace.

---

[102] Rechenschaftsbericht über die nachrichtendienstliche Arbeit des Referates VI G 2 für das Jahr 1940, BA-DH, ZR 920/57.
[103] Rechenschaftsbericht über die nachrichtendienstliche Arbeit des Referates VI G 2 für das Jahr 1940, BA-DH, ZR 920/57.

This list, then, mostly reflected Nazi ideology that constructed a difference in opinion with the "leader" as an at least potentially treasonous act. And, ultimately, this section's name-dropping primarily indicates the group's failure at the nuts and bolts: the creation and maintenance of an extensive intelligence network providing reliable information about the country. Yet undeterred by any doubts, the section reported early successes in influencing the media as well as semiofficial and private organizations, opining that it would soon be able to influence public opinion in much the same way the British did. Convinced that the United States presented a society without any "real ideals and higher goals," in which politics was "first and foremost a business transaction," those involved in this approach – from the V-man to the specialist all the way up to Heydrich and Himmler – believed in its eventual success.

The situation was less abysmal in countries and regions closer to Germany, for example, Switzerland and Scandinavia. With the beginning of the war, it became clear that Switzerland would yet again become the main playing field for all intelligence services, as it had been during the Great War. In addition, "as one of the few neutral states," Switzerland was to become the center of the world economy.[104] But even there problems abounded: the section's existing contacts were ill-prepared to address the changing situation and plans to expand the intelligence-gathering network failed for a lack of qualified personnel. However, the section established several of its men under the cover of the German legations in Switzerland.[105] The report stressed the existence of an intelligence network reaching into ministries, the economy, and into the most relevant organization of the country. The section was also to prepare general situation reports; reports on important events with special focus on political changes; on the economy; on bilateral and cultural organizations as possible conduits of foreign propaganda; on personnel changes in the relevant state and economic agencies; and on national parties and groups. In addition, it was to watch over the country's relations to France and England. It was furthermore to engage in "intelligence service-related work:" recruit additional V-men; keep tabs on the French and British intelligence services; report on people working for foreign services; investigate the foreign services' methods; and examine the possibilities of working into enemy countries. Considering the section's low

---

[104] Nachrichtendienstliche Arbeit des Referates VI F 3 nach der Schweiz [1940], BA-DH, ZR 920/64.
[105] Nachrichtendienstliche Arbeit des Referates VI F 3 nach der Schweiz [1940], BA-DH, ZR 920/64; Rechenschaftsbericht des Referates VI F 1 für das Jahr 1940, BA-DH, ZR 920/64.

staffing levels in Switzerland, the list of tasks primarily showcases the office and the section's ambition while its relationship to reality remains hazy.

In an alleged close cooperation with the Auswärtige Amt the section also attempted to influence Swiss policies for Germany's benefit. Good connections purportedly existed with pro-German groups and with a number of high-ranking Swiss officers. Indeed, this might have been the section's main focus, especially as it was believed that these officers would be at the forefront of the "struggle for the change of Swiss policies." An associated fencing club was regarded as the "cadre of a later to be established SS;" its members were selected based on SS qualifications.[106] There was a clear expectation that Switzerland would become a National Socialist country, whether voluntarily or by force, and Office VI believed itself to be laying the political groundwork for this. The nuts and bolts associated with the establishment of a functioning intelligence service took a distant second, but compared to other countries, Office VI's activities in Switzerland were considered successful.

Office VI's activities in Scandinavia were considered another bright spot.[107] In late 1939 and early 1940, SD representatives were installed in the various Scandinavian capitals, where they were to create intelligence networks. In the spring of 1940, the section established a transmitter in Copenhagen; a second transmitter in Oslo was in the works when German troops occupied the country. Denmark and Norway now fell under the domestic intelligence service, Office III. Within a few weeks in early 1940, then, the responsibilities of VI G 3 were cut in half.

Sweden and Finland presented more difficult territories, though. Both countries restricted the travel of foreigners and, particularly in Sweden, or so the report claimed, German citizens as well as ethnic Germans were under constant surveillance. However, as their capitals were the centers of political, cultural, and economic life, the section was determined to create intelligence connections there.[108] Sweden was assigned a particular role in the New Order that Germany strove to create. Swedes were considered "Nordic," and many Nazi leaders presumed political affinities based on presumed racial commonalities. Aside from these racial constructs, many leading and ordinary Swedes held pro-German

---

[106] Nachrichtendienstliche Arbeit des Referates VI F 3 nach der Schweiz [1940], BA-DH, ZR 920/64.

[107] Rechenschaftsbericht über die nachrichtendienstliche Arbeit des Referates VI G 3 für das Jahr 1940, BA-DH, ZR 920/63.

[108] Rechenschaftsbericht über die nachrichtendienstliche Arbeit des Referates VI G 3 für das Jahr 1940, BA-DH, ZR 920/63.

sympathies. Sweden's proclaimed wartime neutrality also tilted toward a pro-German stance and entailed close economic relations with Germany. The country profited handsomely from the conflict.[109] Germany, for its part, was interested in maintaining stable relations with Sweden; however, it also indicated its willingness to move against Sweden militarily if the need arose.[110] Yet as long as all remained quiet and leading Swedish circles maintained their pro-Germany, pro-business stance, Germany had no interest in antagonizing Swedish officials. This German assessment of its needs and the situation in Sweden impacted foreign intelligence matters. As a neutral country that, at least in theory, traded with all belligerent countries, in whose capital all the belligerent countries maintained legations, and that would serve as a protecting power for various European countries occupied by Germany, Sweden – and its capital – presented the ideal playing field for intelligence services. Furthermore, Sweden's location allowed for Office VI to reach into other countries as well, at least in theory. The activities of enemy intelligence services in Sweden were therefore part of the section's focus. It professed, however, even more interest in other areas of surveillance:

1. Government, state leadership, and political parties;
2. Print Media, Jewry, Freemasons, High Finance as well as industry and economy;
3. Foreign diplomacy, under special consideration of the British, Soviet-Russian and Norwegian legations;
4. Swedish conduct and efforts regarding occupied Denmark and Norway;
5. Sweden as a contact point for possible British–Soviet–Russian rapprochement efforts;
6. Sweden as a power factor in case of possible Finnish–Soviet–Russian warlike clash;
7. Sweden in view of the coming new European order.[111]

Two central tenets of Office VI's approach can be discerned from this list. Ideology defined targets, for how else to explain the prominent inclusion of "Jewry, Freemasons" as a main field of inquiry in a country with a minuscule Jewish population?[112] Second, the section took a page from

---

[109] On Sweden during the Nazi Era: Stig Ekman and Klas Åmark, *Sweden's Relations with Nazism, Nazi Germany and the Holocaust: A Survey of Research*, Stockholm Studies in History, vol. 66 (Stockholm: Amquist and Wiksell International, 2003).

[110] Gunnar Åslins "Sweden and Nazi Germany," in Ekman and Åmark, *Relations*, 94–97.

[111] Rechenschaftsbericht über die nachrichtendienstliche Arbeit des Referates VI G 3 für das Jahr 1940, BA-DH, ZR 920/63.

[112] It has been estimated that around 1940 approximately 7,000 Jews lived in Sweden. By the end of the war, the Jewish community in Sweden had doubled. Most notably, Sweden took in almost all Danish Jews.

the domestic intelligence service's playbook, as witnessed in points one and two. One clearly wanted to gain a total picture.

The section took pride in the completion of various individual activities, such as a review of the Norwegian Embassy's foreign intelligence efforts, the procurement of court files about a British agent, and the registration of enemy services' operatives. Allegedly, it had also played a part in the reorganization of the Swedish National-Socialist Workers' Party and had been active in the surveillance and the eventual shutdown (*Abstellung*) of associations and contact points of emigrants, refugees, and Jews. In addition, the report claimed that the section had secured information about the organization and capabilities of Swedish coastal fortifications, admittedly an issue outside of the service's immediate mandate. But, then, broadly conceived intelligence gathering bred opportunities and Office VI was not in a position to pass those up. Scandinavia was clearly easier for Office VI to handle than, for example, the United States. Proximity provided possibilities, as did the presence of ideological fellow travelers. Yet their role amplified an issue with which the office grappled: what to report on. In Sweden – as well as in Finland – reporting reflected the ideological surveillance embraced by the SD's domestic intelligence section; the countries, too, were treated as "living sphere abroad." To quite some extent, Office VI functioned as an, albeit disjointed, ideological watchdog abroad.

Office VI's problems and inconsistencies did not escape notice. During a conference of the Security Police and the Security Service in summer 1941, almost two years into its existence, Jost found himself on the defensive. Clamoring for sympathy and support from the leadership of the other RSHA offices, Jost's speech was tinged with desperation.[113] He enumerated the office's problems and, based on Heydrich's earlier demand that the RSHA offices should collaborate better, suggested broad solutions. Jost admitted that his office's relations with numerous government agencies – the Auswärtige Amt was cited as an example – were poor. But he also stressed that men suitable for intelligence work were not assigned to Office VI and that those active abroad lacked the needed support. He also complained that Office VI, despite its role as a clearing house, was not given all information on foreign countries, thus making it difficult to collate "factually accurate reports" for Heydrich and the various ministries. Echoing Heydrich, Jost, too, called for closer collaboration as well as better communication and a willingness to share information. He implored his colleagues to exhibit "particularly the good will to really

---

[113] Vortrag SS-Brigadeführer Jost auf der Tagung der Sicherheitspolizei und des SD, Berlin, June 12, 1941, BA-DH, ZR 920/59.

serve the cause and not to react aggressively to every small incident that had been done wrong." Listing a few accomplishments – among them the alleged creation of a courier route via Finland to the United States and the recruitment of Finnish volunteers for the SS, hardly an intelligence-related task – Jost emphasized that Office VI did, indeed, work. "You will recognize from this that even Office VI fulfills its responsibility and duty, and that it is surely worth the support by other offices and departments, if this is possible in the first place." Sounding rather desperate, Jost added that the members of the political foreign intelligence service were "as good National Socialists as the members of the other offices." Problems with the office's performance, Jost stressed, were due to a lack of funding and its recent establishment; however, these shortcomings could be neutralized by better interagency collaboration.

Any institution needing to emphasize that work is actually done is in dire straits and Jost's Office VI was no exception. He was correct that some of the reasons for the office's lackluster performance were to be found outside of his control, for example the office's late establishment, which coincided with the beginning of the war. Other problems were of the office's own making. Buying into a skewed notion of how the British Intelligence Service functioned, namely as a loose net of patriotic volunteers working for a great and shared cause, and infusing this with the ideological zest of National Socialism, Office VI relied almost exclusively on ideologically trustworthy German citizens or ethnic Germans. If foreigners were used for intelligence gathering, they were ideological fellow travelers. This, in turn, curtailed the information accessible to the office: it was better informed about ethnic German communities or pro-German, National Socialist movements abroad than about anything. Only in countries ideologically or geographically close, preferably both, was the service able to make any inroads. Otherwise Germany's ideological spies were rarely in any position to learn anything worthwhile.

Structural flaws made the situation even worse. Office VI's mandate remained exceedingly defined or phrased so broadly that just about anything could be considered worth the office's attention. More often than not, Office VI found itself engaged in broadly construed fishing expeditions for anything that could be considered valuable, completely void of a clear focus or workable approaches. This was part of the office's unrestricted approach to intelligence gathering and its intent to achieve totality, but it led to a situation in which the office's personnel created concreteness on the fly and fell back on dealing with foreign countries in a manner similar to that of the domestic intelligence service; foreign countries became "living spheres abroad." Extremely fragmented information, gathered based on ideological preconceptions, was then formed into an ideologically driven idea of a complete picture.

Competition with state agencies exacerbated an already bad situation. Prone to attempts to conduct its own foreign policy, a propensity even more pronounced in later years, Office VI had a tendency to run afoul of Ribbentrop's Foreign Office. In January 1941, for example, it provided support for the revolt of the radical Iron Guard, led by Horia Sima, against General Ion Antonescu in Romania; it was one of the office's first attempts at conducting an independent foreign policy. Antonescu guaranteed, however, stability in areas needed for Germany's war economy, especially in light of the coming war against the Soviet Union. Antonescu therefore had Hitler and Ribbentrop's support for his policies and, coming under pressure by the Iron Guard, inquired with Hitler whether he still had his backing. This Hitler confirmed. He also suggested that Antonescu remember how he had dealt with Ernst Röhm and the SA in 1934. The Romanian general took Hitler's advice and squashed the revolt; all the SD could do at this point was to rush Sima and his closest collaborators out of the country.[114] But this was the tip of the iceberg in the deteriorating relationship between Office VI and the Auswärtige Amt. With its broad reporting on foreign countries, Office VI also trespassed on the traditional tasks of the Auswärtige Amt. SD men embedded in diplomatic posts abroad created another layer of problems, for they sometimes reported on the ideological trustworthiness of the German diplomats around them. Jost did little to mitigate these problems and a lot to accentuate them – especially with Office VI's Romanian adventure. Internal RSHA competition did not help matters. In German-occupied countries, Office VI competed with the Gestapo, and with the domestic intelligence service as well. The better Germany was doing militarily, the more problematic Office VI's the standing became. And between 1939 and summer 1941, Jost's years at the helm of the office, Germany's military was doing exceptionally well. Consequently, Office VI's reach was ever shrinking. After the war, several ranking members of Office VI, including Schellenberg, agreed that the service's performance under Jost had been a failure. Their reasoning differed, as they alternately described it as "nothing but – for the matters at hand – an insignificant, badly staffed and corrupt office," or as in wild disarray at every level and not even meeting minimum requirements. Some former officials also blamed others, such as the Auswärtige Amt or Heydrich personally, for the office's negligible

[114] Heinz Höhne, *Der Orden unter dem Totenkopf. Die Geschichte der SS* (Munich: Bertelsmann, 1967; reprint, Augsburg: Weltbild Verlag, 1998), 267–268.

impact. The former did not care for its work and Heydrich, the argument went, simply withheld reports with which he disagreed.[115] Schellenberg shared these assessments and, after the war, related the shortcomings of Jost and Office VI – and particularly the conflict with the Auswärtige Amt – in great detail, noting that both Heydrich and Himmler had to justify the office's activities on a regular basis. In addition, Schellenberg pointed to disagreements with other Reich authorities.[116] Schellenberg attributed Office VI's inefficiency to Jost personally. His predecessor, he maintained, took a lax approach; worked only a few hours a day; let his subordinates wait; and did not exercise proper oversight. Work was duplicated. Schellenberg also believed that many of the people working in Office VI were simply inept – "all these characters were too off for me."[117] Put differently: Schellenberg saw nothing wrong with the ideologically charged ways in which Office VI conducted its business but rather believed that it needed professional leadership and oversight.

Schellenberg's interest in a leadership position in foreign intelligence or "even with the Foreign Office" was well known. For a man of Schellenberg's social background and lack of ties to Foreign Minister Joachim von Ribbentrop the latter was largely out of reach. But by 1941 Schellenberg had positioned himself for a leading position in Office VI. His exploits in Venlo and then in the Gestapo's counterintelligence department, combined with his liberal interpretation of what counterintelligence was to entail, made Schellenberg a more obvious choice for a position at the helm of Office VI. Moreover, Schellenberg's foreign policy aspirations fit in with the ambitions of the SD. Schellenberg claimed that he approached Heydrich and Canaris with his wish to head Office VI in the spring of 1941. If Schellenberg is to be believed, his was a well-timed pitch; allegedly, Canaris was concerned about the poor performance of Office VI.[118] Around the same time, questions about the personal and financial integrity of some leading Office VI members, tenuously implicating Jost, surfaced. Shortly thereafter, he was linked to an embezzlement charge. Financial problems stemming from the insolvency of a Berlin Import/Export firm – meant to serve as a cover for intelligence work abroad – added to the office's and Jost's woes. Department IV E 2, part of Schellenberg's domain, conducted the subsequent investigation,

[115] Affidavit, Dr. Theodor Paeffgen, March 12, 1948, NA, RG 238, M 897, Reel 114, Frame 913; Interrogation Report Nr. 15, NA, RG 319, IRR, XE 000882 Hoettl.
[116] Final Report on the Case of Walter Schellenberg, NA, RG 319, IRR, XE 001725, Walter Schellenberg, Folders 7 and 8 [hereafter: Final Report.]
[117] Interrogation of Walter Schellenberg by Dr. R.W.M. Kempner, November 13, 1947, IfZ, ZS291/V, 00031.
[118] Final Report.

Image 4.1 Portrait of Walter Schellenberg, September 1943. Bundesarchiv. [Signature: Bild 101III-Alber-178–04A]

which, as Schellenberg insinuated after the war, was driven by Heinrich Müller who did not care for a foreign intelligence service outside the Gestapo, disliked Jost, and wanted him dismissed.[119] Others emphasized Schellenberg's direct involvement in the investigations of Jost and stressed that Heydrich's wish to rid himself of Jost, who also had close links to Werner Best, drove the investigation. Schellenberg then – yet again – did Heydrich's deed and turned a minor embezzlement charge into a full-fledged affair that led to Jost's dismissal. Schellenberg's appointment as

---

[119] Final Report. Through an "aryanized" bank in Prague, which Office VI had "helped acquire" in the first place, members of Office VI received loans at favorable interest rates. In turn, they gave out credits at higher rates. From the net profits, Jost allegedly bought a house in Berlin. According to postwar reports, Office IV E 2 conducted the investigation.

the acting head of Office VI was his door prize.[120] He was designated *Amtschef*, office head, in February 1943.[121] By then, Schellenberg had impressed many, including some of his life-long critics. It was said that he had made "an exact science" or "really something" out of an intelligence service that had seemingly been beyond redemption.[122] Whether this was indeed the case or whether Schellenberg was a masterful illusionist, fooling others and himself, is the focus of the following chapters.

[120] SS Sturmbannfuehrer Dr. Wilhelm Hoettl, A Character Sketch of Schellenberg: Chief of Germany's Espionage Service, July 12, 1945 NA, RG 226, Entry 199A, Box 55, Folder 1602; Interrogation Report Nr. 15, NA, RG 319, IRR, XE 000882 Hoett.

[121] CdS to RFSS, SS-Personalhauptamt, Schellenberg, September 8, 1941, IfZ, FA 74; Himmler to Schellenberg, February 25, 1943, NA, RG 242, BDC, A 3343, SSO, Reel 074B, Frame 247.

[122] SS Sturmbannfuehrer Dr. Wilhelm Hoettl, A Character Sketch of Schellenberg: Chief of Germany's Espionage Service, NA, July 12, 1945, NA, RG 226, Entry 199A, Box 55, Folder 1602; Excerpts, Interrogation of Karl Wolff, February 26, 1947, Interrogation #476-d, Mr. Lyon-Flick Case, IFZ, ZS 317/III, 00001.

5 Competing Visions
Office VI and the Abwehr

It took three minutes out of a busy day: on June 22, 1941, the first full day of the German invasion of the Soviet Union, Reinhard Heydrich appointed Walter Schellenberg Acting Head of Office VI of the Reich Security Main Office.[1] Schellenberg was 31 years old and while his ascent had been spectacular thus far, he was surely convinced that the best was yet to come. A career in foreign intelligence had been one of his dream jobs, and it is likely he eagerly anticipated the challenges ahead. Schellenberg took over a foreign intelligence service in disarray, but soon established himself firmly at the helm of Office VI and created a semblance of efficiency, activism, and a sharpened vision for his new domain. The latter set Office VI on a collision course with other German intelligence and security entities, but this was not unintended.

The most obvious rivalry existed between Office VI and the military intelligence service Abwehr, headed since 1935 by Admiral Wilhelm Canaris; it is the focus of this chapter. Much has been written about this conflict, which ended with Office VI's incorporation of the better part of the Abwehr in February 1944 and Canaris' arrest in July of the same year, but often to a curious historiographical effect. These postwar writings remade Office VI into just another ordinary foreign intelligence service while bestowing the nimbus of a victim of Nazism on the Abwehr. Yet, as Reinhard Doerries notes, both entities were "Nazi intelligence services" and both competition and cooperation defined their relationship.[2]

An investigation of the rivalry between Office VI and the Abwehr is important still. Tarnished by real and talked-up intelligence failures and suspected of defeatism, if not treason, the Abwehr became comparatively easy prey for its rival. Intermittent cooperation and the friendly relationship between Schellenberg and Canaris notwithstanding, Office VI

---

[1] Walter Schellenberg, *The Labyrinth: Memoirs of Walter Schellenberg, Hitler's Chief of Counterintelligence*, trans. Louis Hagen (New York: Harper & Brothers, 1956; reprint, Cambridge, MA: Da Capo Press, 2000), 208.

[2] Reinhard C. Doerries, *Hitler's Intelligence Chief Walter Schellenberg: The Man Who Kept Germany's Secrets*, intr. by Gerhard L. Weinberg (New York: Enigma Books, 2009), 367.

sharpened its profile as the standard-bearer of a new, radical approach to foreign intelligence in the realm of military intelligence and in its rivalry with the Abwehr. Much of the eventual success of Office VI was prepared on the ground, for example in the Soviet Union, where the office established predominance by bringing a radical, ideological approach to Germany's intelligence efforts. It did not yield better results but captured the imagination of the decision makers. Indeed, the demise Abwehr was all but a foregone conclusion well before it became reality in 1944. Despite intermittent conflicts of personality and vision, Schellenberg, Heydrich – later Kaltenbrunner – and Himmler achieved their shared goal and moved closer to their envisioned superagency. It is in the aftermath of the Abwehr's usurpation that Schellenberg's vision for the new service – the centralized, ideologized, morally unbound intelligence service of the "Uncompromising Generation," comes into view most clearly.[3] This, in turn, calls into question Schellenberg's later assertions that he had stayed free of ideology or long stopped believing in the National Socialist project.

Schellenberg's appointment was Heydrich's attempt to salvage the field of foreign intelligence for the RSHA. Schellenberg, for his part, approached his new assignment with his customary gusto and ostensibly ended the inefficiency of the Jost years. He first dealt with the remnants of the office's decentralized approach: while finding additional qualified men remained as difficult as it had been for Jost, experienced personnel, for example from Vienna, was transferred to Berlin.[4] Prone to micromanagement, Schellenberg came, however, close to over-centralizing Office VI, involving himself not only with the office's important endeavors but unimportant ones as well.[5] Whereas Jost had been too removed from his subordinates and their activities, Schellenberg was front and center. There is no indication that this approach was more useful, but it gave the impression that Schellenberg was in control.

Schellenberg's reorganization of Office VI had a similar effect. As Jost had done before, Schellenberg hoped it would translate into better intelligence work. Thus, from mid-1941 to 1942, VI A was the

[3] Schellenberg to Kaltenbrunner, Vortrag Schellenberg, vorgelegt zur Genehmigung, May 10, 1944, RGVA, Fond 500, Opis 1, 1164. The Uncompromising Generation is the title of the English version of Michael Wildt *Generation des Unbedingten. Das Führunngkorps des Reichssicherheitshauptamtes* (Hamburg: Hamburger Edition, 2002).
[4] Counter Intelligence War Room, Situation Report No. 10, Amt VI of the RSHA Gruppe VI E, NA, RG 319, IRR, Box 1, XE 002303 [hereafter: Situation Report No. 10]; Final Report on the Case of Walter Schellenberg, NA, RG 319, IRR, XE 001725, Walter Schellenberg, Folders 7 and 8 [hereafter: Final Report.]
[5] Protokoll über die Referentenbesprechung, am Donnerstag, den 4. Dezember 1941, vormittags 9 Uhr, USHMM, 14.016 M, 428.

administrative section of Office VI; VI B dealt with Slovakia, Hungary, Romania, Yugoslavia, Greece, Turkey, Iran, Iraq, and Afghanistan; and VI C focused on Russia, Japan, China, Finland, and the Baltic States. VI D concerned itself with Great Britain, the British Empire, the United States, South America, Sweden, Denmark, and Norway, and VI E investigated France, the Low Countries, Spain, Portugal, Italy, and Switzerland. The Technical Department, designated as VI F, and "Ideological Enemies Abroad," VI G, rounded out Office VI. In 1942, Office VI was reshuffled. VI B now concentrated on France, the Low Countries, Switzerland, Spain, and Portugal; Russia, the Near East, and the Far East fell under VI C. VI D dealt with the "Anglo-American sphere," while VI E focused on Central Europe, the Balkans, Italy, and Scandinavia. "Ideological Enemies Abroad," mostly an exercise in redundancy, was disbanded.[6] Office VI's performance did not improve. Rather, these structural changes are indicative of deep-seated problems that masked uncertainties: Did it make more sense to investigate Italy in the context of France, the Low Countries, Switzerland, and the Iberian Peninsula or should this country be combined with Central Europe, the Balkans, and Scandinavia? Did the Near East belong with Central Europe or with Russia and the Far East? Nobody seemed to know, but the constant reshuffling of sections created an illusion of activism and professionalism – while likely weakening further the already under-performing service, for it did not matter where the investigation of the Far East was located on a flow chart if no substantial gains were made either way.

Schellenberg's efforts were, however, received favorably and his activism even earned him the praise of some of his detractors. Schellenberg made "an exact science out of intelligence work," opined Wilhelm Höttl, even though he also likened Schellenberg's personnel transfer to a purge, because experienced group leaders were replaced with "young, inexperienced men whose talents lagged considerably behind the enthusiasm they brought to the job." Karl Wolff, initially Chief of Himmler's Personal Staff and later Highest SS and Police Leader in Italy, who was not well-disposed toward Schellenberg either, conceded that he did "really make something" out of Office VI.[7] Schellenberg's activism earned him praise from unexpected quarters.

---

[6] Situation Report No. 10, Appendix I, Chart of the Distribution of Work in Amt VI from 1939–1945. This postwar chart does not appear completely accurate, but illustrates my point.

[7] SS Sturmbannfuehrer Dr. Wilhelm Hoettl, A Character Sketch of Schellenberg: Chief of Germany's Espionage Service, July 12, 1945, NA, RG 226, Entry 199A, Box 55, Folder 1602; Excerpts, Interrogation of Karl Wolff, February 26, 1947, Interrogation #476-d, Mr. Lyon-Flick Case, IFZ, ZS 317/III, 00001.

By late 1941, Schellenberg was in reasonable control of his office but frictions remained. Schellenberg's leadership style oscillated between threats and praise, occasionally with a decidedly passive-aggressive bend. In a staff meeting in November 1941 Schellenberg noted, for example, that he did not care for gossip about the circumstances of his appointment, apparently a sore topic for him, and tartly complained about his subordinates' tardiness, noting that the competition, the Abwehr, did not sleep. He also remarked that if his subordinates felt insecure about their positions, the reason might be their knowledge that they were not doing their jobs well. Some weeks later, explanations replaced admonishments: acknowledging a lack of trust between himself and his subordinates, Schellenberg defended the personnel changes he had instituted and explained, "[e]verything the deputy office head does, is done only in fulfillment of the great tasks and in the interest of all the office's members." But even when striking a conciliatory note, Schellenberg employed well-placed threats: if the office failed to shape up, he would be forced to suggest its dissolution to Heydrich. The threat to abolish Office VI, if not successful within a year's time, came likely from the outside, though.[8] Its use in a staff meeting spoke volumes about Schellenberg's determination to succeed and leadership style: he remade a threat against himself into one against his subordinates and used it to boost his own standing, as it conveyed his close relationship with Heydrich.

Office VI found itself in a constant state of tension with state, military, and party entities, but as the war moved into its third year, problems between Office VI and the Abwehr, identified in staff meetings as the prime competitor, were mounting. Relations, one should recall, were still regulated by the prewar Ten Commandments, but a new agreement was needed. Heydrich's long-term intentions, despite his negligible interest in foreign intelligence per se, were straightforward: he wanted to relieve Canaris of his position, shut down the Abwehr in its current form, and move its tasks into the RSHA. Accordingly, Heydrich exploited any Abwehr failures to the fullest while insinuating – even if he was as of yet unable to prove so – that leading Abwehr personnel were in close contact with resistance circles.[9] In the short term and after lengthy discussions

---

[8] Protokoll über die Referentenbesprechung, am Donnerstag, den 6. November 1941, vormittags, 8 Uhr; Protokoll über die Referentenbesprechung, am Donnerstag, den 22. Dezember [1941], nachmittags 16 Uhr, USHMM, 14.016 M, 428. Other documentation suggests that the threat to abolish the Office VI came from the outside. See: Situation Report No. 10; Eighth Detailed Interrogation Report on SS Sturmbannführer Huegel, Dr. Klaus, June 26, 1945, NA, RG 226, Entry 119A, Box 71, File 1829.

[9] David Kahn, *Hitler's Spies: German Military Intelligence in World War II* (New York: Macmillan, 1978; reprint, Cambridge, MA: Da Capo Press, 2000), 267–268.

marked by Heydrich's annoyance and Canaris' reticence, the two men agreed on an amendment to the Ten Commandments in March 1942.[10]

The old agreement, concluded when the power differential between Sipo/SD and Abwehr had been substantial, was regarded as imprecise – disadvantageous to the former. The new agreement gave a better-defined and more prominent role to Heydrich's men, even if its basic terms remained stable: Sipo and SD were tasked with the surveillance of and the fight against all enemies of the Volk and the state, preventively or postfactum, and the Abwehr focused on the procurement of military information from enemy states and potential enemy states and on military counterespionage. The *Geheime Meldedienst*, Secret Military Intelligence Service, was with the Abwehr; Sipo and SD were to share pertinent information with it and to provide assistance. Conversely, the Abwehr was to share relevant political information it gathered with Office VI – or other relevant RSHA office – but not to assist them. The same distinction between military and political information prevailed for counterespionage matters. However, as enemy services did not differentiate their approach into military and political matters the way Germany did and also engaged in "political, subversive, sabotage-related and terrorist activities," Sipo and SD took on a bigger and better-defined role in counterintelligence. This put the Gestapo's counterintelligence department, Schellenberg's old office, on surer footing.[11] The agreement confirmed the overall set-up that had been in place for years – the Abwehr focused on military matters, espionage, and counterespionage and Sipo and SD focused on political matters and counterintelligence – but it reflected the two outfits' changing fortunes. Sipo and SD had grown stronger.

A conference between leading members of the two organizations to discuss the new arrangements and their practical implications was held

---

[10] See the exchange between Heydrich and Canaris in early 1942, BAL, NS 19/3514. Key documents are printed in *Das Amt Ausland/Abwehr im Oberkommando der Wehrmacht: Eine Dokumentation*, bearbeitet von Norbert Müller unter Mitwirkung von Helma Kaden, Gerlinde Grahn, Brün Meyer, Tilman Koops (Koblenz: Bundesarchiv, 2007), Nrs. 133, 134, 139, 140. See also: Horst Mühleisen, "Das letzte Duell: Die Auseinandersetzungen zwischen Heydrich und Canaris wegen der Revision der 'Zehn Gebote'," *Militärgeschichtliche Mitteilungen* 58/2 (1999), 395–458.

[11] CdS, Zusammenarbeit zwischen den Dienststellen der Sicherheitspolizei und des SD. und den Abwehrdienststellen der Wehrmacht, April 6, 1942, BA-DH, ZR 920/149. Heydrich's negotiator for the agreement had been Walter Huppenkothen, Schellenberg's successor in the Gestapo's counterintelligence department, explaining the department's gains. Heydrich to Canaris, February 5, 1942, BAL, NS 19/3514, 141–145. Doerries notes that the final agreement was signed by Heydrich and Canaris and not by Canaris and Schellenberg. As the agreement impacted several RSHA offices, this only made sense. Doerries, *Intelligence Chief*, 52. For the agreement as such, see: *Dokumentation*, Nr. 140.

at the Hradčany in Prague in early May 1942.[12] City and palace were now Heydrich's main places of business; Hitler had appointed him Reich Protector of Bohemia and Moravia in September 1941. Much like the imperial venue showed Heydrich's might, the conference reflected a new balance of power: Sipo/SD and Abwehr met as equals. Both Heydrich and Canaris addressed the assembled intelligence and policing bureaucrats, and their remarks indicated the two men's respective strengths. Heydrich asserted the Sipo/SD demand for political leadership [*politischen Machtanspruch*] and, having reached the agreement, Heydrich looked toward the future. Canaris, on the other hand, stressed the Abwehr's willingness to "collaborate honestly" and offered a different interpretation of the agreement: with its clear regulations all conflict had come to an end.[13] Canaris appeared relieved enough to have the present sorted out. The conference then broke into sections that held separate consultations. Schellenberg read his paper "The Political Secret Intelligence Service and Its Working Method," unfortunately now lost, to his Sipo and SD peers. Toward the end of the conference, Heydrich extolled the virtues and the importance of Office VI in a speech. As Schellenberg reported to his subordinates with pride and relief, "[Heydrich] expressed the view that Amt VI was the most important department in the R.S.H.A. and that it was in no way to be regarded as a freak but as an Amt possessing equal status to the rest."[14] Put differently, Office VI was no longer considered an underperforming oddity, but had been recognized as a contender and as of central importance to the RSHA. Heydrich had pronounced Schellenberg's attempt to turn around the service – whether it was real, the trick of master illusionist, or a figment of the collective imagination – a success.

Schellenberg's report on the conference was positively giddy. During a staff meeting, he gave a detailed account of the events, highlighting Heydrich's assertion of the Sipo and the SD's political primacy as well as his spirited defense of the Einsatzgruppen, at this point deep into their murderous campaign in Eastern Europe. Schellenberg also mentioned Canaris' contrite admission that better collaboration was needed and emphasized Heydrich's praise for the work of Office VI. Schellenberg was also clearly enamored with the success of his own "important" paper, which he believed to have served as a wakeup call with an

---

[12] CdS, Zusammenarbeit zwischen den Dienststellen der Sicherheitspolizei und des SD. und den Abwehrdienstellen der Wehrmacht, April 6, 1942, BA-DH, ZR 920/149; Final Report.

[13] Amt VI, Protokoll der Referentenbesprechung am Mittwoch, den 27.5.1942, 9 Uhr 30, USHMM, 14.016 M, 482.

[14] Final Report.

immediate effect: a greater willingness to engage in additional work was evident after his speech, he claimed. Never afraid to toot his horn, Schellenberg had the speech read during a later staff meeting.[15] But the afterglow of the conference, Heydrich's praise, and Schellenberg's claptrap notwithstanding, fundamental problems remained: Office VI's mandate was as poorly defined as it has been under Jost.

"It is the task of the political foreign intelligence service to collect information abroad," began a decree issued in the aftermath of the Prague meeting in May 1942. Meant to strengthen and to define the role of Office VI, its summary was an exercise in vagueness:

The questions that relate to the German AND. [Allgemeiner Nachrichtendienst, General Foreign Intelligence Service] are no exception to what is to be said for a political intelligence service in general. The mentioned points are just a small selection of them. They are multifaceted, like the manifestations of life itself. This variety brings with it that it is not possible to write down or even discuss all the tasks, functions, possibilities for success and failure as well as all the methods and techniques for offense and defense. The attachment to this decree attempts to discuss the most pertinent issues, as far as this is possible without the personal, actual reaction of the listener. Nevertheless, many issues – that necessarily escape the written form – remain; therefore, meetings, which will happen in Berlin in Office VI on a regular basis or will be brought on by particular events, will solve the questions emerging from the interaction between the center and the front. In addition, it has to be understood that the intelligence service carries with it numerous issues that deserve secrecy and cannot be endangered by committing them into writing and sending them by mail.[16]

Put pointedly, Office VI had an unclear mandate and planned to improvise – in secret, if necessary.

The decree's attachment did not clarify matters. It described, in grandiose terms, Office VI's overarching goals and approaches and defined, yet again, its relationship to other intelligence entities. It also detailed the minutiae of the work, stating a good many foreign intelligence truisms. Office VI's approaches were divided into three steps: acquisition of information, transmission of information, and its evaluation and use. Office VI planned to acquire and disseminate information that was "unobjectionably accurate," "true," or at least "probable." Information was to be as complete and current as possible and to be

[15] Amt VI, Protokoll der Referentenbesprechung am Mittwoch, den 27.5.1942, 9 Uhr 30, USHMM, 14.016 M, 482.
[16] CdS, Geheimer politischer Nachrichtendienst im Ausland; (AND.), May 31, 1942, BA-DH, ZR 920/59; Anlage zum Erlaß vom 31. Mai 1942, VI B. Nr. 0490/41 g.Rs., BA-DH, ZR 920/59. An earlier decree stated that a political foreign intelligence service existed and defined its position in the RSHA. CdS, Geheimer politischer Nachrichtendienst im Ausland, December 10, 1941, BA-DH, ZR 920/63.

transmitted quickly and safely; it had to be designated as fact or rumor; there should be an indication whether confirmation would be possible or whether a confirmation process was already underway and what the process was; whether the source was reliable; and, lastly, whether and why another office had received the same information. The main office's task was to go beyond that of a collection point: it was to contextualize and to evaluate information and, if needed, to gather additional information. Yet the mass of information was seen as a double-edged sword: the decree took a dim view of the prevalent reports on moods and attitudes abroad, which provided much useless information. That said, any information was considered relevant still.

On what type of information did the service concentrate? Office VI was to focus on "objects" in foreign countries and in their domestic and foreign policies:

The goal [*Objekt*] are events, situations, plans, which are not officially accessible, but rather in contrast to official pronouncements; knowing about them, though, in their actual form, can be vital for the German state and military leadership [. . .] The moveable, the future is in the foreground. The present, the seemingly still, is an illustration and a worthy addition. The internal situation of a country, the availability of consumer goods and raw materials, ideological movements, the political character of the governing regime [. . .] The AND. has to pay attention to all these questions, but as it was said, not exclusively, but as a base and corrective [. . .]

In other words, only "pure military matters" and everything under the authority of the Gestapo's counterintelligence department fell outside the responsibility of Office VI. But again, there were caveats: "of course" the political foreign intelligence service was to gather all the information it could and then to share it with other entities, thus dampening down the conflict with the Abwehr and within the RSHA. The decree, however, stressed Office VI's overall responsibilities:

The AND. exclusively has to take care that the surveillance of foreign countries works, that dangers for the Reich are recognized in a timely manner in order to use this for the policies of the Reich or to enable the Abwehr to disarm [neutralize] them in their area. The AND. is a weapon in the broadest sense. It attacks the enemy in its own territory using the weapon of surveillance, not preventive violence. Its task is fulfilled with the report and the subsequent surveillance.[17]

The main office was to evaluate information in its context and to assemble the mosaic: the decree made clear that neither subordinate offices nor other agencies could fulfill this task, as "the AND. [General Foreign

---

[17] Anlage zum Erlaß vom 31. Mai 1942, VI B.Nr. 0490/41 g.Rs., BA-DH, ZR 920/59.

Intelligence Service] has to function preventively. [...] Information about the future is the ideal to strive for." In other words, Office VI had to be an absolutely reliable foreign intelligence, preferably able to predict the future. To heighten the drama, the decree suggested that its performance would reflect upon the entire Reich Security Main Office.[18]

Office VI laid a broad claim. The decree lacked precision, was full of vague grandiosity, and raised the stakes but it apparently sold. Tone and style, as well as its vaguely holistic approach, suggest that Schellenberg authored the decree and its attachment, which was approved by Heydrich shortly before his death. It is equally likely that the paper Schellenberg gave during the conference was similar to the decree. Ultimately, though, little was said here that had not been said before. Decree and attachment confirmed and explicated earlier agreements about the role and the scope of Office VI and attempted to buttress its relevance. If it could not be done in deed, then it had to be in word. Office VI had long existed in obscurity and had been regarded, prominently by Heydrich and Schellenberg, as full of unrealized potential; these pronouncements, in all their vagueness and grandiosity, put it on the map. In addition, they allowed for the SD to claw its way into the areas of responsibility of others, notably the Abwehr. The slow demise of Canaris' service gathered momentum with the agreement concluded in Prague. Office VI's meddling was now officially sanctioned and it wasted no time waiting. The Abwehr existed for another two years, but the vultures were circling.

In the short term, the assassination of Heydrich threw into turmoil the RSHA, but the leaderless year until the appointment of Ernst Kaltenbrunner as the head of the RSHA provided Schellenberg with opportunities to strengthen his position. Heydrich died on June 4, 1942 from wounds he had suffered less than a week earlier during an assassination attempt by a Czech commando, trained and equipped by the British foreign intelligence service MI 6. The retaliation for Heydrich's death, epitomized by the fate of the inhabitants of Lidiče, was horrendous even by Germany's standards. Counterespionage, counterintelligence, and old-fashioned security had clearly failed. But as these fields were not part of Schellenberg's portfolio, at least not anymore, he did not seem to have worried.[19] For the RSHA Heydrich's assassination represented a "far-reaching caesura;" as a whole, it never again reached the level of

[18] Anlage zum Erlaß vom 31. Mai 1942, VI B.Nr. 0490/41 g.Rs., BA-DH, ZR 920/59.
[19] See Robert Gerwarth, *Hitler's Hangman: The Life of Reinhard Heydrich* (New Haven: Yale University Press, 2011); Günther Deschner, *Reinhard Heydrich: A Biography* (New York: Stein & Day, 1981); Jan G. Wiener, *The Assassination of Heydrich* (New York, NY: Grossmann, 1969); Schellenberg, *Labyrinth*, 289–293. In his memoir Schellenberg insinuated that the assassination might have been an inside job.

success it had under Heydrich. The RSHA remained without a full-time leader for almost a year, while Himmler stepped in as stop-gap measure. Yet Himmler was not short of work and during this time, in particular, much of his attention was focused on the Holocaust, in Wildt's words the "genuine" task of the RSHA. Consequently, Himmler did not execute much oversight over the office heads.[20] For Schellenberg, this meant a free hand in the conducting his business and the supportive patronage of Himmler.

Himmler was the last and most influential of Schellenberg's impressive string of powerful mentors and patrons; his peers were both well aware and occasionally reminded of Schellenberg's special status. Schellenberg's close relationship to Himmler was not a recent development. As early as 1939, and more so as the head of the Gestapo's counterintelligence department, Schellenberg's access to Himmler had been remarkable; in many ways, he was Himmler's golden boy. After the war Schellenberg told a remarkable story about how Himmler showed his support for Schellenberg during Heydrich's funeral and while it is unclear how much of this is true, it indicates Schellenberg's special status among his peers. Before Heydrich's state funeral Himmler allegedly assembled all the office heads of the RSHA, admonished them to cooperate, not to succumb to interoffice jealousy, and, for good measure, threatened them with punishment by Hitler. Himmler then gave most office heads a "severe dressing down," laced "with biting irony that emphasized their characteristics and defects." The one exception was Schellenberg, or so he claimed. Drawing attention to the difficult nature of Schellenberg's assignment and his comparative youth, Himmler berated the others for making Schellenberg's tasks more difficult and for resenting his youth and high party number. Himmler also stressed that Heydrich had considered Schellenberg suitable for the position he held and that he, Himmler, concurred; indeed, he considered Schellenberg "incorruptible." Himmler then dared the assembled office heads to disagree with his views on Schellenberg; nobody took the bait. Finally, Himmler extended his particular support to Schellenberg. Casting himself as the biblical patriarch and Schellenberg as his youngest and most beloved son, Himmler dubbed him the "Benjamin of our leadership corps." And this son was special indeed: Himmler wanted Schellenberg to "work closely with him" and emphasized "he needed [Schellenberg's] abilities, and wished [Schellenberg] to report to him as frequently as possible."[21] Himmler thus carved

---

[20] Wildt, *Generation*, 680–693.
[21] Schellenberg, *Labyrinth*, 293–294. Slightly differently: Final Report. At this point, Office VII, Ideological and Scientific Research, with Alfred Six at its helm, had been

out a special position for Schellenberg in the RSHA and in Himmler's immediate entourage. Or so Schellenberg claimed after 1945. After Heydrich's death, the two men consulted frequently.[22] Unlike Heydrich, Himmler shared Schellenberg's interest in foreign intelligence matters and presumably appreciated Schellenberg for the same reasons that had swayed Heydrich: his abilities, industriousness, and loyalty. For Schellenberg the direct access to Himmler was a useful boost and insurance in interoffice rivalries. In the coming years, Schellenberg came to function as one of Himmler's key advisors, especially in matters of foreign policy.

The RSHA's leaderless year ended on January 30, 1943, when Himmler appointed Ernst Kaltenbrunner as its new head.[23] The appointment of Kaltenbrunner, plucked out of relative Austrian obscurity, was one of Himmler's more unexpected moves. Contemporaries wondered how a man lacking the police experience, personal connections, and patronage needed to succeed in this environment wound up in this position; they eventually concluded that Himmler had been concerned by Heydrich's increasing power and therefore chose as a replacement a man whose main trait was his personal loyalty to Himmler. This is too shortsighted a view. While Kaltenbrunner's loyalty was an asset, Himmler saw the leadership of the RSHA as a political position that needed to be filled, as Peter Black put it, by an ideological soldier with an administrative background.[24] Kaltenbrunner fit the bill.

Personal relationships, patronage systems, and relationships of mutual assistance – or mutually assured destruction – could make or break careers in Nazi Germany. Schellenberg, who had had more supporters than detractors during his ascent in power, knew that as well as anyone. Initially pleased with Kaltenbrunner's appointment, as it ended the "terrible interregnum," Schellenberg and Kaltenbrunner's honeymoon period ended quickly and their relationship grew sour. Kaltenbrunner

---

added to the RSHA. Only five of the seven office heads were in attendance, Wildt, *Generation*, 683 note 247.

[22] Wildt, *Generation*, 683 note 248. Himmler met most frequently with Streckenbach, the head of the RSHA's Personnel Office and Himmler's special assistant during the "interregnum" and with Heinrich "Gestapo" Müller. Still, Schellenberg's access to Himmler was exceptional; in the second half of 1942, they met seventeen times, see: Peter Witte et al., *Der Dienstkalender Heinrich Himmlers, 1941/42* (Hamburg: Christians, 1999), 715.

[23] Schellenberg contends in his memoirs that he came up as a possible successor to Heydrich and was relieved when he was not chosen. Schellenberg, *Labyrinth*, 296–297. Peter Black, *Ernst Kaltenbrunner: Ideological Soldier of the Third Reich* (Princeton: Princeton University Press, 1984), 128–129; Wildt, *Generation*, 694 note 287.

[24] Many historians share Black's view. Curiously, while basing his narrative on Black, Wildt maintains that the reasons for Himmler's decision remain unclear. Black, *Kaltenbrunner*, 129 note 75; 129–133; Wildt, *Generation*, 695.

was keen to establish his leadership of the RSHA; Schellenberg, for his part, was anxious to maintain his "short string" [*kurzen Draht*] to Himmler.[25] Postwar testimonies make clear their disdain for each other. In Schellenberg's statements, Kaltenbrunner appears as a boorish, drunk, mean Austrian hick and as a fanatical ideologue, unconditionally obedient and loyal. Schellenberg also diagnosed Kaltenbrunner with a Heydrich complex and suggested that Kaltenbrunner blamed Heydrich for his lackluster career after the annexation of Austria in 1938 and, after Heydrich's death, transferred his bitterness to Schellenberg. Schellenberg made himself into the victim of the bully Kaltenbrunner. For his part, Kaltenbrunner regarded young Schellenberg as a careerist who lacked an early party pedigree and was politically unreliable.[26] In Schellenberg's view, his relationship and virtually unfettered access to Himmler suffered in the aftermath of Kaltenbrunner's appointment. Contemporaries told a different story: the relationship between the two men deteriorated because Schellenberg "maintained direct contact with Himmler even after the arrival of Kaltenbrunner."[27] Either man saw his polar opposite in the other, neither one was pulling punches, and Schellenberg circumvented the hierarchies of the RSHA, did not subordinate himself to his new boss, but rather maintained, at times flaunted, his relationship with Himmler.

Disliking each other, the two men fought about their differences in opinion and approaches but also found areas of agreement. Part of Schellenberg's problem was that he had found a serious rival in Kaltenbrunner, who, earlier in his life, had been involved with the collection of intelligence. He took interest in these matters; considered himself an expert; and, different from Heydrich or Himmler, contested Schellenberg's unquestioned expertise. Kaltenbrunner was a force to reckon with but Schellenberg still had Himmler's ear and support, much

---

[25] Gruppenleiterbesprechung am 14. December bei VI/V, NA, RG 242, T-175, Reel 458, Frame 2975422–297523; Protokoll über die Gruppenleiter- und Referentenbesprechung des Amt VI, February 10, 1943, cited in Black, *Kaltenbrunner*, 178 note 4; Interrogation Paeffgen, January 8, 1948, NA, RG 242, M 1019, Reel 51, Frame 0859.

[26] Schellenberg, *Labyrinth*, 331–334; Black, *Kaltenbrunner*, 108–110. See also: Final Report. "There is little doubt that, at least on Schellenberg's side, there was from the very beginning a strong feeling of enmity between the two men. Kaltenbrunner for his part accuses Schellenberg of being insatiably ambitious and inordinately jealous of his position which he charged him with coveting for himself, nevertheless he states that relations between them were correct but cool."

[27] Interrogation of Paeffgen, April 14, 1947, NA, RG 242, M 1019, Reel 51, Frame 0809. Schellenberg attempted to convey both tales, see: Final Report. He also maintained that Kaltenbrunner laced the RSHA with Austrians loyal to him personally: Schellenberg, *Labyrinth*, 333.

to the former's chagrin.[28] These conflicts, which became prominent during the postwar trials and impact the perception of Kaltenbrunner, should not distract from the fact that in practical terms and for the most part the two men worked together well. They agreed on many things, so, for example, the need to expand Office VI's role into military intelligence.

Operation Zeppelin, Office VI's only substantial espionage and effort against the Soviet Union, provides one example, even if it originated before Kaltenbrunner's appointment and saw little direct involvement of the office head Schellenberg.[29] Zeppelin was a function of Office VI's relationship to the military intelligence efforts of other agencies and part and parcel of the battle for dominance in this area. It was fought by ideological means and won handily by Office VI, even though its results were not better than those of other intelligence agencies. In fall 1941, with the German advance in the Soviet Union stalling, it became clear that earlier intelligence about the Soviet Union, largely assumptions based on ideology – the tropes of anti-Bolshevism and Judeo-Bolshevism – had been patently wrong. Germany was in dire need of reliable strategic intelligence. Dr. Heinz Gräfe of Country Group VI C, "Russian–Japanese Sphere of Influence," suggested gathering more current information on the Soviet war economy, its overall potential, and the country's stability by interviewing Soviet prisoners of war. These initial interviews led to the understanding that the Soviet Union would be capable of continuing the war despite the German onslaught. Gräfe therefore suggested attacking the Soviet Union's "moral potential."

Operation Zeppelin was to be the weapon: the idea was to tap into the huge reservoir of Soviet POWs, to recruit them as intelligence operatives or "activists," and to send them into Soviet territory in massive numbers. Additional activists, Gräfe believed, could be found among civilians living in German-occupied Soviet territories, especially national and religious minorities, and among Russian émigrés living across the continent. Focusing on any group with possible anti-Bolshevik leanings, Gräfe even considered contacting – in an undefined manner and five years after the

---

[28] Final Report.

[29] Little more than the bare outlines of the operation and the fact that some of the "activists" were killed when they fell ill during their training were known about Operation Zeppelin until a few years ago. After 1989, more material became available. Klaus-Michael Mallmann, "Der Krieg im Dunkeln: Das Unternehmen 'Zeppelin' 1942–1945," in Michael Wildt, ed., *Nachrichtendienst, Politische Elite und Mordeinheit: Der Sicherheitsdienst des Reichsführers SS* (Hamburg: Hamburger Edition, 2003), 324–346. The RGVA in Moscow holds significant documentation in Fond 500, but Mallmann's article is based on copies of these materials available in German archives. On Gräfe, see Mallmann, "Krieg Im Dunkeln," 325 note 7.

Great Terror, which had defined opposition very broadly – anti-Bolshevik Communist groups in the Soviet Union. Gräfe was convinced that anyone in opposition to the Soviet system could be considered a potential activist for Operation Zeppelin and would be willing to work for Germany and envisioned a plethora of tasks for them: from the collection and transmission of intelligence, to sabotage, to assassinations, to the apprehension of Soviet agents, to the dissemination of national, social, and religious propaganda, to the instigation of localized revolts.[30] Primarily, though, Zeppelin was to obtain concrete information about the Soviet Union:

> The essential elements of information to be obtained by the UZ [Unternehmen Zeppelin] group concerned the status of the food supply within the USSR, possible increases in agricultural production by state farms in the USSR, the potential of the Soviet coal and petroleum industries, significant anti-Soviet movements within the USSR, and the best means of using anti-Soviet propaganda within the USSR.[31]

The operation brought to the fore the three main strands of Office VI's activities in a way that was never directly addressed in directives and decrees but clearly observed by the Western Allies; "Amt VI of the RSHA is at the same time a political intelligence department, a political warfare executive (whispering campaigns, press and radio propaganda) and a special operations section."[32]

Gräfe's ideas soon gained the approval of Heydrich and, eventually, Himmler. The latter brought the matter to Hitler's attention and gained his support. The endeavor came from an entity with the appropriate ideological background and Gräfe's ideas were broad and visionary. Gräfe recreated common approaches, the basic idea to use POWs for intelligence gathering, in an exciting and colossal fashion. An Operation Zeppelin member summarized Office VI's approach pointedly after the war, "[t]hey [military intelligence] had more experience and we more imagination."[33] Imagination carried the day: the OKW and the Gestapo advised their personnel of the project in March 1942 and by July 1942 the latest, the OKH, High Command of the Army, was on board as well. The impetus for Operation Zeppelin notably came from below, from inside Office VI. It did not originate with Himmler, as Schellenberg and others

---

[30] Mallmann, "Krieg Im Dunkeln," 326.
[31] Counterintelligence Special Report 61, Operation Zeppelin, NA, RG 319, IRR, Box 6, XE 003374 [hereafter: Special Report 61.]
[32] R.I.S. 16/27.9.43, NA, RG 226, Entry 108 B, Box 286, Folder: RIS Reports.
[33] Otto Kraus quoted in Mallmann, "Krieg Im Dunkeln," 323 note 21. Postwar reports stress that the two entities mainly duplicated each other's work; Special Report 61.

claimed after the war.[34] Office VI was front and center: its members initiated, conceptualized, and set into motion Operation Zeppelin.

Office VI shrewdly used the stalled military situation at the East for its gain. The Abwehr and other entities, such as *Fremde Heere*, Foreign Armies, had failed to predict accurately the situation Germany's military forces were to encounter upon the invasion; the notion of the Soviet Union as a giant on clay feet had determined the pre-Barbarossa discourse. With Operation Zeppelin, Office VI expanded officially and with the blessing of the highest Reich authorities into military intelligence, indicating the ongoing power shift in Germany's foreign intelligence universe: Zeppelin commenced in earnest around the same time, the first half of 1942, that the new version of the Ten Commandments went into effect.[35] The ink on the agreement was barely dry but Office VI was probing its boundaries and embarking on activities that made a mockery of it. But then for Office VI agreements between the different branches of Germany's foreign intelligence universe and intelligence work on the ground existed independently from each other. What Gräfe planned and Schellenberg, Heydrich, Himmler, and, ultimately, Hitler approved, namely the de facto intrusion into core tasks of military intelligence, was one thing; agreements had little to do with it. Office VI upheld agreements only if they were to its advantage.

The basic ideas of Operation Zeppelin were by no means new but standard procedure; POWs and disaffected citizens of occupied countries had been used for the collection of frontline – tactical – intelligence since time immemorial. Primarily in charge of the evaluation of military intelligence at the Eastern Front was *Fremde Heere Ost* (FHO), Foreign Armies East. General Reinhard Gehlen headed FHO between 1942 and 1945; it was tied to the High Command of Army.[36] By spring 1942, FHO

---

[34] Mallmann, "Krieg Im Dunkeln," 325–327; Schellenberg *Labyrinth*, 261; Final Report; also Doerries, *Intelligence Chief*, 113–114, 260–261. Doerries suggests that Schellenberg did not know about details that Gräfe collaborated closely with Müller and the Gestapo, especially when it came to interrogations and "certain measures behind the Russian lines." As an Office VI operation, it was still Schellenberg's responsibility.

[35] Mallmann, "Krieg Im Dunkeln," 327. The discussions between Heydrich and Canaris began in February 1942 the latest. BAL, NS 19/3514, 131–145.

[36] David Thomas, "Foreign Armies East and German Military Intelligence in Russia 1941–1945," *Journal of Contemporary History* 22 (1987), 263. On Gehlen and FHO, see Kahn, *Spies*, 428–442. On his postwar career: Timothy Naftali, "Reinhard Gehlen and the United States," in Richard Breitman et al., eds. *U.S. Intelligence and the Nazis* (Washington, DC: National Trust Fund for the Nazi War Crimes and Japanese Imperial Government Records Interagency Working Group, 2004), 373–418; Mary Ellen Reese, *General Reinhard Gehlen: The CIA Connection* (Fairfax, MD: George Mason University Press, 1990). See also Gehlen's voluminous CIA files, NA, RG 263, Entry ZZ 18, Boxes 39–41.

had acquired operational direction over the Abwehr and its intelligence collection efforts in this theater of war, as the Abwehr's performance before the German invasion of the Soviet Union and during the first few months of the war was considered abysmal. Generally speaking, FHO managed to become well acquainted with the Red Army's capabilities but knowledge "did not vouchsafe better understanding of intentions."[37] FHO also used Soviet POWs but on a smaller scale than the one proposed by Office VI.

Operation Zeppelin's recruitment tapped into a reservoir of recalcitrant Soviet citizens. Klaus-Peter Mallmann shows that Zeppelin recruits shared characteristics: many had lost loved ones during the Russian Civil War, the collectivization and the famine of the late 1920s and early 1930s, or the purges of the 1930s. Others were at odds with Soviet life and ideology for ethnic or religious reasons.[38] The organizers of Operation Zeppelin were convinced that they could translate the recruits' disaffection from, or hate for, the Soviet regime and their survival instinct into support of National Socialist Germany and its imperial project. But Nazi ideology was a hard sell to people who were considered subhuman under it and had little to gain from their collaboration. Ideological training consequently honed onto the lowest common denominator: anti-Semitism and anti-Bolshevism.[39] Bolshevism should not be identified with any "ethnic group or race," like Russians or Asians, Gräfe suggested, but should be exclusively tied to "international Jewry."[40] In short: "Judeo-Bolshevism" was to be ticket to convince Soviet POWs to take up Nazism's cause.

Operation Zeppelin's distinguishing characteristics were its mass approach and the plan to use those activists far in the Soviet hinterland.[41] The goal was to go beyond the collection of tactical intelligence and acquire strategic intelligence that would allow for the formation of policies

[37] Thomas, "Foreign Armies East," 289. Gehlen's detailed knowledge about the Red Army's capabilities did not prevent him from misinterpreting its intentions; Foreign Armies East missed several major Soviet attacks, as Gehlen was wedded to his misconceptions about the Soviet Union, even in the light of counterevidence. "Gehlen is proof that the greatest deception senior intelligence officers suffer is from their own opinions," as Thomas points out. In addition, Foreign Armies East fell prey to Soviet deception; even its most reliable agents were either double agents or conduits for Soviet misinformation, *maskirovka*. See Kahn, *Spies*, 441–442. On FHO: Magnus Pahl, *Fremde Heere Ost: Hitler's Feindaufklärung* (Berlin: Ch. Links Verlag, 2012).
[38] Mallmann, "Krieg Im Dunkeln," 329–330.   [39] Special Report 61.
[40] Quoted in Mallmann, "Krieg Im Dunkeln," 344 note 111.
[41] However, there is mass approach and then there is mass approach. Thomas suggests: "per annum, the Soviets committed roughly 40,000 well-trained agents and perhaps twice as many poorly trained mass agents." Thomas, "Foreign Armies East," 274.

and broader military planning.[42] Zeppelin ultimately also distinguished itself from similar operations, past and present, through its complete and racially motivated disregard for its recruits. The mass approach initially netted a substantial number of candidates; recruitment ended in the summer of 1942 due to its success. However, these men were hardly volunteers. Recruitment rested with the Einsatzgruppen, as they represented Sipo and SD locally. POWs, starving to death in nonprovisioned holding pens and sleeping on the bare ground, confronted a life-or-death decision when being recruited and many chose possible survival. Screened for health and overall political reliability, the men then went through a series of training camps. Next to the tricks and trades of their future deployment, ideological education was central.[43]

In his memoir, Schellenberg presented Operation Zeppelin as a meeting of anti-Stalinist minds. He conjured up the image of Soviet POWs in German army uniforms, provided with the best of the best: " . . . .best food, clean quarters, lecture films, and trips through Germany," and screened for their political convictions: " . . . whether they only wanted to enjoy the advantages of the plans; whether they had really turned against the terrors of the Stalinist system; or whether, racked by inner conflicts, they were hovering between the two ideologies Nazism and Stalinism."[44] Schellenberg's stories had nothing to do with reality. Hundreds of recruits who fell ill during their training were murdered at Auschwitz, while others were murdered for insubordination or for their lack of enthusiasm.[45] Being with Operation Zeppelin was a dangerous livelihood.

The recruits' situation got only worse once operations commenced in late June 1942 and Office VI gained little. Most activists were parachuted into their target area; others crossed the frontlines clandestinely. Most groups were consisted of four to five people with one man serving as the radio operator. Missions of particular importance included two radio operators. If a group's task included propaganda, they also carried with them enormous quantities of propaganda material, sometimes

---

[42] I follow basic definitions of strategic and tactical intelligence here. Norman Polmar and Thomas B. Allen, *Spy Book: The Encyclopedia of Espionage* (New York: Random House, 1997), 538, 545.

[43] Mallmann, "Krieg Im Dunkeln," 328–332. On the situation in the POW camps, see: Christian Streit, *Keine Kameraden: Die Wehrmacht und die sowjetischen Kriegsgefangenen 1941–1945* (Suttgart: Deutsche Verlagsanstalt, 1978). The recruitment drive was so successful that the RSHA established two volunteer units consisting of Soviet citizens not qualified for activists' work. These units assisted the Einsatzgruppen.

[44] Schellenberg, *Labyrinth*, 264. Note how Schellenberg serves postwar sensibilities with this statement.

[45] Mallmann, "Krieg Im Dunkeln," 341. At Schellenberg's trial, Kasimierez Smolen, a former prisoner employed in the camp's administration, testified to the murders at Auschwitz; Doerries, *Intelligence Chief*, 260–261.

several thousand pamphlets or magazines.[46] Mallmann counts a total of 126 activists targeting the Caucasus alone between June and November 1942; many more were available for deployment. Estimates have five to eight hundred Zeppelin "activists" behind enemy lines on any given day between 1942 and 1944 but the overall yield was small. Office VI also had no capabilities to double-check the information it received. Weekly reports were submitted to Operation Zeppelin's central administration, and information deemed particularly important was disseminated immediately within the RSHA. General intelligence assessments dealing with Ukraine were, on occasion, shared with the military; however, this procedure was soon halted. One of the biggest successes in the Soviet Union was an act of sabotage against one of the main train stations in Leningrad, but the city was already under a tight German siege. Other planned acts of sabotage, especially in the Urals, did not come to fruition, as airplanes and fuel became scarce in Germany. And many recruits simply disappeared once they had crossed the frontlines while others sent inaccurate information or tried to make it through the maze by sending a mixture of accurate messages and inventions. Men waiting for weeks on end for deployment, on the other hand, became "nervous and mistrustful," drank too much, and became, in the opinion of their German masters, easy prey for Soviet agents. Schellenberg tried to secure additional funding from Himmler, but to no avail. By March 1943 the more ambitious parts of Operation Zeppelin had, for technical and financial reasons, come to all but a standstill.[47]

In February 1943, Gräfe took an accounting of the operation. He concluded that some information had been gained but noted that sabotage activities had been "less complete."[48] Foreign Armies East and the Abwehr were equally misinformed, though. Ultimately, they all supplied the same distorted information. Gräfe identified three main reasons for his operation's lackluster results: technical difficulties; the distracting attempt to be active on the entire Eastern Front; and the success of Stalin's propaganda. Subsequently, sabotage took a backseat to intelligence gathering and soon long-range intelligence gathering took a backseat to frontline espionage – tactical intelligence instead of the strategic intelligence one had initially set out to collect. In addition, Zeppelin men were increasingly used for other activities: many became auxiliary troops in Germany's bloody campaign against real and imagined Soviet partisans and anyone who could possibly be accused of collaboration with the

[46] Special Report 61.
[47] Mallmann, "Krieg Im Dunkeln," 335–336; 338–340; Special Report 61.
[48] Mallmann, "Krieg Im Dunkeln," 336 note 69.

partisans.[49] Office VI's ambitious plans in military intelligence, which had initially captured the imagination of Himmler and Hitler, were being downscaled every step of the way. Erstwhile Zeppelin recruits now primarily supplemented the Sipo and SD in its "genuine" task: race war.

There was little doubt that as an intelligence operation Zeppelin had failed. Heinrich Fenne, involved with it in the South of the Soviet Union, after the war proposed seven reasons for the project's resounding failure: higher officials had no understanding of the country and its problems and failed to understand that even disaffected people might not be willing to revolt; its security was poor; the Germans assigned to lead treated the activists as inferiors; too much time was spent on hatching fantastic plans; German planes could not reach distant targets; German propaganda worked only while the country held the upper hand in the war; and the lack of cooperation between the RSHA and the military intelligence.[50] Some of Fenne's reasons belie his postwar effort to blame someone else – superiors or subordinates – but others are indubitably accurate. Ultimately, a ragtag team of Soviet POWs, pressed into service in the most dire of circumstances, perceived and treated as subhumans, exposed to mixed ideological messages, and trained haphazardly was how Germany's ideological vanguard tried to gather information on the political and military viability of the Soviet Union. None of this appears as a recipe for success. But then Operation Zeppelin had never been about the collection of military intelligence alone. It was at least as much about Office VI's protracted turf war for primacy in matters of intelligence with the Abwehr and Fremde Heere Ost. When their failures became evident in late 1941, Office VI rushed to fill the void – with an approach similar to the one taken by FHO and the Abwehr, but in a new and radically Nazified key. The official usurpation of the Abwehr's functions remained a matter of time and timing, but Office VI's success in gaining support for Zeppelin indicates that, as early as 1942, strategic military intelligence was down for the count. Its demise was not yet a forgone conclusion, but had become a definite possibility.

Office VI officially usurped the Abwehr in early 1944. Hitler's order was issued on February 12, 1944 and achieved what Office VI, Schellenberg, Heydrich and later Kaltenbrunner, and Himmler had worked and schemed for since the early 1940s: the inclusion of the Abwehr into the RSHA. The four men, as well as Müller of the Gestapo, who was interested in the Abwehr's counterintelligence functions, did not agree

---

[49] Mallmann, "Krieg Im Dunkeln," 337–339; Kahn, *Spies*, 360. Schellenberg remembered Zeppelin men infiltrating partisan groups rather than as auxiliaries in the race war; Schellenberg, *Labyrinth*, 264.
[50] Special Report 61.

on all the details of the incorporation but worked together well to achieve the basic fact. The eventual set-up, which amalgamated Office VI and the Abwehr under the leadership of the former and under Himmler's oversight, corresponded with Schellenberg and Himmler's plans. The Abwehr was broken into its constitutive pieces and distributed among different offices of the RSHA, with the biggest and most important components going to Schellenberg's domain.[51] Doerries' suggestions that there existed a fundamental difference between Himmler and Schellenberg, as the former wanted to bring "all police, security, and intelligence functions in Germany under his control" while Schellenberg wanted to create an independent, centralized, and efficient service relies largely on Schellenberg's postwar statements.[52] Schellenberg might have dreamt of such a service but there is little indication that he was tempted to antagonize his patron Himmler then. As it was, Schellenberg was the developments' main beneficiary. Office VI almost doubled in size and importance and became, at least on paper, the unified, all-encompassing foreign intelligence service that he had envisioned heading for many years.

Ranking members of the RSHA had been suspicious of the Abwehr and Canaris for years. It was generally believed that in the winter of 1939, Abwehr members had attempted to make contact with the Western Allies, trying to sound out attitudes toward a peace offer by a German government without Hitler. It was also assumed that early in 1940 Abwehr members had leaked German plans for the attack on the Western European countries. These allegations were true.[53] Canaris' personal loyalty had been questioned even earlier; allegedly, he had provided the British Navy with information about German submarine construction before his appointment to the Abwehr in 1935. This was likely "a figment of Schellenberg's (and perhaps also Heydrich's) imagination," but indicates the general atmosphere of suspicion and distrust.[54] After the beginning of the war, intelligence failures, such as the Abwehr's poor performance in the Soviet Union, its failure to predict the Allied landing

[51] Black, *Kaltenbrunner*, 193–194; Decree Hitler, February 12, 1944, NA, RG 242, T-78, Reel 497, Frame 6485650.
[52] Doerries, *Intelligence Chief*, 52; 131–132. It is a stretch to suggest that there is a no clear indication that Schellenberg wanted to destroy the Abwehr from the start. As Schellenberg wanted to head a centralized, unified service, the Abwehr's destruction was implicit in his plans.
[53] Black, *Kaltenbrunner*, 190–191; Schellenberg, *Labyrinth*, 348–349. For a short overview on the Abwehr's contacts to the Vatican: Wolfgang Benz and Walter Pehle, eds., *Lexikon des Deutschen Widerstandes* (Frankfurt/Main: S. Fischer Verlag, 1994), 294–297. For Canaris' contacts with the German resistance: Heinz Höhne, *Canaris*, trans. by J. Maxwell Brownjohn (New York: Doubleday & Company, 1979), 388–423.
[54] Black, *Kaltenbrunner*, 190–191 note 24.

in North Africa, or its inability to run agents in Great Britain or the United States began to pile up. Canaris' formerly fine relationship with Hitler and other Nazi leaders deteriorated perceptibly.[55] Canaris' position was becoming tenuous and the same was true for the organization he headed.

Suspicions of disloyalty, even treason, and an unseeming ideological distance to the party state notwithstanding, Schellenberg had a good relationship with Canaris. It dated back to Schellenberg's years in the Gestapo's counterintelligence department and continued when the two men headed their different intelligence services and over the years much has been made of Schellenberg's postwar – and self-serving – hints that he and Canaris spoke openly about their allegedly shared disillusionment with the state they served.[56] After the war, Schellenberg drew an intriguing picture of Canaris and the Abwehr, which was meant to make sense of and to justify the development of the 1940s. He stressed Canaris' pessimistic, fatalistic, and elusive attitudes, his nervousness, and also commented on his mystical streak. The latter Schellenberg tied to Canaris' fascination with Catholicism, its organization, and strength of faith. In Schellenberg's view, the Vatican unduly influenced the Protestant Canaris and his conspiratorial activities had to be blamed on the influence of the "Roman Papacy"; Schellenberg's capacity for ideological reasoning had clearly not diminished. But he still "could not help liking the Admiral."[57] The men's relationship, Schellenberg stated, allowed him to observe closely the Abwehr and he shared with his postwar audiences his observations, which he deemed impartial as he "quite soberly regarded the facts." These spoke against Canaris and the Abwehr:

He [Canaris] was overinflating his organization, indiscriminately enrolling serious workers and dubious riffraff; reforms were feebly attempted and then allowed to peter out. To me this whole organization was a nightmarish oppression for how was the general situation to develop if no efficient work was done in this important sector of military intelligence?[58]

Regarding him as "far too humane," Schellenberg also considered Canaris the pawn of his subordinates, unwilling to take strong measures or to see them through. In short, Canaris was a pessimistic weakling and the Abwehr was a failure. But Schellenberg always knew that the solution could be found in the integration of the two services into one unified intelligence organization under his oversight.[59]

[55] Doerries, *Intelligence Chief*, 131; Kahn, *Spies*, 268.
[56] Doerries, *Intelligence Chief*, 52, 52 note 122.   [57] Schellenberg, *Labyrinth*, 193, 347.
[58] Schellenberg, *Labyrinth*, 353.   [59] Höhne, *Canaris*, 372.

It remains impossible to determine who wanted to get rid of Canaris. At different times different RSHA personalities – Himmler, Heydrich, Müller, Kaltenbrunner, and Schellenberg – led the charge but the envisioned end result was the same: Canaris' disposal and the end of his organization as independent from the RSHA. Schellenberg used the Abwehr to rouse his subordinates into action, admonishing them to "continually increase our influence in the ministries and to try to outstrip the predominant position of the Abwehr."[60] Kaltenbrunner's appointment brought the campaign against Canaris, which had simmered on the backburner during the leaderless year after Heydrich's death, to the fore again. The new head of the RSHA shared the belief that Canaris and his organization were treasonous as well as incompetent; in addition, and different from Heydrich and Schellenberg, he also despised Canaris.[61] The usurpation of the Abwehr was close to Kaltenbrunner's heart and the overall situation developed in his favor.

An isolated arrest on currency charges in August 1942 had led the Gestapo to an anti-Hitler group in the Abwehr; by April 1943 several members of the Abwehr were relieved of their positions and arrested. Himmler did not take the matter to Hitler, but passed it on to the military authorities.[62] Canaris' Italian activities in the fall of 1943 were dubious as well, but again Himmler did not move against Canaris and his organization. While never averse to broadening his own purview, Himmler possibly did not believe to have Hitler's support in the expected showdown.[63] Apparently, Himmler's zeal to incorporate the Abwehr

---

[60] Protokoll über die Gruppenleiter und Referentenbesprechung des Amt VI, 19 September 1942 cited in Black, *Kaltenbrunner*, 191 note 26; Protokoll über die Referentenbesprechung, am Donnerstag, den 6. November 1941, vormittags, 8 Uhr, USHMM 14.016 M, 428.

[61] Black, *Kaltenbrunner*, 192.

[62] In August 1942, German customs officials arrested Major Wilhelm Schmidhuber, a Bavarian businessman with connections to the Abwehr office in Munich, for a currency violation. When denied assistance by Canaris, Schmidhuber hinted at Abwehr attempts to make contact with the Western Allies via the Vatican in 1939–1940. This turned it into a Gestapo matter that by February 1943 had led into the heart of the Abwehr. Black, *Kaltenbrunner*, 193; Benz and Pehle, eds., *Lexikon*, 294–297; Höhne, *Canaris*, 498–509; Richard Breitman, "Nazi Espionage: The Abwehr and the SD Foreign Intelligence," in Richard Breitman et. al., eds., *U.S. Intelligence and the Nazis* (Washington, DC: National Trust Fund for the Nazi War Crimes and Japanese Imperial Government Records Interagency Working Group, 2004), 108.

[63] Shortly after Mussolini's ouster and arrest, Canaris met with the head of the Italian military intelligence service, Cesare Amé. Amé alerted Canaris that the Badoglio government was trying to sue for a separate peace with the Western Allies. Purportedly, Canaris hoped that other German Allies would follow suit. In the meantime, Canaris ensured that the German military in Italy believed in Badoglio's assertions that the new Italian government would stay in the war. The information Schellenberg received was

was not immediate but, fortified with ample evidence, Himmler bid his time until he could be reasonably assured of Hitler's support.

In early 1944, the situation came to a head. In the second week of January, the Gestapo arrested several leading members of a resistance circle in Berlin, among them a ranking member of the Abwehr, Major Otto Kiep.[64] Shortly thereafter, Allied troops landed behind German lines at Anzio, Italy; military intelligence had pronounced such a landing unlikely. And before the month's end, an Abwehr agent in Istanbul and his wife, spooked by the recent arrests in Berlin, defected to the British. To add insult to injury, Kaltenbrunner, stoking Hitler's ire, reported some ten days later that the man, Erich Maria Vermehren, had been working for the British Intelligence Service for some time. And the Turkish Abwehr exodus was not over yet: two more operatives working under cover in Istanbul, Willy Hamburger and Karl Kleczkowski, made off into the open arms of US intelligence. There is indication that all three men brought with them valuable German documents and the British press had a field day reporting on Vermehren's defection.[65] Within a short time the Abwehr had suffered three major blows: it had missed, yet again, a significant military development; ranking members had been arrested for treason; and personnel abroad had defected. And at least one of the defectors was rumored to have been a double agent. Things would have looked dire for the Abwehr even without other agencies circling the waters.

An Abwehr bomb planted on a British ship carrying Spanish oranges proved to be the straw that broke the proverbial camel's back, as the Abwehr was under orders not to engage in sabotage efforts that would harm Spanish interests. Earlier German acts of sabotage had hurt the relationship between Germany and Spain, and in 1943 Francisco Franco had moved the country from nonbelligerence to neutrality. Germany needed Spain for its wolfram supplies and along its coastline German submarines were resupplied. The Auswärtige Amt reasoned that any further sabotage activities would bring Spain even closer to the West. Upon receiving the news of the attack on British and Spanish interests, on ship and oranges, and egged on by Himmler's liaison at his headquarters, SS Brigadeführer Hermann Fegelein, Hitler became livid

---

diametrically opposed and actually accurate. Schellenberg, *Labyrinth*, 354–356; Black, *Kaltenbrunner*, 193–194. Höhne, *Canaris*, 531–534; Breitman, "Nazi Espionage," 107. For details on Italy, see below.

[64] Black, *Kaltenbrunner*, 194. On the "Solf Kreis:" Benz and Pehle, eds., *Lexikon*, 298–300; Höhne, *Canaris*, 538.

[65] Black, *Kaltenbrunner*, 194; Höhne, *Canaris*, 539, 547–548; Doerries, *Intelligence Chief*, 132–133.

and decided to create a unified intelligence service and be done with Canaris and the Abwehr once and for all.[66]

Hitler's initially verbal order led to several conferences and negotiations with differing casts of characters. An initial conference took place among Himmler, Kaltenbrunner, Müller, Walther Huppenkothen, Schellenberg's successor in the Gestapo's counterintelligence department, Schellenberg, and his confidant Martin Sandberger, bringing together RSHA officials who had a vested interest to break up the Abwehr and who stood to benefit from it. They discussed the basics of the planned merger from the viewpoint of the RSHA. Subsequently, Kaltenbrunner began discussions with Generals Alfred Jodl and Wilhelm Keitel of the OKW; they designated General August Winter as their chief negotiator. A conference at Zossen in early March 1944 then hammered out the most relevant details. Kaltenbrunner, Müller, Huppenkothen, and Schellenberg represented the RSHA; the OKW/Abwehr was represented by Winter, Colonel Georg Hansen, and the leadership of Abwehr II and III, Espionage and Sabotage. Kaltenbrunner's and Müller's plan, agreed upon during the earlier RSHA-only meeting, was simple: they intended to incorporate fully the Abwehr's espionage and sabotage departments into Office VI and its counterespionage department into Office IV, the Gestapo. The first part of the plan has been likened to a tiger's attempt to swallow an elephant; Office VI was a quarter of the size of those two Abwehr departments. Schellenberg, presumably to the surprise of the others, opposed the straightforward absorption of these two entities into his office but advocated the establishment of a separate *Militärisches Amt* or *Amt Mil*, Military Office, consisting of the espionage and sabotage departments of the Abwehr. This new office was to work side by side with the existing Office VI. The Abwehr representatives eagerly embraced this suggestion, which would allow them to maintain some independence from the RSHA.

As told by Schellenberg, Kaltenbrunner and Müller were aghast at his plan, which remained below the possible: the full integration of the Abwehr into Office VI. Summoned to Himmler to explain his support for the lesser alternative, Schellenberg argued that if the Abwehr departments were to be fused with Office VI right away, Office VI and ultimately the RSHA would be responsible for all military matters, for example, warnings about Allied landings. Both men knew that the Abwehr had failed repeatedly on this account and earned Hitler's wrath. Schellenberg

[66] Black, *Kaltenbrunner*, 194; Höhne, *Canaris*, 552–553; Doerries, *Intelligence Chief*, 138, suggests that Keitel also lobbied Hitler for the break-up of the Abwehr. Decree Hitler, February 12, 1944, NA, RG 242, T-78, Reel 497, Frame 6485650.

had no interest to have his office tainted by Abwehr failures and Himmler, ever concerned about Hitler, "saw the wisdom" of Schellenberg's reasoning and supported it.[67] For Schellenberg, his plan combined the best of two worlds: Office VI would gain access to the resources of the Abwehr departments forming Amt Mil and could take credit for its successes. Yet it would still be able to disavow Amt Mil's failures. In addition, Schellenberg's willingness to entertain something less than a complete integration of the Abwehr garnered him some goodwill among Abwehr officials now adrift. It established him as the reasonable RSHA representative willing to pick battles with Kaltenbrunner and Müller and able to win them through Himmler's backing. There is little indication that Schellenberg's plan was meant "to protect the Abwehr against falling fully into the power sphere of Heinrich Müller, the Gestapo Chief" for the sake of the Abwehr and its personnel.[68] Schellenberg regarded the inclusion of the Abwehr into his sphere as his birthright as the chief of foreign intelligence and his careful approach had little to do with protecting the Abwehr. However, Schellenberg's savvy moves made a fruitful future collaboration between his office and the Abwehr and its personnel much more likely.

The same was true for the agreement between Schellenberg and the designated leader of Amt Mil, Colonel Georg Hansen. As the two offices were to exist next to each other and have departments dealing with the same matters, the two men agreed to deputize for each other. This policy was extended to the lower levels as well. While some have seen this as "the realistic beginnings of a fruitful cooperation" that included "even attempts at some organized socializing to improve relations between the officers of the two services," Schellenberg and Office VI ultimately held the advantages.[69] Amt Mil, formerly known as the Abwehr, had lost its independence and had been moved under the purview of Office VI. No social occasion or show of cooperative duality was to change this, even if Schellenberg's willingness to postpone the official pronouncement of complete victory must have smoothed some ruffled feathers. The realities were clear: Schellenberg had Himmler's ear and was, in his relationship with Hansen, *primus inter pares*. The new, combined intelligence service was an integral part of Himmler's universe with Schellenberg at its helm.

On May 23, 1944, after intense discussions with Wilhelm Keitel, the commander-in-chief of the OKW, Kaltenbrunner issued the decree that finalized the destruction of the Abwehr.[70] The personnel and administrative departments of the Abwehr were incorporated into the corresponding

---

[67] Final Report; Kahn, *Spies*, 269; Black, *Kaltenbrunner*, 196; Doerries, *Intelligence Chief*, 138–140.

[68] Doerries, *Intelligence Chief*, 139.   [69] Doerries, *Intelligence Chief*, 140.

[70] Black, *Kaltenbrunner*, 196–197.

offices of the RSHA; the pertinent sections of the Abwehr's counterespionage department were transferred to the comparable Gestapo offices;
and the espionage and sabotage departments of the Abwehr now formed
Amt Mil of the Chief of the Security Police and SD, Kaltenbrunner. Amt
Mil and its offices and personnel abroad now fell under the authority of
Schellenberg; the take-over came into effect on June 1, 1944. Yet Amt
Mil's semi-independence was a temporary arrangement, for Schellenberg
was tasked to prepare the eventual "fusion" of the two offices.[71] In the
short term, though, the arrangement's wisp of compromise preserved the
peace and made the transition more agreeable for Abwehr personnel. Yet
few could have doubted that the RSHA would swallow completely the
Abwehr eventually. In fact, Schellenberg had set his aims even higher.

On May 14 and 15, 1944, in conjunction with Himmler and Keitel
signing the final agreement about the absorption of the Abwehr, a conference for intelligence services' leading personnel took place in Salzburg.
Little is known about this conference that was meant both to commu-
nicate and to cement the new structures and to allow the officers from
the two organizations to socialize and to get to know each other better.
Himmler delivered the concluding keynote speech, which, as Augustinovic and Moll argue, set out to confirm his leadership, to intimidate
critics of the restructuring, and to bring the Abwehr officers in line.
The roster of speakers is indicative of the change of guards: Colonel
Hansen represented the former Abwehr, even though General Keitel also
addressed the assembled officers. The other speakers were: Kaltenbrunner as the head of the RSHA; Müller of the Gestapo; Eugen Steimle
and Theodor Paeffgen representing Office VI Country Groups; and an
additional member of Office VI.[72] As the head of Office VI and the main
beneficiary of the changes, Schellenberg, too, delivered a major speech;
he had shared the manuscript with Kaltenbrunner for approval a few
days prior.[73] Only Himmler and Schellenberg's speeches seem to have
survived, but these and the line-up of the other speakers indicate that
Abwehr officers were to be inducted into the structures of the RSHA and
its foreign intelligence and Gestapo counterintelligence components.

---

[71] Black, *Kaltenbrunner*, 196–197; Decree Kaltenbrunner, May 23, 1944, NA, RG 242,
T-78, Reel 497, Frame 6485655–6485658.
[72] Werner Augustinovic and Martin Moll, "Heinrich Himmlers Rede vor den
Nachrichtenoffizieren im Mai 1944: Eine Dokumentation," *JPSS* 6 (2/2012), 139.
I thank Florian Altenhöner, Berlin, for alerting me to this Himmler speech and for
sharing with me his knowledge of the speakers lined up.
[73] Schellenberg to Kaltenbrunner, Vortrag Schellenberg, vorgelegt zur Genehmigung, May
10, 1944, RGVA, Fond 500, Opis 1, 1164. For the context of the agreement, see above
and Black, *Kaltenbrunner*, 195–196.

In his speech Schellenberg laid out his vision for Germany's future intelligence and information service [*Geheime Meldedienst*] and its mandate. It is one of the few surviving documents in which Schellenberg talks to this at length in front of his peers. Schellenberg laid out his vision of a service – emerging from the SD – that closely integrated domestic and foreign spheres, was total in its approach, ideologically bound, and on a collision course with the Auswärtige Amt. He began his speech with a dual salvo at the formerly independent Abwehr and the Auswärtige Amt, noting that entities had failed. He declared that there existed the need for an intelligence and information service – by which he meant a unified service with a total approach, as there had been no shortage of intelligence and information services – but noted that Germany had come to this realization only slowly during the war. The lack of prewar interest had led to German disadvantages, as he illustrated by focusing on the German lack of preparation in the United States. German intelligence, Schellenberg argued, had not capitalized on the many advantages it had held initially: diplomatic personnel and businessmen were in the country until May 1942 and there also existed a huge reservoir of ethnic Germans and German nationals in the United States. In addition, there had been no preparation to use neutrals countries for intelligence work in case of a war with the United States. German intelligence, Schellenberg argued, had seesawed too long between "correct realizations" and "consequences not taken." The bill had been paid with the "biological and material substance of the Volk." This needed to change. Schellenberg regarded as important for an intelligence service the "ethical strength and military-soldierly superiority" but emphasized that these "virtues, grown out of traditions, strongly grounded and newly defined by National Socialism" had to be supplemented by the "truth-loving insights of an intelligence service which, working on a broad basis, is led with good political instincts." Germany needed a Nazified, politically led intelligence service.

To make his case, Schellenberg discussed the history of several intelligence services, including the German one, always tying their structure to the country's history and presumed racial character. Vague notions of racism and visions of organic, natural developments provide the undercurrent of Schellenberg's historical overview, in which he argued that every people had the intelligence service that fit its voelkisch character and history. Consequently, "practical doing" and the "life laws of the island" – and not theory – defined the British service, which had been created simultaneously to the colonial empire. The Poles, on the other hand, had long experienced subjugation and had therefore developed a "natural proclivity towards conspiracy." The Russian service, he suggested, was defined by centralization, meant to organize the "continental space" and the "racial substance" as a basis for the Communist idea. Germany was no exception to the rule. The country and its service had been defined by political disunity, a weak economic position, "tension and release of tension from East to West on the continent," a lack of global experience, and the "eternal idea of the Reich." The new service was to rectify any shortcomings that originated in the past. Its mandate was to inform as quickly as possible the political leadership of the German Volk about any relevant political, military, economic, and technical matters relating to foreign countries that were needed for the continued existence of the Volk and the maintenance of the space it dominated, and that had not or could not be collected by the official organs of the state.[74] In other words, the envisioned service was to be all-encompassing and able to go beyond anything any other state authority could accomplish. Schellenberg followed this vision for the future with a critique of the "authorized services" of the past and showed his understanding for Hitler's cool reception of their efforts. These services had presented Hitler with a "rubbery-like collection of 20 to 30 reports," without "properly and methodically evaluating" them and creating a "responsible, comprehensive statement [. . .] about the situation," argued Schellenberg. Put differently, Hitler's rejection of information emanating from the "authorized services" – Schellenberg clearly did not include his own in this group – was based on the services' poor performance, their inability to evaluate information, and their leaderships' lack of political instinct. It had nothing to do with Hitler's aversion to intelligence.

Schellenberg then discussed proper methods and fields of inquiries for a successful foreign intelligence service that could also outperform the Auswärtige Amt. His frame of reference remained the surveillance of domestic living spheres, and he argued that the understanding of foreign living spheres would help the service to understand its "objects." His example showed the ideological approaches of both Office III and VI in a nutshell. It was possible to "deduct from Mr. Eden's kinship his basic political tendencies, his attitudes," but of equal importance, according to Schellenberg, was "the influence of his private life (heart

---

[74] This is a paraphrase of Schellenberg's tortuous prose: "Die Führung des deutschen Volkes muss durch den Geheimen Meldedienst über alles in politischer, militärischer, wirtschaftlicher und technischer Hinsicht so schnell wie möglich unterrichtet werden, was für den Bestand des deutschen Volkes und der Erhaltung des von ihr zu beherrschenden Raums erheblich ist und in irgendeiner Beziehung zur übrigen Außenwelt steht und von den offiziellen Organen (außen- wie innenpolitische Ressorts des Reiches) nicht zur Kenntnis gebracht wird, bezw. gebracht werden kann."

problems, bisexual pp.)" in understanding the man and his politics. Office VI's reliance on the approaches of the domestic intelligence service and biologistic approach were rarely pronounced as clearly. Indeed, Schellenberg argued that the integration of domestic and foreign intelligence collection and evaluation would ensure the service's strength and its dominance over other agencies, most notably the Auswärtige Amt. The collection of intelligence – domestically as well as abroad – was to be subsumed under a unified, central leadership, and eventually, the same would happen to its evaluation. Foreign intelligence was to be solidly anchored in the domestic space, the *Heimatraum*. With this seemingly innocuous statement, Schellenberg moved to his explanation why the Auswärtige Amt would never succeed in its attempt to create an intelligence and information service. The Auswärtige Amt did not "understand" or "dominate" the domestic sphere.[75] Furthermore, it was dependent on the political situation and the environment in the various host countries, as it wanted to use "diplomatic-political opportunities." The Auswärtige Amt's very function restricted its abilities, even if "a completely new form of National Socialist Diplomacy" – which clearly did not yet exist – were to develop. Ultimately, Schellenberg argued, diplomacy was a profession, and diplomats moved among their peers. A proper intelligence service it was not and could never become. Against this, Schellenberg set his vision of an intelligence service as a "detached" entity that worked "coldly as ice" and was not defined by the political needs of the day or driven by emotions. Rather, it penetrated societal and living spheres abroad and was restricted only by the "coldest reasons of state [*kühlste Staatsraison*]." These reasons of state, in turn, provided the "ethical basis for [the service's] activities" and made them "morally unimpeachable" even if "in reality they were beyond good and evil." As such, the service worked like a "secure and well-oiled machine," took note of "people, developments, situations and most secret connections," and provided them to its "own leadership, and, as much as needed, also to the department of the Auswärtige Amt." The subsequent use of the information was not the service's concern. This was the vision of the morally unbound service worthy the RSHA's "unbound generation."

Schellenberg also previewed the envisioned service's structure. As had been the case before, collection would be organized geographically. Within these geographical sections four subsections would be created: the "intelligence section," the "secret service," the "scientific-systematic

---

[75] Schellenberg used the verb *beherrschen* that can mean both: to dominate and to understand.

section," and the "technical-systematic section."[76] The intelligence section was to be staffed by personnel coming from domestic organizations, who would provide the service with means, ways, and information. As Schellenberg noted, "honorary members recruited on the basis of ideology have proved themselves very well." The intelligence section would also keep recruiting agents of "foreign racial stock," but, along with informers and trusted men, they would occupy the hierarchy's lowest rungs and kept on the periphery. The leadership of the intelligence section was to be staffed by men of "German or Germanic stock" with "secure political instincts." Theirs was an "honor service of the nation [*Ehrendienst der Nation*]." In contrast, the "secret service section" was to be staffed by trained specialists who were full time employees. The "scientific-systematic sections" – one for each country – were to focus on the collection of information from open sources, while the "technical-systematic section" was to deal with technical matters like transmissions or decoding. The entire edifice was to be held together and led – strictly and centrally – by a "leadership center." Schellenberg did not elucidate how he expected to pull of this feat, but firmly set forth his maxim: "The Center needs to know everything." An Evaluation Section deemed indispensable and divided up into political, military, economic, and technical subsections was to round out the future service. Its focus was to be the collection of information in one place, its interpretation, and the development of its potential utilization. Schellenberg claimed that the service had no interest in how information was used but the tasks of the planned Evaluation Section suggest differently, as it was to provide – at least – suggestions for political measures. Schellenberg's vision for the intelligence and information service of the future was broad and ambitious: it was to be unified, total in its approach, and defined by ideology.

The defining role of ideology is particularly obvious in the speech's last section. Discussing the "political education problem," Schellenberg stressed the ideological convictions of the entire service and emphasized that the "political development, directed by our leader, has opened the eyes of the German Volk for the European space." Schellenberg regarded this as a step toward "world experience [*Welterfahrenheit*]." This ideological conviction, Schellenberg emphasizes, would be particularly important in the coming peace and in the "exploitation of the space gained in the East in a German Europe," as ideology guaranteed secure instincts. Indeed, Schellenberg deemed "a clean National Socialist, Germanic world view" the basis of the intelligence service, especially in the

---

[76] The German original uses the following terminology: Intelligence Sektor; Geheimdienstlicher Sektor; Wissenschaftlich-methodischer Sektor; Technisch-methodischer Sektor.

context of "moral and material freedoms" given to it. Ideology was key –
not only in the service that already existed, but also in the future service
that Schellenberg described vividly in his talk. These are hardly the words
of a man racked by doubts about the National Socialist project.

Himmler's concluding keynote, which ran for about two hours, amplified some of the points Schellenberg also made; however, compared to
Himmler's speech, Schellenberg's was a beacon of moderation.[77] Presumably, this was not lost on the Abwehr officers in the audience. Himmler, too, spent much time on a historical overview of intelligence services,
making in even starker terms the point that there exists a correspondence between a service's structure and the race, blood, and nature of
the people who created it. Himmler, for example, opined that Heinrich
I. must have had a voelkisch intelligence service and conversely assumed
that the Mongol Khans knew about everything "due to an intelligence
service based exclusively on the meanness corresponding to their blood
and their subhuman-ness." Race, blood, and instinct based on blood –
and not rules and regulations – Himmler argued, should guide the service's way and show what is right: "[c]onsequently, all question of life
can only be evaluated by the most intensely racially and instinctually
secure members of the people in the intelligence service, and these need
to follow – instinctually secure – their blood." The second precondition
for an intelligence service is the state, he went on, and the state's will
to internal power and to imperial endeavors; there is nothing defensive
about it. "Blood and race and state form and imperial will; those are the
preconditions for an intelligence service. Only when both are there and
coming together – if the Reich is the Reich of this blood – only then are
the preconditions created that an ideal intelligence service for this Reich
can be brought to life and keep on living." Clearly, only the SS/SD could
be this ideal service.

Himmler attempted to dispel concerns Abwehr officers might have
had, especially about the SS; "if one wants to know what the SD is,
one need to know first, what the SS wants." He provided an overview
of the organization's basic tenets – blood and race, commitment to the
Reich, loyalty to the Führer, clan community, *Sippengemeinschaft*, and
knowledge and ability – and made sure that it was understood that this
was the SD's pedigree and background. The SD, Himmler stressed, "took
a stand on all matters based on ideology (*Weltanschauung*) and from the
racial perspective of a German." It is a service of honor in which, short
of a few exceptions – "if I want to get something out of a Jewish meeting,
I can not show up with a trusted man from Schleswig-Holstein but need

---

[77] Augustinovic and Moll, "Himmlers Rede," 141–160.

well to buy myself a Jew" – paid agents have no place. Rather, the SD is a place where people of special character work behind the scenes, not thirsting for glory but simply doing their duty for Germany.

Himmler discussed the integration of the services and the need to achieve this seamlessly and without any stoppages and frictions; he then detailed his expectations for the new entity. These ran the gauntlet: he discussed loyalty; obedience; comradeship; truthfulness; trustworthiness; secrecy; and the role of the service's members as convinced carriers of the race, the idea of the Reich, and loyalty to the Führer. He also devoted time to trusted men and to SD service as an honor service – "to be as honorable [a service], as it is honorable in England"; to how to deal with people, especially of other races; to the need to be hard against oneself; to have good nerves; and not to be pessimistic but firm, "with a clear eye and a strong heart." Himmler also made sure to stress that the service's only customer was Hitler – and the Reich – and that it was not supposed to make policy: "We are the obedient instrument, eye, and hand of the Reich and its Führer." He ended his speech, which was as programmatic and ideological as it was divorced from reality, with a view into a future when the German Empire was secure based on this generation having done its duty "in those years, however difficult they might [have] be[en]."

Both Himmler's grand ideological visions and Schellenberg's slightly more concrete, but still heavily ideologized approach to the future of the foreign intelligence put Abwehr officers on notice. Commenting on the "tertiary, ideologically motivated, and odd (*abwegig*) question with which the intelligence amateur Himmler relished his highly professional audience," Augustinovic and Moll note that "if it is correct that the situation 'on top' always reflect the situation 'down below', the German intelligence service must have been in a truly sad shape at the beginning of [its] last year."[78] There is no way of knowing what the assembled Abwehr officers thought of the speeches, but they were in accordance with each other. And that is what mattered in May 1944, for Schellenberg was now in charge. The Officers' Plot of June 20, 1944, some eight weeks after the Salzburg Conference, helped the RSHA to expedite the cowing and integration of Amt Mil and its personnel. Georg Hansen was implicated in the plot and arrested, and so was Canaris – by Schellenberg himself. Amt Mil was integrated fully into Office VI, allowing the latter unrestricted access to Abwehr personnel.[79] As far as bureaucratic

---

[78] Augustinovic and Moll, "Himmlers Rede," 139.
[79] Fifth Detailed Interrogation Report on SS Sturmbannführer Huegel, Dr. Klaus, June 14, 1945, NA, RG 226, Entry 174, Box 39, Folder 307. For a chart of Office VI after the integration of Amt Mil, see: Appendix B, Diagram Showing the Extent of the Amalgamation of RSHA Amt VI and Amt Mil as at Beg 45, Fifth Detailed Interrogation

successes go, they do not come much bigger. And the biggest beneficiaries were Schellenberg and his expanding, but still curiously unformed and uninformed foreign intelligence service.

It has been argued that Kaltenbrunner's wish to take over the Abwehr was ideologically motivated whereas Müller and Schellenberg were driven by personal ambition.[80] Whatever their individual reasons, they shared the wish and determination to see the Abwehr's independence ended and pushed aside their rivalries to reach their goal. The demise of the Abwehr was by no means a sudden development of late 1943 and early 1944, or a function of the Abwehr's intelligence failures, or of the anti-Nazi activities of some of its members. Instead, the RSHA as a whole – and Office VI in particular – actively and aggressively tried to gain purchase in the Abwehr's core tasks while calling into question its abilities as an intelligence service. Operation Zeppelin serves as a fine example, as it tried to capitalize on the Abwehr's failure to procure strategic intelligence and suggested a radical and ideological approach to achieve exactly that. Schellenberg's ambitions knew no bounds and he doubtlessly had set his sights on leading the state's one and only foreign intelligence service. His ideological convictions, on the other hand, have frequently been doubted and he was surely less vocal than others. However, his May 1944 speech on the future of a unified German intelligence service shows a man who thought and argued ideologically, saw Nazi ideology as the basis of the future service, and displayed no doubts about the future. Indeed, the speech showed that the de facto incorporation of the Abwehr into Office VI was but a first step. Schellenberg's sight was now set on the Auswärtige Amt.

Schellenberg was also an able, politically savvy tactician. His long-term goals notwithstanding, he was pragmatic – and always calculating his own potential gain – when dealing with Abwehr officers who did not share Himmler's zest for ideological reasoning or found themselves at the receiving end of Kaltenbrunner's ideological force. Colonel Hansen and others must have been thrilled at Schellenberg's willingness to settle for less than the maximum possible, but Schellenberg had his own interest in clear view: the incorporation of the Abwehr into Office VI without being responsible for all of the former's shortcomings. Schellenberg got

Report on SS Sturmbannführer Huegel, Dr. Klaus, June 14, 1945, NA, RG 226, Entry 174, Box 39, Folder 307. Canaris was interrogated for months and eventual sentenced to death by an SS court-martial. He was executed at Flossenbürg on April 9, 1944. See: Schellenberg, *Labyrinth*, 357–359 and, regarding the curious fact that Heinrich Müller appeared to have ordered Schellenberg to arrest Canaris: Doerries, *Intelligence Chief*, 145–146.

[80] Black, *Kaltenbrunner*, 198.

it all and managed to retain the goodwill of Abwehr personnel now adrift. In many ways Schellenberg was the perfect chameleon. He was the reasonable, pragmatic bureaucrat and the solid ideologue rolled into one, showing colors according to his environment. Ultimately, this made him difficult to deal with but it allowed Schellenberg to achieve what he wanted without making too many enemies.

6 Doing Intelligence
Italy as an Example

> Though information from various sources had indicated the possibility
> of the overthrow of the Fascist government, the actual event, coming
> when it did, was a surprise to the Amt.
>
> Interrogation Dr. Klaus Huegel June 26, 1945

Italy must have appeared an easy target for political foreign intelligence work. Hitler's Germany and Mussolini's Italy were joined in an extensive, although not always unproblematic, political, military, and ideological alliance. German travel to and from Italy was easy and frequent, as was postal communication. The Italian police showed no particular interest in German citizens traveling or living in the country. And after the German annexation of Austria in early 1938, Italy and Germany shared a border. Northern Italy was also home to a sizeable ethnic German minority in South Tyrol. On the other hand, and most probably in order to protect this alliance, any German intelligence work against Italy was initially explicitly banned.[1]

Italy is an ideal nutshell in which to investigate Office VI as an intelligence service.[2] First, there are intelligence efforts in and against an allied country that should have been easy but turned out to be anything but.

---

[1] A substantial number of ethnic Germans in South Tyrol opted for resettlement; Götz Aly, *"Endlösung": Völkerverschiebung und der Mord an den europäischen Juden* (Frankfurt/Main: Fischer Taschenbuch Verlag, 1999), 170–177. It is not clear who was responsible for the prohibition of intelligence work against Italy; postwar statements suggest that it originated with Hitler. Wilhelm Höttl, *Die Geheime Front. Organisation, Personen und Aktionen des deutschen Geheimdienstes* (Linz & Vienna: Nibelungen, 1950), 388; Wilhelm Höttl, *Einsatz für das Reich* (Koblenz: Verlag S. Bublies, 1997), 274; Eighth Detailed Interrogation Report on SS Sturmbannführer Huegel, Dr. Klaus, June 26, 1945, NA, RG 226, Entry 119A, Box 71, File 1829. Some contemporaneous documents indicate that the order came from Heydrich; VI C 1 Vermerk, January 24, 1940, BA- DH, RSHA Film B 200001–200007; Stand der Nachrichtenverbindungen nach und über Italien - Pläne zum Ausbau der ND-Verbindungen.

[2] For examples outside of Europe, see: Adrian O'Sulivan, Nazi Secret Warfare in Occupied Persia (Iran): *The Failure of German Intelligence Services, 1939–1945* (Basingstoke, UK: Palgrave Macmillian, 2014); Richard L. McGaha, "The Politics of Espionage: Nazi Diplomats and Spies in Argentina, 1933–1945" (Ph.Diss. Ohio University, 2009).

Secondly, there is the period around Mussolini's ouster in the summer of 1943 when Office VI scrambled first to understand and then to get ahead of the developments. Third, there is a period, beginning in the fall of 1943, when Italian authority had fallen to the wayside and various German authorities – while battling each other – pushed through their agendas. The role of Office VI underwent numerous changes over the years, but its problems as an intelligence agency remained the same: operatives and agents were ideologues; poorly trained and equipped; moved largely in pro-German circles; looked for and found anodyne information based on shared ideological assumptions; regarded the country as a homogenous entity; and furnished reports that closely resembled those of the SD's domestic branch, treating Italy as a living sphere abroad. In addition, Office VI wasted resources battling other German authorities abroad, such as the Auswärtige Amt or the military, and engaged in protracted intramural fights with other RSHA offices active in Italy, most notably the Gestapo. Doing intelligence in Italy was a three-ring circus. A semblance of cooperation, at least among the RSHA offices, was achieved after Mussolini's establishment as the head of the German puppet government of the Republic of Salò. Cooperation also came more easily in the realization of core SS and SD policies, notably the deportation of the Italian Jews and the policing and looting of the country. The collection of intelligence ceased to be Office VI's focus but remained on the agenda. Office VI became part of a unified, executive RSHA security and intelligence complex: its operatives were considered experts on Italy and provided intelligence rationales for planned policies.[3] Ultimately, these men, who frequently also had taken part in German atrocities, began to use their contacts and their location close to Switzerland to sound out possibilities for a separate peace, discussed in detail later on. Here, the focus is on Office VI as an intelligence-gathering entity – and the many ways in which it failed.

Office VI was always active in Italy.[4] A 1940 draft report to Heydrich mentioned the prohibition of intelligence work directed against Italy but described it as the base of intelligence work against enemy countries in Europe and overseas. A report by the Country Group, dated around the same time, stated that with the outbreak of the war, a reliable and

---

[3] Compare to Andrej Angrick, "Otto Ohlendorf und die SD-Tätigkeit der Einsatzgruppe D," in Michael Wildt, ed., *Nachrichtendienst, Politische Elite und Mordeinheit. Der Sicherheitsdienst des Reichsführers SS* (Hamburg: Hamburger Edition, 2003), 267–302.

[4] The locus of the Italian Department in Office VI changed several times, see: Appendix 1, Chart of Distribution of Work in Amt VI from 1939–1945, Counter Intelligence War Room, Situation Report No. 9, Amt VI of the RSHA Gruppe VI D, NA, RG 319, IRR, Box 1, XE 002303. To simplify matters, I use "Italian Department."

multifaceted net of operatives, most of them volunteers, had been created and efforts to centralize the collection of information were underway. The report stressed that the operatives' main task was the transmission of messages from other countries to Berlin office.[5] This was the official explanation for Office VI's contacts in Italy and the solicitation of reports from travelers but there is ample evidence that these men mainly gathered information on Italy.[6]

In the early phase of the war, local intelligence operatives in Italy were selected along the lines that Office VI and its predecessor had established in the 1930s. The office restricted its recruitment to politically and ideologically reliable candidates, preferably German citizens and ethnic Germans. These requirements extended to about everyone; even the lowest-level *Zubringer*, feeders, were vetted accordingly and the office preferred volunteers over paid informers – presumably for ideological and budgetary reasons.[7] A report of the SD Outpost Innsbruck in June 1941 captures the screening and recruitment process.[8] The ideological and political backgrounds of the candidates and their commitment to the cause were central and trumped their intelligence potential. If possible, the Italian Department vetted them; if it was unable to ascertain a person's political and ideological reliability, it established ideological guarantees and verifications through personal connections. One of the intelligence networks created in Northern Italy in 1940 provides a perfect example: one man had worked for the illegal Austrian intelligence service before 1938; another one was deemed "unobjectionable" by two reliable men already working for the department. The next man on the list had proven his loyalty by opting for resettlement to Germany and yet another worked as the secretary of a local NSDAP/Auslandsorganisation, NSDAP Abroad, and had been in this position when his employer, the German Consulate, had still prohibited such activities. He, in turn, suggested yet another candidate. Additional V-men were found among South Tyroleans who had opted for resettlement to Germany and among people suggested by local NSDAP groups. Informers of Italian extraction

---

[5] Vortrag, January 1940, BA-DH, ZR 920/57; Bisherige Tätigkeit und Aufgaben der Gruppe VI C, RSHA VI C, January 22, 1940, BA-DH, ZR 920/57; Stand der Nachricht-enverbindungen nach und über Italien - Pläne zum Ausbau der ND-Verbindungen, VI C 1 Vermerk, January 24, 1940, BA- DH, RSHA Film B, 200001–200007.

[6] See, for example, Mil und Mil Polit. Spionage gegen Italien 1939–1940, BA-DH, RSHA Film B, 400. For a permanent contact in Italy, see "S" I-II, VM 6841=Schwend alias "Wendig." Berichte, BA-DH, RSHA Film D, 650.

[7] Organisation u. Aufgaben des SD-RFSS, n.d., [post 1939], BA-DH, ZR 920/48; Allge-meine historische Entwicklung des Nachrichtendienstes, n.d., BA-DH, ZR 920/ A59.

[8] Dienstreisebericht des SS-O'Stuf Schubernig, SD Innsbruck to RSHA, Amt VI, June 10, 1941, BA-DH, RSHA Film A, 110001–110018.

were evaluated in a similar fashion, as "old and convinced Fascists" or as decorated war heroes.[9] Conversely, people deemed ideologically unreliable were not used or eventually dismissed: reasons for rejection ranged from Catholic-school education to having served the enemy in the mercenary and "racially mixed" French Legion.[10] In short, the application of firm, yet intuitive recruitment standards created a homogenous and effectively self-selected group of intelligence operatives – brought together and bound together by shared politics and personal connections. The nature of the recruits had, in turn, an effect on their reporting.

The informers reported on a wide variety of issues: popular moods and attitudes, the population's relationship to Nazi Germany, the economic situation, the state of the Italian army and the war effort, living conditions, and musings about the political future of Italy and its leadership as well as the future of the German–Italian alliance figure prominently.[11] The better reports focused on clear issues influencing Italian moods and attitudes and described them in great detail, developed through longstanding contacts and frequent visits to the country.[12] The worst reports were largely gossip, innuendo, and travel reports, leading to irritation in Office VI.[13] A draft letter described these reports as "completely useless" and a "waste of time" and noted that some reports, written without any understanding of the department's needs, did not go beyond the description of "meals consumed." The Italian Department requested that informers be, first, politically reliable and, second, knowledgeable

[9] BdS, Belgien und Nordfrankreich, Abteilungsleiter Zschunke to VI E 1, Höttl, August 13, 1943, BA-DH, RSHA Film C, 500052; Vermerk, RSHA VI 1, Juli 1942, BA-DH, RSHA Film B, 180076. See also Beurteilung Barilli, BA-DH, Film B, 180078–79. Here Barilli is described as an old fighter and friend of leading personalities in Italy and Germany.

[10] In one case, a woman's education in Catholic school shed doubt on her politics. SD Aussenstelle München to VI E 1, October 26, 1940, BA-DH, RSHA Film C, 556259. Also interesting is the case of Hans Theo Perschbacher, who was drafted into the RSHA in 1940. Perschbacher, generally praised as a daredevil, was a member of the SS; he had lived abroad and spoke several languages. It eventually became clear that, first, he had served with the French Foreign Legion and, second, not disclosed this information. Perschbacher's supervisors had been willing to overlook his poor test results in training but balked now: the dearth of suitable candidates for assignments abroad did not override ideological considerations. Lebenslauf, RG 242, A 3343, RS, Reel E 0520; "S" Antiitalienische Spioagenten PA II, VM Perschbacher, BA-DH, RSHA Film C, 556; Perschbacher, BA-DH, ZR 666/13.

[11] For a wealth of reports, see BA-DH, RSHA, Film A-F.

[12] SD Leitabschnitt Stuttgart to RSHA, Amt VI E, Reisebericht des Vertreters des Hösch-Konzerns für Italien, Ernst Mailänder, February 21, 1941, BA-DH, RSHA Film A, 150276–150286.

[13] SD-Abschnitt Klagenfurt to RSHA VI E 1, Reisebericht aus Italien des SS-Untersturmbannführer Hahn und des SS-Scharführers Zarka, May 1940, BA-DH, RSHA Film A, 150176–150186; SD Innsbruck to VI, August 7,1941, BA-DH, RSHA Film A, 110163.

about the country due to frequent visits.[14] Political reliability came in ahead of familiarity with the country still.

The informers' backgrounds notwithstanding, similarities prevail in the reports. They focus on generic Italian moods and attitudes and on the question whether Italy would remain pro-German – pro-Nazi – or whether the country would switch sides. Most informers held that the issue was tied to living conditions in Italy, which they regarded as tainted by corruption and nepotism, commonly described as quintessential Italian problems. Occasionally, difficult living conditions were tied to Jewish influences.[15] The reports also discussed the competency – or the lack of competency – of Mussolini and his immediate circle. Informers also reported on the state and performance of the Italian military and its draft system, which was deemed unfair and corrupt. Conversely, the reports habitually noted the Italian admiration of Germany, especially its better living conditions, fairer rationing system, and powerful army, and some suggested that the Italians were hoping for Hitler to create order in Italy or wishing for a German intervention. Others reported on the fear of a German occupation.[16] Only a few reports focused on the activities of other intelligence services in Italy, allegedly the department's mainstay.[17] Italy and its population were conceptualized entirely in terms of their relationship to Nazi Germany and the war, but as the informers were recruited on account of their ideological convictions, their frame of reference does not surprise.

Having received little to no instruction – as should be recalled, Office VI was vague on the focus of its work but might have provided its operatives with questions – the informers used their imagination and their understanding of the culture and purpose of their organization to fill this vagueness with meaning. Most reports surveyed the various Italian living spheres much like Office III, if less formulaic, reported on Germany. Indeed, some members of the Italian Department identified this as the

[14] Reiseberichte aus Italien, n.d. [1940/1941], BA-DH, RSHA Film B, 18001–18005.
[15] Deapoli Bericht, December 14, 1940, BA-DH, RSHA Film A, 050230.
[16] SD Leitabschnitt Düsseldorf to VI, Bericht des Kaufmannes Max Müller [. . .] über Italienreise im Mai 1940, May 29, 1940, BA-DH, RSHA, Film A 150032; SD Innsbruck to VI, Nachrichten aus Italien, July 3, 1941, BA-DH, RSHA Film A, 110123–110124; SD Innsbruck to VI, July 15, 1941, BA-DH, RSHA Film A, 110160; SD Innsbruck to VI, June 20, 1941, BA-DH, RSHA Film A, 110155; Innsbruck to VI, February 6, 1941, BA-DH, RSHA, Film A, 110262.
[17] Auslandsberichterstattung Italien, laufend, March 24, 1941, Nh 11733, BA-DH, RSHA Film A, 001068–69. Many reports dealing with enemy services in Italy delved into the possibilities of sabotage. Of particular interest are the reports by Friedrich Schwendt alias "Wendig;" "S" I-II, VM 6841=Schwend alias "Wendig," Berichte, BA-DH, RSHA Film D, 650.

best approach.[18] But the informers did not understand the living spheres abroad particularly well: they, for example, made no allowance for the country's geographical and social differences. They wrote about "Italy" and "Italian" while reporting on industrial Northern Italy and Rome, regions vastly different from each other, let alone from the rural South. The Italian Department shared this understanding of an Italy easily measured by one yardstick. And instead of analyzing the information received, the Italian Department simply split the reports into different subjects and labeled them *Vermerk*, notation, under its department's designation.[19] Personal impressions of informers selected for their ideological reliability thus became Office VI's foreign intelligence record.

Systematic foreign intelligence activities in Italy were, until late summer 1943, centered in Rome. A number of operatives were active there and an SD Main Representative, attached to the German Embassy, oversaw and directed them.[20] The Italian Department also attempted to establish full-time, covert operatives in Rome. However, its approaches were haphazard – indicative of a service in search of its place and mandate – and more invested in intramural German conflicts than in gathering intelligence. The story of Hans-Joachim Böttcher's posting to Rome serves as a telling example. In early 1940, aware that he was about to lose his position with Hermann Göring's Forschungsamt, an agency devoted to the surveillance of phone and wireless communication, Böttcher set out to get a new job. He applied to the three institutions gathering foreign intelligence: the Abwehr, the Auswärtige Amt, and Office VI. Böttcher, who had lived in Italy and spoke the language, lacked prior intelligence expertise but understood the culture of the organizations and marketed himself accordingly: he emphasized his political reliability over his language capabilities. Office VI, aware that the competition had received Böttcher's application as well, began to woo Böttcher with far-reaching promises for the future. Having agreed to settle in Rome posing as a German newspaper correspondent, Böttcher was dispatched immediately. He was all but completely unprepared for his covert assignment: his journalist accreditation was still pending, and while he knew that he

[18] Gedanken und Anregungen zur Gestaltung der ND-Arbeit des Referates VI B 5 (Aufgabengebiete – Arbeitsrichtlinien und VM-Einteilung – Verwertung) von SS-Obersturmführer G. Zimmer, VI B 5, May 1941, BA-DH, RSHA Film B, 350001–350016.

[19] For example: BA-DH, RSHA Film A, 160087–160091; "S" I-II VM 6852 Böttcher alias "Oettinger" – PA, BA-DH, RSHA Film D, 750.

[20] It is not clear whether there was an official SD representative posted to Rome before summer 1941; Counter Intelligence War Room, London, Liquidation Report No. 7, Amt VI of the RSHA, Gruppe VI B, NA, RG 226, Entry 116 A, Box 24, Folder 628 [hereafter: Liquidation Report No. 7.]

was to report about Italian and foreign press circles and on any information from the Italian ministries, he had no established courier routes for his reports and received his first instructions on basic counterintelligence methods three months into his Roman stint. In addition, the Italian Department had yet to resolve how to finance him.[21] In essence, Böttcher's quick deployment took precedence over any decent preparation of the mission or of the man for his mission. Despite his lack of preparation, Böttcher did well initially. His reports were deemed good, sometimes even superior, and praised for displaying clear and independent judgment. Some of Böttcher's reports were furnished to Heydrich, and they featured prominently in the *Auslandskurzmeldungen*, Short Foreign Reports, a daily publication of Office VI that highlighted individual reports.[22] Böttcher quickly became the Italian Department's beacon of hope in Rome, giving an indication of how poorly the foreign intelligence service must have been performing if a layman without instructions or training could make such an impact.

The calm was not to last. Soon, Böttcher became entangled in the competition between various RSHA offices and party organizations in Rome, a situation made only more complicated by the embassy's involvement. Rome was one of the first places where a police attaché was installed after the agreement between Foreign Minister Joachim von Ribbentrop and Heydrich – discussed below – was signed in October 1939. Police attachés ostensibly liaised with the police forces of the host country but also oversaw German police and intelligence activities in their host countries and reported directly and secretly to the RSHA. However, as they operated under the oversight of the Auswärtige Amt and its local representatives, they had to share their information with it. While police attachés could be either Sipo or SD men, they mostly came from Office IV of the RSHA, the Gestapo. This was true for Herbert Kappler, the police attaché in Rome.[23] Kappler defined himself as a member of the Gestapo and was wary not to jeopardize for the benefit of Office VI his position in the embassy or the amenable relationship with the Italian security forces. Yet Kappler took seriously his mandate as the police attaché, which included a foreign intelligence component; he gathered information for Office VI and submitted "regular but unofficial reports . . . on Italian politics and

[21] Katrin Paehler, "Ein Spiegel seiner selbst: Der SD-Ausland in Italien," in Michael Wildt, ed., *Nachrichtendienst, Politische Elite und Mordeinheit. Der Sicherheitsdienst des Reichsführers SS* (Hamburg: Hamburger Edition, 2003), 258.

[22] Paehler, "Spiegel," 258–259.

[23] Interrogation Report on SS Obersturmbannführer Kappler, Herbert, June 8, 1945, NA, RG 226, Entry 194, Box 63, Folder 280 [hereafter: Interrogation Kappler].

morale."[24] First and foremost, though, Kappler represented the Gestapo representative, and Office VI was the competition.

Kappler learned quickly that Italian security forces were convinced that Böttcher was a "Gestapo-man," the common shorthand for any RSHA member active abroad. Aware that covert German activities went against the existing agreements between the two countries and fearful for his own position, Kappler tried to curb Office VI activities by bringing the matter to the attention of the head of the Gestapo, Heinrich Müller. The latter wasted no time in addressing the issue with Heydrich, coyly suggesting that the Italians should be notified in general terms about the activities of Office VI in the country. Office VI's Italian Department was not amused by this idea, for it would have made a mockery out of its secret activities. It countered with its reading of the situation based on information provided by Böttcher. The response held that Böttcher had always acted professionally and rejected the idea to divulge the department's activities and operatives to the Italian police, predicting that such an admission would effectively end its activities in Italy.[25] This was, however, exactly what Kappler must have had in mind when he brought the matter to Müller's attention. Kappler and the Gestapo intended to monopolize information gathering in their office and hold Office VI at arm's length.

The Gestapo was a tough match for Office VI, as its political and ideological reliability could not be challenged as easily as that of other entities. Competition was intense and the Gestapo had tried to curb the radius of Office VI frequently – sometimes meeting with success, sometimes not. The Gestapo and Office VI were, however, mostly on the same side in the conflict with the Auswärtige Amt, which was deeply suspicious of professional RSHA members in its midst. Accordingly, Office VI tried to accommodate the police attachés to an extent, as their existence benefitted the intelligence service as well. In earlier cases Office VI had recalled operatives to protect Kappler's position.[26] However, that did not mean that it served at the Gestapo's pleasure. In this particular case, Office VI balked at recalling Böttcher.

Made by the Italians and the object of a tug of war between Offices IV and VI, Böttcher was soon caught up entirely in Germany's intramural fights; foreign intelligence took a distant second. But then bureaucratic infighting was territory more familiar to everyone involved; in this case, it simply happened abroad. In late 1940, Böttcher was offered a position in the press office of the NSDAP-Auslandsorganisation in Rome, yet

---

[24] Liquidation Report No. 7.   [25] Paehler, "Spiegel," 259.
[26] Paehler, "Spiegel," 259.

another organization interested in restricting the influence of the political foreign intelligence service in Italy. Despite – or maybe because of – the two organizations' antagonistic relationship, Böttcher accepted the position, even without prior approval from his supervisors in Berlin. Böttcher reasoned that he should take the job, as he did not want the head of the Auslandsorganisation in Italy, Otto Butting, an SS member himself, to become suspicious about his exact activities in Rome. He also believed that the position would allow him to get close to Butting and learn more about his politics and activities. The Italian Department, aware of Butting's antagonism toward Office VI and assuming that Butting provided information to the Abwehr and the party leadership, concurred with Böttcher's assessment. One hoped that Böttcher's new position would allow him to prove that the Abwehr collected political intelligence in Italy.[27] This information would undoubtedly constitute a bargaining tool in the ongoing conflict with the military intelligence service. Within a few months, then, Böttcher's position in Italy underwent a fundamental shift; rather than focusing on Italian and foreign press circles or trying to ascertain what was going on in Italian ministries, his mandate when he was deployed in April 1940, the end of the year found Böttcher almost ensnarled in the competition among various German agencies active in Italy. The German political turf battle was in full swing but the turf was Italian.

Conflict was not confined to the outside. Böttcher also found himself doing battle with another covert operative of the Italian Department in Rome, Prince Friedrich zu Hohenlohe-Bartenstein. A member of a well-known European aristocratic family and regarded as politically reliable by Office VI, the Italian Department wanted to capitalize on his society connections; Hohenlohe, under the cover of a business consultant, began reporting in early 1941.[28] Hohenlohe must have aroused the suspicions immediately on arrival; his file is full of documents questioning whether this cover remained intact.[29] An informer of

---

[27] VI E 1 Vermerk, Hans-Joachim Böttcher, hauptberuflicher SD-Mitarbeiter in Rom – Neue Arbeits- und Tarnungsmöglichkeiten, December 7, 1942, BA-DH, RSHA Film D, 750128–750131.

[28] BA-DH, RSHA Film D, 690002; VI, B 5 c, Vermerk, Antwort Friedrichs auf das letzte hiesige Schreiben vo. 7.5.41, May 23, 1941, BA-DH, RSHA Film D, 690054–690055. There is indication that Hohenlohe had worked for the society service, *Gesellschaftsdienst*, of the German Embassy in Rome earlier, but embassy personnel regarded him as "too stupid" for the task and lacking basic manners. Hohenlohe had also served as a low-level informer of VI H, Ideological Enemies Abroad; VI E 1, Friedrich zu Hohenlohe-Bartenstein, November 1, 1942, BA-DH, RSHA Film D, 690089–690100.

[29] "S" Personalakten (PA) und Berichte des VM Prinz Hohenlohe-Bartenstein, BA-DH, RSHA Film D, 690.

Hohenlohe's, a White Russian émigré, Nicolaus Alexejeff, also known as T-100/2 and supposed to work against US circles, summed up the situation in all its confusing details.[30] Stressing that his personal impressions of Hohenlohe were positive and that he was neither inept nor careless, Alexejeff cautioned that many different groups in Rome – from the Italian nobility, whose circles Hohenlohe was to penetrate, to the police – assumed Hohenlohe to be an intelligence operative and that the Italians were contemplating Hohenlohe's expulsion. Hohenlohe therefore endangered the entire network and Alexejeff noted that he had begun to use Böttcher to transmit his information.[31] In addition, he let Berlin know that Hohenlohe and Böttcher did not get along, much to the detriment of any work in Rome. Alexejeff likened the situation between Böttcher and Hohenlohe, fighting for professional superiority in the Italian capital, to a "subterranean civil war."[32]

Its resolution fell to SS-Hauptsturmführer Guido Zimmer. Zimmer had been a member of the Italian Department for a while and was sent to Rome as the SD Main Representative in August 1941. Attached to police attaché Kappler's office, Zimmer was approved by and embedded with the German Embassy. Reporting to Berlin under the aliases Peterman and Reinecke, Zimmer brought with him an able secretary fluent in Italian, Hildegard Beetz, then still Burckhardt.[33] On Hohenlohe, Zimmer soon arrived at the same conclusion that the Italian Department had reached earlier: he had to go. Zimmer's report clearly summarized the haphazard, uncoordinated, and unprofessional conduct of Office VI's

---

[30] Nicolaus Alexejeff, known as T-100/2, was born in Moscow in 1895. His supervisor seems to have been T-100, identified by Schellenberg as a certain Rittmeister von Petrow, conceivably called Wladinir Feodorowitsch in Alexejeff's letters. Schellenberg indicated that T-100 visited Rome sometime in 1941 to meet an old V-man, maybe Alexejeff. This man was later arrested by the Italian police, creating an overall unpleasant situation, as the Amt VI representative in Rome, Dr. Groebl, was also involved. Schellenberg fired Groebl; Appendix XXIII, Miscellaneous Personalities, Final Report on the Case of Walter Schellenberg, NA, RG 65, Entry A 1–136 Z, Box 3, Folder: Bulky 39; Saint BB8 to Saint Amazon, Subject: Zimmer, Guido, November 28, 1945, NA, RG 263, Entry ZZ-18, Box 144, File: Zimmer, Guido, 1 of 2.

[31] Letter to T-100, aus dem Russischen, April 11, 1941, BA-DH, RSHA Film D, 690044–690046.

[32] Letter from A [Nicolaus Alexejeff], Aus dem Russischen, April 25, 1941, BA-DH, RSHA Film D, 690060; Letter from A. to Wladimir Feodorowitsch, April 25, 1941, BA-DH, RSHA Film D, 690061.

[33] Saint BB8 to Saint Amazon, Subject: Zimmer, Guido, November 28, 1945, NA, RG 263, Entry ZZ-18, Box 144, File: Zimmer, Guido, 1 of 2; Translation of Statement handed in by Schellenberg on 20.8.1945, NA, RG 263, Entry ZZ-18, Box 112, File: Schellenberg, Walter, Vol. 1, 2 of 2. Richard Breitman, Analysis of the Name File of Guido Zimmer, http://www.nara.gov/iwg/declass/zimmer.html. See also BA-DH, RSHA Film G Zvláštni Archiv, Archivbestände des RSHA-Amt VI for Film E.

men in Rome.[34] The Roman intelligence network had disintegrated into a charade of backstabbing operatives forging constantly shifting personal alliances. Little to no time was spent on the collection and transmission of any information.

Zimmer was to establish a functioning intelligence-gathering network and to transmit reports to Berlin, but his tenure in Rome was short-lived. His secretary claimed after the war that she did most of the work, for Zimmer was "stupid with his work." A political blunder of epic proportions in October 1941 validates Beetz' assessment of Zimmer.[35] Suddenly oblivious to political intricacies and his office's delicate relationship with the Auswärtige Amt – the role and rights of the police attachés were just being renegotiated in Berlin and the AA held the upper hand – Zimmer did not relay Alexejeff's information about a planned attempt on Mussolini's life to Berlin via Kappler but informed the chargé d'affaires of the German Embassy, Otto von Bismarck. Bismarck recognized an opportunity when he saw one and shared his knowledge with the Italian police. In one fell swoop Bismarck managed to unmask Alexejeff and to expose Zimmer and his network to the Italians, making it likely that Zimmer would have to leave the city and his embassy posting.[36] Zimmer was, indeed, recalled to Germany and so was his secretary, who disavowed any part in this gaffe and later claimed to have counseled Zimmer to "report through channels but he failed to heed her advice," thus creating an "embarrassment."[37] The offending network in Rome was dismantled and Böttcher was also recalled; he was eventually entirely let go from Office VI.[38] The Roman intelligence operations, which had never been in the best of shape, were now a complete shambles.

There were additional repercussions to Zimmer's bungle. The *Auslandsmeldungen*, Foreign Reports, of October 3, 1941 noted "[t]he Italian administration has created a special intelligence service whose exclusive task it is to keep all Germans in the country under surveillance. In particular, all connections between German diplomatic missions and Italians are

---

[34] VI B 5 c, Vermerk, Friedrich, July 16, 1941, BA-DH, RSHA Film D, 690069–690079. It took the Italian Department some effort to rid itself of Hohenlohe. For an incomplete rendition of the story, see: [Answer Friedrich], May 23, 1941, BA-DH, RSHA Film D, 690054–690055; VI E 1 Vermerk, Friedrich von Hohenlohe-Bartenstein, November 1, 1942, BA-DH, RSHA Film D, 690089–690100; Erklärung, August 21, 1941, BA-DH, RSHA Film D, 690076.

[35] Addendum to Lebenslauf written by H.B., May 28, 1946, RG 263, ZZ-16, Box 5, Beetz, Hildegard, Vol. 3 [hereafter: Addendum H.B.]

[36] Saint BB8 to Saint Amazon, Subject: Zimmer, Guido, November 28, 1945, NA, RG 263, Entry ZZ-18, Box 144, File: Zimmer, Guido, 1 of 2.

[37] Addendum H.B.

[38] Entlassung des Vertragsangestellten Hans-Joachim Böttcher, Berlin, November 11, 1941, BA-DH, RSHA Film D, 750549–750550.

being observed."[39] The nightmare scenario of which the Italian Department had warned months earlier, when Kappler had suggested informing the Italian security forces about Böttcher, had come to pass. The poor judgment that led to this had been Zimmer's, yet the offending report to the Italians had originated with Bismarck and thus the Auswärtige Amt. Office VI chose to blame the latter.

The intelligence network created in the aftermath of Zimmer's slip and Bismarck's tale was tied more closely to police attaché Kappler, but did not meet with Greater success. For about a year – year one of Schellenberg's tenure at the helm of Office VI – no SD Main Representative was posted to Rome. Rather, Kappler performed Office VI tasks on the side. In August 1942, SS-Sturmbannführer Helmuth Looss arrived in Rome; designated as the new Main Representative, he was attached as an assistant to Kappler. Looss' qualifications for his posting were mainly ideological. He had worked for "Ideological Enemies Abroad," focusing on the so-called political churches, and had led an Einsatzkommando, a murder squad, in the Soviet Union.[40] There is some indication that Looss was on an unidentified special mission from Schellenberg, but he primarily collected general political information and kept in contact with various individuals recruited for Office VI. He was meant to pick up where Zimmer had left off and even brought the self-same secretary, Beetz, with him. Receiving little assistance from Berlin, left to his own devices, and, in Beetz' words, "not interested in his work," Looss was useless and soon alerted the Italian police to his activities. Schellenberg, who had been involved in Looss' posting to Rome, later claimed to have recalled him "for his dogmatic and completely inflexible attitude; he was of no use to the Meldedienst." Looss, for his part, seemed to have "desired to leave" as well. His Roman stint ended in December 1942 or January 1943. His next position was with the *Beauftragter der Sicherheitspolizei* (BdS), Representative of Security Police, in Minsk, surely a better fit for him.[41] The cost–benefit analysis presumably conducted by Office VI must have revealed that the creation and maintenance of an intelligence network in Rome, headed by an SD Main Representative and focused on the activities of the Italian government, was difficult: Main Representatives were not up to the task, and the German Embassy as well as the police attaché

[39] Auslandsmeldungen, October 3, 1941, BAL, R 58/7725.
[40] Wildt, *Generation*, 404–405, 549.
[41] Preliminary Interrogation Report on Oberfuehrer Eugen Dollmann, no date, NA, RG 319, IRR-Personal, Box 40, XE 138128, Dollmann, Eugen, 1 of 3; Interrogation Kappler; Addendum H.B; Liquidation Report No. 7; Translation of Statement handed in by Schellenberg on 20.8.1945, NA, RG 263, Entry ZZ-18, Box 112, File: Schellenberg, Walter, Vol. 1, 2 of 2.

Kappler put up a stiff resistance against independent Office VI work. At the same time, Kappler did some work for Office VI – as did Beetz, who remained in Rome after Looss left. Now assigned as a secretary to Kappler, Beetz still focused on foreign intelligence issues.[42] Rendered all but invisible by her gender and her subordinate position, and not perceived as a threat by either the Auswärtige Amt or the police attaché Beetz, in all but name, became Office VI's main representative in Rome.

Under Schellenberg's oversight, Office VI took less confrontational approaches to its appointment policies and to the creation and maintenance of intelligence networks. Rome is a good example, as is Sweden, discussed below. For one, Schellenberg's stance provided for surface cooperation with the Auswärtige Amt; many Office VI representatives were embedded with the German legations abroad and they, as well as Schellenberg, seemingly strove to adhere to the existing with the Auswärtige Amt. The new approach also probed the agreements' boundaries by seeing just how many men (and sometimes women) Office VI could embed in a given legation abroad. Similarly, Office VI tried to create and maintain good working relations with already established Police Attachés. After all, these men did some foreign intelligence work and were useful partners when it came to finding positions for Office VI members in their legations. The less confrontational stance did not leave Office VI in the dark: despite his misgivings, Kappler, for example, provided information to the office and let Beetz do her work. In addition, "free agents" in Italy, such as Himmler's personal representative, Eugen Dollmann, with his stellar connections to high-ranking Fascist circles, offered additional avenues of information gathering.[43] Other men were sent to Italy with special assignments, such as Dr. Willi Groebl, who arrived in Rome in late 1942 under the cover of a travel agency. His primary mandate was to create a postoccupational network in Sicily and Calabria.[44]

---

[42] Addendum H.B.
[43] Preliminary Interrogation Report on Oberfuehrer Eugen Dollmann, no date, NA, RG 319, IRR-Personal, Box 40, XE 138128, Dollmann, Eugen, 1 of 3; Translation of Statement handed in by Schellenberg on 20.8.1945, NA, RG 263, Entry ZZ-18, Box 112, File: Schellenberg, Walter, Vol. 1, 2 of 2; Frederick W. Deakin, *The Brutal Friendship: Mussolini, Hitler, and the Fall of Italian Fascism* (New York: Harper & Row, 1962), 232. Dollmann posed in Italy as a correspondent of the SS magazine "Das Schwarze Korps"; VI E 1, Nachrichtendienstliche Tätigkeit in Italien [no date], BA-DH, RSHA Film C, 555021–555022. By 1943, the Allies were aware of Dollmann as "Himmler's political observer," who "enjoyed the confidence of the most prominent Fascist personalities in Rome, and so was better informed about political trends than the accredited Ambassador;" The German Intelligence Service, October 25, 1943, NA, RG 226, Entry 108 B, Box 286, Folder: The German Intelligence Service.
[44] Second Detailed Interrogation Report on SS Sturmbannführer Huegel, Dr. Klaus, May 1945, NA, RG 263, Entry ZZ-16, Box 26, File: Huegel, Klaus; Translation of Statement

What type of information came out of all these efforts in Rome and elsewhere? Was there clearly defined, concrete Roman intelligence, which was qualitatively different from information collected elsewhere in Italy? There is no indication of that. Office VI disseminated its insights in the RSHA in two main formats: the *Auslandskurzmeldungen*, Short Foreign Reports, and the *Auslandsmeldungen*, Foreign Reports.[45] The Auslandskurzmeldungen, published every weekday and three to five pages long, were the less sophisticated format. Providing the informer's cover number and location, they were simple, paraphrased compilations of selected reports organized by county group; for Italy, they spotlighted the rare report, about one a day, that dealt with Italian political decisions and decision makers, governmental appointments, the national economy, contacts between Italian and Western allied officials, and military matters.[46] The Auslandskurzmeldungen seem to have functioned primarily as an informer showcase and should be regarded as a function of the rivalries within the RSHA. They provided proof positive that Office VI was active in Italy and did acquire political information.

The Auslandsmeldungen, published twice weekly at around twenty to thirty pages per issue, were more sophisticated. They surveyed, and to some extent analyzed, the political, economic, and social developments in countries not occupied by German forces. They combined various sources, among them informer reports, press clippings and other open sources as well as, in all probability, information from non-SD sources. These reports presented Office VI's view on developments abroad and occasionally alluded to its foreign policy visions. In the case of Italy, the population's changing moods and attitudes toward Germany were of major concern – as they were in the reports on which the Auslandsmeldungen were based. By focusing on the Italians' German-friendliness or the lack thereof, the reports sought to gauge Italy's trustworthiness as an ally. In that context, Italian military campaigns became a matter of importance beyond the purely military question, as they influenced popular moods and attitudes.[47] Much space was devoted

handed in by Schellenberg on 20.8.1945, NA, RG 263, Entry ZZ-18, Box 112, File: Schellenberg, Walter, Vol. 1, 2 of 2; Interrogation Kappler. Groebl is sometimes referred to as the SD Main Representative.

45   Beginning in 1943, the Auslandsmeldungen were published as Allgemeine Auslandslagemeldungen. For 1940, a separate category of Auslandslageberichte can be found, which were also published twice weekly. Either these reports were discontinued or I have only found part of the collection. The Auslandslageberichte rely heavily on press reports and informers' reports. BAL, R 58/7728.

46   See Auslandskurzmeldungen, Spring and Summer 1940, BAL, R 58/7726; and Auslandskurzmeldungen, Winter and Summer 1941, BAL, R58/7727.

47   Auslandsmeldungen, August 13, 1940, BAL, R 58/7723; Auslandsmeldungen, May 20, 1941 and June 6, 1941, BAL, R 58/7724; Auslandsmeldungen, August 22, 1941, October 3, 1941, and April 2, 1942, BAL, R 58/7725.

to the discussion of Italian living conditions, food supplies, and the issue of corruption.[48] The alleged Italian loyalty toward Italian Jews and their consequent "lax" treatment was another issue of much concern in the Auslandsmeldungen.[49] Anti-German attitudes were surveyed in great detail, as, for example, in the Auslandsmeldungen of August 22, 1941. In this case, operatives purportedly "systematically" collected "sayings and thoughts of anti-Fascists, fragmentary remarks and comments of Catholics and former Freemasons, Democrats, and Socialists regarding a reorganization of Europe from an anti-German vantage point." Without any analysis, these opinions were then partially blamed on skillful "Anglo-American propaganda," playing on the Italian "mentality."[50] Similarly, certain areas of the country, such as Sicily, were simply defined as "Anglo-friendly."[51] The perceived problems with Italian moods and attitudes were also tied to a lack of Italian propaganda.[52] By the standards of Office VI, Italy and its population were not considered trustworthy.

The Auslandsmeldungen offered ideological interpretations of complex societal situations. Incidentally, they could also serve as a political program for Italy and a blueprint for future action. In the collective mind of the SD, as seen here through the lens of Office VI, the matter was simple: if only the SD were in charge, all would be better. It could bring justice to Italy's corrupt food distribution or recruitment system and alleviate the greatest problem of many ordinary Italian while a crackdown on anti-German circles would end rumors as well as alleged Italian plans to desert Germany's war effort and bring the Italians into line. A better, German, effort to curb enemy propaganda would do the same. And the influence of the Jews on the Italian population could be easily dealt with if the SD were in charge. By applying Nazi ideology to the collection and evaluation of information on Italy and to a reporting effort that treated Italy solely in terms of its relationship to Germany, Office VI procured "useful news," indeed, even if in the short term nothing came out these reports. Like many other entities Office VI doubted Italy's allegiance to Germany and its stability – and had ample intelligence reports for evidence. Yet in the short run, no apparent reason, let alone political or military support, existed for an intervention. But if the situation were to change, Office VI's Auslandsmeldungen could provide the needed rationales.

[48] Auslandsmeldungen, August 26, 1941, BAL, R 58/7724; Auslandsmeldungen, August 29, 1941, September 5, 1941, October 17, 1941, BAL, R 58/7725; Auslandsmeldungen, March 19, 1942 and August 4, 1942, BAL, R 58/7729; Auslandsmeldungen, July 2, 1942, BAL, R 58/3485.

[49] Auslandsmledungen, April 16, 1941, BAL 58/7729; Auslandsmeldungen, May 15, 1943, BAL, R 58/7730.

[50] Auslandsmeldungen, August 22, 1941 and October 17, 1941, BAL, R 58/7725.

[51] Auslandsmeldungen, September 26, 1941, BAL, R 58/7724.

[52] Auslandsmeldungen, April 22, 1941, BAL, R 58/3485.

The Allied landing on Sicily on July 10, 1943 changed the military situation in Europe. This was not the Second Front for which Stalin had pleaded, but a first chink in Germany's European hegemony. German suspicions and concerns that Italy would drop out of the war and abandon the Axis reached a new level.[53] The Italian High Command was considering surrender, a group of old Fascists in the Fascist Grand Council was pondering a coup, and Mussolini seemed more unreliable than ever. Even a meeting between Hitler and Mussolini at Feltre on July 19 did not calm the waters, for against expectations and earlier experience, Hitler was unable to boost Mussolini's morale and to convince him that an Axis victory was on the horizon. The Allied bombs that fell on Rome that day surely did not help Hitler to make his case.[54]

On the day that Hitler and Mussolini met, a concrete warning of an imminent coup against Mussolini, carefully tuned to Himmler's and his organization's political and ideological dispositions, crossed Himmler's desk. It was an unabashed attempt to garner the support of a man and an organization known to be interested in conducting foreign policy in support of the most radical faction in any given country. Despite earlier and almost constant but generalized reports about defeatist moods and attitudes in Italy, the information blindsided Office VI but Himmler did not waste time. Eager to impress on Hitler as well as on Foreign Minister Joachim von Ribbentrop the need for his intelligence service, Himmler rushed the information to the Auswärtige Amt and the Party Chancellery. The message, which Himmler indicated to have received via "secure intelligence service routes," was alarming. A coup against Mussolini was imminent, and its planners expected to install Pietro Badoglio, "a known exponent of Freemasonry in Italy," as the head of the future war cabinet. But not all was lost: pro-German Fascists had created a Council of Five and asked for Germany's support. The Council promised to devote itself to a "decidedly anti-Freemasonry, anti-Jewish and pro-German policy, a radical removal [*Beseitigung*] of all traitors of all kinds [...] the creation of a joint military command for the Axis forces."[55] In other words, after labeling Badoglio a Freemason, the Council of Five promised to conduct future Italian policies in a fashion close to Himmler's heart. If Germany were to support the Council of Five, it could move Italy even closer to Germany's orbit and engender the radical political changes that Mussolini had thus far avoided.

[53] Gerhard L. Weinberg, *A World At Arms: A Global History of World War II* (Cambridge: Cambridge University Press, 1994), 587–589.
[54] Paehler, "Spiegel," 263.
[55] Fernschreiben Himmler to Bormann, June 19, 1943, NA, RG 242, T-175, Reel 53, Frame 2567176–2567177.

Himmler received the information too late for it to become actionable intelligence, but he was able to use it in his ongoing conflict with the Ribbentrop and Auswärtige Amt. The embassy in Rome relayed similar information two days later only.[56] Himmler and Office VI appeared superior but this superiority was mainly a function of careful wording. Himmler's message implied that the foreign intelligence service had received this information over the course of its routine activities. This was decidedly not the case. Himmler owed the information to Dr. Siegfried Fuchs, incidentally the same man who two years prior had helped install Böttcher in Butting's office. Fuchs, an SS man, was an archeologist living in Rome; his SS affiliation was presumably common knowledge.[57] Any connections to Office VI were unofficial; at best he was considered an *ehrenamtlicher Mitarbeiter*, honorary member. A representative of the Council of Five had approached Fuchs information about a possible coup on July 17, 1943 and Fuchs had initially suggested transmitting it to Himmler via the embassy in Rome. Fuchs' Italian counterpart argued vehemently against this proposition, convinced that the embassy would leak the information to the anti-Mussolini conspirators. Fuchs eventually agreed to serve as a courier; he traveled to Klagenfurt and asked the *Gauleiter*, the party district leader, to forward the information to Himmler. Within five hours, Himmler transmitted the information exactly as he had received it.[58] In short: Office VI had missed the most important development in Rome, but an individual SS member with good contacts in Italy and Germany saved the day. And Himmler made shrewd use of the fact that he had received any information at all to showcase the alleged capabilities of, and need for, his foreign intelligence service. With equal parts of luck and panache, Himmler turned a potential intelligence disaster into the illusion of a success.

The coup against Mussolini still happened. On July 25, the Fascist Grand Council forced Mussolini to step down and subsequently arrested him. With it, the first distinct phase of Office VI's activities in Italy came to an end. The service had failed on every level for reasons such as the competition between the different state and party agencies in Rome and Berlin, the rivalries among different RSHA offices and the intense competition between individual service members. The ideologically based

---

[56] Josef Schröder, *Italiens Kriegseintritt 1943: Die deutschen Gegenmaßnahmen im italienischen Raum: Fall "Alarich" und die "Achse"* (Göttingen: Musterschmidt Verlag, 1969), 196.
[57] See Fuchs' RuSHA questionnaire, NA, RG 242, BDC, RuSHA, Reel 543, Frame 956–957. Although Fuchs held a voluntary position with the Roman branch of the NSDAP-Auslandsorganisation, his loyalties were with the SS, as his earlier assistance to Böttcher indicates.
[58] Paehler, "Spiegel," 264–265.

recruitment of operatives and informers, introduced in the early years of the SD's activities in Italy, harmed the foreign intelligence service additionally, as it limited the service's human potential and the radius of its intelligence-gathering efforts. Germany's foreign intelligence efforts in Italy remained restricted to pro-Nazi and government circles, and even there, operatives and informers were not privy to the most important information. It was a stroke of amazing luck that the coup against Mussolini originated among these groups. But even so, it was not the foreign intelligence service that gathered information about the looming coup, but a serendipitous individual loosely attached to it.[59] Office VI had failed resoundingly in the most comfortable environment any intelligence service could wish for – an allied country. Anything beyond this would be an uphill battle at best.

The role of Office VI transformed with the changing political landscape in Italy in the aftermath of the coup. Former dividing lines between the RSHA offices became porous, and Office VI eked out a role more substantial than it was normally afforded in occupied countries. In this process, its nature changed. A poor intelligence collection agency before the late summer of 1943, the Italian Department of Office VI now combined intelligence gathering, sabotage activities, looting, and racial and political persecution under one roof, creating an altogether new and decidedly executive service.

Upon the ouster and arrest of Mussolini, who was held at a secret location, a new Italian government was formed under Pietro Badoglio, as Himmler's informant had predicted. It promised to continue the war at Germany's side, and the Germans pretended to believe the Italian remonstrations. Based on information furnished to him by Dollmann and Kappler, Himmler expected this to be a ruse. The German military, on the other hand, counseled to trust the new Italian government but eventually moved troops toward Italy.[60] These developments notwithstanding, both Hitler and Himmler were adamant that the Duce had to be liberated. Finding Mussolini became the first order of business and an Office VI command unit under Otto Skorzeny was sent to Rome to see to the Duce's liberation. Skorzeny's orders originated with Hitler personally.[61]

---

[59] Paehler, "Spiegel," 266.
[60] German Policy toward Italy, NA, RG 226, Entry 171 A, Box 80, Folder 891 [hereafter: German Policy Italy.]
[61] Deakin, *Brutal Friendship*, 543–546; Glen B. Infield, *Skorzeny: Hitler's Commando* (New York: St. Martin's Press, 1981), 30–31. From August 1943 on, Skorzeny headed Office VI-S of the Reich Security Main Office as a special section for sabotage missions and assassinations; Counter Intelligence War Room. Liquidation Report No. 13, Amt VI of the R.S.H.A. Gruppe VI S, NA, RG 319, IRR, Box 1, XE 002666.

A central role in this and other Sipo and SD activities of the coming months fell to police attaché Kappler. Shortly before the coup, Kappler had moved his radio transmitter into the German Embassy and maintained constant contact with the RSHA in Berlin. The German radio traffic was regularly intercepted and decoded by the Western Allies; the intercepts now provide detailed insights into Germany's Italian concerns and developments on the ground.[62]

The search for Mussolini threw into sharp relief the differences of opinion and approach between the SD and the military. Initial German attempts to locate the Duce did not meet with success and the military, represented by the commander of an air corps stationed near Rome, General Karl Student, came out against additional attempts to locate and rescue Mussolini at the present time. The RSHA representatives, however, remained in hot pursuit.[63] In the second half of August, Kappler notified Berlin that he had learned that Mussolini had been transferred to the island of Maddalena off the northern tip of Sardinia, likely in reaction to the ongoing German search.[64] Skorzeny's reconnaissance mission confirmed Mussolini's location, but his plane crashed into the sea. Yet luck was on the German side; Rome radioed to headquarters in Berlin, "All crew saved. Skorzeny only slightly injured." Mussolini, however, was moved again, as Kappler learned from an Italian contact a few days later. The Duce's new location was in Gran Sasso, high in the Abruzzi Mountains, as Kappler was able to confirm. Himmler now ordered to "liberate Mussolini at all events" and, irate about General Student's earlier refusal to divert paratroopers for the task, Himmler advised, "that no other Stellen [sic; authorities] were to be acquainted

---

[62] Richard Breitman with Robert Wolfe, "Case Studies of Genocide," in Richard Breitman et al., eds. *U.S. Intelligence and the Nazis* (Washington, DC: National Trust Fund for the Nazi War Crimes and Japanese Imperial Government Records Interagency Working Group, 2004), 76–77.

[63] German Policy Italy. According to Richard Breitman, this document is of British origin; he dates it to October 1943; Breitman, "Case Studies," 76 note 11. The actual date of the report appears to be late November 1943, as it references a November 6, 1943 communication. Kappler insisted that he deemed the idea to reestablish Mussolini a "fatal mistake." He claimed that he suggested the moderate Fascist Tassinari, a contact of Himmler and Dollmann's, as the potential head of a new government and persuaded Himmler, who brought up the matter with Hitler. Eventually, the plan was dropped; Interrogation Kappler.

[64] German Policy Italy. In 1962, Deakin noted that there was no indication of a battle of wits between the German and Italian intelligence services; the new documents indicate some small-scale competition. Deakin also mentioned that it is not clear how the German tracked down Mussolini, but reported on "bribery on a massive scale." The new documents indicate that Italian Fascist Pagnozzi was Kappler and Dollmann's main source of information. Deakin, *Brutal Friendship*, 545.

with the whereabouts of Mussolini."[65] If Mussolini were to be liberated, as Hitler had ordered, Himmler and Office VI's commando unit under Skorzeny wanted to claim all the glory.

In the meantime, on September 3, 1943, the Badoglio government and the Western Allies reached a ceasefire agreement – the official announcement of Italy's surrender came five days later – and the situation in Italy took a turn for the chaotic. The agreement coincided with the beginning of the Allied landing in Italy proper. Not wasting any time, German troops occupied the better part of the Italian peninsula and disarmed Italian troops. Badoglio, his government, and the royal family fled south toward the Allied troops. And while British and American forces established a foothold on Italian soil, most of Italy, including Rome, became a German-occupied country.[66]

Office VI asserted its role in Italy with two successful operations. First, there was Skorzeny's liberation of Mussolini. Postponed briefly due to military developments, for German troops around Rome were involved in the occupation of the city and Skorzeny needed the support of a battalion of General Student's paratroopers after all, Kappler eventually notified Berlin that the mission was scheduled for September 12. Himmler then issued his instructions to Schellenberg. Noting the centrality of the mission, his expectations for his men, and alluding to General Student's earlier hesitation, Schellenberg signed the operation's final "go":

It is the primary and most important task of the Sicherheitspolizei and the S.D. to devote themselves to the liberation of the Duce. All other assignments and activities are to be postponed. Everyone is to obey this order with all prudence and bravery. Any excuse made under General Student's authority will not be accepted. Skorzeny and his men are expected to exert themselves to the utmost.[67]

Exert themselves they did. In an exploit often described as daring, Skorzeny and his commando used gliders to reach Mussolini at Grand Sasso; he purportedly greeted Mussolini with "The Führer sent me." As a heavy Skorzeny used a light plane to transport a heavy Mussolini, the overload almost spelled disaster. Another plane wreck was avoided narrowly.[68] Ultimately, all worked out and Mussolini, accompanied by Skorzeny, left the same evening for the Reich. Reminiscent of the hero's welcome

---

[65] German Policy Italy. The translation "liberate Mussolini at all events" appears to be a clumsy attempt to translate the German phrases "auf alle Fälle" or "unter allen Umständen."

[66] Weinberg, *World at Arms*, 593–601.

[67] German Policy Italy; Breitman, "Case Studies," 78.

[68] Heinz Höhne, *Der Orden unter dem Totenkopf: Die Geschichte der SS* (Munich: Bertelsmann, 1967; reprint, Augsburg: Weltbild Verlag, 1998), 504; Deakin, *Brutal Friendship*, 546.

Image 6.1 Friedenthal, Commando Skorzeny. Walter Schellenberg (left) and Otto Skorzeny in conversation, October 1943. Bundesarchiv. [signature: Bild 101III-Alber-183–33]

Schellenberg had received four years prior after the abductions at Venlo, Hitler congratulated Skorzeny on a mission accomplished.[69] Mussolini subsequently announced and headed the Fascist Republic of Salò. A German puppet state, Mussolini gave it a veneer of legitimacy; however, the real power rested with the Germans. The same day that Mussolini was taken from Gran Sasso, a second RSHA commando freed several important Italian Fascists from the Italian prisons; they, too, were flown to Germany. Kappler was thus able to report on another resounding success in his message to Berlin; "Most important Fascists personalities, who are reliably pro-German, illegally freed by S.S. Commando. No losses. They are in the German Embassy."[70] September 12, 1943, was shaping up to be a very good day for the RSHA and Office VI in particular. The liberation of the Duce was a tremendous success for Office VI and the freeing of the "Fascist personalities" on the same day an added bonus. Office VI had asserted its importance beyond intelligence gathering and evidenced its willingness to undertake missions at which the German military balked – and be successful.

[69] Infield, *Skorzeny*, 45.   [70] German Policy Italy.

In the aftermath of the German occupation of the country – and the establishment of the Republic of Salò notwithstanding – Kappler strove to create a firm German rule, masterminded and executed by Gestapo or Office VI personnel, over Rome. Kappler assumed the leadership of the Einsatzkommando Rome, which combined the RSHA's main functions: ideological policing and intelligence, both defined in the broadest sense.[71] The Roman population – and the same held true for Italy in general – was less than enthusiastic about the reinstallation of Mussolini and many of his old cronies; discontent was widespread and not restricted to anti-Fascists. Kappler, for his part, distrusted any and all Italians, saw enemies everywhere, and acted accordingly. For example, he had a number of high Italian officials, including old Fascists, arrested.[72] Kappler also moved against the Italian *carabinieri*, the regular police, allegedly still loyal to the king and rumored to be monitoring the movements of German troops around the city. Kappler proposed to Berlin their disarmament and deportation to Germany as forced workers. He suggested the same approach for all higher Italian Army personnel not planning to join the new Fascist government.[73] The disarmament and arrest of the carabinieri took place on October 6, 1943; Kappler requested transport facilities for approximately 8000 men. The Italian Colonial Police, more loyal to the new German masters, took over for the deported carabinieri.[74]

Even before the deportation of the carabinieri and the threatened deportation of high army officials, Kappler and his RSHA associates embarked on the realization of Germany's core project in Rome: the deportation and eventual murder of the Roman Jews. Kappler likely received his orders soon after September 12, 1943, the day of Mussolini's liberation.[75] It might have been that Karl Wolff, who arrived in Rome on September 17, 1943, transmitted them. Wolff held a key role in the new Italian state as *Höchster SS and Police Führer* (HSSPF), Highest SS and Police Leader, and thus Himmler's personal representative. His task was the coordination of the different police and SS forces and

[71] The RSHA in Occupied and Neutral Countries, Early 1945, NA, RG 263, Entry ZZ-17, Box 2, German Intelligence Service, Vol. 1, 1 of 2.
[72] German Policy Italy.
[73] Decode 7184, Kappler to Berlin, October 5, 1943, NA, RG 226, Entry 122, Box 1, Folder 5.
[74] Decode, Kappler to Berlin, October 6, 1943, NA, RG 226, Entry 122, Box 1, Folder 5.
[75] For an evaluation of the deportation of the Roman Jews and an investigation of Kappler's postwar justifications, see Richard Breitman "Case Studies," 76–84. Using selected decodes, Robert Katz takes a different stand on Kappler's role, following Kappler's protestations that he attempted to save the Roman Jews. He does not convince. Robert Katz, *The Battle for Rome: The Germans, the Allies, the Partisans, and the Pope, September 1943–June 1944* (New York: Simon & Schuster, 2003), 61–78.

the maintenance of Mussolini's government.[76] Wolff did not come to Rome empty-handed, but set the stage for Kappler's success in rounding up the Roman Jews: he transferred to Rome one hundred policemen normally stationed in Northern Italy, which made Kappler independent from Italian police forces. Wolff might have also notified Kappler about his latest promotion, boosting his morale.[77] On September 24, the RSHA informed its branches that the deportation of the Italian Jews was imminent. The same day Kappler warned Berlin that a large number of Jews might try to escape Rome on a train for Spanish diplomats; he claimed the Vatican had provided the necessary visas.[78] His postwar claims notwithstanding, by September 24 at the latest, Kappler knew that the Roman Jews were to be deported. And he did his best to allow for no escapes.

On October 6, 1943, Kappler confirmed to headquarters in Berlin that SS-Hauptsturmführer Theodor Dannecker, the widely traveled RSHA expert on deportations, had arrived in Rome.[79] However, he also reported on a troubling development that seemed to bring together two rivals of the RSHA to foil its plans: the military and the Auswärtige Amt. Kappler noted that some German officials in Rome were engaged in talks with Generalfeldmarschall Albert Kesselring, the commander of the German military forces in Italy, trying to gain his support for their suggestion to use the Roman Jews as laborers in the country rather than to deport them. Members of the German Embassy in Rome also tried to forestall the deportations by contacting Minister Ribbentrop and forwarding the same message, the so-called Möllhausen Telegram, to Hitler.[80] The telegram had, as Vatican Embassy Secretary Albrecht von Kessel testified after the war, three objectives: to prevent a German "loss of dignity;" to secure the Pope's neutrality; and to save the Jews – presumably in that order. During the ensuing discussions, several ideas on how to prevent the deportations were kicked around; forced labor was high on the list of possible solutions.[81] Trouble seemed to be on the horizon for Kappler and the RSHA.

---

[76] Kerstin von Lingen, *SS and Secret Service: "Verschwörung des Schweigens": Die Akte Karl Wolff* (Paderborn: Ferdinand Schöningh, 2010), 28–29.

[77] Richard Breitman, "New Sources on the Holocaust in Italy," *Holocaust and Genocide Studies* 16 (Winter 2002), 404; Breitman, "Case Studies," 78.

[78] Richard Breitman, "Holocaust in Italy," 79; Claudia Steur, *Theodor Dannecker: Ein Funktionär der "Endlösung,"* (Essen: Klartext Verlag, 1997), 115.

[79] Decode 7244, Rome to Berlin, October 6, 1943, NA, RG 226, Entry 122, Box 1, Folder 5. Dannecker arrived in Rome in late September or early October. Steur, *Dannecker*, 113–128.

[80] Breitman, "Holocaust in Italy," 405; Katz, *Rome*, 78–85.

[81] Katz, *Rome*, 77–78. As the German Ambassador to Italy, Rudolf Rahn, was absent, Eitel Friedrich Möllhausen was in charge.

Five days later, on October 11, 1943, Kaltenbrunner sent a message to Kappler that left no doubt that the deportations were to go forward. Kaltenbrunner described the planned deportations as a matter of "special interest of the present internal political situation and the general security in Italy." Any delays, argued Kaltenbrunner, would lead to more Jews leaving the country or going into hiding. He also stressed that the order originated with Himmler.[82] The message's firm tone might have been linked to Kappler's initial involvement with the discussion that led to the Möllnhausen Telegram, even though it remains unclear which position Kappler took. Aside from his postwar protestations, there is no indication that he intended to save the Roman Jews. If Kappler had ever asked Kaltenbrunner for anything in relation to the deportations, odds are that he asked for a short-term postponement until after the "carabinieri and the Italian army officers have been removed," and that Kaltenbrunner's message was a reaction to this request.[83] As the carabinieri had been arrested on 6 October, Kappler's concern that the round-up of the Roman Jews could not be conducted efficiently was now a moot point. In addition, Dannecker had arrived. The pieces for the successful execution of the deportation order were in place.

Kappler now proceeded quickly; the round-up of the Roman Jews took place on October 16, 1943. 1,259 Roman Jews – male and female, young and old – fell prey to the operation and were imprisoned in a military school in close proximity to the Vatican. The operation began in the early morning hours and ended at 2 p.m., leaving the RSHA commando enough time to screen the arrested Jews. Some were subsequently released: non-Jews arrested by mistake, spouses in mixed marriage, and Jews from countries where deportations had not yet begun. 1,002 people remained. Kappler's after-action report to Berlin was as triumphant as it was defensive: he reported on the operation's success but also listed reasons why the catch had not been bigger.[84] On October 18, 1943, 1,007 Jews were put on a train that was accompanied by a police escort, which was exchanged twice along the way. The train's final destination

---

[82] Cited in Richard Breitman, "Holocaust in Italy," 405; Katz, *Rome*, 77.
[83] Katz, *Rome*, 77–78.
[84] Breitman, "Holocaust in Italy," 405; Decode 7668, Rome to Berlin, October 16, 1943, NA, RG 226, Entry 122, Box 1, Folder 5. It is generally assumed that the message originated with Kappler, as his signature is on the copy that can be found among Himmler's documents, see NA, RG 242, T-175, Reel 53, Frames 2567133–2567134. Steur indicates, however, that Kappler might have been accurate when he attributed the message to Dannecker, who had prepared such reports in similar situations. Steur, *Dannecker*, 121–122. I thank my former student Bradley Marcy for opening my eyes to useful military terminology.

was Auschwitz.[85] Of the slightly more than 1,000 people on the train, only 196 Jews were not gassed immediately upon their arrival. Of those 196, only 15 were alive at the end of the war.[86] In other words, the survival rate was about 1.5 percent. Kappler, Dannecker (who left Rome for similar activities in Florence a few days later), and their superiors might not have been too pleased with the absolute number of people rounded up that day – the defensive tone of the after-action report indicates as much – but this deportation had an enormous murderous depth.[87]

After the war Kappler claimed that he tried to stall the deportation of the Roman Jews by turning to extortion, but his attempts at blackmail belong in the broader context of the looting of postoccupation Italy.[88] On September 26, 1943 Kappler met with two leading members of the Italian Jewish community in Rome. He demanded fifty kilograms of gold within the next 48 hours, threating to deport 200 Jews to Germany otherwise.[89] This was not Kappler's attempt to spare the Jewish community in Rome from deportation, but rather the beginning of the outright plunder of Germany's former ally, Italy. On the same day Kappler reported that "gold from Jews" was being shipped to Kaltenbrunner, he also discussed the completion of the removal of the Italian state gold and problems connected with the storage of 110 tons of gold. Two days later Kappler returned to the issue of "Jewish gold," noting that this loot should take care of "foreign currency for our purposes." He was clearly thinking of Office VI's ongoing financial problems.[90] Various messages to Berlin also indicate a keen German interest in art treasures, mostly for Göring's collections, and other valuables, such as shoe leather.[91] "The

---

[85] Decode 7754, Dannecker to RSHA IV B 4, October 21, 1943, NA, RG 226, Entry 122, Box 1, Folder 5. Steur counts 1,002 people on the train and describes that when Dannecker reported to Kappler, the latter taunted him with Jews living in his, Dannecker's, Roman hotel. Dannecker then arrested them. Steur, *Dannecker*, 121. These additional arrests might account for the different numbers provided to Berlin. The destination of the train was read clearly by the British; Decode 7732, Harster to Berlin, October 20, 1943, NA, RG 226, Entry 122, Box 1, Folder 5.

[86] Breitman, "Holocaust in Italy," 406–407.

[87] Decode 7834, Kappler to Berlin, October 23, 1943, NA, RG 226, Entry 122, Box 1, Folder 5.

[88] Katz, *Rome*, 61–77.

[89] Breitman, "Holocaust in Italy," 404. Or, depending on the account, Kappler threatened to deport all Roman Jews; Katz, *Rome*, 69.

[90] Decode 7185, Kappler to Berlin, October 5, 1943, NA, RG 226, Entry 122, Box 1, Folder 5. Initially stored in a bank in Milan, the state gold was moved eventually to Franzenfeste, a fortification in South Tyrol. In the last months of the war, it was transported to Switzerland; Decode 7265, Kappler to Berlin, October 7, 1943, NA, RG 226, Entry 122, Box 1, Folder 5.

[91] Decode 7873, Rome to Berlin, 25 October 1943, Decode 7913, Kappler to Berlin, October 26, 1943, NA, RG 226, Entry 122, Box 1, Folder 5. See also R.I.S. 20/

S.D. is now pillaging Rome," noted Allied intelligence reports and suggested that, "Himmler has sent S.S. men who have had experience of this work in Russia to Rome."[92] Kappler's extortion of the Roman Jewish community was part and parcel of the country's overall plunder.

Factions that had fought each other before cooperated much better in the country's purge and plunder, but differentiation and difference between the RSHA offices remained. As did organizational problems. After the liberation of Mussolini, Karl Hass returned to Rome and took over intelligence matters.[93] Considered the "chief assistant to Kappler," Hass, along with a certain Schubernigg, another long-time member of the Italian Department, began to prepare postoccupational networks in Rome and Southern Italy and to plan for sabotage activities.[94] The changing military situation should have made such plans a priority, but preparations remained marred by the basic problems. But then postoccupational networks had never been Office VI's forte.

As early as March 1943 Schellenberg had "ordered" Kappler to prepare a postoccupational network for Sicily; as will be recalled, Groebl had received similar orders for Southern Italy even earlier.[95] Their realization remained a problem. In January 1943, for example, Schellenberg had to request the help of Karl Wolff, then still the Chief of Himmler's Personal Staff, in gaining the release of a certain wireless expert from the military; Schellenberg emphasized that the order to establish an intelligence network in preparation for a possible invasion had come directly from Himmler.[96] Progress reports, customarily blurring the lines between the planned and the achieved, focused on the networks' great potential and the office's far-reaching plans for it. One report claimed that a network

31.10.43, The Sicherheitsdienst, Recent Developments – II, Italy, October 31, 1943, NA, RG 226, Entry 108B, Box 286, Folder – RIS Reports. "Two special transports have left Rome by rail with wagon-loads of loot for Göring." Decode 7945, Priebke (by order) to Berlin, October 27, 1943, NA, RG 226, Entry 122, Box 1, Folder 5. An informant had provided the information about the leather.

[92] R.I.S. 18/9.10.1943, The Sicherheitsdienst, Recent Developments – I, October 9, 1943, NA, RG 226, Entry 108B, Box 286.

[93] Karl Hass left Six's initial RSHA office early on, spent some of 1940–1941 as a member of Office III in the Netherlands, and subsequently worked for Office VI. After the war, Hass escaped Allied custody and helped fellow war criminals to escape to South America on the so-called Rat Line. Hass also worked with the CIA and later for the Italian secret service. The Italian prosecutors managed to track down Hass, who was listed as deceased, for the second trial of Erick Priebke in 1997. Hass as well as Priebke received prison sentences; Hass died in 2004 while under house arrest in Italy. He was 94. Katz, *Rome*, 341–342; NA, RG 263, Entry ZZ-18, Box 44, File: Hass, Karl Alfred.

[94] Interrogation Kappler; Card 3, no date; Information regarding network Los Angeles, February 1949, NA, RG 263, Entry ZZ-18, Box 44, File: Hass, Karl Alfred.

[95] Interrogation Kappler; Liquidation Report No. 7.

[96] Schellenberg to Wolff, January 8, 1943, BA-DH, ZR 920/78.

under construction would be able to tap into "a large group of people all over Italy that is action-ready [*einsatzbereit*] and 100 percent on Germany's side." It was assumed that the same group of people would engage in acts of sabotage on Germany's behalf.[97] Ultimately, early plans for a postoccupational network in Southern Italy failed for mundane, technical reasons. Kappler, for example, indicated after the war that he had been able to make the needed contacts in Sicily, but that Italian-speaking wireless operators and wireless sets, which he requested in Berlin, were not available.[98]

Matters did not improve after September 1943; simply retaining proficient radio operators remained a problem. On October 7, 1943 an exasperated Kappler cabled Wolff, now the HSSPF in Italy, that two recently assigned wireless operators were about to be recalled and all but begged for their continued presence in Rome. Kappler also took proactive steps to ensure that wireless sets were available. Through a long-standing contact of Office VI, the director of the Anti-Semitic Institute in Rome, Kappler commissioned an Italian expert to build wireless transmitters. At the same time, Rome and Berlin were trying to determine basic procedures, such as the language of transmission, the frequency, and the complexity of the cipher system.[99] Perhaps to circumvent the problems connected to establishing and equipping new networks, Office VI also tried to take over existing networks.[100] Results were mixed at best. In one case, Hass was to use a contact in the Vatican to extend an existing network without divulging his RSHA association; he was to claim that he "work[ed] for German diplomats in Rome."[101] In Southern Italy, Hass took over one of Groebl's operatives and sent him to Naples, about to be overrun by advancing Allied troops. The man was never heard from again.[102] Another Office VI man trying to be overrun by Allied forces

---

[97] VI E 1, Aufbau des I-Netzes, May 31, 1943, BA-DH, ZR 920/78.

[98] Interrogation Kappler.

[99] Decode 7258, Kappler to Berlin, October 7, 1943, NA, RG 226, Entry 122, Box 1, Folder 5; Interrogation Kappler. The transmitters caught the fancy of the headquarters in Berlin; five hundred were commissioned but never carried out for a lack of time and material. Decode 7253, Berlin to Rome, October 7, 1943, Decode 7753, Kappler to Berlin, October 21, 1943, NA, RG 226, Entry 122, Box 1, Folder 5.

[100] Decode, Hoettl to Rome, October 29, 1943, NA, RG 226, Entry 122, Box 1, Folder 5.

[101] Decode 7215, Berlin to Rome, October 6, 1943, NA, RG 226, Entry 122, Box 1, Folder 5.

[102] This was the same man whose release from the Wehrmacht Schellenberg had requested from Wolff in January 1943. Johannes Kallmeyer, whose relationship with Office VI was longstanding, was dispatched to Rome on June 18, 1943. His cover had been a veritable stumbling block. Kallmeyer received a French passport, but the Technical Section cautioned the Italian Department that French citizens were not exactly

in the South failed in several attempts. First, he sought sanctuary in a cloister posing as an Austrian refugee but could not stay behind without blowing his cover when it was evacuated. In a second thwarted attempt, he hid with a troupe of actors, but this ruse failed, too. His third attempt saw him posing as a beekeeper. Having found the right spot for his planned activities – keeping bees and radioing information – he developed back problems. The mission was aborted and he was sent back to Berlin.[103]

The creation of sabotage networks taxed Office VI and confusion reigned supreme. In late October 1943, the realization dawned that people had to be found for such networks as well as trained, preferably in Germany.[104] In early November, Himmler indicated that the time had come to prepare for sabotage operations and directed both Kaltenbrunner, as the head of the RSHA, and Wolff, the HSSPF Italy, to do so. Independently from each other, both men designated a person responsible for sabotage. Kaltenbrunner's man, Walter Hammer, came from the Italian Department of Office VI, while Wolff ordered Kappler to take care of sabotage matters. Hammer was sent back to Germany.[105] Incidentally, the erstwhile police attaché Kappler was not trained in sabotage and eventually Kappler and Hass went to an SD sabotage school to learn ropes. Yet after the war Kappler claimed that the responsibility for the sabotage network rested with Hass and his subordinates from Office VI.[106] Either way, the preparation for sabotage activities got a late and poorly coordinated start and was impacted by dual command structures and competing personalities.

Office VI also tried its hand at a propaganda campaign. On October 19, 1943 a communication advised the representative of Office VI in Rome, presumably Hass, that Schellenberg had accepted a "special assignment." Office VI representatives were to seek instances of "ill-treatment of Italian nurses or similar persons by the Anglo-Americans" and make all efforts to "uncover suitable cases." Accuracy was not

traveling to Italy. Anwerbung eines Studenten, Johannes Kallmeyer, stud jur, studiert an Fremdenuniversität Perugia, Bericht 248, BA-DH, RSHA Film D, 65051; VI F 4 to VI E, Ausstellung eines französischen Passes für Joh. Kallmeyer, BA-DH, ZR 920/78; VI E 1, Vermerk: Funker Johannes Kallmeyer, June 18, 1943, BA-DH, ZR 920/78.

[103] Interrogation Kappler.
[104] Decode 7936, Hammer to Rome, October 27, 1943, NA, RG 226, Entry 122, Box 1, Folder 5.
[105] Interrogation Kappler. An Allied report of November 24, 1943 stated, "Sturmbannführer Hammer was sent to Italy to carry out a special assignment for Himmler; this assignment was exclusively concerned with the preparing of a Fifth Column and a Sabotage network." See R.I.S. 22/24.11.43, Sicherheitsdienst (Amt VI) Operations, NA, RG 226, Entry 108B, Box 286, Folder – RIS Reports.
[106] Interrogation Kappler.

Schellenberg's primary concern, "[t]he case can be greatly exaggerated, but it must contain at least a grain of truth."[107] Kappler responded with some information about the situation in the American-occupied parts of the country, highlighting that the population of Naples was prohibited from locking their doors at night.[108] As an atrocity, this surely fell short.

The RSHA regime in Rome, with its generous number of Office VI members, was least efficient when it came to foreign intelligence and sabotage matters and most efficient when it came to terror and murder. On March 24, 1944, a RSHA killing squad executed 335 male Italian civilians in the Adreatine Caves outside the city. A day earlier partisans had attacked an SS Battalion on the Via Rasella in Rome, killing 33 men. Hitler called for a bloody revenge and suggested executing thirty to fifty Italians for every German victim. German military and police authorities in Italy, with Kappler and Kesselring working side-by-side, decided that a ten to one ratio would work just as well. Kappler assembled a list, selecting for execution people imprisoned on racial and political grounds. In short, the list comprised Jews and men with actual or perceived anti-German and anti-Fascist attitudes; 320 men were on it. The Italian police added further men to the list. RSHA personnel executed them.[109] Hass was part of the killing squad.

After Mussolini's ouster, then, a mixture of tasks defined the role of Office VI in Rome, but it was not alone in these endeavors. Rather, it found support from and gave support to other entities of Himmler's universe. Bona fide intelligence activities, such as the preparation of post-occupational networks, intermingled freely with commando activities, the planning of sabotage missions, the looting of the country, the preparation of propaganda campaigns, the deportation of political and racial enemies, and murder. In the Roman context, Office VI largely ceased to exist as a foreign intelligence section but its members found their purpose in the broader, integrated RSHA structure that emerged. Internal operations reflected these new realities. In September 1943 an Allied report stated, "[t]he Amt VI Intelligence Officer is Kappler [...] He recruits and directs the main S.D. network of agents and is responsible for political reports. His judgment is good; he has not encouraged

---

[107] Decode 7721, Waneck to Rome, October 19, 1943, NA, RG 226, Entry 122, Box 1, Folder 5.

[108] Decode 7762, Kappler to Berlin, October 21, 1943, NA, RG 226, Entry 122, Box 1, Folder 5.

[109] Katz, *Rome*, 217–254. After the war, Kappler portrayed his decision to refrain from randomly rounding up Italian civilians as a humane act, in much the same way as he construed the existence of a Führer order.

illusions. He comes under the orders of Schellenberg."[110] The report reflected the new realities on the ground well. Kappler, indeed, represented Office VI and ran and directed networks. And while he was not under Schellenberg's authority, a new spirit of cooperation was palpable.

Developments in Northern Italy took a roughly similar path; however, as long as the front remained in the south, Office VI tried to maintain a level of independence from other RSHA and SS entities active in the region. In the early days after the Italian armistice, intelligence and sabotage networks were created in Northern Italy and the usual technical and administrative problems ensued. The commando of "Operation Saxony," for example, was run directly by Office VI. Dispatched to Northern Italy on the same day that German troops entered the country, it was led by SS-Obersturmführer Reissmann, the head of the Vatican department of Office VI; Schubernigg assisted. Schellenberg signed the telegram apprising the SS authorities in Bolzano of the commando.[111] The commando was to install a transmission station and to report on developments in Northern Italy, seemingly a mundane task.[112] The first report reached the Italian Department the moment the unit arrived in Bolzano. While generally upbeat, it mentioned problems with the procurement of gasoline. Other technical problems added to the commando's woes: assigned wireless times were to start only four days later and the commando asked headquarters to secure earlier transmission times.[113] Technical problems were already impacting the unit's ability to function.

Conflict with other entities of Himmler's widespread universe was not far behind. Himmler's designated local representative in Verona, the *Beauftragter der Sicherheitspolizei und des Sicherheitsdienstes* (BdS), Representative of Security Police and Security Service, Wilhelm Harster displayed a keen interest in learning the identities of the informers on whom the commando planned to rely. The unit's leaders refused to divulge this information, arguing that the net had been created for the express purpose of foreign intelligence and constituted a connection to the South. In communications with Berlin, the unit's leaders emphatically promised to guard their independence.[114] Harster, however, remained

[110] R.I.S. 15/17.9.43, The Abwehr and Sicherheitsdienst in Italy, Part II, NA, RG 226, Entry 108B, Box 286, Folder – RIS Reports.
[111] Schellenberg to Sonderbeauftragte des RFSS und Chef der deutschen Polizei, SS-Brigadeführer Brunner, Bozen, September 9, 1943, BA-DH, RSHA Film B, 220001.
[112] Unternehmen Sachsen to Amt VI, September 14, 1943, BA-DH, RSHA Fim B, 220010–220012.
[113] Telegram to Amt VI, Hoettl, September 11, 1943, BA-DH, RSHA Film B, 220005–220006.
[114] Telegram to Amt VI, Hoettl, September 11, 1943, BA-DH, RSHA Film B, 220005–220006.

intent on learning more. The unit kept evading his questions and maintained that any collaboration with visible German authorities, such as Harster's office, would jeopardize its informers. Messages to Berlin grew more exasperated as time went on. It was even suggested that the matter should be brought to Kaltenbrunner's attention, so that – "finally, for once" – the unit could function without interference.[115]

The reports of this unit, which was in the country for about two weeks, closely resembled those received by the Italian Department years earlier; they still focused on moods and attitudes. And the mood was bad: Italians were deeply unhappy with the reinstallation of Mussolini. More strongly than before the reports advocated political solutions: renaming the Fascist party; providing better German propaganda able to "touch the Italian soul;" and the installation of an Italian leadership that was not visibly dependent on the German authorities. The reports also provided information needed to destroy preventively potential centers of resistance, for example by radio jamming. And as if further encouragement was needed for anti-Jewish measures, the report stressed that Jews furthered the anti-German propaganda emanating from the Allies. However, the unit emphasized that arrests were difficult, as these Jews were "Italianized and not easily recognized as Jews." Thus, the cooperation of the Italian authorities was needed.[116] Other reports commented on the anti-German attitudes coming to the fore, detailed anti-German gossip at length, and noted that the Italians eagerly devoured Allied propaganda. Some reports intimated that the behavior of the German troops in Italy contributed to anti-German sentiments but frequently fell back on ideological interpretations still: discontent was blamed on the growing importance of Jews and Freemasons or the ready availability of British propaganda. Suggested remedies ranged from the requisitioning of all radios to the deployment of Einsatzgruppen and the establishment of "firm German control (beyond the end of the war)."[117] For what they were – reports focused on moods and attitudes – they were reasonably

---

[115] Unternehmen Sachsen to Amt VI, September 14, 1943, BA-DH, RSHA Film B, 220012.

[116] Unternehmen Sachsen to Schellenberg, September 21, 1943, BA-DH, RSHA Film B, 220043–220045; RSHA, VI E 1, Abberufung des Unternehmen Sachsen, September 23, 1943, BA-DH, RSHA Film B, 220013.

[117] For example: Telegram to RSHA, attn. Kaltenbrunner and Ohlendorf, September 7, 1943, BA-DH, RSHA Film C, 420058–420062; Telegram, Schubernigg [Operation Saxony] to VI E, BA-DH, Film RSHA C, 500101–500103; Schellenberg to Kaltenbrunner, Echo auf die Befreiung des Duce in Italien, September 14, 1943, BA-DH, RSHA Film C, 50007; Schellenberg to Kaltenbrunner, Stimmung in Rom, September 30, 1943, BA-DH, RSHA Film C, 4200228; Bericht Oscar Ebner von Ebenthal, September 24, 1943, BA-DH, RSHA, Film, C 500113–5000127. Similar reports: BA-DH, RSHA Film C, Höttl. Antiital. Tätigkeit.

perceptive but later self-congratulatory remarks that "even during this period reports from Italy were usually rather objective and exposed some illusions" are rather droll.[118] The Italian desperation about the occupation of the country must have been hard to overlook and the proposed solutions were firmly entrenched in ideology, especially anti-Semitism.

The establishment of a permanent German presence in Northern Italy led to more formalized intelligence structures and networks. Yet despite reams of Allied reports and interrogations of those involved, many details remain in the dark or are difficult to verify – partly for a lack of contemporaneous documentation, partly due to postwar obfuscation. Harster was appointed Beauftragter der Sicherheitspolizei, BdS, and established his headquarters in Verona. His office included an *Abteilung VI*, Section VI, in charge of intelligence matters with Klaus Huegel at its helm. There also existed various smaller posts and, in addition, Einsatzkommandos. Aside from Rome, Einsatzkommandos were deployed in Florence under Groebl (who was eventually killed by partisans), in Milan under Walther Rauff, and in Trieste under a certain Weinman. In Northern Italy a third category of foreign intelligence entities, under the authority of Office VI, existed: *Sonderkommandos*, special commandos, supposed to engage in "offensive espionage and political subversion" and answerable to the local commanding officers. These special commandos were "almost completely independent" from the existing structures.[119] Into this third category fell, for example, a group that was to don Allied uniforms and operate behind Allied lines as well as a special commando under an "old faithful" of the service in Italy, Friedrich Schwendt, alias Wendig. Wendig's association with the political foreign intelligence service dated back to at least 1939. Back then, Wendig's many schemes at the intersection of foreign intelligence, business, sabotage, and murder had not come to fruition; by 1944, Wendig had created a perfect niche for himself. He procured whatever Office VI needed – equipment, food, weapons – and laundered money; to be precise, Wendig laundered forged money. Supposedly, Wendig's group was also to collect intelligence but this task

---

[118] Interrogation Report No. 18, July 16, 1945, NA, RG 263, Entry ZZ-18, Box 54, File: Hoettl, Wilhelm, Vol. 2, 1 of 2.

[119] On the Security Police and SD apparatus in Northern Italy: Carlo Gentile and Lutz Klinkhammer, "Gegen die Verbündeten von Einst: Die Gestapo in Italien," in Gerhard Paul and Klaus-Michael Mallmann, eds., *Die Gestapo im Zweiten Weltkrieg: 'Heimatfront und besetztes Europa* (Darmstadt: Primus Verlag, 2000), 521–540. The RSHA in Occupied and Neutral Countries, early 1945, NA, RG 263, Entry ZZ-18, Box 2, German Intelligence Service, Vol. 1, 1 of 2; Third Detailed Interrogation Report on SS Sturmbannführer Huegel, Dr. Klaus, May 19, 1945, NA, RG 226, Entry 174, Box 39, Folder 307.

was routinely neglected.[120] Other SD members active in Italy and supposed to prepare postoccupational networks developed other interests as well: in Milan, Guido Zimmer – the same man who had blundered his Roman assignment three years prior – failed to set up postoccupational networks.[121] He busied himself with the trafficking of sequestered – stolen – goods and, eventually, people. Zimmer brought back Italian nationals interned in Germany but with a discerning eye: they had to be rich. For Zimmer this was almost a step up. In Genoa, he had tracked down Jews for deportation.[122]

As the BdS, Harster kept in contact with the RSHA in Berlin and with the Italian Department of Office VI. He was to keep the office abreast of developments in Northern Italy and provide information about Allied-occupied Italy. The former information was also given to Office III of the RSHA; with the German occupation of the country, the domestic intelligence service was officially in charge. Yet in view of the deteriorating military situation, these distinctions – bitterly fought over when Germany was still victorious – became less important. With the country divided into two parts, one occupied by Allied troops and the other by German forces, Italy had become a frontline country and the presence of a unified intelligence service a necessity. However, this did not preclude Office VI and Office IV from quarreling over their contacts in the Vatican.[123] Old habits died hard.

According to Harster, Section VI, under the direction of Huegel, began operations in March 1944, but it appears that an approximation of functionality was only achieved in the fall. In addition to its regular tasks, the section was also in charge of Unit IDA, yet another intelligence network, and an espionage school. Hass and Schubernigg, the same men who had failed to establish a postoccupational network in Rome (and subsequently in Florence), were responsible for Unit IDA in Parma.

[120] Third Detailed Interrogation Report on SS Sturmbannführer Huegel, Dr. Klaus, May 19, 1945, NA, RG 226, Entry 174, Box 39, Folder 307. Huegel indicated that money came from the German Reich mint, the plates, however, were created by concentration camp inmates. On Wendig: Richard Breitman, "Follow the Money," in Richard Breitman et al., eds., *U.S. Intelligence and the Nazis* (Washington, DC: National Trust Fund for the Nazi War Crimes and Japanese Imperial Government Records Interagency Working Group, 2004), 121–127.
[121] Interrogation Report on SS Standartenführer Rauff Walter, May 29, 1945, NA, RG 226, Entry 194, Box 63, Folder 279.
[122] File Traces on Zimmer, Lt. Dr. Guido, NA, RG 263, CIA Name Files, Box 8, Folder Zimmer.
[123] Interrogation Report on SS Gruppenführer Dr. Harster, Wilhelm, May 20, 1945, NA, RG 226, Entry 194, Box 63, Folder 219. On Germany's intelligence efforts against the Vatican: David Alvarez and Robert A. Graham SJ, *Nothing Sacred: Nazi Espionage Against the Vatican, 1939–1945* (London: Frank Cass, 1997), especially chapter 2.

By focusing on basic line crossing into enemy territory and shorter missions – the most extensive excursion led an agent to Rome – Hass found his way back into his superiors' good graces, even though some of his colleagues considered his network useless. Technical problems remained: when a shipment of wireless sets arrived in January or February 1945, Hass realized that it was impossible to reach the contact station in Bamberg. Incidentally, the espionage school, in which wireless operators were to be trained, never received wireless sets at all, thus making training rather difficult.[124] Around the same time, a sabotage organization/training entity, *Unternehmen Zypresse*, Operation Cypress, under Otto Begus, was moved to Verona. Conceptualized as a sabotage entity – especially against Allied supply lines – it was to use only Italians for its activities and, if possible, to collect political information as well. A technical unit was to be in charge of forgeries and other technical demands; incidentally, Begus noted after the war that this unit had to be kept secret from Office VI's technical department in Berlin.[125] Even within the office, rivalries abounded.

After the war Huegel gave his interrogators detailed insights into attempts to create intelligence networks in Northern Italy in the last eighteen months of the war and especially after the Allied liberation of Rome on June 6, 1944.[126] He portrayed a system in disarray, trying to get by on a shoestring while entertaining grandiose plans: the more things changed, the more they stayed the same. Candidates for missions in Italy were commonly recruited by Italians and only sometimes by the German representatives of the RSHA; if credentials were in doubt, Section VI in Verona or Unit IDA vetted them by focusing on their political and private affairs, their motives, and their contacts in Allied-occupied Italy. Those suitable for espionage work began their training; others were assigned to sabotage missions. Recruitment valued quantity over quality: the more agents were dispatched, the more would return. And only few did. Between August and November 1944, for example, Huegel's Section VI sent twelve agents into Allied-occupied territory; one returned. The

---

[124] Interrogation Report on SS Gruppenführer Dr. Harster, Wilhelm, May 20, 1945, NA, RG 226, Entry 194, Box 63, Folder 219; Interrogation Reports on SS Hauptsturmführer Schoenepflug, Egon, May 22, 1945, NA, RG 263, Entry ZZ-16, Box 26, File: Huegel, Klaus.

[125] Interrogation Report on SS Gruppenführer Dr. Harster, Wilhelm, May 20, 1945, NA, RG 226, Entry 194, Box 63, Folder 219; First Detailed Interrogation Report on SS Sturmbannfuehrer Begus, Dr. Otto and SS Untersturmführer Strauss, Otto, August 7, 1945, NA, RG 263, Entry ZZ-18, Box 126, File: Steimle; Organizational Charts in NA, RG 263, Entry ZZ-16, Box 26, File: Huegel, Klaus.

[126] Third Detailed Interrogation Report on SS Sturmbannführer Huegel, Dr. Klaus, May 19, 1945, NA, RG 226, Entry 174, Box 39, Folder 307.

returnee rates for Unit IDA were slightly better: four of eighteen agents returned, a considerable success. Furthermore, only few contacts existed in the South, indicating the shortsighted work of the foreign intelligence service in the early years of the war, and basic technologies – particularly wireless transmitters–were in short supply.

Huegel also emphasized the difficulty inherent in trying to convince anyone to spy against an enemy that is apparently winning. Most of the men were mercenaries, a development that was diametrically opposed to how the SD had initially envisioned its intelligence networks. Few people joined out of anti-Allied convictions, and even then, they "were not always in ideological agreement with the policy being carried out by Germans in Northern Italy," but Office VI was cognizant that "there was little that could be done about [the lack of agreement]" and consequently threatened agents with reprisals against their families if they abandoned their missions. Huegel claimed that reprisals were never carried out, but knowing the German track record against civilians, it is unlikely that Italian espionage recruits took the threats lightly.

The agents' training was, according to Huegel, divided into three parts. The first dealt with the mission, the second with the agents' cover story, and the third with the situation in the Allied-controlled territories. Huegel also detailed the various shortcomings of these approaches. The establishment of the cover stories, which the prospective agents made up on their own and kept simple by design, included mock interviews. A number of them broke down during these. Insufficient knowledge about the realities in the Allied-occupied part of the country made the situation worse and left the agents poorly prepared. The practice of training agents in large groups, borne of a lack of instructors and time, created another security risk. One captured agent was could possibly unravel a complete network, if not several.

The agents' deployment raised other problems. The German military disliked dispatching agents across the lines on Office VI's timetables. If detained on the other side, agents would frequently give detailed information about German military positions to shore up their own value to the Allies. Military authorities occasionally held back agents until their crossing was in sync with military needs. Some agents parachuted into target areas, but few had the necessary training and aircraft for the drops were in short supply and had to be set up well in advance. Once in Allied territory, the agents were left to their own resources. Section VI representatives were content if they had not made matters worse, as when they had outfitted all agents with brand-new and identical suits and wristwatches. Agents' returns were not easy either: specific crossing times and passwords were not always shared with the military and returning agents were, much to the frustration of Section VI that eagerly awaited them, detained.

Agents were then debriefed in detail and two different reports were created. The "technical details" of the mission focused on the agents' routes, difficulties encountered, Allied countermeasures observed, and a general overview of their movements and activities. These technical reports went to Office VI in Berlin, Section VI of the BdS Verona, and Unit IDA and sometimes to the sabotage unit active in Northern Italy. The second report focused on the information obtained during the mission, dividing it into military and political information. The former was given to the military authorities in Italy without any indication of its origin. The latter part was forwarded to the RSHA, the German Embassy, and, by way of the Liaison Officer of the Fascist Republican Party, to Mussolini. Focusing on political and economic information in Allied-occupied Italy, this section also covered the activities of the various Italian political parties, the relations between Allied troops and the Italians, and relations among various Allied forces. Section VI was also supposed to issue bimonthly reports on the situation in Southern Italy; however, Huegel noted that before the collapse of the German power structure in Italy, these summaries had been created only twice. Harster was not pleased with these reports. Commenting on those Unit IDA provided, he noted that they always contained the same information regardless of the section of the front from which they originated. Without fail, they focused on "civilian control, morale, prices, political situation, prostitution of women, relationship between troops and civilians, etc."[127] In January 1945, Harster instructed Huegel and his counterpart from Section III to locate more suitable agents but nothing came of it. In short, it was the same old story.

Huegel provides an instructive look behind the scenes of Office VI's operations in Northern Italy in the last months of the war. Even if he had a vested interest in downplaying the office's importance and effectiveness, his interrogations show an intelligence service scrambling to make do at the worst possible time. Random recruits, vetted quickly and frequently recognized as mercenaries, were sent on vaguely defined missions, for which they were barely trained. Their superficial reports were proudly sent onward to the highest authorities in the Reich. Analysis did not happen; the foreign intelligence service, desperate for information, was hanging on by a thread. To say that planning for a postoccupational period was shoddy and contributed to Office VI's poor performance would be a serious understatement. Trying to make sense of Office VI's

---

[127] Interrogation Report on SS Standartenführer Rauff Walter, May 29, 1945, NA, RG 226, Entry 194, Box 63, Folder 279.

poor performance after the war, Huegel volunteered that nobody dared to plan for "total collapse," a notion supported by other postwar interrogations.[128] But something else was at work as well: nobody was planning on losing the war and there was a vague sense that the war was either still winnable or that it would at least be possible to avoid complete defeat – be it by the deployment of new secret weapons or by creating a split between the Allies. To this end Office VI worked as well. There was little interest in the Italian government per se, but Office VI regarded it as a mirror in which to observe divisions among the Allies and the various levels of Allies influence. The little intelligence gathering that happened honed into these potential faultlines: "[Huegel] was instructed to brief his political agents to obtain information on the principal causes of dissension between the Allies and the principal causes of discontent on the part of the Italians." The plan was to create even more dissent. Very little of this came to pass, but Office VI was blinded by its beliefs.

As an intelligence-gathering entity active in Italy, Office VI was a resounding failure. It did not do any better with the creation and maintenance of stay-behind networks or sabotage activities. The reasons for this failure were numerous and remained stable despite fundamental political shifts on the ground: poorly trained, poorly equipped personnel – with their ideological blinders firmly in place – took on poorly conceived missions. Reports were and remained exercises in ideologically correct vagueness. The office's strength was to be found primarily in its ability to engage, to be successful, and to benefit from the ongoing conflicts with other German entities active in Italy. Among them the competition with Office IV, the Gestapo, represented in Rome by police attaché Kappler, was the most difficult to handle, yet eventually a *modus vivendi*, which served both Kappler and Office VI well, was found. Foreign intelligence in Italy was a multi-ring circus. Ultimately, Office VI and its personnel made the greatest impact in Italy after its occupation, when its purge and plunder took precedence over everything else. These activities were part and parcel of the new, Nazified security and intelligence service that came into being in those years. It was yet another aspect of Germany's New Order.

[128] Second Detailed Interrogation Report on SS Sturmbannführer Huegel, Dr. Klaus, May 1945, NA, RG 263, Entry ZZ-16, Box 26, File: Huegel, Klaus; Appendix No. 10 to Final Interrogation Report of Steimle, Eugen, SS Standartenfuehrer, Chief Grupe VI B an Abtlg. Mil B, RSHA, December 12, 1945, RG 263, Entry ZZ-18, Box 126, File: Steimle, Eugen.

7   Alternative Universes
Office VI and the Auswärtige Amt

[A] perennial conflict existed between this service and the Foreign Office. The constant state of open war was interrupted by occasional periods of external armistices.

Wilhelm Hoettl,
Interrogation Report No. 18, July 16, 1945[1]

[B]ut the SD wanted to make foreign policy, which he could not allow. A serious struggle with the SD therefore developed in the last few years.

Report on Ribbentrop Interrogation of June 30, 1945[2]

The Abwehr, Germany's military intelligence service, always serves as Office VI's main historiographical foil, for the agencies' contentious relationship defines the scholarly literature. Office VI's self-definition as a foreign intelligence service, its claim for totality, and its usurpation of the Abwehr in 1944 account for this focus. Yet as the preceding chapters have shown, it was comparatively easy for Office VI to paint the Abwehr as insufficiently ideologized and to take it over. A closer investigation indicates, however, that Office VI's main rival was not the Abwehr, but the Auswärtige Amt under minister Joachim von Ribbentrop. Confrontations between Office VI and the Auswärtige Amt were endemic to Office VI's understanding of its role at the intersection of intelligence gathering and ideological foreign political activism. The tensions between the two entities only grew as Schellenberg, who fancied himself a foreign policy expert and a politician, came into his own as the head of Office VI and deliberately encroached on the sphere of the Auswärtige Amt.

The Auswärtige Amt reported on political and economic developments abroad; this had been a key task of diplomatic posts since time immemorial. With its concentration on political and economic information and its poorly defined mandate, Office VI was set to infringe on Auswärtige Amt

---

[1] Interrogation Report No. 18, July 16, 1945, NA, RG 265, Entry ZZ-18, Box 54, File: Hoettl, Wilhelm, Vol. 2, 1 of 2.

[2] Report on Ribbentrop Interrogation of June 30, 1945, NA, RG 319, IRR-Personal, Box 241 B, File: Ribbentrop, 1 of 5.

territory – initially by default but increasingly by design. However, conflict was not restricted to Office VI's information gathering. Ribbentrop attempted to make the collection and evaluation of information central to his office and even though he targeted primarily information gathering in Goebbels' Propaganda Ministry, Office VI was affected as well.[3] Schellenberg, for his part, made several attempts to unseat Ribbentrop and to draw foreign policy into Himmler's universe; they all failed. Unlike the Abwehr, Ribbentrop's Auswärtige Amt could not easily be branded as ideologically unreliable since, quite simply, it was not. Hitler trusted and backed Ribbentrop. Eventually, Schellenberg settled on a different tack: he created an alternative Foreign Office and strove to conduct foreign policy through it.

Schellenberg held strong opinions about Germany's foreign politicians. He was still with the Gestapo's counterintelligence department when he concluded that most had "little understanding of countries other than their own." To counteract this, he imagined "forming a central information office for foreign countries from which information on political-economic questions could be collected and disseminated." As far as Schellenberg was concerned, such a center, knowledgeable about "formative political and economic forces" at work abroad, did not exist. Allegedly, Himmler shared his view.[4] Schellenberg made these statements in Allied custody when he had ample reason to portray Office VI as less of an intelligence agency and more of a foreign policy think-tank at the intersection of information gathering and foreign policy and himself as a politician instead of an ideological soldier. Yet Schellenberg always held this vision of an alternative foreign policy office with himself as Himmler's foreign minister and had labored to create it. Foreign intelligence was Schellenberg's work, and, as will be recalled, not his office's strong suit. A partial explanation for this failure – and many of the office's peculiarities – can be found in the fact that Schellenberg deemed foreign policy his calling and used Office VI accordingly.

Many issues of contention existed between the Auswärtige Amt and Office VI – and the RSHA as a whole – but the status of SD personnel abroad and their relationship to the German missions was among

[3] Michael Geyer, "National Socialist Germany: The Politics of Information," in Ernest R. May, ed., *Knowing One's Enemy: Intelligence Assessment Before the Two World Wars* (Princeton: Princeton University Press, 1984), 313–314; Eckart Conze et al., *Das Amt und die Vergangenheit. Deutsche Diplomaten im Dritten Reich und in der Bundesrepublik.* Unter Mitarbeit von Annette Weinke und Andrea Wiegershoff (München: Blessing Verlag, 2010), 146–145.
[4] Final Report on the Case of Walter Schellenberg, NA, RG 319, IRR, XE 001725, Walter Schellenberg, Folders 7 and 8 [hereafter: Final Report].

the most important.[5] Were these men under the authority of the mission or did they operate independently, answering to their SD superiors? In the fall of 1939, this long-simmering conflict came to a first boil. After Ribbentrop and his office gained Hitler's backing, proclaiming the Auswärtige Amt superior to all other organizations in matters of foreign policy, Reinhard Heydrich entered negotiations. In October, Heydrich and Ribbentrop came to an agreement, which Schellenberg claimed to have drafted.[6] Despite the strength of the Auswärtige Amt, the arrangement was evenhanded and typical for Nazi Germany, in that each party had its most important demands met and could regard itself the winner; only time would tell which organization would come out on top. Ribbentrop accepted Office VI's right to gather political information abroad; agreed to the inclusion of Security and Intelligence Service (SD) or Security Police (Sipo) representatives into foreign missions as police attachés; and granted them the privilege of reporting directly and secretly to their main office in Berlin. Furthermore, the Auswärtige Amt promised to turn a blind eye on "illegal tasks" undertaken abroad. Ribbentrop was not unexpectedly generous; from behind the scenes Hitler apparently supported Heydrich. The minister, in return, received the guarantee that all political foreign intelligence collected would be evaluated, examined, and ultimately approved by *Abteilung II Deutschland*, Department II Germany, which also housed the Information Division.[7]

The installation of the police attachés began right thereafter. Most came from the Gestapo, Office IV, as in the case of Herbert Kappler in Rome, discussed above.[8] These appointments fit the official fiction that the police attachés were to liaise with their host countries' police forces. In reality, their tasks included foreign intelligence matters, much like military attachés did more than their briefs held. V-men and informers in the field reported to the police attachés, and they forwarded this

---

[5] The SD sometimes gained embassy personnel as V-men; these men often reported more on their colleagues than their host countries. The Auswärtige Amt tried to close their missions' doors to SD members; 090 SD-Berlin, Antiital. Tätigkeit, BA-DH, RSHA Film A.

[6] Peter Black, *Ernst Kaltenbrunner: Ideological Soldier of the Third Reich* (Princeton: Princeton University Press, 1984), 179. Walter Schellenberg, *The Labyrinth: Memoirs of Walter Schellenberg, Hitler's Chief of Counterintelligence*, trans. Louis Hagen (New York: Harper & Brothers, 1956; reprint, Cambridge, MA: Da Capo Press, 2000), 247.

[7] Black, *Kaltenbrunner*, 179–180. The department, headed by Rudolf Likus with Werner Picot serving as his deputy, dealt with the affairs of the Reichsführer SS, Reich Security Main Office, international police cooperation, and freemasonry. For a chart of Luther's department: Christopher R. Browning, "Unterstaatssekretaer Martin Luther and the Ribbentrop Foreign Office," *Journal of Contemporary History* 12 (1977), 321.

[8] For a list of police attachés in August 1940: Schriftverkehr mit den Sonderbeauftragten des Sicherheitspolizei bei den deutschen Auslandsvertretungen, August 29, 1940, USHMM 14.016 M/837, 1.

information, plus their own impressions about the country – and sometimes about embassy personnel – to Berlin.[9] Representatives of Office VI, the so-called SD Main Representatives, were frequently attached to the police attachés as assistants or the like. A workable solution had been established.

This fragile balance fell apart after the Iron Guard Revolt against the Romanian dictator General Ion Antonescu in January 1941. Office VI and its representative in Bucharest, Hauptsturmführer Otto von Bolschwing, supported the revolt led by Horia Sima. Neither the Auswärtige Amt nor Ribbentrop nor Hitler were amused; in their estimation, Antonescu guaranteed stability in a country whose oil fields were important to the German war effort, especially in light of the planned invasion of the Soviet Union. With Hitler's backing, Antonescu put down the revolt. What was left for the Bolschwing and an SD commando was to spirit Sima and his closest associates out the country.[10] Emboldened, Ribbentrop now pressed for more oversight of the police attachés and other RSHA representatives active abroad.

Himmler and Ribbentrop signed a new agreement dealing with the role of RSHA representatives abroad in early August 1941, shortly after the invasion of the Soviet Union and Schellenberg's appointment to Office VI. With the Soviet Union seemingly on the verge of collapse, Germany was approaching the height of its power. It was a good time for Ribbentrop to straighten out the ground rules and to establish that foreign policy decision were not to be made by the erstwhile party intelligence service. The new agreement established that RSHA representatives abroad were to refrain from any activity that could harm Germany's foreign policy. They were also prohibited from any involvement with domestic policies in their host countries and any special tasks – sabotage – had to be approved by Ribbentrop ahead of time. Yet, police attachés were to be installed in all countries where the RSHA was active and German missions existed; it was their task to control and to take the responsibility for local RSHA activities and to keep informed the mission chiefs. Indeed,

---

[9] Compare to BA-DH, RSHA, Film A, 090. These documents consider in great detail the alleged Jewish ancestry of the German ambassador in Rome.

[10] Heinz Höhne, *Der Orden unter dem Totenkopf: Die Geschichte der SS* (Munich: Bertelsmann, 1967; reprint, Augsburg: Weltbild Verlag, 1998), 267–268; Reinhard R. Doerries, *Hitler's Intelligence Chief Walter Schellenberg. The Man Who Kept Germany's Secrets* (New York: Enigma Books, 2009), 49. It is correct that the Romanian adventure contributed to Jost's downfall, as Doerries suggests; however, Heydrich likely had decided to rid himself of Jost no matter what. On Bolschwing and his postwar transformation: Timothy Naftali, "The CIA and Eichmann's Associates," in Richard Breitman et al., eds., *U.S. Intelligence and the Nazis* (Washington, DC: National Trust Fund for the Nazi War Crimes and Japanese Imperial Government Records Interagency Working Group, 2004), 343–354.

any RSHA member active abroad would fall under the authority of the respective diplomatic mission; independent RSHA offices abroad were to close. For countries in which RSHA representatives were active but no German missions existed, Ribbentrop and Himmler agreed to find a solution by which another individual would fulfill the police attaché's tasks. Reporting was also organized better: reports by RSHA representatives were to be forwarded, via the mission, directly to their offices for evaluation and analysis; any information about foreign policy would then be shared with the Auswärtige Amt. How to use the information was the Auswärtige Amt's prerogative.[11]

The new agreement attempted to tie the hands of the RSHA outside Germany and to shore up the position of Ribbentrop and his diplomats. However, the service regulations for the police attachés contained important caveats. In matters of extreme importance, the police attachés could report directly to Himmler and Heydrich; they had a separate set of codes. The regulations also stressed that, despite their formal subordination to the mission chiefs, the police attachés remained responsible to Himmler.[12] The RSHA took additional steps to maintain control over its personnel: emphasizing the primary relationship between the police attachés and the RSHA, a Police Attaché Group directly subordinate to its head, was created a year later.[13] However, the Auswärtige Amt also exercised its powers; reams of visa requests for RSHA representatives traveling abroad indicate clearly the intention to keep the SD on a short leash, even if most requests were granted without much ado.[14] On occasion Ribbentrop asserted his power, for example by telling Himmler that a planned trip to Italy needed approval by the Auswärtige Amt. He also displayed his savvy when he tapped into a pool of former SA men for diplomatic positions in South-Eastern Europe.[15] Ribbentrop could be assured that these "survivors" of the Röhm purge of 1934 would do their utmost to keep SS ambitions in check.

Ultimately – and surprisingly, considering Ribbentrop's superior position in the aftermath of the SD's Romanian disaster – the agreement and service regulations of August 1941 represented a draw. Subordinated to

[11] Grundsatzvereinbarung vom 8. August 1941, Führerhauptquartier, August 8, 1941, Ribbentrop and Himmler, BAL, NS 19/178.
[12] Dienstanweisung für die einigen deutschen Botschaften und Gesandtschaften (Missionen) zugeteilten Polizeiattachés, August 28, 1941, BAL, NS 19/178. In the weeks before, Heydrich fought for the independence Office VI; CdS to Weizäcker, June 20, 1941, BAL, NS 19/178.
[13] Black, *Kaltenbrunner*, 180–181.
[14] Auslandsreisen des SD [1940–1945], Politisches Archiv des Auswärtigen Amtes (PAAA), R 100803-R 100808.
[15] Höhne, *Orden*, 269; Conze et al., *Amt*, 165–166.

the mission chiefs, the police attachés were still there and the regulations governing their role were phrased just broadly enough for them
to remain useful. Ribbentrop asserted his privilege to be kept informed,
but the RSHA retained the ways, means, and rights to bypass the minister. The latter became standard procedure. After the war Klaus Huegel
stated, "since 1942 signals and dispatches coming to Amt VI were only
passed to the Foreign Office once Amt VI had received notification that
Himmler had read them. If Himmler thought fit, certain information
never reached the Foreign Office."[16] On the surface, Office VI played
by the rules; under Schellenberg postings of Office VI members abroad
were discussed with the Auswärtige Amt in great detail and with an eye
toward the discussion's placating effects.[17] Open warfare ceased. Historians argue that Ribbentrop drew a line that Himmler was unable to
cross while Himmler, for his part, recognized the futility of Ribbentrop's
victory: foreign policy did not matter anymore.[18] Put differently, Himmler gave up on foreign policy and never looked back. This was not the
case. Office VI under Schellenberg took on the Auswärtige Amt and
Ribbentrop in various ways and direct attacks on the minister were one
of them.

In late 1942, Schellenberg joined forces with Unterstaatssekretär Martin Luther of Abteilung II Deutschland in an effort to depose Ribbentrop.
As Schellenberg told the story after the war, he had tried to convince
Himmler as early as August 1942 that the war was not going to end in
Germany's favor and suggested exploring options for a separate peace
with the Western Allies. Schellenberg believed Ribbentrop unacceptable
to the West and regarded himself as a better negotiator.[19] Schellenberg
found a perfect partner in the intrigue against Ribbentrop in Martin
Luther, at least if one ignores that Luther had ministerial ambitions himself. Disenchanted with Ribbentrop, his standing in the ministry deteriorating, and allegedly pushed by a group of younger men in his office to
depose Ribbentrop and to explore options for a separate peace, Luther,
too, was looking for ways to oust the minister. It is not clear how either
man learned of the other's plans and who made the first move. In one
version of the story, Luther approached Schellenberg to gain Himmler's
support; in another Schellenberg, aware of Luther's misgivings about
Ribbentrop, begged Luther for additional material against the minister
and assured him that, with Himmler's backing, he would be able to bring

[16] Fourth Detailed Interrogation Report on SS Sturmbannführer Huegel Dr. Klaus, June
   10, 1945, NA, RG 226, Entry 174, Box 39, Folder 307.
[17] Auslandsreisen des SD [1940–1945], Politisches Archiv des Auswärtigen Amtes
   (PAAA), R 100803-R 100808.
[18] Höhne, *Orden*, 269.   [19] Schellenberg, *Labyrinth*, 299–316.

about Ribbentrop's downfall.[20] The plot failed utterly and landed Luther in a concentration camp while Schellenberg, agile as ever, extracted himself unharmed.

Schellenberg and the conspirators in the Auswärtige Amt related the reasons for the plot's failure differently. The conspirators in the Auswärtige Amt held that the chain of events was set into motion in January 1943. While they were still trying to gain additional partners for their plan, Schellenberg insisted that they had to expedite their efforts, intimating that there was progress to be made with the Americans.[21] In this version of the story, during a meeting at the Italian Embassy in February 1943, Himmler let Luther know that he would support Ribbentrop's removal. Upping the ante, Schellenberg called Luther and assured him that Himmler was on board and ready to convince Hitler to get rid off Ribbentrop. Schellenberg requested the conspirators' plans and arguments in writing.[22] In other words, Schellenberg pushed his co-conspirators into a breakneck pace and asked for – and received – written proof of the conspiracy. In Schellenberg's version, Luther drove the action and made costly mistakes. Schellenberg claimed that during a chance meeting at the Italian Embassy at the end of 1942, Luther, behaving like an "ill-bred upstart," approached Himmler, "buttonholed" him "as though they were bosom friends and began to talk shop."[23] As their respective phone calls to Schellenberg the next day made clear, Luther and Himmler had experienced their meeting differently: Himmler was annoyed, but Luther assumed that his encounter with Himmler had gone splendidly and opined that Ribbentrop could "lump it now." During their next meeting, Schellenberg admonished Luther for his behavior toward Himmler and made him promise not to make another move without his approval, as only he would know when Himmler would be ready. Luther ignored Schellenberg's sage advice and began showing around and distributing a file that called into question the minister's job performance and sanity.[24] This raises the question where the plot against Ribbentrop originated. Most historians agree that this file, which has

---

[20] Browning, "Luther," 334–335; Schellenberg, *Labyrinth*, 324.

[21] Doerries ties the Luther-Schellenberg affair directly to contacts between Schellenberg's confidant Max von Hohenlohe and Allen Dulles, the OSS representative in Switzerland, discussed below. Two reasons speak against a direct connection: the timing does not work out, as the meetings in Switzerland and the plans for the plot in Berlin took place almost simultaneously; Schellenberg liked his successes more predictable. Secondly, Schellenberg never made the direct connection in his postwar testimonies. He only intimated that there was a chance for progress with the Americans. Schellenberg was not a truthful man but he never missed an opportunity to present himself in a good light. Doerries, *Intelligence Chief*, 88.

[22] Browning, "Luther," 338.   [23] Schellenberg, *Labyrinth*, 324.

[24] Schellenberg, *Labyrinth*, 324–326; Final Report.

not surfaced after the war, came out of the Auswärtige Amt. Doerries, on the other hand, draws attention to one witness, a Luther confidant, who recalled that Luther and Schellenberg dictated information to one of Schellenberg's secretaries.[25] If true, this indicates a close collaboration between the two men but does not negate the plot's origins in the ministry. Schellenberg attempted to profit from it but had no intention of taking incalculable risks. Luther showing around the file was such as risk; he was jumping the gun while Schellenberg was not yet convinced that Himmler would go along with the plans. Cautious as ever, he made sure not to commit to Luther's plans "prematurely" or "foolish[-ly]." Rather, Schellenberg made his commitment conditional on Himmler's decision, but promised Luther that he would raise the issue with Himmler immediately. This he did. As Himmler dithered about whether to support Luther – Schellenberg believed that he was about to give his approval – Karl Wolff, then Himmler's Chief of Personal Staff, a friend of Ribbentrop, and a man who wholeheartedly despised Luther, joined the meeting and took on Ribbentrop's cause.

But, Herr Reichsfuehrer, you cannot let SS Obergruppenfuehrer Joachim von Ribbentrop, one of the highest ranking members of our order, be kicked out by this scoundrel Luther. It would be a grave infringement of the roles of the Order. I am certain you would never get Hitler's approval.

With this appeal to the importance of the SS and the warning that Hitler would not approve, Wolff swayed Himmler. Instead of using the file to demonstrate to Hitler that Ribbentrop was no longer up to his position, it was turned over to him.

Ribbentrop now cleaned house, but the affair's fall-out remained comparatively mild. The weeks after the surrender of the Sixth Army at Stalingrad, when Propaganda Minister Joseph Goebbels was working overtime to strengthen the population's commitment to "total war," were not a good time for the plot's thorough investigation. Luther carried the aftermath's brunt; he was arrested on February 10, 1943 and sent to the concentration camp Sachsenhausen.[26] Luther's department was split into two groups directly under Ribbentrop; Gruppe I kept the contact with the party while Gruppe II, under SS-Standartenführer Horst Wagner, liaised with the SS. The growth of Gruppe II to 55 men should surely be seen as an indication of the SS growing relevance in matters of foreign policy as well as of its many activities. The Information Division was placed directly under a new State Secretary, Baron Gustav Bruno Steengracht

[25] Doerries, *Intelligence Chief*, 88.
[26] Schellenberg, *Labyrinth*, 327–328: Browning, "Luther," 334–335, 339.

von Moyland.[27] Schellenberg and his office escaped the affair unharmed and actually came out ahead. There were no repercussions for Schellenberg personally but rather found himself in a position in which he tried to use "his influence with Müller" [sic!] to secure better treatment for Luther. Secondly, the dissolution of Abteilung II Deutschland and the new administrative locus of the Information Division were to the RSHA's advantage. Luther had created problems of his own for the Sipo and SD and now he was gone. As Huegel put it:

Himmler was delighted at the turn of the events, as it gave him an opportunity of having Luther removed which at the same time greatly weakened Ribbentrop's position, as instead of the powerful personality of Luther, he received in his place the colourless Steengracht, who was appointed State Secretary when Luther was arrested.[28]

With Luther in a concentration camp, a much weaker man in part of his position, and Ribbentrop slightly damaged, the field had shifted in favor of Himmler and the RSHA. This is exemplified by a meeting between Horst Wagner, Steengracht von Moyland, and Kaltenbrunner in November 1943.[29] The three men discussed yet again the proper channels for foreign intelligence reports and Steengracht von Moyland adamantly defended the earlier agreement that required all reports to be examined by the Auswärtige Amt before being forwarded to Hitler. Kaltenbrunner agreed, but reserved the right to deviate from this standard procedure in "exceptional cases." The new men were no real matches for Kaltenbrunner.

Office VI also tried to use its activities abroad to unseat Ribbentrop. In 1943 and 1944 Office VI members in Italy spent much time and energy on obtaining the papers of the former Italian Foreign Minister Galeazzo Ciano, which were rumored to contain damming material on Ribbentrop and other German leaders. The objective of this mission was "to unseat Ribbentrop and put a candidate of their own – Schellenberg was mentioned – into his place."[30] Ciano, who was married to Edda Mussolini, had been important in the creation of the Axis Rome-Berlin but was, unlike his father-in-law, less inclined to involve Italy too deeply in the war. The relationship between the two men cooled and in February

---

[27] Black, *Kaltenbrunner*, 182; Conze et al., *Amt*, 145–146.
[28] Fourth Detailed Interrogation Report on SS Sturmbannführer Huegel Dr. Klaus, June 10, 1945, NA, RG 226, Entry 174, Box 39, Folder 307.
[29] Black, *Kaltenbrunner*, 182–183.
[30] SCI Detachment Weimar, L.E. de Neufville, The RSHA and the Death of Count Ciano, Source: Interrogation of Frau Hildegard Beetz, June 14, 1945, NA, RG 263, Entry ZZ-18, Box 9, File: Beetz, Hildegard, Vol. 1, 2 of 2 [hereafter: RSHA/Death Ciano].

1943, the Mussolini dismissed Ciano from his position. In July, Ciano voted for the ouster of Mussolini; in the eyes of Mussolini, his remaining Italian supporters, and the Germans Ciano thus sided with the "traitors." In the unstable situation after the Mussolini's ouster – defined by the new Italian government's attempt to reach a deal with the Western Allies, suspicious Germans ready to occupy Italy, and German attempts to find, liberate, and reinstall Mussolini as the head of a puppet government – Ciano feared arrest. In this context his wife, presumably making the appropriate noises about the value of his papers, approached Himmler's man in Rome, Eugen Dollmann and with the help of police attaché Kappler, Office VI arranged for the Ciano family's escape from Rome. In late August 1943, the Cianos found themselves under thinly veiled house arrest in Allmannshausen in Southern Germany, while one was trying to figure out how to proceed further.[31] Office VI and Ciano eventually reached an agreement: Ciano was to trade the coveted papers for his and his family's freedom in Spain. But when Edda Ciano tried to gain Hitler's approval for the deal, it fell through.[32] Ciano was transferred to a prison in Verona in October; he was to stand trial for treason in the new Fascist Republic, headed by his estranged father-in-law under the oversight of the Highest SS and Police Leader (HSSPF) Karl Wolff. A death sentence was almost a forgone conclusion. Not incidentally, the Auswärtige Amt had its hands in Ciano's transfer to Italy.

Office VI did, however, not give up on the acquisition of Ciano's papers. Hildegard Beetz, the same woman who had served as a secretary for a string of inefficient SD Main Representatives in Rome and then filled the position herself, played a central role in these attempts. Her own ambiguous role notwithstanding, she masterminded and executed a plan that – had it not been for her superiors' zest of "working towards the Führer" (Ian Kershaw) – almost led to success. Having already served as the Cianos' translator in Allmannshausen, and tasked by Office VI to find out more about Ciano's political views, she now flew to Berlin and implored her superior, Wilhelm Hoettl, then in charge of Italian matters, to send her to Verona. This Hoettl did. Beetz was "to make contact with Ciano and find out from him where he had hidden

[31] Lorie Charlesworth and Michael Salter, "Ensuring the After-Life of the Ciano Diaries: Allen Dulles' Provision of Nuremberg Trial Evidence," *Intelligence and National Security* 21/4 (2006), 547 note 66.

[32] Ray Moseley, *Mussolini's Shadow: The Double Life of Count Galeazzo Ciano* (New Haven: Yale University Press, 1999), 186–187; Howard McGraw Smyth, *Secrets of the Fascist Era: How Uncle Sam Obtained Some of the Top-Level Documents of Mussolini's Period* (Carbondale: Southern Illinois University Press, 1975), 28–29; Edda Ciano, *My Truth, as told to Albert Zarca*, translated from the French by Eileen Finletter (New York: William Morrow and Company, Inc., 1977), 200ff.

the papers."[33] Kaltenbrunner' expected the same: Beetz was to learn more about "[Ciano's] materials, including all details in its most specific form," as well as "details, most importantly every statement directed against Germany and, especially again, against Ribb.[entrop]," paying special attention to allegations which documentary evidence could confirm. Beetz, who was given ready access to Ciano in prison, was to explore "possibilities for us with him." She soon had promising things to report: she had heard about materials against Ribbentrop, including "funny episodes that are not always indicative of an above average intelligence," but also knew to report that Ciano's materials were "less directed against Germany than against the war," did not contain anything against the "Führer himself," and emphasized that "surprisingly" Ciano showed "sympathy for the Reichsführer SS."[34] Ciano had the goods against Ribbentrop and little animus toward Hitler or Himmler. He was trustworthy.

Beetz suggested a solution that would meet needs of both the office and Ciano. Before his transfer to Verona, Beetz stressed, Ciano had wanted to leave Italy for a neutral country and live there pleasantly; he was not interested to remain active politically. Rather, he had intended to ready for publication after the war his books, for he needed money. Ciano had planned ahead, she reported: if he were to be executed, his books would be published abroad immediately to secure his children's future. Despite the bleak description – Office VI had no idea where Ciano had hidden the diaries – Beetz conclusion was upbeat: Ciano held no animosity against Germany would gladly "sell the books to us," thus making the money without publishing them. "We have practically two options," Beetz, building a straw man to knock it down, opined: "a) to insist that he be executed, b) to conclude an agreement with him." She predicted that the first option would win the approval of the small but valuable milieu of fanatical fascists but also make Ciano into a national martyr, and trigger the publication of the diaries, which would harm German interests. Beetz, using to the hilt her knowledge of Ciano, had another suggestion, "[i] f we buy the books for a generous price, and secure the needed guarantees [from Ciano], we will be able to prevent this type of propaganda and get the useful knowledge ourselves."

---

[33] RSHA/Death Ciano; Graf Ciano, October 26, 1943, NA, RG 263, Entry ZZ-16, Box 5, File: Beetz, Hildegard; Richard W. Cutler, "Reminiscence. Three Careers, Three Names: Hildegard Beetz, Talented Spy," *International Journal of Intelligence and Counterintelligence* 22 (2009), 516. Cutler misrepresents the timeline and part of Beetz' mandate.

[34] Hoettl to Harster, December 1, 1943; Memorandum/Letter [Beetz], [no date],NA, RG 263, Entry ZZ-16, Box 5, File: Beetz, Hildegard.

She expected it possible to buy "not only his books but also him and have him be useful for us, at least on the margins [am Rande] and in society circles," and predicted that Ciano could "provide us a great service." The crux of the matter was Ciano's intent to live in a neutral country, but Beetz was convinced that he had no intention "to cross us." Keeping him in prison indefinitely, a sure-fire way to prevent the publication of the diaries and maybe to find out their location eventually – surely an option on the mind of her superiors – would not solve the problem, Beetz counseled, predicting that Ciano would commit suicide eventually.[35] Beetz' reasoning, bolstered by her assurance that Ciano's papers would not affect negatively Himmler or Hitler but could be used against Ribbentrop to devastating effect, fell on eager ears.

The plan to have an Office VI commando spring Ciano from prison, bring him to Switzerland and thus trade his life, freedom, and some money for the diaries took shape in December 1943. Postwar sources suggest that the idea originated with Hoettl and Kaltenbrunner – Schellenberg was not directly involved in this matter although he was mentioned as a replacement for Ribbentrop – but Beetz took a more active role in its instigation and formulation than commonly assumed. In early December, Beetz traveled to Berlin for a meeting with Hoettl during which she suggested the springing Ciano from prison; Hoettl saw the plan's benefits and asked Beetz to draft for Kaltenbrunner a letter outlining "the possibilities of using Ciano's papers to expose Ribbentrop's shortcomings." This she did.[36] Beetz also kept up the pressure, letting Hoettl know that Ciano had noted, "the Germans will soon learn the content of my papers, either amongst themselves or in serialized form on the first page of United Press and there will be plenty of surprises [. . .] the Führer will be surprised when he reads the words with which Mussolini reacted to the attempt on his life in Munich." Plans to spring Ciano took center stage, and Beetz confidently explained to Hoettl that it would be "very simple" and that there was not backlash to fear.[37]

A meeting between Kaltenbrunner, the head of the RSHA, Harster, the Representative of the Security Police (BdS) Verona, Hoettl, representing Office VI, and Beetz, representing both Office VI and Ciano, in Innsbruck on January 2, 1944 kicked the plan to spring Ciano, ultimately meant to depose Ribbentrop, into high gear. A de-facto contract, consisting of four steps, was drawn up: as a sign of good faith, Ciano was

[35] Memorandum/Letter [Beetz], [no date], NA, RG 263, Entry ZZ-16, Box 5, File: Beetz, Hildegard.
[36] RSHA/Death Ciano.
[37] Beetz to Hoettl, December 18, 1943; Beetz to Hoettl, December 27,1943, NA, RG 263, Entry ZZ-16, Box 5, File: Beetz, Hildegard.

to disclose the location of the Foreign Office materials. These materials were not Ciano's crown jewels but likely to be immediately useful in Office VI's battle against Ribbentrop. An SS/SD commando would then free Ciano from prison and take him and his family to Switzerland; Beetz would accompany them. Ciano was then to hand over his diaries, the most valuable part of his papers, to Beetz and, lastly, receive an undefined amount of money. Kaltenbrunner did not sign the agreement but promised to honor it.[38] Beetz now jumped into action: she met with Edda Ciano, learned the location of the Foreign Office materials, collected them, and handed them over to Harster; they were flown to Kaltenbrunner in Berlin. Ciano had kept his end of the bargain and Beetz had scored a tremendous success, as Office VI now had in its hands a good portion of Ciano's paper with more soon to come.[39] Taking her inspirations from ideas that were in the air – Ciano's freedom for his diaries – Beetz had come up with a concrete and daring plan that achieved everyone's objectives and had brought everyone on board. Beetz, who was anything but a smitten secretary, had created a win-win situation: Office VI would get everything it wanted and Ciano would live.[40] However, her superiors' ultimate point of reference was Hitler and it was in this focus, that Beetz' plan fell apart.

It is unclear how Hitler came to know of the plan in the first place but he did not approve. Hoettl suggested that Kaltenbrunner and Himmler began to fear their own courage and asked for Hitler's permission to go ahead. They were rebutted. Another version of the story has Hitler learning about the plan from Ribbentrop, its target, or from Propaganda Minister Joseph Goebbels, a Ribbentrop ally. In either scenario the result was the same: Hitler did not give his permission and threatened dire consequences if someone went against him. Kaltenbrunner reneged on his earlier grandstanding promise that he was willing to go against Hitler in this matter.[41] This serves as a nice reminder of Hitler's power as the

---

[38] RSHA/Death Ciano. Everybody at the meeting pretended to be unaware that Ciano's children had fled to Switzerland weeks ago. Moseley, based on secondary sources and postwar memories, provides a different timeline. Moseley, *Shadow*, 213–214. It seems to be more reasonable to assume that Beetz got right the dates just two years after the events.

[39] RSHA/Death Ciano. Beetz was accompanied by Emilio Pucci, Edda Ciano's confidant. Per Cianos' request, he concealed additional documents (labeled Germania) and stored them at Ramiola. Moseley, *Shadow*, 214–215; Smyth, *Secrets*, 37–39. Smyth is the one author cognizant of Beetz' successes.

[40] Much of the literature seeks to explain Beetz' engagement for Ciano by pointing to an affair with the incarcerated man, a noted playboy and womanizer. Beetz always denied an affair. I am working on a book on Beetz that will also discuss the issue of gender in her professional life as well as in the writing about her.

[41] RSHA/Death Ciano; Moseley, *Shadow*, 216; Smyth, *Secrets*, 39–40; Ciano, *Truth*, 230.

final arbiter: high-ranking SS members were not only unwilling to go against Hitler's expressed wishes but also hesitated – or attempted to solicit his approval – if they deemed their plans on a collision course with what they assumed to be Hitler's wishes. They were not held back by an ideological Hitler, as they put it after the war. Keen on maintaining their Führer's approval, they gladly let go of any plans for it.

Ciano's trial commenced on January 8, 1944; death sentences were handed down two days later. Legally, the trial was an Italian matter, and Mussolini had to decide about Ciano's clemency appeal. He was not simply considering the fate of a convicted traitor but also held in his hands the life of his daughter's husband and his grandchildren's father. The Duce consulted with Karl Wolff, the HSSPF Italy and, as will be recalled, a defender of Ribbentrop's. Wolff kept up the pressure on Mussolini, intimating that Himmler and Hitler expected that Mussolini would not have the stomach to go forward with the death sentence. But Mussolini did, and the execution was carried out early in the morning hours of January 11, 1943. By all accounts, it was a disorganized mess. German diplomats evidently liked their executions to be cleaner, for one of them remarked, "It was like the slaughtering of pigs."[42]

The Ciano affair, which ended with the execution of the Italian and the transfer of his diaries to Switzerland by his wife – warned by Beetz, who increasingly developed dual loyalties – is often seen as the last full-scale attempt of the RSHA to remove Ribbentrop.[43] This is not accurate. For one, Office VI kept trying to obtain Ciano's diaries from his widow or to ensure at least her silence. Beetz was sent to Switzerland for that purpose. And in the summer of 1944, Beetz led her supervisors to another cache of Ciano papers still in Italy, making her haul, despite her protection of the Cianos, impressive. By the late summer of 1944, the RSHA and Office VI were in possession of two-thirds of Ciano's papers; only the diaries of the war years remained elusive. And the hunt was still on. Office VI was even able to find a sliver of hope if the diaries were to be published abroad: "there was also the hope that the British would publish the dairies, and so smear Ribbentrop in the way [. . .] desired."[44] In late 1943 and early 1944, when the war was turning against Germany on all fronts, substantial Office VI resources, including one able operative – maybe the most able one – were tied up in an attempt to remove Ribbentrop from

---

[42] Moseley, *Shadow*, 230–235.
[43] Black, *Kaltenbrunner*, 186; Moseley, *Shadow*, chapter 19; Wilhelm Höttl, *Einsatz für das Reich* (Koblenz: Verlag S. Bublies, 1997), 300–305.
[44] The RSHA and Edda Ciano in Switzerland, Source: Interrogation of Frau Hildegard Burckhardt Beetz, June 16, 1945, NA, RG 263, Entry ZZ-18, Box 9, File: Beetz, Hildegard, Vol. 1, 2 of 2; Smyth, *Secrets*, 56.

his position. Foreign intelligence this was not. And in fall 1944 Office VI launched another full-scale attack against Ribbentrop. The playbook came from the take-over of the Abwehr earlier that year.

Before this came to pass, the incorporation of substantial parts of the Abwehr into the RSHA and Office VI necessitated the confirmation and slight redefinition of the rules that governed the relationship between the new foreign intelligence universe under Schellenberg and the Auswärtige Amt. Despite the incessant attacks, the Auswärtige Amt remained strong and the agreement concluded in June 1944 indicates as much. In many ways, it restated what had agreed on earlier and extended the arrangement to Amt Mil: the Foreign Minister retained access to the unified foreign intelligence service under Himmler and was allowed to task it with intelligence-gathering and other jobs. And while the service was to share all information pertaining to foreign policy matters with the Auswärtige Amt, the latter was to keep the intelligence service abreast of developments abroad and share the intentions of the Germany's foreign policy. Presenting materials to Hitler remained Ribbentrop's privilege but not exclusively so; Himmler could bring directly to Hitler's attention important information while simultaneously informing the Auswärtige Amt. The intelligence service was to refrain from any activities abroad that could harm Germany's foreign policy, but if such activities were planned, the minister had to approve of them. The Auswärtige Amt, on the other hand, was to extend every possible support to members of the intelligence service abroad. In accordance with the guidelines for the police attachés established in 1941, one local member of the intelligence service took responsibility for all its members in country and kept informed the mission chief of all their activities. To ensure the collaboration, a special liaison was established between the Auswärtige Amt and Office VI and the two entities were to engage in "comradely and loyal collaboration"[45] Hidden in this list is one true gem indicative of the changing landscape: the Auswärtige Amt was to share its foreign policy intentions with the intelligence service. This had not been the clearly defined case before.

Earlier, failed attempts to get rid of Ribbentrop notwithstanding, after the Abwehr's absorption Himmler came to believe that the Auswärtige Amt was the smaller and more easily digestible entity. "I feel like a big snake," he allegedly remarked, "which has just swallowed an ox and is still working it down his throat (i.e., Admiral Canaris), and now all I

---

[45] Vereinbarung ueber die Zusammenarbeit zwischen dem Auslandsnachrichtendienst und dem Auswaertigem Amt vom Jahre 1944 (Dokument SD 1 USSR aus dem IMT-Prozess), Schellenberg Document Nr. 63, NA, RG 238, M 397, Roll 114, F 1169–1168; Final Report; Black, *Kaltenbrunner*, 185 note 16.

have in front of me is a rabbit whose turn will come as soon as I have digested the ox."[46] The absorption of the Abwehr had whetted Himmler's appetite and it provided the blueprint for the renewed attack on the Ribbentrop. The Officers' Plot against Hitler on July 20, 1944, during which Schellenberg had given his all to play the field and remain in everyone's good graces, provided the opportune pretext: some conspirators had direct connections to the Auswärtige Amt while others had personal and familial connections to it.[47] In the earlier case, connections of Abwehr personnel to resistance circles – with the associated accusations of ideological unreliability, defeatism, and treason – had served as the catalyst for its eventual absorption into Office VI. Now was the time to perform the same neat trick on the Auswärtige Amt: create a damming and detailed report that called into question the diplomats' ideological commitment and tar Ribbentrop's reputation. Once presented to Hitler, Ribbentrop would be unseated and his sphere of power would be transferred to Himmler and his foreign intelligence service. But the rabbit turned out to be a fighter.

Receiving his instructions from Himmler, Schellenberg took the lead in this renewed effort to depose Ribbentrop and subsequently defended with vigor his preeminent role in the mounting attack. The Ciano affair had been the doing of the so-called Austrian group around Hoettl and Kaltenbrunner and had not involved Schellenberg prominently, but the Berlin-based bureaucratic intrigue against Ribbentrop fell, much like the earlier Luther affairs, into Schellenberg's area of expertise. The conflict and rivalry between Schellenberg and his men on the one and the Austrian group on the other hand, so relevant in postwar accounts, should not obscure that one agreed on essential issues. That Ribbentrop had to go and that SD men were better equipped to conduct Germany's foreign policy was one of them. On August 28, 1944, five weeks after the Officers' Plot, Schellenberg noted that Himmler had asked him to collect information on a number of prominent representatives – a few of them, such as Emil von Rintelen, Friedrich Gaus, and Karl Ritter mentioned by name – of the Auswärtige Amt. Schellenberg and his office were to cooperate with Office III, the domestic intelligence service, meant to spearhead the effort, and Office IV, the Gestapo.[48] Put differently: a few days after the liberation of Paris, at a point when the Eastern Fronts were moving westward steadily, and the Warsaw Uprising was about to

---

[46] Fourth Detailed Interrogation Report on SS Sturmbannführer Huegel Dr. Klaus, June 10, 1945, NA, RG 226, Entry 174, Box 39, Folder 307.

[47] On Schellenberg during the coup, see: Doerries, *Intelligence Chief*, 143–144.

[48] Vermerk, Amtschef VI, August 28, 1944, RGVA, Fond 500, Opis 1, Film 1155.

enter its fifth week, Himmler ordered half of the RSHA into a show-down with the Auswärtige Amt. Germany's foreign policy options might have been seriously restricted, but Himmler was certain that he and his men were better equipped to deal with them than Ribbentrop and his diplomats.

Soon the Auswärtige Amt was under intense pressure from several sides, as other party organizations joined the feeding frenzy initiated in the RSHA. Under orders from Martin Bormann, the *NSDAP Ausland-sorganisation*, NSDAP Abroad, also began to evaluate politically German diplomats; the plan was to share, via the Party Chancellery, these findings with Schellenberg's Office VI. The head of the Auswärtige Amt's person-nel department, Hans Schroeder, began to assemble lists of personnel with connections to the nobility or abroad as well, presumably trying to identify potential targets ahead of time and to stave off the assault. Schel-lenberg was suspicious of Schroeder's initiative and expected it to lead to cases of "preventive treason," defection to the Allies, by implicated German diplomats.[49] Distrust and suspicion hung over the Auswärtige Amt and potential beneficiaries fanned the flames. In late September Schellenberg reissued his directive to gather all available information on "non-reliable civil servants in the diplomatic service;" emphasized yet again that the order originated with Himmler; and noted and that, while Office III was to lead, his office was to assist the investigation "based on its experience and as much as possible." Schellenberg pulled out all the stops: he praised subordinates for information they had brought conveyed already, but implored them to check their files again and to report back additional findings within the next two-and-a-half weeks.[50] Schellenberg's communications on this matter did not include the Amt Mil. As it was, some former Abwehr members, among them Schellen-berg's deputy Hansen or the deposed Canaris, had been implicated in the coup and arrested.[51] In light of a coup that had originated with the German military elites, former Abwehr personnel were not to be trusted. The attack on the German diplomatic elites, a primary objective of Ger-many's foreign intelligence service in fall 1944, was to be an Office VI endeavor undertaken by its ideological soldiers.

Office VI went into overdrive. Ample information arrived in Berlin, sometimes on individuals, sometimes nicely bundled on every suspect in

---

[49] III A 6 to VI, Sandberger, Auswärtiges Amt, September 27, 1944, Gruppenleiter VI A, Listen über negative Beamte im AA, September 16, 1944, RGVA, Fond 500, Opis 1, Film 1155.
[50] Amtschef VI to Gruppenleiter, September 25, 1944, RGVA, Fond 500, Opis 1, Film 1188.
[51] Doerries, *Intelligence Chief*, 144–146.

a given consulate or region. A number of districts and outposts saw the need to report that they had nothing to report; the importance of the matter was clearly understood in the field.[52] A draft report by one of the Country Groups is indicative of the attack's gist. Dealing with German personnel in Switzerland, the report focused on the diplomats' professional inabilities, *fachliches Unvermögen*, their lack of character, and their political unreliability. Spotlighting individual cases, the report took note of short working hours, "peace-time" vacation schedules, breaks spent in Swiss spas, boozy social events, and dalliances. In sum, it portrayed the German diplomatic personnel in Switzerland as capricious, removed from the realities of war-torn Germany, and unable to appreciate these realities. The report also indicated the possibly grave repercussions of this behavior, as it left the host country with wrong impressions about Germany's current state. Giving, for example, the indication that foreign currency was still in ample supply, the report suggested, hurt German economic interests in Switzerland. What could have been construed as an attempt at deception became, in this rendition, boorish behavior at best and treason at worst. The report counseled that a number of diplomats should be recalled for their conduct, noting that "too many [people]" were posted to Switzerland at any rate.[53] Schellenberg requested additional information and also noted individuals of interest. Time was apparently wasting, as Schellenberg set the deadline for the next day.[54] Office VI was clearly attuned to the need for speed and all-encompassing approaches: Martin Sandberger, the then-head of Group VI A, Administration, and close to Schellenberg, urgently requested the lists prepared in Bormann's office. He also suggested that Martin Luther, still incarcerated in Sachsenhausen, be interrogated on the matter.[55] The assumption was that Luther would be able and willing to provide additional, damaging information on the Auswärtige Amt and its personnel.

Schellenberg prepared a first summation of his efforts, presumably for Himmler, on October 16, 1944. Apparently finding the task difficult, he opened with several disclaimers: important materials had been destroyed during an air raid; there had never been a systematic surveillance of

---

[52] Such reports, some compiled as late as early 1945, are interspersed among the following films: RGVA, Fond 500, Opis 1, Films 1151, 1152, 1155, 1171, 1175, 1177, 1181, 1182, 1184, 1185, 1186, 1187, 1195, 1196, 1197, 1198, 1200.

[53] VI B 3, Entwurf für Vorlage an RFSS, Verhalten von Angehörigen der deutschen Diplomatie einschließlich der Abwehr, der KO, der AO und sonstiger Beauftragter des Reiches in der Schweiz, October 4, 1944, RGVA, Fond 500, Opis 2, Film 260.

[54] VI B 3, Deutsche Diplomaten in der Schweiz, October 4, 1944, RGVA, Fond 500, Opis 2, Film 260.

[55] See Sandberger's correspondence, especially around October 9, 1944: RGVA, Fond 500, Opis 1, Film 1155.

the Auswärtige Amt and its personnel; the elitism of the groups now
under suspicion had made it hard for the intelligence service to penetrate them; and the Auswärtige Amt had been particularly careful over
the preceding year. Schellenberg still promised two reports. The report
for Himmler was to be a "SD-typical structural report" that evaluated
individual cases in their "sociological and political structures." According to Schellenberg, this was the only way to understand the implicated
individuals' activities. Schellenberg's pseudo-scientific approach to intelligence gathering, which had gained him accolades from Himmler and
others over the years, was on full display – as was its much-vaulted rigor,
for Schellenberg opined that this report would be too harsh to share with
Ribbentrop. Consequently, he promised a second, milder version for sub-
mission to the minister. Schellenberg pointedly introduced Himmler to
some of the report's sources: information from the 20 July Special Commission headed by Kaltenbrunner, interrogations of Martin Luther, and
"intelligence connections thus far not fully explored."[56] He was whetting
Himmler's appetite.

An internal Office VI communication dated October 19, 1944 – presumably the structural report – divulged key findings, their repercussions, and offered solutions.[57] Part of the report dealt with the 20 July
conspirators, particularly Adam Trott von Solz, who, before his execution in August, had been a ranking member of the Auswärtige Amt.[58]
By way of Trott, the report cast the Auswärtige Amt as a center of the
conspiracy, staffed with only seven reliable diplomats and described it
as a fundamentally alien milieu of professional diplomats, tightly connected to each other by birth and background, who lacked "political
conscience and responsibility" or loyalty to Reich and Führer. The seven
men deemed reliable were, short of one, SS or SA members whom
Trott had distrusted.[59] As there were more diplomats with strong "party
and movement ties," the report clearly reasoned along an-enemy-of-my-
enemy-is-my-friend-lines. Ultimately, this report was the racial-political

[56] RSHA VI A 7 [Schellenberg],. Politisch negative Strömungen im Deutschen Diplomatischen Dienst,October 16, 1944, RGVA, Fond 500, Opis 2, Film 261. On the Gestapo
Special Investigative Commission; Black, *Kaltenbrunner*, 160–167.
[57] Gruppenleiter VI A to Gruppenleiter im Haus, Negative Tendenzen im Auswärtigen
Dienst des Deutschen Reiches [gez Sandberger], October 19, 1944, RGVA, Fond 500,
Opis 2, Film 260.
[58] On Trott and resistance circles *in* (and not *of*) the AA; Conze et al, *Amt*, 298–316.
[59] The seven are the ones Trott did not trust: Gustav Adolf Baron Steengracht von Moyland, Wilhelm Keppler, Hans Schroeder, Franz Alfred Six, Günther Rühle, Schmidt
[presumably Karl Paul Schmidt], and Andor Hencke. Of the seven men, six were
members of SS or SA; the only exception was Andor Hencke. However, no one ever
doubted Hencke's devotion to the National Socialist State; a career diplomat, Hencke
was arrested at Dönitz headquarters in May 1945; Conze et al., *Amt*, 339–341.

community's indictment of Germany's traditional elites who, allegedly in fundamental opposition to National Socialism, presented a grave danger to the state. The importance of these findings, the report counseled, was not simply a matter of policing but explained Germany's foreign policy failures. Solutions were at hand, though. The report suggested replacing the "old guard" and filling "key positions" with men who have "unconditional devotion to the Führer, to the Reich, and to the movement and [who] combine self-assured trust in the German victory, personal character, [and] political experience with experiences abroad that are absolutely necessary in one of the most important Reich ministries." The report, an indictment of the Auswärtige Amt and its personnel, was a bid for power: the men so eloquently described could be found – at least in its leader's estimation – in Office VI.

A second report presented similar information in a different format; presumably, this version was meant for Ribbentrop.[60] It broke down the personnel and the activities of the Auswärtige Amt into five categories: 20 July Circle, Defectors, Treason and High Treason, Defeatist Statements, Other Cases, and also contained a special section on "leading personnel." Accusations ranged from political to racial offenses and created a picture of widespread political unreliability. Less obviously a bid for power by Office VI, it still conveyed the indictments' gist. In addition, Himmler prepared his *pièce de résistance*: a letter to Ribbentrop.[61] The confrontation forced the Auswärtige Amt's hand: plans to dismiss some 190 men and to create the basis for intensive cooperation with the SS became known quickly.[62] The assault was paying dividends, but not as handsomely as Schellenberg and Himmler had hoped.

In the first days of November Schellenberg and Himmler had to confront the reality that Ribbentrop retained Hitler's backing and would be impossible to depose. Through the interoffice grapevine the Auswärtige Amt let it be known that Hitler had thrown his support behind Ribbentrop; identified fully and completely with the current German foreign policy; would take attacks on Ribbentrop and the Auswärtige Amt personally; and would counter them "in the sharpest possible form."[63] An emboldened Ribbentrop indicated that he would respond to attacks on his authority with all means at his disposal; however, he also noted his

---

[60] Einschätzungen der Mitarbeiter des deutschen diplomatischen Dienstes, (1944), RGVA, Fond 500, Opis 1, Film 263.

[61] RFSS to RAM, Entwurf, October 17, 1944; RFSS to RAM, no date, RGVA, Fond 500, Opis 1, Film 1165.

[62] VI Pers to VI A, AA Bericht 27. Oktober 1944, October 31, 1944, RGVA, Fond 500, Opis 1, Film 1181.

[63] VI Pers, Vermerk, November 4, 1944, RGVA, Fond 500, Opis 1, Film 1155.

willingness to cooperate more closely with the RSHA. A meeting between Gustav Steengracht von Moyland, representing of the Foreign Minister's Personal Staff, and Schellenberg to hammer out details was to take place soon.[64] Once again, an attempt to replace Ribbentrop had failed, despite the ample evidence marshaled by Schellenberg and his colleagues. It was easy enough to tar individual members of the Auswärtige Amt, especially if they represented the proverbial traditional Wilhelmsstrasse. Yet, this did not mean that such an attack would also affect the minister; as it was, Ribbentrop frequently considered the same people of dubious loyalty. But, as Schellenberg and Himmler learned, painting the minister as insufficiently ideological was rather impossible. Ribbentrop was, as Hitler's intervention clearly shows, above suspicion and not going anywhere. Office VI had to remain doing what it had done for years now: work with the Auswärtige Amt and its minister, work around it and him, or upstage it. Schellenberg did it all, occasionally simultaneously.

It is in this context that Schellenberg's contacts with Roger Masson, the head of the Intelligence Service of the Swiss General Staff, and Henri Guisan, the Swiss Chief of Staff – contacts that Schellenberg almost exclusively connected to his wish to open lines of communication to the Western Allies – should be considered. Over the course of a number of meetings between fall 1942 and spring 1943 Schellenberg secured from the Swiss Chief of Staff a note of neutrality, thus besting Ribbentrop and honing his emerging persona as a diplomat. Much remains unclear about these contacts, but it is evident that Schellenberg's initial point of entry was SS Sturmbannführer Hans Wilhelm Eggen, a well-connected buyer for the Waffen SS. Eggen traveled to Switzerland regularly, enjoyed close contacts with Swiss commercial and military circles, and – as discussed below – served as Schellenberg's personal representative in the country.[65] Through his commercial activities, Eggen made contact with Dr. Paul Meyer-Schwertenbach and Paul Holzach, officers of the Swiss Intelligence Service connected to Masson, and Henry Guisan Jr., the son of the Swiss Chief of Staff. The first meeting between Schellenberg and his Swiss counterpart Masson took place in Waldshut on September 8, 1942. The meeting likely originated with the Swiss, who were concerned about a possible German attack and numerous smaller issues to discuss to as

---

[64] VI Pers, Vermerk, November 4, 1944, RGVA, Fond 500, Opis 1, Film 1155.

[65] Saint London to Saint Washington, Amt VI of the RSHA, Liquidation Reports No. 7, Gruppe VI B, October 26, 1945, NA, RG 263, Entry ZZ-16, Box 13, File: Eggen, Hans Wilhelm; Richard Breitman, "Follow the Money," in Richard Breitman et al., eds., *U.S. Intelligence and the Nazis* (Washington, DC: National Trust Fund for the Nazi War Crimes and Japanese Imperial Government Records Interagency Working Group, 2004), 127–132; Doerries, *Intelligence Chief*, 54–57.

well.[66] Schellenberg connected the meeting to his wish to open lines of communication to the Western Allies. Postwar recollections by Eggen – who, like Meyer-Schwertenbach, had been there yet not been privy to the talk between the two spymasters – focused on the Swiss fear of a German attack; Masson himself speaks largely of concrete issues: he wanted a Swiss intelligence officer, a certain Dr. Ernst Mörgli, freed from a German prison; a German visa for Heinrich Rothmund, the Chief the Police Section of the Department of Justice and Police; the pro-Nazi Germany campaign of the *Internationale Press Agentur* (IPA), International Press Agency, stopped; and Swiss citizens living in Germany allowed to return to Switzerland to do their military service. Schellenberg quickly attended to the first three issues. Yet Masson also noted that "[w]ithout spelling things out, it was my understanding that Schellenberg wanted to find a solution to bring the war to an end ...." A second meeting took place in October or in December 1942. Organized by Meyer-Schwertenbach and his wife at Wolfsberg Castle on the Swiss side of the border, it was also a social event; Masson joined the group for one day. Schellenberg was working on establishing good relations – "Masson and his colleague, Dr. Meyer were the contacts with whose help I hope to bridge the gap either to the British or the American military attaché" – and Schellenberg apparently signaled that he would gladly do this part to secure Swiss neutrality.[67]

Swiss neutrality and the German promise not to invade the country subsequently became key issues, and Schellenberg scored a diplomatic success. Using as his intermediaries Eggen and Meyer-Schwertenbach, Schellenberg made it known that there was German interest in a binding Swiss guarantee of neutrality and that he was interested in meeting with General Guisan, the Swiss Chief of Staff, if Hitler and Himmler approved. They apparently did, as a series of meetings began at Wolfburg Caste on March 2, 1943. On March 3, Schellenberg, Eggen, and Meyer-Schwertenbach met with Masson in Zurich and then went on to Biglen outside of Bern for the meeting between Guisan and Schellenberg. The details of the talk remain unclear, but the two men evidently discussed the German concern that the Switzerland would join the allied war effort as well as the Swiss concern that Germany was set to invade the country. The talk's results, on the other hand, are clear. Schellenberg asked for a note of assurance that the Swiss would defend themselves against any force entering the country. This Guisan delivered a few days

---

[66] Schellenberg discusses these meetings in his memoir and in the Final Report. I follow Doerries' description here but not his conclusions. Doerries, *Intelligence Chief*, 56–73; Final Report.

[67] Cited in Doerries, *Intelligence Chief*, 64, 65; Final Report.

later.[68] The two men regarded "their talks [. . .] as successful steps in the right direction," but Guisan apparently noted the German tendency to underestimate the Soviet Union's potential. Be that as it may, Schellenberg rushed back to Berlin and, based on Guisan's note, persuaded Himmler that there was no need to violate Swiss neutrality. Intriguingly enough, weeks after the meeting between Schellenberg and Guisan the Swiss learnt that the OKW was yet again considering an invasion of the country. Doerries raises the possibility that Schellenberg used whatever type of discussion had taken place in the OKW, first, as a "menacing threat" and, second, "as an opportunity to polish his standing," as he was soon able to assure the Swiss that all was well and under control.[69] Schellenberg's final meeting with Masson in October 1943 also dealt with the question of Swiss neutrality; this time, he brought Himmler's assurance that neutrality agreements still stood.

Doerries, in his careful recounting of the series of meetings, wonders about the political significance of the agreement between Schellenberg and Guisan, and in the broader context of the war this is a point well taken. Yet in the context of Schellenberg's contentious relationship with Ribbentrop and the Auswärtige Amt and his expressed wish to conduct an independent foreign policy, the agreement with Guisan counted as an undeniable success, for in securing this note he had done exactly that and upstaged Ribbentrop as well. The Foreign Minister, for his part, was not amused that the head of Office VI was conducting diplomacy, and the German Minister in Berne did not appreciate his exclusion either. Schellenberg's much-professed goal of opening lines to the Western contacts in Switzerland, on the other hand, came to naught. Either way, what transpired had more to do with diplomacy than with political foreign intelligence efforts.

Ribbentrop, conversely, took opportunities to demand foreign intelligence from Office VI, pushing it into missions that were unlikely to succeed and would make visible its shortcomings as an intelligence service. In spring 1943 – a connection to the dealings in Switzerland cannot be established but tempting to assume – Ribbentrop called in Schellenberg for a meeting. He asked for information about the upcoming presidential election in the United States and the effects of German radio propaganda on it. Schellenberg and Ribbentrop apparently came to blows over the lack of first-hand information from the United States and who was to blame for it. "An unexpected intervention of the Auswärtiges Amt" pushed Schellenberg to put together at least one, if not two submarine

---

[68] For the text of the note, see: Doerries, *Intelligence Chief*, 67.
[69] Doerries, *Intelligence Chief*, 68, 69.

missions to the United States.[70] Ribbentrop had managed to catch Schellenberg flat-footed and to send him scrambling.

VI D, the Country Group dealing with England, North and South America (and intermittently also Scandinavia) was Office VI's problem child. Schellenberg's reforms in 1941 and 1942 had largely bypassed it, mostly for the lack of qualified personnel. Schellenberg had removed Jost's appointee Hans Daufeldt from his leadership position and installed in his stead Ernst Schambacher, who had worked for him in the equivalent section in the Gestapo's counterintelligence department. In August 1942, Theodor Paeffgen replaced Schambacher.[71] Paeffgen was one of the few people in Office VI who had actually spent time abroad; he had studied law in Geneva, Bordeaux, and Edinburgh. Postwar Allied reports conceded a "smattering of foreign languages, a fair knowledge of geography," even though the existence and the exact whereabouts of Houston, Texas, escaped him. But Paeffgen's "indefatigable industry" was undeniable as was his loyalty to Schellenberg, which must have made up for more tangible shortcomings. Tagged as "[a]n uncompromising Nazi," his interrogators found that Paeffgen "had no qualification whatever for intelligence work," but acidly noted that "[u]nder a political system that put a premium on the absence of critical faculties Paeffgen was slated for success."[72] Personal loyalty and ideological conviction trumped qualifications.

None of the sections subsumed under Country Group VI D did well, but the ones dealing with the United States and the United Kingdom, were least successful.[73] Country Group VI D

---

[70] Prisoner O/Stubaf Paeffgen, Theodor, Leiter VI-D, RSHA, December 29, 1945, NA, RG 263, Entry ZZ-16, Box 39, File: Paeffgen, Theodor [hereafter: Paeffgen/December 1945]; Interrogation of Walter Schellenberg by Henry Schneider, Lt. Herbert DUBois [sic] (In German), Interpreter: Lt. E. Holton, Palace of Justice, Room 163, Nuremberg, Germany, December 19, 1945, 10.50 A.M., IfZ, ZS 291/I, 8 [hereafter: Schellenberg/December 1945.]

[71] Counter Intelligence War Room, Situation Report No. 9, Amt VI of the RSHA Gruppe VI D, NA, RG 319, IRR, Box 1, XE 002303 [hereafter: Situation Report No. 9]; Paeffgen/December 1945. On Paeffgen, Daufeldt, and Schambacher; Michael Wildt, *Generation des Unbedingten: Das Führunngkorps des Reichssicherheitshauptamtes* (Hamburg: Hamburger Edition, 2002), 164–165, 403, 940, 942.

[72] Paeffgen, Dr. Theodor, SS Obersturmbannführer, Group Chief VI D, RSHA, September 1945, NA, RG 65, Entry A1–136 Z, Box 3, Folder Bulky 34X; Situation Report No. 9.

[73] For Office VI's fairly successful efforts in South America, see Situation Report No. 9. Also: Südamerika, IfZ, ED 90/5. This handwritten document can be found among Schellenberg's handwritten memoir draft; however, there can be no doubt that someone else wrote this treatise. On activities in South America: Stanley E. Hilton, *Hitler's Secret War in South America, 1939–1945: German Military Espionage and Counterespionage in Brazil* (Baton Rouge: Louisiana State University Press, 1981); Leslie B. Rout Jr. and

was essentially an evaluatory Gruppe [sic], since in the countries where it should have possessed organisations [sic] in the Field for the collection of intelligence these were completely lacking [. . .] for [. . .]U.S.A. and Great Britain, VI D was very dependent on material supplied by other Gruppen [sic]. This material was always scanty and rarely offered the possibility of any continuity of work.[74]

There was not a single active agent in the United States or the United Kingdom.[75] Schellenberg pressured Paeffgen to establish contacts in the United States but that was easier said than done; for Paeffgen, language issues alone presented an almost insurmountable problem.[76] Office VI kept looking for opportunities but contended with poor preconditions: no groundwork had been laid earlier and US countermeasures, while heavy-handed and indiscriminate, had plugged many of the inroads Office VI would have taken. And the one group that would have been a natural pool of potential agents, *Rückwanderer*, ethnic German returnees from the United States, who represented the perfect intersection between *völkisch* and ideological qualifications based on which Office VI preferred to recruit, displayed "too wholesome a respect for the FBI to wish to risk returning to the that country as German agents [. . .]".[77] The United States was all but impenetrable for Office VI.[78]

The situation seemed to improve shortly after Ribbentrop and Schellenberg's confrontation. In the summer of 1943, a German merchant seaman, a certain Sievers, offered his services. Sievers had spent time in the United States and was willing to go back and set up an intelligence network; he even named potential associates. The planning for Operation Rösl, under the oversight of Paeffgen and the leader of VI D 1, Sturmbannführer Friedrich Carstenn, took the better part of a year, as problems abounded. Schellenberg commented after the war that this group "was very well trained and [the operation] well planned and under normal circumstances [the men] should have found refuge in the United States,"

John F. Bratzel, *The Shadow War: German Espionage and United States Counterespionage in Latin America during World War II* (Frederick, MD: University Publication of America, Inc., 1986); Richard McGaha "The Politics of Espionage: Nazi Diplomats and Spies in South American, 1933–1945," Phil. Diss, Ohio University, 2009.

[74] Appendix II, Final Report on the Case of Walter Friedrich Schellenberg, NA, RG 65, Entry A1–136 Z, Box 3, Folder Bulky 39; Paeffgen/December 1945.

[75] Situation Report No. 9.

[76] Interrogation of Paeffgen by Barr, April 14, 1947, NA, RG 242, M 1019, Reel 51, Frame 0809.

[77] Situation Report No. 9. The Foreign Office and the NSDAP Organization Abroad (*Auslandsorganisation*) alerted Office VI to returnees with intelligence potential. However, these returnees frequently argued that they should have been contacted before leaving the United States. Interrogation of Paeffgen by Barr, April 14 1947, NA, RG 242, M 1019, Reel 51, Frame 0807–0811; Paeffgen/December 1945.

[78] The Abwehr enjoyed some success in the United States; see Kahn, *Spies*, 327–336.

but the training as clandestine radio operators, for example, proved to be too demanding for the two initial recruits, who "were found unsuitable and were dropped." Sievers found replacements. Financing the mission was another problem. Initially, Office VI was to pay for it out of its regular budget but Schellenberg regarded this as "too great a burden for me," especially as the mission planners insisted on carrying along gold. On Himmler's orders, Kaltenbrunner negotiated with the Minister of Economy, Walther Funk, who eventually approved the demands in return for all "foreign exchange that was confiscated by the Security Police under Kaltenbrunner."[79] Schellenberg was evasive on the issue of finances after the war and implied that most of the money came from captured foreign agents. It seems likely, though, that other captured funds, such as the gold and currency stolen in Rome in 1943, strengthened Kaltenbrunner's bargaining position and allowed for certain missions of Office VI to take place.[80] As planning went on, Ribbentrop's interest waned: the likelihood that the mission would arrive early enough to report on the pre-election campaign diminished. Subsequently, its primary objective became to "secure political intelligence since we had no direct contact with the United States."[81] In the end, all the meticulous planning did not matter. The submarine that was to bring the men to the United States left in spring 1944 but soon found itself in the middle of a heavy air attack in the Bay of Biscay. After eight weeks without any communication,

[79] Schellenberg/December 1945; Situation Report No. 9; Paeffgen/December 1945.
[80] Compare to the preceding chapter. According to Katz the 50 kilograms of gold extorted from the Jewish community in Rome, which Kappler shipped to Kaltenbrunner personally, were never put to any use. It was found in an unopened crate in a corner of Kaltenbrunner's office at war's end. Robert Katz, *The Battle for Rome: The Germans, the Allies, the Partisans, and the Pope, September 1943-June 1944* (New York: Simon & Schuster, 2003), 77. The financing of the political foreign intelligence service was always a problem. Incidentally, some of its agents and contacts, such as the famed Cicero in Ankara, were paid with counterfeit money. Kahn, *Spies*, 340–346. Large amounts of foreign currency as well as document blanks were forged by concentration camp inmates in a special Office VI project, "Unternehmen Bernhard." For a sensational account of the forgery activities by a dubious source, see Walter Hagen [Wilhelm Höttl], *Unternehmen Bernhard. Ein historischer Tatsachenbericht über die größte Geldfälschaktion aller Zeiten* (Wels: Verlag Westermühl, 1955). See also Lawrence Malkin, *Krueger's Men: The Secret Nazi Counterfeit Plot and the Prisoners of Block 19* (New York, NY: Little, Brown and Co., 2006); Kahn, *Spies*, 300–301. For a scholarly assessment, see Breitman, "Money," 121–127. Operation Bernhard has also become the subject of an award-winning movie: *Die Fälscher*, dir. Stefan Ruzowitzky (Germany/Austria, 2007). See also: Schellenberg/December 1945.
[81] Schellenberg/December 1945. Schellenberg's demeanor in these interrogations appears lukewarm; it seems that he took no personal interest in the mission. In 1942, Canaris' organization landed eight men on a sabotage mission in the United States. Within days, these men were captured. Doubtlessly, this knowledge gave Schellenberg "a pause;" Kahn, *Spies*, 6–7.

the High Command of the Navy declared the ship lost and all aboard dead.[82]

In the summer of 1944, the Country Group's problems became so glaring that Schellenberg and Paeffgen reorganized it completely. But "reorganization" was little more than a euphemism for the dissolution of certain sections; those dealing with the United States and Great Britain "abandoned any further pretense at independent" missions. "In the light of past experiences," Schellenberg and Paeffgen realized that "further espionage enterprises into the United States became improbable." Only "as a matter of form" were some of the sections' functions transferred to the South American section.[83] Carstenn was relieved of his position and sent to Copenhagen; if need arose, a member of Office VII took over his tasks.[84] The Collection Section of VI D, dealing with the "Anglo-Saxon world," was apparently completely disbanded while the Evaluation Section was streamlined and its personnel assigned to new tasks. The head of this section was, for example, dispatched to the Oberursel Prisoner of War Camp to interview POWs on "British and American morale" and to mine the field for potential agents. These reassignments were also a way of "finding redundant officers something to do" and presumably to prevent them from being sent to the front.[85] Ultimately, this so-called reorganization of Country Group D and its component parts as well as the reassignment of personnel amounted to a de-facto dissolution of two central sections.

Yet at this point Office VI embarked on another, marginally more successful attempt to bring agents into the United States; it appears that Ribbentrop's pressure was still felt. This mission, code-named "Operation Magpie," had been its early stages when the initial attempt to bring agents into the United States ended on the bottom of the Bay of Biscay. As the section for the United States had been disbanded, the South American section, which had successfully landed agents via submarine,

---

[82] Situation Report No. 9; Schellenberg/December 1945.

[83] Paeffgen, Dr. Theodor, SS Obersturmbannführer, Group Chief VI D, RSHA, September 1945, NA, RG 65, Entry A1–136 Z, Box 3, Folder Bulky 34X. "The American Referat was now practically dissolved . . . ;" Situation Report No. 9.

[84] Appendix II, Final Report on the Case of Walter Friedrich Schellenberg, NA, RG 65, Entry A1–136 Z, Box 3, Folder Bulky 39; Paeffgen/December 1945; Saint, London to Saint, Germany, Subject: Carstenn, Gottlieb Friedrich, NA, RG 263, Entry ZZ-16, Box 9, File: Carstenn, Friedrich. Carstenn intimates that he was in charge of the "archival section," but according to others, he ran VI D-1.

[85] Situation Report No. 9; Paeffgen/December 1945. I thank Gerhard Weinberg for relentlessly impressing on me that any office job with the RSHA in Berlin – or as a concentration camp guard for that matter – was for most people vastly preferable to fighting in an actual war.

ran it.[86] This time the group consisted of two men, the German Erich Gimpel and the American William C. Colepaugh, and their story is known. The two men reached Frenchman Bay, Maine in late November 1944 and, skirting quick detection, proceeded to New York City. They made some attempts to set up their espionage activities, but also enjoyed the city. Having lived the high life for a few days, Colepaugh admitted his espionage activities to an old friend and, after the holidays, Colepaugh contacted the FBI and furnished the information needed to detain Gimpel. Both men were charged with espionage, tried in military court, and sentenced to death. President Truman eventually commuted the death sentences.[87]

Colepaugh's appearance in Europe must have seemed as an answer to the Office VI's collective prayers. Born in the United States, he was eager to work for Germany. His only connection to Germany were his maternal grandparents, but he was enamored with all things German – and Nazi Germany in particular – and had made earlier attempts to collect information for Nazi Germany or to reach the country. A sailor, he jumped ship in Lisbon in early 1944 and made contact with the German consul there. There was, however, much concern that he was a double agent; Office VI checked him thoroughly and declared him trustworthy in late June 1944, the month of the British-American landing in Normandy.[88]

Erich Gimpel, on the other hand, fit the mold of men on whom Office VI relied for its missions, even though his qualifications exceeded those of most others. He had lived abroad, spoke a foreign language, and had done low-level intelligence work before. Originally from Merseburg, Gimpel moved to Peru in 1935. In Lima, he reported on ship movements and cargos to the German legation. After January of 1942, when the diplomatic relations between Germany and Peru were severed and ethnic Germans were returned to Germany via the United States, Gimpel found himself interned in Texas.[89] He arrived in Germany in early August 1942. Eventually Office VI approached him; he was to collect technical information pertaining to his specialty, radio, in neutral countries. During a meeting, Paeffgen tried to convince Gimpel to go to the United States

---

[86] Situation Report No. 9.
[87] Kahn's treatment of this mission is a great read; Kahn, *Spies*, 1–26; Erich Gimpel, *Agent 146: The True Story of a Nazi Spy in America*, foreword by Charles Whiting (New York: St. Martin's Press, 2003). Gimpel was deported to Germany in 1955; Colepaugh was paroled in 1960.
[88] Kahn, *Spies*, 7–9.
[89] Max Paul Friedman, *Nazis & Good Neighbors: The United States Campaign Against the Germans of Latin America in World War II* (New York: Cambridge University Press, 2003).

as an agent. Gimpel was dubious about this proposition but agreed to sample spy training.[90]

Sources vary on the exact nature of the men's assignment. In one version they were to acquire "technical data on shipbuilding, airplanes, rockets, and any other information particularly from the engineering field, that would be of value to Germany" through open sources.[91] Statements by people other than Gimpel and Colepaugh themselves tell a different story: they were to set up an intelligence network in the United States, and, using Gimpel's experience, establish radio contact with Germany and with German spy networks active in South America.[92] They were also tasked to "further intelligence" and to gather "political news." The reasons were, in Schellenberg's words, plain, " . . . we had nothing on North America and they were supposed to establish a basis for intelligence." But apparently Schellenberg also regarded the missions to North America, and this one in particular, as a futile exercise or, at best, as a proverbial Hail Mary – "weak attempts due to the lack of proper personnel."[93] Why then did Office VI invest time and money into them, especially after VI D's "reorganization"?

The answer can be found in the rivalry between Office VI and the Auswärtige Amt. This competition, more than anything else – such as the feasibility of an operation or the availability of qualified personnel – propelled forward the missions to the United States. In the first case, Operation Rösl, Ribbentrop's pressure was immediate and Schellenberg was in no position to ignore what amounted to an order by the Foreign Minister. Ribbentrop asked for foreign political intelligence, and Schellenberg headed the political foreign intelligence service. Admitting that this mission would be impossible was not an option, as it would have been an acknowledgement that the political foreign intelligence service was a failure. This Schellenberg could not afford. With Operation Magpie – launched when the office's relevant section was effectively dissolved – Schellenberg seized a serendipitously arising opportunity that presented Schellenberg and his office as viable, vibrant, and daring. A success, even a temporary one, would have upstaged Ribbentrop and made evident the importance of Office VI. Missions were determined not by what was

[90] Kahn, *Spies*, 9–11.
[91] Kahn, *Spies*, 13. Kahn bases his rendition on statements made by Gimpel and Colepaugh to the FBI in December 1944 and January 1945 and an FBI press release dating to 1954. Kahn adds some strong words of caution about Gimpel's memoirs, originally published in the 1957 in Great Britain; Kahn, *Spies*, 553–554.
[92] Situation Report No. 9.
[93] Schellenberg/December 1945.

feasible but often by internal conflicts and by the reputation that could be earned.

Schellenberg's interest remained the neutralization of Ribbentrop. But rather than contending with him or deposing him through one intrigue or another, Schellenberg began to create an alternate foreign policy universe with himself as the alternate foreign minister, serving at Himmler's pleasure. After the war, Klaus Huegel noted that Office VI "developed more and more in the political as opposed to the intelligence plane" and argued that this "change to active political work was necessitated by the comparative inactivity of the Foreign Office."[94] Huegel's observation was sounder than his reasoning. Office VI's increasing intrusions into plain foreign policy were a matter of design. By the middle of the war, the Auswärtige Amt was largely engaged in maintaining the status quo: active in countries allied with Germany, it tried to keep them in line and at war. It also exerted much energy to get deported to the extermination camps Jews still alive in those countries. Schellenberg, for his part, was clearly interested, as discussed below, in focusing attention on Germany's enemies – especially the Western Allies. There is no indication that Schellenberg held a clear foreign policy vision but seemed to believe that it should be possible to shake something loose that could upend the status quo.

Key to Office VI's inroads into foreign policy were the SD representatives abroad. Initially created under Jost, these representatives were attached to the German missions – by way of the police attachés, mostly Gestapo members – and reported through the structures of the Auswärtige Amt. Some SD representatives worked under of the cover of German companies operating abroad.[95] As mentioned earlier, these men frequently focused their reporting on developments among groups and communities favorably disposed toward Germany and saw foreign countries as living spheres abroad. Only rarely did they focus their attention on the activities of Germany's enemies. This shifted under Schellenberg, mostly around 1942/1943, when a rough equilibrium had been achieved with the Auswärtige Amt and, as Huegel noted, "neither Himmler nor Schellenberg were concerned with the worsened relations." On the one hand, the SD representatives' position was strengthened. On the other, a new category of personal representatives or *Sonderlinien*, special lines, was created. Especially in the neutral countries at the northern and southern edge of the European continent, the SD representatives began to use their

---

[94] Eighth Detailed Interrogation Report on SS Sturmbannführer Huegel Dr. Klaus, June 26, 1945, NA, RG 226, Entry 119 A, Box 71, Folder 1829 [hereafter: Eighth Report/Huegel].
[95] Eighth Report/Huegel.

positions to gain a better understanding of the Allies.[96] After all, this was where representatives of the belligerent countries could still encounter each other.

Schellenberg's personal representatives or special lines functioned as his proxies abroad and provided "the means of checking on the activities of [. . .] subordinates and the reliability of the information received." These special lines of the "System Schellenberg" expanded substantially his range of possibilities; "Schellenberg did not allow himself to be bound by recognised [sic] channels, and when the official channels of Amt VI fell short of his standards, [he] established where possible his own sources of information."[97] This set-up allowed Schellenberg to circumvent or to supersede the existing agreements between Office VI and the Auswärtige Amt as well as the two entities as such. And in a roughly analogous fashion, Country Group leaders attempted to establish private lines as well. Personal connections and relations began to define the foreign intelligence service. Less encumbered by established structures, it came to function as the information service of an alternative foreign policy universe, and, ultimately, as a possible avenue to open communication with the Western Allies. Any institution, yet particularly in a society organized on the leadership principle, is a reflection of its leader and his ambitions. Schellenberg's ambition was to make foreign policy; the longer he was at the helm of Office VI, the more it came to resemble a foreign policy entity.

Several members of Office VI believed that it had the best representation in Spain, a hospitable, pro-German neutral country. Office VI barely worked through the German Legation there, as the police attaché, SS Sturmbannführer Winzer, was fearful of jeopardizing his position, but used a commercial connection: SS Oberführer Johannes Bernhard headed the German–Spanish firm Sofindus. After a meeting with Schellenberg in Berlin in the summer of 1943, Bernhard and his firm began to work with Office VI. Code-named "Grille" [Cricket], it was "agreed to put [Bernhard's] information on politics and economics – gained through social contacts – at the disposal of Amt VI." Bernhard was close to Ramon Serrano Suner, Spain's former Foreign Minister, and this and other contacts supposedly allowed Bernhard and his subordinates to gather information on internal Spanish affairs and on the Spanish government's attitudes toward Germany. Bernhard also busied himself with attempts to sound out Allied outlook on peace negotiations. Eventually, the former

[96] Eighth Report/Huegel.
[97] Eighth Report/Huegel; Annex III Schellenberg's Special Sources of Information to Paeffgen/December 1945; Saint London to Saint Washingon, Amt VI of the RSHA, October 26, 1945, NA, RG 263, Entry ZZ-16, Box 13, File: Eggen, Hans Wilhelm.

head of section VI B 4, Eugen Mosig, was transferred to Spain as well and began to work as a director of Sofindus. With the later assistance of a certain Lackner, he was to gather information on politics and economics; apparently, the two men had a large net of informers. They also threw large parties at Bernhard's home. The men managed "to obtain fairly comprehensive political and economic information not only on Spain but also on England and the United States, inasmuch such information was available to Spanish individuals." Bernhard's and Mosig's work as such was regarded as valuable and promising. Neither a net nor contacts into the United Kingdom or the United States, for which one had apparently hoped, existed at the end of war, but this was blamed on the comparative newness of the endeavor and information on the United States was gathered through additional operatives. Karl Arnold, for example, was sent to Spain to inaugurate a courier system to South America; at the time, Arnold established contact with employees of the Brazilian and the US embassies in Madrid. The latter contact yielded a substantial amount of information, but its low quality made it of little use for the intelligence service.[98] Schellenberg also had personal representatives in Spain, most notably Prince Max von Hohenlohe and his secretary Reinhard Spitzy. Spitzy, who had earlier been an aide to Ribbentrop, reported directly to Schellenberg on political matters. His reports were deemed "analytical" and not simply a "reproduction of factual information;" and, presumably due to a large circle of acquaintances, Spitzy was able to compare "notes with unusually well-informed personalities."[99] This special line notwithstanding, a fairly new network, made up of people doing business with Germany and trading in party gossip, was the best Office VI could do in a friendly country. And the praise for Spitzy's "analytical reports" is also indicative of the regular reports' low quality. Office VI's yield in Spain was, at best, mixed and haphazard.

The situation in Lisbon appears to have been even more problematic, and the duality of representatives defined the scene there, too. No police

---

[98] Eighth Report/Huegel; Appendix Nr. 7 to Final Interrogation Report of Steimle, Eugen, SS Standartenführer, Chief Gruppe VI B and Abt. Mil. B, RSHA, December 12, 1945, NA, RG 263, Entry ZZ-18, Box 126, File: Steimle, Eugen. Appendix Nr. 14 to Final Interrogation Report of Steimle, Eugen, SS Standartenführer, Chief Gruppe VI B and Abt. Mil. B, RSHA, Berlin, December 12, 1945, NA, RG 263, Entry ZZ-16, Box 5, File: Steimle, Eugen, 3 of 3. Regarding very early peace soundings via Suner, see also: To Schellenberg, August 27, 1942, BA-DH, ZR 920/61.

[99] Notes on information obtained from PW CS/2244, SS Ostuf Schueddekopf, Zentral Buero, Amt VI A 7, RSHA, captured Braunschweig, May 17, 1945, NA, RG 226, Entry 119 A, Box 24, Folder 628; Annex III Schellenberg's Special Sources of Information to Paeffgen/December 1945. See also Spitzy's self-serving autobiography, Reinhard Spitzy, *So haben wir das Reich verspielt, Bekenntnisses eines Illegalen*, 4th ed. (München: Langen Müller, 1994), 437–483.

attaché was stationed in Portugal, but police liaison officer SS Sturm-bannführer Schroeder reported to Office VI. SS-Sturmbannführer Adolf Nassenstein and a certain Sturmbannführer Vollbrecht were attached to the consulate as scientific assistants and maintained nets of informers, reporting to Berlin independently of Schroeder. Nassenstein also pro-cured "a steady supply of South and North American publications of all kinds."[100] Stealth was not among Nassenstein's strong suits, though; the FBI misspelled his name but was well aware of his acquisition of US publications.[101]

On Europe's northern periphery, in Sweden, the situation was more complex. SS-Hauptsturmführer Hans Hendrik Neumann was slated to become the police attaché in the Swedish capital in late 1941. He was temporarily pushed through – against the wishes of the Swedish gov-ernment – in cooperation between the Auswärtige Amt, the Gestapo, and Office VI. Despite various German shenanigans to keep him in the country, the Swedes eventually prevailed and Neumann was recalled to Germany.[102] Before the recall, Schellenberg used the apparently bored Neumann, whom he knew due to his former position as Heydrich's adjutant, for Office VI tasks. Neumann was to establish a relationship with the Swedish Nazi Party and to "employ every means for intelli-gence activities on behalf of Germany."[103] For all his confrontational competitiveness, Schellenberg was quite able to work within the exist-ing structures. In Neumann's case, Schellenberg effectively piggybacked on the efforts of the Gestapo. The approach yielded some intelligence results and decreased the tension between Office VI and the Auswärtige Amt; indeed the common target, Sweden, allowed for their coopera-tion. Eventually, Schellenberg moved forward his own men, for example SS Sturmbannführer Regierungsrat August Finke. The man's qualifi-cations – Finke spoke neither Swedish nor Finnish – were clearly not

---

[100] Situation Report No. 9; Appendix Nr. 14 to Final Interrogation Report of Steimle, Eugen, SS Standartenführer, Chief Gruppe VI B and Abt. Mil. B, RSHA, Berlin, December 12, 1945, NA, RG 263, entry ZZ-16, Box 5, File: Steimle, Eugen, 3 of 3.

[101] American Embassy, London to Director, FBI, May 19,1944, NA, RG 65, Entry A1-136 P, Box 43, File 47826.

[102] Inland II g Schweden: Tätigkeit des SD, d. Abwehr, d. Agenten und der Polizeiattaches, 1940–1943, PAAA, R 100775, Fiche 1977. Neumann was initially sent to the country without an official appointment and on a special, short-term task, which was then, in an apparent attempt to wear down the Swedes, extended. The German expectation was clearly Neumann's eventual appointment as police attaché.

[103] Final Report. See also the telegrams between Schellenberg and Neumann; Inland II g Schweden: Tätigkeit des SD, d. Abwehr, d. Agenten und der Polizeiattaches, 1940–1943, PAAA, R 100775, Fiche 1977. On the broader intelligence game in Sweden: C.G. McKay, *From Information to Intrigue: Studies in Secret Service Based on the Swedish Experience 1939–1945* (London: Frank Cass, 1993); Doerries, *Intelligence Chief*, 95–102.

Schellenberg's primary concern. His presence was in Sweden. The German consulate was dubious about Finke's appointment as Legation Secretary; it argued that the Swedes would realize quickly that Finke was not what or who he claimed to be.[104] Yet, ultimately, the Auswärtige Amt was willing to accommodate Schellenberg and found a slightly less obviously fake position for Finke. Finke arrived in Stockholm in late May 1942 and remained there until February 1945, when the Swedish government expelled him.[105] Finke's appointment opened the floodgates. Over the course of the next year, the German consulate in Stockholm agreed to the appointment of several other Office VI members to its staff, eventually bringing their number to six.[106] Numerically, this was doubtlessly a success.

Most of these appointments were negotiated and justified by Schellenberg personally, a surprising level of micromanagement for a man in charge of all of Germany's political foreign intelligence efforts and engaged in a multitude of intramural conflicts. Yet Schellenberg always pursued his goals in numerous ways; cooperation, competition, and conflict were never mutually exclusive. And as the number of appointments indicates, Schellenberg's efforts paid off. This phenomenon was not restricted to Sweden; the files of the Auswärtige Amt are full of visa requests for agents, lengthy exchanges about them, and justifications of appointments abroad.[107] Schellenberg's willingness to compromise and to withdraw men completely disagreeable to the Auswärtige Amt must have made him appear a reasonable enough man with whom to negotiate. Yet the suspicion remains that Schellenberg also saw benefit in burying under a mountain of paperwork those responsible in the Auswärtige Amt. Be that as it may, none of the Office VI appointments in Sweden, one of the main intelligence hotbeds of World War II, aroused the interest or the suspicion of Ribbentrop. Things were getting done *auf dem kleinen Dienstweg*, on the lower-level track. And this track led to success.

---

[104] Situation Report No. 9; Inland II g Schweden: Tätigkeit des SD, d. Abwehr, d. Agenten und der Polizeiattaches, 1940–1943, PAAA, R 100775, Fiche 1978.

[105] HICOG Bonn, Biographic Data, Finke, August Hermann, February 8, 1952, NA, RG 263, Entry ZZ-18, Box 30, File: Finke, August. McKay suggests that Finke was initially slated to become the police attaché; McKay, *Intrigue*, 198.

[106] Inland II g Schweden: Tätigkeit des SD, d. Abwehr, d. Agenten und der Polizeiattaches, 1940–1943, PAAA, R 100775, Fiche 1978; 1979. The initial appointment was that of an assistant (*Hilfskraft*) whose language capabilities (Swedish and Finnish) were stressed. In that sense Finke's unpreparedness for his position allowed for additional appointments. The appointment of two women over the span of nine months is an interesting development and gender politics are not to be ignored; male assistants with SD and SS ranks might have raised some eyebrows.

[107] Auslandsreisen des SD, PAAA, R 100803-R 100808.

The value of the information these men gathered was a matter of debate. Schellenberg wanted to use neutral Sweden for espionage against the United States, the United Kingdom, and the Soviet Union. Finke, however, reported mainly on the internal situation in Sweden and his work received, at best, mixed reviews. Described sometimes as "Schellenberg's best agent in Sweden," Schellenberg held that Finke's reports were always good and timely.[108] Paeffgen, on the other hand, deemed Finke's reports as deficient and requested his recall several times. Finke was, indeed, summoned to Berlin for instruction several times, but as Office VI was understaffed – and presumably also due to Finke's long tenure with the office and his established position in the embassy – he always returned to his post.[109] Finke's reporting remained tied to the old ways of Office VI. He ran a net of some thirty V-men made up of members of Swedish Nazi groups, German journalists, the representative of a German shipping company, the director of a haulage company as well as other business contacts, and a Soviet defector to Sweden who boosted his "'insider's views' of Soviet political strategy and tactics." Finke apparently also had the support of two members of the German Legation in Stockholm.[110] His reports focused on internal Swedish conditions. A piece of his military intelligence – on convoys between Great Britain and the Soviet Union – provoked Allied chuckles after the war and called into questions the soundness of his information gathering efforts. "Finke's alleged source was a German named Schmidt who had an affair with an English girl who in turn had an affair with an Irish priest. The priest was supposed to have been the British Ambassador's father confessor. This is hardly plausible, especially since the British Ambassador was a Scotch Presbyterian."[111]

Other members of Office VI in Sweden provided additional information, but for a service largely unable to procure high-level intelligence, information deemed "too good" raised doubts. This happened in the case of Dr. Hans Heinz Krämer, code-named Josephine. Until 1943, Krämer reported to both the Abwehr and Country Group VI D. Office VI,

---

[108] Final Report; Appendix XI "Schellenberg's Relations with the Swedish Intelligence Service," in Reinhard Doerries, *Hitler's Last Chief of Foreign Intelligence: Allied Interrogations of Walter Schellenberg* (London: Frank Cass, 2003), 266–267. The document can also be found here: Appendix XXIII, Final Report on the Case of Walter Friedrich Schellenberg, NA, RG 65, Entry a 1–136 Z, Box 3, Folder Bulky 39; Index Card, June 28, 1945, NA, RG 263, Entry ZZ-18, Box 30, File: Finke, August; Saint to Saint Stockholm, Reference Interrogation Report on Paeffgen, Theodor, May 15, 1945, NA, RG 263, Entry ZZ-16, Box 39, File: Paeffgen, Theodor.

[109] Appendix XXIII, Final Report on the Case of Walter Friedrich Schellenberg, NA, RG 65, Entry A1–136 Z, Box 3, Folder Bulky 39.

[110] McKay, *Intrigue*, 198–200.   [111] Paeffgen/December 1945.

however, decided to let go of Krämer, as it regarded his reports as unreliable. With the amalgamation of the Abwehr and Office VI in 1944, Krämer came back into the fold; Schellenberg was particularly interested in him. Described as "the dean of the GIS [German Intelligence Service] agents" in Sweden, Krämer mainly reported on the labor situation and domestic and foreign policies in Great Britain and the United States, but, per Schellenberg's request, also gathered political information. He apparently provided a fine report on the Allied conference in Yalta in early 1945.[112] Incidentally, Krämer created most reports from open sources, which he "played back," and through good contacts with the Japanese Military Attaché in Stockholm, Makato Onodera, who "ran a veritable clearing house of intelligence." Krämer also had contacts among Germans living in Sweden who, in turn, had good contacts abroad, for example in Spain and Hungary. The richness of his reports made Krämer suspect. McKay intimates that Krämer was "part of the enemy's decoy plan" without being controlled by it but concludes, "the particular alchemy of his espionage remained the professional secret of Dr. Krämer alone." MI 5, which monitored Krämer's reports, deemed them a "smart mixture of intelligent speculation and of refutable or uninteresting facts."[113] Schellenberg was initially dubious about Krämer's allegiance, and at one point Paeffgen asked Finke to investigate Krämer. It was, however, the Gestapo's Heinrich Müller who strongly believed Krämer to be an Allied spy. Schellenberg, on the other hand, eventually resolved to trust Krämer. Impressed with his political reports, he established closer contact with him and "supported him to the hilt," claiming that he saved Krämer from being arrested by the Gestapo. Schellenberg saw the tussle about Krämer as a proxy conflict between him and Müller and reasoned that by raising doubts about Krämer the head of the Gestapo intended to undermine him. Schellenberg's decision to support Krämer was thus, at least partially, a function of his conflict with Müller. In addition, Schellenberg also liked what Krämer had to report. He used the information in the so-called Egmont Reports discussed below.[114]

---

[112] Situation Report No. 9. Other documents give Krämer's first names as Karl Heinz: Appendix XXIII, Final Report on the Case of Walter Friedrich Schellenberg, NA, RG 65, Entry A1–136 Z, Box 3, Folder Bulky 39; Saint to Saint Stockholm, Reference Interrogation Report on Paeffgen, Theodor, May 15, 1945, NA, RG 263, Entry ZZ-16, Box 39, File: Paeffgen, Theodor.
[113] McKay, *Intrigue*, 180–184.
[114] Appendix XXIII, Final Report on the Case of Walter Friedrich Schellenberg, NA, RG 65, Entry A1–136 Z, Box 3, Folder Bulky 39; Saint to Saint Stockholm, Reference Interrogation Report on Paeffgen, Theodor, May 15, 1945, NA, RG 263, Entry ZZ-16, Box 39, File: Paeffgen, Theodor; Major Friedrich Busch, February 7, 1946/July 6, 1955, NA, RG 263, Entry ZZ-18, Box 112, File: Schellenberg, Walter, Vol. 2, 1 of 2;

The decision to embed Office VI personnel in German legations abroad and to keep them independent from the police attachés, commonly Gestapo members, had an important side effect, indicative of the office's transformation from a secret intelligence service to an alternative foreign office open for business. Schellenberg's men in German legations abroad were included in the local diplomats' lists; in other words, they were known to the local authorities. The Swedes, for example, must have been aware of the men's real occupation, in particular, as their diplomatic covers were paper-thin. In the case of Finke, the Swedes got on his tail almost immediately after his arrival in Stockholm.[115] This reality seriously circumscribed intelligence opportunities. Yet it established Office VI as an official player on the Swedish scene. Indeed, Neumann introduced Schellenberg to the head of the Stockholm Security Police during Schellenberg's first visit to Sweden in November 1941.[116] This was clearly one of Schellenberg's goals; there is no indication that Schellenberg lost sleep over the lack of covert operatives in Sweden.[117]

Another country paramount to Office VI's attempts to learn more about the Allies was Switzerland.[118] Office VI's activities in Switzerland initially held a dual purpose: to collect information on the host country and on Great Britain as well as on neutral countries, which, until December 1941, included the United States. At the beginning of the war Office VI relied on V-men from the SD Outposts close to the Swiss–German border but began establishing permanent representatives in the country in 1940. Dr. Ernst Peter, formerly the head of department VI in the SD Lead District Stuttgart, was appointed as the cultural attaché at the

---

Cable from Ustravic, London, July 7, 1945/June 1, 1955, NA, RG 263, Entry ZZ-18, Box 112, File: Schellenberg, Walter, Vol. 1, 1 of 2.

[115] McKay, *Intrigue*, 201.

[116] Final Report; Inland II g Schweden: Tätigkeit des DS, d. Abwehr, d. Agenten und der Polizeiattaches, 1940–1943, PAAA, R 100775, Fiche 1977. Different sources describe Martin Lundquist's position differently ("head of the Swedish Intelligence Service" or "Chief of the Swedish Police" or "Stockholm controller of the Security Service," respectively). I am following Fleischauer's designation; Ingeborg Fleischauer, *Die Chance des Sonderfriedens: Deutsch-Sowjetische Geheimgespräche 1941–1945* (Berlin: Siedler Verlag, 1986), 52.

[117] A postwar document contains the following curious sentence: "It must be remembered that a good source has said that Schellenberg has for some time considered that the officers of Amt VI must be known to the Allies." As the sentence is taken out of its context, the meaning – especially taken into consideration that the "good source" likely spoke German – remains unclear. Did Schellenberg assume that the Allies must have known the officers' identities; or did Schellenberg consider it useful for them to be known? War Room Summary (monthly) # 2, June 4, 1945/July 1, 1955, NA, RG 263, Entry ZZ-18, Box 112, File: Schellenberg, Walter, Vol. 1, 1 of 2.

[118] Sixth Detailed Interrogation Report on SS Sturmbannführer Huegel Dr. Klaus, June 21, 1945, NA, RG 226, Entry 119A, Box 71, Folder 1828. Huegel's account appears truthful enough to serve as the basis for the narrative here.

Legation in Berne. That summer Dr. Hans-Ulrich Reiche became an employee at the Consulate in Geneva, and Dr. Wilhelm Groebl took on a similar position in Zurich. Over the course of the next eighteen months, the Swiss authorities uncovered the men's activities and had them recalled to Germany. By the middle of 1941, Office VI's efforts in Switzerland were untenable; "practically no information of value was obtained on the neutrals or Great Britain. Work directed against Switzerland itself had led to bad relations between that country and Nazi Germany, and to the suppression of the Swiss Nazi Movements."[119] In short, the work of Office VI in Switzerland was a failure and had worsened relations between the two countries.

After he took over the office, Schellenberg laid down the law. Office VI was to focus on the collection of information about Great Britain and the neutrals and not to report on Switzerland anymore. In addition, all activities in favor of the Swiss Nazi Movement were banned. Killing two birds with one stone, Schellenberg also installed the former head of Office VI D and Jost-man, Hans Daufeldt, as the new representative of Office VI in Switzerland. Daufeldt became vice-consul in Lausanne and remained in this position until March 1945, when the Swiss expelled him. Daufeldt created a net of informers and, depending on the source, either collected useful information on the Allies and their intentions or did not produce any results. Schellenberg used Hans Wilhelm Eggen as his personal representative in Switzerland, capitalizing on Eggen's connections, as was the case in the meetings with Masson and Guisan in 1942 and 1943.[120] In 1943, Schellenberg attempted to increase the number of permanent SD representatives in Switzerland, but despite torturous discussions with other German entities, nothing came out of this plan – either because they did not support the Office VI's plans or because no suitable candidates could be found.[121] Eggen remained Schellenberg's key line into Switzerland.

These sources contributed to the reports Himmler received from Office VI. With some astonishment, the Allies listed them:

In January 1942 a report on Saldago and the Green shirt movement is passed to him for a decision: in December 1942 it is 'considered essential' that he

[119] Fifth Detailed Interrogation Report on SS Sturmbannführer Huegel Dr. Klaus, June 14, 1945, NA, RG 226, Entry 174, Box 39, Folder 307.
[120] Fifth Detailed Interrogation Report on SS Sturmbannführer Huegel Dr. Klaus, June 14, 1945, NA, RG 226, Entry 174, Box 39, Folder 307; Saint London to Saint Washington, Amt VI of the RSHA, Liquidation Reports No. 7, Gruppe VI B, October 26, 1945, NA, RG 263, Entry ZZ-16, Box 13, File: Eggen, Hans Wilhelm.
[121] Fifth Detailed Interrogation Report on SS Sturmbannführer Huegel Dr. Klaus, June 14, 1945, NA, RG 226, Entry 174, Box 39, Folder 307.

should be informed of the Cossack question: he received constant reports on the development of the S.D.'s Persian enterprise: he is asked for a decision about the German minority in Hungary: he demands an urgent interim report about the invention of a new gas incendiary bomb: on the success of sabotage in North Africa. In addition, whenever there is an important development of the more obvious kind, the S.D. is required to furnish an immediate report for the Reichsführer; a governmental change in Spain in August 1941: the French crisis in November 1942, the murder of Darlan, the murder of General Lukoff in Sofia. When an important Finn or Hungarian or Italian offers his collaboration, Himmler decides whether or nor the offer is to be accepted.[122]

Aside from specialized reports, Himmler also received the *Auslandsmeldungen*, Foreign Reports, of Office VI. These were a curious mélange. On the surface, they appear as straightforward reports on internal conditions in various countries across the globe, meant to keep the RSHA abreast of developments abroad. On closer inspection they reveal an ideological tunnel vision of the countries under investigation. The case of the German ally Hungary is particularly instructive in this context. In April 1941, the Auslandsmeldungen stressed that the population wished nothing more than a government willing to dispose of the large landholders and the Jews.[123] In stark contrast to popular attitudes, leading personalities in Hungary, the Regent Admiral Miklos Horthy in particular, were "Jew-friendly," which explained the elite's negative attitudes toward Germany. The only resistance to Horthy came from the fascist Arrow Cross organization whose leaflets carried the "naked truth to the public." Accordingly, the SD expected the Arrow Cross movement to be banned shortly. Until Adolf Eichmann's arrival in Budapest in the early spring of 1944, the Hungarian Jews remained a thorn in the SD's side and the most prominent issue in reports on Hungary.[124] The reports also provided the perfect ideological excuse, as all problems Germany encountered in its dealings with its Hungarian ally were blamed on this alleged Jewish influence. Sober foreign intelligence this was not.

On the southern edge of Europe, the Auslandsmeldungen identified the undiminished influence of the Catholic Church as the source of Spain's problematic relationship with Germany.[125] Yet the report also

---

[122] R.I.S. 16/27.9.43, Himmler und der Sicherheitsdienst, NA, RG 226, Enrty 108 B, Box 286, Folder RIS Reports.
[123] Auslandsmeldungen, April 22, 1941, BAL, R 58/3485.
[124] Auslandsmeldungen, March 2, 1942 and July 17, 1942, BAL, R 58/3485; Auslandsmeldungen, August 26, 1941, August 29, 1941, September 12, 1941, and September 19, 1941, BAL, R 58/7725.
[125] Auslandsmeldungen, July 8, 1941, BAL, R 58/3485. Christian Leitz, *Sympathy for the Devil: Neutral Europe and Nazi Germany in World War II* (New York: New York University Press, 2001), 114–143.

noted that the lack of food was the population's most pressing need and ventured that the "right man in the right position" was missing in Spain, counseling that a German invasion would not encounter resistance. It, indeed, suggested that the Spanish population hoped for a German invasion – the sooner the better – and expected provisioning to improve substantially thereafter.[126] This was a marked change from an evaluation a year earlier, when the Auslandsmeldungen had opined that the undisciplined Spaniards were afraid of a German occupation, for discipline would come in its wake.[127] In the end, though, the Auslandmeldungen steadfastly maintained that the Catholic Church was the main cause for any problems between Germany and Spain. Not only was its influence increasing, but the heads of the British and US diplomatic missions in Spain were alleged to be in close contact with its representatives as well. The SD also reported on rumors that Franco had changed his pro-German attitudes – as long as he was in office, the SD also watched carefully the pro-German leanings of Foreign Minister Serrano Suner – suggesting that this would signify a total victory for the Church.[128] As in Hungary, Office VI identified the ideological enemy as the main source of any and all problems with and in Spain.

In Portugal, Office VI reported, the situation was similar to Spain but teetering on worse. Aside from the influence of the Church, the anti-German emigrants living in the country strengthened its negative attitudes. British propaganda added to the mix.[129] However, there was no anti-German protest; the country remained neutral. Indeed, the Auslandsmeldungen indicated with relief that moviegoers preferred German newsreels to British ones, suggesting that German propaganda was beginning to be effective, even if Germany still had a long way to go in a country that had been economically dependent on Great Britain for centuries.[130]

The reports on Switzerland focused on the country's vacillating attitudes toward Germany, which depended on Swiss perceptions of the course of the war.[131] In January 1941, for example, the Auslandsmeldungen stressed that as long as the country retained its independence, Switzerland seemed to be getting accustomed to the idea of a German-led Europe, noting with relief, "emotional cramp [*Krampf*] in regards

---

[126] Auslandsmeldungen, August 8, 1941, BAL, R 58/7725.
[127] Auslandsmeldungen, August 13, 1940, BAL, R 58/7723.
[128] Auslandsmeldungen, July 2, 1942, BAL, R 58/3485; Auslandsmeldungen, October 3, 1941, BAL 58/7725; Auslandsmeldungen, August 27, 1940, BAL, R 58/7723; Auslandsmeldungen, June 6, 1941, BAL 58/7724.
[129] Auslandsmeldungen, August 12, 1940, BAL, R 58/7725; Auslandsmeldungen, August 19, 1940, BAL, R 58/7725; Leitz, *Sympathy*, 144–174.
[130] Auslandsmeldungen, August 26, 1941, BAL, R 58/7725.
[131] Auslandsmeldungen, July 17, 1942, BAL, R 58/3485; Leitz, *Sympathy*, 10–48.

to all that is German has largely dissipated." "Objective and accurate" statements about Germany could be heard and a police action against Swiss Freemasons, another ideological enemy in Office VI's crosshairs, was a distinct possibility.[132] In September 1941, the Auslandsmeldungen focused on the conclusion of the German–Swiss economic negotiations that led to Germany receiving a de facto interest-free credit. And a few months after the German invasion of the Soviet Union, the Auslandsmeldungen noted that the "better classes" of Swiss society saw Germany as a protective wall against Bolshevism.[133] As the war wore on, though, Switzerland began to see itself in the role of a mediator between the belligerent nations.[134]

Sweden, on the other hand, was regarded as heavily influenced by British propaganda, which – the argument went – fit the "Swedish mentality" and its "exaggerated humanist leanings."[135] The reports nervously enumerated anti-German activities and noted that the Swedish population paid careful attention to the behavior of the German occupiers in neighboring Norway.[136] In early October 1941, the reports devoted substantial space to "increasingly grotesque reactions" in Sweden and noted "pro-English and even pro-Russian agitation." Later that month, a report stressed that the Swedes had reacted negatively to the recent introduction of the Star of David in Germany and other anti-Jewish measures.[137] German propaganda – which should have counteracted these Swedish attitudes – completely lacked the understanding of the Swedish mentality the British propaganda efforts displayed, or so the Auslandsmeldungen opined. Indeed, the argument went, any pro-German attitudes in Sweden were based on necessity and an increasing fear of the Soviet Union. The Swedes were also obstinate: even if they followed certain German examples, they never admitted to it.[138] Ultimately, the Auslandsmeldungen detected intense anti-German propaganda at work in Sweden and expressed doubt that it would ever diminish.

---

[132] Auslandsmeldungen, January 17, 1941, BAL, R 58/7724; Auslandsmeldungen, June 6, 1941, BAL, R 58/7724. Doerries suggests that Daufeldt's focus on Freemasons (and Jews) seems to be indicative of "routine Gestapo work" and not of foreign intelligence. This is a dubious assessment, as Office VI regarded Freemasonry as an ideological enemy and a secret intelligence entity. Doerries, *Intelligence Chief*, 56.

[133] Auslandsmeldungen, September 12, 1941 and September 26, 1941, BAL 58/7725.

[134] Auslandsmeldungen, June 2, 1942, BAL, R 58/3485.

[135] Auslandsmeldungen, May 20, 1941 and June 6,1941, BAL, R 58/7724; Auslandsmeldungen, August 19, 1940 and September 23, 1941, BAL, R 58/7725; Leitz, *Sympathy*, 49–84.

[136] Auslandsmeldungen, September 16, 1941, September 19, 1941, September 23, 1941, and September 26, 1941, BAL 58/7725.

[137] Auslandsmeldungen, October 3 and October 17, 1941, BAL 58/7725.

[138] Auslandsmeldungen, May 20, 1941, BAL, R 58/7724.

The Auslandsmeldungen on the United States and Great Britain focused on the countries' domestic situation, their future ambitions, and their will to be successful in the war. In the case of Britain, allegedly fresh intelligence parroted insights from the Invasion Handbook of 1940 while reports on the United States focused on the country's industrial and political strength and on Roosevelt. One report held that despite German air raids on London, the population, although doubtful of a victory, was determined to hold on until Germany would "recognize the futility of the fight," while another maintained that the success of the German submarines had undermined the British belief in its Navy, thus harming the country's will to fight back.[139] Living and working conditions in Great Britain were carefully scrutinized and compared unfavorably to those in Germany.[140] At one point, the reports even detected a "revolutionary Bolshevik mood."[141] On the other hand, the reports noted that crude anti-German propaganda was rampant and Jewish influence overwhelming. But then again, in the summer of 1942, there were hopeful reports that the population's trust in Churchill was fading. At the same time one detected indications of an increasing collaboration between the Anglican Church and the Jews and assumed that the establishment of a social-democratic government was the collaboration's goal.[142] Jews allegedly also influenced heavily British postwar planning and were involved in all major developments on the Isle.[143] The reports on the United States focused on the war industry and, before the country's entry into the war, rearmament efforts on the one hand and the isolationist movement on the other.[144] US activities in the Western hemisphere, especially in South America, were scrutinized and decried as imperialism.[145] In 1942, Republican dissent with President Roosevelt's policies was recorded in much hopeful detail.[146] Conversely, the president's "almost dictatorial

[139] Auslandsmeldungen, November 29, 1940, BAL, R 58/7723.
[140] Auslandsmeldungen, September 12, 1941, September 16, 1941, and September 26, 1941, BAL 58/7725; Auslandsmeldungen, June 6, 1941, BAL, R 58/7724.
[141] Auslandsmeldungen, September 9, 1941, BAL, R 58/7725.
[142] Auslandsmeldungen, March 2, 1942, June 17, 1942, June 2, 1942, July 2, 1942, and July 8, 1942, BAL, R 58/3485
[143] Auslandsmeldungen, July 17, 1942, BAL, R 58/3485; Auslandsmeldungen, June 10, 1941, BAL, R 58/7724.
[144] Auslandsmeldungen, June 17, 1942, BAL, R 58/3485; Auslandsmeldungen, May 16, 1941, BAL, R 58/7724; Auslandsmeldungen, August 29, 1941, September 19, 1941, and September 26, 1941, BAL, R 58/7725.
[145] Auslandsmeldungen, June 17, 1942, BAL, R 58/3485; Auslandsmeldungen, May 16, 1941 and May 27, 1941, BAL, R 58/7724.
[146] Auslandsmeldungen, July 17, 1942, BAL, R 58/3485; Auslandsmeldungen, August 19, 1940, BAL, R 58/7725.

powers" were discussed and seen as indicative of the Western democracies' hypocrisy.[147]

Everything that was wrong with Nazi Germany's political foreign intelligence service is evident in these reports. Random information on the domestic situation in various countries coming from undefined sources in undefined countries and information likely culled from open source were molded into authoritative narratives generously infused with ideology while intermittently hinting at alternative policies that Germany could or should embrace. Ultimately, though, there was little to learn from them. Under the guise of foreign intelligence reporting and analysis, they confirmed preconceived notions about the world in general and individual countries in particular, such as the influence of Catholicism in Spain and Portugal, democracies' hypocrisies, and the existence of a worldwide Jewish conspiracy. Office VI's intelligence efforts abroad always found what they came looking for: explanations in sync with basic Nazi ideology.

In 1943, Office VI reporting underwent a change, symptomatic of its ongoing transformation from a political foreign intelligence service to foreign policy think-tank or alternative foreign office, and "[t]he reports submitted to the Reichsführer often took the form of a diplomatic dossier."[148] The change in reporting coincided with the implementation of the "System Schellenberg" of personal representatives. The new breed of reports focused more clearly on foreign policy, put them in a global perspective, and paid particular attention to the state of the anti-Hitler alliance and possible cracks in it. Ideological thinking remained but was less overt and joined by wishful thinking. The report of March 10, 1943, six weeks after the Casablanca Conference, discussed, for example, the points of conflict between Great Britain and the United States as well as the Soviet Union and emphasized the closer alignment between the latter two. It stressed the utilitarian nature of the coalition between Great Britain and the Soviet Union and noted that many British politicians were wary of the United States' postwar ambitions. These observations captured the shifting, uneasy alliance between the Big Three but exaggerated its immediate relevance. The insinuation that the coalition could not hold was a product of Office VI's wishful interpretation of the situation – the Casablanca Conference had made Germany's unconditional surrender to all Allies an official policy – than of the realities observed. And about a month after the loss of the 6th German Army at Stalingrad,

---

[147] Auslandsmeldungen, January 17, 1941, BAL, R 58/7724; Auslandsmeldungen, August 29, 1941, BAL, R 58/7725; Auslandsmeldungen, August 13, 1940, BAL 58/7723.
[148] Eighth Report/Huegel.

a report stressed that information received from the Japanese Embassy at Kubishev confirmed that the current offensive of the Red Army "was this time, for sure, the last desperate attack of the Russians." If "for sure" was not assurance enough, Office VI also found this information confirmed by the good authority of "serious Turkish circles."[149]

A report a few weeks later, dealing with differences in opinions and ultimate goals for the postwar period among the Big Three, displayed the same proclivity to focus on developments detrimental to the anti-Hitler coalition and to suggest that Germany had many options.[150] The report noted that debates about the postwar, and the Soviet Union's role in Eastern Europe, were not yet settled; it also discussed US and British attitudes toward a negotiated peace with Germany. Either misinformed about the decisions at Casablanca or willfully ignoring that the Allies expected Germany's unconditional surrender, the report stressed that the British, expecting a total collapse of Germany, rejected any negotiations, while the Americans remained willing. The report held that the Americans, in particular Republicans, understood that "the folkish-ness (*Volkstum*) of the people of the smaller states on the continent is not equal to that of the German people. They came to this decision based on their experience with immigrants." Therefore, they understood that smaller European peoples would have to accept German leadership. The report also counseled that most Americans saw Japan as their "decisive enemy" and would happily accept a "generally satisfying end of the European conflict." The United States and Great Britain were also clearly at odds about their goals regarding Europe: Great Britain had no interest in a prolonged US presence on the continent and was therefore reluctant to engage the United States' complete military power. Incidentally, the report also insinuated that Great Britain was not eager to establish a Second Front, which would divert German troops from the East; rather, Great Britain intended to maintain the current balance on the Eastern Front, thereby weakening the Soviet Union before the war's end and rendering it ineffectual in peace negotiations. In short, Great Britain meant to create an equilibrium that would not hurt its imperial expectations. These collided, however, with American intentions at hegemony. The Soviet Union, on the other hand, tried to keep its options open.[151] This new type of report was certainly an improvement over earlier ones, and they took on the veneer of a foreign policy entity – but key problems remained: the information available was vague at best, and while

[149] Auslandsmeldungen, March 10, 1943, BAL, R 58/3486.
[150] Auslandsmeldungen, May 15, 1943, BAL, R 58/7730.
[151] Auslandsmeldungen, May 15, 1943, BAL, R 58/7730.

the focus had changed from the domestic situation in various countries to a consideration of foreign policies, evaluation and analysis remained defined by Nazi ideology and wishful thinking.

These reports were the forerunner of the so-called Egmont Reports that Schellenberg and Giselher Wirsing prepared between September 1944 and March 1945. Wirsing, a member of the NSDAP, the SS, and on the payroll of the Auswärtige Amt, was a well-known and highly regarded author, editor, and publicist.[152] Widely traveled, he published on foreign affairs and foreign countries, espousing a view of German superiority and mission. As his interrogators put, he

interpreted Nazi expansion in terms of renascence of German 'Kultur':–his theme was German hegemony in Europe, cloaked in the deceptive verbiage of a 'Federal Europe'. The mission of German Kultur, the degrading nihilism of "Amerikanismus", the mechanistic barbarism threatening from the East, the decadence and hypocrisy of British Imperialism, all these were recurrent topics in his writings, served with a seemingly rational erudition in which shared historical and social analysis, insidious half-truth and astonishing fallacies constantly intermingled.[153]

Wirsing's books were widely read by Nazi Germany's elite. Hitler owned Wirsing's books while Propaganda Minister Joseph Goebbels noted that "[t]he material [. . .] was truly shattering. Roosevelt is one of the worst pests of modern culture and civilization," and concluded, "[i]f we were not able to completely defeat the enemy, which joins Bolshevism, plutocracy, and lack of civilization, then the world would approach the darkest darkness."[154] Schellenberg, too, was one of Wirsing's readers. Despite his occasional contrarian streak that at various points created problems with Goebbels and Ribbentrop and might have even irritated Hitler – and which Wirsing touted after the war – his views fell squarely within the acceptable; he was published into 1944. Indeed, his contrarian streak and alleged independence from NSDAP, which he joined in 1940, made him valuable, for he "share[d] in laying the ideological foundations upon

---

[152] Wirsing's publications included *Deutschland in der Weltpolitik* (1940); *Engländer, Juden, Araber in Palästina* (1933); *Köpfe der Weltpolitik* (1934); *Der Krieg 1939–1940 in Karten* (1940); *Hundert Familien beherrschen das Empire* (1940); *Der Masslose Kontinent: Roosevelt's Kampf um die Weltherrschaft* (1942), and *Stalinism: Soviet Policy in the Second World War* (1944). Otto Köhler, *Unheimliche Publizisten: Die verdrängte Vergangenheit der Medienmacher* (München: Knaur, 1995), 290–327; Norbert Frei, *Karrieren im Zwielicht: Hitler's Eliten nach 1945* (Frankfurt/Main: Campus Verlag 2001), 263–266; Conze et al., eds., *Amt*, 150–151. His CIA files are instructive: RG 263, Entry ZZ-16, Box 57, File: Wirsing, Giselher and RG 263, Entry ZZ-18, Box 140, File: Wirsing, Giselher.

[153] Final Report on Sturmbannführer Giselher Wirsing, no date, RG 263, Entry ZZ-16, Box 57, File: Wirsing, Giselher.

[154] Wildt, *Generation*, 823 note 290.

which the conservative elements of Germany could submerge their dis-like of the many repugnant aspects of the Nazi regime." A disgusted allied interrogator called Giselher Wirsing an "intellectual war criminal of the highest order."[155]

In mid-September 1944, around the time that Himmler and Schellen-berg commenced their attack on Ribbentrop, Schellenberg and Wirsing met for the first time and agreed to collaborate. As Wirsing related the story after the war, the two men discussed the political situation in Ger-many, the war, and Germany's diminishing political options, agreeing that the information Ribbentrop received and on which Hitler based his decisions was deficient. They decided that Wirsing should write reports that gave an "unvarnished picture of hopelessness" and "pro-pose[d] specific measures" to save Germany as an alternative sources of information for Hitler, Himmler, and a select group of party functionar-ies. Next to Kaltenbrunner his close associate, the Reich Commissioner for the Netherlands, Arthur Seyss-Inquart received the reports. Two men deemed to have influence on Hitler were also among the recipients: Himmler's liaison at Hitler's headquarters, SS-Gruppenführer Hermann Fegelein and Ribbentrop's equivalent there, Ambassador Walther Hewel. Ribbentrop and Goebbels were not to receive them. Hewel apparently had to sign a statement that he would not share the reports with his Ribbentrop but Goebbels might have received them after all. Schellen-berg believed that Kaltenbrunner forwarded the reports to "all kinds of people."[156]

To make possible the preparation of "unvarnished" reports, Schel-lenberg pulled out all the stops. He provided Wirsing – who became an honorary Office VI member and took on the pen name of Egmont in a misplaced reference to Goethe's Egmont who stood in the way of a king making the first mistake – with all the information available to him: information from international news agencies; American and British newspapers and magazines procured via Stockholm and Lisbon; embassy reports; information from German personalities – journalists and diplo-mats – abroad; information from foreign personalities; all available Amt VI materials, sometimes in their raw format, including those from the various country groups (Wirsing was partial to Krämer's reports from

---

[155] Draft Report from MFIU, No. 3, July 30, 1945, RG 263, Entry ZZ-16, Box 57, File: Wirsing, Giselher.
[156] Draft Report from MFIU, No. 3, July 30, 1945, RG 263, Entry ZZ-16, Box 57, File: Wirsing, Giselher; Progress Report in the case of Schellenberg, July 17, 1945, NA, RG 319, IRR, Box 195; Eidesstattliche Erklärung, Dr. Giselher Wirsing, December 29, 1947, NA, RG 238, M 897, Reel 114, Frame 09720989; Eidesstattliche Erklärung, Walter Schellenberg, February 10, 1948, IfZ, ZS 291/VII.

Stockholm); the monitoring reports from the decoding service *Seehaus*; still code-named reports from sources abroad; and decoded messages if available. During their meetings Schellenberg also summarized information available to him alone via his special lines and contacts he had

both in Germany and abroad, e.g. Swiss Federal Councillor Mussi (Musy); members of the Japanese Embassy in Berlin, particularly its Naval Attaché Admiral Koshima; and the Swiss and Swedish ambassadors. Schellenberg had a line into France [. . .] He frequently received reports from a Spanish source, either a diplomat or an industrialist who appeared well versed in Vatican affairs.[157]

Giselher Wirsing received it all.

The purpose of the reports was "didactic;" they were meant to "enlighten[. . .] their readers on the true state of affairs." There were subtle contradictions, however, as to where this enlightenment should lead. On the one hand, the reports were clearly directed against Ribbentrop. It is clear, and in accord with Schellenberg's other activities, that he "aimed to counteract Ribbentrop's influence and, if possible, to oust Ribbentrop from his position. . . ." Other postwar statements suggest that Schellenberg and Wirsing wanted Hitler to disappear from the political scene in one way or the other as well. Wirsing believed that if Hitler had "a spark of responsibility left," he would step down and Schellenberg purportedly regarded Hitler as a "medical case," unable to accept reality. At a minimum, Schellenberg – and Wirsing – thought it possible to "maneuver [. . .] Hitler into a political stalemate where no alternative was left him [sic] but to resign." At least until November 1944, though, when Schellenberg reported to Wirsing that Hitler did not take the reports into consideration, neither man had completely given up on their Führer. On the other hand, the only person with the power base to move Hitler into a political stalemate was Schellenberg's patron, Himmler and Wirsing and Schellenberg apparently agreed that after the Officers' Plot of July 20, 1944, whose aftermath had broken the remaining power of the military, the "only group capable of bringing about the required changes were Himmler and his SS." In effect, then, the reports were to induce Himmler to sideline Hitler and to take power in the country. In Wirsing's estimation Schellenberg wanted to convince Himmler that he was "the man of the hour and that Hitler had to go." As Schellenberg related it after the war, Himmler largely agreed with the reports but was unable to make headway with Hitler. Wirsing

---

[157] Abstract of Document being Cross Filed, Egmont Reports, October 1, 1945, NA, RG 263, CIA Name Files (Reference Collection), Box 45, Schellenberg, vol. 1; Appendix A to FR 105, Giselher Wirsing, The 'Egmont' Reports, October 25, 1946, NA, RG 263, Entry ZZ-16, Box 57, File: Wirsing, Giselher.

purportedly believed that any Himmler-government would be short-term, but he also went on the postwar record stating, "Schellenberg never committed himself to that length and most likely envisaged Himmler's ascendancy as a more lasting solution."[158] In short, if everything went as Schellenberg planned, Himmler would be the head of state and Schellenberg his Foreign Minister and trusted advisor.

Twelve or thirteen Egmont Reports were authored by Wirsing between October 1944 and March 1945; sometimes, Schellenberg and Wirsing discussed and edited Wirsing's initial drafts. During their first meeting in September 1944, the men supposedly came to several general agreements that provided the basis for the reports. They agreed that Germany's position was "militarily and politically" hopeless and that the last chance to negotiate a separate peace with the Soviet Union had passed. Both wanted to end the war but had concluded that "equal negotiation" was out of the question. They agreed on the need to ascertain whether the Allied demand for an unconditional surrender "left room for a change in government, acceptable to the Allies across the table." The ouster of Hitler was one of these changes, but the reports also carried additional recommendations on "which negotiations with the Allies could be launched:" the solution of the "Jewish question" and the "Catholic Church question." Thus, there were plans to release all Jews "still in German concentration camps," lest they would be "liquidated."[159] In their concrete implementation these ideas are discussed below, but the clear point was to curry Allied goodwill.

No complete copy of an Egmont Report seems to have survived the war, but in 1946 Wirsing summarized the gist of the reports for the benefit of his interrogators and he also reconstructed an almost complete version of the last Egmont Report of 1945 from memory while in Allied custody. In both, Wirsing clearly played to his new audience.[160] The reports for October and November noted that open conflict between the United States and the Soviet Union could not be expected before Germany's defeat, but also stressed that no complete agreement on Germany's future had yet been reached. Taking into account the "stabilization of the Western front," which had come as a surprise to the Western military leaders, there was an opportunity to initiate negotiations with the

---

[158] Appendix A to FR 105, Giselher Wirsing, The 'Egmont' Reports, October 25, 1946; Draft Report from MFIU, No. 3, July 30, 1945, NA, RG 263, Entry ZZ-16, Box 57, File: Wirsing, Giselher.

[159] Draft Report from MFIU, No. 3, July 30, 1945, NA, RG 263, Entry ZZ-16, Box 57, File: Wirsing, Giselher.

[160] Appendix A to FR 105, Giselher Wirsing, The 'Egmont' Reports, October 25, 1946; Draft Report from MFIU, No. 3, July 30, 1945, NA, RG 263, Entry ZZ-16, Box 57, File: Wirsing, Giselher.

Western Allies. In November, the report also stressed the urgent need for "early negotiations with Eisenhower" and subsequent reports pushed this reasoning, noting that the relatively successful Battle of the Bulge "has proved that [Germany] still exist," repeating the call for negotiations. The February report analyzed the Yalta Conference and concluded that Germany's last chance had passed; "There can no longer be any hope of a separate Anglo-American policy . . . ". The March report called for the dissolution of the NSDAP and suggested that former chancellor Heinrich Brüning, living in Swiss exile, create a new government. Wirsing's postwar summaries forefronted the interest in peace negotiation over the foreign affairs' razzle-dazzle clearly in evidence in the reconstructed March 1945 report, but Wirsing's and Schellenberg's reports were only slightly more realistic in their assessment of the world situation than what was in regular German circulation. Even if one believed in miracle weapons, Germany's situation looked a tad bleak but the reports maintained well into 1945 that a small chance for a negotiated peace remained. Schellenberg, for his part, assumed – apparently well beyond March 1945 – that the Americans would be willing to negotiate an agreement that would allow Germany to maintain its territorial integrity under a central German government, presumably led by Himmler.[161]

Schellenberg was, indeed, planning for this future. Having used the earlier changes, in the wake of the absorption of the Abwehr, to create an inner circle or personal cabinet of immediate advisors meant to coordinate better the work of the office, Schellenberg now considered cutting the office's personnel by 30 percent and maintaining the service only on German controlled "islands."[162] The Western Allies later noted that Schellenberg held "the ambition to have a 'gentlemanly' secret service" that would be "similar to the English service."[163] Ultimately, Schellenberg was caught in his preconceived notions just as much as Hitler and Ribbentrop; his were simply slightly different preconceptions.

Most relevant about the Egmont Reports is their existence, as they show Schellenberg taking on the responsibilities of a Foreign Minister. Relying on the alternative foreign office he had created over the preceding years and in which his personal representatives served as his ambassadors,

[161] Eidesstattliche Erklärung, Walter Schellenberg, February 10, 1948, IfZ, ZS 291/VII.
[162] German Intelligence Service, March 7, 1945/June 19, 1955; CI War Room Publication – Amt VI, August 11, 1945/June 16, 1955; No date/June 10, 1955, NA, RG 263, Entry ZZ-18, Box 112, File: Schellenberg, Walter, vol. 1, 1 of 2. Allied reports sometimes label the department VI *Verwaltung* (VI Administration) and sometimes *Zentralbüro* (Central Office).
[163] Shaef CI War Room, London, May 1945/July 7, 1955; SCI France-Paris Base, SS Brigadeführer Schellenberg, November 11, 1944, NA, RG 263, Entry ZZ-18, Box 112, File: Schellenberg, Walter, vol. 1, 1 of 2.

while completely ignoring the existing Auswärtige Amt, which he deemed a failure, Schellenberg, tacitly backed by Himmler, took his ambition to a new level. It was one of Schellenberg's main detractors in Office VI, Wilhelm Hoettl, who provided the Allies – and historians – with clues to the reports' role

> The Egmont reports were no mere 'Lageberichte', but political acts of an order usually prepared at the highest level of policy-making agencies. Had they emanated from the German Foreign Office, they would have passed as routine surveys designed to keep the Foreign Minister posted and to enable him to make up his mind what to do next. What lifts the Egmont reports out of the ordinary is the fact that in publishing them and lining up behind their findings and recommendations the authority of men like Schellenberg, Kaltenbrunner, and Himmler, the RSHA arrogated to itself policy-making functions in the field of foreign policy which by rights belong to the German Foreign Office.

Indeed, Hoettl saw a "specific program aiming at Hitler's overthrow and Himmler's accession to power" and noted that the reports were a "blueprint for Germany's foreign policy" for that case.[164] Yet the full potency of the Egmont Reports reveals itself only in their context. This was neither a late nor a spurious attempt by Schellenberg and Himmler to forge Germany's foreign policy in the moment of defeat, but the culmination of a long-standing and multifaceted attack on Ribbentrop and his ministry. Schellenberg's political foreign intelligence service had long ceased to be only that. Instead, he attempted to create an alternative foreign office, serving at Himmler's pleasure. If Himmler ever chose to engage in foreign policy, the basic structures for such an endeavor existed. Yet for an outright usurpation, the "rabbit" of the Auswärtige Amt – ideologically firm and consistently backed by Hitler – proved to be more than a mouthful.

---

[164] Draft Report from MFIU, No. 3, July 30, 1945, Egmont Berichte, Source: SS-Sturmbannführer Dr. Hoettl, Gruppe VI E, RSHA, June 30, 1945, RG 263, Entry ZZ-16, Box 57, File: Wirsing, Giselher.

8   Schellenberg, Himmler, and the Quest for "Peace"

> I mentioned back then among my friends that only praetorians were in the habit of toppling the Caesars.
>
> Dr. Giselher Wirsing
> Affidavit, December 29, 1949

Walter Schellenberg wanted to be the man who ended the war. He claimed time and again that he broached the idea of peace negotiations with Himmler as early as August 1942 and made several attempts to contact the West, only to be held back by Himmler at the last moment. It was not until the last months of the war that Himmler agreed to pursue careful peace soundings that later morphed into similarly conditional surrender offers; Schellenberg served as his emissary. To establish and maintain contacts with the West, Schellenberg displayed a willingness to possibly release even large groups of Jewish and Gentile prisoners.[1] This was Schellenberg's and Himmler's alternative foreign policy at its height. Ultimately, he failed to deliver but succeeded in saving his own skin. War's end found Schellenberg in Sweden, living under the protection of Count Folke Bernadotte, a member of the royal family, the vice president of the Swedish Red Cross, and Schellenberg's partner in the last set of negotiations.

---

[1] For the most thorough and self-serving accounts see: Final Report on the Case of Walter Schellenberg, NA, RG 319, IRR, XE 001725, Walter Schellenberg, Folders 7 and 8 [hereafter: Final Report]; Brigadeführer Schellenberg, Amtschef VI, Autobiography compiled during his stay in Stockholm, June 1945, NA, RG 226, Entry 125A, Box 2, Folder 21 [hereafter: Autobiography/Sweden]; Walter Schellenberg, *The Labyrinth: Memoirs of Walter Schellenberg, Hitler's Chief of Counterintelligence*, trans. Louis Hagen (New York: Harper & Brothers, 1956; reprint, Cambridge, MA: Da Capo Press, 2000). Schellenberg wrote the so-called Autobiography at the behest of Bernadotte to portray his side of the story; the version available at NARA is in English. A German copy is at IfZ, ED 90/7. On the whereabouts of some of Schellenberg's autobiographical writings: Reinhard R. Doerries, *Hitler's Last Chief of Foreign Intelligence: Allied Interrogations of Walter Schellenberg* (London: Frank Cass, 2003), 43 note 202 as well as Reinhard R. Doerries, *Hitler's Intelligence Chief Walter Schellenberg: The Man Who Kept Germany's Secrets* (New York: Enigma Books, 2009), 293–295.

There are two uncontested facts. First, beginning in late 1944, Schellenberg began humanitarian negotiations with representatives of Switzerland and Sweden, respectively. Over the course of these activities, over 20,000 concentration camp inmates – including many Jews – were released.[2] Secondly, in late April 1945, Himmler, after much prodding and cajoling by Schellenberg and via Swedish intermediaries who had initially come to Germany to negotiate for the release of prisoners, offered conditional surrender to General Dwight Eisenhower. Beyond this, much remains a matter of debate. What did Schellenberg want to achieve with his various initiatives and how much agency did he have? Is Schellenberg's claim that he wanted to bring about peace with the West as early as summer 1942 – when Germany was close to the height of its power – and worked tirelessly and relentlessly toward this goal only to be thwarted by Kaltenbrunner, Himmler, and others to be believed? Is his self-portrayal as an altruistic humanitarian, willing and eager to negotiate for the freedom of Jews and other victims of Germany without expecting much in return, truthful? Or did he see the release of Jews and others as the entry fee into peace talks, convinced by the ideological precept that the "Jewish World Conspiracy" could sway British and American political and military leaders? Did Schellenberg want to achieve an actual peace with the West or did he intend to break up the anti-Hitler alliance, thereby gaining a new lease of life for the state he so diligently served? And how much were Schellenberg's activities driven by his own quest for survival?

Reinhard Doerries, while not uncritical, follows Schellenberg's accounts. He focuses on Schellenberg's various alleged peace initiatives and humanitarian activities and emphasizes the risks he took, ultimately describing a man almost outside the Nazi hierarchy. Richard Breitman and others see Schellenberg's activities more critically, regard them as attempts to sow dissension among the Allies, and evaluate his humanitarian efforts as cynical, ideology-driven attempts to rouse Allied interests in him and Himmler.[3] Strikingly, it is the release of a substantial number of concentration camp inmates that makes the debate about Schellenberg's motives uncomfortable, for, as Gerhard Weinberg remarks, "Those saved were unlikely to have been troubled at the time by the prior activities of those who kept them from being slaughtered."[4] And they surely must have been equally untroubled about having become pawns in

---

[2] Doerries, *Intelligence Chief*, 214.

[3] Doerries, *Intelligence Chief*; Richard Breitman, "Nazi Espionage: The Abwehr and the SD Foreign Intelligence," in Richard Breitman et al., eds., *U.S. Intelligence and the Nazis* (Washington, DC: National Trust Fund for the Nazi War Crimes and Japanese Imperial Government Records Interagency Working Group, 2004), 94–120.

[4] Gerhard Weinberg "Introduction," in Doerries, *Intelligence Chief*, x.

negotiations about different issues or even in one man's quest for glory or survival. However, this does not absolve the historian from asking questions about Schellenberg's plans and motivations, their various contexts, or his personal and political expectations at different points in time.

Schellenberg's quest for a separate peace dated back to the late summer of 1942, he claimed. He gave several renditions of a meeting with Himmler at his headquarters in Zhitomir, Ukraine in August 1942. Facing Himmler's ire, consternation, but ultimately gaining his tentative approval, Schellenberg allegedly proposed suing for peace from a position of military strength. Concerned that the US entry into the war would make victory, Schellenberg planned to strengthen Germany's bargaining position by exacerbating the frictions in the anti-Hitler alliance; he also claimed to have presented Himmler with plans for a compromise with the West and a timeline for the ouster of Ribbentrop, whom he regarded as the stumbling block on the road to peace. Schellenberg expected to establish contact with the West through the "political sector of the Secret Service" and not "through official channels of conventional diplomacy."[5] Himmler was cautious: he promised to try to convince Hitler to let go of Ribbentrop but made it clear that Schellenberg was on his own – "if you make a serious error in your preparations I will drop you like a hot coal." The two men parted in the wee hours of the morning, or so Schellenberg claimed, even though no independent confirmation of this long meeting exists.[6] By Schellenberg's account then, he proposed using Office VI personnel as diplomatic emissaries and offered to serve as Himmler's foreign minister.

There is indication that in the meeting's aftermath, Schellenberg began to use his emerging system of personal representatives to sound out possibilities for separate negotiations. The first serious attempt happened in fall 1943, a year after the meeting in Zhitomir, when Schellenberg met with the American Abram Stevens Hewitt in Stockholm.[7] Schellenberg and his men were well-known entities in Sweden. Schellenberg was acquainted with Martin Lundquist, the head of the Stockholm Security

[5] Schellenberg, *Labyrinth*, 306–315. According to Schellenberg, the two men also discussed the set-up of Europe after a compromise peace; Schellenberg suggested that Himmler was willing to give up all territorial gains in the West. On the meeting in Zhitomir, also: Final Report.

[6] Schellenberg, *Labyrinth*, 300–301; 311; 315; Final Report; Autobiography/Sweden. See Himmler's appointment book for 1942, NA, RG 242, T-581, Reel 40a. Himmler's *Dienstkalendar* indicates a meeting in Zhitomir from 4.45 to 6.30 pm on August 12, 1942. Peter Witte et al., eds., *Der Dienstkalendar Heinrich Himmlers 1941/42* (Hamburg: Christians, 1999), 514–515.

[7] Richard Breitman, "A Deal with the Nazi Dictatorship? Himmler's Alleged Peace Emissaries in Autumn 1943," *Journal of Contemporary History* 30 (1995), 413–430. I follow Breitman's description, but not all of his conclusions.

Police, since late 1941; he habitually visited him when he was in Stockholm, discussing matters of a "general political nature." After the war Schellenberg made sure to emphasize that he "never received any political or military information from [Lundquist]" and that the Swede had refused the type of collaboration Schellenberg had in mind, "arising from his experiences and knowledge of Russia, on the basis of a common anti-Communist attitude."[8] In Sweden Schellenberg behaved not like a spymaster but like a well-positioned politician working his connections.

Schellenberg was deeply involved in the fate of the so-called Warsaw Swedes, a group of seven Swedish businessmen who were arrested by German authorities in Warsaw in April 1942 for maintaining contacts between Polish resistance circles there and their counterparts in Swedish exile. These men were representatives of Swedish industry and banking, which meant that they worked for the Wallenberg family; Swedish businessmen in occupied Poland were commonly referred to as "Wallenbergers."[9] Some six months after their arrest, the General Director of the Swedish Match Company, Axel Brandin, contacted Schellenberg with a request for help for the men expecting their trial – and death sentences – in Germany. Subsequently, Schellenberg went to work. He allegedly achieved improvements in their prison diet and, by stressing the toll the men's fate could have on Swedish–German relations, pushed forward the trial date and secured Himmler's promise that expected harsh sentences would be mitigated. Schellenberg claimed to have been instrumental in having commuted five death sentences to life in prison and to have guided, shortly before Christmas 1944, Himmler "to effect their release."[10]

Schellenberg's activities on behalf of the Warsaw Swedes necessitated several meetings with Brandin and Alvar Moeller, the Berlin representative of the Swedish Match Company, and led to additional contacts with important Swedes. In June 1943, Schellenberg met with Brandin in Stockholm and in September 1943, Brandin and a colleague visited Himmler at his headquarters in East Prussia. They lobbied for the release of their countrymen, but to no avail. Schellenberg, for his part, shared the men's trial transcripts with Brandin, who, according to Schellenberg,

---

[8] Final Report; Translation of Statement handed in by Schellenberg on 20.8.1945, NA, RG 263, Entry ZZ-18, Box 112, File: Schellenberg, Walter, vol. 1, 1 of 2.

[9] Harold Remblom, "Sweden and the Holocaust from an international perspective," in Stig Ekman and Klaus Ámark, eds., *Sweden's Relations with Nazism, Nazi Germany and the Holocaust: A Survey of Research Stockholm Studies in History*, Vol. 66 (Stockholm: Almquist & Wiksell International, 2003), 237–238. Also see: C.G. McKay, *From Information to Intrigue. Studies in Secret Service Based on the Swedish Experience 1939–1945* (London: Frank Cass, 1993), 89–90.

[10] Final Report.

was duly convinced of the men's guilt and became even friendlier toward Schellenberg. Brandin and Moeller were Schellenberg's initial connection to Marcus and Jacob Wallenberg, which in 1944 allegedly helped Schellenberg "to renew trade agreements with Sweden, even though the Swedish government was reluctant to do so because of Germany's grave military situation."[11] His work for the so-called Warsaw Swedes also facilitated Schellenberg's contacts with the Swedish Ambassador to Berlin, Arvid Richter, who was unhappy with the treatment he and other diplomats received from Ribbentrop and "was convinced that in me [Schellenberg] he had found a silent helper."[12] As far as important Swedes went, the Wallenbergs were the biggest catch.

Schellenberg apparently first met Jacob Wallenberg between October and December 1943, when relations between the two countries were tense: Germany was in need of ball bearings but the Swedes were displeased by the treatment of Scandinavians in German camps. Schellenberg yet again found the right tone in his interactions with Jacob Wallenberg, leaving Wallenberg with the impressions that the he "understood our points of view [on the mistreatment of neighboring countries and their citizens, KBP] and expressed his disapproval of such brutal measures. He declared his willingness to use his entire influence with Himmler to achieve an end or at least a moderation of such measures."[13] By way of his activities for the Warsaw Swedes and by behaving like a diplomat or a reasonable and well-connected power-broker, Schellenberg made new and influential contacts in Sweden. His opposition to Ribbentrop and his less confrontational approach were presumably part of Schellenberg's charm, but his biggest asset was undoubtedly his close connection, his role as a gatekeeper to Himmler. This proximity allowed Schellenberg to do more than to negotiate; he was also able to deliver. It is unsurprising then that some of Schellenberg's Swedish contacts considered him the man who might be interested in meeting with Hewitt and who could sway Himmler's opinions.

Abram Stevens Hewitt was the scion of a well-connected American political family. Educated in law at Oxford and Harvard, Hewitt was also part of New York society. In wartime Stockholm, he worked on economic warfare for the OSS, Office of Strategic Services, which led to connections with Jacob Wallenberg. In late summer 1943, Wallenberg

---

[11] Annex IV, Amt VI Peace Feelers, Prisoner: O/Stubaf Paeffgen, Theodor, Leiter Amt VI-D RSHA, December 29, 1945, NA, RG 263, Entry ZZ-16, Box 39, File: Paeffgen, Theodor. Also: Doerries, *Intelligence Chief*, 103–104.

[12] Final Report; Translation of Statement handed in by Schellenberg on 20.8.1945, NA, RG 263, Entry ZZ-18, Box 112, File: Schellenberg, Walter, vol. 1, 1 of 2.

[13] Statement under Oath, Jacob Wallenberg cited in Doerries, *Intelligence Chief*, 106.

inquired whether Hewitt would be interested in making contact with the German resistance; he was. However, when Hewitt inquired about such a meeting sometime later, Wallenberg noted that the resistance had been liquidated; only the German military or Himmler remained as alternatives to Hitler. Wallenberg then brought the American into contact with the Himmler's masseur Felix Kersten, who had recently relocated to Sweden. Himmler relied on Kersten's treatment and also bestowed them upon those close to him, such as Schellenberg.[14] Soon, Kersten, who dabbled in politics, began treating Hewitt as well, attempting to persuade him that Himmler presented an alternative to Hitler and that Hewitt should travel to Germany to meet with Himmler.[15]

Hewitt had no mandate to negotiate with the Germans, but apparently gave the impression that he did and that "he knew President Roosevelt personally." This might have been a misunderstanding between two men without a common language.[16] Or Hewitt might have misspoken or Kersten might have misheard – by mistake or on purpose – but the idea that Hewitt had a direct, personal connection to Roosevelt and consequently a mandate stuck. Schellenberg bought the story hook, line, and sinker and maintained that Hewitt was Roosevelt's man until the end of his life: "Mr. Hewitt was Roosevelt's special representative for European affairs," who "[a]pparently, [. . .] had *decisive* [emphasis added] influence on Roosevelt in all matters concerning Europe."[17] Historians' verdicts on the relationship between Hewitt and Roosevelt remain ambiguous, but there is no concrete evidence that Hewitt was anything but a lawyer with good

[14] I use the term masseur loosely here; he could also be described as a quack: Breitman, "Deal," 414. Final Report; Schellenberg, *Labyrinth*, 304–305; Translation of Statement No. 6 by Schellenberg, July 16, 1945, NA, RG 226, Entry 125 A, Box 2, Folder 21. Kersten, too, had pleaded the case of the Warsaw Swedes with Himmler; apparently, the Swedes permitted Kersten's residency due to these efforts. Kersten's role and influence is shrouded in mystery and depends on how much stock one puts into the veracity of his memoirs, allegedly based on wartime diaries. Felix Kersten, *The Kersten Memoirs, 1940–1945*, trans. Constantine Fitzgibbon and James Oliver (New York: MacMillan, 1957). For opposing takes, see Raymond Palmer, "Felix Kersten and Count Bernadotte: A Question of Rescue," *Journal of Contemporary History* 29 (1994), 39–40 and Breitman, "Deal," 414. Positively on Kersten: John H. Waller, *The Devil's Doctor: Felix Kersten and the Secret Plot to Turn Himmler against Hitler* (New York: John Wiley & Sons, 2002). Kersten, certainly important during negotiations involving Sweden, appears to have exaggerated his own significance.

[15] Kersten, *Memoirs*, 188–197. Palmer indicates that Kersten and Hewitt "agreed on a blueprint for peace," which was mailed to Himmler with a request to send Schellenberg to Stockholm; Breitman notes that there is no record of such a letter. Palmer, "Question," 41; Breitman, "Deal," 414–415, 417.

[16] Breitman, "Deal," 414. Kersten, though, noted: "I had a long conversation today with Hewitt, who also speaks German, so that we can understand each other very well." Kersten, *Memoirs*, 188.

[17] Final Report; Schellenberg, *Labyrinth*, 370–371.

connections among East Coast Democrats, now working for the OSS in Sweden.[18] Schellenberg was also impressed by Hewitt's social background, "It was also said that he had been formerly married to a Vanderbilt, was married now to a Haghesson and had influence with Mrs. Roosevelt."[19] He was convinced that he had found his way into East Coast society and the antechambers of the Oval Office, displaying an attitude reminiscent of Office VI reports on its US connection in 1940 or of the examples he gave in his speech in Salzburg in May 1944. Indeed, Schellenberg never conceded that he had conducted peace talks with someone who acted on even less authority than he did. And Schellenberg's authorization dating back to the alleged tête-à-tête in Zhitomir, had been vague.

Schellenberg and Hewitt met twice during Schellenberg's stay in Stockholm in November 1943; they then attempted to rouse interest in their home countries.[20] During their meetings, which apparently opened with both men noting their lack of authorization, they agreed on the need to establish an understanding between Germany and the West to avoid the "Bolshevization of large parts of the European continent."[21] Schellenberg's plan was to "strengthen the Waffen S.S. by this organisation taking over, and withdrawing the greater part of the army from the West, and thereby ending the war against the Western Powers."[22] He was convinced that the common loathing and fear of the Soviet Union could be translated into an agreement between Germany and the Western powers; the fundamental difference between them and the Nazis' racial–ideological hatred in the assessment of Bolshevism did not enter into his considerations. The two men eventually agreed on a plan of action, borne out of their lack of mandates: Hewitt was to return to the United States, test the waters for the proposal, and signal general approval through a

---

[18] Palmer states that Hewitt posed as President Roosevelt's special representative; Palmer, "Question" 41. If Hewitt did so, he was overstepping his mandate; Breitman, "Deal," 414 note 15. Waller, for his part, maintains that Hewitt was Roosevelt's confidant; Waller, *Devil's Doctor*, 133, 137–139 as does Doerries, *Intelligence Chief*, 106.

[19] Final Report; Translation of Statement by Schellenberg (Nr. 21), August 6, 1945, NA, RG 226, Entry 125 A, Box 2, Folder 21.

[20] Translation of Statement by Schellenberg (Nr. 21), August 6,1945; Translation of Statement No. 6 by Schellenberg, July 16, 1945, NA, RG 226, Entry 125 A, Box 2, Folder 21. For part of the meetings Kersten was present as well, but the extent his role is a matter of debate. Schellenberg indicates that he was under strict orders not to use Kersten for intelligence work, as Himmler was afraid that Kersten would be arrested, and that he only introduced the men. Schellenberg portrayed Kersten as a man dealing in real and imagined information, which he mostly received from a numerous lady friends. Schellenberg, whose moniker for Kersten was "good fatty," appeared baffled by Kersten's success with women.

[21] Final Report; Breitman, "Deal," 418.

[22] Translation of Statement No. 6 by Schellenberg, July 16, 1945, NA, RG 226, Entry 125 A, Box 2, Folder 21.

Swedish newspaper in the first half of February 1944. If Hewitt were to receive concrete support, he would contact Schellenberg via the German Embassy in Lisbon. Schellenberg, for his part, was to go back to Germany at once to gain Himmler's support, for, if he were amenable, Hewitt's position in the United States would be strengthened. In Berlin, Schellenberg reported to an unreceptive Himmler. The Reichsführer either rejected the plan outright or suggested the need to confer with Kaltenbrunner, which, due to Kaltenbrunner's stance, amounted to the same.[23]

Hewitt did not fare much better with US representatives in Stockholm or stateside. When he informed the American Minister in Stockholm, Hershel V. Johnson, about his meetings with Schellenberg and Kersten, Johnson did not pull any punches. He "informed the American citizen [Hewitt]...that proposal such as Dr. Kersten's were completely unacceptable..." and the State Department "confirmed the Minister's understanding that the only terms which the government of the United States is prepared to give are those of unconditional surrender, and that under no circumstances would peace proposals from Himmler be considered." Intent on not jeopardizing the alliance, let alone by one individual's unauthorized talks, the State Department also shared with Great Britain – and apparently with the Soviet Embassy in DC – the curious developments in Sweden. Doerries suggests that Johnson's reprimand of Hewitt was "probably largely for the record," but as the US minister in Sweden and the State Department spoke loudly and with one voice, and adhered to the inter-Allied information-sharing agreement, this is unlikely.[24] They meant to shut down Hewitt's activities. The proposal did, however, reach President Roosevelt in March 1944. This is what Schellenberg had hoped for but it was too little and too late.[25]

Nothing had come out of them, but the Stockholm peace soundings present a fascinating picture. Two men of different stature in the intelligence world met; one was a fairly low-ranking member of the new US service while the other headed Germany's rising political foreign intelligence service. But rather than remaining in the shadows, Schellenberg, in accordance with the image he had crafted for himself with influential Swedish power-brokers, took a visible role, his thin disguise as a member of the German military notwithstanding. In effect, he functioned as Himmler's foreign political envoy. Even if Himmler was not on board,

---

[23] Schellenberg, *Labyrinth*, 371; Final Report; Breitman, "Deal," 418–420. The suggestion that Schellenberg was lucky to have avoided "serious consequences" does not appear to be grounded in reality; Doerries, *Intelligence Chief*, 109.

[24] Documents cited in Doerries, *Intelligence Chief*, 108; see also 108 note 227.

[25] Breitman, "Deal," 422–423.

the alternative foreign office was coming into its own and emerging on the international scene.

Schellenberg had attempted to use his emerging alternative foreign policy universe to establish contacts with the West even before meeting Hewitt. One point of contact was the British Consul General Eric Grant Cable in Zurich who apparently made it known that he would be interested in meeting a German interlocutor. Himmler allegedly allowed Schellenberg to develop this contact but ultimately shared the information with Ribbentrop. The disquieted foreign minister informed Hitler, who prohibited intelligence personnel from making contacts with political personalities abroad.[26] In summer 1943, Schellenberg tossed around the idea of initiating contacts with the Western Allies in Spain; Schellenberg imagined approaching the former British foreign minister and now ambassador to Spain, Sir Samuel Hoare, who had played a decisive role in the partition of Ethiopia after the Italian aggression against the country. Schellenberg's personal representatives in Spain, Prince Egon Max zu Hohenlohe-Langeburg and his secretary Reinhard Spitzy, asked for concrete directions and an endorsement by Himmler. Schellenberg promised these, but suggested that Hohenlohe and Spitzy should simply start working on making the contact.[27] Von Hohenlohe, an Austrian nobleman, was no novice at sounding out Western attitudes. Frequently described as an SD freelancer, he was part of Schellenberg's network of private contacts; he had been involved in the Cable business but had dabbled in contacts with Western representatives as early as the fall of 1939. And a few months before Schellenberg devised the plan to make contact with Hoare, Hohenlohe met Allen Dulles, the representative of the OSS in Berne.[28]

Hohenlohe's contact with Dulles emerged seemingly independently of Schellenberg's machinations but its genesis remains patently unclear.

---

[26] Final Report. The timeline and the genesis of the contact with Cable are not as clear as Schellenberg made them out to be. Huegel indicated that the contacts dated back to the spring of 1942 and that Schellenberg initiated them without Himmler's approval and suggested the reasons for the contact with Cable were the especially favorable military situation, the attitude of Ribbentrop, and Schellenberg's weak position vis-à-vis Himmler. Himmler feared the negative reaction "German Peace Feelers" would elicit from Hitler and the idea was dropped, then picked up again in spring 1943, only to be dropped once more. Sixth Detailed Interrogation Report on SS Sturmbannführer Huegel, Dr. Klaus, June 21, 1945, NA, RG 226, Entry 119A, Box 71, File 1828.

[27] Final Report.

[28] On Hohenlohe and his attempts to establish contact between Allen Dulles, the representatives of the OSS in Berne, and Himmler and Schellenberg: Breitman, "Deal," 418–419; Peter Black, *Ernst Kaltenbrunner; Ideological Soldier of the Third Reich* (Princeton: Princeton University Press, 1984), 220; Heinz Höhne, *Der Orden unter dem Totenkopf Die Geschichte der SS* (Munich: Bertelsmann, 1967; reprint, Augsburg: Weltbild Verlag, 1998), 479–484; Doerries, *Intelligence Chief*, 79–82; Final Report.

The two men were apparently acquainted from before the war and their meeting went well; Hohenlohe reported that he found Dulles thoroughly reasonable and a kindred spirit. He noted that Dulles saw Germany as a key to postwar stability and rejected portioning Germany or detaching Austria from the Reich but wanted to restrict Prussian influence in Germany to a reasonable degree. Dulles was not interested in the Czech issue, Hohenlohe relayed, and envisioned pushing Poland eastwards, while retaining Romania and a strong Hungary as a *cordon sanitaire* against Pan-slavic and Bolshevik influences. Overall, or so Hohenlohe reported, Dulles envisioned a federalized Greater Germany, which, closely aligned with a Danube Federation, would guarantee stability in Central and Eastern Europe. And if that was not reason enough to rejoice, Hohenlohe was convinced that he had found a fellow anti-Semite in Dulles.[29] Whether Dulles was playing to his counterpart's interest and beliefs, whether his own anti-Bolshevism, anti-Semitism, and elitist attitudes got the better of him, or whether Hohenlohe spun Dulles' statements for the benefit of his audience, Hohenlohe's report inspired hope that a negotiated peace with the West was, indeed, feasible.

The second meeting between the men in April 1943 was equally encouraging. Dulles intimated that an agreement about Germany's future could be found but for the Nazi hardliners, yet also noted that time was running out. Put differently, Hitler needed to be removed. Allegedly, Dulles also confided his concerns about a German–Soviet rapprochement.[30] The discussions ended when the British became aware of them and reminded their American partners of the agreement reached at Casablanca a few months prior: Germany was to surrender unconditionally to all members of the anti-Hitler alliance.[31] It remains an intriguing fact that the meetings between Dulles and Hohenlohe are barely mentioned in Schellenberg's many postwar testimonies. He must have been involved in them but maybe not as closely as he would have wished; it is also worth recalling that the initial meeting between Dulles and Hohenlohe took place around the same time that Schellenberg and Martin Luther were plotting the removal of Foreign Minister Ribbentrop. This, in turn, serves as a fine reminder that Schellenberg, despite his eagerness to stylize himself as the man completely focused on ending the war – a notion picked up by historians, was a busy man. Making

---

[29] Black, *Kaltenbrunner*, 221; Höhne, *Orden*, 483–484; Doerries, *Intelligence Chief*, 85–90. See also the documents in BA-DH, ZR 920/60.

[30] Black, *Kaltenbrunner*, 221.

[31] Höhne, *Orden*, 484. Note Kaltenbrunner's take on the conversations; as they could not ask Hitler for the approval of his own dismissal, the RSHA chief suggested using the "Soviet bugaboo" to press for American concessions. Black, *Kaltenbrunner*, 222.

contact with representatives of the West was, at best, one of his many interests. That said, it is a reasonable conjecture that Schellenberg used Hohenlohe's impressions about Dulles and his views to strengthen his arguments that, first, the Americans were still willing to negotiate with Germany and, secondly, that the anti-Hitler alliance was, indeed, a fragile one.

Focusing on the talks in Stockholm in fall 1943, others have argued that they provide two fundamental insights into Schellenberg's role: first, Schellenberg was their "driving force." Second, neither Schellenberg – nor Kersten – had a mandate from Himmler, "let alone Hitler." Rather, the two men "hoped to generate enough of a show of interest by the West to tempt Himmler to take risks with or without Hitler" through their activities.[32] This is undoubtedly correct but not the whole story either: Schellenberg believed to have Himmler's tacit approval to test the waters; he "felt justified in pursuing these attempts because of Himmler's attitude in their discussion at Zhitomir."[33] It is also likely that Schellenberg took the information provided by Hohenlohe, which arrived before the contacts in Sweden got under way, as an independent confirmation of his understanding of the global situation, thus justifying his engagement. Conversely, though, Schellenberg was too much of a company man and too focused on his career to move against Himmler's wishes. He also knew – and had experienced it on occasion, for example during the Luther affair when Karl Wolff's objections allegedly derailed his plans – that Himmler could change his mind quickly, most notably when Hitler announced his displeasure or when Himmler believed or was persuaded that Hitler might be displeased. Schellenberg was therefore cautious in his dealings with Himmler, waiting for the most opportune moment. Lastly, and contrary to what Hohenlohe had heard Dulles say, Allied policies regarding Germany and the demand for unconditional surrender to all the Allies were, by fall 1943, locked in place. Johnson's reprimand of Hewitt and the ensuing exchange with Great Britain – and seemingly the Soviet Union as well – only support this basic fact. The anti-Hitler alliance was not without friction and in that sense Schellenberg's intelligence assessments were on target, but he seriously overestimated Germany's opportunities. Rather the opposite was true, as the State Department's reactions to Hewitt's initiative indicate: there was no inclination to threaten the at times fragile alliance for low-level contacts of doubtful pedigree. Himmler might have presented an alternative to Hitler, but not by much. And at least at their highest levels, the Western Allies were aware of the murderous scope of Himmler's universe;

---

[32] Breitman, "Deal," 426, 424.   [33] Final Report.

the Soviets could witness it on their soil.[34] Even though the anti-Hitler alliance was an uneasy one, its break-up was not quite on the horizon.

What, then, was Schellenberg trying to achieve? After the war Schellenberg rendered, in teleological fashion, one consistent story: from late summer 1942 onwards, he had focused all his energy, considerable talents, and many contacts on his efforts to secure a separate peace. For example, Schellenberg discussed in this context a meeting with the head of the Swiss Intelligence Service, Roger Masson, in December 1942, during which he claimed to have broached the issue of a separate peace and gained Masson's agreement.[35] Aside from apparently misdating the meeting with Masson, Schellenberg dissembled about the focus of these meetings: the Swiss' well-founded fear of a German invasion. Schellenberg might have hoped that his contacts in Switzerland would eventually help him establish contacts to the West and to gain information about Allied plans from Masson. It is worth noting that the Americans were not enthused about this "perilously close" connection, as they feared information leakage.[36] Schellenberg's personal representative in Switzerland, Eggen, was more candid in his assessment of Schellenberg's motives:

Schellenberg created, as far as I know, the connection to the Swiss General Staff and to the head of the Swiss Intelligence Service in collaboration with Heydrich and later with Himmler and Kaltenbrunner. It was later also used to bring the office of Admiral Canaris [. . .] into Office VI of the Reichssicherheitshauptamt and replace Canaris.

But upstaging the Abwehr was not all. As discussed above, Schellenberg also planned to use "the Swiss connections [. . .] to enable peace negotiations with the Allies and to appear as a strong contender to the Foreign Ministry (that is Ribbentrop) and, if possible, to replace him with a man to the liking of the Reichsführer-SS."[37] In other words, Schellenberg had

---

[34] See: Richard Breitman, *Official Secrets: What the Nazis Planned, What the British and Americans Knew* (New York: Hill and Wang, 1998).

[35] Final Report. Authoritatively on these contacts: Pierre-Th. Braunschweig, *Geheimer Draht nach Berlin: Die Nachrichtenlinie Masson-Schellenberg und der Schweizerische Nachrichtendienst im Zweiten Weltkrieg* (Zurich: Verlag Neue Züricher Zeitung, 1989).

[36] Braunschweig, *Draht*, 205–230; Doerries, *Intelligence Chief*, 56–70. Eggen's recently declassified CIA files suggest a Schellenberg–Masson meeting in spring 1942 and November and December 1943. First Detailed Interrogation Report on Sturmbannführer Hans Wilhelm Eggen, December 1, 1945, NA, RG 263, Entry ZZ-16, Box 13, File: Eggen, Hans Wilhelm. Cable from Bern, Switzerland March 15, 1944/June 21, 1955, NA, RG 263, Entry ZZ-18, Box 112, File: Schellenberg, Walter, vol. 1, 1 of 2.

[37] Cited in Braunschweig, *Draht*, 303. The translation is mine. First Detailed Interrogation Report on Sturmbannführer Hans Wilhelm Eggen, December 1, 1945, NA, RG 263, Entry ZZ-16, Box 13, File: Eggen, Hans Wilhelm.

several reasons for forging contacts with members of the Swiss Intelligence Service, while his Swiss counterparts – correctly, as Schellenberg delivered on occasion – deemed him "sufficiently powerful to be able to effect [sic] something." His eagerness for professional advancement, whether in foreign intelligence or foreign policy, was the most important among Schellenberg's reasons; the constant rumors in Office VI that he had a special representative of high standing in Switzerland served this purpose well.[38] Potential lines to the Western Allies seem to have been a positive side effect of Schellenberg's Swiss dealings. After the war, and in tune with his defense strategies, Schellenberg provided one single and seemingly unimpeachable purpose for all his foreign contacts, even though they were undertaken initially for a different reasons at various times.

Schellenberg was not only interested in contact with Western Allies, even if that was his narrative focus after the war. In 1943, Schellenberg also tried to establish contacts with the Soviet Union via Stockholm, and there are indications that he attempted the same through Japanese intermediaries in Switzerland in late summer or fall 1944.[39] Schellenberg's anti-Soviet attitudes were well known; he made many a derogatory comment about German officials whom he suspected of having dealings with the Soviet Union. He clearly favored the so-called Western solution: an agreement with the West and joint German–Western efforts against the Soviet Union. The fear of Bolshevism and Soviet control of Europe was one ideological tenet Nazi Germany and the Western powers had in common; Schellenberg planned to capitalize on it. Not surprisingly, Schellenberg stated after the war that he had planned to use his Soviet soundings to scare up attention in the West.[40] However, Schellenberg's intelligence reports, in particular the Auslandsmeldungen, Foreign Reports, bring to the fore another explanation for Schellenberg's activities in fall 1943, when he put considerable effort into contacting any

[38] Schellenberg's Schweizer und Schweden-Verbindung, no date, NA, RG 263, Entry ZZ-18, Box 54, File: Hoettl, Wilhelm, vol. 3, 1 of 2.
[39] Braunschweig, *Draht*, 303 note 52. Braunschweig states that Schellenberg was dealing with Raoul Wallenberg, the young Swedish diplomat who was later posted to Budapest where he saved many Hungarian Jews, but it appears more likely that Schellenberg was dealing yet again with Jacob Wallenberg, Raoul Wallenberg's banker uncle. Chief, Munich Operations Group to Chief [redacted], Chief [redacted], chief of Base, Frankfurt Attn: [redacted], Chief of Station, Germany, Subject: German Intelligence-Soviet Contacts, WW II, September 10, 1962, NA, RG 263, Entry ZZ-16, Box 10, File: Daufeldt, Hans. See also the documents on Nace Sakai in Eggen's CIA file; Sakai was "to explore the possibilities of establishing direct and confidential contacts with the staff of President Roosevelt and Premier Stalin." NA, RG 263, Entry ZZ-16, Box 13, File: Eggen, Hans Wilhelm.
[40] Braunschweig, *Draht*, 303 notes 51; 53.

member of the anti-Hitler alliance: his preferred option was not to sue for a separate peace but to exacerbate existing rifts and eventually topple the anti-Hitler alliance entirely. Had he succeeded, he would have become the man who staved off defeat for Nazi Germany. A separate peace seems to have been the proverbial Plan B.

After the flurry of activities in the fall of 1943, Schellenberg's peace efforts, to use loosely the term, lay dormant for almost a year.[41] 1944 was a busy year for Schellenberg; the absorption of the Abwehr took up much of his time and the final, frontal assault on Ribbentrop and his office also fell into that year. By the fall of 1944, Schellenberg was at it again, but the basic preconditions had changed. Schellenberg's plan to negotiate from a position of strength, feasible in 1942 – if he, indeed, had it then – was already dubious when Schellenberg met Hewitt a year later. US and British forces were slowly making their way up the Italian peninsula and the political situation had changed as well: Allied postwar policies had been announced and repeated. No "engraved invitations" for peace negotiations would be sent out to German officials anytime soon.[42] By the fall of 1944, Germany's situation had gone from bad to worse. The Italian front was north of Florence and Pisa. American and British troops, having landed in Normandy in June, had liberated France. The Red Army had crossed the Vistula and was poised to enter East Prussia.[43] Yet Germany's defeat was not a forgone conclusion, and its leaders were not continuing the war for lack of a better option or out of inertia. Hitler and his supporters were convinced that the war could still be won even after the "mini-blitz" against Great Britain had failed: a new generation of U-boats, being developed and tested in the Baltic Sea, was to enable Germany to interrupt Allied supply lines.[44] In addition, Germany was mobilizing its last reserves. Sufficient for but one major offensive, they were then used in the Battle of the Bulge, which began in mid-December 1944 and reminded the Western Allies – especially the United States – that the war was far from over.[45] The conviction that

---

[41] There is, however, the Modelhut Mission in late 1943 and early 1944. The initiative seems to have come from Coco Chanel, who already had Abwehr contacts. Hal Vaughan, *Sleeping with the Enemy: Coco Chanel's Secret War* (New York: Alfred A. Knopf, 2011), chapter 10.

[42] Breitman, "Deal," 419.

[43] Gerhard L. Weinberg in *A World at Arms: A Global History of World War II* (Oxford: Oxford University Press, 1994), 667–721.

[44] Gerhard L. Weinberg, "German Plans for Victory, 1944–1945," in *Germany, Hitler, and World War II: Essays in Modern German and World History* (Oxford: Oxford University Press, 1995), 284–285.

[45] The Battle of the Bulge was directed mainly against American forces. German preconceptions, palpable in the Auslandsmeldungen and the Egmont Reports, held that the American home front was weak and might crack under the impact of a major defeat.

the war could still be won was by not restricted to Germany's political leadership and ideological die-hards; the Officers' Plot of July 20, 1944 indicated that Germany's military leadership was, at best, divided on this matter. Most plotters came from Germany's highest military echelons – which frequently coincided with Germany's aristocracy – and they and their families paid grievously for the attempt on Hitler's life.[46] However, once the coup failed, it became evident that most military leaders did not share the conspirators' view that Germany would be better off without Hitler and that the war was lost, for they decided to obey the orders emanating from Hitler's headquarters.[47] Over the years, there has been speculation about the extent of Himmler's advance knowledge of the plot and whether he planned to join the conspirators after a successful coup. No evidence to connect Himmler unambiguously to the resistance exists, but these speculations illuminate the enigma that was Himmler. For all his devotion to Hitler, Himmler was a more realistic and more pragmatic man than his Führer.[48] This did not include active participation in Hitler's demise; benefiting from it, however, would have been acceptable. On the other hand, Himmler's reluctance to act against Hitler even extended to the Führer's implied wishes. Schellenberg, for his own reasons, described Himmler's vacillating behavior in much detail: able to understand and appreciate the deteriorating military situation, Himmler would perpetually shrink away from taking decisive steps against Hitler.[49] Much had changed for Schellenberg and his alleged peace efforts, but his patron Himmler remained the same.

In the summer and fall of 1944 contacts between high-ranking members of the RSHA, apparently tacitly backed by Himmler, and representatives of the West became a widespread phenomenon, even if the

The German offensive was directed at the port city of Antwerp, which, according to Weinberg, confirms Hitler's strategy to hold on to the major port cities for the renewed naval campaign. Weinberg, "German Plans," 285.

[46] Peter Hoffmann, *The History of the German Resistance, 1933–1945*, trans. Richard Barry (Cambridge, MA: MIT Press, 1977). The investigation of the plot fell to Kaltenbrunner and Müller; they performed ruthlessly. Black, *Kaltenbrunner*, 160–167.

[47] Weinberg, "German Plans," 283.

[48] Hedwig Maier, "Die SS und der 20.Juli 1944," *VfZ* 14 (1966), 299–316. Höhne, *Orden*, 448–498, devotes a chapter to these contacts, constructing a close collaboration between the SS and the resistance that affords Schellenberg an important role. Schellenberg's own representation of his contacts with the German resistance is curious. Postwar, he suggested that he had frequent contacts with resistance members and was considered for government positions. In his memoirs, available to a wider readership including actual surviving resistance members, Schellenberg's description of these contacts is much more muted, once more an indicator of his opportunistic relationship to the concepts of truth, half-truth, and lies. Final Report; Schellenberg, *Labyrinth*; Breitman, "Deal," 418.

[49] This is a constant theme in all of Schellenberg's writings and statements about Himmler. For its most prominent display: Autobiography/Sweden.

choreography had changed.[50] Instead of broaching the issue of a separate peace right away, as Schellenberg had done with Hewitt, initial contacts centered on the release of Jews whom German negotiators perceived as bargaining chips or their entry fee into negotiations. The "blood-for-truck" negotiations during what has been termed the Hungarian Holocaust is the best-known incident of this sort. In March 1944, German troops entered Hungary. Miklos Horthy remained the country's regent, but the German presence ensured that his new government – past incarnations had been intransigent and dabbled with contacts to the West – would do the Germans' bidding. The existence of a large Jewish community of around 800,000 people was a particular thorn in the side of the planners and executioners of the Holocaust. Since 1938, the Hungarian Jews had experienced a constantly worsening situation, but Horthy had not allowed for their wholesale deportations to the extermination camps. This changed within weeks of the German take-over: SS-Brigadeführer Edmund Veesenmeyer, reporting primarily to Ribbentrop but close to Himmler as well, was installed as the Plenipotentiary for Hungary and Obergruppenführer Otto Winckelmann, answering directly to Himmler, served as the Highest SS and Police Leader (HSSPF). With them arrived a number of SS men, including Adolf Eichmann, who had one goal: to deport to their deaths in Auschwitz as quickly as possible all Hungarian Jews. Starting in the outlying provinces and initially sparing the approximately 200,000 Jews living in Budapest, Eichmann and his helpers – relying on the assistance of the Hungarian state – deported around 440,000 people between mid-May and July 7, 1944. On that day, Horthy, under increasing pressure from abroad and reacting to the unstable domestic situation, halted the deportations. In April or May 1944, with the deportations getting underway, Eichmann made a striking offer: he would spare the Hungarian Jews if the Western Allies were to deliver to Germany ten thousand trucks and other goods needed. In an acerbic nod to the anti-Hitler alliance, he promised that these supplies would only be used against the Soviet Union.[51]

There has been a lively debate about Eichmann's proposal for years. Did it present a real chance to save Jews, which was thwarted by the

---

[50] Richard Breitman and Shlomo Aronson, "The End of the 'Final Solution'?: Nazi Plans to Ransom Jews in 1944," *Central European History* 25 (1993), 177–203; Meredith Hindley, "Negotiating the Boundaries of Unconditional Surrender: The War Refugee Board in Sweden and Nazi Proposals to Ransom Jews, 1944–1945," *Holocaust and Genocide Studies* 10 (1996), 52–77. For general overviews: Yehuda Bauer, *Jews for Sale? Nazi–Jewish Negotiations* (New Haven: Yale University Press, 1995); Shlomo Aronson, *Hitler, the Allies, and the Jews* (Cambridge: Cambridge University Press, 2004).

[51] The basic terms of the deal are covered in any number of publications; for example: Breitman and Aronson, "End," 177–203.

Western Allies unwilling to negotiate with Nazi officials and not that interested in saving Jews, as Bauer suggests? Was it a German attempt to jump-start peace negotiations with the West? Was it an attempt to throw a monkey wrench into inter-Allied cooperation? And with whom did the offer originate and who approved of it on the German side? As Breitman shows, newly declassified documents support the reading that the Eichmann offer was a cover for a German attempt to open lines of negotiations to the Western Allies.[52] The idea to stave off or delay the deportations, however, apparently originated in the Hungarian Jewish community; after all, there was a decent possibility that the war might be drawing to a close. Through various bribed SS intermediaries, Rudolf Kasztner, as a representative of the Hungarian Jews, eventually made contact and then met with Eichmann.[53] During this meeting, Eichmann proposed the so-called trucks for blood deal; he then used Joel Brand, "a Hungarian Jewish activist," to convey the offer to Western representative in Istanbul. With Brand traveled a certain Bandi Grosz, a smuggler with contacts to various intelligence services: the Abwehr, when it still existed as an independent entity; later Office VI; but also the Hungarian intelligence service; and the US network "Dogwood," run out of Istanbul. His was the real mission: Otto Klages, representing Office VI, and other SD men had given Grosz the task to make contact with Western representatives – either through his Zionist or US intelligence connections – and arrange for a meeting between SD officials and British and US representatives. Grosz was a known entity to the Allies but, against German expectations, this was a strike against him: by June, the OSS had identified him as an "unscrupulous double-agent" and all around bad news.[54] The mission failed, and Brand and Grosz eventually found themselves in British custody in Cairo. Official, high-level negotiations – about the fate of the Hungarian Jews or about an end to the war – were not on the horizon.

It is unclear who masterminded either the Brand or the Grosz mission on the German or how they related to each other. It is unlikely that Eichmann took it upon himself to make such a far-reaching offer or that other local SD officials acted on their own recognizance. Logic and structure of the RSHA bureaucracy suggest that Himmler must have

---

[52] Richard Breitman, "Other Responses to the Holocaust," in Richard Breitman et al., eds., *U.S. Intelligence and the Nazis* (Washington, DC: National Trust Fund for the Nazi War Crimes and Japanese Imperial Government Records Interagency Working Group, 2004), 54–57.
[53] Eichmann took several million pengoes in advance of the negotiations as well; Breitman, "Responses," 54.
[54] Breitman, "Responses," 49–53, 55.

given at least his tacit approval. Indeed, Aronson and Breitman read the Hungarian activities as Himmler's attempt at "moving Hitler toward a more realistic course, not at overthrowing him" and as such indicative of Himmler's more pessimistic outlook on the development of the war.[55] Recently, Breitman unearthed an intriguing document by the German deserter Karl Marcus who, in British interrogations, claimed that the Brand mission was "approved by Schellenberg himself, and that its main purpose was to split the alliance against Germany." Breitman suggests that Eichmann would have gone along to sow dissension among the Allies, happily overlooking the fact that Schellenberg had no jurisdiction over Jewish matters.[56] This is the only document that directly connects Schellenberg to the blood-for-trucks deal, and the fact that Schellenberg does not mention any involvement in it or subsequent negotiations in Hungary in postwar testimonies suggests that he was not involved in any substantial fashion. After all, Schellenberg could have spun this as yet another attempt to act as a humanitarian and to reach an agreement with the West – only to be thwarted by the Allies yet again.

Schellenberg's personal involvement or this plan's endgame aside, its basic hope was to open a line to the Western Allies, especially to the United States. This approach was rooted steadfastly in Nazi ideology and its anti-Semitic tenet that the United States was firmly in the thrall of a world Jewish conspiracy that determined the country's policies. Therefore, the thinking went, the United States could be swayed into a negotiated peace by the promise to save Jews. This was another variant of Schellenberg's assessment of Hewitt and his familial and political connections, which had excited him a year prior. And as with these contacts, the question remains whether their ultimate goal was a separate peace or, as the interrogation of Marcus intimates, the break-up of the anti-Hitler alliance. Forging contact with the Western Allies, especially in Hungary, indubitably meant sowing distrust in a coalition that was experiencing strain – over the issue of Poland and its political future. It is therefore likely that the break-up of the anti-Hitler coalition was Schellenberg's ultimate goal, and his foreign intelligence assessments and foreign policy counsel to Himmler actively fostered an understanding that allowed the latter to conclude that a break-up of the anti-Hitler alliance was still within reach or that it would be possible to modify the conditions for a German surrender. The Egmont Reports of fall 1944, allegedly unvarnished and prepared to wean Hitler off Ribbentrop's assessments or to induce Himmler to break with Hitler, left open the possibility of reaching a negotiated peace with the Western Allies, inter-allied agreements notwithstanding.

[55] Breitman and Aronson, "End," 203.   [56] Breitman, "Responses," 57.

Schellenberg made liberal use of documents that suggested that the Americans were willing to "modify" the policy of unconditional surrender; were not interested in "fighting for every German village;" and were willing to alter their approach as soon as political changes in Germany were on the horizon.[57] Other information Office VI received fed into Schellenberg's narrative. A report of VI D in November 1944 indicated, for example, that Dulles was inclined to negotiate and had counseled Roosevelt accordingly. The report suggested that the "moral and military German resistance" against the Soviets – the word choice alone speaks volumes about German self-perception, as it construes Germany as the victim of Soviet aggression – had impressed the Americans.[58] The Americans noted after the war that Schellenberg "failed to see these contacts in their right perspective, viz against the backdrop of Germany's inevitable military defeat" and "followed this particular tack with [. . .] much fanatical zeal (*Verbissenheit*)."[59] Schellenberg clearly decided to see the perspective that worked best for him. He believed it possible to break free of the demand for unconditional surrender, thereby effectively destroying the anti-Hitler alliance. And he was convinced that one way of achieving this goal would be to keep up the fighting, especially on the Eastern Front, as it impressed the Americans. He counseled Himmler accordingly.[60]

By late fall 1944 Schellenberg was personally back to his efforts to make contact with the West. Having given up his former strategy of forging contacts with Western political representatives, he instead took a page from the Hungarian playbook of the preceding summer: "humanitarian concerns" were to lead the way. This was easier said than done. As the head of the political intelligence service and foreign minister in waiting, Schellenberg was at a distinct disadvantage: He had no high-level agents to exchange and despite his closeness to Himmler, Schellenberg's involvement with the Holocaust had been less "hands-on" than that of many of his peers. He held no collateral, no lives to trade. But without a change in his approach, Schellenberg would not be able to break free from what must have been an utterly frustrating cycle for this ambitious man: without an endorsed offer by Himmler, he was unable to garner interest among Western representatives. Conversely, without Western interest, or a *fait accompli*, as Schellenberg phrased it, he was

---

[57] Eidesstattliche Erklärung, Abschrift von Abschrift, Walter Schellenberg, February 10, 1948, IfZ, ZS 291/VII.

[58] CdS, VI D, Betr. Amerikanische Haltung gegenüber Deutschland, November 4, 1944, USHMM, 10.016 M, 1119.

[59] Saint, Washington to Saint, London, Transmittal of Interrogation Report, October 3, 1945, NA, RG 263, CIA Name Files (Reference Collection), Box 45, Schellenberg, vol. 1.

[60] Final Report.

not able to gain a commitment from Himmler.[61] Schellenberg needed to find "humanitarian questions" to which he could attend.

Various Western organizations working on relief programs for POWs and concentration camp inmates were active across Europe in late 1944. This was to some extent an aftereffect of the Brand/Grosz mission. The Western Allies had publicly rejected the "trucks for blood" deal, but the US War Refugee Board was willing to go along with negotiations between Jewish representatives, Americans or of other nationalities, and German officials to save Jews and other victims of Nazism – and be it by protracted negotiations. A number of different organizations and individuals, willing to establish and to maintain contacts with any German who seemed suited for these talks and appeared prepared and able to deliver, jumped into the fray as well.[62] They clearly understood the multiple German desires for such contacts – from the opportunity to engender eventual peace soundings to attempts to reduce individual culpability to a mixture of several reasons, now couched in the language of humanitarianism – and were eager to capitalize on them. In the coming months, Schellenberg seized every chance to establish contacts with the West through these humanitarian organizations. Aside from being possible conduits to the West, they also held out the possibility for Schellenberg to hone an international identity distinct from his official one as the head of Germany's political foreign intelligence service; these contacts could help him to become a diplomat or a humanitarian or, in the best of all worlds, both.

Just such an opportunity presented itself in October and November 1944. The former federal president of Switzerland, Jean Marie Musy, visited Germany.[63] His reputation tarnished by earlier association with the Nazis both in Germany and in Switzerland, Musy renewed his prewar contact with Himmler.[64] Acting on behalf of Agudath Israel and the

---

[61] In December 1943, Himmler unexpectedly approached Schellenberg and inquired whether he could reconnect with Hewitt, who had long since left Sweden. Translation of Statement by Schellenberg (Nr. 21), August 6, 1945, NA, RG 226, Entry 125 A, Box 2, Folder 21. Breitman links Himmler's change of mind to a conference with Hitler in December 1943, during which possible contacts with the British might have been a topic; Breitman, "Deal," 421. Surely, Schellenberg regarded this as another mandate of Himmler's to go forward with his peace soundings. On the need for a *fait accompli*: Final Report.

[62] Breitman, "Responses," 57.

[63] For the Musy episode, see Schellenberg, *Labyrinth*, 378–383; Final Report. On Musy and the genesis of the meeting with Himmler from Musy's viewpoint: John Mendelsohn, ed., *The Holocaust: Selected Documents in Eighteen Volumes, Vol. 16, Rescue to Switzerland: The Musy and the Saly Mayer Affairs* (New York: Garland Publishing, 1982); Doerries, *Intelligence Chief*, 172–186.

[64] Schellenberg claimed that it took him weeks to coax Himmler into a meeting with Musy. The truth was much simpler: Musy simply wrote Himmler and asked for a meeting.

Union of Orthodox Rabbis in the United States and accompanied by his son, Benoit Musy, he was intent on rescuing Jews. He also carried with him a list of individuals imprisoned in Germany whose release he wanted to achieve. The first meeting between Himmler and Musy took place in near Breslau in October 1944 and he achieved the release of the individuals on his list. Subsequently, Musy asked Himmler to release all inmates of the women's camp Ravensbrück, most of them French, and suggested that all Jews interned in Germany "for religious reasons" should be transported to Switzerland; the Swiss government, he explained, would eventually send them to the United States. Himmler gave the impression of being interested in a deal, but – echoing the Hungarian negotiations of the preceding summer – asked for ransom: "tractors and trucks," according to Musy; "tractors, cars, medicine, and other things of which we were badly in need," according to Schellenberg.[65] Musy cautioned that it would be difficult to barter war materiel and "emphasized that Himmler should not act like a meat salesmen, [and] he should be satisfied with a sensible amount of foreign currency," a statement at odds with Musy's impression that "the *Reichsführer* SS either was or acted as of he were tired 'of the entire question . . . they could have them all'."[66] Ultimately, Himmler agreed to Musy's proposal but, insisting that he preferred material compensation, asked his Swiss contact to explore this possibility. Himmler clearly wanted to have insurance in case his apparent readiness to release Jews was questioned; after all, Hitler had earlier indicated his willingness to exchange some Jews for war materiel. Himmler's promise to release immediately of a number of prominent Jewish and French individuals identified by Musy was, on the other hand, likely a show of good faith and supreme power. Its execution, as well as the exploration of the discussed release of women from Ravensbrück, fell to Schellenberg, who charged his assistant Franz Göring with this matter.[67]

Schellenberg, *Labyrinth*, 378; Testimony of Jean Mary Musy, October 26, 1945, in *Rescue to Switzerland*, Document 2.

[65] It is not clear whether Schellenberg was in the room during the initial meeting, even though he gave that impression. Final Report; Schellenberg, *Labyrinth*, 378; Testimony of Jean Mary Musy, October 26, 1945, in *Rescue to Switzerland*, Document 2; Doerries, *Intelligence Chief*, 175.

[66] Affidavit, Jean-Marie Musy, May 8, 1948, NA, RG 238, M 897, Reel 114, Frame 1069 [hereafter: Affidavit Jean-Marie Musy]; Doerries, *Intelligence Chief*, 176.

[67] As Doerries points out, Musy asked for the release of a number of individuals – such as the family of the French General Henri Honoré Giraud, the Polish General Bor [Tadeusz Komorowski], Edouard Herriot, and Paul Reynaud. In the case of the Giraud family, the initial request might have come from General Masson and thus taken particular import for Schellenberg. Doerries, *Intelligence Chief*, 154–155, 175, 177. Schellenberg claimed that he managed to improve the prisoners' living conditions substantially. The younger Musy indicated that a few people, mostly Frenchmen, were released before January

There is little indication that Schellenberg made these efforts his top priority, but the named individuals, held by the Gestapo, were freed.

Musy returned to Switzerland for negotiations on the deal's details, informing Himmler about his progress on November 18, 1944. He also suggested meeting immediately. Himmler, by now also the commander in chief of Army Group Upper Rhine, which Peter Black reads as a renewal of Himmler's loyalty to Hitler, took his time responding.[68] Public relations benefits, cash rewards, or the chance of opening lines to the West notwithstanding, the release of Jews was not among Himmler's priorities. While Himmler let Musy cool his heels, the Swiss' main contact in Germany was Schellenberg. And if the latter is to be believed, the two men used the interim period to settle "the minutest details of the arrangement."[69] Almost two months to the day after Musy's letter, Himmler agreed to meet again.

This meeting took place at Wildbad in the Black Forest in January 1945. Schellenberg's postwar account describes a straightforward transaction: twelve hundred Jews would be transported to Switzerland on "first-class trains" every fortnight. In exchange, the Jewish organizations with which Musy worked would "give active support in solving the Jewish problem according to Himmler's suggestions," worldwide 'anti-German' propaganda would cease, and ransom would be tendered – not in goods but in money. Musy was to serve as the trustee of the ransom account.[70] The actual meeting was more complicated. Himmler opened it by questioning Musy's credentials. Another one of Himmler's subordinates, Obersturmbannführer Kurt Becher, was in contact with Saly Mayer, a Swiss businessman who acted on behalf of the American Jewish

---

1945. Schellenberg, *Labyrinth*, 378; Affidavit, Benoit Musy, May 8, 1948, NA, RG 238, M 897, Reel 114, Frame 1075 [hereafter: Affidavit Benoit Musy]. Schellenberg's assistant Franz Göring stated that Schellenberg ordered him to locate certain Jews whose release Himmler had promised to Musy in October 1944 on January 22, 1945. Eidesstattliche Erklärung, Franz Göring, February 24, 1948, NA, RG 238, M 897, Reel 114, Frame 1016 [hereafter: Erklärung Göring]. Doerries emphasizes that Göring "fearlessly went into concentration camps." Göring was indubitably fulfilling a difficult and gruesome mission for his boss; however, Göring was part of the system – it was not that a camp commander would have or could have kept him for bad behavior. He did, after all, represent Walter Schellenberg.

[68] Musy to Himmler, November 18, 1944, NA, RG 242, T-175, Reel 118, Frame 2643521–2643523; Black, *Kaltenbrunner*, 229.

[69] Final Report; Affidavit, Jean-Marie Musy, May 8, 1948, NA, RG 238, M 897, Reel 114, Frame 1070.

[70] The date of this meeting is not clear. Schellenberg wrote in his memoirs that it took place on January 12, 1945; Musy did not address the issue and Himmler's files contain a written summary, suggesting that it took place on January 15, 1945. Schellenberg, *Labyrinth*, 379; Niederschrift, 18.1.1945, NA, RG 242, T-175, Reel 118, Frame 2643515–2643516; Further Testimony of Jean Marie Musy, October 29, 1945 in *Rescue to Switzerland*; Affidavit Jean-Marie Musy.

Joint Distribution Committee and had the support of Roswell McClelland, the representative of the War Refugee Board; these contacts had grown out of the Hungarian negotiations in summer 1944. Both Musy and Mayer claimed that their respective organizations had excellent contacts within the US administration, and Himmler wanted to get to the bottom of the matter. Which of the two Jewish organizations had the most influence? Or, in Himmler's words: "Is it the Rabbinical Jew or is it the Jiont [sic]." Himmler's primary interest was not the relief mission but establishing contact with the West, and if that meant dealing with members of the "Jewish World Conspiracy," he at least wanted to ensure that he picked its most influential representative.

Himmler then elaborated on the fate of the Jews. He told Musy that they had been deployed for heavy work in the preceding years; mortality had been high. Since the negotiations had commenced, Himmler stated, Jews were being used, like Germans, for regular, war-related work. There is little need to note that this is a lie, but it is intriguing to see Himmler spin a story for the benefit of negotiations with Musy. Himmler intimated that he would be glad to let the Jews leave, but only if they were completely removed from the German sphere of influence. Not to impose Germany's problem on kindred spirits, Himmler expected assurances that Jews would never be allowed to immigrate to Palestine; "we will not stand for such an indecency [*Unanständigkeit*], to send to these poor people [Arabs], tortured by the Jews, additional Jews."[71] Lastly, Himmler stressed again that he expected goods: "tractors, trucks, and machine tools." Himmler's fixation on war materiel clearly took into account Germany's strained war economy, but it also protected him from charges of defeatism or even treason. While personally negotiating with representatives of "the Jews," Himmler remained firmly within the guidelines established by Hitler and his own ideological comfort zone.

Himmler was in a combative mood during this meeting. Humanitarian concerns were window dressing and the promised mass release of Jews – if envisioned at all – was an entryway into bigger issues and not his primary concern. Even if Himmler's memorandum for the files took a more swaggering tone than the meeting warranted, his interaction with Musy were confrontational. He wanted it to be understood that he was not a pushover when it came to a central tenet of Nazi Germany's policy and ideology, and he strove to ensure that his ultimate goal, establishing contact with the US government, would be achieved. He needed to be absolutely certain that he would enter negotiations with the part of the "Jewish World Conspiracy" that had the best contacts in Washington and

---

[71] Niederschrift, 18.1.1945, NA, RG 242, T-175, R 118, Frame 2643515–2643516.

thus asked Musy to provide written proof from the Americans that his organization was more prominent than Saly Mayer's. A true ideologue, Himmler believed himself in possession of a commodity sought after by Washingtonian officials – Jews – and his memorandum indicated that Musy agreed: "He [Musy] stressed several times that the Jewish question is a side issue [*Nebensache*], because the main point would be to initiate a greater development through this."[72] Both men regarded these humanitarian negotiations as the insignificant launching pad for altogether different negotiations. McClelland came to a similar conclusion: "Himmler must be interested in negotiating for something more important [...] than the release of Jews....Musy is in even closer contact with Schellenberg than with Himmler and . . . Schellenberg is very willing to assist in questions such as the Jewish [one] . . .".[73] Schellenberg ordered his assistant Franz Göring, already working to secure the release of the individuals whom Musy had requested in October, to organize the transports negotiated during the second meeting. Göring went to Theresienstadt (Terezín) and, despite some obstacles, got a train on its way to Switzerland. It arrived there on February 7, 1945 with Göring "announcing: 'In the name of the Reichsleiter Himmler you are now free'." A second group of people was to come from the Bergen-Belsen camp.[74] This transport never materialized, as Kaltenbrunner interceded.

   The rivalry between Kaltenbrunner and Schellenberg had become increasingly intense, especially when it came to their respective access to and influence over Himmler. The two men, whose official relationship was not one of equals since, strictly speaking, Schellenberg answered to Kaltenbrunner, agreed on little short of their distaste of Ribbentrop. Both believed themselves able to do better than the Foreign Minister. And both men disliked any person coming between them and Himmler. Then, they tended to unite, only to resume their infighting once they had disposed of the interloper. In November 1944, Kaltenbrunner brought to Hitler's attention Himmler's indirect contacts, via Kurt Becher, to Rudolf Kasztner and Saly Mayer. Kaltenbrunner had known about them since

---

[72] Niederschrift, 18.1.1945, NA, RG 242, T-175, R 118, Frame 2643515–2643516; Doerries, *Intelligence Chief*, 181. Doerries evaluates Musy's motivations differently; he does, however, not use this memorandum by Himmler.

[73] Breitman, "Nazi Espionage," 111–112.

[74] Erklärung Göring; I am following the Erklärung here; the "diary" is largely identical. Initially, not many volunteers could be found, for most inmates assumed that they would be transported to their deaths. Doerries, *Intelligence Chief*, 183. For Bergen-Belsen; Alexandra-Eileen Wenck, *Zwischen Menschenhandel und "Endlösung": Das Konzentrationslager Bergen-Belsen* (Paderborn: Schöningh, 2000). On last-ditch rescue efforts, with particular focus on Kersten's alleged role, see 362–371. Wenck's misdates the meeting between Himmler and Musy; it took Schellenberg a week, and not a day, to set Franz Göring's activities in motion; it was a *Nebensache*.

the late summer but had not seen the need to alert Hitler eventually, however, the interloper Becher became too much to bear. Yet Hitler's reaction was not what Kaltenbrunner expected: he did not hold these contacts against Himmler. By focusing on ransom in-kind, Himmler had chosen the proper path to stay clear of Hitler's anger. Schellenberg was presumably not thrilled by Becher's negotiations either: he had no part in them, they later impacted the negotiations with Musy, in which he had invested much time and effort, and they made a sham of his privileged role as Himmler's foreign policy advisor. But Schellenberg was apparently less perturbed than Kaltenbrunner by these negotiations or the possible release of a few people, whereas Kaltenbrunner smarted about it and the pending release of another thousand whom he regarded as "dangerous enemies" of the Reich. As Black notes, "Kaltenbrunner's ideological make-up was not as subtly flexible as that of Himmler."[75] Schellenberg might well have been the most flexible of the three.

The relationship between Schellenberg and Kaltenbrunner kept deteriorating and the self-ascribed humanitarians of the RSHA remained busy with internecine battles for Himmler's and Hitler's attention and their personal advancement. Kaltenbrunner apparently decided to "sabotage any peace initiatives coming from Himmler that did not provide him with a major protected role." The Musy talks fell into this category. Excluded from them and propelled by "hatred and jealousy" of Schellenberg as well, Kaltenbrunner interfered with the planned release of Jews in January 1945. However, Schellenberg was not simply a victim of Kaltenbrunner's machinations; a few months earlier, Schellenberg might have been the reason that a similar scheme, set into motion by Kaltenbrunner in Sweden, had failed.[76] Shortly after the second meeting between Himmler and Musy, Kaltenbrunner struck gold in his efforts to undermine Schellenberg and – by default – Himmler. Kaltenbrunner got hold of a message from Charles de Gaulle's Spanish intelligence center that indicated that Himmler and Musy had also negotiated asylum for "250 Nazi leaders." He informed Hitler who subsequently threatened with execution "any German who helped a Jew, or a British, or an American prisoner to escape." Franz Göring's affidavit suggests a more underhanded course of events: Kaltenbrunner ordered Becher to have Saly Meyer discredit the Musy negotiations in the press. Soon after the arrival of the first transport of Jews in Switzerland, press reports began to link it to asylum negotiations for "200 leading Nazis in Switzerland."

---

[75] Black, *Kaltenbrunner*, 228. No record of Schellenberg's attitude toward the Becher negotiations exists.
[76] Black, *Kaltenbrunner*, 228–230.

Through Mayer and Becher, Kaltenbrunner received these reports quickly and presented them to Hitler who issued his dictum.[77] Göring's affidavit contains some inconsistencies in terms of timing and collaboration – it described Becher doing Kaltenbrunner's bidding a few weeks after Kaltenbrunner had used Becher's activities as the proverbial Exhibit A with Hitler – and might have well been the parting shot of a former competitor. But even if the details remain murky, Kaltenbrunner indubitably played a leading role in scotching further dealings with Musy, and Hitler laid down the law. In this humanitarian competition – on which Schellenberg rested his hopes for opening a line to the West – Schellenberg and Musy came out in "second place:" Becher and Mayer had brought more than sixteen hundred Jews to Switzerland, and Becher had even managed to meet McClelland, the War Refugee Board's representative in Switzerland. The human cargo aboard the Schellenberg–Musy train, on the other hand, amounted to slightly more than twelve hundred people. And no US representative in Switzerland wanted to deal with Schellenberg.[78]

Despite his plans hitting a wall, Schellenberg maintained contact with the Musys, keeping options open. His confidant Franz Göring and the younger Musy managed to secure the release of additional individuals, but the broader release of Jews, now made difficult by Kaltenbrunner's intervention and Hitler's clear statement, remained a side issue to Schellenberg and Himmler.[79] The elder Musy, on the other hand, kept plodding away, apparently still hoping for a breakthrough. Breitman pronounces him "undeterred" and convinced that Himmler would come to a rescue agreement if offered exile somewhere. In conversations with US diplomats, Musy also raised the specter of chaos and Communism instead of a strong central government reigning in Germany. Schellenberg's dual strategy of humanitarian negotiations and fearmongering had not just "taken on an independent life" but found actual foreign champions. As late as the end of March 1945, Musy tried to arrange a personal meeting with Himmler, but to no avail.[80] Schellenberg was less coy about

[77] Schellenberg, *Labyrinth*, 379–380. This version is the commonly accepted one; Black, *Kaltenbrunner*, 229–230; Wenck, *Bergen-Belsen*, 366 note 118. In the Final Report, no mention is made of the asylum negotiations; Hitler's ban on further transports of Jews is linked exclusively to press reports; Final Report; Erklärung Göring.

[78] Breitman, "Nazi Espionage," 111–112.

[79] Schellenberg, *Labyrinth*, 380–382; Affidavit, Jean-Marie Musy; Affidavit, Benoit Musy. Schellenberg's and Musy's plan of a four-day truce to escort all prisoners through the lines, allegedly concocted in early April 1945, generally approved by Himmler, and decisively rejected by Kaltenbrunner, seems to belong in the realm of Schellenberg's fantasy. Erklärung Göring.

[80] Breitman, "Nazi Espionage," 112. Breitman refers to a document by McClelland in his private possession. For excerpts of seemingly the same document, dated two

getting together with Musy than the Reichsführer and a meeting between them in late March 1945 supposedly led to an order by Himmler not to "evacuate" the concentration camps – that is, not to send their inmates on death marches across the remaining German territories – but to allow for the approaching Allied forces to overtake the camps. This concession was tied to one condition: concentration camp guards were to be treated as Prisoners of War and not to be "shot on the spot." Himmler's alleged initial condition – that no black soldiers were to be used in the occupation of Germany – was rejected and in talks with McClelland, Musy claimed this as his achievement.[81] Himmler's order was not followed uniformly: some commandants "evacuated" their camps while others stayed put. Schellenberg – and men writing in his wake, such as Franz Göring – placed the blame for the failure to carry out Himmler's order at Kaltenbrunner's feet, but this straightforward explanation is problematic. After March 7, Kaltenbrunner found himself in an isolated spot in Austria and his impact muted.[82] However, blaming Kaltenbrunner served Schellenberg well: it absolved him from any responsibility for the failure to release the Jews, a release Himmler had promised Musy and whose execution had been assigned to Schellenberg while allowing him, in his guise as a humanitarian, to take credit for those who were freed.

The eager attempts to make contact with the West and to blame Kaltenbrunner for any problem were only part of Schellenberg's activities in late 1944 and early 1945, for he also actively scuttled initiatives to make contact with Western intermediaries that did not involve him and threatened his. The activities provide telling insights into Schellenberg's thinking about negotiations, his professed humanitarianism, and his political and personal ambitions. Schellenberg, for example, appears to have blocked a proposal that came to Himmler from Stockholm via Kaltenbrunner. Bruno Peter Kleist, a member of the Auswärtige Amt with good contacts in Scandinavia, had been contacted by Hillel Storch, a representative of the World Jewish Congress. Storch offered several

months earlier: Conversation with Musy concerning his most recent trip to Germany, April 9–10, 1945/June 10, 1955, NA, RG 263, Entry ZZ-18, Box 112, File: Schellenberg, Water, vol. 1, 1 of 2.

[81] Erklärung Göring; Affidavit, Jean-Marie Musy; Affidavit, Benoit Musy; Conversation with Musy concerning his most recent trip to Germany, April 9–10, 1945/ June 10, 1955, NA, RG 263, Entry ZZ-18, Box 112, File: Schellenberg, Water, vol. 1, 1 of 2. Breitman, "Nazi Espionage," 112–113.

[82] Final Report; Erklärung Göring; Affidavit, Benoit Musy. Musy's affidavit clearly indicates that he received that bit of information from Schellenberg. Göring stated that Kaltenbrunner went around Himmler to Hitler, convincing the latter that concentration camp inmates should be taken out of the reach of the Allies to serve as hostages later on. Black emphasizes that it is debatable that Kaltenbrunner sabotaged the orders due to his then location: Black, *Kaltenbrunner*, 232 note 28.

million dollars for some forty-five hundred Jews of different nationalities held in Estonia and Lithuania; he also intimated that President Roosevelt was interested in offering a negotiated end to the war in exchange for the 1.5 million Jews assumed to be still alive in German captivity. Kleist rushed to Berlin to report to Kaltenbrunner. Intrigued by the amount of money and the promise of a political breakthrough, Kaltenbrunner informed Himmler, who allegedly approved the contact and indicated that Germany had, indeed, 2.5 million Jews to trade. Kleist was to return to Stockholm to conduct the negotiations and, as a door prize of sorts, he was to bring one thousand Jews with him, presumably to persuade Storch and Roosevelt of Himmler's sincerity. Ultimately, neither the trip nor the negotiations came to pass: Himmler withdrew his approval. Kleist was convinced that Schellenberg had persuaded Himmler not to pursue this angle.[83] Despite Storch's masterfully laid breadcrumbs to the White House, nothing came of it: Schellenberg was not interested in any rescue operations or negotiations that did not involve him. Put differently, humanitarianism, peace soundings, even the chance to break the anti-Hitler alliance only interested Schellenberg if he held a prominent role. The contact with Musy, then in its beginning stages, must have seemed the much better bet. Schellenberg likely also understood better than others that Storch's offer was just too good to be true: it served on a silver platter at the beginning of a process what Schellenberg hoped to see as its end result. A masterful manipulator himself, Schellenberg might have recognized Storch's offer for what it was: a desperate bluff meant to garner attention. Where Schellenberg offered Jews he could not deliver for contacts in the White House, Storch offered undeliverable White House contacts while wanting Jews. However, Schellenberg was nothing but thorough. After scuttling Kleist and Kaltenbrunner's contacts with Storch, he tried to establish his own line to Hillel Storch.

Schellenberg did not restrict his sabotage efforts to so-called humanitarian efforts but also torpedoed peace overtures. In fall 1944, an Italian industrialist approached Wilhelm Harster, the Representative of the Security Police and Security Service (BdS) in Verona, with the idea of using his contacts in Switzerland to establish a line to the Allies. The Italian wanted to ensure that the Northern Italian industries would not be destroyed by the Germans or the Allies once the war moved through these territories. Harster was intrigued, hoping that these contacts would lead to even more. At the end of October, shortly after Schellenberg began

---

[83] Black, *Kaltenbrunner*, 230; Wenck, *Bergen Belsen*, 366–368. Wenck has Kersten as the main intermediary here. On Kleist and on the Hesse mission: Doerries, *Intelligence Chief*, 100–101, 158–162, 194–195.

negotiating with Musy, Harster and his Office VI representative, Klaus Huegel, visited Berlin to discuss with Kaltenbrunner the operation they had codenamed "West-Wind." Kaltenbrunner asked them for a written report that was then discussed in a meeting between Müller, Kaltenbrunner, and Schellenberg. The strongest objections against "West-Wind," which incidentally never reached Himmler, came from Schellenberg. He argued that the Allies would soon be surprised by a major offensive in the West; that, if successful, Germany would be in a stronger position to negotiate; that the Russians would be beaten in Poland or Silesia; that an indiscretion by the Allies or the Swiss would harm Germany's standing with Japan; and that there was insufficient evidence that the plan would succeed. Huegel opined after the war that Schellenberg rejected the proposal due to Harster's prominent role in it and noted that, shrewdly, he had his nemesis, Heinrich Müller, do his bidding during the meeting. Schellenberg was certainly no friend of Harster's, whom he saw as part of Kaltenbrunner's clique, and this certainly contributed to his negative response. Schellenberg's alleged statements also indicate that he did not believe defeat to be inevitable, but still expected to be able to negotiate from a position of – relative – strength: The Soviets could be defeated in one place or the other, and the Western Allies would come to the negotiating table if shown that Germany was still a force to reckon with; "the key to the outcome of the was [war] is in the West."[84] Schellenberg reasoned that the anti-Hitler alliance could still be split and preferred negotiations in which he played a primary role; he was, after all, the foreign expert.

Later attempts by SD members in Italy to make contact with Western representatives in Switzerland were more successful, as Schellenberg's bid to scuttle them failed. During a meeting called by Huegel in Verona in November 1944, the everlasting Guido Zimmer, who had been involved with Office VI operations in Italy for years, suggested using Baron Luigi Parrilli, an Italian who had formerly represented the American company Kelvinator & Nash, to forge contacts in Switzerland. General approval for this, known as "Operation Wool," came in late November. By the end of January, Berlin signaled that Parrilli should be sent on his mission soon; precise instructions would follow by courier. Parrilli ultimately went without directives from Berlin, but with the support of the highest-ranking Nazi official in Italy, Highest SS and Police Leader (HSSPF) Karl Wolff. Parrilli saw Allen Dulles and his assistant around the middle of February;

shortly thereafter Zimmer, Parrilli, and Eugen Dollmann called on Paul Bloom, the OSS representative in Lugano. And on March 8, 1945, Wolff met with Dulles. "Operation Sunrise," which led to the end of the war on the Italian front a few days before Germany's unconditional surrender at Reims, was under way.[85] Already deeply engaged in negotiations with Dulles, Wolff was ordered to Berlin to report to a doubtful Kaltenbrunner and a sidelined and unenthusiastic Schellenberg. During the meeting, Kaltenbrunner allegedly took the role of the main questioner while Schellenberg remained cordial, but after the war Wolff was adamant that Schellenberg was the man behind the curtain attempting to orchestrate his downfall. Wolff surmised that Schellenberg was jealous of his contact with Dulles, as Schellenberg – despite his position and the rumored millions at his disposal – had never managed to establish personal contact with the OSS representative. Wolff was also convinced that Schellenberg still believed Himmler to be acceptable to the West and a break-up of the anti-Hitler alliance possible. Schellenberg, for his part, deemed Wolff out of his depth; he claimed to have on good authority that Dulles would only negotiate with someone who had an actual mandate to do so.[86]

Wolff's diagnosis that Schellenberg suffered from a case of Dulles Envy was not far off, as Schellenberg exerted tremendous energies to make direct contact with Dulles but to no avail. Even before Parrilli's meeting with Dulles, Schellenberg's personal representative in Switzerland, Eggen, met US diplomat Frederick R. Loofborough. Eggen attempted to get Loofborough's attention by trading in worst-case scenarios: Germany had no other option than to fight until the end, even if no German would survive, and then Bolshevism would triumph in Europe. He proposed a meeting between Schellenberg and Dulles, promising that

---

[85] Sixth Detailed Interrogation Report on SS Sturmbannführer Huegel, Dr. Klaus," June 21, 1945, NA, RG 226, Entry 119A, Box 71, File 1828; Breitman, "Nazi Espionage," 108–111. On "Operation Sunrise": Bradley F. Smith and Elena Agarossi, *Operation Sunrise: The Secret Surrender* (New York: Basic Books, 1979). Breitman asserts that Zimmer's declassified files indicate that Operation Wool preceded and facilitated Operation Sunrise, thus making the Italian surrender "as much a German initiative as it was an American coup." Richard Breitman, "Analysis of the Name File of Guido Zimmer," http://www.nara.gov/iwg/declass/zimmer.html. On Wolff and Dulles: Kerstin von Lingen, "Conspiracy of Silence: How the 'Old Boys' Network of American Intelligence Shielded SS General Karl Wolff from Prosecution," *Holocaust and Genocide Studies* 22 (Spring 2008), 74–109 and *SS and Secret Service "Verschwörung des Schweigens": Die Akte Karl Wolff* (Paderborn: Ferdinand Schöningh, 2010), chapters 1 and 2.

[86] See Wolff's various interrogations in the fall of 1947 on that matter at IfZ, ZS 317/IV. Wolff stated that Schellenberg provided Kaltenbrunner with a wireless report to paint Wolff a traitor and alleged that Schellenberg had confessed to him that the report originated with the head of the Swiss Intelligence Service, Roger Masson, making him into a traitor as well. Appendix 1 "Statement by Schellenberg regarding Wolff," Final Report.

Schellenberg would bring proof positive of the Soviets' duplicity. Dulles was intrigued by Schellenberg's plea for attention but did not rush into action to meet the man. And once the Parrilli contacts began to take on momentum and led to a meeting between Dulles and Wolff, "the Americans had not need for Schellenberg."[87] In both his actual role as the head of German foreign intelligence and his assumed role as an able diplomat, Schellenberg must have felt shunned by his US counterpart. But he was nothing if not persistent: in February 1945, an envoy of Schellenberg's, likely Eggen again, called on Roger Masson, to whom Schellenberg, in American estimations, was "perilously close." The envoy indicated Schellenberg's interest in seeing "me," that is Dulles.[88] Nothing came of it. In March 1945, almost simultaneously to the meeting between Dulles and Wolff, Eggen approached his Swiss contacts again, still wanting to arrange a meeting between Schellenberg and Dulles "to explore jointly [. . .] the possibilities of bringing the war to an early conclusion." Yet again Eggen raised the specter of a "communization of Germany" and opined, "Nazism and Communism are closely related and [. . .], with the exception of the upper ten thousand, the country was ripe for Communism." He was told that there was no point in such a meeting unless Schellenberg had a plan that fit into the general framework of Germany's division as agreed upon at Yalta in February 1945. Eggen protested that it would be impossible for anyone to seize power in Germany, sue for peace, and get nothing from the West in return. His contact expressed his hope that there existed "a man strong enough to seize the power and wise enough to see that unconditional surrender was now the best policy for the German people." Eggen's contact was clearly not willing to deal, but, pleased with the development, noted, "if it was ever wanted by us a direct channel now exists to Himmler." The OSS might have been intrigued, but the gig was up. Eggen was seen as yet another German trying to split the alliance, and it was deemed dangerous to give even the impression that one was willing to engage with the likes of him. He was simply not the right man.[89] But Schellenberg kept at it. In April, Masson inquired again. This time, Dulles' cable reporting on the matter was positively irritated and indicated that he had deftly put both men in their place:

[87] No title, January 18, 1945/June 22, 1955, NA, RG 263, Entry ZZ-18, Box 112, File: Schellenberg, Water, vol. 1, 1 of 2; Breitman, "Nazi Espionage," 109.
[88] Cable from Bern, Switzerland, February 4, 1945/June 21,1955, NA, RG 263, Entry ZZ-18, Box 112, File: Schellenberg, Water, vol. 1, 1 of 2.
[89] 224 [D'Oench] to 110 [Dulles], Interview with Heinrich Wilhelm Eggen at Wolfberg on the Bodensee, Present 224, Eggen and Wolf, Sunday, March 4, 1945, March 7, 1945; Evaluation of Eggen, March 21, 1945; Saint to Saint, Subject: Hans Wilhelm Eggen, March 21, 1945, NA, RG 263, Entry ZZ-16, Box 13, File: Eggen, Hans Wilhelm.

I replied that our interest was unconditional surrender of German forces and that any contact with Shellenberg [sic] seemed quite futile, Shellenberg's idea was apparently time worn one of opening West Front. I told Masson that West front was already opened up without Schellenberg's help. [. . .] Schellenberg is obviously attempting to buy immunity as he has just delivered Gen. Giraud's family to Masson [. . .] and is apparently prepared to release further women and children.[90]

Despite his persistence, Schellenberg had little success in his attempts to contact Dulles. When it came to Dulles, Wolff had him beat. Derailing Wolff's plans was no longer possible while supporting him would have placed Schellenberg in an unacceptable tertiary role. Schellenberg, in search of a starring role, tried to gain back the initiative: concurrent to making his final attempts to reach Dulles and with the Musy talks stalling, Schellenberg cast around for other options.

Just such an option opened up in February 1945, when Count Folke Bernadotte, the Swedish vice president of the International Red Cross, announced through diplomatic channels his intention to visit Germany.[91] The trip was humanitarian. Bernadotte came to supervise the collection of widowed Swedish-born women and their transfer to Sweden. By 1944, Allied pressure on Sweden, which had been neutral during the war but had done brisk business with Germany, was mounting; Bernadotte's visit was also an attempt to test the waters for more significant humanitarian endeavors. Incidentally, the Bernadotte mission began to take shape around the time that the first and only "Musy-Train" reached Switzerland and he also hoped to gather Scandinavian internees in Germany and transfer them to Sweden, where they would remain interned for the duration of the war.[92] And if the opportunity arose, Bernadotte was to expand his efforts to other people in German captivity as well. With the pending arrival of the Swede, Schellenberg was propelled into a prominent role. His good contacts in Sweden were known, and Ribbentrop originally assumed that Schellenberg had initiated Bernadotte's visit. This was not the case.[93] Yet, when it came to Sweden and Swedish representatives,

---

[90] Cable from Bern, Switzerland, April 5, 1945/June 28, 1955, NA, RG 263, Entry ZZ-18, Box 112, File: Schellenberg, Water, vol. 1, 1 of 2.
[91] Count Folke Bernadotte, *The Curtain Falls: Last Days of the Third Reich*, trans. Count Eric Lewenhaupt (New York: A. Knopf, 1945); Ted Schwarz, *Walking with the Damned: The Shocking Murder of the Man Who Freed 30,000 Prisoners from the Nazis* (New York: Paragon House, 1992); Kati Marton, *A Death in Jerusalem* (New York: Arcade Publishing, 1996); Sune Persson, "Folke Bernadotte and the White Buses," *Journal of Holocaust Education*, 9/2–3 (2000), 237–268.
[92] Bernadotte, *Curtain*, 10–20.
[93] Schellenberg, *Labyrinth*, 382–383; Bernadotte, *Curtain*, 19–20; Doerries, *Intelligence Chief*, 155; 187–190. Doerries holds that the background of Bernadotte's first trip to Germany remains unclear.

Schellenberg could not be ignored. He was a known entity among influential Swedes – as an assumed humanitarian, as Germany's spymaster, and as Himmler's foreign policy advisor – and had proven his worth in his earlier efforts. He had also established a reputation as a reasonable man with whom a self-respecting, prominent Swede could do business. Schellenberg was soon to take an important role in contacts with Bernadotte. His carefully nurtured Swedish connections were bearing fruit.

Bernadotte's visit to Germany was initially beset with questions of diplomatic protocol. Schellenberg wanted to meet with Bernadotte and informed Himmler and Kaltenbrunner about the opportunity, but, as this was an official visit, Hitler's approval was needed but unlikely to be granted. The ensuing diplomatic dance, stage-managed by Schellenberg, was meant either to gain Hitler's approval or to circumvent him while covering everybody's back and is indicative of the grip Hitler still had on his subordinates. After attempts to gain Hitler's consent failed, a complicated series of talks was set into motion, meant to implicate Ribbentrop and the Auswärtige Amt into contacts prohibited by Hitler and to make the latter as culpable as the RSHA.[94] Once the maneuverings were over, Himmler and Bernadotte met at Hohenlychen on February 17, 1945. There, they agreed on the transfer of all Scandinavian prisoners to one camp, but Himmler did not allow their transport to Sweden.[95]

---

[94] The plan went as follows: Kaltenbrunner met Ribbentrop, while Schellenberg met Ribbentrop's assistant Wagner. The goal was to persuade Ribbentrop to meet with Bernadotte. Ribbentrop was not to be informed that Hitler had objected to a meeting with Bernadotte. After a meeting between Ribbentrop and Bernadotte, Kaltenbrunner and Schellenberg would then meet with Bernadotte. Himmler wanted to "have time to see how the affair was developing before committing himself officially." Incidentally, Bernadotte threw a monkey wrench into these finely calibrated plans; a phone call by Bernadotte led to a situation where the meeting with Kaltenbrunner and Schellenberg preceded his meeting with Ribbentrop; Schellenberg, *Labyrinth*, 383. Black states that Himmler ordered Kaltenbrunner to meet with Bernadotte, hoping that this would co-opt Kaltenbrunner into the pending talks. Kaltenbrunner, uneasy with the proposition, phoned Hitler's headquarters and was informed that Hitler saw the meeting as idiocy. The meeting went ahead anyway. Black, *Kaltenbrunner*, 231.

[95] Schellenberg, *Labyrinth*, 384–385; Final Report; Autobiography/Sweden; Bernadotte, *Curtain*, 43–59. Bernadotte, misdating the meeting to 12 February, wrote that he initially wanted to see the Scandinavians assembled in two camps. This plan raises another problem with the various accounts. Felix Kersten stated after the war, relying on his purported wartime diaries, that he negotiated this agreement on either 2 or 8 December 1944; Kersten, *Memoirs*, 229–232. Kersten's account found its way into the historiography: Black, *Kaltenbrunner*, 231 or Wenck, *Bergen-Belsen*, 363. There is little to no evidence that Kersten's account is true, and while Wenck's comments are well taken – certain letters by Kersten are confirmed by their responses – they fail to convince in this context. The only person to insist that this agreement was concluded on December 8, 1944 is Kersten. The animosity between Bernadotte and Kersten is legendary and found its best expression in a scholarly controversy about an apparently forged letter, which sought to establish Bernadotte's anti-Semitic attitudes: Gerald Fleming, "Die Herkunft des 'Bernadotte-Briefs' an Himmler vom 10. März 1945," *VfZ* 26 (1978), 571–600.

There was stiff opposition to this scheme from various people, most notably Kaltenbrunner and Heinrich Müller, who held that a transfer was unfeasible since the camp in question, Neuengamme, was already overcrowded. Schellenberg, intent on making the best out of the contact with Bernadotte, assigned Franz Göring to the task, but it took Göring and an army of Swedes until the end of April to transfer most of the imprisoned Scandinavians to Neuengamme.[96] But these were future problems; the contact between Bernadotte and Himmler was off to a promising start. Bernadotte even remembered that Himmler indicated his willingness to release Jews to the Allies.[97]

Schellenberg pushed forward a more ambitious agenda, or so he later claimed. He suggested to Himmler that it was time to use the Swedish intermediary to offer surrender to the Western Allies, urging Himmler to ask Bernadotte to fly to Eisenhower's headquarters with a personal surrender offer from Himmler. He also implored Himmler to free himself of Hitler – if needed by force. Trying to drum up Allied interest in Himmler based on his humanitarian acts, Schellenberg conversely asked Bernadotte to inform Eisenhower about Himmler's order – or at least his intent – not to "evacuate" the concentration camps.[98] Despite Schellenberg's fervor, or maybe because of it, Himmler allowed him to maintain only superficial contact with Bernadotte.[99] Put differently, while Schellenberg's humanitarian activities – the support he rendered to Musy and Bernadotte – helped to save a substantial number of lifes, rescue remained the side issue to Schellenberg.[100] His focus was on opening lines of communication with the Western Allies and on persuading Himmler to make use of them.

By February 1945, it was obvious to anyone paying attention that Himmler was entertaining foreign visitors with humanitarian proposals on a regular basis. He became a go-to person for any person or organization hoping to negotiate the release of individuals held in Germany. A veritable revolving door emerged. In mid-March the President of

---

[96] Schellenberg, *Labyrinth*, 385; Erklärung Göring. Doerries makes much of Schellenberg's efforts, calling him "plucky" and suggesting that he had planned ahead to defuse possible roadblocks. He also indicates that Schellenberg might have had an informant in the Swedish Embassy in Berlin, allowing him to anticipate the Bernadotte's needs. Doerries, *Intelligence Chief*, 191–192; 196–199.

[97] Bernadotte, *Curtain*, 58. It is not clear whether Himmler made this statement during the 17 February meeting or later; Schellenberg suggested that such a hand-over was discussed in late March. Schellenberg *Labyrinth*, 387; Final Report.

[98] Bernadotte, *Curtain*, 58; Schellenberg *Labyrinth*, 387; Final Report.

[99] Schellenberg claimed that he was engaged in a fight for Himmler's soul, and the Faustian metaphor Schellenberg employed in his writing is instructive. If Himmler is Faust and Hitler the devil, then Schellenberg cast himself as God. Schellenberg, *Labyrinth*, 386; Final Report; Autobiography/Sweden.

[100] For a more positive evaluation of Schellenberg: Doerries, *Intelligence Chief*, 193.

the International Red Cross, Dr. Carl Burckhardt, let it be known that he was interested in meeting Himmler. Himmler was less interested – maybe because he feared Hitler's reaction or maybe because his interests were in his with Bernadotte, eloquently and eagerly proffered by Schellenberg. Himmler therefore ordered Kaltenbrunner to meet with Burckhardt; Kaltenbrunner made extensive promises only to then drag his feet.[101] Himmler took greater interest in another group of emissaries, most prominently among them Hillel Storch, that sought better treatment for concentration camp inmates as well. Himmler's interest likely stemmed from Kersten's involvement in it, as he spoke for Storch. But Storch, who had made a stunning offer for ransom and contacts to the White House a few months earlier, was a known entity. It is unclear what transpired between Himmler and Kersten, but in a letter to Storch in mid-March Himmler promised, yet again, not to evacuate the camps.[102] At this point, then, Himmler had given virtually the same assurance to any humanitarian negotiator he had encountered; the order not to evacuate was, however, not implemented across the board. Command and communication structures were breaking down, but it also stands to reasons that the execution of these orders was of little interest or urgency to Himmler or, for that matter, Schellenberg. Its haphazard execution also allowed the deflection possible internal criticisms, as it could be used to show that Himmler was playacting for his foreign contacts. Conversely, any delays could easily be blamed on Kaltenbrunner or Germany's general state of disintegration, as Schellenberg did on Himmler's and his own behalf after the war. Ultimately, these promises afforded Himmler and Schellenberg with the perfect opportunity to maintain contact with Western representatives – effectively stringing them along – while keeping their bargaining chips in a tight grip. Promises were cheap and humanitarian gestures means to an end.

For all the contacts that had been established with Western representatives by spring 1945, Schellenberg found himself with the same old problem: Himmler. The SS leader listened to Schellenberg's plans, agreed and went along with them for a while, but his bond with Hitler remained unbroken. And Schellenberg remained without a mandate to do anything beyond setting up yet another meeting between Himmler and

---

[101] Final Report; Autobiography/Sweden. Schellenberg claimed that he was in contact with Burckhardt through Swiss friends who told him that Burckhardt was interested in meeting with Himmler to discuss political prisoners – especially French and Polish – as well as Jews. Other authors suggest that the initiative for the meeting came from Himmler. Also: Black, *Kaltenbrunner*, 239–249.

[102] Kersten, *Memoirs*, 275–292; Palmer, "Question," 39–51; Doerries, *Intelligence Chief*, 201–202; Final Report.

another individual focusing on humanitarian issues. Himmler could not be persuaded to act against Hitler, no matter what Schellenberg tried.[103] He was not one step closer to persuading Himmler to negotiate a separate peace or to offer surrender, effectively breaking up the anti-Hitler alliance, than he had been six months earlier, or in the fall of 1943, or, if Schellenberg is to be believed, in the summer of 1942. Schellenberg was getting nowhere fast.

In the third week of April, with Germany's military situation beyond precarious – the Red Army was closing in on Berlin and British and American troops were advancing rapidly through Western Germany – two Swedish delegations arrived on Himmler's doorstep. Himmler's willingness to entertain foreign representatives involved in humanitarian matters had them beating a path to his door, despite the deteriorating circumstances in war-ravaged Germany, and even though Himmler had not made good on most of his promises. Indeed, alongside many smaller camps, US and British troops had liberated Buchenwald and Bergen-Belsen, on April 11 and April 15, 1945 respectively. Yet the negotiators kept arriving. The first group consisted of Kersten and Norbert Masur, Storch's replacement as the representative of the World Jewish Congress; the other one was Bernadotte's, who was back in Germany for another meeting with Himmler.[104] Himmler's endgame remains a matter of speculation: it is unclear whether he still believed that he would be able to trade Jews for money or goods or whether he accepted Schellenberg's assessment that it might remain possible to broker a separate peace. It is likely, though, that the constant stream of representatives, now including a representative of the World Jewish Congress, affirmed Himmler's conviction that Jews in German hands remained a valuable commodity.

In the early morning hours of April 21, 1945, Himmler – returning from celebrating Hitler's birthday in Berlin – met with Kersten and Masur. Himmler saw the need to justify himself and opened the meeting with an attempted monologue on the "Jewish question" – much to Schellenberg's chagrin, who had allegedly advised Himmler to "determine shortly and precisely what had to be done to save those who could still be saved" and to "accentuate" his "open contradiction and disobedience to Hitler making amends in this manner for his own personal conduct." Himmler, though, launched into his defense: going back to pre-1933, he described Jews as foreign elements; discussed his attempt

[103] Schellenberg, *Labyrinth*, 389–390; Final Report; Autobiography/Sweden; Lutz Graf Schwerin von Krosigk, *Memoiren* (Stuttgart: Seewald, 1977), 239–240.
[104] Palmer, "Question," 39–51; Hindley, "Negotiation," 52–77. On Masur as Storch's replacement and Himmler's concern about taking a meeting with a Jew: Doerries, *Intelligence Chief*, 203–204.

to solve the "Jewish question" through emigration, which was foiled by the world and some of his party comrades; labeled Jews as carriers of epidemics and partisans; and justified the creation of ghettos and the use of crematoria to dispose of those who had died of natural causes. Himmler did not acknowledge outright mass murder but tied the fate of the Jews to the – preventive – war against the Soviet Union and the partisans' brutal warfare. He also noted, "if the Jewish people suffered from the severity of the fights, one should not forget that the German people was not spared either." Masur interrupted Himmler several times but commented later that it seemed as if Himmler had the "need" to give his defense in front of a Jew; Masur's recollections of his trip and of Himmler's attempted justification provide a remarkable glimpse into Himmler's pathology at the time, indeed. Masur eventually voiced his requests and, according to Schellenberg, requested Himmler's assurance, first, that no more Jews would be killed; second, that the Jews were to be kept in the camps and that death marches, the so-called evacuation, would cease; and, third, that the names and places of the camps would be made public. The agreement was put in writing, but Himmler insisted that he had given the pertinent orders already.[105] He had indeed, but there is no indication that Himmler ensured their uniform execution. And the reality on the ground made a cruel mockery out of Himmler's assurances: dying people on death marches crisscrossed the charred countryside with the bodies of the dead marking their passage.

Masur's recollections differ in noteworthy ways. In addition to what Schellenberg mentioned, he recalled asking for the release of Jews held in camps close to Switzerland and Scandinavia and permission to bring them across the border. He furthermore requested for everybody else to be kept in place, treated and fed well, and eventually handed over to the approaching Allies. Masur also recalled asking Himmler for the number of Jews still remaining in the camps, and Himmler's inflated numbers and overall comments throw an interesting light on his mindset. For one, Himmler claimed that 150,000 Jews were in Auschwitz when the Red Army liberated the camp in January 1945 – instead of the approximately 7000 people the Red Army actually found – thereby laying the responsibility for their alleged disappearance on the Soviets. Himmler also stressed that he had left, and Masur is attuned to the fact that Himmler uses the first person in this and other comments, around 450,000 Jews in Budapest, ignoring Masur's interjection that this also

---

[105] Schellenberg, *Labyrinth*, 393; Final Report; Autiobiography/Sweden; Norbert Masur, "Ein Jude spricht mit Himmler," in Niklas Günther und Sönke Zandel, eds., *Abrahams Enkel: Juden, Christen, Muslime und die Shoa* (Stuttgart: Steiner, 2006), 133–144; Doerries, *Intelligence Chief*, 207–208.

meant that some 400,000 people were "missing." Lastly, Himmler noted that he had planned to hand over the camps to the approaching Allies and had done so in the case of – recently liberated – Buchenwald and Bergen-Belsen where 6000 and 50,000 Jews, respectively, should have been. But, Himmler emphasized, he was "rewarded foully," as the Allies had used these camps for propaganda and was therefore disinclined to hand over other camps. Himmler also kept mentioning the 2700 Jews from Terezín who had been brought to Switzerland in fall 1944 – the Becher/Mayer and Schellenberg/Musy deals discussed above – and stated that the international press had claimed he wanted to secure an alibi: "I do not need an alibi. I have always done what I deemed right for my people and I stand by it." Masur tried to defuse the situation by pointing at positive press reactions at the prisoners' reasonable health, the freedom of the press in democracies, and the need to go forward with rescue regardless of the press. He also brought to bear logistical arguments, noting that "evacuations" clogged German streets even further. The meeting, Masur recalled, eventually came down to business. Afraid that the deteriorating situation or Allied news reports about the horrifying situation in the liberated camps could spell doom for Jews remaining in German hands, Masur was keen on precise agreements and hoped that the presence and involvement of Schellenberg, Kersten, and Himmler's adjutant Dr. Rudolf Brandt, would ensure Himmler's follow-through. Schellenberg and Masur left the room while the other three hammered out the details. Himmler then informed Masur that he would allow the Red Cross to collect 1000 Jewish women from Ravensbrück; he also agreed to release from the same camp fifty French women who were on Masur's list and was willing to do the same for a number of Dutch Jews identified by name. Fifty Jews held in Norwegian camps were to be brought to the Swedish border; the cases of twenty Swedes found guilty by German courts and imprisoned in Germany were to be reviewed sympathetically and, if possible, they would be released; he promised the same for a number of Norwegians held as hostages. However, all Jewish women to be released from Ravensbrück had to be labeled as Polish and their departure from Germany and arrival in Sweden had to be kept absolutely secret. When it came to ending the "evacuations" and handing the camps to the Allies, though, Himmler simply stated that "he would do his best to fulfill these wishes."[106]

Kersten and those historians who base their accounts on his memoirs regard this agreement as "monumental," and the later meeting with Bernadotte, which prominently involved Schellenberg, as focused on its

---

[106] Masur, "Jude," 134–144.

technical execution.[107] The issue at stake is an important one: who was to take credit for the agreement? Primarily a question of political credibility – and maybe vanity – for Masur and Bernadotte, it was an issue of survival for Schellenberg and Kersten. Both men feared that their close association with Himmler would spell disaster for them once the war ended, and both were using humanitarian issues, discovered conspicuously late, to cover their bases and to secure the goodwill of neutral representatives. Schellenberg regarded the meeting with Masur, facilitated by Kersten, as little more than a nuisance in a full day. His short description of the two-and-a-half-hour meeting is telling, as it highlighted statements by Himmler that allowed Schellenberg to drive home Himmler's willingness to help, without asking for anything in return, and his inability to break with Hitler. Yet getting together with Masur prevented, in Schellenberg's estimation, Himmler from giving his full attention to the meeting with Bernadotte that Schellenberg had facilitated. And Schellenberg's reputation – maybe even survival – rested on the latter.

From the discussions with Kersten and Masur, Schellenberg and Himmler drove to a breakfast meeting with Bernadotte. Schellenberg hoped for a breakthrough, but little was achieved even though the meeting took intriguing turns. Bernadotte's wish to take the assembled Scandinavians to Sweden came to naught; Himmler kept dithering but agreed not to "evacuate" them from the Neuengamme when the front neared. On the other hand, Himmler allowed Bernadotte to "transport the women internees from Camp Ravensbrueck to Sweden," effectively letting go the same women twice – once for Masur's and once for Bernadotte's benefit. Schelleneberg postwar statements indicate something curious about this matter, for where the Final Report mentions "women internees," his Autobiography calls them "Polish women from Ravensbrueck" and identifies it as a "new offer." Incidentally, both documents suggest that this release had Hitler's approval and was a "gesture against Russia." Schellenberg claimed that Benoit Musy had given him a list of Polish women, originally put together by Prince Radziwił in Geneva. Schellenberg asserted to have pushed repeatedly with Himmler for the women's release and made the strange claim that he tried to impress on Himmler the "racial qualities of the Polish people," using his own wife as a case in point. Be that is it may, Schellenberg stated that Himmler gained Hitler's approval for the release of the women by suggesting that their arrival in Sweden would be a gesture against the Soviet Union.[108] It is

---

[107] For the opposing ends of the debate, see: Palmer, "Question," 45–48; Marton, *Death*, 263–268; Doerries, *Intelligence Chief*, 207.

[108] Final Report; Autobiography/Sweden. Bernadotte, *Curtain*, 101–102.

not clear whether Hitler approved of this or whether Schellenberg made up this tale from whole cloth. However, Himmler was clearly willing to fiddle with the margins by releasing some people. And gender played a role. When the Red Cross convoy, now a joined operation of Masur and Bernadotte with the Swedish Foreign Ministry functioning as a relay center, arrived at Ravensbrück it was, according to Masur, allowed to pick up "all" women – some 7000, about half of them Jewish.[109] A few days later, the Red Army liberated the camp. The overall number of people rescued from Ravensbrück and other camps through these operations cannot be determined, but is substantial.[110] Intriguingly, Schellenberg was not interested in numbers but focused his postwar recollections on the lack of progress toward a separate peace: the clear endgame of his humanitarian endeavors.

After the meeting Schellenberg accompanied Bernadotte for part of his return; however, the two men's recollections of their conversation differ. Schellenberg claimed that he told the Swede that Himmler expected him to persuade Bernadotte to fly to Eisenhower's headquarters and to try to arrange for a meeting between the General and Himmler.[111] But Bernadotte's parting comments left no doubt that he believed that the time for negotiations had long since passed, telling Schellenberg that Himmler should have taken matters into his own hands after Bernadotte's earlier visit. By now, he, Bernadotte, was in no position to do anything for Himmler and he also advised Schellenberg to take care of his personal affairs and survival.[112] Bernadotte's account of the conversation differs markedly from Schellenberg's: it took place at the beginning of April rather than at its end and he also disabused Schellenberg of the notion that Himmler would be an acceptable partner for the Western Allies. Bernadotte advised Schellenberg that he

must rid his mind of any illusions that the Allies would ever enter negotiations with Himmler. Himmler could not conceivably head the government for more than a short period of transition, after which it would be taken over by the Allied occupation authorities. . . . [113]

---

[109] Masur, "Jude," 143.
[110] For a serious attempt at a detailed accounting: Doerries, *Intelligence Chief*, 212–214, especially note 411 as well as Persson, "Buses," 241–244. Persson also addresses the questions if and how prisoners were prioritized for rescue to Scandinavia.
[111] Schellenberg, *Labyrinth*, 394; Final Report; Autobiography/Sweden; Bernadotte, *Curtain*, 102. Kersten, *Memoirs*, 229–232. Palmer, normally following Kersten's lead, offers a third version and suggests that Himmler made these concessions in his earlier meeting with Masur and under the influence of Kersten. Palmer, "Question," 45.
[112] Schellenberg, *Labyrinth*, 394; Final Report; Autobiography/Sweden.
[113] Bernadotte, *Curtain*, 92.

Bernadotte conceded, however, that Himmler's involvement might prevent Germany from falling into complete chaos and presented the conditions under which he would be willing to go to Eisenhower. First, Bernadotte expected an announcement by Himmler that Hitler had stepped down for medical reasons and had chosen Himmler as his successor. Second, Himmler was to dissolve the party, remove all of its functionaries, and order the cessation of all Werewolf – Nazi guerrilla – activities. Lastly, Bernadotte expected Himmler's permission to transfer all Norwegian and Danish concentration camp prisoners to Sweden. To Bernadotte, fulfilling these conditions would have spelled Nazi Germany's end, and he never imagined that Himmler would be willing to accept them. He was thus surprised when Schellenberg "did not hesitate. He told me that he would try to induce his chief to accept them."[114] If Bernadotte's timeline is to be believed, Schellenberg had known since the beginning of April that Himmler would not be acceptable as a negotiator to the West. Yet he continued to convey to Himmler the contrary, but then this message matched with the Egmont Reports: if only Himmler would break with Hitler and take matters into his own hand, all would be well. Schellenberg played a double game. Few of his intentions were purely humanitarian and he could nolonger have truly believed Western representatives would negotiate much of anything with Himmler. But he was willing to bet that if he were the one to persuade Himmler to make a surrender offer, something beneficial would shake loose.

Developments picked up pace again. Schellenberg met with Himmler and the two men planned, in vague terms, for the time after Hitler's death, or so Schellenberg claimed. On April 22, 1945, after another round of discussions, Himmler stated that he was willing to request that Bernadotte transmit to the Western powers a surrender offer in his name.[115] Schellenberg left for the Baltic port city Lübeck and eventually managed to phone Bernadotte, who was on the Danish side of the border; they met in the Swedish Consulate in Flensburg the next day. Bernadotte was pleased by Himmler's change of mind, but conveyed his doubts that the Western Allies would be willing to accept a partial – conditional – surrender offer. He also restated that, "there is no question of Himmler playing any part in the Germany of the future. At most, the Allies might want to use his services to carry out the surrender." Schellenberg assured the Swede that he understood and would inform Himmler accordingly; it is not clear if

---

[114] Bernadotte, *Curtain*, 93.
[115] Schellenberg, *Labyrinth*, 397; Final Report; Autobiography/Sweden; Appendix C to FR 105, Giselher Wirsing, Prisoner's last meeting with Schellenberg at Flensburg, April 29–May 1, 1945, NA, RG 263, Entry ZZ-16, Box 57, File: Wising, Giselher [hereafter: Wirsing/Last Meeting Schellenberg.]

he did so. And there is, yet again, an interesting divergence in the recollections. Schellenberg remembers that Bernadotte did not see the need to meet again with Himmler, as "the terms of capitulation could be drafted in a letter addressed to Eisenhower," but Schellenberg insisted on a face-to-face meeting. Bernadotte, for his part, recalled that he saw no point in flying to General Eisenhower's headquarters as Himmler's emissary. Rather, he saw more sense in conveying Himmler's offer to the members of the Swedish Government, "who could then, if they were willing, transmit them to the representatives of the Western powers."[116] In other words: Schellenberg envisioned making direct contact with Eisenhower – and entertained the notion that this bit of diplomatic showmanship could include himself – while Bernadotte attempted to slot the offer into the norms of wartime diplomacy.

The Swedish Count and Himmler met later that night at the Swedish Legation in Lübeck. In a meeting interrupted by air raids and lighted by candles, Himmler declared that he had the authority to offer surrender as he expected Hitler to be dead within days. Yet he emphasized that his offer did not extend to the Soviet Union, but stressed that the German military would keep fighting in the East – an "East" now located in Berlin's neighborhoods – until the arrival of British and American relief troops.[117] Bernadotte expressed his doubt that the Western Allies would be willing to accept conditional surrender and stressed that it would be "quite impossible to carry out a surrender offer on the Western front and continue fighting at the Eastern front. It can be looked upon as quite certain that England and America will not make any separate settlement with Germany." In short, he reminded Himmler, who was by now willing to meet with Eisenhower and "prepared to surrender unconditionally on the Western front," of the conditions laid out at the Casablanca Conference more than two years prior. Himmler, for his part, argued that he wanted to save millions of Germans from Russian occupation, and was therefore restricting his surrender offer to the Western powers. Obvious differences notwithstanding, Bernadotte agreed to transmit Himmler's message to the Swedish Minister of Foreign Affairs, who would then forward it to Eisenhower. Bernadotte added one condition: Himmler was to include Denmark and Norway in the surrender.[118] Himmler agreed and proceeded to write down his offer.

---

[116]   Final Report; Bernadotte, *Curtain*, 105–106.
[117]   Schellenberg, *Labyrinth*, 397–399; Final Report; Autobiography/Sweden; Bernadotte, *Curtain*, 108–112.
[118]   Bernadotte, *Curtain*, 108–113; Final Report; Autobiography/Sweden; Doerries, *Intelligence Chief*, 210.

The conditions under which Himmler made his final bid are worth considering, as he squared a circle that allowed him to make contact with the West and remain loyal to his Führer. Expecting Hitler to be dead within days, Himmler consoled himself that "Hitler should fall fighting against Bolshevism, the fight against which, [sic] he had dedicated his life" and considered himself the Führer's rightful successor. Himmler's alleged break with Hitler was nothing of the sort; instead, Himmler simply assumed power before its preconditions – Hitler's death and Himmler's official ascent – were fulfilled. Secondly, Himmler's surrender offer was not unconditional, even if the term was used. It was restricted to the Western powers, and he expected the Western Allies to join the Germany in its battle against the presumed common enemy of Bolshevism. Himmler's proposition was firmly rooted in Nazi ideology and practice and constituted his last attempt to break up the anti-Hitler coalition. And he proceeded exactly along the lines that Schellenberg had suggested in the preceding months. This was a success for Schellenberg, for no matter what would happen next, he was the man who persuaded Himmler to make this offer of – conditional – surrender.

Himmler's proposal created a temporary stir among Allied leaders but was quickly rejected.[119] Schellenberg learned in a meeting with Bernadotte on April 27, 1945 that his efforts had failed, as Himmler was not an acceptable negotiator to the West. Schellenberg's renditions of the event indicate astonishment over this development and, despite having pushed the "Himmler option" with tremendous single-mindedness over the preceding months, Schellenberg lays the responsibility its failure at Himmler's feet. This is indicative of Schellenberg's pathology, for he had done more than "reinforced the unrealistic expectations (i.e., that he was acceptable) of his chief," as Doerries suggest.[120] Schellenberg had created them. And he now tried to divest himself of the plan's failure, but expected to be commended for having dragged Himmler to the negotiating table still. Yet Himmler was only part of the offer's problems and the smaller one at that, as its conditionality negated a deal as well.

---

[119]   Himmler's offer of surrender was the topic of a telephone conversation between Churchill and Truman on April 25, 1945; the two Western leaders decided to inform Stalin immediately. In his reply of April 26, 1945, Stalin made it clear that the offer should also be extended to the Soviet Union according to the policies adopted at Casablanca. The same day, Truman requested the American Minister in Sweden, Hershel Johnson, to "inform Himmler's agent that the only acceptable terms of surrender by Germany are unconditional surrender on all fronts to the Soviet Union, Great Britain, and the United States." *Foreign Relations of the United States, Diplomatic Papers 1945, Volume III, European Advisory Commission, Austria, Germany* (Washington, D.C.: GPO, 1968), 759–769.

[120]   Doerries, *Intelligence Chief*, 215.

Schellenberg reported to Himmler a day later. Allegedly initially afraid of Himmler's reaction, especially as the international press was picking up on the developments, Schellenberg did just fine: Himmler still expected to be appointed Hitler's successor within a day or two, and Schellenberg received another special assignment from Himmler. He was to negotiate with the Swedish government the cessation of hostilities in the Northern Sector, Denmark and Norway. During an earlier meeting, Bernadotte had indicated Swedish interest in that matter; Schellenberg made it his concern, won Himmler's support, and received a de facto appointment as "special envoy."[121] Things were looking up for Schellenberg. Rather than to stay in Germany and wait for what was to come, Schellenberg began to travel between Northern Germany and Denmark.[122] He had remade himself a diplomat.

Office VI, on the other hand, was slipping through his fingers. Returning from Denmark to Flensburg early on May 1, 1945, Schellenberg was greeted by Giselher Wirsing bringing news from Kaltenbrunner. The head of the RSHA had reorganized or "streamlined" Office VI and appointed his close associates, Wilhelm Waneck and Otto Skorzeny, to head the two parts of Amt VI. As Kaltenbrunner's new Office VI made no mention of Schellenberg, he was dismissed "by implication." In Hoettl's estimation, Kaltenbrunner had reason enough to rid himself of Schellenberg: he disliked Schellenberg; felt double-crossed by Schellenberg; was afraid that Schellenberg would use the Bernadotte connection for his and Himmler's benefit alone; believed that there would be no "Austrian solution" – a preferential, separate deal for Austria – under Schellenberg; and was concerned that Schellenberg would interfere with Kaltenbrunner's emerging connection to Dulles. Hoettl's comments, which foreground the personal animus between the two men, notwithstanding, there is also indication that Kaltenbrunner was streamlining the office for postoccupation resistance and considered himself the civilian commander-in-chief of the planned Alpine Redoubt.[123] Either way, Kaltenbrunner had finally made the foreign intelligence service his. Schellenberg remained undeterred by a "'Lilliputan rebellion' that

[121] Schellenberg, *Labyrinth*, 402–403; Final Report; Autobiography/Sweden; Bernadotte, *Curtain*, 117.
[122] Final Report; Doerries, *Intelligence Chief*, 216.
[123] Headquarters Third US Army, Intelligence Center, Interrogation Section to 12th Army Group, Subject: Meeting between Wirsing and Schellenberg at end of April 1945, July 25, 1945, NA, RG 263, Entry ZZ-16, Box 191, File: Wirsing, Giselher [hereafter: Meeting Schellenberg Wirsing April 1945]. Hoettl's comments are part of the above document. No title, no date, NA, RG 319, IRR-Personal, Box 191, XE 000855, Sandberger, 2 of 4. The same statements by Sandberger show up in numerous documents in this file; they are also referenced in Wirsing's file. Autobiography/Sweden.

resulted in [his] ouster." Concerned with "high policy," he had "little interest in what Kaltenbrunner might be doing in Bavaria" – an acerbic Prussian takedown of both the man and his location – and regarded "Amt VI as a thing of the past." However, Schellenberg was neither ready nor willing to relinquish his powers. A few weeks earlier, he and his group leaders had discussed an office reorganization to "maintain a secret intelligence service when only islands of military would remain in Germany," in effect deliberating then what Kaltenbrunner had done now. In conversations with Wirsing, Schellenberg made it clear that "neither Himmler nor himself recognized Kaltenbrunner's orders." Indeed, Schellenberg expected Himmler to countermand them by wireless soon. For the time being, however, Schellenberg had relegated Office VI "to a matter of secondary importance."[124] Diplomacy was on his mind.

Driving to Himmler's headquarters near Travemünde, Schellenberg informed Wirsing about the failed surrender offer and identified Himmler – who had waited too long and was unable to "take the right decision at the right moment" – as the main culprit, but also expressed dismay at Churchill's "categorical refusal" of the offer. Yet Schellenberg still did not believe that all was lost. He now wanted to create "domestic conditions" that would allow for a resumption of the negotiations and "still had hopes of arriving at some agreement with the Western Powers, using the German occupation of Norway as his trump card."[125] Schellenberg was still trying to bargain. Now, humans had been replaced by real estate, but his general approach remained the same: use whatever leverage was available to circumvent the Allied demand for unconditional surrender.

At Himmler's headquarters Schellenberg and Wirsing encountered astonishing news: Hitler had committed suicide and had appointed Admiral Karl Dönitz as his successor. An adherent of *Durchhaltestrategie*, keep on fighting as deliverance would somehow materialize, Dönitz had just sent several hundred cadets to Berlin to protect Hitler and was readying troops for battle. Hitler also saw Dönitz as "a dedicated Nazi who would never surrender."[126] When Schellenberg arrived, Himmler had already tried to ingratiate himself with Dönitz, but to no avail. He had, however, persuaded Dönitz to depose Ribbentrop and appoint Lutz

---

[124] Meeting Schellenberg Wirsing April 1945; Wirsing/Last Meeting Schellenberg; Schellenberg, *Labyrinth*, 404; Final Report; Autobiography/Sweden; Subject Sandberger, Internal Memorandum, June 10, 1955, NA, RG 263, ZZ-18, Box 112, File: Schellenberg, vol. 1, 1 of 2.

[125] Meeting Schellenberg Wirsing April 1945; Wirsing/Last Meeting Schellenberg.

[126] Howard D. Grier, *Hitler, Dönitz, and the Baltic Sea: The Third Reich's Last Hope* (Annapolis: US Naval Institute Press, 2007), 198–202; 212–223; Weinberg, "Plans for Victory," 274–285.

Graf Schwerin von Krosigk in his stead, even though "in the Grossad-miral's purely military circles Himmler's political steps with the Western Powers was not understood."[127] Himmler, Schellenberg, and Wirsing drove to Dönitz' headquarters at Plön, where intriguing discussions that led to intriguing plans took place. While Himmler met with Dönitz, Schellenberg, who was to be Schwerin von Krosigk's "immediate assis-tant on foreign policy," and Wirsing penned a memorandum that dis-cussed "the next German move in light of Hitler's death and the Truman and Churchill communiqué of the night before." It was to inform the new Foreign Minister of his new deputy's previous activities.[128]

Schellenberg and Wirsing's report recounted the recent developments for Schwerin von Krosigk and maintained that even though "uncondi-tional surrender to all three Allies was now inevitable," room for mod-ifications remained. They counseled that "[t]he Russians must be held as long as possible, thus allowing German troops and civilians to evac-uate to Central and Western Germany [. . .] For this purpose nego-tiations with the USSR must be protracted" and maintained that "[i]n spite of the 'unconditional surrender' clause, concessions could be wrung from the Allies; the most important would be the retention of a central government."[129] In December 1943, the British ambassador in Moscow had informed his US colleague that his government had received a com-munication indicating that Himmler's interest in learning the exact mean-ing of the phrase "unconditional surrender." The British Government had signaled back that the phrase was self-explanatory.[130] Apparently, it was not. Schellenberg still believed this conditional surrender to be possible.

Wirsing prepared an additional memorandum for the new deputy For-eign Minister that reiterated elements of the Egmont Reports of March and early April. One hoped to be able to preserve a central government by using the exiled former German chancellor Heinrich Brüning as its head and to placate the Allies by dissolving the NSDAP, the SS, and its affiliated organization, by disbanding the Gestapo, and by banning all Werewolf activities. Wirsing's report also added a new and intriguing consideration that prefigured postwar debates; he suggested that "[i]n view of Allied disclosures of conditions in the concentration camps,

---

[127] Schellenberg, *Labyrinth*, 404; Final Report; Autobiography/Sweden; Wirsing/Last Meeting Schellenberg.

[128] Wirsing/Last Meeting Schellenberg. Doerries describes Schellenberg's position as that of an "official emissary of the post-Hitler German government" with "the title of *Gesandter* (Minister)," reads the situation as less advantageous for Himmler and Schel-lenberg, and makes no mention of Wirsing and his role. Doerries, *Intelligence Chief*, 218.

[129] Wirsing/Last Meeting Schellenberg.   [130] Höhne, *Orden*, 485.

a <u>German</u> [underlined in original] definition and prosecution of 'war criminals' was advisable." He was not alone with that idea. Schellenberg, who had protested to Wirsing that he had nothing to do with the camps, "mentioned Müller, Amtschef IV and Ogruf Pohl as the chief war criminals."[131] Postwar was arriving.

Schellenberg spent the war's last days in a frenzied shuttle diplomacy. On May 2, 1945, he went back to Copenhagen and resumed contact with Erik von Post of the Swedish Foreign Office to discuss his plans to "surrender the Northern sector without fighting." On May 3, he met with Himmler and Schwerin von Krosigk, and then with the new Foreign Minister alone. Schellenberg stressed that Schwerin von Krosigk was glad to have him for consultations and as his first *Mitarbeiter,* coworker, and agreed that Schellenberg should pursue the question of the Northern Sector. Schellenberg noted that they discussed unconditional surrender but this "came to nothing at that time" due to the situation in Bohemia-Moravia "where the Heeresgruppen of Generalfeldmarschall Schroener and Generaloberst Rendulic – about a million men, equipped with munitions and provisions for another 7 weeks, were still intact and on the whole more than holding their own on this part of the Eastern front." Indeed, and likely related to the military situation in the Czech lands and in Norway, which they also regarded as a good card to play still, Schwerin von Krosigk agreed that in addition to his mission for the Northern sector, Schellenberg "had to endeavor under all circumstances to arrange a meeting with General Eisenhower for [him]self or a representative of the Government, whether through the Swedish Government or through the Swedish Red Cross." Direct, separate negotiations with Eisenhower remained the ultimate goal, and Schellenberg received a carte blanche to do whatever was needed to "prise open General Eisenhower's firmly shut door."[132] Later that day, Schellenberg met with Dönitz, who needed to be persuaded of the course of action on which he and Schwerin von Krosigk had settled, as Dönitz' military advisors had pointed out the good strategic positions of the German army and navy in Norway and had no intention of "abandoning Norway and interning German troops in Sweden for the duration of the war." Schellenberg alleged that he stressed the long-term gains to be found in "saving in the 'biological substance' of the German people and what remained of the reputation of the Reich." Besides making a race-based argument, Schellenberg purportedly also stressed that in the view of the collapse of the Reich, there

---

[131] Meeting Schellenberg Wirsing April 1945; Wirsing/Last Meeting Schellenberg. See also, with slight difference in timing: Autobiography/Sweden.
[132] Autobiography/Sweden.

was no "moral or traditional justification" of continuing the war in Denmark or Norway. Doing so held no "political or other value."[133] Once more, then, Schellenberg presented himself as the voice of reason and pragmatism trying his best to persuade reluctant superiors of the errors of their ways. Dönitz dithered overnight, but signed Schellenberg's appointment as *Gesandter* with "plenary powers to negotiate with the Swedish government" the next morning.[134] In early May 1945, then, Schellenberg became a foreign politician – Schwerin von Krosigk's deputy and a Gesandter with plenary powers–but in a government and for a country much different from what he must have imagined earlier.

Schellenberg left for Denmark immediately. He had taken his final leave from Himmler, his primary patron of many years, the evening before. Himmler allegedly noted "[i]f only I had listened to you sooner" but also held hopes for his longtime foreign policy advisor: "perhaps you are the first German to be permitted to do something positive for your poor 'Vaterland' again." Schellenberg's Scandinavian counterparts, however, grew increasingly puzzled by Schellenberg's activism. On May 3, one of them stated that the cessation of hostilities in Scandinavia was becoming an academic question; it was patently obvious that Germany's complete and unconditional surrender was a matter of days away, if that long. But Schellenberg kept insisting to the Dönitz Government and the Swedes that something would be gained by continuing negotiations and that he was the only person who could possibly do so, for he held the needed diplomatic credentials. Schellenberg's frenzied activities had taken on a distinctively surrealist flair, though: a meeting in the Swedish Embassy in Copenhagen on May 4 took place amid jubilant, singing crowds that expected the official announcement of the end of hostilities any minute now.[135]

On May 5, 1945, Schellenberg boarded Bernadotte's plane to Sweden. Four days earlier, he had offered to arrange a trip to Sweden for Wirsing, if he "cared to quit Germany."[136] Keeping up the pretense of negotiations, Schellenberg cared to quit Germany, but did so as a diplomat – newly minted but always by inclination – and with his cover and credibility as a reasonable and able negotiator intact. Unable to end the war, whether by breaking up the anti-Hitler alliance outright or via a separate peace, he had created a new identity for himself: as a diplomat, humanitarian, and as the man who had cajoled Himmler into a surrender offer. Even though Schellenberg had it on good authority that this surrender offer would be

[133] Autobiography/Sweden.   [134] Autobiography/Sweden.
[135] Schellenberg, *Labyrinth*, 406–412; Final Report; Autobiography/Sweden; Wirsing/Last Meeting Schellenberg; Doerries, *Intelligence Chief*, 222.
[136] Meeting Schellenberg Wirsing April 1945.

rejected well before Himmler made it, he neither could nor would believe Bernadotte's assertions. Schellenberg trusted more his own, ideological analysis of the situation, which held that it would be possible to use shared anti-Bolshevist beliefs to negotiate a peace – or at least a surrender – with the Western powers. He also trusted his own knack for self-preservation. There he never failed.

In the end none of it mattered. The preliminary capitulation was signed at Eisenhower's headquarters in Reims, France on May 7, 1945; General Eisenhower wore "a battle dress and a hat."[137] On May 8, 1945, the Dönitz government finalized Germany's unconditional surrender. The document was signed that night at Karlshorst, near Berlin. General Georgi Konstantinovich Zhukov represented the Soviet Union.

---

[137] See: Memorandum for Secretary General Staff, Subject: Trip to Berlin, NA, RG 331, Box 115, File No. 387/1, Germany Vol. 1, August 1944–11 May 1945.

9 Postwar

Amt VI was a world of illusion and naivety, not of sinister design; but, unlike the old Abwehr, its illusions were powerfully represented and contributed to the general ruin. Himmler believed in Schellenberg until the end.

The Geheime Meldedienst was a fiction of Schellenberg's own mind, and he had neither the time nor the official support necessary to make it a reality.

Counter Intelligence War Room London
War Room Monthly Summary No. 4
July 23, 1945

Schellenberg was neither unprepared for the future when he arrived in neutral Sweden nor alone for long. Outwardly still negotiating the cessation of hostilities in Scandinavia, or, more precisely, German surrender there, he was soon joined by several companions. His secretary Marie-Luise Schienke, her assistant Christl Erdmann, SS-Obersturmbannführer Heinz Renau, Renau's wife and daughter, and Franz Göring arrived in Sweden on May 6–7, 1945.[1] Schellenberg's family – his pregnant wife and three children under four – remained in Bavaria; his recent activities had not included fetching them. The group arrived in Stockholm with some means: enough cash to pay salaries for three months and a forged US passport for Schellenberg. As the Swedes

---

[1] Reinhard R. Doerries, *Hitler's Last Chief of Foreign Intelligence: Allied Interrogations of Walter Schellenberg* (London: Frank Cass, 2003), 43 note 203; Reinhard R. Doerries, *Hitler's Intelligence Chief Walter Schellenberg: The Man Who Kept Germany's Secrets* (New York: Enigma Books, 2009), 224–225, 226. Doerries notes that Heinz Renau "seems to have been a personal adjutant to Gestapo Chief Heinrich Müller," assigned to the assist with Bernadotte's operation by his request. Göring and Schienke were engaged, either secretly or officially; Schellenberg took the then still married Göring on his personal staff on Schienke's recommendation. Final Report on the Case of Walter Schellenberg, NA, RG 319, IRR, XE 001725, Walter Schellenberg, Folders 7 and 8 [hereafter: Final Report]; Internal Memorandum, August 10, 1945, NA, RG 226, Entry 119 A, Box 26, Folder Schellenberg.

furnished him with papers, this item was not needed.[2] The group clearly had no intention of returning to Germany anytime soon. Schellenberg had "quit Germany."

Between May 5 and 7, Schellenberg, true to his mandate, engaged in negotiations about the surrender of the German troops in Norway with representatives of the Swedish Foreign Office. He also still tried to arrange for a meeting with Eisenhower, claiming that he had received instructions to do so from Schwerin von Krosigk. No such meeting was forthcoming. The Dönitz government had established direct contact with the Allies for the purpose of surrender and the Swedes kept Allies representative abreast of Schellenberg's activities and "ongoing activities." An end run by Schellenberg that excluded the Soviets had little chance, even though there was no lack of trying.[3] Interestingly, arranging the surrender of the German troops in Norway turned out to be more difficult than expected. General Franz Böhme was unwilling to give up and have his troops interned; was hard to reach by phone; did not take a meeting with visiting German Minister Hans Thomsen; and doubted Schellenberg's authority. To complicate matters further, Dönitz appears to have been intransigent about Böhme's "fresh, strongly entrenched" soldiers who were, in the General's words, "sufficient in number to hold out for nine months." Germany's unconditional surrender eventually resolved this situation: when Schellenberg reached the Dönitz headquarters, likely on May 7, hoping to persuade the Admiral to contact Böhme and vouch for Schellenberg, Schwerin von Krosigk told him that, while there were still some negotiations underway, Germany had "declared total capitulation."[4]

Now a man without a mission, Schellenberg decamped to Bernadotte's home near Stockholm. There he sought to recover from the "constant journeys and negotiations" and began contemplating his future – with Bernadotte and other, unidentified "Swedish friends."[5] Schellenberg probably consulted with members of the diplomatic community and maybe Martin Lundquist of Sweden's civilian Security Service came calling too. Later, he met with Alvin Möller and Axel Brandin; he conceivably also met with one Wallenberg or the other. Never one to pass up an opportunity, Schellenberg also met the President of the Swedish Royal Court of Justice and prominent Swedish Red Cross members. Soon, the consultations came to a promising conclusion: Schellenberg

---

[2] Richard Breitman, "Nazi Espionage: The Abwehr and the SD Foreign Intelligence," in Richard Breitman et al., eds., *U.S. Intelligence and the Nazis* (Washington, DC: National Trust Fund for the Nazi War Crimes and Japanese Imperial Government Records Interagency Working Group, 2004), 113.
[3] Doerries, *Intelligence Chief*, 222–223.
[4] Final Report; Doerries, *Intelligence Chief*, 223–224.   [5] Final Report.

decided that he would stay in Stockholm for the time being and would try
to obtain work with the "German Administration for the British Military
Government, should the British wish to employ him" later. Schellenberg expected a quid pro quo; he expected to trade information about
his "previous intelligence work" in return for employment. Schellenberg
and his interlocutors sincerely believed him a viable candidate for a position in postwar Germany; Jean Marie Musy had floated similar ideas
with Roswell McClelland of the US War Refugee Board in Switzerland
earlier. As it was, Schellenberg fell under Allied Automatic Arrest Category, but since he was in Sweden, this was of no immediate concern. It
is also likely that Schellenberg and his Swedish associates assumed that
individual exceptions could be made, especially in light of Schellenberg's
much-touted humanitarian achievements and with his many foreign contacts.[6] Out of the reach of the Allies and initially under no pressure to
return to Germany, Schellenberg had time to evaluate his options and
vie for the best opportunity. The war was barely over but things were
decidedly looking up.

In his own assessment, Schellenberg had done little wrong. His self-
image was defined by a benign reading of his role in Nazi Germany:
propelled by his legal training and professional drive, but devoid of overt
ideological attachments, he had worked as a legal advisor to state and
party leaders. He had then headed a professional and unbiased foreign
intelligence service that had competed valiantly with its counterparts
during an intense six-year war. Ignoring personal risks and speaking
truth to power, he had realized early on that the war could not be won
and had counseled the most powerful man he knew, Heinrich Himmler,
accordingly. His efforts had failed due to Himmler's ambivalence, even
though he ultimately, but too late, had convinced Himmler to offer surrender. However, Eisenhower had presided over a "firmly shut door" that
Schellenberg had been powerless to "prise" [sic] open. Uninvolved with
genocidal policies, he had negotiated for the release of "Jewish prisoners" and had helped various individuals to evade prison terms and worse.
And he had foreign friends to vouch for his efforts.[7] His career and conduct, Schellenberg was convinced, had been honorable. A comment to

---

[6] Final Report; Conversation with Musy concerning his most recent trip to Germany,
April 9–10, 1945/June 10, 1955, NA, RG 263, Entry ZZ-18, Box 112, File: Schellenberg, Walter, vol. 1, 1 of 2. For a different assessment, consider Doerries: "How anyone
might have thought that Schellenberg could have worked for the British Military Government in Germany, as indicated here, remains an enigma." Two years later, Schellenberg
considered relocating to Sweden and practicing law there, which Doerries regards as a
more realistic idea. Doerries, *Last Chief*, 43 note 202.

[7] Final Report. For a positive reading of Schellenberg's humanitarian efforts, Doerries,
Hitler's Last Chief, 31–41; Doerries, *Intelligence Chief*, passim.

his interrogators some time later affirms this self-perception: upon learning that the British intelligence officials, Best and Stevens, abducted by Schellenberg and his posse from Venlo in November 1939, were still alive, he expressed profound relief. This, Schellenberg opined, was his only activity that could be considered a war crime. Yet Schellenberg was far from naïve: he believed in his activities' righteousness but also knew that Allied officials would not necessarily agree with him. He needed to create a coherent story that was supported independently. Schellenberg needed to fashion a usable past.

Schellenberg soon put pen to paper, but, feigning disinterest, claimed that Bernadotte persuaded him to write down "the events leading up to the capitulation" while his memories remained fresh. He also had time on his hands. On May 15, 1945, after increasing press interest in Nazi Germany's spymaster residing in Stockholm, Schellenberg moved from Bernadotte's residence to a house in Saltjoe-Duvnaes, outside of Stockholm, which belonged to a certain Captain Ancgarkrona, who had headed the earlier Red Cross Delegation to Germany.[8] Trying to escape the "tedium of his forced inactivity," Schellenberg obliged Bernadotte; he also reckoned that Göring and Schienke could help him recall "the exact order of events."[9] He held that he initially envisioned creating the outline for a book but, realizing that he was soon to face American and British interrogators, settled on an autobiographical summary. The format allowed Schellenberg to focus the text precisely to his liking: more than nine-tenths of it discuss his good deeds, in particular his collaboration with Bernadotte, which began in February of 1945.[10] Thus came into being the *Urfaust* of Schellenberg's defense.

The Red Cross-connected residence morphed into a writers' collective of contaminating closeness that benefited Schellenberg. While Schellenberg dictated his recollections to Schienke, Bernadotte and Franz Göring also committed their memories to paper. There have been

---

[8]   Schellenberg's various residences during his stay in Sweden are difficult to sort out. According to the Final Report, Schellenberg stayed in Bernadotte's house near Stockholm from May 8 to May 15, 1945; then resided at Saltjoe-Dunvas from May 15 to June 10; and returned to Bernadotte's house from June 10 to June 17, 1945. His staff moved to a small hotel used by the German Embassy in Trosa. While Schellenberg's Autobiography Compiled in Sweden is frequently called the "Trosa Memorandum," the author never stayed there. Final Report. For a different account that has Schellenberg living at Trosa: Doerries, *Intelligence Chief*, 228.

[9]   Final Report.

[10] Brigadeführer Schellenberg, Amtschef VI, Autobiography compiled during his stay in Stockholm, June 1945, NA, RG 226, Entry 125A, Box 2, Folder 21 [hereafter: Autobiography/Sweden.] In the immediate aftermath of the war, different parties were interested in obtaining it; the document can be found in several place; Doerries, *Last Chief*, 43 note 202.

enduring suggestions that Bernadotte's account was ghostwritten by Schellenberg; Doerries puts this to rest once and for all.[11] Had that been the case, Schellenberg surely would have done better smoothing over the accounts' differences. However, the two men had doubtlessly grown close over the preceding weeks and likely discussed their writing efforts and potential differences in their recollections, ultimately sorting out many of them. Conversely, Bernadotte's presence, and the impending publication of his book, likely reined in inclinations at overreach Schellenberg might have entertained. He needed Bernadotte, his contacts, and his influence; there was nothing to be gained from contradicting or alienating the Swede. Schellenberg was surely aware of the asymmetrical nature of their relationship: he needed Bernadotte more than the Swede needed him. Bernadotte's book was published in London in October 1945, coinciding with the beginning of the International Military Tribunal at Nuremberg. Complimentary of Schellenberg, it included passages that were taken verbatim from Schellenberg's Autobiography. Put differently, as early as fall 1945, the English reading public could access Schellenberg's version of the events – validated by its inclusion into Bernadotte's book.

The third party to the writers' collective was Franz Göring, Schellenberg's trouble-shooter during the efforts to transfer into Swedish custody concentration camp prisoners. With Göring, the power differential was set to Schellenberg's advantage. He was Göring's boss and the only reason that Göring found himself – and in the company of his fiancée – on a Swedish estate and not in a prisoner of war camp in Germany. When Schellenberg "asked him [Göring] to write an eye witness account, in order to supplement and confirm certain parts of his [Schellenberg's] story," Göring must have taken seriously Schellenberg's wish and its implications.[12] Göring also had independent reasons to hitch his

---

11 This issue of ghostwriting is most pronounced in Trevor-Roper's introduction to Kersten's memoirs; other authors relying on these follow Trevor-Roper's lead. H. R. Trevor-Roper, "Introduction," in Felix Kersten, *The Kersten Memoirs 1940–1945*, trans. Constantine Fitzgibbon and James Oliver (New York: MacMillan, 1957), 17; Raymond Palmer, "Felix Kersten and Count Bernadotte: A Question of Rescue," *JCH* 29 (1994), 39–51. Circumstantial evidence suggests that Hugh Trevor-Roper (Lord Darce) was among Schellenberg's interrogators; he apparently disliked him immediately and pegged him liar.
      Doerries also points out that Schellenberg was not in Sweden long enough to impact Bernadotte's writings; Doerries, *Last Chief*, 44. It is, however, a slim book. Charles Whiting makes the baseless claim that Schellenberg's memoirs were ghostwritten by the British Intelligence service; Charles Whiting, *Hitler's Secret War: The Nazi Espionage Campaign against the Allies* (London: Leo Cooper, 2000).
12 Final Report. Göring's account is known under two different titles; the documents also resonate in Göring's affidavit for Schellenberg. Franz Göring, Auszug aus meinem Tagebuch über die Befreiung von Menschen aus deutschen Konzentrationslager, PRO, FO 371/46749; Annexe written by Hauptsturmführer Göring to Schellenberg's report

wagon to Schellenberg's horse: Schellenberg's last-ditch humanitarian efforts had helped Göring to better his own record as well. Schellenberg undoubtedly set the tone for both accounts, effectively establishing much of what will ever be known about the negotiations. Taken together with Bernadotte's account, a strikingly coherent and difficult to dislodge narrative emerges.

The Swedish writers' collective has occasionally been identified as the moment when the rewriting of history began.[13] The texts did not emerge in a vacuum but in a short period of time and in close quarters and cannot be taken as independent confirmation of each other. However, "rewriting of history" only partially captures the realities and delusions under which Schellenberg penned his piece. He certainly had a vested interest in putting his best foot forward and needed his account and those of his closest collaborators to be in general agreement. Yet there was more to it. Schellenberg considered himself an honorable man; he believed that he had done nothing wrong and achieved much good. That the Autobiography written in Sweden anticipates Schellenberg's posthumously published memoirs in tone and interpretation is a point as well taken as it is apparent. But to learn about Schellenberg's image of self and his pathology, there exists a better foil.

In 1939, Schellenberg went through a divorce. While the proceedings were still underway and a protracted legal battle a distinct possibility, he authored a lengthy piece that contained details about the Schellenbergs' married life.[14] The matters discussed here could not be further apart from his postwar writing, but the resemblances are striking nevertheless. Both accounts claim to establish events truthfully but also anticipate legal proceedings that could make or break the author. The similarity in tone is eerie; in both pieces Schellenberg established himself as a man who did nothing wrong and tried his best only to be foiled by forces outside of his control. In the account of his marriage, Schellenberg portrays himself as the respectable husband, keen to start a family, who sought to raise his wife – older than him and of lower social standing – to his levels of society and respectability. His efforts and intentions coming to naught and his health deteriorating, he eventually saw no other recourse than to divorce her, only to find himself in the middle of an embarrassing and exhausting legal battle. In short, he behaved honorably. His political

---

on his transactions with Count Bernadotte and events in the last weeks of the German Reich, NA, RG 226, Entry 125 A, Box 2, Folder 21; Eidesstattliche Erklärung, Franz Göring, February 24, 1948, NA, RG 238, M 897, Reel 114, Frame 1016–1031. See also: Doerries, Intelligence Chief, 357–362 [Appendix II]; 230–231.
13 Breitman, "Nazi Espionage," 113.
14 BAL, R 58, Anhang I/49. The National Archives in Washington, DC also holds these files and I thank the late Robert Wolfe for the information.

autobiographical writings follow a similar tack. Here he is the ultimate insider, cosmopolitan diplomat, humanitarian, and thwarted bringer of peace whose positive initiatives were sabotaged by forces beyond his control. Schellenberg regarded himself as beyond reproach; he was a man with a pathologically clean conscience and his belief in his own righteousness was staggering. There is no indication that he ever doubted his narrative, even when he had to retract details. But this also explains why he managed to stay on message: in his view, he never lied – certain things he just had to explain more forcefully or without providing all the details, as nobody would be able to appreciate them properly.

The twenty-odd-page Autobiography was Schellenberg's initial and successful attempt to control the story. It garnered early interest and Schellenberg handed out several copies while in Sweden. Bernadotte received one, as did the Swedish Foreign Minister, Christian Ernst Günther. Schellenberg gave another copy to Hillel Storch, the representative of the World Jewish Congress; at Storch's request, Schellenberg initialed each page to dispel any suggestions at forgery. Doerries suggests that Norbert Masur and Storch "may have had a particular influence on the still young German SS leader who in his function and through his position had supported the programmed mass murder of Jews and others," but there is no support for this.[15] At 35, Schellenberg was still young, but he had cut his teeth and been successful in Nazi Germany's intramural fights and, indeed, the opposite might have well been the case: while still in Sweden, Schellenberg foisted onto a number of influential foreigners his interpretation of his character and the events. Schellenberg, in effect, became his own character witness.

US intelligence agencies had been tracking Schellenberg since late April 1945 and were keenly interested in his transfer into Allied hands. They located him in Copenhagen on May 1 but still believed him there six days later when he was already in Sweden. There was no secret about his whereabouts after May 8, 1945, and OSS documents indicate annoyance at Schellenberg's disappearing act, noting that he "succeeded in escaping to Sweden and now is living in 'supervised liberty' in the Stockholm suburb of Saltjoe-Duvnaes." The Western Allies planned to demand his extradition as a war criminal.[16] But as Bernadotte took a lively interest in his well-being, Schellenberg's situation developed advantageously: his earlier Swedish activities paid off handsomely and in unexpected ways, as he piqued the benevolent curiosity of Colonel Charles E. Rayens,

---

[15] Doerries, *Last Chief*, 43 notes 205 and 206; Doerries, *Intelligence Chief*, 229–231; Final Report.
[16] Index Cards, June 5, 1945 and June 16, 1945, NA, RG 263, Entry ZZ-18, Box 112, File: Schellenberg, Walter, vol. 2, 2 of 2.

the US Assistant Military Attaché in Stockholm. The two men met in Bernadotte's home on May 27 and a day later at Rayens' residence. Rayens – and maybe Bernadotte – suggested that Schellenberg should submit to interrogation and Rayens was to discuss arrangements with higher authorities.[17] Schellenberg was not unknown to Rayens, who had heard about Schellenberg and his efforts on behalf of the Warsaw Swedes from Alvar Moeller of the Swedish Match Company as early as 1943. Moeller had described Schellenberg as "a young SS general" who had "the courage to speak his mind, one whose constant endeavor was to influence Himmler in the right direction." Subsequently, Rayens learned that Bernadotte had worked with Schellenberg during his mission to Germany and, later, that Dönitz' special minister "empowered to capitulate for the German forces in Norway" was "the same SS General who had befriended Mr. Moeller and Count Bernadotte." Through Moeller, Rayens inquired whether Schellenberg would be willing to part with information about German–Japanese relations, exchange of scientific data, and other issues pertaining to Japan, which, with the Pacific war ongoing, was of great interest to the US authorities. Schellenberg played his cards well. Using Moeller and Bernadotte as his intermediaries, he assured Rayens that he "was willing to tell everything he knew regarding German-Jap [sic] relations, and he was also disposed to answer any questions, or help the Allied authorities in any way to get Germany on the right path." Schellenberg also let it to be known that he did not want anything in return but "was answerable for himself" and simply wanted to do something "for the good of Germany and his people." Even before he met with Rayens, Schellenberg had, in effect, set the meeting's tone and, as much as possible, predetermined its outcome. He had established his credentials as a courageous, honorable man and German patriot; indicated his willingness to assist the Americans; and, by seemingly humbly emphasizing that he "asked for no special considerations," suggested that he had knowledge worth trading.

Schellenberg's meetings with Rayens were dress rehearsals for his later approaches and defense strategies. They went well. Rayens' report to Major General Clayton Bissell, Assistant Chief of Staff G-2 in Washington, oozes goodwill and portrays Schellenberg in the best light.[18] Rayens reported that Schellenberg had been a good influence on Himmler and tied this to Schellenberg's religious identity that began to appear in

---

[17] Rayens to Bissel, Assistant Chief of Staff, G-2, Washington, May 30, 1945, NA, RG 226, Entry 119 A, Box 26, Folder 29. The Final Report gives a short overview but is unreliable on the exact dates; Final Report.

[18] Rayens to Bissel, Assistant Chief of Staff, G-2, Washington, May 30, 1945, NA, RG 226, Entry 119 A, Box 26, Folder 29.

postwar statements; "Schellenberg, a Catholic, employed an approach that appealed to the Catholic teaching of Himmler's youth." Schellenberg's influence over Himmler increased as the latter's star was descending, the report held, and, against the advice of the German military, Schellenberg persuaded a vacillating Himmler to surrender Norway and Denmark. He even convinced Rayens that Himmler took Hitler prisoner and killed him with a slow-releasing toxin. Schellenberg also suggested that his enemy Kaltenbrunner might have killed Schellenberg's wife and children while he, Schellenberg, had attempted to bring peace. Schellenberg thus fingered an official in whom the Allies had great interest and who, after Himmler's suicide, was the highest-ranking RSHA member in Allied hands. His name connected to the feared, yet largely imaginary "alpine redoubt," Kaltenbrunner was considered a security threat, a potential postwar player, and was on every arrest list. Thus, Schellenberg's "right internal enemies" helped him to establish his bona fides as one of the few Nazi officials with whom self-respecting American officials could still deal.[19] His right enemies helped Schellenberg to counterbalance his wrong friends, most prominent among them, Heinrich Himmler. Asked by Rayens why he had not renounced Nazism, Schellenberg explained that he had been afraid for his family, as he knew that he would have been killed and had therefore decided "to remain at his post and do what he could for Germany and humanity from inside the Party." He also noted that he did not take Musy's advice to flee to Switzerland and that the former Swiss president agreed that he "could do more from his position in the Party in Berlin." Schellenberg had his explanations and interpretations straight and Rayens took the bait: he believed Schellenberg and counseled in his report to Washington that Schellenberg's statements could be easily counter-checked. As his interrogators would learn in the coming years, this was easier said than done with a dissembler of Schellenberg's stature.

Schellenberg expertly capitalized on American fears, sold an illusion, and gained advantages from it. Rayens' preoccupation with the Pacific war was both apparent and unsurprising and Schellenberg stressed that he had always opposed an agreement between Japan, Russia, and Germany, a standpoint that had made him enemies among the Japanese diplomatic personnel in Germany. He thus created a commonality with Rayens and made a suggestion that Rayens could hardly afford to refuse: "Schellenberg believed that his Japanese section, personnel, specialists and records, could be assembled for the benefit of our army." Rayens

---

[19] Breitman, "Nazi Espionage," 113; Peter Black, *Ernst Kaltenbrunner: Ideological Soldier of the Third Reich* (Princeton: Princeton University Press, 1984), 260.

must have been thrilled; little did he know that Schellenberg's Japanese section was largely a mirage and that little concrete could come out of this offer. Rayens suggested that Schellenberg surrender himself to the Allied military authorities, and Schellenberg agreed, stressing that "he was not in Sweden as a refugee, but rather that fate found him here . . . ." As Bernadotte was planning to travel to Germany to discuss Red Cross business at the Supreme Headquarters of the Allied Expeditionary Force, SHAEF, in Frankfurt in the middle of June, Rayens and Bernadotte – and Schellenberg – concluded that Bernadotte should bring Schellenberg there and vouch for him. For Schellenberg the contacts to Rayens were an unadulterated success: the Americans were willing to deal, while his Swedish friends were doing much of the legwork and vouching for his character and intentions.

Rayens' straightforward plan for Schellenberg's transfer into American custody did not work out as smoothly. British military authorities were also interested in Schellenberg – as were the Soviets. But short of kidnapping the man, there was little the Soviets could do. Between the Western Allies, competition, if not conflict, developed.[20] Eventually, a compromise was reached: Schellenberg was to be brought to London for interrogations but with a stop at SHAEF Forward Headquarters in Frankfurt first. Schellenberg, for his part, believed that he had placed "himself at the disposal of the American authorities;" after the promising meetings with Rayens, British custody had become second choice. When Schellenberg boarded his plane for Frankfurt on June 17, 1945 – after almost six weeks in Sweden – Rayens, who had negotiated the transfer and seemed reasonably taken by the German, was with him. Also on board was Bernadotte, who was willing to vouch for him and who wanted to ensure that all went well.[21] Schellenberg carried his calling card: additional copies of his Autobiography.

The negotiated surrender to the Western Allies explains Schellenberg's unusual trajectory upon his arrival in Frankfurt. After registration at SHAEF, he was initially stashed away in one or several safe houses. Doerries notes with surprise that Schellenberg was not transferred to an Allied detention center for Nazi bigwigs and site of interrogations about the structure and nature of Nazi Germany, but then he had been the head of the foreign intelligence service. It made sense to interrogate Schellenberg separately and exclusively by members of the Allied. The interrogations began ten days after Schellenberg's arrival in Frankfurt and

[20] Doerries, Last Chief, 43.
[21] Final Report; Index Card, June 18, 1945, NA, RG 263, Entry ZZ-18, Box 112, File: Schellenberg, Walter, vol. 2, 1 of 2.

were summarized in a lengthy report, described as "not overly impressive in analysis and conclusion but densely packed with information and data gathered in the obviously rewarding sessions with Schellenberg."[22] The interrogations were off to a promising start.

About a fortnight later, Schellenberg was transferred to London, where his soon-to-be interrogators were giddy with anticipation: "Schellenberg is entirely co-operative and is particularly willing to denounce Kaltenbrunner."[23] Flying into London on a beautiful summer day, Schellenberg took in the sights, searching for the devastation brought upon it by German air raids. Finding little in the view available to him, he whispered: "I can not understand – no destruction at all."[24] What he saw was not in sync with what he expected to see. Schellenberg was then brought to Camp 020, an internment center theoretically under the oversight of the British Home Office but practically run as an MI 5 interrogation site; he was also interrogated at other places, most notably the Counter Intelligence War Room in London, a central intelligence office jointly organized, staffed, and led by members of the British and the US foreign intelligence services.[25] Having been treated with the care by Bernadotte and other prominent Swedes and then with much consideration by Rayens, Camp 020 was a rude awakening to Schellenberg. Its commandant, Lieutenant-Colonel R.W.G. Stephens, who scathingly described Schellenberg as a "priggish little dandy, fetched up rakishly" who was "shocked by his stern reception and sulked peevishly until he was brought face to face with the reality of British contempt for him and his evil works" clearly did not care for Schellenberg.[26] At Camp 020, the

---

[22] Doerries, *Intelligence Chief*, 233–234; Report on Interrogation of Walter Schellenberg, 27th June to July 12, 1945, NA, RG 226, Entry 125A, Box 2 [hereafter: Interrogation/June–July 1945]. Thus, the first interrogation took place on June 27, 1945, a detail Doerries confirms in a reference to the actual interrogation (as opposed to the summary report) but notes that "Schellenberg was kept inactive as long as fourteen days at the safe house in Frankfurt." Schellenberg, however, arrived on June 17; Doerries, *Intelligence Chief*, 234 note 453; 235. Schellenberg left for London on July 7, 1945 and July 12, 1945 presumably refers the report's completion. The report contains tidbit about Schellenberg's flight to London and might also include information from interrogations there.

[23] Doerries, *Last Chief*, 45–46; SHAEF Forward to War Room, July 2, 1945, NA, RG 226, Entry 119 A, Box 26, Folder Schellenberg.

[24] Interrogation/June–July 1945.

[25] Doerries, *Last Chief*, 47 note 229; Doerries, *Intelligence Chief*, 239. Doerries indicates that Schellenberg, who had been dealing with diffuse ailments for years, was already very sick when he was brought to London. Upon arrival, Schellenberg was given a thorough medical examination and pronounced healthy (enough); there is no indication that British authorities misrepresented his medical status. Final Report.

[26] *Camp 020. MI5 and the Nazi Spies. The Official History of MI5's Wartime Interrogation Centre*, introduced and edited by Oliver Hoare (Richmond: Public Record Office, 2000), 365.

interrogation of suspected spies and others had been made into an art during the war: interrogators used psychological intimidation, sensory deprivation, and played the mystique of the omnipotent British Secret Service to their advantage. However, recent research provides strong circumstantial evidence that during the war some prisoners were tortured.[27] Schellenberg had always regarded the British Secret Service as the epitome of the ideal service – and the service on which his organization should be modeled – and it is reasonable to assume that he, too, was convinced that the British knew everything that needed knowing already. There is no indication that Schellenberg was tortured but he was certainly treated more poorly than he expected; he later noted that he disliked the "light, being hollered at, cold water baths" and felt "finished." After eight weeks in a dark cell, he had been ready to kill himself but did not find the opportunity to do so.[28]

This picturesque despair stands in stark difference to his eagerness to talk; "[t]he first interrogation of Walter Schellenberg left nothing to be desired and justified reasonable hope that complete answers will be received to all queries which Schellenberg will be competent to answer." Nothing suggests that interrogators had to "force [information] out of Schellenberg," as Doerries suggests. He was, indeed, so eager to please, "playing the skin saving-game with foppish elegance," that conflict arose.[29] Counterintelligence wanted to keep him in London for further interrogations, surmising that if he were to be sent to Nuremberg for the trials under preparation there, he would lose his value as a witness; they also reckoned that Schellenberg would end any cooperation if he concluded that he might become a defendant in Nuremberg. The lawyers preparing the International Military Tribunal, on the other hand, wanted him in Nuremberg: he was a fountain of insider information, especially on Kaltenbrunner, and, possibly, a defendant.[30] Ultimately, it was decided that he was to be sent to Nuremberg eventually.

Understanding the man and the intelligence service he led and arresting any developing security threats that might still emanate from it were the interrogations' main objectives. Schellenberg and Office VI remained a mystery to the Allies – and had been a source of anxiety for years. Now

---

[27] Ian Cobian, *Cruel Britannia: A Secret History of Torture* (London: Portobello Books, 2012), 2–74.

[28] Interrogation Walter Schellenberg by R.W.M. Kempner (in German), November 13, 1947, IfZ, ZS 291/V.

[29] Interrogation/June–July 1945; *Camp 020*, 365; Doerries, *Intelligence Chief*, 240.

[30] Doerries, *Last Chief*, 47–48; Doerries, *Intelligence Chief*, 241. Doerries also raises the question why Schellenberg was never brought to the United States and surmises that the officials in the Counterintelligence War Room concluded that sending Schellenberg to Nuremberg was the lesser of two evils.

was the time to get to the bottom of matters. However, the realities revealed were a definitive and exasperating letdown, for neither the service nor the man lived up to Allied expectations.

His demeanour at this camp has not produced any evidence of outstanding genius as appears to have been generally attributed to him. On the contrary his incoherency and incapability of producing lucid verbal or written statements have rendered him a more difficult subject to interrogate than other subjects of inferior education or humbler backgrounds.[31]

Schellenberg's sagging performance has been connected to his declining health or to the interrogation procedures becoming less efficient.[32] A third possibility seems more likely: Schellenberg and his foreign intelligence service, shrouded in mystery and connected to the center of terror, had occupied British and US intelligence officials for years. Initially, little had been known but Schellenberg's proximity to Himmler as well as the fact that this new entity swallowed and transformed substantial parts of the venerable Abwehr had created the mystique of a formidable foreign intelligence service with a wiz kid spymaster at its helm.[33] Such anxieties had been unfounded, "the concern [. . .] about the absence of fresh information on the H.Q. of the Mil.Amt was needless; there was in fact little new to learn."[34] Allied ignorance had been a function of the German service's inabilities, not of its superiorities.

In October 1944, when the military intelligence section of SHAEF, G-2, prepared a lengthy report on the German intelligence service indicative of Allied concerns, that had not yet been known. Noting that Allied knowledge was small and recent – the earliest Allied knowledge about Office VI dated to winter 1940 – the report painted an ominous picture. It was a rising entity of great danger and of great personal interest to Himmler; its active espionage was "the most secret of all RSHA's activities," and the office controlled "centers of espionage in every capital city of Europe, both occupied and unoccupied, and throughout South America." It also supported Fifth Column activities and its respective representatives "may play an active part in the politics of a foreign country, acting as intermediary . . . ." G-2 appeared particularly concerned about the office's potential, for it was not content with "having established a political information service of some merit," but was "making a sustained effort first to curtail and finally to supplant the local influence of

[31] Final Report.   [32] Doerries, *Last Chief*, 47.
[33] See, for example, various R.I.S. reports: NA, RG 226, Entry 108B, Box 286, Folder – RIS Reports.
[34] Counter Intelligence War Room, London, War Room Monthly Summary No. 4, July 23, 1945, NA, RG 319, IRR, Box 195 [hereafter: War Room Summary No. 4].

the German Ambassador and his staff." The report also commented on the "enthusiasm" of the agents, who, even if unsuccessful, were indicative of the "growing importance and self-assertiveness of SD." G-2 expressed particular concern about Himmler's personal representatives, noting that political intelligence "at its most effective depends more on personal contact than on paid agents." The report also commented on various attempts to ferment disorder, for example in North Africa and Persia, and on the "impressive scale" of the office's activities in Russia, even if success was hard to gauge. The ideological coherence of the service was another cause for concern: a fusion of party and state organizations, bound together by common membership in the SS, unified headquarters, and shared commandos "have together produced a well organized and experienced security and espionage service, bound by faith and work to the Nazi scheme of things."[35] In short, it was feared that Office VI and its ideologically committed and enthusiastic members were a force to reckon with and could become a source of unpleasant and unanticipated surprises for the Allied forces.

The reality was a disappointment, but in the best possible way. Leading members of Office VI, including Schellenberg, talking freely and exhaustively, demystified Schellenberg and the organization and put to rest Allied fears of an omnipotent service that would remain a problem in the future. By mid-August 1945, a self-congratulatory tone snuck into a progress report that held that a so-called Schellenberg Report, presumably the Final Report, "comes close to exhausting the essential information on Amt VI as seen from its headquarters. [It] causes no particular change in our views of the subject. In fact, our previous knowledge of Amt VI organization is rather greater than what Schellenberg can now remember."[36] Two weeks earlier, the Counter Intelligence War Room in London issued War Room Monthly Summary No. 4. Programmatically entitled "Obituary of the G.I.S." it was charitable neither on the service nor on its mastermind. Its purpose was to "wind up [the] history of the G.I.S. [German Intelligence Service] as an intelligence service," made possible by Schellenberg's and Sandberger's recent, exhaustive testimonies. Not mincing words, the report declared that "[i]t would be neither profitable nor honest to occupy ourselves any longer with this once over-rated institution." It noted that Schellenberg had dreamt of a big service, fashioned after "what he believed to be the English model,"

[35] SHAEF, G-2 German Intelligence Service, October 4, 1944, NA, RG 319, Entry 134 A (Impersonal), Box 5, XE 003641, German Intelligence Service, 1 of 3.
[36] Cable from Ustravic, July 13, 1945/June 1, 1955; Progress Report, August 13, 1945/June 3, 1955, NA, RG 263, Entry ZZ-18, Box 112, File: Schellenberg, vol. 1, 2 of 2.

but that the service was largely "a fiction of Schellenberg's own mind," and that he "neither had the time nor the official support" to make his dream reality. Stressing Office VI's "tradition of failure and incompetence," another Allied report scathingly described "a number of insignificant agents [who] were recruited to no purpose by officers who had little or no knowledge of what they wanted." Himmler, however, had advertised isolated successes, thereby camouflaging the office's overall failures. Office VI had realized Allied deceptions too late, had no direct sources in the United States or the United Kingdom, and, when it actually possessed accurate information, believed that being played by the Allies. In addition, Western intelligence agencies had been aware of all of Office VI's most relevant activities. Consequently, Office VI "never materially affected the fortunes of the war." Even Schellenberg's late 1944 attempts to better the situation through the creation of the Central Office, meant to be the "brain of the organization," had not made a difference, for "the brain still lacked the limbs and nerves which could execute its purposes." The Allied reports also noted that Office VI had received no support from German military authorities and that his colleagues in the RSHA, particularly Kaltenbrunner and Heinrich "Gestapo" Müller, had regarded Schellenberg and his office with "jealous hostility." Indeed, "the reality was a service in almost every part corrupt and stupid."[37]

On the man himself, the summary was no more generous:

The Amtschef had been described by almost all our sources as able, ambitious and coldly calculating; from obscurity he had risen to be the youngest Major-General in the SS. For a German he had a unique opportunity of objective study of actual conditions outside of Germany, and he had the most naïve and ridiculous conceptions of English and American policy and method. [. . .] neither Schellenberg nor any of the officers under his command had the capacity to evaluate the political and other intelligence which it was their function to collect, to discriminate between sense and nonsense, good sources and bad [. . .].

Neither the man nor the service were what they had been rumored to be. Yet Schellenberg and Sandberger apparently managed to shift some blame, as the report also noted, "their advice would have been rejected by their infatuated leaders." Ultimately, the report recognized Schellenberg's role in the creation of this largely imaginary intelligence service and the impact it – and he – had on Himmler, " . . . Amt VI was a world of illusion and naivety, not of sinister design; but, unlike the old Abwehr,

---

[37] War Room Summary No. 4; The German Intelligence Service and the War, [no date], NA, RG 319, Entry 134 A (Impersonal), Box 5, XE 003641, German Intelligence Service.

its illusions were powerfully represented and contributed to the general ruin. Himmler believed in Schellenberg until the end."[38]

The realization that neither Schellenberg nor Office VI had been paeans of professionalism – even if there had been no shortage of sinister designs – held immediate benefits for the Allies. There had been concern about "Stay-Behind" or "Post-Surrender" Networks and the security of Allied troops in Germany. The interrogators realized quickly that such networks had been discussed, but "never matured," or, for networks planned for neutral countries, had been dependent on the continuance of a central authority, "which of course no longer exists."[39] The Allies were equally pleased that, beginning with the disintegration of the Reich and fully after its surrender, Office VI simply ceased to exist. Already by the summer of 1945, the Allies' interest – aside from US concerns about German spies in the Southern hemisphere, the situation on the Iberian Peninsula, and a few individuals – was historical. The relief was palpable and tempered by contempt and, maybe, the realization that in its focus on Office VI, Allied intelligence had been chasing a mirage: "The post-mortem is now complete; further dissection of the limbs of the corps is pointless." Indeed, there was more concern about Amt IV, the Gestapo, which had proven to be "more experienced and professionally competent at running agents" than Schellenberg's office. And while the latter had "largely surrendered," the former "will need to be found."[40] Based on the respective experiences Allied interrogators had made with members of Office IV and VI, they concluded that policemen "are less easily made to tell the truth than intelligence officers." The mystique surrounding Schellenberg, his office, and its members had clearly vanished – as did the Allies' detailed interest in all things Office VI.

Schellenberg was brought to Nuremberg in fall 1945.[41] Exploiting status as the quintessential insider, he initially and with compelling lucidity – notably different from his lackluster performance at Camp 020 and in London – served as a witness for the prosecution. But then the situation at the Nuremberg Palace of Justice must have been much more agreeable to Schellenberg. He was housed in the witness wing of the building and interrogated in view of the upcoming trial against the major war

---

[38] War Room Summary No. 4.
[39] Cable from Ustravic, July 13, 1945/June 1, 1955; C.I. War Room Publication – Amt VI, August 11, 1945/June 16, 1955, NA, RG 263, Entry ZZ-18, Box 112, File: Schellenberg, vol. 2, 2 of 2; War Room Summary No. 4.
[40] War Room Summary No. 4.
[41] The date of Schellenberg's transfer to Nuremberg is unclear; Doerries, *Last Chief*, 48 notes 235, 236; Doerries, *Intelligence Chief*, 242–243. Doerries notes that the C.I.C. still interrogated Schellenberg and took him on unexplained trips in the US Occupation Zone.

SCHELLENBERG

Image 9.1. Half-length portrait of Walter Schellenberg, ullstein bild/ gettyimages.

criminals. Trained in law, Schellenberg likely felt much more at home under these circumstances while his role as a witness for the prosecution allowed him to flaunt his knowledge of the system's inner workings and its leading personalities and to keep honing his new persona as a friend of the Allies. "The best thing Schellenberg had going for him after the war was that he had developed the right internal enemies," Richard Breitman quips shrewdly, describing precisely a fortuitous situation Schellenberg exploited to the hilt.[42] Among his right enemies were Ernst Kaltenbrunner, the head of the RSHA and Schellenberg's superior; Foreign Minister Joachim von Ribbentrop; the Gestapo chief Heinrich Müller, who had disappeared at war's end; and sabotage expert Otto Skorzeny – all men the Allies planned to prosecute. As

---

[42] Breitman, "Nazi Espionage," 113.

Schellenberg's luck had it, these were the men with whom he had inter-
acted closely, competed viciously, and whom he had grown to dislike
intensely over the years. He had much to say about them and none of
it was good. They counterbalanced nicely Schellenberg's late "wrong
friends," a category in which Heydrich and Himmler took pride of place.
However, by brandishing his insider credentials – he had been close to
positions of power since the mid-1930s – Schellenberg established himself as the resident expert on many matters structural and organizational
issues of great interest to the Allies and under these particular circumstances his wrong friends transformed into assets, for his professional and
personal proximity to them lent his statements even greater credibility.
Schellenberg transformed two proverbial albatrosses around his neck into
assets.

Catering toward their interests and preoccupations while whitewash-
ing and obfuscating his record, Schellenberg delivered on Allied expectations. This was particularly true when it came to Kaltenbrunner, whom
historians have pronounced Schellenberg's "most dangerous enemy,"
arguing that Schellenberg "cooperated [with him] out of necessity."
Whether this captures realities – the two men had worked well together
for some time and had agreed on many issues – remains questionable, but
the assessment certainly reflects Schellenberg's view. Already at Camp
020 it was well known that no love was lost between them, providing
amusement to their interrogators: Schellenberg "was found anxious to
indict his former chief. Kaltenbrunner [. . .] responded with gratifying
tu quoques."[43] However, the Allies regarded Kaltenbrunner, who – as a
visual bonus – fit the image of the proverbial ugly German down to his
dueling scars, as particularly unsavory; there was no doubt that he would
stand trial.[44] Schellenberg never passed an opportunity to lay blame at
Kaltenbrunner's doorstep but deftly sidestepped their substantial cooperation over the years. Traces of this strategy can, indeed, already be
found in reports on Schellenberg's conversations with Jean-Marie Musy
and Count Bernadotte in late 1944 and early 1945 and his later talks with
Rayens; it came to full fruition thereafter.[45] It is impossible to quantify
the relevance of Schellenberg's testimony for Kaltenbrunner's conviction,
but it indubitably helped. The corollary of Schellenberg's eagerness to
tar Kaltenbrunner was that it accentuated his independent spirit and his

[43] Doerries, *Intelligence Chief*, 241; *Camp 020*, 81; 363.
[44] Black, *Kaltenbrunner*, 258–276.
[45] Katrin Paehler, "Auditioning for Postwar: Walter Schellenberg, the Allies, and Attempts
      to Fashion a Usable Past," in David Messenger and Katrin Paehler, eds., *From Nazis
      to West Germans: Self Invention, Recast Identities, and the Politics of the Past after 1945*
      (Lexington: The University of Kentucky Press 2015), 29–56.

Postwar   335

good deeds, both of which allegedly irked Kaltenbrunner. Indeed, by its constant retelling, Schellenberg's role as a humanitarian and thwarted bringer of peace, supported by affidavits from Bernadotte, Musy and Masson, began to overshadow anything else: his years as Heydrich's and Himmler's right-hand man or his long tenure at the helm of Office VI. These activities also served as an explanation for Schellenberg's close association with Himmler, as he presented a coherent and teleological narrative according to which he had begun to plant the seeds of negation with Himmler as early as late summer 1942, but had to wait for them to come to fruition in April 1945. Lastly, Schellenberg took on the mantle of a diplomat and cast himself not as the nefarious spymaster of an SS agency but as a diplomat representing an alternative to Ribbentrop's Foreign Office. In short, there was no reason to prosecute Schellenberg.

Schellenberg believed for more than two years that he would be able to avoid standing trial but, at long last, the US authorities found a case in which to include him.[46] He became one of the twenty-one defendants in *Case No. 11: United States of America vs. Ernst von Weizsäcker et al.*, also known as the Wilhelmstrasse-Trial or the Ministries-Trial. Case 11 was a late, judicial mopping-up operation by US prosecutors and as the trial's monikers indicate, Schellenberg was indicted alongside members of the old bureaucracy and the Auswärtige Amt, among them luminaries and rumored resisters such as State Secretary Ernst von Weizsäcker.[47] This was already a victory for Schellenberg and evidence of the dexterity with which Schellenberg had managed to recast himself – no mean feat for an early and influential member of the SD and the RSHA and a close associate of Heydrich and Himmler.

The trial opened in early January 1948 and went on for fifteen months. Schellenberg was indicted on four counts, a situation that Doerries regards as better than that of other defendants but "potentially very dangerous."[48] Yet considering Schellenberg's former roles and positions, the indictment alone provides clear evidence of the court's commitment to the rule of law: both the indictment and the eventual verdict highlight

---

[46] Indictments were handed down of November 4, 1947; Doerries, *Intelligence Chief*, 251; 253.

[47] Eckart Conze et al., *Das Amt und die Vergangenheit: Deutsche Diplomaten im Dritten Reich und in der Bundesrepublik* (München: Karl Blessing Verlag, 2010), 380–391, esp. 382.

[48] Doerries, *Intelligence Chief*, 253; Doerries, *Last Chief of Foreign Intelligence*, 49–50. In the latter, Doerries indicates surprise that Schellenberg was not indicted under Count IV, "Crimes against Humanity: Atrocities and Offenses Committed against German Nationals on Political, Racial, and Religious Grounds from 1933 to 1939", "in spite of his brief service in Amt IV." Schellenberg began his service with the Gestapo's counterintelligence department in late fall 1939; an indictment would not have made a lot of sense for a court that followed the law to the letter. Schellenberg had also managed to steer Allied interest away from his tenure with the Gestapo.

the court's measured approaches. Count I concerned "Planning, Preparation, Initiation and Waging Wars of Aggression and Invasion of Other Countries" and Schellenberg was indicted due to SS and SD membership, the Venlo incident, and the Einsatzgruppen negotiations in 1941. The complex issue of the Einsatzgruppen negotiations fell largely by the wayside in the court's deliberations on this count, to be taken up elsewhere. Ultimately, Schellenberg was acquitted on Count I. "Venlo" not withstanding, he could not be convicted of the preparation of war in the proper sense. And like all his co-defendants charged under Count II, "Planning and Committing Crimes against Peace, War Crimes, and Crimes against Humanity," Schellenberg was acquitted, for the court concluded that "a conviction of the defendants in a common plan and conspiracy" was not warranted.[49]

On Count V, "War Crimes and Crimes against Humanity: Atrocities and Offenses committed against Civilian Populations," the court came to a mixed result. The indictment mentioned Schellenberg's role in the Einsatzgruppen negotiations of spring 1941, but the court chose to acquit, a testament to the court's high standards. There was no doubt about the role Schellenberg had at Heydrich's behest – he had testified to that matter extensively, if guardedly – but the court's decision rested on the issue of knowledge. Reasonable doubt remained about Schellenberg's knowledge of the Einsatzgruppen's precise mission, despite his involvement in the negotiations. The court voiced suspicions about the defendant's narrative – Schellenberg claimed to have been sent out of the room when Heydrich and Army Quartermaster General Wagner discussed a secret Führer Order – but remained staunchly committed to the cornerstones of Western jurisprudence: *in dubio pro reo*: "While we doubt that Schellenberg was as ignorant of the mission of the Einsatzgruppen as he now asserts, the proof that he had knowledge does not convince us to a moral certainty. We therefore give him the benefit of the doubt . . . ."[50] Schellenberg was acquitted on this charge. The court was nothing if not deliberate.

The murders committed in the context of Operation Zeppelin – the deployment of Soviet POWs as spies on the Eastern Front – were a different matter. Schellenberg's involvement with Operation Zeppelin had been less direct than with Einsatzgruppen deliberations, but it had been under his jurisdiction; when asked point-blank in court, Schellenberg's answer was to the point: "Zeppelin was subordinated to me." There was also testimony by Auschwitz survivor Kasimierz Smolen about the

---

[49] Doerries, *Intelligence Chief*, 255.
[50] Doerries, *Last Chief*, 50–52; Doerries, *Intelligence Chief*, 256–257.

execution of Zeppelin men. Smolen, who worked in the camp's "political department" and saw the attendant paperwork, could not recall having seen a decree signed by Schellenberg, though. Most of the murders originated with the Gestapo, but Office VI was informed.[51] In short, Zeppelin was Schellenberg's responsibility and he regularly received information about the execution of "used-up" agents. What ultimately transpired with this charge is the flipside of Schellenberg's acquittal when it came to the Einsatzgruppen and not, as Doerries implies, the result of the prosecution's success in tripping up Schellenberg. Not having held any official responsibility worked to his benefit in the former situation – regardless of the function he had fulfilled and the knowledge he must have had. For Operation Zeppelin the opposite was true: it was subordinate to Schellenberg and the responsibility was his. Lastly, Schellenberg was found guilty of "Membership of a Criminal Organization." His membership in SS, SD, and Gestapo caught up with him.[52] The indictment had suggested a judicious court and the verdict bore it out; Schellenberg benefitted mightily from rule of law and the growing US interest in West German public opinion.

Schellenberg and his defense provided the court with a staple of affidavits, colloquially called *Persilscheine*, a pun on a German slogan for a popular detergent: "Persil washes whiter than white." These affidavits, noting that a person had never been a real Nazi or had helped victims of persecution, were a valuable commodity. Schellenberg made the best out of his humanitarian endeavors and provided some truly valuable affidavits that spoke to his achievements and bore the signatures of foreigners and, even more impressively, in one instance of a Jew. They surely factored into the court's sentencing.[53] Among the people who wrote affidavits on his behalf were both Musys – father and son – Count Bernadotte, and Isaac Sternbruch of the Union of the Orthodox Rabbis of the United States of America and Canada. The Swedish Minister to Berlin, Arvid Richter, wrote for Schellenberg, praising him for having assisted the Swedes in all matters, as did Alvar Moeller and Jacob Wallenberg. Intriguingly, both Richter and Moeller claimed to have approached Schellenberg to get the Gestapo off the back of Swedish diplomat Raoul Wallenberg in Budapest in 1944, but no reference to this can be found elsewhere. Richter and Moeller also stated that they had offered Schellenberg refuge in Sweden only to be turned down by him. And Bernadotte made sure to have it known that Schellenberg "neither requested nor received" anything from

---

[51] Doerries, *Intelligence Chief*, 260–262.
[52] Doerries, *Last Chief*, 52–53; Doerries, *Intelligence Chief*, 262–263.
[53] Doerries, *Intelligence Chief*, 264.

Image 9.2 The Defendants of the Ministries Trial sit in the dock. First row, left to right: State Secretaries Ernst von Weizsäcker, Gustav Adolf Steengracht von Moyland, Wilhelm Keppler, and Ernst Wilhelm Bohle. Second row: Press Chief Otto Bohle, SS General Gottlob Berger, Intelligence Chief Walter Schellenberg, and Reich Finance Minister Lutz Schwerin von Krosigk, circa 1947. United States Holocaust Memorial Museum. [Photograph # 66035]

the Swede for his assistance during the Swedish rescue missions in early 1945. Roger Masson, retired and largely disgraced in Switzerland, supported Schellenberg's assertion that he prevented a German invasion of Switzerland, a statement Henri Guisan confirmed with a handwritten note. To this Schellenberg was able to add affidavits by people who had worked with or for him, such as Franz Göring or his driver Hugo Buchwald or Emil Bernsdorff of the Gestapo who noted that Schellenberg never sent people into protective custody.[54] And in the face of prosecution by the Allies, old animosities among Nazi Germany's elites were

---

[54] Doerries, *Last Chief*, 53; Doerries, *Intelligence Chief*, 264–270. See also the various affidavits found in NA, RG 242, M 897, Reel 114. Published works, such as Bernadotte's and Kersten's memoirs, Dulles' book on the German resistance, and Trevor-Roper's book on the last days of Hitler, were also presented in Schellenberg's defense.

shoved aside: old enemies like Werner Best and Otto Skorzeny wrote on Schellenberg's behalf, if less glowingly than his new friends.[55] These affidavits – sometimes described as "sensitive personal statement[s] of recognition" or as remarkable since a Jew wrote "in favor of a ranking SS leader" or as indicative of Schellenberg's "different side" – should not be taken at face value. Basic factual information is likely to be correct, but the affidavits were part of an economy of exchange. This is a truism when it comes to German officials who wrote for Schellenberg. They could rest assured that he would return the favor and the milder Schellenberg's sentence, the greater the value of his future affidavits. The Swedes and Swiss who made the Court aware that Schellenberg "was respected and accepted by these cultured and internationally known personalities from the world of business and diplomacy," as Doerries phrases it, were involved in a different economy of exchange.[56]

They had dealt with the devil and sometimes also looked back on individual and collective cooperation with Nazi Germany. Establishing their negotiation partner as not completely despicable but as a cultured and sensible man driven by humanitarian concerns, helped to varnish their reputations in turn. Everybody won.

The court's final verdict, and the treatment of the ailing Schellenberg thereafter, was a testament to its fairness and to the changing political environment. The sentence of six years' imprisonment was handed down on April 14, 1949. Time served since June 17, 1945, the day Schellenberg arrived at SHAEF Headquarters in Frankfurt after his Swedish sojourn, was applied, making him eligible for release on June 17, 1951. This was a mild sentence, indeed, and the defendant, like many others, had benefitted from the timing of the trial. By 1947 and 1948, the Cold War was heating up; the Berlin Blockade began during the trial. Prosecuting Nazi war criminals was no longer a priority. By the late 1940s, Schellenberg was also an extremely sick man who had been diagnosed with cholangitis and cholecystitis, basically progressing ailments of the gall bladder that led to additional complications such as liver damage, jaundice, and generally poor health. In October 1948 already, a prison physician felt unable to make a prognosis about Schellenberg's possible recovery or life expectancy. Recuperating from gall bladder surgery and allegedly kept alive by strong doses of penicillin, Schellenberg did not attend his sentencing in April 1949. Additional surgery was deemed necessary, but the prisoner remained weak and his prognosis abysmal and was therefore never transferred to the Landsberg prison. Instead, he was

---

[55] NA, RG 242, M 897, Reel 114.
[56] Doerries, *Intelligence Chief*, 266; 267; 270; 272.

held in a guarded room in the Nuremberg City Hospital. He must have been in dire shape, as a February 1950 report stated that Schellenberg was bed-ridden and no flight risk. On March 27, 1950, the US High Commissioner for Germany, John J. McCloy, signed Walter Schellenberg's medical pardon.[57] He had not even served five years.

Recreating Schellenberg's postpardon life is surprisingly difficult, even though US intelligence, sometimes with the help of the Gehlen organization – the nascent West German intelligence service led by Reinhard Gehlen, formerly of Foreign Armies East, kept an eye on him. US intelligence held a general interest in Schellenberg, but was keen to learn his thoughts about Gehlen. This does not contradict the 1945 British assessment of the man as "not of outstanding genius," for even those who are not may hold relevant or interesting information – especially under changed circumstances. After his release, Schellenberg moved to another medical facility; he was then traced to a hospital in Iburg and described as "very, very sick."[58] But he apparently recovered well enough and between fall 1950 and summer 1951 Schellenberg's whereabouts remain unclear. The CIA reported a visit to Spain in May 1951, during which he was alleged to have contacted Skorzeny, who was involved with in various Nazi and Fascist networks. However, little concrete is known about this trip: there might have been talk about the creation of a "militarily organized protection force" and financial issues were discussed as well.[59] The sources remain tantalizingly vague.

Reinhard Doerries has, on the other hand, unearthed an intriguing memoir by a Swiss country doctor, Francis Lang, that provides seemingly reliable detail on Schellenberg's location and situation between fall 1951 and his death in March 1952.[60] In May 1951, Roger Masson contacted Lang; he had received Lang's name from an acquaintance, who was friends with the doctor. Masson wanted Lang to care for Schellenberg and Lang agreed to do so at the hospital of Billens, Switzerland. Lang and his

---

[57] Doerries, *Last Chief of Foreign Intelligence*, 53; 53 note 277; Doerries, *Intelligence Chief*, 273–276.

[58] In June 1950, the CIA traced Schellenberg to a hospital in Iburg, near Osnabrück. Heidelberg to Special Operations, June 26, 1950, NA, RG 263, Entry ZZ-18, Box 112, File: Schellenberg, vol. 2, 2 of 2. Additional materials that indicate US interest in keeping tabs on Schellenberg as well as the involvement of Gehlen and his men can be found here. Doerries, *Intelligence Chief*, 278–279.

[59] Special Operations to Pullach, Karlsruhe, 16 May 1951, NA, RG 263, CIA Name Files (Reference Collection), Box 45, Schellenberg, vol. 2. For a redacted account of this meeting, indicating that Skorzeny was talking to CIA members: NA, RG 263, Entry ZZ-18, Box 112, File: Schellenberg, vol. 2, 2 of 2. This version indicates that. Doerries, *Intelligence Chief*, 280–282.

[60] Doerries, *Intelligence Chief*, 282–287.

wife apparently also socialized with Schellenberg and encountered several situations when Schellenberg, who was in the country illegally, was
recognized on Swiss streets. The pressures on Schellenberg were mounting and Lang eventually tried to marshal the help of Guisan and Musy.
Guisan, afraid of repercussions, demurred but Musy went all out, trying
to arrange refuge for Schellenberg in the Vatican, or so Lang remembers. All of this is curious, as Lang initially contacted Guisan because he
wanted to transfer Schellenberg to a better hospital in Lausanne. Lang
eventually located a clinic right across the border in Italy willing to take
Schellenberg. Outfitted with a fake Swiss passport and driven by "Masson's man Sven Hinnen," Schellenberg was driven to Pallanza on the
Lago Maggiore where his wife joined him. In March 1952, travelling on
the train with his wife, possibly to see a doctor in Turin, Schellenberg
experienced a medical emergency. Subsequent surgery did not save his
life, but gave him a few days during which Lang found a priest to give
Schellenberg his last rites. Apparently, Schellenberg returned to Catholicism – the religion in which he had been raised – during his stay at
Nuremberg: "in Switzerland and Italy he wore a cross and took commu-
nion regularly." In his deathbed confession Schellenberg made sure that
the priest knew about "all the things he did for Switzerland." He died of
heart failure, liver cirrhosis – there is no indication that he had been a
heavy drinker – and an infection of the spleen on the last day of March
1952.[61]

It remains an open question how Schellenberg paid for his and his
family's upkeep and his presumably substantial medical expenses. Schellenberg had been working on his memoirs for some time, even though
his exact work schedule remains a matter of dispute.[62] It is known that
Schellenberg was already considering writing his memoirs when he was in
Sweden in summer 1945 and likely expected it to be a source of income.
One is reminded of Galeazzo Ciano who, too, believed that his and his
family's financial wellbeing rested on his memoirs. But Schellenberg did
not sell the manuscript before his death. Lang, in this context, relates

---

[61] Doerries, *Last Chief*, 52–53; Doerries, *Intelligence Chief*, 287; Klaus Happrecht, "Vorwort," in Walter Schellenberg, *Aufzeichnungen: Die Memoiren des letzten Geheimdien-
stchefs unter Hitler*, ed., Gita Petersen (Wiesbaden: Limes, 1979), 7–20. Happrecht
dates Schellenberg's death to the beginning of March 1952. Chief [redacted] to Chief
WE, Specific – Walter Schellenberg, October 20, 1952, NA, RG 263, CIA Name Files
(Reference Collection), Box 45, Schellenberg, vol. 2. André Brissaud, who later wrote
The Nazi Secret Service (New York: W.W. Norton, 1974), seemed to have chanced on
Schellenberg in Italy.

[62] Doerries suggests that he worked on it while in the hospital in Nuremberg. The Institut
für Zeitgeschichte (IfZ) in Munich, which holds the files, dates them to 1951/1952.
Doerries, *Intelligence Chief*, 274.

a titillating story, as does a recent biography on French fashion icon Coco Chanel. Meeting with Schellenberg, Lang noted that he had laid out 20,000 Swiss Francs over the preceding months, a minor fortune. Schellenberg subsequently contacted Coco Chanel who eventually called on Schellenberg – in a black Mercedes nonetheless – and handed him 30,000 francs. Indeed, it appears that Chanel had already given Schellenberg a substantial sum in June 1951, after learning that he intended to publish his memoir. Chanel had collaborated with both Abwehr and SD – including yet another ill-fated attempt to make contact with the Western Allies, in this case the British in 1943 – and might have hoped to keep her name out of Schellenberg's book. Schellenberg's widow Irene, who eventually handled the book's publication, stated, "Madame Chanel offered us financial assistance in our difficult situation and it was thanks for her that we were able to spend a few more months together."[63] Someone footed the bill – be it Chanel or several people – but it surely was not Schellenberg.

Among the last people who spent uninterrupted time with Schellenberg was the German journalist Klaus Happrecht, who was working with Schellenberg on his memoirs. Happrecht provided a fascinating sketch of a broken man, an opportunistic parvenu, eager to please, and trying to bathe in the afterglow of bygone glory while harboring ill-will against Reinhard Gehlen, who was creating the West German intelligence service under American tutelage. Schellenberg never understood that it was not "for the time being," as he wrote in his memoirs, that his "services were not required anymore." And he oscillated between frustrations that the Italians were not interested in his activities and the conviction that various services were keeping him under close surveillance.[64] He might have been on to something, even though the surveillance was less close than he assumed. A document in the CIA records, dating to February 1952, reported that Schellenberg led an information service, called, curiously, "Anbeter der absoluten Macht," Admirers of Absolute Power, which allegedly attempted to establish international connections, "especially in

[63] Doerries, *Intelligence Chief*, 284. On Chanel's association with German foreign intelligence, but with some interpretative issues: Hal Vaughan, *Sleeping with the Enemy. Coco Chanel's Secret War* (New York: Alfred A. Knopf, 2011), 205–207, chapter 10 "A Mission for Himmler."

[64] Happrecht, "Vorwort," 7–20; Timothy Naftali, "Reinhard Gehlen and the United States," in Richard Breitman et al., eds., *U.S. Intelligence and the Nazis* (Washington, DC: National Trust Fund for the Nazi War Crimes and Japanese Imperial Government Records Interagency Working Group, 2004), 375–418. Doerries raises interesting questions as to when and where Happrecht met with Schellenberg; Doerries, *Intelligence Chief*, 285. Walter Schellenberg, *The Labyrinth: Memoirs of Walter Schellenberg, Hitler's Chief of Counterintelligence*, trans. Louis Hagen (New York: Harper & Brothers, 1956; reprint, Cambridge, MA: Da Capo Press, 2000), 412.

Austria," after having already established such in Spain and North Africa. And in early March, an unidentified person with connections to the West German intelligence service, the *Bundesnachrichtendienst* (BND), let it be known that he had been invited to visit Schellenberg at the latter's expense.[65] It is unsurprising, then, that the intelligence services received the news of Schellenberg's death with some disbelief; ideas of a faked death and of Schellenberg as a potential key figure in a nascent European fascist movement made their rounds. CIA and BND officials worked hand in hand to confirm Schellenberg's death and eventually settled on the veracity of the news.[66] After his death, his widow and the children returned to Germany.[67]

[65] Information Service: Anbeter der absoluten Macht, February 7, 1955/June 24, 1955; [No title], March 5,1955/July 25, 1955, NA, RG 263, Entry ZZ-18, Box 112, File: Schellenberg, vol. 2, 2 of 2.

[66] Redacted to Chief, WE, Walter Schellenberg, 20 October 1952, NA, RG 263, Entry ZZ-18, Box 112, File: Schellenberg, vol. 2, 2 of 2.

[67] 25 to 30, Betrifft: Schellenberg, 8 May 1952, NA, RG 263, CIA Name Files (Reference Collection), Box 45, Schellenberg, vol. 2.

10 Concluding Thoughts

Schellenberg is hard to grasp. To some extent this has to do with a lack of sources, as no documents of Schellenberg exist that do not have an implicit public audience or are means to an exculpatory end. There are no unguarded letters or diaries that allow for an unvarnished view of the man or smoking guns that reveal hidden truths. Schellenberg was inordinately ambitious but then, so were many. And many young men made formidable careers in Nazi Germany – a state led by comparatively young men – but Schellenberg's career stands out still.[1] Was he simply, as his former subordinate Wilhelm Waneck mused in the 1970s, "at the bottom of his heart [...] never a National Socialist, but an eager swot for power and influence?"[2]

The story of his marriages perhaps illustrates best the depths of Schellenberg's overall ambitions, his eagerness to achieve what he believed he deserved and was owed, his personal make-up, and his corresponding Achilles' heel. Schellenberg's premarital relationship with his first wife is best described with an untranslatable German term: it was a *Bratkartoffelverhältnis*, a cohabitant relationship in which an older woman caters to the financial – and sexual – needs of an ambitious younger man, hoping to gain married respectability and status eventually. It is a risky relationship for the woman; in economic parlance, it is a future's market. For several years after the end of his studies and while advancing rapidly in the SD, Schellenberg did not hold up his end of the bargain. He did not marry her. Yet once his supervisors began to pressure him to legalize his long-standing relationship, he obeyed and brought his private life in line with his public persona as one of the rising stars of the SD. The marriage did not last. Schellenberg realized that his new wife, a former seamstress – described by him as older, unsophisticated, unglamorous, and after years of cohabitation still without child – would be a dead weight in his effort

---

[1] Götz Aly quoted in Harald Welzer, *Täter: Wie aus ganz normalen Menschen Massenmörder werden*. Unter Mitarbeit von Michaela Christ (Frankfurt: Fischer Taschenbuch Verlag, 2013), 53 note 94.
[2] Wilhelm Waneck, Der Auslandsnachrichtendienst, ms., 1970s, IfZ, ZS 1597/II.

to rise professionally and socially. He began to contemplate divorce. But Frau Schellenberg was not going to go quietly, and she was well aware of her husband's vulnerabilities: reconciliation was possible, she reckoned, if her husband's supervisors would issue the appropriate orders and if he were to fear professional costs. Consequently, she sought appointments with Heydrich and Himmler, succeeding with the former. In the end, her hopes came to naught and the divorce took place, although not without causing her husband a good measure of embarrassment.[3] Schellenberg's second marriage was far more suitable; his bride was young, from a good family – even though she had distant Polish relations – by all accounts attractive, and bore several children in short order. No one should pass judgment on another person's marriages, especially not based on fragmentary information, but it is apparent that even Schellenberg's matrimonial life was connected to his professional ambitions. He always did what was best for him and his career. Careerism, opportunism, ambition, and the desire to curry favor with those who could be of use to him defined Schellenberg. But ultimately these attributes alone cannot account for his success.

Schellenberg's political and ideological convictions remain surprisingly hazy. There are no telltale signs of epic proportions. Put differently, he was neither Werner Best, whose programmatic writings make it possible to discern Best's ideological make-up, nor Otto Ohlendorf, who led an Einsatzgruppe and later discussed freely his activities.[4] Yet by investigating his writing and actions, one can arrive at a good approximation of Schellenberg's ideological make-up and show him as an able bureaucrat and occasional activist rooted firmly in National Socialist ideology and practice. Slightly younger than his peers who led the other RSHA offices – Himmler's "Benjamin" – Schellenberg was still right out of central casting for Nazi Germany's elite. His biographical background, from his earliest childhood experiences to not having engaged in National Socialist student politics before January 1933 and having joined party and SS in 1933, was common.[5] It then remains intriguing, though, that he began his SD career as an ideological speaker. But Schellenberg's time in Marburg – a choice – was not devoid of politics. The town, the university, and

---

[3] BAL, R 58, Anhang I/49.

[4] Ulrich Herbert, *Best: Biographische Studien über Radikalismus, Weltanschauung und Vernunft 1903–1989*, 2nd ed. (Bonn: Dietz, 1996); Hilary Earl, *The Nuremberg SS-Einsatzgruppen Trial: Atrocity, Law, and History* (New York: Cambridge University Press, 2009).

[5] Gerhard Paul, "Von Psychopathen, Technokraten des Terrors und 'ganz gewöhnlichen Deutschen': Die Täter der Shoah im Spiegel der Forschung," in Gerhard Paul, ed., *Die Täter der Shoah. Fanatische Nationalsozialisten oder ganz normale Deutsche?* Dachauer Symposium zur Zeitgeschichte, Bd. 2 (Göttingen: Wallstein Verlag, 2002), 45.

Schellenberg's corps Guestphalia were known for their anti-republican and anti-Semitic disposition. As an ideological speaker in Bonn, Schellenberg took these prevalent ideas to the next, more radicalized level and there is no reason to assume that he found it difficult. "Ideological conjunctions" – shared assumptions, values and beliefs, defined by anti-liberal, anti-Marxist, nationalist, racist, and anti-Semitic mentalities – between "radically racist Nazis" and a broader swath of conservative Germans, which George Browder proposes, made such moves not only possible but easy and altogether unremarkable. These conjunctions, Browder argues, ultimately "suck[ed] in vast number of allies."[6] They did even more: they also netted people of great ability. Schellenberg liked to note after the war that some of his peers found his high party number suspicious but his activities and writings at the time give no indication that he was concerned about his lack of pre-1933 activism or overcompensated for his ideological and biographical shortcomings by being particularly ideological, as has been suggested for Arthur Greiser and Reinhard Heydrich.[7] Schellenberg appears self-assured and at peace with himself.

There is no reason to conclude that Schellenberg kept his distance from National Socialist ideology or practice, a notion he intimated after 1945 and which permeates the literature. Even if Schellenberg was not the most convinced National Socialist in 1933 or even 1934, he was surely in basic agreement with its core policies. Claudia Koonz, among others, suggests that to understand National Socialism's mass appeal, one should regard it as an "ethnic revival" or "ethnic fundamentalism," in which the German *volk*, the racial community, brought together by its shared traits and convictions, was pitted against its racial–ideological enemies. The wellbeing of Aryans became the "benchmark for moral reasoning."[8] Schellenberg's postwar writings make clear that he shared the belief in a need for an ethnic revival and in a state organized by the *Führerprinzip*, leadership principle, for the benefit of the racially defined folk. Schellenberg questioned neither the state nor its organizations. Ultimately, knowing and slightly sardonic postwar remarks about individuals – primarily his rivals – and the way in which they ran their fiefdoms were the long and short of Schellenberg's proudly proffered critical distance to the state. He served this state diligently.

---

[6] George C. Browder, *Hitler's Enforcers: The Gestapo and the SS Security Service in the Nazi Revolution* (New York: Oxford University Press, 1996), 7.

[7] Catherine Epstein, *Model Nazi: Arthur Greiser and the Occupation of Western Poland* (Oxford: Oxford University Press, 2010), 8–9; Robert Gerwarth, *Hitler's Hangman: The Life of Heydrich* (New Haven and London: Yale University Press, 2011), xviii–xx.

[8] Claudia Koonz, *The Nazi Conscience* (Cambridge, MA: The Belknap Press of Harvard University Press, 2003), 4–13.

If Schellenberg distinguished himself from some of his peers it was by a lack of ideological obsessiveness and a higher level of ideological pragmatism. Ideology was key but not a straightjacket. This facet of Schellenberg's personality and ideological make-up are particularly apparent when it comes to the core concept of anti-Semitism. He was not a rabid anti-Semite and there is no indication that *Judenpolitik*, Jewish policy, as defined by Peter Longerich, was of central interest or importance to Schellenberg.[9] Rather, anti-Semitism and Judenpolitik were unquestioned facts of life. During his divorce proceedings, for example, Schellenberg contemplated pacifying his estranged wife with a recently "aryanized shop or something of that sort;" Office VI's building in Berlin-Schmargendorf was a former Jewish Old People's Home whose residents had been deported East shortly before Schellenberg and his men took over the facility in 1941.[10] And at several crucial points in his career Schellenberg took on important tasks related to Judenpolitik and became directly involved with bureaucratic measures that facilitated the persecution and then murder of European Jewry. In May 1941, he signed an order that regulated Jewish emigration and a few weeks earlier he had played – by his own recounting – an important role in the Einsatzgruppen negotiations prior to their deployment, as mobile killing squads, in the Soviet Union. At that point, Schellenberg's involvement with Einsatz-gruppen issues was already longstanding: for all intents and purposes, he had been a member of one in Vienna in March 1938. A few months later, he was involved with the Einsatzgruppen deployment in Czechoslovakia. And less than a year later, he was among the men who gathered in Hey-drich's apartment to discuss the Einsatzgruppen deployment in Poland. His role in the negotiations with Wagner in spring 1941 was a logical continuation of his earlier involvement. Yet Schellenberg never gave any indication that he knew about the exact function of the Einsatzgruppen in the Soviet Union – or cared about it in any fashion if he indeed, knew. The closest he ever came to acknowledging that anything might have been askew, was when he related that Heydrich and Wagner retreated to a different room to discuss a secret Hitler order for the Einsatzgruppen. Yet Schellenberg must have known more and, in light of the apparent radicalization of the Einsatzgruppen mandates even before the invasion of the Soviet Union, his protestations of ignorance ring hollow. He must have realized that the Einsatzgruppen would implement measures that

[9] Peter Longerich, *Holocaust: The Nazi Persecution and Murder of the Jews* (Oxford: Oxford University Press, 2010), 4–5.
[10] Report about Schellenberg's marriage, BAL, R 58 Anhang I/49; www.berlin.de/ ba-charlottenburg-wilmersdorf/ueber-den-bezirk/geschichte/gedenktafeln/artikel .125614.php, accessed June 3, 2015.

were in accord with ideology and went to its core policies – the removal of Jews by whatever means available. It is, indeed, highly likely that Schellenberg knew much more than that, and Richard Breitman's frustration that Schellenberg successfully obfuscated his precise knowledge about the so-called genesis of the Final Solution is palpable.[11] But unless new documentation surfaces, these questions cannot be settled, for there is not enough hard evidence to support reasonable assumptions.

Schellenberg himself saw no need to explain specifically his ideological stance and his involvement in Judenpolitik. He presented the elements that involved him as bureaucratic issues – orders that needed signatures or deadlocked negotiations in need of able mediators. The content, he intimated, was not his concern or he was, as during the Einsatzgruppen negotiations of spring 1941, not present when the discussion turned to incriminating details that went beyond what he had negotiated. Conversely, at Nuremberg Schellenberg implicated the military in the Einsatzgruppen's activities. Part of this must have been a strategic decision, for it complicated the prosecution's understanding of the Einsatzgruppen deployment. But Schellenberg's statements also pointed to a larger truth: some groups and individuals pushed Judenpolitik more than others but all major constituencies were on board or could be brought there by an able negotiator. In short, anti-Semitism and Judenpolitik did not propel Schellenberg but were part and parcel of his life and helped him to make his career. Indifference to and disinterest in the concrete consequences of his engagement accomplished the rest. Ian Kershaw famously remarked, "[t]he road to Auschwitz was built by hate, but paved by indifference."[12] Schellenberg possessed both in sufficient quantities.

Schellenberg's own anti-Semitism can – ironically – be found in instances often read as indicators of his ideological aloofness. Schellenberg's eventual willingness to free racial and political enemies of Nazi Germany is often seen as a sign that he was less beholden to Nazi ideology than others. This line of reasoning is flawed. Schellenberg's plan

---

[11] Breitman notes that Schellenberg must have known more about the decision making process of the Final Solution and its timing. He proposes that Schellenberg's use of the term "final solution" in the May 1941 order already meant "exactly what it later became" and was a conscious allusion to Heydrich's plans which were solidified by spring 1941. However, the term "final solution" turns up in many a document dealing with Jewish issue and oftentimes does not refer to the murder of all European Jews. In addition, the order did not originate in Schellenberg's department and was most probably authored by someone else. Richard Breitman, *Official Secrets: What the Nazis Planned, What the British and Americans Knew* (New York, NY: Hill and Wang, 1998), 35 note 33; Yaacov Lozowick, *Hitler's Bureaucrats: The Nazi Security Police and the Banality of Evil*, trans. by Haim Watzman (London: Continuum, 2002), 52, 74.

[12] Ian Kershaw, *Popular Opinion and Political Dissent in the Third Reich* (Oxford: Clarendon Press, 1983), 277.

to use Jews to gain the goodwill of the Western Allies – and Washington in particular – sits at the center of anti-Semitic beliefs in the existence of a Jewish World Conspiracy. To be sure, and it needs to be emphasized, real people survived due to the negotiations between Schellenberg and Bernadotte. Yet the fact remains that Schellenberg considered these men and women his entry fee into negotiations with the Western powers and assumed that advantages – for Germany and himself – could be purchased thusly. There is little indication that the conscience of a "guilty participant," who saw no way out and feared "his entire family's and his personal extermination [sic!]" led to Schellenberg "assist[ing] the victims when approached."[13] Rather, there is every indication – going back to his talks in Stockholm in fall 1943 with Hewitt, who was noted to have Jewish relations and connections – that Schellenberg's latter day humanitarianism and his show of ideological pragmatism were predicated on his conviction that there existed a Jewish World Conspiracy that had the power to sway US policies.

In evaluating Schellenberg's ideological make-up, off-hand comments he made after the war are instructive. His ideological reasoning shines through and, paradoxically, most when he tried to distance himself from Nazi ideology and practice. For example, when he was interrogated about the emigration ban he signed in 1941, Schellenberg stated that the ban had nothing to do with broader plans for the murder of Europe's Jews, but was simply necessitated by Jewish black-marketeering and espionage activities. Similarly, when discussing Admiral Canaris' personality, Schellenberg claimed that Canaris' taste for conspiracy was a function of Vatican influence. And Schellenberg's anti-Bolshevist and racist attitudes were in evidence whenever he discussed real or imagined Soviet policies, but most obviously when he tried to blame "German atrocities" on the Eastern Front on Soviet agents infiltrating local German military posts and duping them into action. In effect, Schellenberg tried to hold Soviet agents responsible or Germany's racist rampage in the East.[14] But these statements, oscillating between laughable – when it comes to Canaris – and seriously delusional – when it comes Soviet agents conning German soldiers into murder – are the justifications of a man who is trying to put his best foot forward, to sound reasonable and thoughtful. These ideologically grounded statements were meant to show that Schellenberg was no ideologue at all. This was clearly not the case, no matter how much

---

[13] Reinhard R. Doerries, *Hitler's Intelligence Chief Walter Schellenberg: The Man Who Kept Germany's Secrets* (New York: Enigma Books, 2009), 248.

[14] Walter Schellenberg, *The Labyrinth: Memoirs of Walter Schellenberg, Hitler's Chief of Counterintelligence*, trans. Louis Hagen (New York: Harper & Brothers, 1956; reprint, Cambridge, MA: Da Capo Press, 2000), 265–266.

Image 10.1 Profile of Walter Schellenberg, Nuremberg, July 1, 1946.
United States Holocaust Memorial Museum, courtesy of Gerald (Gerd)
Schwab. [Photograph # 94530]

Schellenberg would have liked the world to believe so and apparently
believed it himself.

Schellenberg struck similar notes in the document he created in the
middle of his divorce. He portrayed himself as a clear-eyed and righteous
man who always did his best, even under the most trying circumstances,
but found himself thwarted by forces outside of his control or harmed by
his enemies' malicious intent. Also in evidence is a strong undercurrent
of self-pity and more than a hint of martyrdom. These same attitudes
permeate his postwar statements, in which he portrayed himself as a victim of Kaltenbrunner and others, all men unable to see the righteousness
of his path and his moral character. Schellenberg was a man with a pathologically clean conscience. This self-delusion must have helped him to
stay on message during his interrogations and in writing his memoir.

Schellenberg's self-perception was no exception. Students of history – and of the human condition – have long been puzzled by the self-perception of many Nazi officials. But "[t]he road to Auschwitz was paved with righteousness," as Koonz states, and inhumane policies directed against the enemies of the Volk were recast as defensive acts void malicious intent.[15] Similarly, in his work on the perpetrators of mass murder, Harald Welzer argues that to probe the perpetrators' perceptions of themselves as moral, one needs to consider their frames of reference – in broad, societal terms, in the concrete situation, and on the individual level. Rather than analyzing perpetrators as men whose morals had "decayed," one should consider the "contemporaneous normative orientations" that allowed them to consider themselves morally upstanding while committing mass murder.[16] Put differently, new norms defined a new morality and the perpetrators' evaluation of their actions should be analyzed in that context. This is not a call for moral relativism. Yet only by making "National Socialist morality" part of the equation is it possible to gain an understanding of perpetrators' perceptions of themselves as ordinary and decent men – and their subsequent ability to retain this image of themselves.

Schellenberg was not a murderer himself, but his bureaucratic activities facilitated the Final Solution. He had converted, to use Peter Fritzsche's term, to the norms of the particularistic National Socialist morality that was predicated on the "fundamental inequality" of peoples, which translated into danger for the presumed "higher group" and the conviction that a Jewish Question existed and needed to be solved. This conviction was not simply a matter of ideology, but also one of societal practices and of a new reality. It entailed a vision of a future in which Jews were imagined as "already extinct." Judenpolitik was the central "relay station" of what Welzer, in a pithy nod to Jürgen Habermas, calls the "National Socialist transformation of the public sphere." Welzer argues that the "realization of the utopian creates a lot of work," and notes the joy and pride that many felt for their engaged participation in this "historical project" and their willingness to go above and beyond the call of duty. "[This was]," Welzer writes, "the fatal strength of the National Socialist system and the mobilization was only possible as the participants were deeply convinced

[15] Koonz, *Conscience*, 3–13.
[16] Welzer, *Täter*, 15–17, 29. On female perpetrators: Wendy Lower, *Hitler's Furies: German Women in the Nazi Killing Fields* (Boston: Houghton Mifflin Harcourt, 2013); Elisabeth Kohlhaas, "Revision of Life Story/Revision of History: Gertrud Slottke, from National Socialist Coperpetrator to Expellee Official," in David Messenger and Katrin Paehler, eds., *From Nazis to West Germans: Self Invention, Recast Identities, and the Politics of the Past after 1945* (Lexington: The University of Kentucky Press 2015), 249–270.

by the significance of their trying tasks and willing to give it their best."
National Socialist morality, hinging on Judenpolitik, "anticipated killing
and approved of it," provided plausible reasons for murder, allowed men
to fill their roles comfortably, as murderers or bureaucrats, and to remain,
in their mind, "decent" [anständig], especially if they did their jobs without "malice."[17] Schellenberg regarded himself as a decent man: he did
his jobs, did them well, and without malice.

Schellenberg's speech at the intelligence conference in Salzburg in May
1944 indicates his understanding of National Socialist morality. Stressing
that earlier intelligence mistakes had been paid with "the biological and
material substance of the Volk," he stressed the need for the "ethical
strength and military-soldierly superiority" of the service and highlighted
that these "virtues, grown out of traditions, [were] strongly grounded
and newly defined by National Socialism" and needed to "be led with
good political instincts." And he maintained that the raison d'être of the
National Socialist state made activities "morally unimpeachable" even if
"in reality they were beyond good and evil."[18] Schellenberg's reference
to "reality" is not an indication of moral decay. Converting to National
Socialism's particularistic morality, which valued the well-being of the
race above all, did not mean that people had forgotten that a different,
universal morality existed. It only meant that it did not apply.

Thinking about National Socialist morality also offers a way to understand how and why Schellenberg could claim ideological distances.
Deviations from the pure doctrine – and Schellenberg's ideological
pragmatism lent itself to those – could be construed as such, especially
after the war and with audiences that conceived of Nazi Germany
as a top-down, totalitarian police state. However, at the end of the
day, National Socialist morality was a fairly wide tent; the "conjunctions" (Browder) were many and so were the "conversion processes"
(Fritzsche). For functionaries of Schellenberg's stature – and in light
of his patron Himmler's solid support – it would have taken a bit to
end up in an irreversible predicament. And as I have shown, as an
able political operator who knew how to handle rivals, how to smooth
bureaucratic kerfuffles, when to argue ideologically and when to use
seemingly pragmatic approaches, Schellenberg avoided problems he
could not handle. And Himmler had his back.

Schellenberg's career was not defined by deviations but shows him
as an able bureaucrat and occasional activist firmly rooted in National

[17] Welzer, *Täter*, 31–69; Peter Fritzsche, *Life and Death in the Third Reich* (Cambridge: The
Belknap Press of Harvard University Press, 2009), chapter 1: "Reviving the Nation."
[18] Schellenberg to Kaltenbrunner, Vortrag Schellenberg, vorgelegt zur Genehmigung,
May 10, 1944, RGVA, Fond 500, Opis 1, 1164.

Socialist ideology and practice. And he had set his sights high, earning speedy promotions. Schellenberg performed well and tended to be the right man at the right time and in the right place. By January 1938, he was the head of the SD's Main Department I/II, having replaced his mentor Herbert Mehlhorn. He was a rising star and Heydrich's rumored patronage only added to his luster; it also led to his prominent role in formulating the future shape and trajectory of the SD and Security Police. Schellenberg was soon doing Heydrich's ideological bidding in the latter's conflict with Werner Best about Sipo and SD career paths. However, for all of Schellenberg's eagerness to impress Heydrich, Schellenberg sat on the fence for some time when it came to the question whether political soldiers or political jurists were better suited to lead Sipo and SD. Schellenberg himself fell into the latter category, but he soon realized that the way to go was Heydrich's, for even if the conflict was to end in a draw, as it did, Heydrich would be the better patron to have. Indeed, almost simultaneously to the debate about career paths, Schellenberg received the bureaucratic assignment of a lifetime: he was to draft the plans for the amalgamation of the Security Service and Security Police into the Reich Security Main Office. As before, Schellenberg's ideological leanings were carefully calibrated and far from overt, but unmistakably there to benefit him, and Schellenberg morphed into Heydrich's legal expert of choice when it came to complicated bureaucratic issue related to the envisioned integration of the normative and the prerogative state. And along the way, Schellenberg tried to theorize the SD's unique characteristics as well as its role and mandate: a total political intelligence service, firmly grounded in ideology, that dealt with offenses that could not be addressed judicially but put volk, the racial community, and state in the gravest danger. The SD was also more important than the police.

Schellenberg reaped his commitment's initial benefits with his appointment as the head the Gestapo's counterintelligence department, IV E, of the RSHA. In this position, he established himself as a bona fide intelligence doer with the abductions at Venlo; worked on the invasion handbook for Great Britain; and attempted to run IV E according to a new, Nazified definition of counterintelligence, which he formulated. Germany's enemies were defined in political and racial terms, and Schellenberg and his department took a prominent role in their – preventive – removal, and, frequently, their murder, as in the A-B Aktion in Poland. This was a broad and unusual understanding of counterintelligence and if Schellenberg had any compunction about his approach, it did not show; instead, his position and tasks afforded him an increasingly closer relationship with Himmler. As its head, Schellenberg tried to make IV E into a close approximation of the total intelligence service he envisioned and theorized. IV E's mainstay was counterintelligence, *Spionageabwehr* – the domestic defense against the efforts of enemy services – but Schellenberg was intended to bring into his realm counterespionage, espionage, and, if possible, intelligence collection as well. He wanted it all; heading "half of an intelligence service" was not what he had in mind for his future. Encroaching on the tasks of the Abwehr or Office VI, then still headed by Heinz Jost, was part of the course. Alas, in July 1941, Schellenberg was appointed acting head of Office VI. Seen as an underperforming entity headed by a lightweight, it was considered a blank canvas of great potential. Schellenberg meant to make the RSHA's political foreign intelligence department into "something." His ambitions matched the task.

Office VI was the post-1939 incarnation of the SD-Ausland, the foreign section of the SD, initially – and recently – created as the intelligence service of the SS. Put differently, both the SD and its personnel came out of Nazi Germany's self-appointed ideological elite; they had no background in intelligence. In the early 1930s the SD slowly expanded in size and went through numerous structural changes while negotiating and establishing its role in relation to both the police and the Abwehr. The SD's claim to fame was its ideological prowess and its envisioned total approach to intelligence and security that, in the minds of the decision makers, set it apart from the police and the Abwehr – organizations frequently deemed ideologically unreliable – and made it a better choice for the tasks at hands. It was, however, not so much the actual activities that gained the SD its reputation, but its SS pedigree and its leadership's bureaucratic wrangling skills that allowed the SD to entrench itself in the National Socialist security, intelligence, and policing complex and to establish itself as an alternative to the existing agencies. Yet, both the SD and its foreign department were entities in the making. They came out of nothing – invented by Himmler and Heydrich, underfunded, and understaffed. Amateurs, long on political allegiance to the Nazi movement and ambition but short on intelligence experience, made up the organization, but they shared their leadership's ambition to make the SD into Germany's foremost intelligence agency, at home and abroad. And what was to become Office VI of the RSHA remained the SD's smallest department, grossly understaffed despite its ambitious structure. It nevertheless gradually found its way into matters of foreign intelligence – via an expanding role in counterintelligence matters and by laying claim to the complete surveillance of all living spheres abroad, thus emulating the approach of the SD's domestic intelligence service. Totality and ideology were key and the emergence of Main Department III 3 in 1938 – a department that was short-lived – indicates long-term plans for the creation of an active and unfettered foreign intelligence service.

Some of Office VI's problems between 1939 and 1941 came out of its reconceptualization as part of the RSHA at the beginning of the war against Poland. The creation of intelligence networks and courier routes, to pick but one example, became even more difficult than it would have been in peacetime. Yet the preconditions for these problems had been created before 1939, as the then SD-Ausland – moving beyond counter-intelligence and toward intelligence and espionage by creating networks reaching across Germany's borders – relied almost completely on ideologically trustworthy German citizens and ethnic Germans who moved in pro-German – pro-Nazi – circles. Consequently, Germany's ideological spies were rarely in a position to learn anything worthwhile about the countries on which they reported but knew much about German communities abroad and their infighting – and oftentimes supported the most radical faction in these conflict. As it was, the SD-Ausland did some of its most useful work in the run-up to the annexation of Austria and the take-over of the Sudeten territories in 1938, when it prepared handbook-like indices that focused on securing and policing the acquisitions in political and racial terms. Mandates, on the other hand, were so broadly defined that it defied reason and personnel fell back on their ideological understanding of the world and the surveillance of broadly conceived living spheres. To put it pointedly: fragmented information, collected by people whose primary qualification was their National Socialist convictions and who approached the world accordingly, was pressed into an ideologically driven picture of the world by the ideologues who staffed the center.

Office VI had a tendency to run afoul of the Auswärtige Amt and its minister without having anything to show for it once the dust settled and also found itself ensnared in conflicts with Office IV, the Gestapo, and Office III, the domestic surveillance service, as Germany's ongoing occupation of new countries between 1939 and 1941 reshuffled Office's VI's areas of responsibility. But for Heydrich – and presumably Himmler – the crux of the matter was that the ideologically firm intelligence service for which they held such high hopes did not live up to expectation. It did not make accessible the secrets of Germany's enemies but provided poor information and was a source of friction in the RSHA's relationship to other agencies. They laid much of the blame at Jost's doorstep. Jost's Office VI was a no-value added albatross around the RSHA's neck.

Schellenberg's appointment to the leadership of Office VI was meant to change this and while the new head of the office created an oftentimes magnificent illusion of a professional and successful foreign intelligence service, led by a whiz-kid spymaster – which captured the imagination of some of his peers and of the Western intelligence community – the office's fundamental shortcomings remained the same. Ideology remained key on every level of the service's operations, and it was still staffed by intelligence amateurs who were mostly political soldiers. Office VI selected operatives on all levels based on ideology. Report topics were selected according to ideology, and, although there was no central evaluation division, incoming material was evaluated ideologically. However, the office's personnel certainly believed that their reporting was unobjectionable; indeed, "unobjectionable" was the word most frequently used to describe the operatives and their work. Like true ideologues, these men did not believe that their judgment was impaired by their worldview and knowing that some of their activities did not gain Hitler's or Himmler's support, or even evoked their ire, only strengthened their – postwar – conviction of having been above the ideological fray. Nothing can be further from the truth. The office's decidedly ideological approach to foreign intelligence remained its main claim to fame and distinguished this new service from older, better established, and better-funded foreign intelligence entities. National Socialism was not a system that stymied initiative. Rather, the right idea at the right time could open all kinds of doors. And nobody ever claimed that "working towards the Führer" (Kershaw) was easy. What differentiated Schellenberg's from Jost's Office VI, then, was the former's adeptness at projecting ideology, professionalism, and daring, even if their basic approaches were similar – and similarly unsuccessful. Schellenberg was something Jost was decidedly not: a masterful illusionist and salesman. He sold to Himmler and others the illusion of a functioning and useful National Socialist intelligence service. The absorption of the better part of the Abwehr in 1944 was the illusion's highpoint. It also confirmed, at home and abroad, Schellenberg's status as a force to reckon with.

Office VI is commonly investigated as a regular foreign intelligence agency alongside other intelligence entities active in Nazi Germany. This approach falls short and blinds one to the office's realities: its many idiosyncrasies can be understood only if Office VI is evaluated as an organization that originated with the SS and the SD and conceived of itself in these terms. At best, Office VI was an ideological reporting and (occasional) policing organization operating abroad; its primary loyalties – and Schellenberg's loyalty – were with Himmler and his universe. Himmler, as the primary customer of Office VI's intelligence and the source of Schellenberg's power and influence, was Schellenberg's ultimate vantage point. In addition, it is worth noting and taking seriously that most of the activities that Schellenberg described after the war had little to do with the collection of foreign intelligence per se but were attempts to create an alternative foreign policy agency for Himmler, intent on realizing

Himmler's wishes or what Schellenberg presumed them to be. Others have remarked that under Jost Office VI already had the propensity to conduct foreign policy. Under Schellenberg this was taken to a new level: there was a concerted effort to depose Foreign Minister Ribbentrop or, failing that, to create a framework to work around him. And this independent foreign policy – especially Schellenberg's efforts to enter negotiation with the West – was predicated on the existence of Jewish World Conspiracy. Office VI was more than a foreign intelligence service and less: it never provided reliable foreign intelligence nor was it particularly successful at forging an independent foreign policy. However, under Schellenberg, Office VI provided the powerful illusion of being both. And, as the role former SD agents played later in West German services showed, the illusion of a reliable service carried into the postwar period.[19]

Office VI was certainly not the first intelligence service, past or present, that failed to live up to expectations; that was guided by state ideology – witness the Soviet case; made up largely of amateurs – witness the OSS; or that fell victim to wishful thinking or preconceived notions. The hunt for WMDs, weapons of mass destruction, in the run up to the second Iraq War and the slanted interpretation and reinterpretation of the available raw intelligence make obvious that even in a democracy political demands and convictions have the power to guide intelligence. Perfectly functioning services with reasonable actors as producers and customers of foreign intelligence remain the domain of International Relations theory.[20] And heads of foreign intelligence services as well as station chiefs, as the example of Allen Dulles' negotiations with Highest SS and Police Leader Karl Wolff about the surrender of the Italian front in spring 1945 illustrates, have conducted operations that swayed substantially into foreign policy. Put differently, all intelligence services, all their operations, all their personnel are products of their time, their place, and their culture, and these conditions impact what services do and how they do it; and many a spymaster has interpreted his brief broadly, emboldened by the conviction that he understood the situation on the ground better than his customers. And yet, there was something decidedly different about the SD-Ausland/Office VI.

[19] Norman A. Goda, "The Gehlen Organization and the Heinz Felfe Case: The SD, the KGB, and West German Counterintelligence," David Messenger and Katrin Paehler, eds., *From Nazis to West Germans: Self Invention, Recast Identities, and the Politics of the Past after 1945* (Lexington: The University of Kentucky Press 2015), 271–294, esp. 271–276.

[20] Richard K. Betts, "Analysis, War, and Decision: Why Intelligence Failures are Inevitable," *World Politics: A Quarterly Journal of International Relations* 31 (1978/1979), 61–89; Michael I. Handel, *War, Strategy, and Intelligence* (London: Frank Cass, 1989).

Foreign intelligence never held a prominent place in Germany, and Office VI was meant to change this. Foreign intelligence customarily meant military intelligence but it was not much of a priority either and beset by a whole set of problems, which had its origins, as Rebecca Ratcliff argues, in German military, intelligence, and cultural traditions. These characteristics predated Nazism but were also exacerbated by it: the German penchant for decentralization and specialization; rivalries for funds and personnel; the wish to hire the "right people;" and the low priority intelligence – and its practitioners – held in the minds of the decision makers who focused on tactical intelligence.[21] SD-Ausland/Office VI – in the minds of its champions – was meant to overcome these shortcomings by taking a decidedly National Socialist approach to foreign intelligence. In the new state, foreign intelligence was to be centralized; the "organic" and total understanding of the world for which National Socialism provided the tools was to supersede specialization; its pedigree with the SS was to provide priority when it came to staffing and funding needs; and the "right people" would finally truly be such, as race and commitment to the cause would trump and cut across class and traditional networks of power and influence. This new service, with its racially and ideologically screened personnel, would be capable of handling the broad strategic questions and able to produce intelligence of utter import to the state's leadership.

Realities did not match visions. Office VI – like the SD-Ausland before – remained understaffed and underfunded, and it certainly never evolved into the centralized service with broad influence one had imagined. As Michael Geyer suggests, centralization of intelligence collection and assessment could have come only out of a consensus or at least a debate "over the direction of the Third Reich." This was not going to happen – yet another indication of National Socialism as a tent wider than commonly acknowledged, at least until decisions were made – and thus information remained a lever in the struggle for credibility, power, resources, and access to Hitler.[22] Office VI's main claim to fame – ideological and racial firmness – made for stunningly homogenous personnel at each and every level of its operations, a tremendously restricted reach abroad, slanted interpretations, ideologically defined contempt for the enemy, and few options as to how to fill with meaning vague mandates. It also made an excellent weapon in the internal battles that

---

[21] Rebecca A. Ratcliff, *Delusions of Intelligence: Enigma, Ultra, and the End of Secure Ciphers* (Cambridge: Cambridge University Press, 2006).

[22] Michael Geyer, "National Socialist Germany: The Politics of Information," in Ernest R. May, ed., *Knowing One's Enemy: Intelligence Assessment Before the Two World Wars* (Princeton: Princeton University Press, 1984), 338; 340.

defined Nazi Germany and gave reason for hope. Maybe once the next rival was beaten – and its most useful parts gobbled up – Office VI would reach the potential its ambitious head was already selling as a reality. And Schellenberg needed these potentials to be realized if he did not want to lose the hard-fought ground, on which his and his service's reputation was based and which was meant to lead to the service's broad future roles.

Office VI was a world on its own. Some of its characteristics, activities, and failures are reminiscent of other foreign intelligence services – past and present, in democracies and dictatorships alike. But in Office VI the combination of traits created a perfect storm that spelled disaster. And ideology took pride of place. Good, reasonably reliable foreign intelligence relies on the operatives' and analysts' ability to see and appreciate options and alternatives that might be in stark contrast to their pre-conceived notions. Nazi ideologues made particularly poor intelligence officers, as the ideological rejection of the racial and political "other" created a service seriously blinded to any development that did not con-form to ideology. Ideological convictions coming from within the office and permeating all its crevices appear as the most important reason for Office VI's failure as an intelligence service. Other reasons, such as the nature of Nazi Germany's bureaucracy or the unwillingness of the leader-ship to appreciate foreign intelligence – not that Office VI provided much of that – contributed to the failure of Nazi Germany's foreign intelligence efforts.[23] But in the final analysis, it was the reliance on Nazi ideology at every level of the service and in all its major activities that doomed Office VI – and its predecessor – from the start.

Any intelligence service can see only what it knows, and in the case of the SD and later Office VI this knowledge – by pedigree, training, and conditioning – was ideology. This made the SD blinder than other services, and much blinder than the Western services. Openness is key. Diversity is key. There is comfort in the realization, also proposed by Ratcliff, that diversity – racial, political, social, and sexual – in all its sometimes so frustrating messiness has the ability to help us see.

[23] David Kahn, *Hitler's Spies: German Military Intelligence on World War II* (New York: Macmillan, 1978; reprint, Cambridge, MA: Da Capo Press, 2000), 524–536.

Appendix

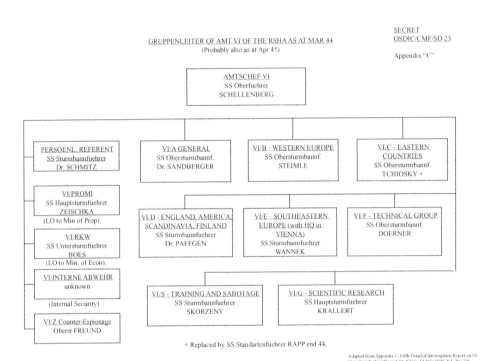

GRUPPENLEITER OF AMT VI OF THE RSHA AS AT MAR 44
(Probably also as at Apr 45)

AMTSCHEF VI
SS Oberfuehrer
SCHELLENBERG

PERSOENL. REFERENT
SS Sturmbannfuehrer
Dr. SCHMITZ

VI/A GENERAL
SS Obersturmbannf.
Dr. SANDBERGER

VI/B - WESTERN EUROPE
SS Obersturmbannf.
STEIMLE

VI/C - EASTERN COUNTRIES
SS Obersturmbannf.
TCHIOSKY +

VI/PROMI
SS Hauptsturmfuehrer
ZEISCHKA
(LO to Min of Prop).

VI/RKW
SS Untersturmfuehrer
BOES
(LO to Min. of Econ).

VI/INTERNE ABWEHR
unknown

(Internal Security)

VI/Z Counter-Espionage
Oberst FREUND

VI/D - ENGLAND, AMERICA, SCANDINAVIA, FINLAND
SS Sturmbannfuehrer
Dr. PAFFGEN

VI/E - SOUTHEASTERN EUROPE (with HQ in VIENNA)
SS Sturmbannfuehrer
WANNEK

VI/F - TECHNICAL GROUP
SS Obersturmbannf.
DOERNER

VI/S - TRAINING AND SABOTAGE
SS Sturmbannfuehrer
SKORZENY

VI/G - SCIENTIFIC RESEARCH
SS Hauptsturmfuehrer
KRALLERT

+ Replaced by SS Standartenfuehrer RAPP end 44.

Adapted from Appendix C, Fifth Detailed Interrogation Report on SS Sturmbannfuehrer Huegel, Dr. Klaus, 14 June 1945, NA, RG 226, Entry 174, Box 39, Folder 307

"Gruppenleiter of Amt VI of the RSHA as at March 44 (Probably also as at April 1945)." National Archives and Records Administration. [NARA, RG 226, Entry 174, Box 39, Folder 309, Fifth Detailed Interrogation Report on SS Sturmbannführer Huegel Dr. Klaus.]

Glossary

I have tried to use the translations that are commonly accepted but have chosen different translations if those convey meanings and mandates better or more accurately carry German connotations.

Abteilung VI (in context of BdS)   Section VI
Abteilung Fremde Heere   Foreign Armies Branch
Abwehr   Germany's Military Intelligence Agency
Abwehr-Abteilung   Abwehr-Branch
Amt Auslandsnachrichten und Abwehr   Office for Foreign
    Information and Counterintelligence
Amt (in context of RSHA)   Office
Anschluß   Annexation of Austria
Aufbruch Kreis   Departure Circle (Sudeten German organization)
Auslandskurzmeldungen   Short Foreign Reports
Auslandsmeldungen   Foreign Reports
Beauftragter der Sicherheitspolizei und des SD, BdS   Representative
    of the Security Police and the SD
Beobachter   Observers
Deutsche Nationalsozialistische Arbeiterpartei, DNSAP   German
    National Socialist Workers' Party (Sudeten German Organization)
Einsatzgruppe   Mobile Intelligence and Policing Unit; post-June 1941:
    Mobile Killing Squad
Forschungsamt   Research Office
Gauleiter   Party District Leader
Hauptbeauftragte   Main Representative
Hauptamt Sicherheitspolizei   Main Office Security Police
Höherer SS und Polizeiführer   Higher SS and Police Leader
Höchster SS and Polizeiführer   Highest SS and Police Lader
Inspekteur der Sicherheitspolizei und des Sicherheitsdienstes   Inspector
    of Security Police and SD
Kameradschaftsbund   Comradeship Circle (Sudeten German
    Organization)

Kriminalpolizei, Kripo   Criminal Police

Ländergruppe   Country Group

Lebensgebiete   Living Spheres

Ministeramt   Minister Office

Militärisches Amt/Amt Mil   Military Office (Abwehr parts integrated into Office VI in 1944)

Nachrichtenabteilung   Intelligence Branch

Nachrichtenbüro   Intelligence Bureau

Nationalsozialistischer Deutscher Studentenbund   National Socialist German Students' Association

NSDAP Auslandsorganisation (NSDAP-AO)   NSDAP Abroad

Oberkommando des Heeres (OKH)   High Command of the Army

Index

Printed in Great Britain
by Amazon